THE SOCIALIST TRADITION

MOSES TO LENIN

LONGMANS, GREEN AND CO. LTD.
OF PATERNOSTER ROW
43 ALBERT DRIVE, LONDON, S.W. 19
NICOL ROAD, BOMBAY
17 CHITTARANJAN AVENUE, CALCUTTA
36A MOUNT ROAD, MADRAS

LONGMANS, GREEN AND CO.
55 FIFTH AVENUE, NEW YORK 3

LONGMANS, GREEN AND CO.
215 VICTORIA STREET, TORONTO 1

First Published 1946

CODE NUMBER: 15631

Printed in England at THE BALLANTYNE PRESS
SPOTTISWOODE, BALLANTYNE & CO. LTD.
Colchester, London & Eton

PREFACE

It is a chastening thought that some parts of this book have had an ante-natal existence of approximately twenty-two years. When I began the final stage of reducing to writing an unwritten book, I had in mind the production of what should be, in size and otherwise, a companion volume to *The Development of Economic Doctrine*, which apparently has been found to serve a certain purpose in the education of the young economist. Despite my good intentions, however, it has refused to be compressed; and in the end it does not fall far short of attaining twice the modest dimensions originally planned. Possibly the socialists, being in the main dissentients, rebels, and prophets, are a more interesting lot than their orthodox and respectable cousins, the 'economists.'

I make no apology for writing this book. It may not be *the* book which the general reader requires as an introduction to the development of socialist thought, but that at the present moment he does require *a* book on the subject is beyond all question. Kirkup's *History of Socialism* dates from 1892; and since then the literature on the subject has been astonishingly meagre, and—as it may appear to many—grossly disfigured by prejudice on one side or the other. It ought to be possible to write of Socialism without the underlying assumption that socialists alone are right and righteous; that they alone are the true crusaders against the powers of darkness. Equally, of course, it ought to be possible to write of Socialism without assuming that all socialists are fundamentally dishonest, and that Socialism attracts exclusively the world's incompetents and the world's failures. And of this second view, there are also some glaring examples.

Not that any one in these matters can be expected to write without bias: if such a miracle were possible, the result would probably not be worth reading. There is, however, an obvious duty resting on an expositor to try to understand a point of view, even when he disagrees with it. In the present case, my bias—some may say my 'prejudice'—is doubtless sufficiently apparent. I shall be told that I am not sympathetic to Marx and the Marxian tradition. In a Preface an author, having rigorously eschewed the First Person Singular throughout eighteen chapters, may be allowed to talk somewhat more informally to his readers; and accordingly I am prepared to acknowledge that I do not like Marx, and that I do not like Lassalle; just as further back I do not like Rousseau. And though one may admit on high principle that one ought not to allow a small matter of likes and dislikes to influence judgment, those of us who are honest with ourselves will admit that in general it does for all that! It is difficult to imagine any normal person wishing to meet Marx for a third time. Further, if in the intimacy of a Preface I may continue to be indiscreet, Marx irritates me because in the last generation he has so successfully led so many of the 'intellectuals' up the garden path, where at great length they discuss What Marx Really Meant, and say things which would astonish you, as they would certainly have astonished Marx, could he have overheard them discoursing in the garden-house. It is greatly to his credit that Marx, so it is recorded, protested on one occasion that he was not a Marxian. Mr. E. H. Carr, who almost alone in the present generation writes of Marx with balance, comments on the attitude of the pseudo-Marxists in this matter, and their pathetic faith that 'if but one plank can be saved from the discredited platform of Marxism, all will be well.' It is an unedifying spectacle. No one would suggest that Marx was consciously dishonest, but a very great deal of intellectual disingenuousness has gone to the explaining (and the explaining-away) of Marx. Accordingly, all things considered, I do not like the company of Marx.

Spiritually, despite, or because of, their absurdities, I am much more at home with Saint-Simon and Fourier. While I would do much to avoid meeting Marx—for this Diotrephes of the socialist church would merely bark at me in his hot displeasure—I should greatly appreciate a long evening with Fourier in a quiet hostelry; and, if the bar were not too crowded, I believe I could prevail upon him to give his marvellous impersonation of a fox or of a robin or a giraffe, with copious comments on the qualities each of them symbolised. It was a performance which he gave only when his company was entirely congenial.

While I am thus prepared to acknowledge that I have my likes and dislikes among the team here assembled, and while this may have made me in some cases more sympathetic than elsewhere, I do not think that I have anywhere been 'unfair.' At least, within the space available, I have tried to allow my witnesses to say all that they have to say, and to say it in their own words. As a final contribution to 'impartiality,' I have, after searching my heart, confessed herewith that, should we all hereafter forgather in an Elysium, devised by Mr. Eric Linklater, it is only with Marx, Lassalle and Rousseau that I shall hope to avoid being on visiting terms. Having warned the reader of this, my possible bias, he may make the desired correction in the other sense.

The only practical reparation an author can make for writing a book twice the length he had intended is to indicate what parts the reader-in-a-hurry may skip. While, officially, I am bound to say that each chapter contributes something to a comprehension of all the others, in fact most of the chapters are reasonably self-contained, and any one may therefore read the portion in which he is interested. The reader who is exclusively concerned with the problems of Socialism to-day may be tempted to begin at Chapter 12 with Marx; but I would plead with him (unless he is very pressed) to go further back; we do not in this country know enough about the Fathers of Socialism (so-called), and on the human side they are much more interesting than the children they begat. I would therefore suggest that the hurried reader, after running through the Prologue which gives the framework, should begin at Chapter 5, with William Godwin. He might omit Chapter 11, unless, merely for the sake of sampling, he elects to read the sections on two of the English pre-Marxians (let us suggest Hall and Gray). In Chapter 12 he might, if he gnaws at the main joint, omit Lassalle and Rodbertus. In Chapter 13 he could restrict himself to Bakunin, and in Chapter 14 he might prove his insularity by leaving Bernstein aside. The concluding chapter, as it merely contains disconnected and irresponsible comments by the author, may also be neglected by those who seek a 'shortened course.'

I am under great obligations to many librarians who have magnanimously allowed books to go out of their immediate care; perhaps I may be allowed to acknowledge in particular the help received from the Custodians of the Libraries of the Universities of Edinburgh and Aberdeen. To my son, John Gray, I am indebted for assistance in the tasks of proof-reading and of the preparation of the Index.

ALEXANDER GRAY.

Edinburgh,
September 1944.

CONTENTS

THE SOCIALIST TRADITION

MOSES TO LENIN

PROLOGUE AND PLAN

THE purpose of the present volume is to present the outstanding figures in the development of socialist thought, with some estimate of the significance of their several contributions. It does not, it should be observed, aim at being a history of socialist thought: such a task, in its immensity, would probably engage more than the average lifetime of any moderately conscientious student. Nor indeed (though it may savour of heresy) is a history of socialism on a comprehensive scale a primary requirement for the ordinary man, confronted with the problems of to-day. Further, any temptation to be drawn into the history of the socialist movement has, so far as possible, been resisted. It is admittedly a cognate subject; but again, the effort, doubtless incumbent on all of us, to disentangle the confusion of ideas making up the environment in which we live, would not be materially aided by embarking on the vain attempt (for instance) to understand the cross-currents and interrelations among the socialist parties in France in the second half of the nineteenth century. Here we are primarily concerned with 'ideas,' as these ideas have been reflected in the minds of the men who have been most influential in shaping the socialist tradition. As a consequence of this method of approach it is inevitable that many connecting links should be omitted and even some considerable movements ignored. It is suggested, however, with some confidence, that if the ordinary man, who is the bulk of the population, can acquire a knowledge of what Godwin or Proudhon, or Marx or Lenin stood for, he may, without great immediate loss, leave to the academic expert the fascinating pursuit of conjectural sources and hidden influences.

One question barks for an answer on the threshold of our journey; but Prudence and Cowardice (a combination of potent masters) unite in suggesting that the question should meantime be avoided. What, it may at the outset reasonably be asked, are we to understand by socialism? The definitions of socialism that strew the expositions and the criticisms of socialism furnish a depressing prospect. Some are foolish; some are vacuous; some are contradictory; some, which appear commendable up to a point, leave gaping omissions.

There is in short no agreement among the experts as to what socialism is supposed to mean, or what it is that constitutes the *Wesen* of a socialist system of thought. On the other hand, there is not the same disagreement as to who are the 'great socialists,' to fall back on the title of Mr. Muckle's little book [1]—though, admittedly, there are not a few of Mr. Muckle's team who would be entirely excluded on any strict interpretation of most of the most-favoured definitions. For the purpose of our journey through time we shall accordingly guide ourselves, not so much by the application of a definition of socialism postulated in advance, as by accepting somewhat unquestioningly those whom the general consensus of opinion has agreed to designate as 'the great socialists.' When these have gone into the witness-box, and have severally testified to the faith that is in them, it may in a concluding chapter be possible to consider more knowledgeably what is the essence of socialism, and how one brand of socialism differs from another. For the present, therefore, without suggesting that it even remotely foreshadows a definition, we shall accept all who, urged by a passion for justice or equality, or by a sensitiveness to the evils of this present world, seek a better world, not by way of reform, but by way of subversion (using the word in its literal and neutral sense)—or, if it be preferred, by a fundamental change in the nature and structure of society.

It may be convenient if in this Prologue some indication is given of the prominent figures selected to illustrate the development of socialist thought. In the modern western world, our way of thinking derives largely, on the one hand, from the Jews, modified and supplemented later by Christianity, and on the other hand from Greece. These together provide in large measure the pit from which have been dug our thoughts on the relation of man to man, of man to society, of man to God. Inevitably many of the ideas which lie at the root of socialism were foreshadowed (and more than foreshadowed) in the Mosaic Law, in the indignation of the prophets, in the speculations of the Greek philosophers, and in the teaching of the early Church. The first two chapters accordingly seek to determine how far socialism may justifiably appeal to Greek philosophy; how far it may claim that it finds inspiration and support in the Jewish and Christian traditions.

The third chapter may also in a sense be regarded as concerned with background—with the inspirations leading to socialism, rather than with socialism itself. A curious and fascinating side-line in the literature of socialism is concerned with the portrayal of imaginary and ideal societies, where, without any of the pangs of birth (so familiar to Marx), the perfect world is represented, in the guise of fiction, as a going and highly successful concern. The greatest of all Utopias is,

[1] Friedrich Muckle: *Die grossen Sozialisten.*

of course, the original *Utopia* itself, unless indeed Plato's *Republic* is regarded as a Utopia—which, strictly speaking, it is not. The third chapter is accordingly devoted to the *Utopia* of Thomas More (1478–1535); and since Utopias play so large a part in later socialist literature (down to *Looking Backward* and *News from Nowhere*), some attention is devoted to two of the other early Utopias, as represented by Campanella (1568–1639) and Fénelon (1651–1715).

In the fourth chapter we approach the questionings out of which modern socialism has sprung. Here we are concerned with the prelude to the French Revolution, where, of course, the greatest name is that of Rousseau (1712–1778). Rousseau was primarily a political writer, but he was tortured by a passion for equality, by a hatred of property (or of certain kinds of property) and by a vision of class warfare which made him one of the greatest influences in the origins of socialism. In this chapter there is also included some reference to two much smaller pre-revolutionary figures who were, however, great in their time, Mably (1709–1785) and Morelly (?–?). These also thirsted for equality, as did Babeuf (1764–1797), the martyr of the *Secte des Egaux*, who likewise is admitted to this chapter. Though he is hardly at home with these companions, there is also included here a slight account of Fichte (1762–1814), who represents the enlightenment of the late eighteenth century, and who became influential in the authoritarian tradition of Germany.

In the following chapter (5) we meet one of the enigmatic figures of English literature. William Godwin (1756–1836) appears here as the first, and perhaps the greatest and most consistent of the anarchists, and, as such, he opens a line of thought which has ever since been in part intermingled with, and in part opposed to, socialism. Godwin was an anarchist because he was so pre-eminently a man of reason and inhuman logic. An anarchist society is conceivable only if all concerned are the embodiment of reason and restraint. Not merely therefore should an anarchist be a man of reason; he should also combine with his own reason a wholly unreasonable belief that all others are equally reasonable. It is Godwin's distinction that, more successfully than any other, he came within sight of accomplishing this nice balancing feat.

The next stage brings us to the group of writers among whom (in the foolish metaphor) we must look for the father (or the fathers) of socialism. They represent what Marx later called in derision the 'Utopian Socialists'; they have also, again with a touch of contempt, been classed as 'associationists.' They were Utopian because, in the main, this initial phase of socialism represented a naive belief (as it appeared to Marx) that a better world could be engineered by men of good will doing something, by action from above, in the form of an Act of Parliament, the promulgation of a Royal Decree, or the philanthropy of a well-disposed capitalist. They were associationists because (again, in the main) they looked for the realisation of socialism through the formation of groups or associations of people, living on socialist lines within this present tainted world, yet in the course of time gradually leavening the lump.

The representatives of this phase of socialism provide an odd assortment of interesting types, distinguished by a high degree of eccentricity, if not of something more, though in some cases with very doubtful claims to be regarded as socialists at all. Saint-Simon (1760–1825), a turbulent, tumultuous, restless, forward-looking mind, was in himself rather a prophet of big business, of the totalitarian State and of the virtue of leadership; but his followers, the Saint-Simonian school, gave his doctrine a slight modification which had far-reaching effects in making Saint-Simonism a profound socialist influence. Charles Fourier (1772–1837) is likewise a father of socialism in whom the old Adam of individualism dies hard; for he loved property, and he loved inequality and he loved most of the things that a socialist ought not to love. But he let his terrible imagination loose in criticising this poor civilisation of ours, and in his own unbalanced way he preached the gospel of co-operation as a way of escape. Saint-Simon and Fourier have high claims to be regarded as the most interesting and piquant figures in the history of socialism: it is a matter of regret that those who are unquestionably immeasurably more important should also be immeasurably duller.

The third of this group is Robert Owen (1771–1858), who, after being a successful man of business, devoted his fortune to the furtherance of experiments in the establishment of communistic settlements and to much communistic and miscellaneous propaganda. His life, after he ceased to make money as the model employer, may appear to the superficial eye as a series of frustrations; yet his influence is everywhere in the labour movement of the nineteenth century. Lastly there is Louis Blanc (1813–1882), who, though unquestionably an associationist in virtue of his plan of co-operative associations, yet in many ways belongs to a somewhat later era because of his frank acceptance of the existing State as the appropriate machine for bringing the new world into existence. To each of these representatives of the Utopian or associationist stage a chapter is devoted (Chapters 6–9).

Chapter 10 brings us to Proudhon (1809–1865), a writer who refuses to be classified and who, superficially viewed, appears as a mass of contradictions. He was indeed a lone fighter who railed against everyone and anyone whose views he did not at the moment share. As he rather prided himself on arguing on both sides of every question, a consistent body of doctrine can hardly be expected from Proudhon, who, in the admirable phrase of Emile Faguet, 'ne comprenait pas tout à la fois, mais qui, successivement, comprenait admirablement chaque chose.'[1] But if Proudhon *must* be 'placed' for the purposes of this plan, he is best regarded as a continuator of the anarchist tradition, a kind of link between Godwin and Bakunin later, carrying on the same Holy War against all authority and against all authoritarian forms of socialism.

The next stage should bring us to the centre of things and to 'scientific socialism.' On the way to Marx, however, it is well for us in this country to recall a remarkable group of early English socialists—forgotten and rediscovered—who anticipated the Marxian way of thinking, and at times indeed Marxian phraseology, especially with regard to exploitation. So far as mere chronology goes, these writers (Hall: 1740–1820; Thompson: 1785–1833; Hodgskin: 1783–1869; Bray: ?–?; Gray: 1799–?1850) are, at least in their fruitful period, more nearly contemporary with Saint-Simon and Fourier, but spiritually they are on the threshold of Marx. It has accordingly been thought advisable to ignore dates in this matter, and give some account of certain of the members of this remarkable English pre-Marxian group in Chapter 11, immediately before the discussion of Marx; and along with them has been included a brief reference to agrarian socialism in this country, as seen in Spence (1750–1814) and Ogilvie (1736–1819), who had at least this in common with Marxians everywhere, that they popularised the idea of 'theft.'

Having considered these English forerunners, we are free to turn to the main exposition of scientific socialism. The essence of scientific socialism, as distinguished from utopian socialism, is that it bases socialism on a philosophical view of history, usually, but not very happily, described as the 'Materialist Conception of History.' The urge forward in history comes, it is held, not from men's ideals, but from the conditions under which they earn their living. Men's ideals indeed are a result and not a cause; they represent a by-product of their material conditions. Moreover, the Materialist Conception of History finds its expression in an everlasting class-struggle, where exploiters defraud the exploited, and in which one struggle is resolved, merely to give place to another. In the future, however, with the expropriation of the expropriators, there will be inaugurated a condition of affairs, called the 'dictatorship of the proletariat,' leading ultimately to a classless society. Thus, in its classic form as presented by Marx (1818–1883), scientific socialism comprises at least a philosophy of history, embodying the class-struggle; a theory of exploitation, based on presumed economic reasoning, and a vision of the dictatorship of the proletariat. In the enunciation of scientific socialism, Marx was united in indissoluble partnership with Engels (1820–1895), and they are considered together here. Although the Marx-Engels combination is almost sufficiently representative of scientific

[1] Faguet: *Le Socialisme en 1907*, p. 202.

socialism, there are two others who ranked more highly two generations ago than they do to-day, and who even now ought not to be ignored. These are, firstly, Rodbertus (1805–1875), who thought like a philosopher and who lived aloof like a philosopher ; and secondly, Lassalle (1825–1864), who, not without demagogic qualities, largely created the German working-class movement, and who exercised a greater immediate influence than Marx. Marx and Engels, with addenda on Lassalle and Rodbertus, are discussed in Chapter 12.

The post-Marxian development of socialism has been entirely conditioned by Marx. There has been nothing that cannot be interpreted, either as a reaction against Marx, a ' revision ' of Marx, or a return to what is presumed to be the essential core, the pure gold, of Marx. These stages and schools may be briefly indicated. We have already noted the anarchism of Godwin and Proudhon. A large part of Marx's life, especially in connection with the First International, was devoted to the feud with the anarchists, and indeed the First International shipwrecked because of the incompatibility of the authoritarian tendencies of Marxism and the anarchism of Bakunin. Chapter 13 is devoted to some of the representatives of the anarchist tradition, Bakunin (1814–1876), Kropotkin (1842–1921) and Bertrand Russell.

Inside the professedly socialist party, the chief reaction against Marx is found in the Revisionist movement, of which the chief representative was Bernstein (1850–1932). Some such Revisionist movement was natural and probably inevitable. Marxism had comprised a considerable mass of prophecy, which somehow was not being too obviously fulfilled. The worker was not becoming more miserable ; the middle class was not being squeezed out ; to the unaided eye, which did not see by faith, the promised revolution was perhaps even rapidly advancing backwards. Even if Marx were right in his prophecies—it was whispered—was it not possible that he might have been mistaken in the time that would be required for their fulfilment ? And if so . . . ? What should be done meanwhile ? The end-result of Revisionism was thus to eliminate the revolutionary aspect of Marxism and turn it into a gospel of Reform : evolutionary socialism took the place of revolutionary socialism. Substantially the same point of view, without however being due to a reaction against Marx, was represented by the Fabians in this country. Chapter 14 deals with the Fabians and their continental counterpart, the Revisionists.

The next significant movement is that of Syndicalism, and this provides the subject of Chapter 15. Syndicalism was pre-eminently a French and Italian manifestation. It is perhaps best viewed as a protest against Revisionism and the moderating influence of the Second International. Socialism, having become reformist, had also become respectable and middle-class ; the fighting spirit had gone out of it; it was being infected by corroding, bourgeois influences. Inevitably also, being reformist, it had truckled to the State. Syndicalism is thus a call to return to the essence of Marx, which is to be found in the class struggle; it represents a determination to make socialism once again exclusively a working-class movement, looking for and finding the working classes in the trade unions. With this is combined a strong infusion of influences deriving from anarchist sources, making Syndicalism hostile not merely to the existing State but to any State. In short, Syndicalism seeks to revive the purity of Marxism, but in Marxism it sees primarily, if not exclusively, the class struggle, which it embodies in the vision of the General Strike.

Guild Socialism, which occupies Chapter 16, is best viewed as the Anglo-Saxon equivalent of Syndicalism. While in no way falling behind the Syndicalists in violence of language, the Guild Socialists were somewhat less extreme, to this extent at least, that in their reconstruction of things a place was still left for some sort of a rump of a State to represent consumers. On the side of production, the world, was, however, to be refashioned on the basis of trade unions remodelled as Guilds.

Finally, in Chapter 17 we come to Lenin (1870–1924). Leninism has this in common with Syndicalism, that it professes to be a return to the purity of Marx; but again it is difficult to resist the impression that the Marx to whom we are invited to return is a somewhat one-sided Marx. Lenin, in fact, is almost exclusively interested in revolution. The aspect of Marx and Engels on which he concentrates is accordingly that which is concerned with the technique of revolution, and above all with the significance of the Dictatorship of the Proletariat. For Lenin, Marxism means the theory of the Dictatorship of the Proletariat, and of the process whereby, after the establishment of this dictatorship, the State will begin to wither away.

In a concluding section (Chapter 18) some consideration is given to certain general questions relating to the nature of socialism and the position of socialism to-day and to-morrow.

Such is the programme, and such are the representatives, or schools, chosen to reveal the development of socialist thought. Mindful of the high injunction of St. Thomas Aquinas in these matters, it may be as well to ask whether there are any glaring defects or omissions in what is here offered to the public. Realising that round any great name are clustered whole galaxies of other writers both before and after, bearing in mind that seldom have two socialists, even of the same school, entirely agreed, it is clear that in any finite volume, whole cohorts of authors must be treated as though they had not been.

It may, however, be permissible to indicate three non-existent 'infra-marginal' chapters, the inclusion of which might have been in some ways advantageous in completing the picture. Firstly, there is much so-called 'mediaeval socialism,' which is humanly interesting if not economically very instructive. The early writers, Sudre and Thonissen,[1] who held 'le socialisme' and 'le communisme' in undisguised horror, thought it incumbent on them to give a somewhat lengthy account of the Anabaptists and of the debaucheries of Münster, as a horrible warning of the awful consequences that follow from any trafficking with the accursed thing. But indeed the history of the Anabaptists and the fantastic life of John of Leyden, while admirably providing ample material for a crowded historical film, are of doubtful significance in the history of socialism. No doubt, the mediaeval outlook on economic questions is of absorbing interest; and that not merely from the point of view of a history of socialism. Otherwise, however, most of 'mediaeval socialism,' on its more dramatic and picturesque side, is rather a psychological and pathological study in the aberrations that follow certain types of religious mania.

The second infra-marginal chapter might have been devoted to the task of disentangling and defining the many strands of nineteenth-century French socialism. France has been particularly prolific of writers whose names stand for a system of socialism somewhat different from those offered by rival and competing socialists, each with just a little of something the others haven't got. Leroux, Buchez, Pecqueur—and for that matter, Cabet—may be cited from the beginnings of socialism, merely to indicate the nature of the labyrinth. If this challenge has been declined, it is because the questions involved, though doubtless of considerable interest to the French student, are hardly of pressing importance to us in this country. We are not sensibly inconvenienced by an ignorance of Blanqui, even though a 'Blanquist' is a recurrent term of abuse in the writings of Lenin.

The third unwritten chapter comes nearer home. In the great literature of the Victorian era there are a number of writers who reveal something which, if not socialism, is a kind of socialist simmering. A later age has, by a kind of natural reaction, tended to find in the Victorian a figure inviting satire; yet it is well to be fair, even to the Victorians. They had their ideals. Now there is nothing greatly wrong with idealism, so long as high ideals are not advanced in extenuation of low practice. What has brought 'idealism,' in this sense, into disrepute, so that no one under the age of sixty so much as uses the word without blushing, is the gap not infrequently observed between profession and attainment, which somehow seems to import into idealism an element of what crude people call hypocrisy. The best Victorians aimed high; they took themselves seriously. They were

[1] Sudre: *Histoire du Communisme*, 1848; Thonissen: *Le Socialisme dans le passé* and *Le Socialisme et ses Promesses*, 1850. Though necessarily antiquated in their outlook, and although violently hostile to socialism, these two books are still pre-eminently worth reading. The authors had at least conscientiously read the authors whom they criticised.

extremely anxious to do that which is right; they were intent on putting an end to evil.[1] Perhaps, as their grandchildren tend to suggest, they may have been somewhat discriminating in the selection of the evils to which they were sensitive: no generation understands its immediate predecessors. For our purpose it is significant that the Victorian idealism produced a kind of literary socialism, or at least a revolt against the ugliness of industrialism, the selfishness of individualism, the general depravity of 'Manchesterthum'—to borrow a libellous word from the Continent. Hence the socialism (or is it sometimes fascism?) of Carlyle, Ruskin, Kingsley and others. But indeed, though a chapter on the quasi-socialist utterances of some of the great literary Victorians ought to be of interest, it is doubtful whether it would be in place here. Apart from Morris (though Morris is not quite in this company) this 'literary socialism' exercised little or no influence on the general development of socialism, except in so far as it disposed public opinion to a readier acceptance of more virile forms of socialism—or, in the case of Carlyle, may have helped to sow the seeds of fascism.

On their claims, therefore, the three infra-marginal chapters are better left as infra-marginal. But there is a more compelling reason. It may be that poets sing because they must, and pipe but as the linnets sing; but other books are written in the hope that some one will read them, or selected portions of them. Apart from novels, where there is apparently no upper limit, it is to-day distressingly true that no quality so inexorably condemns a book to be classified among the unreadable and the unread as does excessive length. Probably, without John of Leyden and Pecqueur and Ruskin, this volume has already approached that undefined amplitude beyond which even an author's most tactful daughter-in-law will obdurately refuse to have dealings with it.

[1] It may be permissible to recall the words of an eminent, if somewhat fastidious, Victorian regarding his own generation: 'We show, as a nation, laudable energy and persistence in walking according to the best light we have, but are not quite careful enough, perhaps, to see that our light be not darkness' (Matthew Arnold, in *Culture and Anarchy*).

CHAPTER I

THE GREEK TRADITION

At what point a history of socialism should begin is a question which might give occasion to high argument. There are some who hold that we merely becloud our judgment if we allow ourselves to speak of socialism before the middle of the eighteenth century, or perhaps even somewhat later. On this view socialism is essentially a manifestation of the proletarian spirit; or, if socialism is not necessarily proletarian in character and origin, it at least postulates a society which tends to be comprehensive in its membership. Accordingly, it is suggested that a society which assumes for its efficient working the existence of a slave population, denied all rights, may at times speak a language suggestive of socialism, but it can know nothing of socialism as that word has been understood in the nineteenth and twentieth centuries. The existence of a serf or slave population may in certain respects add a complication to life; but in other directions it quite obviously enormously simplifies the social and political problems of existence, as these are presented to that section of the population who are not slaves. On this view, a history of socialism should probably begin among these first ripples and disturbances which presaged the deluge of the French Revolution.

As against this view, which looks on socialism as something which cannot be dissociated from the social and political conditions of the last century and a half, there are some who carry their excavations for the roots of socialism not merely to ancient Greece, but to ancient China and to the early days of the children of Israel, and who accord a place in the socialist temple to Moses, in virtue of certain provisions in the Mosaic Law; and to Isaiah, in virtue of his poetic sensitiveness to the wrongs of this world.

If we are strict, it is probably to the former of these views that we should incline. We shall see presently how futile to our present-day mind is the justice and the equality of a State which attains these elevated aims by building on the slavery and oppression of the overwhelming majority of the population. Yet it does not follow that the history of socialism can exclude all that happened before the eighteenth century. Lycurgus and the polity of Sparta may in fact have little to teach us. The community of life which Minos introduced into Crete may have no point of contact with our modern needs. Plato, to ascend to higher names, may have dreamed a dream which would be but a nightmare to-day, if any attempt were made to realise it. Yet throughout the ages, somewhat surprisingly, the limitations imposed by the assumptions of Sparta and Athens have been overlooked. Plato and Lycurgus, to mention no others, have been permanent influences in moulding communist theory. This is particularly true of Plato, though at times (as in Mably) Lycurgus runs him hard. It would be an unpardonable exaggeration to say that all communism and egalitarianism derive from Plato ; but on the more visionary and utopian side, he is everywhere. Like the fabled tree of the nursery, his evergreen branches have given support and shelter to all manner of strange birds, great and small :

> Tous les oiseaux du monde vont y faire leurs nids.

Even if the ' socialism ' of antiquity has, in its own right, no claim to be considered as an integral element in a history of socialism, its representatives demand attention as inspirers of socialism in others in much later centuries.

This subsequent appeal to Greece, as the presumed holder of the original title-deeds of socialism, has been made on two grounds. On the one hand, Greece, in its highly variegated political life, is presumed to have given examples of the actual functioning of the communistic way of life. Here, of course, it is pre-eminently Sparta that has fascinated later ages ; though Crete also enters into the picture—and to a much lesser extent, Lipara. On the other hand, Greece has supplied the theory and the vision of Communism. On this side, needless to say, it is Plato, in *The Republic* and *The Laws*, who in himself very largely constitutes the legacy of Greece. Before approaching Plato, the begetter of much socialism which he would have disowned, it may be advisable to glance, even if hastily, at Greek communism in practice.

According to tradition, Sparta was the handiwork of Lycurgus ; but what may any one profitably or usefully say regarding this obscure personality, of whom even Plutarch says that there is nothing concerning him that is not the subject of dispute ? This original lawgiver, on whose persuasive powers the socialist laws of Sparta rested, is indeed a shadowy figure—a kind of cross between Moses and King Arthur. If we accept Plutarch's account, Lycurgus was oppressed by the glaring contrast between riches and poverty, the vast number of poor and landless on the one hand, and, on the other, the concentration of wealth in the hands of a few individuals—almost a Marxian vision. And so—although surely external circumstances must have reinforced his arguments—he persuaded the Spartans to agree to a new distribution of lands on a basis of equality, and by other measures he weaned them from the love of silver and gold, and led them to adopt that harsh simplicity of life which the very name of Sparta has come to connote. Plutarch's description is of interest because, waiving the question of its historical accuracy, it gives a very adequate definition of the ideal communistic state, as ideally imagined by countless later generations. In general, he says,

> he trained his fellow-citizens to have neither the wish nor the ability to live for themselves; but like bees they were to make themselves always integral parts of the whole community, clustering together about their leader, almost beside themselves with enthusiasm and noble ambition, and to belong wholly to their country.[1]

Thus Plutarch, of the influence of a man who is after all but the shadow of a shade, and who, it may be, was more or less imagined in order that his influence might explain what was.

Whether or not Lycurgus succeeded in abolishing 'all the mass of pride, envy, crime and luxury' which flowed from the previous state of inequality—indeed, whether or not Lycurgus ever existed—Sparta, with her remarkable system of government and institutions, certainly did exist, and these are in a way something of a portent. The symmetry of her constitution, her clear consciousness of the end for which, in Sparta at least, the State existed, the rigorous discipline imposed on the individual with a view to the realisation of these ends, have, taken together, provoked the eulogies of many simple-minded enthusiasts. The beauty and the stability of Sparta became, to take but one example, something of an obsession with the ineffective Mably. On the other hand, Sir Frederick Pollock has suggested—and one's heart warms to him—that the Spartans were the most odious impostors in the whole history of antiquity. In any event, the Spartan State was probably unique in some respects in the record of political institutions. It is difficult to recall any other State in which the individual was so completely subordinated to the general ends of the community—and such subordination is, of course, of the very essence of socialism in its general sense, as distinguished from that species of socialism generally referred to as communism. From the day of his birth, when he might be not merely subordinated but suppressed for the good of the State, the young Spartan continued to be disposed of in one way or another until death opened up for him a way of escape. The common education, which began at the age of seven, was wholly designed to make good soldiers, to teach men to suffer uncomplainingly the extremes of heat and of cold, of hunger and of pain, and in each was implanted the conviction that he belonged not to himself, but to the State.

With this must be taken another fact no less significant, common indeed to all Greek civilisation, although perhaps specially important in Sparta. When we speak of Sparta, we are not concerned with a homogeneous population. The problem is complicated, as always,

[1] *Life of Lycurgus*, Section xxv (Loeb edition, vol. 1, p. 283).

by one form of the slave question. The Spartan State could continue to exist only so long as the Helots were kept under. Thus the Spartans had to consider not merely their enemies beyond their frontier: they also lived as a governing class amid enemies, vastly more numerous, always sullen, constantly menacing. This is the ultimate explanation of the socialistic aspect of the Spartan State. Pöhlmann has a pregnant saying, written long before 1914, and therefore free from any suggestion that it springs from the misfortunes of the last two generations, to the effect that 'state socialism is the inevitable correlate of the war-like type of society.'[1] Mr. Hawtrey, in our own day, has explained how Collectivism 'emerges as the logical outcome of militarism when pushed to the extreme limit.'[2] A State that is at war, or that is perpetually organised for war, dare not tolerate individual liberties which may be in conflict with the general interest; and if the crisis becomes acute, so that the very existence of the State is in danger, there always has been, and there always will be, a tendency to sacrifice the individual; and this means one or other of two things, either despotism or State socialism.

This then explains much in Sparta. She was perpetually organised for war; inevitably she was organised to subordinate the individual in the interests of military efficiency. This also, it is probable, discloses the significance of the common meals, so striking a feature of the civil life both of Sparta and of Crete. It has been suggested that these common meals, so familiar in More and Campanella, may here be viewed as the last remnants of an older and more primitive agricultural communism. Clearly, this is largely a matter of speculation; but the argument is that if, far back at the beginning of things, there was a time when men worked together on land held in common, they would naturally eat in common also. Diodorus of Sicily, speaking of Lipara (in Book V), says that the people there 'enjoyed their estates in common and fed together in societies,' as if the two were bound together as cause and effect. But indeed no such speculative explanation is necessary. The common meals were merely another consequence of the fact that Sparta was wholly and exclusively organised as a military State, which, even in peacetime and at home, maintained as a symbol and as a discipline the habits of a campaigning army in taking meals together under arms.

In summary, what does the communism of Sparta amount to? There is not, it must be confessed, much to support the moral which it has usually been asked to supply. Despite the original equal division of the soil, differences in material conditions were not excluded; and contact with the larger world in time undermined the more characteristic Spartan virtues, if indeed they were virtues. For the modern

[1] Pöhlmann: *Geschichte des antiken Kommunismus und Sozialismus*, vol. 1, p. 64.
[2] Hawtrey: *Economic Destiny*, p. 187.

communist in search of ensamples there are, on wider grounds, grave stumbling blocks. In the first place, the Spartan State was not so much a State as a military machine. Its sole interest was in training men to suffer and endure, and it pursued this by methods which stand unique in their revolting barbarity. They may have attained equality and community in education, but not much is thereby gained if education is directed to an unholy end. And secondly, to revert to a point which cannot be over-emphasised, if only because the worshippers of Sparta have so frequently forgotten it, there is the horrible obverse of Spartan communism presented by the hunted and harried Helot. It is not merely that communism in Sparta was a communism in use, others having produced. It was a communism of an idle and boastful people, whose government and whose existence demanded an army of Helots, who suffered at their hands a ruthless tyranny without parallel in history. It has too often been forgotten that the Helots also were men. Mably, in his intoxicated enthusiasm for Lycurgus and all his works, does not seem to have thought of this aspect of the question. It would be a fitting Nemesis, if in some reincarnation he were sent to live—as a Helot—in his so greatly adored Sparta.

The case of Crete is not so dissimilar from that of Sparta, despite the efforts of Polybius to show that they had little or nothing in common. The part of Lycurgus is here played by Minos, ' le plus sage et le meilleur de tous les rois '—if we are to believe the undiscriminating Fénelon. The tradition indeed is that Lycurgus learned his statecraft in visiting and studying Crete. Here also there was the same determination that the young ' should grow up accustomed to arms and toils, so as to scorn heat, cold, marches over rugged and steep roads, and blows received in gymnasiums or regular battles.'[1] Here also was the institution of the common dining-table ; but again the communism, such as it was, was a communism bought at a price ; it was the communism of an idle aristocracy, attained at the expense of the many, resting on the ' exploitation of man by man,' to use nineteenth century phraseology. Probably neither the fact nor the phrase would have impressed the Cretans ; nevertheless this consideration, in one form or another, ought to have been sufficiently in the minds of later generations from Fénelon onwards, to have acted as a damper on any yearning to follow too unquestioningly in the footsteps of Minos. It is interesting to recall that in 1793, when Hérault de Séchelles was called upon to produce ' by Monday ' a draft constitution, his first and instinctive step was to call upon all the available librarians to get for him ' sur-le-champ ' a copy of the Laws of Minos.[2] It is a striking example of the abiding influence of the legacy of Greece. Whether in consequence of the insidious influence of the Laws of Minos or by reason of the mysterious

[1] Strabo : Book 10, Section 4.
[2] Cited by Thonissen : *Le Socialisme dans le Passé*, p. 16.

workings of original sin, the ancient Cretans seem to have enjoyed a particularly low reputation among their fellows. The Apostle Paul has most successfully made it a matter of universal knowledge that they were accounted liars, evil beasts, slow bellies. Polybius, in less picturesque language, has said that they were 'the only people in the world in whose eyes no gain is disgraceful'[1]—an odd characteristic in those who are usually cited as having made an obeisance to a communistic way of life.

A third example of the practice of communism, that which for a time existed at Lipara, is in itself vastly less important, but it is of interest inasmuch as the account which has been handed down is more explicit as to the motives prompting to a life in common. The chief source of information on this point is to be found in the fifth book of Diodorus of Sicily, which competent authorities consider may be accepted as substantially correct. He tells us how, somewhere in the sixth century B.C., a number of colonists, under the leadership of Pentathlus, left Cnidus and Rhodes and ultimately settled in the island of Lipara, where they 'received a kindly reception,' and 'were prevailed upon to make common cause with the inhabitants of Lipara in forming a single community there.' The actual description given by Diodorus of what happened is of some importance in disclosing the springs of primitive communism:

> At a later time, because they were being harassed by the Tyrrheni, who were carrying on piracy on the sea, they fitted out a fleet, and divided themselves into two bodies, one of which took over the cultivation of the islands which they had made the common property of the community, whereas the other was to fight the pirates; their possessions also they made common property, and living according to the public mess system, they passed their lives in this communistic fashion for some time. At a later time they apportioned among themselves the island of Lipara, where their city also lay, but cultivated the other islands in common. And in the final stage they divided all the islands among themselves for a period of twenty years, and then they cast lots for them again at every expiration of this period.[2]

The words of Diodorus are particularly interesting, both as explaining the reason for, and the extent of, this communistic experiment. It is clear that communism was not something that the colonists brought with them in their blood, an inheritance from their past life. It was only *at a later time*, when circumstances compelled them to prepare a fleet for their defence, that the step to communism was taken; and in the course of time this was again departed from. In the first place, the main island was divided into private property; later, all the islands were divided, subject to a redistribution every twenty years. But the important point is that the impulse to communism came from the necessity of constant military readiness against an external enemy.

[1] Polybius: Book VI, 46.
[2] Diodorus Siculus, Book V, Chap. 9 (Loeb edition, vol. 3, p. 123).

Nowhere is perpetual preparedness so necessary as against an enemy who comes from over the sea, and the explanation of the system of communism in Lipara is very briefly that the inhabitants, in face of this ever-present danger, were driven to a systematic division of the work of the community among the whole population. Some manned the fleet; some tilled the ground. It is merely a further exemplification of the influence of war conditions in moulding the structure of society in a 'socialistic' direction.

It is, however, time to turn from these tentative approximations towards communistic practice, in order to consider very briefly certain theories propounded elsewhere in these matters. Here it is, of course, primarily Plato—indeed, almost exclusively Plato—who demands attention. In approaching Plato and the place which he occupies in the development of socialism and as an inspiration of socialism, we are confronted with a very obvious difficulty. There is an immensity of Plato, as there is an immensity of Shakespeare and of Adam Smith, and to seek to detach a fragment of this immensity is probably a course that would be frowned upon by austere scholars. In short, the communism advocated by Plato, such as it was and limited as it may have been, is but a part of his general theory regarding the State, and doubtless it should be discussed in connection with the main body of his political theories. A chapter on the 'Politics' of Plato has, however, its proper resting-place in a book with a somewhat different title-page from that which this volume bears. Here, though it may be a difficult and not wholly satisfactory course, we must endeavour to walk gingerly through the Platonic forest, choosing the path which will best disclose his views on the topics which are relevant to our purpose.

But at least the framework may be indicated. The liberalism of Pericles had aimed at the many-sided development of the Athenian citizen. With progressive democratisation, there had emerged an unrestrained individualism. The sophists, on the theoretical side, had represented a disintegrating influence, teaching, among other things, that justice was the interest of the stronger, that it was merely that which was ordained by law, that each man was the measure of all things. All this tended to the subjectivism of philosophical anarchism. Nor were things any better on the side of the practical administration of affairs. As Plato (or Socrates) saw things, the State suffered from two main defects. In the first place, it suffered from disruptive tendencies. There was strife; there was envy; there was division. And secondly, it suffered from the democratic assumption (pushed to its absurd extreme in election by lot) that all men were equal, and that anyone could do anything as well as anyone else.

Such were the maladies from which Plato's world suffered, and his suggested remedies corresponded to the diagnosis. To cure disruption, unity must be implanted at the centre of things ; the State (or that part of it which matters) must become One, with all causes of dissension removed. To cure the cult of incompetence, inherent in Democracy, it must be made abundantly clear that government is a matter for the expert ; and indeed, not merely in the field of government, but everywhere, people must stick to their job, and not interfere with others. The world and all its affairs must be run by experts. It is primarily with the first of these points—the lack of union and the cure for disunion—that we are here concerned.

Plato's own statement of the overriding importance of the general principle of unity is almost as important as the machinery for its realisation. A short extract from the fifth book of *The Republic* may be given. Socrates is speaking, Glaucon supplying the responses.

> Can there be any greater evil than discord and distraction and plurality where unity ought to reign ? or any greater good than the bond of unity ?
>
> There cannot.
>
> And there is unity where there is community of pleasures and pains—where all the citizens are glad or grieved on the same occasions of joy and sorrow ?
>
> No doubt.
>
> Yes ; and where there is no common but only private feeling a State is disorganised—when you have one half of the world triumphing and the other plunged in grief at the same events happening to the city or the citizens ?
>
> Certainly.
>
> Such differences commonly originate in a disagreement about the use of the terms ' mine ' and ' not mine," ' his ' and ' not his.'
>
> Exactly so.
>
> And is not that the best-ordered State in which the greatest number of persons apply the terms ' mine ' and ' not mine ' in the same way to the same thing ?
>
> Quite true . . .
>
> . . . and I agree with you that in the best-ordered State there is the nearest approach to this common feeling which you describe.
>
> Then when any of the citizens experiences any good or evil, the whole State will make his case their own, and will either rejoice or sorrow with him ?
>
> Yes, he said, that is what will happen in a well-ordered State.[1]

Such is the programme in its general terms : we must eliminate (in places where it matters) the distinction between ' meum ' and ' tuum.' The first person singular in all its forms—I, me, my and mine—must be excoriated. Property therefore must go ; for it is the obvious embodiment of ' mine ' and ' not mine ' ; but no less logically, though more courageously, the home and the family must also go, for in the family are the springs of all individualism. There must be community of possessions and community of wives. No one must know his offspring, just as no one must know his father or his mother. A generation will beget a generation.

[1] Plato : *The Republic*, Book V, 462 (Jowett's edition, vol. 3, p. 156).

This, however, is rather a summary statement, in general terms, of the vision to which Plato tends. To appreciate the motives of Platonic communism and the limitations by which it is hedged, we must go back and assist in the construction of the city, observing at what point and with what objects the condition of communism is imposed. The State, as Socrates unfolds it, springs from the needs of mankind: in the language of a later age, it is based on division of labour. 'The barest notion of a State must include four or five men' [1]; and in its first stages there is a husbandman, a builder, a weaver and a shoemaker. It sounds like an echo of that other fragment of oriental wisdom that the chief thing for life is water and bread and clothing and a house to cover shame. But obviously, beyond this primitive embryo of four essential workers, the State must expand, and it does so with the suggestion of a possible stopping-place where all the natural and simple needs of mankind are satisfied. If we pass beyond this 'healthy State,' the addition to the population and the list of occupations will be represented by luxury trades. Also in such a world of clutching States, countries which 'exceed the limit of necessity, and give themselves up to the unlimited accumulation of wealth' [2] will each covet a slice of their neighbour's land, and wars will become inevitable. Thus, faced with the necessity of defence, we encounter the guardians.

In the Platonic State, the guardians, who are later sub-divided into 'guardians in the fullest sense' (the rulers) and 'auxiliaries' (the soldiers) occupy a place of very considerable importance. Inevitably, for the discharge of their duties a peculiar combination of qualities is required. The guardian must unite in himself philosophy and spirit, and swiftness and strength: he is to be spirited towards those without and gentle towards those within, and he must be educated and trained with those objects in view. Education indeed is one of the chief instruments for fashioning the right guardian, and accordingly *The Republic* resolves itself, over long stretches, into a treatise on education. Yet education alone, even if it is shaped on the somewhat peculiar lines laid down by Plato, is not sufficient to produce the perfect guardian. There remains a danger. May not the guardians, being stronger than the citizens, become a menace? May they not become savage tyrants instead of friends and allies? May not the watch-dog worry the sheep instead of the wolf? The solution of this difficulty is found in the institution of communism. That the guardians may not be thus corrupted they must be a class apart, consecrated to high and noble ends; they must be in the world but not of it; they must not be as other men, entangled in secular affairs. Hence not only their education, but their habitations and their whole environment should be such as will not impair their virtue as guardians, nor tempt them to prey upon the other citizens. It is so important that Plato should

[1] *Republic*, Book II, 369. [2] Book II, 373.

not be misrepresented on this fundamental issue, that the actual words used in instituting communism should be quoted.

Then now let us consider what will be their way of life, if they are to realize our idea of them. In the first place, none of them should have any property of his own beyond what is absolutely necessary; neither should they have a private house or store closed against any one who has a mind to enter; their provisions should be only such as are required by trained warriors, who are men of temperance and courage; they should agree to receive from the citizens a fixed rate of pay, enough to meet the expenses of the year and no more; and they will go to mess and live together like soldiers in a camp. Gold and silver we will tell them that they have from God; the diviner metal is within them, and they have therefore no need of the dross which is current among men, and ought not to pollute the divine by any such earthly admixture; for that commoner metal has been the source of many unholy deeds, but their own is undefiled. And they alone of all the citizens may not touch or handle silver or gold, or be under the same roof with them, or wear them, or drink from them. And this will be their salvation, and they will be the saviours of the State. But should they ever acquire homes or lands or moneys of their own, they will become housekeepers and husbandmen instead of guardians, enemies and tyrants instead of allies of the other citizens; hating and being hated, plotted and being plotted against, they will pass their whole life in much greater terror of internal than of external enemies, and the hour of ruin, both to themselves and to the rest of the State, will be at hand.[1]

This is indeed a strange communism! The guardians, using the phrase in the wider sense to include the auxiliaries, are, in a phrase beloved of the Physiocrats, a *classe stipendiée*. They are supported by the third estate, and although it is said that they are to receive a fixed rate of pay, it is clear in fact that all they get is sufficient to provide for the common table. Indeed it is perhaps inaccurate to describe this as a system of communism at all; for of possessions, singly or collectively, they have none. It is made clear at the beginning of the next book that 'they are only fed, and not paid in addition to their food, like other men.'[2] In short, they are boarded out, and no pocket-money is allowed. This, if it be a type of communism, is a communism of poverty and of asceticism, of abnegation and renunciation. It represents an economic disability, not a privilege—a badge of poverty, imposed as a condition of efficiency. The motive is thus poles asunder from that which inspires communism in any of its modern forms from Thomas More downwards. Others have preached communism, tormented by the frightful inequality of the rich and the poor; they have been haunted by the enormity that, as Rousseau puts it, a handful of people are stuffed with superfluities, while the famished multitude lacks what is necessary. Here then Plato stands completely apart from the main stream of communistic thought; and in its way it is somewhat curious, for the other aspect of the question was not absent from his mind. He realised, in a frequently quoted sentence,

[1] *Republic*, Book III, 416–417 (Jowett, vol. 3, p. 106). [2] Book IV, 420.

the danger that the city might be not one but two, a city of the rich and a city of the poor. Yet in his advocacy of communism, there is no hint of this; communism is instituted solely in order that those to whom it applies may escape the entanglements of this world.

The second point of interest that arises is concerned with the extent to which the system of communism is to be applied throughout the Platonic State. A straightforward perusal of the passage from the close of the third book cited above would certainly leave with any reader, not given to over-ingenious sophistication, the impression that the system of communism is limited to the relatively small class of the guardians and the auxiliaries, and that it is not intended to be applied to the much more numerous third estate, whom for convenience we may call the husbandmen. Certain it is that in *The Republic*, when once Plato has mentioned the husbandmen, they fade from the picture with an astonishing celerity and completeness: it is the education and the way of life of the two higher ranks that alone have power to engage his attention. Consequently it has been generally assumed that communism is advocated only for the soldiers and officials, and that the workers are left to an unregenerated family life, and to the burden and care of wife and children. This view, however, has not been universally accepted. Thus Mr. Beer, in his *Social Struggles in Antiquity*, observed:

> A superficial reading of the *Republic* gives the impression—which is, in fact, shared by many writers—that Plato recommends communism solely for these upper sections, and leaves the remaining class of the people in the old conditions. This interpretation, however, is wholly erroneous. From the quotations we have given above it is quite clear that Plato advocated communism for all Hellenes. Otherwise, there would be no point in the entire social criticism which he levels, in both his works, against the economic, political and moral conditions of his country.[1]

Aristotle is, of course, one of the more eminent of those superficial readers of *The Republic*, and he promptly seized on the point that 'the main body of the State consists not in the guardians but in the mass of other citizens, about whom nothing is determined.'[2] He complained that Plato had not made it clear whether the system of communism was to extend to husbandmen as well as to guardians. If yes, how would the classes differ? If no, there would in fact be two States within the State. Among our modern authorities on Plato, Sir Ernest Barker, rivalling Aristotle in his superficiality, roundly states that 'neither the communism in respect of goods, nor that in respect of wives, which are both advocated by Plato, touch the third or economic class. How indeed could a system which means the abnegation of desire touch the class which represents the element of desire?'[3]

[1] Beer: *Social Struggles in Antiquity*, p. 97.
[2] Aristotle: *Politics*, Book II, Chap. v.
[3] Barker: *Political Thought of Plato and Aristotle*, p. 140.

The argument that Plato did not in his statement overlook the position of the husbandmen will be found heavily advanced in the course of Pöhlmann's two ponderous volumes.[1] Briefly, it is, in the first place, urged that the fact that Plato makes minute provision for the way of life of the husbandmen in *The Laws*, which is concerned with the second-best State, clearly proves that he cannot have intended to exclude them from the advantages of the best State. The second-best State cannot in fact be more enlightened than the best State. Secondly, and perhaps more cogently, it is contended that the omission of details as to the precise manner of the application of the fundamental principles to the whole population was deliberate, was indeed forced upon Plato by the scheme of his work, and that he foresaw Aristotle's arguments and met them in advance. In the fourth book, Socrates declines to go into a great many matters of detail on the ground that all these things are, comparatively speaking, 'trifles,' and that they will settle themselves, or at least be easily settled if the main thing, the education and the training of the governing class, is secured: 'If our citizens are well educated and grow into sensible men, they will easily see their way through all these, as well as other matters which I omit.' Then a little later he enumerates another host of questions, and asks impatiently: 'But, oh heavens! shall we condescend to legislate on any of these particulars?' and the echoing Adeimantus dutifully replies: 'I think that there is no need to impose laws about them on good men; what regulations are necessary they will find out soon enough for themselves.'[2] Thus the argument is that Plato was concerned with one thing and with one thing only, the training of the guardians and the rulers: it would be for them later to make provision for the regulations governing the population as a whole, by the issue of the appropriate Statutory Rules and Orders within the general framework. Meanwhile, like a discreet junior Government clerk, Plato refrained from expressing any opinion which might later embarrass his Ministers.

When two such eminent authorities as Aristotle and the late Professor of Ancient History in the University of Erlangen are ranged in opposite camps, it behoves the ordinary man to walk warily. Yet if Plato himself be allowed to speak—bearing in mind the legal assumption that words be taken to mean what apparently they do mean—the position as to the extent of this communism should be clear beyond any shadow of a peradventure. The institution is expressly said to be 'the regulations appointed by us for our guardians'; the guardians are to receive a fixed rate of pay *from the citizens*, which is clearly a system of life that cannot be universalised; most conclusive of all,

[1] Pöhlmann: *Geschichte des antiken Kommunismus und Sozialismus*, vol. 1, p. 295 *et seq.*

[2] *Republic*, Book IV, 423, 425.

if they depart from communism in any respect, they will become housekeepers and husbandmen instead of guardians. Moreover, if the motive of Platonic communism is borne in mind, it will be clear that there would be no justification for extending it to the husbandmen. It is possible to provide that one class shall not be too much spotted by contact with the world; but the whole population cannot be so treated. Indeed, apart from the exercise of academic ingenuity, it might have been thought that Plato had been at pains to make it abundantly clear that his communism was designed as the essential distinguishing mark of the two upper classes, marking them off from the third.

To complete the picture of Platonic communism, as presented in *The Republic*, a slight further reference should perhaps be made to the community of wives and children which is dealt with in Book V. It is not necessary here to consider the machinery of marriage, the system of lots, together with the 'considerable dose of falsehood and deceit' introduced with the highest eugenical ends, and all the rest of what may be called the administrative arrangements. Nor need we concern ourselves unduly with the regulations designed to obliterate in the mother all knowledge as to which of the next generation is in fact the fruit of her body, and the means by which what the mathematicians would call a 'one-one relationship' is to be expunged. But it is of some interest to note the object and intention of community of wives (and of husbands) in confirmation of what has already been said. Again the motive may be said to be twofold, blending together. In the first place, there is the (quite mistaken) idea that there will be greater unity if each regards the whole of the next generation as his children, and shares this fatherly feeling with all those of his own. Behold, how good and how pleasant it is for brethren to dwell together in unity; and what greater unity is possible than that prevailing among men of whom it can be said that 'every one whom they meet will be regarded by them either as a brother or sister, or father or mother, or son or daughter, or as the child or parent of those who are thus connected with him?'[1] This is on the point of becoming complicated, but the meaning is clear. There is much justice in the observation of Aristotle that, in a world where every one has a thousand sons, shared with a correspondingly large number of fathers, 'the result will be that all parents will be equally neglectful of all the children.'[2] Proudhon, thinking in terms of universal brotherhood, made the same point more epigrammatically. And mingled with this attainment of unity—or perhaps but another phase of this—is the promotion of greater efficiency: 'Both the community of property and the community of families, as I am saying, tend to make them more truly guardians; they will not tear the city in pieces by differing about "mine" and

[1] *Republic*, Book V, 463. [2] *Politics*, Book II, Chap. 3.

" not mine." ' The very poverty of their communism will make them efficient: 'As they have nothing but their persons which they can call their own, suits and complaints will have no existence among them; they will be delivered from all those quarrels of which money or children or relations are the occasion.' The guardians will be efficient as guardians, just because they will have the carefree existence of those who have no cares, who have rid themselves of the meannesses of life: 'all the pains and pangs which men experience in bringing up a family, and in finding money to buy necessaries for their household . . . the many evils of so many kinds which people suffer in this way are mean enough and obvious enough, and,' says the Greek philosopher, 'not worth speaking of.' [1]

Enough has perhaps been said to indicate the nature of the communism of *The Republic* and to show how unfitted it is to respond to many of the appeals directed to it by subsequent ages. In summary, it is a communism of monastic asceticism and renunciation, a communism of withdrawal from the world and the cares of the world. Despite the efforts of the ingenious, it is further a communism confined to a small part of the community. Again Aristotle's comment is amply justified: 'The necessary consequence is that there will be two States in one and those States mutually hostile.' [2] But indeed this understates the difficulty. The communism established in *The Republic* is a communism of dependence: 'their pay was to be their food, which they were to receive from the other citizens, and they were to have no private expenses.' [3] An age which has been, and is being increasingly, taught the importance of economic power will have little difficulty in deciding which of the two mutually hostile States, in Aristotle's language, will enter the contest with most advantages.

For our present purpose, it may be sufficient to glance at *The Laws*, for, significant as this Dialogue may be in throwing light on Plato's views on many political questions, it may be doubted whether it adds anything of substance, so far as general principles are concerned. *The Laws*, as is well known, was written in Plato's old age, and it has been assumed to betray to a certain extent the disillusionment that frequently comes with the years. For, odd as it may appear, there is a tradition that Plato had believed that the vision of *The Republic* was realisable, and that he had sought, ineffectively, to bring it down to earth. In current jargon, while *The Republic* is revolutionary, *The Laws* is reformist. Acknowledging that the ideal State of *The Republic* was something beyond the reach of frail men, he has now descended to outline the constitution of what is admittedly the second-best State. We are back again in the chill atmosphere of unrelieved monogamy. The constitution and the mode of life which, in some respects, are

[1] *Republic*, Book V, 464, 465. [2] *Politics*, Book II, Chap. 5.
[3] *Republic*, Book V, 464.

outlined in astonishing detail, are primarily directed towards preventing the emergence of unhealthy inequality, by limiting the ratio of the possessions of the richest to those of the poorest. What, however, is of interest—and perhaps this alone concerns us—is that the old faith still burns bright, although the architect has been constrained to compromise with the second-best. In a passage, somewhat tinged with the pathos of vanished dreams, Plato says:

> The first and highest form of the State and of the government and of the law is that in which there prevails most widely the ancient saying, that 'Friends have all things in common.' Whether there is anywhere now, or will ever be, this communion of women and children and property, in which the private and individual is altogether banished from life, and things which are by nature private, such as eyes and ears and hands, have become common, and all men express praise and blame and feel joy and sorrow on the same occasions, and whatever laws there are unite the city to the utmost—whether all this is possible or not, I say that no man, acting upon any other principle, will ever constitute a State which will be truer or better or more exalted in virtue.[1]

To complete the picture of Plato's communism, if only by way of contrast, Aristotle should be allowed to testify on the subject. His views on the community of wives and property, expressed at some length, may be found in the second book of *The Politics*. Aristotle, as is his manner, speaks with the horse-sense which has distinguished men of horse-sense throughout all the ages; in consequence, perhaps, his views may tend to be somewhat familiar, not to say hackneyed and trite, representing, as they do, what plain blunt men have always said. His fundamental criticism is perhaps political rather than economic. It is that Plato misconceives the kind of unity of which a State is capable. A State consists of a number of individuals who are necessarily different in kind. The State possesses an essential plurality; if it becomes a unit in the sense envisaged by Plato, it will cease to be a State at all.[2]

On the question which more immediately concerns us, that of community of property, Aristotle in one place roundly says that 'Life appears wholly impossible on such principles.' Here there is perhaps somewhat too much of the unreasoning instinct of the man of common sense. The arguments on which Aristotle bases this conclusion rest, broadly, on an appeal to common experience. 'The more numerous the joint owners of anything, the less it is cared for.' On the principle that what is everybody's business is nobody's business, men neglect their common possessions, relying on 'the idea that someone else is looking after it.' Nor, as he argues, is there any virtue in the argument that common ownership eliminates contention. On the contrary,

[1] *The Laws*, Book V, 739 (Jowett's edition, vol. 5, p. 121.
[2] *The Politics*, Book II, Chap. 2.

nothing is so difficult as for people to live together and enjoy any worldly goods in common: witness what happens when people travel together and keep a common purse. It is precisely when people try to share that they start to quarrel. Further, Aristotle opens a casement on an unending vista of age-long disputes on the question of stimulus, in conflict with the allurements of sloth: those who think that they consume less and work more (and that, though Aristotle does not say so, is the bulk of humanity) will complain of those who enjoy more and work less. Aristotle, it will be observed, tries to take men as he finds them.[1]

Turning from criticism of communism to what is at least a modified defence of property, Aristotle suggests (and it is a profound observation, capable of many applications) that the evil complained of may spring not from the want of community of property, but from defects of human nature. His argument, in general terms, is that property corresponds to something in human nature: 'there is an unspeakable advantage in the sense of private property.' And again, 'the love each individual bears to himself is not purposeless.' While defending property, because it satisfied a 'natural' instinct—if we may use a much abused eighteenth-century word—Aristotle is not, however, an obfuscated defender of things as they are. He prefers the existing system, but it should be 'embellished by the moral tone of those who live under it, and by a code of wise laws.' In a rather vague way, he suggests that private ownership should be combined with common use, at least among friends, and cites approvingly the practice in Lacedaemon where, without overmuch ceremony, citizens made use of each other's slaves and horses. As a matter of law, tenure of property should be private, but in practice it should be common; and the task of the legislator should be to produce in the citizen a disposition to adopt this course. It has been a familiar solution from time to time in the world's history: in effect, it accepts private property, but seeks to correct its possible abuses by developing a sense of public responsibility, at times indeed of trusteeship, in the owners of property.

From Aristotle, supplying the cold douche of individualist criticism, it is time to turn to the reverse side, the ideas of Plato as seen in burlesque parody. For this we are indebted to Aristophanes, who, in the *Ecclesiazusae* has given us a most excellent skit on women's rights and communistic theories. The *Ecclesiazusae* is, as a matter of mere chronology, slightly older than *The Republic*, but conscientious students have elaborated so many similarities in phraseology, so many passages in the *Ecclesiazusae* which acquire their full meaning only in the light

[1] *The Politics*, Book II, Chap. 5.
[2] *Ibid.*

of something in Plato, that it is difficult to believe that the two works are not connected. Mr. Bickley Rogers, than whom it is impossible to appeal to a higher authority, had no doubt on the point. In modern phraseology, Aristophanes had doubtless in some way a pre-view of *The Republic*.

In the *Ecclesiazusae*, Praxagora, the heroine, wife of Blepyros, who is very much a music-hall figure of a husband, engineers a *coup d'état* which places the control of the State in the hands of the women. The motive of the revolution is that men are wayward and changeable, whereas women are conservative, doing everything as of old, not perpetually in a hurry and trying new plans. Yet despite this, Praxagora's first step is to enact a universal state of communism in possessions, in which there will be no marriage, but where all women and men will be common and free.

In a burlesque one does not look for honest criticism: indeed a parody is almost necessarily a libel and a misrepresentation. The communism of Praxagora is therefore in its essence very different from the communism of Plato. Plato's communism is founded on asceticism run mad; even the curious communism of wives rests on a crucifixion of the flesh. Praxagora's communism is a communism of enjoyment, which expresses itself in the promise of magnificent banquets and in the unseemly brawling of rival hags over the abduction of a desirable young man. Yet, waiving the Aristophanic skulduddery, it is curious that the communism of Praxagora is much more akin to the spirit of modern communism. If one may take seriously what was not meant to be taken seriously, her revolution was designed as a protest against the monstrous inequalities of life, the crying shame of the poverty of the poor, placed cheek-by-jowl with the offensive luxury of the rich. Praxagora thus announces her programme to her downtrodden husband:

> The rule which I dare to enact and declare,
> Is that all shall be equal and equally share
> All wealth and enjoyments, nor longer endure
> That one should be rich, and another be poor,
> That one should have acres, far-stretching and wide,
> And another not even enough to provide
> Himself with a grave: that this at his call
> Should have hundreds of servants, and that none at all.
> All this I intend to correct and amend:
> Now all of all blessings shall freely partake,
> One life and one system for all men I make.[1]

The further conversation between Praxagora and her husband runs on familiar, yet diverting, lines. All property is to be brought to the stores; there will be one fund out of which 'We (the women) will

[1] Translation by Mr. Rogers, p. 89.

feed and maintain you.' But suppose, says Blepyros, on this question of surrender of goods:

> Suppose
> He choose to retain it, and nobody knows;
> Rank perjury doubtless; but what if it be?
> 'Twas by that he acquired it at first.
>
> P. I agree.
> But now 'twill be useless; he'll need it no more.
>
> B. How mean you?
>
> P. All pressure from want will be o'er.
> Now each will have all that a man can desire,
> Cakes, barley-loaves, chestnuts, abundant attire,
> Wine, garlands and fish: then why should he wish
> The wealth he has gotten by fraud to retain?

'But who will attend to the work of the farm?' is another question asked by the anxious Blepyros. The answer is that

> All labour and toil to the slaves you will leave;
> *Your* business 'twill be, when the shadows of eve
> Ten feet on the face of the dial are cast,
> To scurry away to your evening repast.

There will be no more law-suits, no more theft—for why should any one steal what is partly his own? Blepyros imagines that he has cornered his wife when he asks how, in the new world, it will be possible to fine anyone who has committed a common assault, 'when elated with wine'; but Praxagora is ready with her answer, which is not so different from that offered for our acceptance in these latter days:

> Why, his victuals and drink
> Will be stopped by command for a while; and I guess
> That he will not again in a hurry transgress,
> When he pays with his stomach.

It is all vastly entertaining, and there can be little doubt that the house rocked with laughter; yet it is not wholly without its elements of pathos, in that a play well over two thousand years old should be in places so horribly topical. The rest of the play is concerned with the scheme of communism in operation. We see the prudent citizen waiting to see what the others will do in the matter of giving up property, hatching

> some crafty shrewd device
> To keep my goods, and yet secure a part
> In all these public banquets like the rest.

We have the very irksome consequences of State interference in the amatory affairs of the population; and at the end the Chorus urges all and sundry to the munificent public banquet, but (believing in the virtue of private enterprise) adds a wise hint to take a plate and an omelet with them if, notwithstanding the overwhelming menu, they wish to be sure of something to eat.

Those who seek in the inquisitive Greek spirit for foreshadowings of every trend of modern thought have little difficulty in finding prototypes of that other subversive tendency which runs through extreme individualism to something approaching anarchism. A liberal in all ages is one who upholds the rights of the individual against the claims of the State and of authority; and an anarchist is merely a liberal who has gone off the deep end, losing all sense of proportion. The various types of communism so far considered, both practical and theoretical, have all been what we should now call national. Even Plato's Republic was, as has been noticed, organised in its most essential features because, things being what they are, it would inevitably go to war with other States and other States would inevitably go to war with it. Anarchism which denies the authority of the State within its frontiers, necessarily denies the authority of all States, and is thus impelled to a vague internationalism, or the far-off dream of a somewhat nebulous world-state. The tendency towards extreme individualism, anarchism and cosmopolitanism may be found in Zeno and the Stoic school generally.

But not there alone. There is a long line of individualism in Greece, and Pericles is its greatest ornament. Indeed Socrates and Plato exist very largely to protest against the liberalism of Pericles, run to degenerate forms. The Cynics, who have points of contact with the Stoics, were also individualists, at times repulsive individualists, with whom the State counted for little. Moreover, the Greeks did not escape that ubiquitous nostalgia after a primitive state of nature which, Hobbes notwithstanding, has usually been regarded as a blissful, though more populated, Garden of Eden. It is almost impossible to yearn after a vanished state of nature without resenting the shackles which now cause us to stumble. Consequently, the devotees of a state of nature tend to hunger after a freedom, ample and unrestrained.

The professed teaching of Zeno was not indeed marked by that 'churlishness' and that anti-social tendency which traditionally are associated with the Cynics. It is possible, with care, to select extracts which would present the founder of Stoicism as apparently highly conscious of a man's duties to his fellows. The 'wise man,' that ideal figure of the Stoics, 'will take part in politics, *if nothing hinders him*': he will not live in solitude, 'for he is naturally made for society and action.' Thus Diogenes Laertius, reporting on the school[1]; though it may be suggested that the somewhat conditional statement of a duty to participate in politics rather implies a fear that something in

[1] Diogenes Laertius: *Life of Zeno*, Loeb edition, vol. 2, pp. 225–229.

fact may very well hinder the wise man from so behaving. And it need hardly be said that the whole tendency of Stoic doctrine was in the direction of a self-sufficient aloofness. The end, according to Zeno, is 'life in agreement with Nature'; and the natural life, moreover, is the life according to reason.[1] But throughout the ages, those who have sought to live according to reason have naturally lived according to their own reason; and those who have sought to live in agreement with Nature have been impelled to act on their own interpretation of what is natural. The compulsion of circumstances fades away, and each becomes a law to himself, listening to the voice of his own reason. In Zeno's *Republic*, of which Diogenes Laertius has preserved for us some of the high-lights, we are in a world where there is no marriage, no temples, no law courts, no places of education, no currency, no compulsion.[2] This removal of landmarks, placing faith in the guidance of reason, is pure Godwin; and though apparently reached by a different path, it is almost the whole of Godwin.

The injunction to take part in politics, 'if nothing hinders,' becomes indeed rather nugatory, if it is realised that something always does hinder. This hindering something is the nature of States as we know them. One Stoic teacher expressly held (and probably all others would have agreed) that a statesman must either displease the gods or displease the people. Along various lines, then, the Stoic is led to reject the State, and the sum total of States known to men. Here we reach the true significance of the Stoics for our purpose, the point on which they introduced something peculiarly their own in the bubbling cauldron of Greek political speculation. Turning away from the pettinesses and the cares in which the State was enmeshed, they claimed to be citizens of the world. For if reason is the distinguishing mark of man, and if all men are endowed with reason, then all men are, or should be, members of one community which has reason for its common law. Thus we have the vision of a world State—nebulous, it may be, with not a little anarchism at its roots—but representing a significant progress beyond the stage when the world was thought of in terms of Greeks and a vast but inferior horde of barbarians outside. In particular, the contrast with Plato is sufficiently marked; for Plato never quite got above the idea that the foreigner represented a dangerous and insidious element which should be kept remote in order to avoid corruption and contamination. In Zeno, then, we have the foreshadowings of anarchism and cosmopolitanism.

One other phase of socialist literature may, without undue straining, be said to have its precursors in Greek literature. Where precisely the literature of Utopia fades into the literature of Baron Munchausen

[1] Diogenes Laertius: *Life of Zeno*, Loeb edition, vol. 2, p. 195.
[2] *Ibid.* p. 145.

would be an interesting question for discussion elsewhere. As it loses its didactic purpose, as it ceases in intention to contrast the actual and the ideal, a Utopia tends to transform itself into a *Wundermärchen*, a mere fairy tale. Probably, viewed impartially, the Greek stories of far-off happy countries are nearer the fairy-tale end of this ladder. Most of them are not so much known, as known about by fragments and references in other writers; but this, of course, does not prevent these rather shadowy Utopias from making a brave show in German Encyclopædias of Classical Knowledge. Two which are more available will be found embedded in that rich mass of mixed feeding which constitutes the works of Diodorus Siculus. There is, firstly, in the second book,[1] the strange tale of Iambulus, who in some islands conveniently remote discovered a remarkable race, four cubits high, living to the age of 150 years. Having reached this assigned limit, they put an end to their own existence by lying down on a plant endowed with the peculiar quality that whoever lies down upon it imperceptibly and gently falls asleep and dies. These happy islanders live in complete communism, knowing nothing of marriage, but living on that high plane which mankind occupied ere one to one was cursedly confined. Mothers who are suckling their babies hand them round periodically, until they have quite muddled themselves as to which is which. It seems a less satisfactory and less efficient way than that devised by Plato. As a consequence of this confusion of children, 'since there is no rivalry among them, they never experience civil disorders and they never cease placing the highest value upon internal harmony.' It is the familiar story of simple men whose peace is rooted in their simplicity; though it must be added that Nature (after the manner of Utopias) is kind to them and supplies their needs liberally and ungrudgingly. Presumably of no political or social significance, but interesting in illustration of what may be encountered on the other side of the boundary between Utopia and the *Wundermärchen* is one peculiarity of these excellent people. Nature gave them a tongue cleft for some distance, and by artifice they have divided it further back to the base. They are therefore double-tongued, though in no invidious sense. This oddity, however, enables them to carry on two conversations at the same time: an attainment of dubious value to anyone but a ventriloquist. They have also certain remarkable beasts, of which the most interesting is a roundish animal, which has a mouth and an eye at each end of two diagonal yellow stripes intersecting at right angles. The four mouths unite in a common gullet. Underneath, it is amply supplied with feet enabling it to move in any direction. Mr. Facing-both-ways would have been filled with envy. In the fifth book of Diodorus [2] there is the less wonderful account of the

[1] Diodorus Siculus, Book II, 55–60.
[2] Diodorus, Book V, 42–46.

island of Panchaea, a priest-ridden country, where communism is violated only to the extent of a house and garden: 'all the products and the revenue are taken over by the priests, who portion out with justice to each man his share; and to the priests, alone is given two-fold.'

Not much importance perhaps need be attached to such slight Greek fragments descriptive of communistic, happy and simple peoples. But they serve to show the wealth and variety of Greek speculation in these matters, and in some ways they are rather suggestive of 'Utopia made easy,' as disclosed later in parts of Fénelon's *Télémaque*.

CHAPTER II

THE JEWISH AND CHRISTIAN TRADITIONS

(*a*) THE OLD TESTAMENT

If it is from Greece and Rome that Western Europe in large measure derives its ideas with regard to literature, art, philosophy, politics and much more, it is from the Jews and from Christianity that we derive our religion and our morality. Nor is it necessary to differentiate between these two sources: Christianity is the completion of Judaism. Christ professedly came not to destroy the law but to fulfil it[1]; and in a passage which subsequently played a great part in the controversies with which we are concerned—the incident of the young man who had great possessions—he specifically pointed back to the Ten Commandments, as the foundation of all good behaviour and indeed as the key to eternal life.[2] On one side, and that doubtless the most important, the roots of our thoughts on that most difficult problem of how men should live together and behave towards each other are deeply intertwined with the Mosaic Law.

It is therefore not surprising that gallant attempts should have been made to represent Moses in the guise of a primitive socialist law-giver, and to find in the Gospels the seeds of later socialist thought. On all these matters a layman may but speak as a layman, timorously and tentatively; and assuredly no one who could avoid it would willingly allow himself to become entangled in the entangling entanglements of the Books of Leviticus and Deuteronomy. Yet even a layman may perhaps, with reasonable safety, note certain points. In the first place, the Mosaic Code, however it may be viewed, is clearly a monument apart in the history of the world's legislation. Waiving the details which may frequently appear to the modern eye to be concerned with trumpery details, the underlying spirit (which alone matters) is clear and obvious, and, having regard to what the Jews thought of themselves, is readily explicable. The Jews in a very strict sense regarded themselves as the children of one God. This relationship necessarily implied brotherhood; and to a large extent the purpose of the Mosaic Law was to maintain the Jewish people as one family. All should be linked together by a sense of common brotherhood.[3] It was not, however, the brotherhood of children, living under the

[1] Matt. v. 17. [2] Matt. xix. 16–22; Mark x. 17–22.

[3] It is a frequent theme of the prophets. Take, for instance, Malachi: 'Have we not all one father? hath not one God created us? why do we deal treacherously every man against his brother?'

same roof and still eating out of the common pot; it was rather the brotherhood of grown men who have left the old home, each living his own life, yet remembering and acknowledging the claim each has on the other by reason of the past they have shared together. Even with this slight reservation, it may, however, be doubted whether such a prevailing sense of brotherhood could have existed, apart from the unifying conviction that they were a holy people unto the Lord, chosen to be a peculiar people unto himself, above all the nations that are upon the earth. Among other things, their profound consciousness of spiritual superiority tended to unite them, and make them as brothers.

Yet this ' brotherhood,' which it was the final purpose of the Mosaic Code to produce, in no way leads to anything suggestive of the desirability of communism, or of the reprehensibility of private possessions or of private enterprise. On the contrary, the sacredness of private property is an underlying assumption throughout. Probably the Ten Commandments have enjoyed in human history a somewhat unmerited pre-eminence; they represent in the main the negative side of well-doing which consists in avoiding evil-doing. Yet if we take such a commandment as the eighth (on the Anglo-Saxon enumeration), it is obvious (with all respect to Proudhon, who gave a pleasingly revised translation) that stealing necessarily implies the existence of property that may be stolen. ' Respect the property of others ' is not merely the plain sense of the commandment: it is a precept which in a multitude of forms and in a multitude of applications is perpetually recurring in the books of the law. Still remaining within the confines of the Ten Commandments, it is significant that this respect for the property of others is carried so far, that the mere casting of covetous eyes on our neighbour's ass is ranked with the fundamental sins.

When we turn to the confused mass of detailed regulations, the outstanding feature is found in the manifold provision made for the prevention and relief of poverty, for the humane treatment of debtors, for the continuance to each of his property, and, where necessary, for the periodic restitution of property. In a very real sense each man was made his brother's keeper; on each rested the responsibility of seeing that his brother did not suffer want. It may be a trivial matter and of little immediate application to most of us, but it is worth while turning up the 22nd chapter of the Book of Deuteronomy and reading the first four verses, which impose on every one the obligation of taking in, caring for, housing and feeding his neighbour's errant ox, ass or sheep, should it happen in its wanderings to come his way. The spirit of this far transcends mere Scotland Yard regulations. The relief of the poor is put upon each as a duty: ' Thou shalt open thine hand wide unto thy brother, to thy poor, and to thy needy, in thy land.'[1] So also the law with regard to debtors and the taking of pledges was

[1] Deut. xv. 7–11.

hedged round with restrictions and conditions designed to secure the humane treatment of those in distress: 'No man shall take the nether or the upper millstone to pledge: for he taketh a man's life to pledge.'[1] That a worker's distress should not be made the occasion of separating him from his tools indicates the highest economic wisdom. Jesus, the son of Sirach, puts the same point, even more tersely: 'He that taketh away his neighbour's living slayeth him.'[2] More odd is the stipulation that if a neighbour's raiment be pledged, it should be returned before sundown[3]—lest the poor wretch should shiver in the night. Perhaps it is not wholly irrelevant to note that the Mosaic Law throughout also shows a most unusual concern for the humane treatment of animals.

In addition, there was what has come to be known comprehensively as 'The Law of the Corner'—a provision which is surely unique in the world's legislation. It derives its title from the injunction: 'When ye reap the harvest of your land, thou shalt not wholly reap the corners of thy field . . . thou shalt leave them for the poor and the stranger'; but it had different interpretations as applied to corn, vineyards and olive trees, and it regulated the disposal of the gleanings, the fallen grapes and something which is delightfully called 'that-which-is-left-through-forgetfulness.' It is a curious device to make provision for the poor by inciting all and sundry to be somewhat carefully careless in the ordinary affairs of life, the wastage (if it may be so called) being used as a nucleus for poor relief.[4]

It remains merely to point to two institutions whose obvious intention was to prevent the poor from sinking, and to restore every one to his own. The first was the 'release,' a cancellation of debts at the end of every seventh year,[5] to which, of course, there are classical analogies, though doubtless not, as here, conceived as part of a long-

[1] Deut. xxiv. 6. [2] Ecclesiasticus xxxiv. 22. [3] Exod. xxii. 26–27.

[4] The 'Law of the Corner' will be found with slightly different content in the Books of Leviticus, xix. 9–10, and of Deuteronomy, xxiv. 19–21. The Rabbi Maimonides, than whom there could be no greater authority, summarises the position as follows: In a Vineyard, there are four gifts for the poor (fallen grapes; small bunches; the corner; and that-which-is-left-through-forgetfulness); in Corn, there are three gifts (the gleanings; that-which-is-left-through-fortgefulness; and the corner); in Trees, two gifts (that-which-is-left-through-forgetfulness and the corner). But let no one imagine that it is all plain sailing after that. There are nice questions as to when a field is to be deemed to be two fields, calling for two corners. In the case of gleanings, there is (e.g.) the knotty problem of grains of corn found in the receptacle of ants: for who can tell where the ants got them? So, if a sheaf is forgotten by the owner, but not by the labourers, or vice versa, it is not forgotten; it is not a thing-left-through-forgetfulness, until all men have forgotten it. On the other hand, if the owner forgets and later remembers the sheaf when he is in town, this does not suffice to save the sheaf: 'for it is said, "when thou cuttest down thine harvest in the field,"—not indeed in the city.' So, by parity of reasoning, if a strong wind lifts a sheaf into a neighbouring field and it is forgotten, it is nevertheless not a thing-left-through-forgetfulness within the meaning of the Act; for it no longer satisfies the words 'thine harvest in thy fields.' Is it necessary to add that the number of such fine problems approaches infinity?

[5] Deut. xv. 1.

term plan. In addition there is the consecration of the fiftieth year as a year of Jubile, the distinctive feature of which, for our purpose, was that ‘in the year of this jubile ye shall return every man unto his possession.’ [1] What was the relationship, if any, between the year of release and the year of Jubile, whether they were ever effectively enforced, whether (in view of the apparent redundancy of one or other of these provisions) they represent the aspirations of different periods of Jewish history are questions which are easily asked.

Enough has been said to indicate the extent of the ‘socialism’ sometimes attributed to the Mosaic dispensation. The Jewish State was, rather oddly, one in which provision for the poor was more or less the fundamental act of association: it was a State founded on a Poor Law. And the poor were to be succoured by a universal prevalence of benevolence, of ‘charity,’ in the good sense which that word bore before it suffered devaluation. In other respects, however, it is rather a world of rampant individualism, where regard for the property and rights of others is inculcated in a thousand ways.

Needless to say, Israel did not live up to its high professions. It is the recurring theme of most of, if not all, the prophets, who also, by the ingenuous, have been roped into the socialist fold. The prophets were indeed valorous champions of the poor—of whom there ought to have been none, had the Mosaic Law been observed. They were stern in their condemnation of the tyrannous iniquity of the rich in grinding the faces of the poor, and in invoking the judgment of God on those that join house to house, that lay field to field till there be no place. But again the prophets were indignant rather than constructive, or at least they were not constructive with regard to the management of the affairs of this world. With unequalled eloquence they denounced unrighteousness and wickedness, luxury and the abuse of wealth. They called men to repentance. The regeneration they sought was, however, a spiritual regeneration. Beyond this they did not go; nor would they have regarded it as within their province to do so. When, as in Isaiah, there is an idealised vision of the future, it has been suggested [2] that it is more in line with the anarchist dream of a world where all men are good and do good without earthly or political constraint.

(*b*) THE ESSENES

The ancient Jewish world does, however, present one example of an apparently successful communistic way of life, extending over a considerable period of time. The Essenes have been described as the great enigma of Hebrew history and, doubtless because of the fascination of the enigmatic, a considerable literature has gathered round

[1] Lev. xxv. 8–17. [2] As, *e.g.*, by Adler.

them. Seldom have scholars built so much on so little. The ordinary reader will find all he needs to know, and in a sense all there is to be known, in certain pages in Josephus and in Philo. Porphyry, who sometimes figures as a leading authority, is content to reproduce all that Josephus says, with that innocent and honest tendency to plagiarism which former and less sophisticated ages took as a matter of course.[1] Pliny likewise has a few words about the Essenes, as befits a man whose net nothing escapes.[2]

The Essenes, while unmistakably Jews and in the Jewish tradition, nevertheless represent a curious infusion of asceticism which, following a not uncommon sequence, tends towards communism. How the Essenes came to be, what influences went to their making—for that matter, how they ceased to be—are questions to which the experts can give the enquirer no assured answer. In fact, no one quite knows what the word ' Essenes ' may mean: the interpretations offered are many and varied. Rather oddly, there is no mention of a founder. In the matter of their more peculiar characteristics, some speak of Pythagorean influences; some, groping further east, invoke Buddhist doctrine; one of their ritual observances embodies an obvious reminiscence of sun-worship. They regarded the soul as entangled in the prison-house of the body, and their aim was to obtain release from the bonds of the flesh. Holiness, if not dependent upon, was at least thought to be materially stimulated by under-nutrition.

The accounts given by Philo and Josephus, if combined, give a fairly complete picture of a communism which in certain respects has unique features. In numbers the Essenes were never anything but a feeble folk, some four thousand in all at any time, and they lived for the most part in the villages of the western shores of the Dead Sea. The most puzzling and unusual feature in their system of religious communism is, however, that they did not withdraw from the rest of the world. They continued to engage in ordinary secular occupations, working on the land or at their trade, like those around them. They had their houses scattered about among the other houses in the villages where they lived. Nor, although the Essenes were preponderatingly to be found in the area indicated, were they in any way restricted either in their place of habitation, or—generally speaking—in their occupation. Some Essenes lived in Jerusalem; some distinguished themselves as leaders in the war against Rome.

[1] It has been well observed that to-day if a student copies from one book, he is guilty of plagiarism; whereas if he quotes from two books, he is engaged in research. The ancient world had not attained consciousness of this important distinction.

[2] Without pursuing abstruser authorities, reference should be made to Josephus: *Jewish War*, Book 2, section viii, para. 2–13; Philo: *Quod omnis probus liber sit*, sections 12–13; Porphyry: *De Abstinentia*, Book IV, para. 11–13. Pliny; *Natural History*, Book V, para. 15.

But, inside these rather vague frontiers, the Essenes professed to practise complete communism. On being admitted after a rigorous novitiate extending over three years, they surrendered all their possessions to the community. 'In no other community,' says Philo, 'can we find the custom of sharing roof, life and board more firmly established in actual practice.' Further, 'all the wages which they earn in the day's work they do not keep as their private property, but throw them into the common stock and allow the benefit thus accruing to be shared by those who wish to use it.' Consequently, and it is now Josephus who speaks, 'their community of goods is truly admirable; you will not find one among them distinguished by greater opulence than another.'

Communism demands the elimination of the individual home, and this again demands the extinction of the individual wife. This may be achieved either by community of wives (as in many Utopias and in certain extreme and heretical sects), or it may be achieved by pretending that women do not exist. As was natural in an ascetic sect, the second course was that adopted by the Essenes, though with some hesitations. They 'despised' marriage; but they did not on principle condemn it or, apparently, forbid it. They merely desired to avoid what Mr. Thomas Taylor, in translating Porphyry, called the 'lasciviousness of women.' It is almost a Proudhonian intuition. Josephus somewhat unnecessarily adds that the Essenes were 'persuaded that none of the sex keeps her plighted troth to one man.' The community or sect (or whatever it may be called) had thus perforce to be perpetually recruited from outside. On the one hand they received the children of other people, and from a tender age moulded them after their own fashion; on the other hand (the phrase is Pliny's) they received those driven to them through *vitae paenitentia*, the weariness of life. Pliny's brief reference adds nothing to our knowledge; it is chiefly interesting because it is written (or so it may seem to some) in a strain slightly suggestive of satirical scepticism. He describes them as a *gens sola et in toto orbe praeter ceteras mira*—a unique tribe, remarkable beyond all others in the world; and he goes on to add that this 'gens' lives *sine ulla femina . . . socia palmarum*—with never a woman, and with palm trees for company. Thus through thousands of ages, a race, in which no one is born, lives on for ever. It is difficult to resist the impression that here at least Pliny did not believe all he was told.

The metaphysical and religious beliefs of the Essenes do not concern us here, important as they may be elsewhere. Assuming that the accounts given by Philo and Plutarch are fairly reliable in their main outlines—and the best authorities agree that they may be so accepted—the Essenes are of great significance in revealing something like a state of communism, enduring for a considerable period of time, with the added peculiarity that they intermingled curiously with the rest of the population. In themselves they were a special corps of the ultra-pious, more strict even than the strictest of the other Jews in their observance of the Sabbath. They were a moral *élite*, and they so regarded themselves ; and it is fairly clear that in their make-up they had not a little of that spiritual pride and exclusiveness for which the Pharisees (probably unjustly) have become proverbial. In the stream of influences that go to make up the world's history, the Essenes may, without too much imagination, be assigned a somewhat focal place. It is probable that John the Baptist had affiliations, if not with the main body of the Essenes, then at any rate with some of the other less known and somewhat similar sects, which had Essenian characteristics.[1] Also, as we shall see presently, it is extremely probable that Luke's account of the communism in the primitive Church at Jerusalem, if not in fact true of Jerusalem, was a reasonably correct account of the communism of the Essenes ; and it is abundantly clear that this passage, based on and infused with memories of the Essenes, was the inspiration of that line of thought in early Christianity which tended towards communism.

(*c*) THE NEW TESTAMENT

Thomas More represents his Utopians, who were naturally favourable to the community of goods, as eagerly embracing Christianity, 'since they perceived that Christ and his followers lived by that rule.' How far there is an element of socialism in the teaching of the Gospels and in the account of Christian beginnings in the Acts of the Apostles is a question that has given rise to prolonged controversy. At the one extreme are Sudre and Thonissen, devout men, writing at a time when socialism and communism were looked upon as the authentic mark of the Beast ; and to them the spirit and the letter of the New Testament alike give no support to anything so tainted. At the other extreme (to take widely different examples) there are such writers as Cabet and Mr. Beer to whom primitive Christianity means nothing if it does not mean socialism. The question is probably very largely irrelevant in itself ; in any case it is not quite so simple as either of these schools would maintain. It has been seen that the Mosaic Law, while prescribing alms and charity, contained nothing that was communistic or hostile to property. Nor is there in the Old Testament anything that is characteristically ascetic. Asceticism, as Adler suggests (probably rightly), filtered in from the East ; and the results of the ascetic infusion may be seen in the Essenes. As the same writer acutely observes, asceticism may lead to one of two consequences. It may lead to the renunciation of wealth and comfort, and to the

[1] Emile Faguet goes further ; 'A en juger par les Evangiles, Jésus ne fut pas socialiste, et justement il fut essénien' (*Le Socialisme en 1907*, p. 4).

glorification of poverty as in itself a holy state, a sign of virtue. Along this line we have the begging friars and all those who hope to attain blessedness in another world by suffering hunger and self-castigation in this. But the impulse to asceticism may also be satisfied by stopping short at the renunciation of private property, each for himself. This line will lead to the formation of some sort of communistic body, composed of men who have severally renounced the world and who each individually possesses nothing; but the community to which they belong need be in no wise destitute.

In approaching the teaching of the New Testament in these matters, the first point to note is that, whatever may have happened later under various influences, there is no suggestion of asceticism in the earliest enunciation of Christianity. The Son of Man came eating and drinking: contrasting him with John the Baptist, who probably reflected Essene influences, his enemies even derided him as a man gluttonous and a winebibber. In the Gospels themselves it would be difficult to find any passages suggesting that life ought to be a vale of woe, and that we should go out of our way to make ourselves and others unhappy. It is probably equally true to say that so far as the words of Christ are concerned, comparing the different gospels where there is a suggestion of discrepancy, there is nothing anywhere to suggest any condemnation of private property or the structure of society which goes with private property. In large measure he represented the Mosaic Law—which professedly he came to fulfil—carried forward. He taught charity; he emphasised alms-giving as a way to divine favour; he condemned covetousness. Even the acknowledgment that riches may prove a stumbling-block on the way to the Kingdom of God is uttered as a warning rather than as a condemnation. The crucial passage on the subject is the account given of the young man who had great possessions—later the text of the discourse by Clement of Alexandria which probably decided the attitude of the Church on the matter. In view of the large place which this narrative occupies in later discussions of social problems, it may not be unprofitable to examine it with some minuteness.[1] Three points are of special significance. Firstly, in answer to the rich young man's question as to what he must do to inherit eternal life, Christ's original answer is a brief enumeration of the Ten Commandments. The enquirer is in fact referred back to the traditional Mosaic Law, which, as we have seen, involved respect for the property of others. 'Do not steal: defraud not,' as Mark puts it. Secondly, the further and stricter counsel is given only because the young man, protesting that he has kept the commandments from his youth up, insistently presses for something more. It is then that Christ counsels him to sell whatever he has and give to the poor; but if we follow St. Matthew, this instruction is prefaced by the significant

[1] Matt. xix. 16–26; Mark x. 17–27; Luke xviii. 18–27.

words, 'If thou wilt be perfect.' In short there is here the familiar distinction between a precept binding on all, and a counsel of perfection imparted to some and valid in certain circumstances. The third point arises from the account given by St. Mark, in the comment of Christ after the young man had gone away 'grieved,' where there is what at first sight appears a curious repetition. 'How hardly shall they that have riches enter into the kingdom of God,' are Christ's first words to his disciples; and when they were astonished, the difficulties of the rich are restated more guardedly with a slight verbal modification, which, however, profoundly affects the meaning of the phrase. The restatement takes this form: 'how hard is it for them that trust in riches to enter into the kingdom of God.' This, it will be observed, no longer applies merely to the rich, but to all, rich or poor, who put their confidence in the things of this world.

The truth is, or so at least it would seem to some, that there is somehow an element of inappropriateness in microscopically examining the words of Christ in order to find therein an answer to a question in which he was not greatly interested. 'Seek ye first the kingdom of God and his righteousness': this, if one were compelled to choose one text for the purpose, probably best expresses the kernel of Christ's teaching. But it implies, above all in its context, that in the searching light of this exhortation, all other problems fade into insignificance. The true position has been admirably expressed by a writer quoted by Thonissen:

> L'Évangile ne contient pas un mot qu'on puisse tourner contre la propriété; il ne s'élève pas une fois contre les prétendues injustices de l'ordre social; il ne représente pas les riches comme des oppresseurs ni les pauvres comme des opprimés; il se place au-dessus de ces distinctions sans les attaquer, en conseillant aux uns la résignation, aux autres le sacrifice, à tous l'abnégation d'eux-mêmes, la charité et l'amour.[1]

Il se place au-dessus de ces distinctions sans les attaquer: it is probably as just an estimate as it is possible to arrive at in the matter. Even though the lecture containing this phrase dates from 1848, and derives from a forgotten Jew who precariously survives in a quotation in the pages of Thonissen, the words are worthy of perpetuation.

At the same time it is idle to deny, and it is only fair to recognise, that there were mingled with the origins of Christianity certain communistic aspirations, deriving probably from the Essenes, later colouring the day-dreams of the Christian Fathers in their unguarded moments, and erupting periodically as 'heresies' in the first centuries. Among the gospel-writers it is Luke who represents this 'left wing.' It is extraordinarily interesting, as well as extremely instructive as an example of the art of editing, to compare the version of the Sermon on the Mount given by Matthew with the much more summarised version in the gospel of St. Luke.[2]

[1] Thonissen, *Le Socialisme dans le Passé*, p 59. [2] Matt. v.; Luke vi. 20–26.

'Blessed are the poor in spirit,' says St. Matthew; 'blessed be ye poor,' says St. Luke in a conciser phrase.[1] 'Blessed are they which do hunger and thirst after righteousness,' says St. Matthew; 'blessed are ye that hunger now,' says St. Luke. The abbreviating blue pencil converts a spiritual hunger into the pangs of bodily need. If one cared to be fanciful, one might note that Luke slips in (what is not in Matthew) a blessing 'when men shall separate you from their company'—as though Marx and the class war were already pestering to be born. But without being fanciful, it is significant that in Luke the so-called beatitudes are followed by curses and objurgations—against the rich for being rich: 'Woe unto you that are rich! . . . Woe unto you that are full! for ye shall hunger. Woe unto you that laugh now! for ye shall mourn and weep.' This, one feels somehow, is Luke, rather than Christ. It is, on the economic plane and in terms of the physical belly, a denunciation of the full because they are full; a blessing on the empty because they are empty.[2]

It is also to Luke, in the Acts of the Apostles, that we owe that idyllic account of the early days of the Church at Jerusalem, to which appeal has so frequently been made in the subsequent unending discussion regarding riches and poverty. The passage in the fourth chapter of the Acts is among the most familiar in Scripture:

> Neither was there any among them that lacked: for as many as were possessors of lands or houses sold them, and brought the prices of the things that were sold, and laid them down at the apostles' feet; and distribution was made unto every man according as he had need.[3]

It is a fairly typical picture of the golden age; yet to draw from this highly idealised and conventional description of a communism in use the inference that a system of communism prevailed among the early Christians is shown to be erroneous by Luke's own narrative in the passage immediately following. For in the story of Ananias and Sapphira, which is a pendent to this account of primitive communism, it is clear beyond all question that Ananias, having a house, was free to sell or not to sell as he chose; having sold it, he was free to bring the money or retain it for his own use. . He was *not* free to pretend that what he brought was the whole price obtained for the house, when in fact it was not. It is fairly clear that what prevailed at Jerusalem was not in any sense a system of communism: it was rather—as was

[1] The version in the Gospel of Barnabas may be of passing interest: 'Blessed are the poor who truly hate the delights of the world, for they shall abound in the delights of the kingdom of God.'

[2] The Apostle James, it is true (chap. v. 1), exclaims, 'Go to now, ye rich men, weep and howl for your miseries that shall come upon you'; but his view is in fact quite different from that of Luke. James's words lead up to and are part of a denunciation of certain rich men for certain specific acts of exploitation and injustice. To Luke, wealth, as such, and rich men, as such, are offensive.

[3] Acts iv. 34–35. See also Acts ii. 44.

perhaps natural among the members of a new and enthusiastic movement—a condition of unrestrained and voluntary sharing, in which all, in the spirit of the Mosaic dispensation, willingly and gladly helped their neighbours in need. That there was in fact no communism among the early Christian Churches is amply proved by the epistles of St. Paul. Mixed up with much theological doctrine and other things, St. Paul's letters also have, in innumerable passages, the character of begging letters, of appeals for charity. Doubtless they are written in a more impeccable English than most appeals for contributions, but appeals for contributions they nevertheless are—on behalf of distressed Churches. Moreover, it is assumed that what may be ultimately given will be given by individuals and will be, in modern jargon, a 'free-will offering': 'Every man according as he purposeth in his heart, so let him give; not grudgingly, or of necessity: for God loveth a cheerful giver.'[1]

Probably the truth of the matter is that the account of the communistic way of life in the Church at Jerusalem was, for Luke, something of a Sorelian myth. His gospel reveals him as the leveller among the apostles; the passage in the fourth chapter of the Acts, after the manner of myths, served as a rallying cry to all the later egalitarian sects. The account he wrote was, of course, not contemporary with the events described. Looking back through a haze of years, Luke saw at Jerusalem, in the abounding liberality and generosity of the first Christians, something that seemed a reflection of the myth that had been his inspiration; and accordingly he described his ideal golden age, even though within a few lines he was compelled to deny it.

(*d*) THE CHRISTIAN FATHERS: GENERAL CONSIDERATIONS

When we turn to the early Christian Fathers and to their attitude to the problems of wealth, private property and community of goods, it is necessary to trim our course somewhat gingerly round the fringe of an engulfing whirlpool. In a discussion in which the Fathers in their totality may be allotted only one section in a chapter, they cannot expect to be represented by more than a mere random sample. On the general question this much may, however, be said. For at least a hundred years, and perhaps much longer, it has been found an entertaining pastime to bring together explosive dicta from the Fathers,

[1] 2 Cor. ix. 7; but the whole chapter is interesting. See also 1 Cor. xvi. 3. Probably the most explicit and the most egalitarian Pauline utterance on this question has, perhaps rather oddly, been cited with relative infrequency in this long controversy. Even here, however, the underlying principle is that of voluntary liberality, leading in practice to equality: 'For I mean not that other men be eased, and ye be burdened; but by an equality, that now at this time your abundance may be a supply for their want, that their abundance also may be a supply for your want: that there may be equality' (2 Cor. viii. 13–14).

showing their kinship with left-wing revolutionaries. Nor is it a difficult, or even an unamusing task, apart from the fact that the Fathers were in many cases so unconscionably voluminous. Round about 1850, Thonissen obviously found much enjoyment in tearing to shreds a forgotten M. Pelletan, who had compiled such a revolutionary anthology from the Fathers. In our own day, a confiding and unquestioning reader of Mr. Beer would very easily, as indeed he is meant to do, carry away the impression that the term 'Christian Father' merely represents the extreme left of left-wing socialism. On the other hand, Dr. George O'Brien,[1] with much sobriety and conscientious scholarship, has shown that the early teachers in the Church were consistently opposed to what we should now call 'communistic doctrine.' If an alien and an intruder in these fields of scholarship may venture to utter a two-fold word of warning, it would be, firstly, that when any apparently communistic expression of opinion is cited from one of the Fathers, enquiry should be made as to the context, not merely with a view to verifying whether a few words may not have disappeared from the beginning or end of the quotation, but also to ascertain how the quotation is related to the general argument, assuming that there is one; and secondly, such an isolated quotation should be checked against what the Father in question may have said elsewhere on the same subject. This can usually be done without undue labour by looking up the Index under 'Wealth,' 'Property,' 'Riches' or 'Possessions.' If this course be adopted, the judgment of the dispassionate will almost certainly be with M. Thonissen and Dr. O'Brien, rather than with the forgotten Pelletan and Mr. Beer.

Dr. O'Brien very properly indicates certain considerations which ought to be borne in mind in any attempt to assess the true meaning of certain of the apparently more extreme utterances of the Fathers; for indubitably certain isolated expressions may appear to modern ears to bear a revolutionary significance, even if these may be belied by adjacent pronouncements. Three of the points which tend to a frequent misunderstanding of isolated passages may be indicated. There is firstly the altogether extraordinary importance attached to alms-giving in the Old and the New Testaments, and this is quite naturally carried forward to the Christian Fathers. In an age which is increasingly putting its hope of salvation in an indefinite extension of Social Insurance, it is perhaps difficult for us to realise just how fundamental a virtue alms-giving was assumed to be. That alms-giving was the pathway to salvation; that the rich man should open his hand liberally, and regard his wealth as a trust to be used for others; that the rich, in a picturesque phrase, were the dispensers of the treasure of the poor—these were all commonplace propositions in the early days of Christianity. But it is obvious that universal giving is not far

[1] O'Brien: *An Essay on Mediaeval Economic Teaching.*

removed from universal sharing; and it is accordingly not surprising that at times some of the Fathers, not having temperamentally the timorous caution of a civil servant skilled in balanced drafting, should say something that probably appears to mean more than was intended.

A second influence which at times led the Christian Fathers to express a non-communist thought in communist phraseology may be found in the peculiar horror with which the Scriptures regarded the discontented man. Covetousness, no less than murder or adultery, strikes at the framework of society. The greedy, avaricious man who seeks gain is a fool, with a wrong sense of values. He loves this present world, and thus, like Demas, he fails in the supreme test. That we should be contented with what we have is a pervading thought throughout the New Testament. It is one of the boasts of the somewhat boastful Paul: 'I have learned, in whatsoever state I am, therewith to be content.' It is therefore only in the tradition of the prophets and the New Testament that the Fathers should denounce those who make the acquisition of gain the chief end of life; still more those who acquire gain by wrongful and tyrannical means. But again denunciation of the love of wealth may at times appear to imply denunciation of wealth itself; for the impassioned preacher it is a fine line of division that must be observed. It is significant and illustrative to note with what comparative unanimity the Pauline dictum that 'the love of money is the root of all evil' has passed into popular currency in the abridged and quite non-Pauline form that it is money itself that constitutes this root.

The third and most serious cause of misunderstanding of certain of the sayings of the Fathers is more subtle, and indirectly comes from classical sources in the conception of natural law, and the distinction between natural law and positive law. Let us cast aside refinements which vary from the Stoics to the Physiocrats (and beyond). Broadly, natural law reflects the mind and intention of the Creator when he set this globe spinning like a fretful midge and peopled it with men made in his own image. And in this happy state, this Eden, had it but endured, all men would have been equal; there would have been no 'mine' and 'thine'; there would have been communism. Under natural law, God gave all things to all men, to be enjoyed in common; and such would be the position, could we but get back to things as they were 'when they left the hands of the Creator'—in a phrase beloved of Mably in the eighteenth century.

Much, however, has happened since then. We are no longer concerned with man in his innocence, but with fallen man whose heart is deceitful above all things and desperately wicked. And for fallen man something more than natural law is required; he needs, for his restraint, positive law, civil law, civil administration and institutions, all of which would have been unnecessary had he remained in a state of innocence. Thus, under positive law, much may be added to natural law—in a sense modifying it to meet the frailty of man. Property may have to be recognised, a coercive State created and much more. Moreover, what is ordained under positive law is not in itself evil, or worthy of condemnation. These things may indirectly spring from man's sin, but they are devised as a remedy against further sin.[1] It will be seen, therefore, in what sense the Fathers, without condemning property, could yet hold that property is occasioned by, and is the result of, man's evil-doing. When they appear to condemn property, it is frequently the result of an unduly elliptical method of expression. At somewhat greater length they might have said that the recognition of property is a necessary provision in positive law, and that positive law has been rendered necessary because of the hardness of man's heart, which, unfortunately, must be accepted as a permanent hypothesis of the sinful world in which we now live. The Fathers had periodically a nostalgic longing for the world as it might have been under 'natural law'; and in such a mood they describe how happy we would be *if* we could share all things, or live according to Luke's picture (true or imagined) of the early Church at Jerusalem. But in general, it is but a dream dependent on a hypothetical and unrealisable '*if*,' rather than a concrete proposal calling for 'active consideration.'

(*e*) CERTAIN CHRISTIAN FATHERS

Readers who have accepted the foregoing section without demur may perhaps, without great loss, skip the present section. For it is essentially in the nature of an expanded footnote, not perhaps free from a certain amount of repetition. Having stated in general terms the position of the Christian Fathers, it may be as well to give somewhat more concrete form to what has been said, by reference to some of the more frequently quoted passages, where the Fathers are assumed to reveal a communistic tinge. A mere handful of Fathers must suffice; but among these, for reasons which will be apparent presently, Clement of Alexandria must be included. The others must of necessity be a somewhat random selection, cited somewhat summarily to confirm and exemplify the general conclusions of the last section. As, however, they are in substantial agreement, no apology is needed for curtailing the procession of Fathers, or (apart from Clement of Alexandria) reducing to a minimum the time each is allowed to testify.

Clement of Alexandria is here the chief witness, and indeed he occupies a place of peculiar importance in this long controversy. In the main his attitude is the traditional attitude of the early Church;

[1] Compare St. Paul: 'Wherefore then serveth the law? It was added because of transgressions' (Galatians iii. 19).

he holds that riches are a snare and a danger; that we must be on our guard against the love of riches; that they are to be used rightly, and that ultimately riches are a gift of God to be devoted, with a sense of responsibility, to promoting the good of others. In a rather quaint metaphor, he says that 'wealth seems to me to be like a serpent, which will twist round the hand and bite; unless one knows how to lay hold of it without danger by the point of the tail'; and he goes on to say of riches that one must, 'despising them, use them skilfully, so as to crush the creature by the charm of the word.'[1] Moreover, in a phrase which, though sometimes it is taken to mean more than it does, merely emphasises the misery of the miser and the blessedness of unrestrained liberality, he argues that 'it is not he who has and keeps, but he who gives away that is rich; and it is giving away, not possession, which renders a man happy.'[2] Again, in a rather metaphysical argument, which is essentially the same as that underlying Wycliffe's Dominion of Grace, he reasons—as Ruskin might have done—that 'good things are the property only of good men; and Christians are good. . . . Accordingly, good things are possessed by Christians alone.'[3] Stated in this form, there is involved an obvious logical fallacy; in any case, the point is not developed. It is doubtful, however, whether St. Clement is here saying more than that good men alone know how to make a good use of good things, or even know which things are good.[4]

The importance of St. Clement, however, rests on the fact that he wrote a short treatise wholly devoted to the central issue in the question with which we are here concerned. This sometimes bears the title *The Rich Man's Salvation*, which is certainly more concise than the literal translation, *Who is the Rich Man that is being Saved?*. The editor and translator of the *Rich Man's Salvation* in the Loeb series, writing from an English University, opines that it is too long to have been delivered as a sermon on any single occasion: but what do they know of sermons, who only England know? If it were indeed a sermon, then, if one may adapt the title of a frequently donated prize-volume to the young of two generations ago, it certainly deserves to be included among 'The Fifteen Decisive Sermons of the World.' For in some respects it is not too much to say that St. Clement's sermon represents one of the decisive landmarks of the world's history.

For the great miracle of Christianity, however the inexplicable be explained, lies in its ascent to power, authority and influence. It originated among the Jews, a race of outcasts, whose pride it nevertheless was to keep themselves to themselves, as becomes a chosen people;

[1] *The Instructor*, Book III, chap. 6. [2] *Ibid.* [3] *Ibid.*

[4] In fact, whether consciously or otherwise, St. Clement is here virtually quoting the Book of Ecclesiasticus; 'For the good are good things created from the beginning; so evil things for sinners.' Here, however, the implication is that the ordinary things of life (salt, honey, milk, clothing, the blood of the grape, etc.) which are good to the godly, are to the sinner turned into evil.

its first sponsors were for the most part men of mean origin, craftsmen and fishermen ; the gospel, as it was formulated, was a gospel for the poor and downtrodden, counting as naught the powers and principalities of this world. How a movement with such unpromising beginnings came to conquer the Roman world and become the official religion of Europe, wielding a power above kings and emperors, remains something of a riddle, even after the ecclesiastical historians have said their last word. Christianity might very well have remained the faith of an obscure and languishing sect among the poorer Jews—at the most, something like the Essenes, or the Therapeuts, or the Hemerobaptists. The first great obstacle to be overcome lay in its Jewish limitations: the gospel must be extended to the Gentiles. The record of this great controversy runs through certain of the Pauline epistles.

The situation confronting St. Clement was somewhat different. He was stationed in one of the wealthiest cities of the ancient world. In the second century, Christianity, increasing in influence, was making an ever stronger appeal to those who were by no means poor and downtrodden, who could not with any show of reason be called weary and heavy-laden. Clement was in touch with the wealthy and the prosperous: in modern phraseology, he had a west-end congregation. But there was no use blinking the fact that the writers of the gospels (and Luke in particular) had not written at all encouragingly regarding the rich man's prospects of salvation. Above all, there was that incident of the rich young man and the comments attached to it. ' Who then can be saved ? ' the apostles had asked, and it was a question that might well continue to haunt the rich men of Alexandria. Nor had the poorer Christians taken kindly to their richer brethren. Clement implies that they had been behaving with ' insolent rudeness ' to the rich. His mission, conscious or unconscious, was to make Christianity comprehensive: it should be not merely the religion of the poor, but the religion of all. It is unnecessary to emphasise the importance, for the future of Christianity and of Europe, of Clement's pronouncement which made it clear beyond all doubt that Christianity knew no frontiers determined by station or rank in life.

St. Clement's sermon is so illuminating as a considered statement of the attitude of the early Church towards worldly wealth, that a few points in the argument may be noted. The professed purpose of the discourse is to free the rich from their ' unfounded despair,' and to prove to them that they must not regard themselves as irrevocably damned in advance. The text is, inevitably, the story of the rich young man—in this case as given in the Gospel of St. Mark (x. 17–31)—and the problem is to rob of its sting the injunction to ' sell whatever thou hast.' The answer of St. Clement is that the words must not be taken literally. ' It is no great or enviable thing,' he says, ' to be simply without riches.' Nor has the injunction in this sense anything new in it: groping into

Greek history, he cites various instances where men have renounced their wealth for one purpose or another. He will not admit that those who ‘ lie along the roads in abject poverty ’ are, for this reason alone, assured of God’s blessedness. The real essence of the injunction is that we should

banish from the soul its opinions about riches, its attachment to them, its excessive desire, its morbid excitement over them, its anxious cares, the thorns of our earthly existence which choke the seed of the true life.[1]

The fact that it is not the ‘ visible act ’ of parting with goods that matters is again shown by the fact that renunciation of wealth may in fact bring a man no nearer to God. A man who has unburdened himself of his property may be more anxiously minded than before, more occupied with the desire and longing for wealth than when he had it. The command laid upon us to feed the hungry and clothe the naked could not be obeyed, ‘ if each of us were already in want of all these things.’ Consequently, advancing from this ‘ alms argument ’ which cuts little ice to-day (for no one would now admit that the continuance of poverty is necessary in order that alms-giving may flourish), he restates what is, despite deviation, probably the central doctrine of the early Church in these matters:

Wealth too is an instrument of the same kind. You can use it rightly; it ministers to righteousness. But if one use it wrongly, it is found to be a minister of wrong. For its nature is to minister, not to rule.[2]

What matters is not wealth, but the use of wealth. We must extirpate, not possessions which in themselves are neutral, but the passions of the soul which prevent the good use of wealth. Possessions are outward things, and salvation does not depend on outward things. So in the end we come back to liberality on an unbounded scale, with wealth as a trust to be administered with a sense of responsibility. The final statement does indeed speak of a ‘ common stock ’; but it is clear that individual responsibility remains. Christ, he says, ‘ declares that all possessions are by nature unrighteous, when a man possesses them for personal advantage, as being entirely his own, and does not bring them into the common stock for those in need.’ [3]

Let us now call St. Ambrose. One of the most frequently quoted passages in this controversy is that in the seventh chapter of the first book on *The Duties of the Clergy*, where St. Ambrose is concerned with justice and goodwill. The words usually cited are these:

[1] Loeb edition, pp. 291–293. [2] Loeb edition, p. 299.

[3] It is rather surprising that St. Clement does not call in aid the distinction between a counsel of perfection applicable to some, and a precept applicable to all. St. Ambrose, on the other hand, takes the injunction to the rich young man as the classical example of the distinction (*Concerning Widows*, chap. 2).

. . . Nature has poured forth all things for all men for common use. God has ordered all things to be produced, so that there should be food in common to all, and that the earth should be a common possession for all. Nature, therefore, has produced a common right for all, but greed has made it a right for a few.[1]

This occurs in a passage where St. Ambrose is stating and considering the views of certain ' philosophers ' ; and it might be suggested that there is a faint pervading aroma of *oratio obliqua* about the whole argument: it is not clear where St. Ambrose's statement of the views of the philosophers ends, and where his own added comment begins. But, waiving this, the essential point to note in the foregoing extract is that it rests on the distinction between the state of nature and the conditions that supervened later. This is obvious from the fact that the conclusions which St. Ambrose draws from his argument are in no wise revolutionary. Far from suggesting that we should restore the situation as it was when ' nature produced a common right to all,' his recommendations are what we should now call tepidly and mildly reformist:

Thus, in accordance with the will of God and the union of nature, we ought to be of mutual help one to the other, and to vie with each other in doing duties, to lay all our advantages as it were before all, and (to use the words of Scripture) to bring help one to the other from a feeling of devotion or of duty, by giving money, or by doing something, at any rate in some way or other.[2]

This may be criticised on the ground that the guidance it gives to anxious souls (' doing something, at any rate in some way or other ' !) is somewhat nebulous: it certainly cannot be suggested that it is subversive of society.

It may be interesting to apply to St. Ambrose the other test indicated above. What does he say elsewhere, apart from the passages most frequently cited to demonstrate his communistic leanings? Riches, he says, are to be contemned: the love of riches is to be despised; they are unnecessary to salvation. But at the same time, ' riches themselves are not blamable,'[3] if one knows how to direct one's property. All of which is in danger of being trite and commonplace; but at least it reveals that the crucial test is not wealth and possessions, but the use made of wealth and possessions.[4]

[1] *Duties of the Clergy*, Book I, chap. 28 (p. 23 in edition of Nicene and Post-Nicene Fathers).

[2] *Ibid.* p. 23.

[3] Letter 63, p. 470, same edition.

[4] At the same time, in illustration of the intermingling of many lines of thought, perhaps ultimately inconsistent, to which the Fathers, no less than other men, were subject, it may be noted that in one place St. Ambrose cites St. Luke's abbreviated version of the Sermon on the Mount, and comments: ' Thus it is stated as plainly as possible that poverty, hunger and pain, which are considered to be evils, not only are not hindrances to a blessed life, but are actually so many helps towards it ' (*Duties of the Clergy*, Book II, chap. 5). This is the ascetic doctrine, undiluted and undisguised.

Tertullian, in virtue of one passage, is frequently invoked in these questions. In the thirty-ninth chapter of his *Apology*, in describing for the instruction of unbelievers how the Christian community did in fact live, he remarks that 'all things are common amongst us, except our wives.' Waiving the reservation, it is, however, clear that Tertullian's words are not to be taken literally. He was a writer who greatly (and rightly) enjoyed his own rhetoric. Every sentence was fashioned and balanced with an eye to the maximum effect attainable. The whole *Apology* is an example of how a case should be presented to a jury. The significant point here, however, is that immediately preceding the phrase so frequently quoted, Tertullian gives a much more sober account of a way of life which is anything but communistic, but which again represents the prevalence of open-handed liberality among people who recognised private property:

> Even the kind of treasury which we have is not filled up with sums paid under a sense of obligation, as if they were the price of religion; but each one places there a small contribution on a certain day of the month, or when he wishes, providing only he is both willing and able—for the offerings are not compulsory but voluntary.

Thus, he adds, 'we never hesitate to communicate our substance to another.'[1]

Lactantius is another of the early Christian writers frequently cited to prove the essentially communistic features of primitive Christianity—but surely, only by those who are content to accept the stray phrase offered to them, without looking behind and around. For Lactantius indeed condemns what he is summoned to bless. He admits that Plato 'approached nearer to the truth' (i.e. than some others who were more remote from the truth); but in the same sentence he adds that 'no one fell into worse errors, especially because in his books respecting the State, he wished all things to be common to all.' The utmost that Lactantius concedes is that 'this is endurable concerning property, though it is unjust'; and the reason annexed is of the essence of the Manchester School: 'For it ought not to be an injury to any one, if he possesses more than another through his own industry.' But still he admits that 'this is capable of being endured in some way'—an attitude of admirable tepidity, which, needless to say, changes to something else when he contemplates the Platonic community of wives.[2]

Perhaps more significant is a passage in the fifth chapter of the fifth book of the *Divine Institutes*, which is devoted to Justice. Here, Lactantius, with that odd confusion of sacred and profane history which is so charming and disarming a feature of some of the more

[1] *Apology*, chap. 39, pp. 113–115 (Mr. Bindley's translation).
[2] *Epitome of the Divine Institutes*, chap. 38.

scholarly of the early Christians, gives a glowing and approving account of the reign of Justice under Saturnus, before it was banished by Jupiter; and he quotes Vergil, how 'it was not even allowed to mark out or divide the plain with a boundary: men sought all things in common'; and the reason was that

> God had given the earth in common to all, that they might pass their life in common, not that mad and raging avarice might claim all things for itself, and that that which was produced for all might not be wanting to any.

But forthwith he explains that

> this saying of the poet ought so to be taken, not as suggesting the idea, that individuals at that time had no private property, but it must be regarded as a poetical figure; that we may understand that men were so liberal, that they did not shut up the fruits of the earth produced for them, nor did they in solitude brood over the things stored up, but admitted the poor to share the fruits of their labour.[1]

For Lactantius, this golden age is a dream gone for ever; and even the dream did not represent a world of communism, but a world of unbounded liberality, such as had been the ideal of the Mosaic Law, and of all the early Christian teachers without exception.

St. Basil is an interesting witness on these questions, if only because in certain of his homilies (especially 6 and 7) he is unrestrained in his denunciation of the foolish and self-indulgent rich. They keep horses with pedigrees, and 'scarlet cloths make the horses as gay as bridegrooms.' They maintain cooks, confectioners, butlers, huntsmen, sculptors, painters, devisers and creators of pleasures of every kind. They have herds of camels, troops of horses, droves of oxen, flocks of sheep, herds of swine. They paint their walls with flowers and let their fellow-creatures go bare; they have baths in town and baths in the country. And, needless to say, matters are worse when a man has a wealth-loving wife—a common misfortune: 'With all their behests they do not leave their husbands breathing-time. No fortune is vast enough to satisfy a woman's wants—no, not if it were to flow like a river!' In short, 'when will the man have time to care for his soul, who has to serve a woman's fancies.' Isaiah, towards the end of his third chapter, had obviously a glimpse of the truth.[2]

Such is the indictment: the rich man harnesses his horses with splendour, and despises his brother if he is ill-dressed; he lets his wheat rot, and will not feed the hungry. Yet the conclusion to be drawn is anything but communistic. 'Come then,' he says; 'dispose of thy wealth in various directions. Be generous and liberal in thy expenditure on the poor. . . . Do not wait for a famine before thou

[1] *Divine Institutes*, Book V, chap. 5.
[2] Introduction to works of St. Basil (Nicene and Post-Nicene Fathers), p. lxiii.

openest thy barns.' And when Basil is not delivering homilies with an effective popular appeal, but is merely writing soberly to a fellow-bishop, his position is made even more explicit:

> The good man, however, neither turns his heart to wealth when he has it, nor seeks after it if he has it not. He treats what is given him not for his selfish enjoyment, but for wise administration.[1]

It is the orthodox view of the early Church. It is not wealth, but the abuse of wealth that is sinful; the rich man should spend with a sense of his responsibilities.

Many passages might be cited from St. John Chrysostom, a particularly voluminous Father, but one must suffice in a chapter where there is barely room for samples of samples. The quotation selected is from the *Second Homily to the People of Antioch*, where the theme is that it is not riches that are forbidden, but pride; that sin lies not in external possessions, but in the covetous mind. Wealth is not forbidden if wisely used. St. John Chrysostom may himself explain the position in his own words:

> For as I observed, wine is not a bad thing, but drunkenness is so. A covetous man is one thing, and a rich man is another thing. The covetous man is not rich; he is in want of many things, and while he needs many things, he can never be rich. The covetous man is a keeper, not a master of wealth; a slave, not a lord.[2]

The conclusion is that 'the rich man is not one who is in possession of much, but one who gives much.' Wealth is to be wisely used; it is to be a servant, not a master.

Many other Fathers might be summoned, but even if great names have been omitted, enough has been said to clarify the point at issue. And indeed further citation might prove but vain repetition—if indeed that stage has not already been reached. For there is, fundamentally, a singular uniformity in the official and orthodox views of the early Church, even if these views are not always expressed with punctilious prudence. 'Communism' receives no support; it is indeed at times explicitly condemned; but the spokesmen of the Church were very much alive to the dangers inherent in the possible abuse of wealth. Possessions in a sense were indifferent in themselves—neither good nor evil. The essential issue depended on how they were used and how they were regarded. The real evil lay not in wealth, but in being attached to wealth. It was not riches that damned a man; but pride and a covetous heart.

[1] Letter 236.
[2] *Second Homily to the People of Antioch*, p. 41 in Library of Fathers (1842).

While this may be accepted as the 'official' attitude of the early Church, the view taken by responsible Fathers in their responsible utterances, there is perhaps something to be said on the other side. Unquestionably—and it merely shows unreasoning partisanship to deny it—there was a communistic tradition in early Christianity. How far this derived ultimately from the Essenes is largely a matter of speculation. What, however, is not a matter of speculation is the enormous influence and the abiding appeal of Luke's idealised account of the communism of the early Church at Jerusalem. Doubtless, the moment it is read carefully, the inner contradictions reveal that it is but an old man's confused dream of something he has persuaded himself ought to have happened. Yet for centuries one is almost tempted to say that these few verses in the Acts of the Apostles are quoted as frequently as any other passage in the New Testament. Obviously they served as a 'myth,' giving expression, if not to the aspirations of all men, at least to the aspirations of many men in a certain emotional condition. And beyond question the legend of the communism of the Church at Jerusalem served to give continuity to the communist tradition. The manifestations of this tradition are, however, to be found in what without disrespect may be called the underworld, in obscure communistic sects which appeared from time to time, earning the censure of the Church. Probably one such sect was that of the Nicolaitanes, which has the signal honour of a fleeting mention in the Revelation of St. John the Divine, with an expression of the undiluted hatred of the author. In the second century there was the sect founded by Carpocrates and his son Epiphanes, a precocious lad who died (it is said) at the age of 17 and who, rightly or wrongly, is credited with the authorship of a book which no adolescent should have written. The curious will find as much as they require regarding Carpocrates in the second chapter of the third book of the *Miscellanies* of Clement of Alexandria. Carpocrates (or it may have been the precocious Epiphanes) seems to have been moved by a singularly simple logic. The justice of God, it was argued, consists in all things being common, and in all being equal. And just as God makes the sun to shine on all alike, so he made all women for the equal use and enjoyment of all men. Clement was unconvinced and did not approve. It is odd, or perhaps not so odd, to note thus early the apparently inevitable connection between complete communism and promiscuity. The reason is not to be found in the simple faith in God's bounty that appears to have inspired the precocious Epiphanes. There is a much more compelling reason clearly realised by Plato, Campanella, Fourier and many others. It is that women are incorrigible individualists and make men selfish—or if not selfish for themselves, selfish for their wives and children. For the true communist, the home, postulating the supreme devotion of one individual to another, is the nursery of all selfish and anti-social instincts. And even St. Paul dimly sensed this truth.[1]

(*f*) ST. THOMAS AQUINAS

In the concluding section of a chapter dealing with various aspects of the Christian tradition in regard to the questions with which we are here interested, it may be convenient to add a note on the teaching of St. Thomas Aquinas, who, in unusual measure, is a link between far distant centuries. But indeed the significance of St. Thomas lies not so much in the fact that he restates and completes the essential elements of the Christian tradition; it is rather that he combines the Christian and the Greek traditions, aiming at a synthesis of the two great streams of influence in human history. Here, in the nature of things, we are concerned only with a small fragment of the teaching of St. Thomas; and in some ways, as he would himself have thought, the least important. The influence of Christianity had profoundly modified the accepted views on many aspects of human life, so that not a few of the assumptions of Plato and Cicero were no longer axiomatic. Even if slowly, labour was ceasing to be a thing of contempt; even if haltingly, it was being recognised, as in the Jewish tradition, that all men were the children of one God, though doubtless God expressed his will by assigning them to different stations in life. Yet on one point, if for very different reasons, St. Thomas was at one with the leading representatives of Greek thought. Neither Plato nor Aristotle were really interested in economic questions, for the excellent reason that these questions did not really interest them. In their eyes, a taint of lowness and vulgarity adhered to buying and selling, and to 'mankind in the ordinary business of life.' Ethics mattered; and politics mattered. The economic problem, when it appeared in mangled fragments, was a subsidiary by-product of more worthy studies. Nor, could it have been presented to him, would St. Thomas have been greatly interested in the 'economic problem' as such; for the still more excellent reason that it did not matter. Only one thing

[1] Those who are interested in the vitality and the endurance of a tradition may find it illuminating to note how precisely the essentials of the Christian Fathers are produced by a writer as late as Bossuet. One significant passage may provide sufficient illustration: 'Si nous voulions monter à l'origine des choses, nous trouverions peut-être qu'ils (*i.e.* the poor) n'auraient pas moins de droit que vous aux biens que vous possédez. La nature, ou plutôt, pour parler plus chrétiennement, Dieu, le Père commun des hommes, a donné dès le commencement un droit égal à tous ses enfants sur toutes les choses dont ils ont besoin pour la conservation de leur vie. Aucun de nous ne se peut vanter d'être plus avantagé que les autres par la nature; mais l'insatiable désir d'amasser n'a pas permis que cette belle fraternité pût durer longtemps dans le monde. Il a fallu venir au partage et à la propriété qui a produit toutes les querelles et tous les procès: de là est né ce mot de mien et de tien, cette parole si froide, dit l'admirable saint Jean Chrysostome' (*Panégyrique de saint François d'Assise*, vol. 4, p. 434 of edition of 1846).

mattered ; and that was Salvation, Beatitudo, living the Christian life, walking humbly with God now, in order to attain eternal life hereafter. This was the one end ; and all other things were weighed as means to the attainment of this end. If, as we have been told in these latter days, economics is concerned with the application of scarce means to alternative ends, St. Thomas's comment would have been simple and emphatic : There never are and there never can be alternative ends. ' Seek ye first—and indeed seek ye exclusively—the Kingdom of God.'

It is doubtless dangerous to give way to unprovoked generalisations, above all on insufficient knowledge ; yet it may be suggested that perhaps no age has been so completely penetrated with the spirit and the assumptions of Christianity as that of which St. Thomas was the chief ornament. It was an age of moderation and restraint, which not merely accepted the view, but endeavoured to act on the view, that this transient world is but the porch to life everlasting ; that we are indeed but pilgrims, and that in our pilgrimage we should do the right thing by our fellow-wayfarers. The assumptions on which the Middle Ages acted were largely that each should labour unquestioningly at the task assigned to him by Providence ; that no one should take advantage of his neighbour in anything, that greed and avarice are incompatible with a balanced view of the relationship between this world and the next. God, it was held, may give riches ; but riches cannot give God. This may appear, and perhaps is, a somewhat rose-coloured view of the Middle Ages. Possibly the twelfth, thirteenth and fourteenth centuries were as prolific of crime (and other things) as earlier and later ages ; but it is sometimes wise to judge a people by its motives.

In this place we may confine ourselves to the teaching of St. Thomas Aquinas on one point, and one point exclusively. His views on justice in exchange, on the just price and on usury are doubtless not irrelevant, but they are slightly off our path. The central point for our purpose may be subsumed under the heading of the problem of Property—or putting it in larger and more correct terms : ' What should be the attitude of a man seeking the Kingdom of God towards the things of this world ? also what, in respect of these things, should be his attitude to his fellow-men ? ' It is generally said, and on the whole rightly said, that St. Thomas represents in his doctrine, a synthesis of Aristotle and of Christian doctrine, and some have even suggested that he is largely concerned (as in his references to slavery) to carry forward as much as possible of Aristotle. It may be so : but to anyone who reapproaches St. Thomas immediately after a surfeit of the early Christian Fathers, the really arresting point is the close kinship between the Fathers and the Angelic Doctor. St. Thomas indeed is largely the completion, the perfection and the clarification of the early Christian tradition.

The question of the lawfulness of property St. Thomas establishes in two stages. In the first place, he proves that the possession of external goods corresponds to the nature of man. True, all things are under the power of God: the earth is the Lord's and the fullness thereof. But so far as 'use' is concerned, man has a natural power over external things, since, guided by reason and will, he can use them as though they were fashioned expressly for him. The less perfect exists for the more perfect. Thus the Philosopher proves that 'possessio rerum exteriorum est homini naturalis.'[1]

This, it may be said, does not take us very far. It establishes a right in man, made in the image of God, to have 'dominion,' in the phraseology of the first chapter of the Book of Genesis. The really knotty problem remains: may the individual justifiably have individual property? The answer given by St. Thomas is very obviously in line with Aristotle; not so obviously, but nevertheless perhaps more essentially so, it is in line with the Christian Fathers. He is aware of, and indeed quotes in the 'Objections' the apparently communistic utterances of St. Paul and St. Ambrose, which have had such a long run up to, and including, the works of Mr. Beer. But St. Thomas is undeterred. Two rights, he answers, must be distinguished in this matter. There is the power to acquire and administer ('potestas procurandi et dispensandi'); there is the power to use. Now, so far as concerns acquisition and administration, St. Thomas largely follows Aristotle, arguing that private ownership is not merely permissible, but necessary to human life. The grounds advanced are familiar, not to say hackneyed. There is, firstly, the greater care bestowed on individual possessions, compared to that devoted to what belongs to everybody, and therefore nobody; each of us, *laborem fugiens*—such is the nature of the beast—leaves the heavy end of the stick to others. Secondly, things proceed in a more orderly manner, if each has his allotted task and what belongs thereto, as contrasted with the chaos of every one doing, and looking after, everything. And thirdly, a point emphasised by Aristotle in regard to the disputes which spring from the common purse, relations will be more harmonious if each is content with his own possessions. These arguments for private property are, it will be observed, based purely on grounds of expediency and on the imperfection of men. It is not so easy for unregenerate man, *laborem fugiens*, to live in excessive intimacy with his fellows. We need, in all senses, a room of our own. Thus private property is 'necessarium ad humanam vitam,'—not on general principles, but in order to avoid the greater evils which would otherwise result.

While private ownership is thus consecrated on the side of administration, it is otherwise so far as concerns 'use.' On this side it is not permissible to regard possessions as purely private property for personal

[1] *Summa Theologica*, II/II, Quaestio 66, Art. 1.

enjoyment. The Latin somehow sounds more peremptory than most translations: 'Quantum ad hoc non debet homo habere res exteriores ut proprias, sed ut communes.' In form this is substantially Aristotle's counter-proposal to Plato's communism, viz. that the advantages of both systems could be combined by adding to private possessions the mollifying influence of community in use. Yet it is only necessary to read the relevant passage in Aristotle in conjunction with that in St. Thomas Aquinas to realise that in practice the two are poles asunder. In Aristotle the proposal gives effect to the proverb, 'Friends' goods, common goods'; we are, as becomes gentlemen, not to be too particular when our friends make use of what is ours. He cites with approval, as we have already seen, the custom in Lacedaemon where the citizens use each others' slaves, and where the employment of dogs and horses is not too strictly accounted for, when it comes to a hunting expedition. This, with respect to Aristotle, is but to scratch the surface of a deep problem; for this merely represents the camaraderie among members of a governing caste, corresponding to the etiquette of an officers' mess, where one does not wait to be pressed to take another cigarette, where the bottle is for use and not for ostentation, and where the return of Penguins is hardly expected. It is otherwise with St. Thomas Aquinas. There is here no question of free-and-easy sharing with 'friends' and equals. 'Common use' implies that wealth is to be shared easily with those in need; and after the manner of St. Thomas he falls back on the counsel of St. Paul to the rich, that they be 'ready to distribute, willing to communicate.' [1]

We are back, it will be observed, at the great question of alms-giving; and it should be noted that in an age innocent of employers' contributions, and of schemes of social improvement and betterment financed by a progressive income tax, the principle of community in use, of making wealth serviceable to the community at large, could only be effected on the initiative of the possessor of wealth, through the voluntary exercise of alms-giving. In St. Thomas Aquinas, as in the great body of the Christian Fathers, private property is defended, but for its justification it is necessary that almsgiving prevail. Moreover, seeing that the things of this world exist for the use of mankind, there can be no valid right to property, unless the owner by alms-giving makes his wealth available for the purpose for which it was created. It is fairly commonly reported that one of the Christian Fathers said roundly that the rich man is a thief. What in fact he did say was that the rich man, *if he does not give alms*, is a thief. The point illustrates admirably a cardinal element in the views of the Christian Fathers and St. Thomas Aquinas alike. The possessor of wealth is the administrator merely; it may be that in his administration he is responsible solely to his own judgment; but he holds it only on condition that

[1] *Summa Theologica*, II/II, Quaestio 66, Art. 2.

he uses it for the good of mankind, which involves the giving of alms. It is not merely, as the semi-sacred writer said, that alms maketh an atonement for sin. It is necessary to the proper use of wealth; ultimately, the giving of alms alone can justify the existence of property.

The doctrine that wealth exists for the use of those who need it, finds its crucial test in St. Thomas's consideration of the question whether, in extremest need, 'theft' is permissible. He has already explained that the recognition of property is not contrary to natural law, but is something which human reason has added to natural law. But clearly, what flows from human enactment cannot derogate from natural or divine law. Now it is the nature of divine providence that all lower things are designed to meet the necessities of men. No provision regarding private property can therefore be allowed to prevent these lower goods from relieving the necessities of men. In short, what one has in superfluity is, in natural law, due to be applied to the sustenance of the poor. In the extreme case, therefore (where, e.g. death threatens, or help cannot otherwise be got), it is permissible, openly or secretly, to take what is necessary from the possessions of others. Nor has such an action anything in common with theft or robbery.[1]

This, above all if detached from its framework, may sound like the voice of an instigator of anarchy. But, indeed, St. Thomas is cautious and moderate; so far is he from being revolutionary, that there are some who would have us believe that his was the great influence that turned the Church against the socialists and the communists! That alms should be given out of superfluities to those in need is the governing principle which admits of no denial. But as in the case of other general principles, it is easier to enunciate it at large than to apply it to particular cases. It is the need of another that is to be pitted against my superfluities; and (in these days at least) there is a marked disinclination to admit that we possess in superfluity.

The attempt to give the general principle somewhat more concrete form gives interest to St. Thomas's discussion of the question how far one should give alms out of one's necessities. The answer is that, as every text-book knows, the word 'necessaries' may have two meanings. He who merely has that which is necessary, in the sense that he has only enough to keep himself alive—one in the enjoyment of a sort of Ricardian wage—is clearly exempt from the obligation of giving alms, just as for similar reasons he was supposed, in the classical Political Economy, to be able to elude the incidence of taxation. But, on the other hand, 'necessaries' may refer to that provision without which it will be impossible to live appropriately as one's station demands ('secundum conditionem et statum propriae personae et aliarum personarum quarum cura ei incumbit'). Admittedly it is

[1] *Loc. cit.*, Art. 7.

impossible to determine where this line falls. To give alms impinging on this necessary provision is a good work: but it is counsel, not precept (' non cadit sub praecepto, sed sub consilio '). But what is not permissible is that anyone should give so much that with what is left he is unable to lead his life in accordance with his station and the obligations resting on him. And St. Thomas adds, in what is a cardinal thought in the Middle Ages: ' Nullus enim inconvenienter vivere debet.' [1]

The matter is thus in the end left to the individual conscience, and indeed perhaps it cannot be otherwise. Alms-giving, it should be repeated, derived its extraordinary importance in the early Christian and mediaeval periods, from the fact that it was the only method of making provision for social needs; and as it was in its nature voluntary, it was necessary to stimulate the flow of alms by keeping men's consciences tender. But it is obvious that St. Thomas's theory leaves loop-holes. He belonged to an age which believed that men were assigned by Providence to different stations in life and, as has been seen, that it was their first duty to live in accordance with the requirements of that station. He was therefore no egalitarian. He outlined a theory of division of labour by divine decree, according to which one is more drawn to one task than another. But it is of the essence of the doctrine of the ' calling,' that if men are assigned different tasks, then their needs must also be different. Different things are expected of different people, and each must live *convenienter*. If in addition one ropes in dependents (as St. Thomas does), it is obvious that the question whether one has more than is ' necessary,' is a very difficult one, to which very varying answers, according to temperament, may be given. Imagine, in modern phraseology, a middle-class father, ' with a position to keep up ' (which is a free translation of *convenienter vivere*); give him six utterly unattractive and completely feckless daughters, and ask him to determine the point at which he has more than is necessary. If we agree to give him £3000, doubtless the wolf will not be exactly at the door; his answer will be that neither are his six prospective sons-in-law. Nor is it much good telling us to take no thought of to-morrow. Perhaps because of our lack of mediaeval faith, the future nowadays is precisely the one thing we find it impossible to forget. This may seem a trivial example with which to confront Thomist philosophy: concrete examples perhaps always are trivial. The criticism which St. Thomas can hardly wholly escape on this question is that he advances propositions which are somewhat radical in principle; whereas his suggestions as to their application tend to the consecration of things as they are, and to the arbitrament of the flexible and elastic conscience of the individual.

So far as the main issue is concerned, however, the significance of

[1] *Loc. cit.*, Quaestio 32.

St. Thomas Aquinas for our purpose is clear. He represents a continuation of the tradition of the Christian Fathers. Property is defended; but in theory, property is reduced to a right of administration. Wealth is a trust held for the public good, and therefore there can be no arbitrary *jus utendi et abutendi*. The owner is responsible, if only to his own conscience, for the use he makes of his substance. Alms-giving out of superfluity (as in Godwin who, oddly, has much in common with St. Thomas) is not a meritorious act, being merely the discharge of an obvious debt. St. Thomas, however, is much more cloudy than Godwin as to what constitutes superfluity. Lastly, the existence of property is justified only on the assumption of adequate alms-giving. The central dogma that the owner of property is merely the administrator has certain obvious links with some characteristic features of the Feudal System, which also refused to recognise absolute property, but merely usufruct on certain conditions.

CHAPTER III

UTOPIA AND THE UTOPIAS

(*a*) MORE'S *UTOPIA*

SIR THOMAS MORE'S *Utopia* is one of the great books of all time. Reviving the tradition of Plato, it has itself established a tradition for subsequent generations. Yet, when all is said, the book remains and is likely to remain, an enigma, which each reader may interpret as he will. There is certainly no ambiguity about the views expressed in the course of this imaginative fairy-tale by the various participants in the dialogue, above all by that redoubtable traveller, Raphael Hythloday, on whom falls the burden of criticism of this very imperfect world and of the description of a better. But it is a nice matter of speculation to enquire how far what is unquestionably the dominant note of *Utopia* is a reflection of what was in the mind of More when he wrote the work. Clearly a man who writes a play or a dialogue cannot be assumed to hold *all* the views expressed by *all* his puppets. In the present case there are three *dramatis personae*, More himself, Peter Giles, town clerk of Antwerp, and the reporter regarding the blessed island of Utopia, who is also the critic of conditions in England and indeed in Europe generally. Everything of substance is in fact said by Raphael; the other two are, in the main, but a nodding audience. It is, however, perhaps of significance that among the few words More attributes to himself is an orthodox defence of property as against the praise of communism, and the final observation of all on the last page is a caveat that he cannot ' perfectly agree ' to everything that has been related.[1] Is *Utopia* primarily a satire, not intended to be taken too seriously, or is it merely a literary exercise in which a not very convincing flight of fancy provides a series of pegs on which to hang comments on things at large? Or do the devastatingly critical comments of Raphael in fact reflect the mind of More who, confronted with the rather difficult task of living with his contemporaries, chose the path of prudence in giving currency to all this cargo of high explosives in the form of an imaginary dialogue, adding in effect that the editor was not responsible for any of the views expressed by his characters? For, on any interpretation, *Utopia* is a curious book to have come from Sir Thomas More. It was written in 1515–1516, when he was round about thirty-seven years of age. He was already rising in the service of the State, and was to become Lord Chancellor before

[1] Pp. 86, 167 (as printed in *Ideal Commonwealths*, Universal Library). References are to this edition, as probably the most accessible.

tragedy overtook him. To put it no higher, it is unusual for civil servants or Ministers of the State, in the active practice of their profession, to demonstrate, even through the mouth of an imagined Raphael Hythloday, the iniquitous shortcomings of all known States and of most social institutions. One other point may have some bearing on this question. *Utopia* ought to have been one of the great English classics; in fact, it was written in Latin and printed abroad in 1516. An English translation did not appear until as late as 1551, when translations in German, Italian and French were already available. If More undeniably launched on the world a consignment of highly inflammable and revolutionary doctrine, in intention at least he did not address it to Everyman, but only to those who 'had the Latin.'

The devising and the writing of Utopias is a curious weakness of mankind. Were it not that the writer of that *Utopia*, from which all others derive generically their name, was one of the noblest and most courageous of men, one might be tempted to look upon Utopias as the cowards' flight from reality. Doubtless it may be thought that a pleasant tale (assuming that it is pleasant) may reach a wider circle of readers, on the questionable analogy of the efficacy of parables in speaking to the simple:. 'Without a parable spake he not unto them.' We are assured that truth embodied in a tale may enter in at lowly doors. Something may also be allowed to considerations of prudence, as perhaps in the case of More himself, living in the reign of Henry VIII; it may be possible, with greater safety, to present with a coating of fiction what would merely occasion trouble if offered neat. But the weakness of all Utopias is necessarily that they dodge the real difficulty of how to transform this present world into something better. The writers of Utopias take you to a distant island in a magic sea, or to another planet, or to the far future, whence, looking backward, these evil times may be dimly descried, or they even take you into the bowels of the earth. In any event, the reader is called to witness a smoothly working society, which in most cases has worked smoothly for an indefinite period. But the important point for us lies in the practical administrative difficulties of the transition. A Utopia is a kind of Heaven. Easy enough doubtless to live there, once you are there; the whole difficulty is in getting there.

Another point with regard to Utopias is perhaps less surprising than it may appear at the first blush. Viewing them as a group, we have here writers, in many cases of the highest eminence, who set out to describe the ideal State, and to reveal its functioning through ideal institutions; and in all cases we are assured that never was there such a happy population. Yet in fact no Utopia has ever been described in which any sane man would on any conditions consent to live, if he could possibly escape. In spite of all the creature comforts, in spite of (and partly because of) the reduction in the hours of work, there is not one in which life would not be weary, flat, stale and unprofitable. And the reason is not far to seek; it is that in all Utopias life has reached a static stage. Nothing ever happens; no one ever disagrees with any one; the government, whatever its form may be, is always so wisely guided that there may be room for gratitude but never for criticism. 'Life is Colour, and Warmth and Light, and a striving evermore for these.' In all Utopias perfection has, by definition, been attained, and there is nothing left to strive for.

> Etwas fürchten und hoffen und sorgen
> Muss der Mensch für den kommenden Morgen.

But there are no such stimulants to vitality in any known Utopia. The result is that life in any of them would be as devastatingly boring as life in the conventional heaven, where, since the revolt of the angels, nothing has happened to stir the blood or quicken the pulse. Somewhat naively, Raphael says of Utopia that 'he that knows one of their towns knows them all.' It is an understatement. He that knows one inhabitant of any Utopia knows all the inhabitants; and one is almost tempted to add that he that knows one Utopia knows all Utopias. Nothing happens, nothing can happen in any of them.[1]

Yet though the actual description of life in the ideal state—the social gadgets—may appear trivial and puerile, or at best faintly amusing, the ideas inspiring the dream may be of intense interest. Nowhere is this truer than in the case of the original Utopia itself. If *Utopia* survives as a living force, it is not because of its description of the garden city of Amaurot, so pleasantly situated on the river Anider, or because of its account of its rather too rational inhabitants, but because of its comments on the social evils of the times in which it was written, and of its astonishing relevance to much subsequent controversy.

Utopia falls into two 'Books,' the first of which is in the main concerned with the evil conditions prevailing in England round about 1516, though in fact its censures extend to all the princes and potentates of Western Europe. The second 'Book' is devoted, in contrast, to the happy island of Utopia which, through the wise dispensations of a former King Utopus, has escaped the evils from which we suffer. Sitting on a green bank in a garden of Antwerp, More and Peter Giles listen to the tales of Raphael Hythloday, the travelling philosopher. They would fain have a man of his knowledge and experience serve humanity by entering the service of a Prince; but Raphael realises that he would be of no use to the princes of this world, who are

[1] In one of the most insipid of Utopias, *The Coming Race*, Lord Lytton notes the complete extinction of all literature. There is nothing whatever to write about: 'we have no events to chronicle,' nor apparently any emotions to register.

'generally more set on acquiring new kingdoms, right or wrong, than on governing well those they possess.'[1] Raphael, a Portuguese by birth, is extraordinarily well-informed regarding the conditions in England. It was an age of poverty, of homelessness, of robbery and theft due in part to the enclosures, whereby 'your sheep, which are naturally mild, and easily kept in order, may be said now to devour men, and unpeople, not only villages, but towns.'[2] Consequently, honest men were reduced to drifting along the dusty highway in the great company of vagabonds who, by way of theft and robbery, ended on the hangman's gallows. The other great nursery of potential thieves was to be found in the unnecessary retainers of useless nobles, for these, when they lose their occupations, must also take to begging and stealing. As this provides one of the *Leitmotifs* of Utopia, let Raphael Hythloday himself speak:

> There is a great number of noblemen among you, that are themselves as idle as drones, that subsist on other men's labour, on the labour of their tenants, whom, to raise their revenues, they pare to the quick. . . . Besides this, they carry about with them a great number of idle fellows, who never learned any art by which they may gain their living; and these, as soon as either their lord dies, or they themselves fall sick, are turned out of doors. . . . Now when the stomachs of those that are thus turned out of doors, grow keen, they rob no less keenly; and what else can they do?[3]

This leads to a discussion of the effects of the undue severity of the law, as evidenced in the indiscriminate hanging of all thieves; indeed, at one place Raphael's argument is rather directed against all capital punishment, as being an infringement of divine law.[4] Universal bad government, ambitious princes neglectful of their subjects, the abuses of the idle rich, vagabondage, robbery, indiscriminate hanging, neglect of the teaching of Christ—such, briefly, are the distinguishing marks of the world in general and of England in particular, over against which Raphael Hythloday sets the vision of Utopia, of which, after an interval devoted to dinner, his auditors being seated once more on the same green bank, he gives a detailed account in Book II.

Life in Utopia may perhaps be dealt with in this place without overmuch detail and with a large brush, except where the peculiarities of the inhabitants raise points of principle. It is of course a communistic island, where private property has ceased to exist. In morals they appear to have been enlightened followers of Bentham, believing in pleasure, 'using only this caution, that a lesser pleasure might not stand in the way of a greater, and that no pleasure ought to be pursued that should draw a great deal of pain after it.'[5] They seem to have been familiar with the felicific calculus. In matters of religion, 'their priests are men of eminent piety, and therefore they are but few.'[6]

[1] P. 59. [2] P. 64. [3] P. 62.
[4] P. 68. [5] P. 116. [6] P. 156.

It is a country where there are few laws, and no lawyers—'a sort of people whose profession it is to disguise matters, and to wrest the laws.'[1] Other engaging features are that 'they love their ease,' and, rather oddly, 'they take great pleasure in fools.'[2]

Life in Utopia is subject to strict discipline: everything is made to a pattern. The cities are numbered; they are at appropriate distances from each other; the number of families in each city and the size of families are regulated. They have their magistrates—Syphogrants and Tranibors, if such details interest. They have a Prince and a Council; but as in all authoritarian states, it is not for the ordinary citizen to meddle unduly with state affairs; 'It is death for anyone to meet and consult concerning the state, unless it be either in their ordinary council, or in the assembly of the whole body of the people.'[3] That Utopia entails such a vigorous repression of talk in the tavern has perhaps been insufficiently observed. Every one masters two trades, agriculture and one other. All wear the same clothes, except in so far as is necessary to distinguish the sexes, and the married from the unmarried. Moreover, fashions never change. The day is strictly divided up between its various occupations, and the hour-glass is the tyrant of every man's life. All must work, except a few who are exempted because of their aptitude for study, and if these do not make the necessary progress, this exemption is withdrawn. This austerity of life follows them into their leisure, which must be devoted to 'some proper exercise.' The hours of work are, however, only six, three hours before and three hours after dinner. There is a significant passage, the forerunner of much in later literature, arguing that long hours result from the army of idlers which society carries, and that if all did their share, the burden of work could be spread thin, and a few hours' work would suffice. So far from six hours being too little, it is rather too much, for you have but to consider how great a part of all other nations is quite idle:

> First, women generally do little, who are the half of mankind; and if some few women are diligent, their husbands are idle; then consider the great company of idle priests, and of those that are called religious men; add to these all rich men, chiefly those that have estates in land, who are called noblemen and gentlemen, together with their families, made up of idle persons that are kept more for show than use; add to these, all those strong and lusty beggars, that go about pretending some disease, in excuse for their begging; and upon the whole account you will find that the number of those by whose labours mankind is supplied, is much less than you perhaps imagined.[4]

In addition, very few of those who are employed are really engaged on useful work: 'for we who measure all things by money, give rise to many trades that are both vain and superfluous, and serve only to

[1] P. 135. [2] P. 134. [3] P. 95. [4] Pp. 98–99.

support riot and luxury.' It is an idea which later was dear to the heart of Fourier who, with infinite gusto, docketed and classified all the parasitic classes of mankind. And beyond this, there is a point of frequent recurrence in all Utopias, namely, that simplicity of life has its reward. There is less work to be done, when people eschew the luxurious life and shun changes of fashion. 'And thus, since they are all employed in some useful labour, and since they content themselves with fewer things, it falls out that there is a great abundance of all things among them.'[1] In all this More (or Raphael Hythloday) sets a fashion; by a combination of universal labour, the simple life and more effective machinery, there is almost no limit to the shrinkage of the working hours which subsequent writers have suggested as possible.

Within Utopia life is organised on a communal basis, provisions being brought to the four markets in each town, and thence taken freely, firstly for the use of the hospitals, secondly for the public halls, and thirdly by whomsoever will. But in fact they all eat in the public halls, for without good cause no one would willingly eat at home, 'since it is both ridiculous and foolish for any one to give themselves the trouble to make ready an ill dinner at home,'[2] when he might fare so much better eating in public. In an ominous phrase elsewhere, we are told that in Utopia 'all men live in full view.' In that happy island everything may be had in abundance except privacy. Dinner and supper are prefaced by a short 'lecture of morality,' which serves as a text for uplifting conversation[3]; in Utopia this may be an additional reason for shunning the cold domestic joint.

Trade is conducted on rather unusual principles, and with rather unusual results. Seeing that the island abounds in all things, and that little or nothing is needed from abroad, foreign trade is in essence a giving away of superfluities after a two years' supply has been assured. This export is in part a free gift; otherwise they get in return vast quantities of gold and silver. Here indeed is the mercantilist ideal of a country stuffed with bullion. This, however, is combined with a complete contempt for the precious metals and for all other baubles: 'the folly of man has enhanced the value of gold and silver, because of their scarcity.'[4] Accordingly, that the hearts of the Utopians may not be beguiled into worshipping the so-called precious metals, the gold is transformed into vessels of dishonour. It is out of gold that chamber-pots and close-stools are fashioned; so also fetters of gold are made for the slaves, to whom an ear-ring of gold may be attached as a special badge of infamy.

There is thus much gold in the country, even if it is to be found in unexpected places. It is used to hire mercenaries in the event of a war, and this need is also supplied by a certain traffic in the condemned

[1] P. 101. [2] P. 105. [3] P. 106. [4] P. 110.

criminals of other countries who are acquired as slaves. In this fantasy which is called Utopia, we here touch on two points which may offend modern susceptibilities. Firstly, the Utopians do not wage war wholly on approved principles. In this matter they cannot escape the charge of being somewhat imperialistic. If their population exceeds the optimum, they send out colonies to the neighbouring continent, 'taking the inhabitants into their society, if they are willing to live with them.' Otherwise they drive them out of the bounds which they have marked for themselves:

> For they account it a very just cause of war, for a nation to hinder others from possessing a part of that soil, of which they make no use, but which is suffered to lie idle and uncultivated ; since every man has by the law of Nature a right to such a waste portion of the earth as is necessary for his subsistence.[1]

This is the pure doctrine of *Lebensraum*, naked and unashamed, and it is interesting to see the Law of Nature invoked here, and invoked in a logical sense, as applying to the rights of all the inhabitants of the world to all the land of the world, and not merely, for example, to the right which the French people may be supposed to have to the land of France. Wars may of course arise otherwise through loyalty to their friends. When it comes to the waging of war, while the Utopians fight bravely in the last resort, they prefer to hire mercenaries from other nations and to gain victory by dexterity rather than by bloodshed. In practice this means that they stir up fifth columnist activity, and incite enemy subjects to kill their prince.

The second point that may offend is that we are still, apparently, in a world of slavery. Quite apart from the demands of war, the comforts of Utopia demand a slave population whose function it is to render the 'uneasy services' ; they also do the work of the slaughter-house, an occupation which the fastidious Utopians find nauseating. In short, they do everything that is unpleasant, a consideration which ought in itself to make the work of the others more agreeable. Unlike the Utopians who get off with a six-hour day, the slaves 'are kept at perpetual labour and are always chained.'[2] The slaves are a motley crowd ; firstly, there are their own condemned criminals, and secondly, 'which is more common,' condemned criminals of other countries, whom merchants may pick up at bargain prices, or even get for nothing. These are supplemented by the voluntary poor of other countries, who presumably feel that slavery in Utopia is better than freedom elsewhere. These, as indeed they deserve, are better treated than the other classes of slaves. The rebellious slave is treated like a wild beast, and in the last resort is put to death. The implied advocacy of slavery as a punishment represents a protest against the harshness of excessive

[1] P. 102.

[2] P. 129.

hanging; while, on economic grounds, a slave who can be made to do useful work is more of an asset to the community than a hanged criminal. But there is inevitably a flaw in any Utopia that needs slaves for its uneasy services.

Much of this, it may be said, represents but the trimmings of the fairy-tale; and any one who cares may say that this or that is impracticable, or absurd or undesirable. Let it be remembered that More was one of those unfortunate people whose humour is tinged with seriousness, and whose most earnest utterance is illumined by a jest playing in the back of the mind. They are an unhappy race who are sure to be misunderstood: far happier they who announce when they are jesting, or, better still, who refrain from such a dangerous pastime. More was a master of irony, and we are not meant to take literally all that he wrote; if we could but see his eyes as he wrote (or thought) some of the more startling passages, it might help those of us who are specially stupid to a better understanding of what he meant. But there is little irony in what are for us the essential passages, where Raphael Hythloday, with a sombre eloquence, advances a passionate demand for justice, and laments the iniquities, the fruits of selfishness, that spring from man's lust for wealth and power; and argues, in consequence, for the necessity of communism. In order to appreciate the perennial influence of More, it is sufficient to read Hythloday in his more exalted moments, and to note the strange modernity of his utterances. A few extracts—unfortunately too brief—will here be more effective than much exposition. The first relates to the evils of private property, and is a more restrained statement, occurring at the end of Book I, where, in contrast to the evil conditions in England, Hythloday first glances at Utopia:

> Though to speak plainly my real sentiments, I must freely own, that so long as there is any property, and while money is the standard of all other things, I cannot think that a nation can be governed either justly or happily: not justly, because the best things will fall to the share of the worst men; nor happily, because all things will be divided among a few (and even those are not in all respects happy), the rest being left to be absolutely miserable. . . . When, I say, I balance all these things in my thoughts, I grow more favourable to Plato . . . for so wise a man could not but foresee that the setting all upon a level was the only way to make a nation happy, which cannot be obtained so long as there is property; for when every man draws to himself all that he can compass, by one title or another, it must needs follow, that how plentiful soever a nation may be, yet a few dividing the wealth of it among themselves, the rest fall into indigence. . . . From whence I am persuaded, that till property is taken away there can be no equitable or just distribution of things, nor can the world be happily governed: for as long as that is maintained, the greatest and the far best part of mankind will be still oppressed with a load of cares and anxieties.[1]

Towards the end of the second book, a note of passion enters Hythlo-

[1] Pp. 85–86.

day's restatement of the same point. Utopia, he says, is the only commonwealth that truly deserves that name; and he continues:

> In all other places it is visible, that while people talk of a commonwealth, every man only seeks his own wealth; but there, where no man has any property, all men zealously pursue the good of the public: and indeed, it is no wonder to see men act so differently; for in other commonwealths, every man knows that unless he provides for himself, how flourishing soever the commonwealth may be, he must die of hunger: so that he sees the necessity of preferring his own concerns to the public; but in Utopia, where every man has a right to everything, they all know that if care is taken to keep the public stores full, no private man can want anything; for among them there is no unequal distribution, so that no man is poor, none in necessity; and though no man has anything, yet they are all rich; for what can make a man so rich as to lead a serene and cheerful life, free from anxieties; neither apprehending want himself, nor vexed with the endless complaints of his wife? [1]

And on the disputed question of Justice, there is this eloquent denunciation:

> I would gladly hear any man compare the justice that is among them with that of all other nations; among whom, may I perish, if I see anything that looks either like justice or equity: for what justice is there in this, that a nobleman, a goldsmith, a banker, or any other man, that either does nothing at all, or at best is employed in things that are of no use to the public, should live in great luxury and splendour, upon what is so ill acquired; and a mean man, a carter, a smith or a ploughman, that works harder even than the beasts themselves, and is employed in labours so necessary, that no commonwealth could hold out a year without them, can only earn so poor a livelihood, and must lead so miserable a life, that the condition of the beasts is much better than theirs.[2]

Lastly there is this most revolutionary conclusion drawn from the condition of the world at large:

> Therefore I must say that, as I hope for mercy, I can have no other notion of all the other governments that I see or know, than that they are a conspiracy of the rich, who on pretence of managing the public only pursue their private ends, and devise all the ways and arts they can find out; first, that they may, without danger, preserve all that they have so ill acquired, and then that they may engage the poor to toil and labour for them at as low rates as possible, and oppress them as much as they please.[3]

It is such passages as these (all of them, be it noted for what it is worth, spoken by Hythloday) that have made *Utopia* a living book for four hundred years. And if any one cares to cast a forward-looking glance to Marxian revolutionary socialism, he will be able to find in More (or in More's creature, Hythloday) quite a number of significant pointers. They may be worth enumerating. Quite apart from the main thesis of the evils springing from private property, *Utopia* lays emphasis on (i) the evils of the unproductive classes; (ii) our extrava-

[1] Pp. 162–163. [2] P. 163. [3] P. 164.

gance and wrongful use of wealth ; (iii) the evils of money, and in particular the baneful influence of gold ; (iv) the exploitation of the poor by the rich ; and lastly and most surprisingly (v) the conception of the State as a class organisation, a ' conspiracy of the rich.' Somewhat apart from these—in some ways it is more in the anarchist tradition—is the plea for reduction of hours of work by cutting out unnecessary idlers and unnecessary luxuries. Assuredly, whatever may be thought of More, Raphael Hythloday had in him the makings of a very promising revolutionary Marxian socialist.

(*b*) CAMPANELLA : *THE CITY OF THE SUN*

Campanella's *City of the Sun* is not infrequently regarded as a kind of pendent to *Utopia* ; it at least presents an ideal State which is of interest by reason of its similarities and its contrasts. Campanella (1568–1639) was a much tortured, much imprisoned Dominican monk, and *The City of the Sun* is a literary by-product of his imprisonment. It is in stretches a somewhat tedious, not to say boring, production, and more even than most Utopias it is pervaded by a chilling atmosphere of unreality. It is difficult to take seriously a chief ruler called Hoh, assisted by three subsidiary princes named Pon, Sin, and Mor—names admirably devised to fill in the odd corners of a crossword puzzle. Even when these are translated into Metaphysic, Power, Wisdom and Love, they remain somewhat inhuman. It is gratifying to know that in whatever Hoh inclines to, Pon, Sin and Mor are sure to agree. It is a characteristic of all totalitarian States. Nor do we readily acknowledge Magistrates who are called Chastity, Fortitude, Gratitude, Sobriety and so on, through all the known and reputed virtues. There is a somewhat too lengthy description of the city itself, and of its walls. These walls have inscribed on them all knowledge and all science, and thus are the young educated. It is not a wholly absurd idea, for without doubt much wall-space is running to waste in all our cities. A complete course of mathematics displayed on the Underground stations might not be without its effects, though perhaps awkward for those making the journey in the wrong direction.

Here also is a Commonwealth that has risen beyond private property, and has carried community of possessions to the debatable point of community of wives. It is possible to indicate with brevity the few points of significance in Campanella. In the first place, Campanella emphasises, with a clarity and a precision that have seldom been surpassed, the conflict between the individualistic and the social instincts, and he realises that these individualistic instincts are not mere selfishness, but are rooted in the family :

> They say that all private property is acquired and improved for the reason that each one of us by himself has his own home and wife and children.

From this self-love springs. For when we raise a son to riches and dignities, and leave an heir to much wealth, we become either ready to grasp at the property of the state, if in any case fear should be removed from the power which belongs to riches and rank; or avaricious, crafty and hypocritical, if any one is of slender purse, little strength, and mean ancestry. But when we have taken away self-love, there remains only love for the state.[1]

This is a passage of extraordinary importance, and represents a line of thought which extends from Plato to Fourier and beyond. Stripped of unessentials, it means that it is the family that is the stumbling block to the creation of the communistic and the socialist State. Inside this larger community within which all men are to be equals and brothers in a sloppy sense, there is already this other group in which men are brothers in a very peculiar and definite sense: and as Plato and Campanella clearly saw, devotion to the family detracts from that complete devotion and surrender to the State and the public interest which is postulated as desirable.

With this there is also in Campanella an early emphasis on Eugenics, and a realisation that children are produced for and belong to the State, and are not primarily the concern of the parents: 'Indeed, they laugh at us who exhibit a studious care for our breed of horses and dogs, but neglect the breeding of human beings.'[2] More in detail, he argues thus:

Moreover, the race is managed for the good of the commonwealth and not of private individuals, and the magistrates must be obeyed. They deny what we hold—viz., that it is natural to man to recognize his offspring and to educate them, and to use his wife and house and children as his own. For they say that children are bred for the preservation of the species and not for individual pleasure, as St. Thomas also asserts.[3]

The State, therefore, in the person of the mysterious Mor (Love) is responsible for the education of children, since 'individuals for the most part bring forth children wrongly and educate them wrongly.'[4]

The other point of significance in Campanella relates to his attitude to work. In More's *Utopia*, doubtless every one worked; but there were still slaves for the uneasy services. Campanella abolishes slavery, and emphasises the dignity of all work. In contrast with our foolish ideas of nobility, 'they consider him the more noble and renowned who has dedicated himself to the study of the most arts and knows how to practise them wisely,' and they laugh at us in that we consider our workmen ignoble.[5] 'All work they call discipline'; no one thinks it lowering to wait at table or to work in the kitchen. Thus even More's 'uneasy services' are honourable. The working hours which had been six a day in Utopia have contracted to four, and the

[1] *The City of the Sun*, p. 225 (also reprinted in *Ideal Commonwealths*, Universal Library).
[2] P. 224. [3] P. 235. [4] P. 236. [5] P. 228.

rest of the time is spent in 'learning joyously' and in many other diversions. The only prohibition seems to be against games which are played while sitting; on this test, billiards would seem to be permissible, whereas chess is expressly forbidden. Such are the solarians, 'rich because they want nothing, poor because they possess nothing; and consequently they are not slaves to circumstances, but circumstances serve them.'[1]

(*c*) FÉNELON

Among the other writers of early modern Utopias, perhaps a glance should be directed towards Fénelon, who on the strength of certain passages in *Les Aventures de Télémaque* has been claimed as a sympathiser with the communist way of life. Though much admired by the appropriate authorities, *Télémaque* is to our modern eyes a rather odd book. It is a pedagogic romance, written for the instruction of the young Duke of Burgundy; and Fénelon, aiming at two birds with one book, seeks to combine instruction in classical mythology with such moral and political lessons as an Archbishop might properly impart to a pupil of importance. An eminent authority in French literature has declared that to savour the charm of *Télémaque* it must be read 'dans l'innocence de la première jeunesse': presumably the Duke satisfied this condition. There are indeed two Utopias embedded in this morass, the first dealing with La Bétique, at the end of Book VII, the second being concerned with the town of Salente, which is referred to in Books X and XVII. Neither need delay us long.

The happy country of La Bétique is one of those cases in which Utopia is made easy by the special favour of heaven, manifested in an idyllic situation and a climate such as never was on land or sea. The sky is perpetually sweet and serene; the winters are mild, and the heat of the summer is tempered with refreshing zephyrs. Indeed, the whole year is a happy marriage of spring and autumn. Consequently, the soil yields a double harvest every year. The trees by the wayside are perpetually green; the mountains are almost clothed with cattle. It will be conceded that people living under these conditions start off with a certain initial advantage.

Despite all this wealth bursting and sprouting around them, the natives of La Bétique have clung to the simple life. Though they are supplied with gold and silver, these are devoted to the manufacture of ploughs—a more honourable use than in Utopia. The beatific climate enables them to do without houses, just as, apart from certain traditional conventions, it might enable them to dispense with clothes. As a matter of fact, it almost does. They think that we pin ourselves down unduly if we make a house which will outlive us. In this happy

[1] P. 238.

state, they live without dividing the soil, holding all goods in common, moving on with their tents when they have exhausted the fruits and the pasturage around them. Their peace consists in cutting off vain riches and deceitful pleasures. They neither drink, nor wage war, and the list of their virtues is endless. Among all the inhabitants of La Bétique there is neither pride nor haughtiness, nor bad faith nor desire to extend their domination.

All this may have fired the imagination of the Duke of Burgundy in the innocence of his first youth: to our more sophisticated age it sounds rather thin stuff and little better than vacant chaff well meant for grain. A Utopia which rests on a climate which will make possible the scrapping of houses and clothes is not likely to be realised in Surrey's green and pleasant land, still less in the not-quite-so-green but more invigorating land that makes up the Moor of Rannoch. And though it would be unreasonable to ask that the Archbishop should have read the works of Malthus, the Malthusian question of the stability of such a society should have occurred to him. What in fact Fénelon describes in La Bétique is the Garden of Eden, in an enlarged and improved edition; and thither, if only because of the Cherubim with the flaming swords, we may not return.

The town of Salente (Books X and XVII) has been mentioned, but, strictly speaking, the relevant passages give us not so much a description of a Utopia, as instructions for the restoration of a state to a condition of health and well-being. It is, of course, Fénelon, speaking through Mentor, who gives the advice and issues the instructions; and while, in the language of taxation, the impact is on Télémaque and Idoménée (whose city it is), the incidence of the advice is designed to be on the young Duke of Burgundy. Foreign merchandise, tending to luxury, is forbidden; ornaments of gold and silver are banished. A noble and frugal simplicity is restored, and this applies to the delights of the table as to other things. Idoménée (who, after all, is king) is allowed a little *vin du pays*—'mais en fort petite quantité.' Indeed Fénelon, perhaps with his eye on the young Duke, is habitually rather prejudiced in the matter of wine, of which a more inspired and impartial writer has said that it turneth every thought into jollity and mirth, so that a man remembereth neither sorrow nor debt. Effeminate music, superfluous merchants, top-heavy furniture, are all sacrificed to austerity. In consequence, the Salentins, who had complained of their poverty, begin to have the sensation of well-being. 'Deceptive riches had impoverished them, and they became effectively rich in proportion as they had the courage to do without them.' That a feeling of well-being may be attained by restricting the scope of our desires is an old economico-moral lesson which remains ever fresh.

All this would not justify Fénelon's inclusion here; but more importance attaches to certain features, illustrative of Utopian muddleheadedness, confronting us when we turn to the repercussions of these changes on the country around Salente. Here we have an agrarian philosophy, reaching forward to the Physiocrats. The soil has been neglected, and therefore all the superfluous inhabitants of Salente are to be moved back to the land, reinforced by citizens drawn from neighbouring states—to do the hard work, seeing that the banished clerk from the capital would probably not be the most efficient agriculturalist. If they are well treated in the matter of taxes, and encouraged to marry, all will be well. And in support of this, Fénelon argues in a passage which seems to have strayed from a physiocratic treatise:

> The earth is never ungrateful; it always nourishes with its fruits those who cultivate it carefully; and it refuses its gifts only to those who fear to devote their efforts to it. The more children the workers have, the wealthier they are . . . for the children, from their earliest years begin to help them.

There follows a moving picture of rustic felicity, in which not even the shepherd's flute is forgotten. Never, on any stage, was rural life so attractive. And apparently there is no limit to this: 'Nature alone would draw from her fertile bosom all that would be required for an infinite number of moderate and hardworking men.' Could anything be more extravagant? Could there be an easier path to Utopia?

Yet within two pages, Utopia (including, inferentially, the shepherd's flute) is shattered. For Idoménée, pestered by unconscious Malthusian qualms and doubtings, asks whether, if they are thus placed in peace and abundance, they may not be corrupted by *délices*, and turn against their king. To which Mentor, giving evidence of a remarkably short memory, replies that though they will have abundance, they will have only what is necessary; this abundance, moreover, will be diminished by the facility of marriages and by the multiplication of families. Each family, being itself numerous and having little land, will have to cultivate it by 'un travail sans relâche.' In an illuminating phrase, he adds: 'Ils auront du pain, à la vérité, et assez largement; mais ils n'auront que du pain, et des fruits de leur propre terre, gagnés à la sueur de leur visage.'

On all this confused thought Malthus would have thrown himself with glee, inviting the good Archbishop to continue the story of his Salentins for a further trifling period of fifty years. Yet if there is little of positive substance in Fénelon—on this side—he is of interest as showing the natural end of those who make their Utopias too easy. If in your assumptions you are allowed to invoke a miraculous climate and thus increase without limit the bounty of nature; if you may postulate that men, on high moral grounds, are prepared to cut down their enjoyments to unremitting labour and sufficient bread, Utopia should not be so difficult to establish in the imagination. In essence the lesson which Fénelon would seek to convey (and it should never be forgotten that the dish is seasoned for a future King of France) is that luxury is an evil thing, that simplicity is much to be desired, that a prosperous agriculture is essential for a healthy State, and that a large population, living on the land and not in the cities, should be the aim of national policy. Teaching that the plough should be held in honour, he is, on this side of his genius, a Physiocrat born out of due season.

It would be unprofitable, though not uninteresting, to follow further the primrose path leading to a large choice of assorted Utopias. From the time of More to the present day, the years are strewn with them, and not unnaturally most of these are tinged with ideas borrowed from one or other of the schools of socialism. Morris's *News from Nowhere* is wholly charming as a work of literature; Bellamy's *Looking Backward* presents a rather vulgar and unattractive world of state socialism run mad. In Cabet's *Voyage en Icarie*, in its time so influential, the propaganda almost drowns the tale. Hertzka's *Freiland* is another monument of propaganda for a specific purpose, which (judging by sales) made an appeal somewhat incomprehensible to-day. Lord Lytton, who tried everything, had perforce to write a Utopia; and Mr. H. G. Wells is also of the company.

While stoutly refusing to extend this chapter further, one general point may be noted. Utopias tend to become not so much a criticism of our system of government and our social institutions, as a criticism of human nature. Men are so selfish as to prefer their own wives and children to the wives and children of other people; they are foolish and greedy and covetous, and given to unworthy enjoyments; they forget that

> It's no in makin muckle, *mair*,
> To make us truly blest.

Consequently the deviser of Utopias, when he is at it, presents not merely the perfect State, but, more or less, the perfect man. In one sense, this is almost 'cheating,' just because it simplifies matters so enormously for the architects of Utopia. On the other hand, this inferential criticism of human nature may perhaps point to the crux of the whole problem. We have an imperfect world, among other reasons, because we are very imperfect men and very imperfect women. We can have no earthly paradise until we are fit to live in an earthly paradise. Moral and political regeneration are not two problems, but one.

CHAPTER IV

ROUSSEAU AND SOME OTHERS

(*a*) ROUSSEAU

FORTUNATELY, we are here concerned with only one side of Rousseau—assuming, indeed, that it is possible to detach for consideration one aspect of his legacy. Rousseau was primarily a writer on politics, concerned, after the manner of Hobbes and of Locke, in explaining the origins of government by reference to a mythical Social Contract, the terms of which may of course be varied, according to the deductions it is desired to draw from it. He was also a writer, and a writer of influence, on education, though he would doubtless have been a rash parent who sent his daughter to any Ladies' College conducted by Rousseau. He was a prophet of sentiment and sensibility. For that matter, he had views on music. Doubtless even in the most versatile there is a unity linking divergent activities. In the present case, the significance of Rousseau in the development of socialist thought is to be found in the combined and pervasive influence of all his writings on succeeding generations. Yet, within the space here available, it may be permissible, if scarcely defensible, to look on the *Contrat Social* as belonging rather to the history of political thought ; and, accordingly, in searching for his contribution to socialist thought, we shall confine ourselves to those writings which are more exclusively occupied with the perpetual themes of socialist discussion. Briefly, this comes down to a consideration of his *Discourse on the Origin of Inequality among Men*, an essay which was *not* awarded the prize for a dissertation on this subject by the Academy of Dijon.

But before proceeding to the *Discourse on Inequality*, it may be permissible to glance at the earlier essay to which the Academy of Dijon did award its prize, thereby suddenly making Rousseau a celebrity. The subject prescribed for this essay was : ' Whether the restoration (*rétablissement*) of the Sciences and the Arts had contributed to the purification of manners ? ' There is a traditional tale that when Rousseau indicated his intention of competing for the prize, he was warned by a wise acquaintance that if he wished to have any chance of success, he would have to answer the question in the negative, since all the other candidates would be found ranged on the other side. The authenticity of the story may be assessed by Rousseau experts. It is probably entirely apocryphal ; but any examiner of experience will acknowledge, in his cups if not at other times, that if of fifty competing essays, forty-nine say the same thing with varying degrees of lucidity, and the fiftieth says something wholly different, this last cunning candidate has an initial advantage out of all proportion to his deserts, if only because of the difficulty the examiner has in arranging the other forty-nine in ascending order of demerit. In any case, whether because he conscientiously so believed, or because he was instigated by Mr. Worldly Wiseman, Rousseau elected to denounce the baneful influence of the Sciences and of the Arts. As the outlook disclosed is fundamentally the same as in the more effective, but unsuccessful, later essay, it is as well to read the two together.

Later Rousseau affected to regard his *Discourse on the Sciences and the Arts* as mediocre. In substance it is; but there is a certain bravado about this violent and monstrously one-sided attack on civilisation and all its works, which doubtless made it an arresting production on its first appearance, and which obviously carried the Academicians of Dijon off their feet. There is a considerable kinship with the later Discourse, and here already it is obvious that the theme closest to Rousseau's heart is that of inequality and the loss of freedom. The Sciences, Literature, and the Arts, we are told, stifle in men the sentiment of that original liberty for which they seem to have been born, and make them love their bondage.[1] The Sciences and the Arts owe their origin to our vices, and we should be in less doubt as to their advantages if they sprung from our virtues. In explanation he argues that astronomy was born of superstition; eloquence, of ambition; geometry, of avarice (a dark saying, unless he refers to the 'mensuration' of our possessions); physical science, of a vain curiosity[2]; and all are the offspring of human pride. Here we touch the fundamentals of theology, for is there not high authority for the view that Pride is not only the fundamental sin, but the only sin, of which all other sins are merely allotropic modifications? Moreover, this defect in the origin of the Sciences and the Arts is reflected in their aims and objects. What would be the good of jurisprudence without the injustice of man? Where would history be, if there were no tyrants, wars or conspiracies? In an illuminating question which goes to the root of Rousseau's thought or prejudices in these matters, he asks: 'Who would wish to pass his life in sterile contemplation, if each of us, thinking only of the duties of man and the needs of nature, had time only for the fatherland, for the unfortunate and for his friends?'[3] The Sciences, born in idleness, in turn nourish idleness and the vices that spring therefrom. Rousseau, it will be observed, was not the man to allow a regard for truth to deprive him of his paradox.

But, worst of all and most specifically suggestive of the later

[1] P. 4. (References are to the collection of Rousseau's more important works, published by Garnier: this edition is probably the most accessible to the ordinary student.)

[2] P. 13.

[3] P. 13.

Discourse, all these things lead to inequality. With the development of the Sciences and the Arts, tribute is no longer paid to virtue but to ability:

> We no longer ask of a man if he has integrity, but if he has talents; nor of a book if it is useful, but if it is well-written. Rewards are showered on intellect, and virtue remains without honour. There are thousands of prizes for *les beaux discours*, none for *les belles actions*.[1]

So far as there is an ideal here, it is that of a primitive life, so fully occupied with the claims of the fatherland, the unfortunate, and one's friends, that there is no leisure left over in which to become vicious; for an advance beyond this point means the development of opportunities for manifesting superiority based on intellect in place of an imaginary condition of equality in which virtue alone is held in honour.

In the *Discourse on the Origin of Inequality*, dating from 1754, Rousseau gives a philosophy of history, resting on a condensed account of the development of the human race, and the whole essay is saturated with that passionate hatred of inequality which may not unfairly be regarded as the dominant feature of his character. It is almost unnecessary to say that for Rousseau's history there is not the faintest shadow of a particle of evidence. Nor does Rousseau claim that there is; he is indeed engagingly ingenuous on this point. 'Here,' he says, addressing Man at large—'here is your history as I have thought it was to be read, not in the books of your fellows, who are liars, but as it is to be found in Nature, which never lies.'[2] Such a procedure without doubt greatly simplifies the writing of history. In fact, Rousseau is merely imagining what it is convenient to imagine; and, viewed in the cold light of reason, his account of the life of primitive man at times borders on the grotesque and ludicrous.

The *Discourse* falls into two parts, of which the first is devoted to the fairy-tale of Rousseau's primitive man, and the second to the departure, with increasing acceleration, from that happy state. As Rousseau sees him, primitive man takes his fill beneath an oak; he quenches his thirst at the nearest stream, and he finds his bed at the foot of the tree which has given him sustenance; and thus are all his needs satisfied. In this condition, having regard to the rigours of the seasons (for it cannot always be pleasant to sleep, nude, beneath a sheltering oak); having regard likewise to the needs of defence or escape in the matter of beasts of prey, man is, and must be, robust and strong; so also is his progeny. He must use his body, his arms and his legs for everything. When he learns to use an axe, a ladder, a sling, a horse, the convenience is bought at the price of a diminution of strength or agility. Nor does he fear wild animals at this stage; he is a match for them, and if need be, he can climb a tree.[3]

[1] P. 20. [2] P. 41. [3] Pp. 42–43.

Apart from such dangers of the jungle, there are other ineluctable enemies—natural infirmities, infancy and old age. Infancy, of course, is not an infirmity peculiar to man; but on the whole, our remote ancestors scored over other animals by reason of the greater capacity which the female of our species has in carrying about her young. In the matter of old age, Rousseau draws a most rosy and optimistic picture of how things used to be. In old age, the need of victuals diminished with the power of getting them—a singularly beneficent arrangement on the part of Providence; and thus in the absence of gout and rheumatism (unknown to *la vie sauvage*) old people get snuffed out without anyone perceiving that they have ceased to exist, and almost without their noticing it themselves—' ils s'éteignent enfin, sans qu'on s'aperçoive qu'ils cessent d'être, et presque sans s'en apercevoir eux-mêmes.' [1] One would naturally expect that their extinction would be more obvious to the survivors than to the deceased.

As for our other maladies—the rough-and-tumble of a panel practitioner's life—Rousseau indicts society for its sins, and argues that most of our misfortunes are our own work, and that practically all could have been avoided, if we had adhered to the ' simple, uniforme et solitaire ' manner of life prescribed by Nature. As will be seen presently, it is the word *solitaire* that is here the most significant. The history of human diseases is best obtained by tracing the development of civil society. In Rousseau's primitive paradise, no surgeon other than Time is needed to cure a fractured limb; no treatment is necessary other than *leur vie ordinaire*; and all this is accomplished without the patient being tormented with incisions, poisoned with drugs, or wasted with fastings. If primitive man has nothing to hope but from Nature, he has on the other hand nothing to fear but his own illness. So much for the advantages of medical benefit.[2]

Rousseau's dissertation on the origin of language hardly concerns us, except in so far as the conditions of his problem throw light on his conception of the life of the natural and primitive man. For the surprising view emerges, as indicated in the word *solitaire* already emphasised, that Rousseau's primitive men hardly ever met. It is Rousseau's first difficulty in the matter of the origin of language: How could a language arise, or be regarded as necessary among men who had no communication with each other, nor any occasion to have such communication? For in that early phase of human society, any encounter was fortuitous and ephemeral.[3] It is indeed funda-

[1] P. 45. [2] Pp. 45–46.

[3] ' Dans cet état primitif, n'ayant ni maisons, ni cabanes, ni propriétés d'aucune espèce, chacun se logeoit au hasard, et souvent pour une seule nuit; les mâles et les femelles s'unissoient fortuitement, selon la rencontre, l'occasion et le désir, sans que la parole fût un interprète fort nécessaire des choses qu'ils avoient à se dire; ils se quittoient avec la même facilité ' (p. 52).

mental to the development of Rousseau's ultimate thesis, that Nature has taken no trouble to bring men together on the basis of their mutual needs: 'sociability' is not a quality prepared by that mysterious eighteenth-century divinity called Nature. In this primitive condition man had no need of man, and Rousseau intends to emphasise that we must, for our salvation, return to this state of affairs. But though primitive man thus wandered about, for ever solitary except for casual and transient encounters, he was not miserable; for what kind of unhappiness could properly be attributed to a 'free being, whose heart is at peace, and whose body is in health'? [1]

It follows that in this strange world where individuals can, at most, salute each other in passing, where no moral relationships or acknowledged duties unite them, it is impossible to speak of men as being either good or bad. In this lonely and solitary world, no question of virtue or vice can arise. Somewhat oddly, however, and on rather insufficient grounds, Rousseau allows primitive man to have 'Pity,' which is the source of all social virtues. It is this 'Pity' that in a state of nature takes the place of laws, of morals and of virtue.[2]

Clearly also this elimination of the primitive man's fellows delivers him from many of our present-day shortcomings. Having no relationship with others, he knows nothing of vanity, or esteem or contempt for others. Even the sexual instincts, in these happy days, occasioned no jealousy. Rousseau distinguishes between that love which consists in the satisfaction of a physical need, and that love which, if it is permissible to paraphrase, results from the frills which civilisation has added. It is in this type of love alone that jealousy may arise. The primitive man knows only the first kind of love: 'toute femme est bonne pour lui,' and again, 'le besoin satisfait, tout le désir est éteint.' [3]

Thus for primitive man the happy generations passed—an endless wandering in the forests, 'without industry, without speech, without domicile, without war as without union, without any need of his fellows, or any desire to injure them.' If any discoveries were made, 'the art perished with the inventor' in a world where there was no education or progress, and where each succeeding generation set out from the same starting-point.[4]

Rousseau's description of the blessedness of primitive man has been summarised in some detail, because, fantastic as it may be, it is of the essence of his view of things, and it colours his later account of the fall of man from this high estate. At this point, however, it is sufficient to draw attention again to the most astonishing feature in this most astonishing reconstruction of history. The foundation and reason for primitive man's happiness lies in the fact that he had no need of his fellows, in fact had no dealings with his fellows, whom,

[1] P. 57. [2] Pp. 60–61. [3] Pp. 62–63. [4] P. 64.

indeed, to all intents and purposes he never met. Man was never so happy because man was never so much alone.

The second part of the *Discourse* is devoted to tracing the growth of inequality in place of these primitive egalitarian conditions. It opens with a purple passage which has been so often quoted that its further quotation is almost inevitable:

> The first man who, having enclosed a piece of land, took it into his head to say: 'This belongs to me,' and found people simple enough to believe him, was the true founder of civil society. What crimes, wars, murders, what miseries and horrors would have been spared the human race by him who, snatching out the stakes or filling in the ditch, should have cried to his fellows: 'Beware of listening to this impostor; you are lost if you forget that the fruits belong to all and that the earth belongs to none.' [1]

This first unrecorded enclosure was the beginning of property; but in fact it was a culminating point rather than a point of departure. Already, ways and means had been found to take such precautions as were necessary for safety. There had been discoveries and inventions; fire had been brought to earth; the bow and the arrow, as well as hooks and snares for catching animals, had been contrived. All this gave man a sense of superiority over other animals, and implanted in his heart 'the first movement of pride.' [2] Thus, in the triumphant and unseemly gloating of the hunter over his victim, we find the far-off roots of human inequality.

With this also came the distant foreshadowings of co-operation. There were occasions—admittedly rare—when *l'intérêt commun* justified primitive man in counting on the assistance of his fellows. How these ultra-individualistic nomads came to conceive of such a thing as the 'common interest' is, however, not explained. In such a case they united 'by some sort of free association which was binding on none, and which lasted only so long as the transitory need which had occasioned it.' Clearly, however, we have reached a stage when man is not quite so solitary as he once was: the bloom is off the peach. For such occasional acts of mutual assistance as these, no more highly developed language than that of crows or monkeys would be necessary.[3]

In this imaginative history of the human race, the great turning-point, with ramifications in many directions, came when man ceased to sleep 'under the first tree,' and made some semi-permanent shelter or hut, with branches and mud as their basic constituents. For here you have the beginning of the home. Rousseau's primitive man had been extraordinarily successful in shaking off the casual women whom he encountered. But now, enclosed in the same hut, are man and woman, parents and children. Doubtless with this transition, as Rousseau acknowledges, there came the sweetest sentiments known to

[1] P. 67. [2] P. 69. [3] Pp. 69–70.

man, conjugal and paternal love ; but he is able to compile an alarming series of items to be entered on the debit side. Women became sedentary, clinging to the hut, and thus there resulted a division of labour. Also men and women alike became softer, losing something of their ferocity—although in the previous paragraphs Rousseau's primitive man had been depicted as anything but ferocious. Among men living in adjacent huts, language perforce had to arise. More significant is the fact that mere propinquity gave rise to the habit of making comparisons in the matter of merit and beauty. Jealousy awakens with love, and in the highly-coloured language which Rousseau loved: 'Discord triumphs, and the sweetest of passions receives sacrifices of human blood.' [1]

It is an odd picture which Rousseau here draws of the rise of 'distinctions' among men, imposed by their environment. Brought together to live in adjacent cabins, what is there for these attractive primitives to do in the evenings, unless they sing and dance together under a great tree? Now it is a familiar fact that we do not all sing equally well or equally badly, and the same is demonstrably true in the matter of dancing. But, given the circumstances, the man who sings best, who dances best, is most 'considered.' 'Why did she fall for the leader of the band?' is the question put by a later generation, confronted by the same phenomenon. *Es ist*, apparently, *eine alte Geschichte*, *doch bleibt sie immer neu*. In these distinctions, embodied in the judgment of spectators and critics of primitive ball-room behaviour, Rousseau finds the first step towards inequality and towards vice at the same time. One other departure from primitive perfection is significant. From this last idea of 'consideration' paid to any one excelling in any respect, arose the first ideas of civility on the one hand, and on the other the sense of outrage should the measure of respect supposed to be due happen to be withheld. In a world where a man's a man for a' that, and where all are equal, there can clearly be no room for civility.

Despite these first shadows, this was the stage at which Rousseau would have had the human race remain, and he sums up in language of unmistakable clarity his astonishing philosophy of human nature:

> So long as they confined themselves to works which one alone could do, and to arts which did not need the assistance of several hands, they lived free, healthy, good and happy . . .; but from the moment when one man had need of the assistance of another, from the moment when it was perceived that it was useful for one man to have provisions for two, equality disappeared, property was introduced, labour became necessary, and vast forests were changed into smiling fields which it was necessary to water with human sweat, and in which slavery and misery were soon seen to germinate and increase with the harvests.[2]

[1] Pp. 70–72. [2] P. 74.

This indeed is the fundamental idea in this extraordinary *Discourse.* Men may be equal and happy, so long as they never meet, so long as no one needs the assistance of another; but from the moment when they cease to be *solitaire*, from the moment when they begin to live together, help each other, do things together, inequality enters, and from Rousseau's point of view the rest of history is a hastening descent. Waiving his earlier and later history as entirely fictitious, there, is of course, one sense in which Rousseau is merely expressing a platitude in a somewhat allegorical form. On all this question, there is in fact of course no such thing as equality among men, for so it has been ordained by God. Neither in stature, nor in weight, nor in chest expansion, neither in the colour of the eyes or of the hair, neither in strength, intellectual capacity or moral sensibility, are men equal. It is perhaps possible to speak of the equality of men, if there is no possibility of comparison; if, as in Rousseau's primitive conditions, human beings are never brought together except for fortuitous acts of silent copulation—if, in short, the doctrine of equality is never brought to the test. But the whole doctrine of equality in the literal sense breaks down the moment you bring men together and inevitably are forced to compare them, not merely in their capabilities for singing and dancing, as in Rousseau's rather puerile example, but up and down the whole range of human equipment. It is indeed only necessary to view two human beings together in order to realise that in certain respects A is 'superior' to B, and in others B is 'superior' to A; but probably in no respect are they equal. In this sense Rousseau is possibly right in suggesting that the postulated equality of men who are never brought into comparison disappears at once when they live in adjacent huts. It is, however, to be hoped that Rousseau was trying to express more than this dowdy platitude. Also, of course, the admitted inequality of man does not really affect that deeper question as to whether the differences in human endowment furnish grounds for existing differences in rights and rewards.

In the remainder of the *Discourse*, Rousseau warms to the task of denunciation as he traces the growth of inequality. It may not, however, be necessary to follow in detail the development of the argument. The prime impulse towards the furtherance of inequality is found by Rousseau in the arts of metallurgy and agriculture: in more concrete language it is iron and corn that have been the curse of humanity, creating groups of workers dependent on each other.[1] Agriculture likewise led to the partition of land, and consequently to laws to protect the possessor and define his rights. Following Grotius, Rousseau recalls that when Ceres was given the title of 'Lawgiver,' it was to indicate that the partition of land brought with it the necessity of a new kind of law, the law of property, as distinguished from natural law.[2]

[1] P. 74. [2] P. 76.

With industry (typified by iron) and agriculture thus brought on the scene, the stage is set for the development of inequality. Diversity of talent and of capacity bring their natural consequences in diversity of condition. Vice is not far off. It becomes necessary that men should appear to have certain qualities, even when these are absent. 'To be' and 'to appear' have become entirely different matters. Hypocrisy and deceit have arrived. Man is no longer free and independent, since he is dependent on his fellows for the satisfaction of a multitude of needs: 'Rich, he has need of their services; poor, he has need of their assistance; and even mediocrity does not enable him to do without them.'[1] Add to these 'devouring ambition,' and the picture begins to resemble the vision of Marx:

> In a word, competition and rivalry on the one hand, and on the other conflict of interests, and always the concealed desire to make a profit at the expense of others: all these evils are the first effect of property and the inseparable accompaniment of rising inequality.[2]

The final pages of Rousseau's essay are perhaps best viewed as examples of lurid writing rather than of lucid thinking. He defines three main stages in the descent. The first is the establishment of law and the right of property; the second is the institution of the magistrature; the third is the transformation of legitimate into arbitrary power. In somewhat different language, these stages consecrate the distinction between rich and poor, between strong and weak, and between master and slave. Moreover, Rousseau's pessimism is without frontier and without boundary. In surveying the inevitability of human descent, he observes that 'the vices which render social institutions necessary are just those which render inevitable the abuse of these institutions.' What, in short, is the good of anything?

It is a far journey from the innocent picture of men dancing and singing on the grass, beside the primitive mud-covered huts. It was then, when admiration was paid to one and withheld from another, that inequality was born. Into this other Eden, another Serpent entered. The final picture, when the curse has had time to work itself out, is one of unrelieved gloom. Rousseau gives as bitter a picture of modern civilisation as may be found anywhere,[3] and ends with the impassioned declaration that 'it is manifestly contrary to the law of nature, however it may be defined, that a child should command an

[1] P. 77. [2] P. 77.

[3] One short extract may suffice as a sample: 'Au contraire, le citoyen, toujours actif, sue, s'agite, se tourmente sans cesse pour chercher des occupations encore plus laborieuses; il travaille jusqu'à la mort, il y court même pour se mettre en état de vivre, ou renonce à la vie pour acquérir l'immortalité; il fait sa cour aux grands qu'il hait, et aux riches qu'il méprise; il n'épargne rien pour obtenir l'honneur de les servir; il se vante orgueilleusement de sa bassesse et de leur protection; et, fier de son esclavage, il parle avec dédain de ceux qui n'ont pas l'honneur de le partager' (p. 92).

old man, that an imbecile should conduct a wise man, and that a handful of people should be stuffed with superfluities, while the famished multitude lack what is necessary.' [1]

Perhaps Rousseau has sufficiently testified to the faith, or the lack of faith, that is in him, so far as this is manifested in the two *Discourses.* Fundamentally it is a curiously churlish philosophy that is here propounded. Men are represented as happy so long as they live in complete isolation, having no need of each other, and no occasion to meet each other; all evil springs from bringing them together and allowing them to co-operate. Nor indeed is it even a consistent philosophy. Doubtless, Rousseau is careful to explain that his savage in his solitary state has neither virtue nor vices; but he is assuredly a noble beast, endowed with Pity, the mother of all the virtues. Yet as soon as they are brought into contact with each other, it is of the essence of Rousseau's explanation of the decline of man, that forthwith these noble savages seek to take advantage of each other.

Coming more closely to Rousseau's place in the socialist tradition, there are perhaps three points which may be isolated and underlined for their relationship to what has gone before and to what is yet to come. Firstly, property is specifically regarded as the source of all evil, with doubtless a certain emphasis on the case of land. Community in all things is implied—land again receiving special emphasis—though perhaps it should be made clear that by 'community' is rather meant non-appropriation. Secondly, Law for Rousseau is essentially a device whereby those in possession protect themselves against the 'have-nots'; it is in short one of the instruments for the establishment and the maintenance of inequality. In other words, Law (and with it, the State) is an instrument of the governing class. Thirdly, in the contrast between rich and poor, the strong and the weak, masters and slaves, Rousseau preaches, and his words lend themselves to, a vitriolic class-war. But when all is said, it is perhaps truer of Rousseau than of most, that his influence can be traced less to any particular dogma or doctrine which he enunciated than to a pervasive atmosphere which emanated from Rousseau as a whole.

(*b*) MABLY

'Who now reads Cowley?' Probably fewer to-day than when the enquiry was first addressed to the world; but even so, possibly a hundred for every one who reads Gabriel Bonnot de Mably (1709–1785). Mably is one of the most striking examples of swift and irretrievable descent from a position of the highest reputation and influence to a position in which he is less than the dust that strews the paths of the generations of book-worms. A writer who, within a few years of

[1] Pp. 93–94.

his death, enjoys the spectacle of four entirely distinct editions of his collected works (ranging from 12 to 26 volumes according to the format) has no occasion to complain of neglect. Mably, in short, was read and quoted by every one in his own day, and immediately thereafter ; almost a hundred years later, M. Janet was able to testify that, in the frequency of his appearance in the book-stalls along the Quais, he reigned supreme, with the Abbé Raynal as the only possible runner-up. The answer to those who are so hardy as to ask why the world at large does not now read Mably, is that they themselves should try. Without entering into a dangerous controversy, it may be suggested that he is the extreme example of the evil consequences of an undiluted classical education. He was never able to lay the ghost of Plato, and he wrote Platonic dialogues, as they might have been written by Plato, had Plato not been Plato. He worshipped Sparta and all its institutions, real or imagined ; Lycurgus was his constant obsession. It has been suggested that he was acutely sensitive to the social evils, to the inequalities and injustices of his day, when the floods of revolution were gathering to sweep over France. In fact, however, the impression left on a reader of these days is that he sees everything through a haze of classical reading. His heart may have been touched by the wrongs of his time, but he thought and wrote in terms of Lacedaemon. A certain awareness of this paralysing defect seems at times to have knocked dumbly at the portals of his consciousness. In one of his dialogues, one of the speakers (who is more or less Mably) expresses a fear of what his friends may say of him : ' La tête a tourné à ce pauvre homme ; c'est dommage . . . il s'est gaté l'esprit à lire l'histoire des Grecs et des Romains qu'il aimait.' [1] His friends would have been abundantly right ; but they obviously failed to say it effectively.

Mably was destined for the Church, but although throughout his life and subsequently, he has been consistently designated as ' Abbé,' he soon faded away from ecclesiastical activities. He trembled for a time on the fringe of political employment, but this he also abandoned and gave himself up to a life of writing. His works are deplorably numerous and extensive, ranging over the whole field of history, politics, legislation, morals and much more, although always, in his rather pedantic and pedagogic manner, he was chiefly concerned with making man good. For the purpose of ascertaining the relationship which links Plato and More at the one end and Babeuf at the other, a small selection from this numerous brood of publications is sufficient. There is the rather cumbrously entitled *Doutes proposées aux philosophes économistes sur l'ordre naturel et essentiel des sociétés politiques*, which Mably wrote in order to demolish the views on property and other things expressed by Mercier de la Rivière, one of the Physiocrats—not in itself a difficult task. *Des Droits et des Devoirs du Citoyen* is not

[1] *Des Droits et des Devoirs du Citoyen*, p. 295 (vol. XI of edition of 1794–5).

quite a dialogue, though it professes to report conversations with Lord Stanhope. *De la Législation, ou Principes des Loix* is a triangular conversation between an English peer (who figures merely as 'Milord') who, although easily converted, is supposed to represent 'common-sense' views, a Swede who brings vision, and the narrator, who is either markedly silent, or modestly refrains from reporting his own contributions to the discussion. Lastly, for our purpose there is the *Entretiens de Phocion*, professedly a translation of a classical manuscript discovered in a monastery—a fiction as innocuous as the *Entretiens* themselves. It should scarcely be necessary to repeat the warning already hinted at in the case of Sir Thomas More. The *Doutes* are unmistakably straightforward Mably; but in some of the other more important works (e.g. *De la Législation*) he is professedly reporting the discussions of fictitious characters, and in such cases he clearly cannot be held responsible for all the views expressed. Probably in the work cited, Mably would approve in general of the views of the Swede, and he would not always have approved of the views of 'Milord'; but in the nature of things it would have been open to him to disclaim both.

If truth be told, there is not much in Mably that may not be found better expressed elsewhere; he is of interest, partly because of his place in the development of things, and partly because of the strange pessimism which persuaded him that the world was suffering from a disease, or a multiplicity of diseases, for which there could be no effective remedy. Relying on natural law, he believed in the equality of men; looking around him (in the intervals of reading the classics) he was satisfied that private property was the root-cause of all human misfortunes; and (especially after reading the trite moral maxims of antiquity) he was of the opinion that there is much to be said for a simple life. Such, in brief, is the theoretical basis of Mably.

For Mably, the equality of man is part of the design of Nature: 'Nature says to us in a hundred different ways: You are all my children, and I love you all equally . . . the whole earth is the patrimony of each of you; you were equal when you left my hands.'[1] Nature has given us the same needs to be a continual reminder of our equality. It made men *parfaitement égaux*, without rights one over the other, and consequently perfectly free. Nature created neither kings nor magistrates, neither subjects nor slaves, neither rich nor poor. When Nature had finished her work in the creation of man, there was nowhere any principle of inequality.[2] In a frequently recurring phrase Nature destined man to be equal. In one place he opens a wider door, and in words which sound rather like an anticipation of Proudhon, he tells us that this sentiment of equality is nothing other

[1] *Doutes*, p. 15.
[2] E.g. *Doutes*, p. 11; *Droits et Devoirs*, p. 266; *De la Législation*, p. 52.

than the sentiment of our dignity.[1] In amplification, and a dangerous amplification, Mably emphasises the uniformity of Nature. Men are the same everywhere ; he will have nothing to do with the geographical school that holds that men are affected by such trivialities as latitude, temperature and rainfall—as if it were the duty of a legislator, before settling to his task, to consult a thermometer in place of the human heart.[2] If it is urged that men are in fact unequal in endowments, Mably again gives a somewhat Proudhonian reply ; it is education, brutalising some and developing the faculties of others, that persuades us to believe (wrongly) that Providence has established differences among men. At birth all men are substantially alike. The variegated history of any family, where presumably the members have the same heredity, and to a large extent have the same environment and education in essential matters, should provide sufficient comment on this aspect of the argument that humanity is but a tub of undifferentiated and indistinguishable peas.

On the question of the origin of property in the bosom of that primitive society which was so happy as to be propertyless, Mably offers suggestions which are peculiar, and which, if he had paused to reflect, go far towards the torpedoing of all his theorisings on these subjects. For in the *Doutes* where he is writing in his own person and cannot therefore disclaim responsibility, he suggests that property had its origin in the indolence of certain drones, *frelons*, who sought to live at the expense of others, and in whom it had not been possible to inculcate a love of work—*à qui on n'avoit pas l'art de faire aimer le travail.*[3] This same explanation is advanced at greater length by the Swedish philosopher in *De la Législation.* Indolent men, less active than the others, served society with less assiduity and zeal. Their indifference grew because it was not repressed. These idlers were a burden on their fellow-citizens, who complained of their conduct, and presently the Republic was agitated by dissensions. Presumably, society then fell back on the Pauline injunction that if any would not work, neither should he eat. Should this theory of the dronishness of men prove unacceptable, the Swedish philosopher, like an obliging salesman, is quite prepared to offer an alternative solution of the problem of the origin of property. It is that certain of the magistrates retained more than their share in the distribution of the fruits of the earth, or showed an unjust preference towards their friends and relations.[4] On this curious (and, perhaps, in part plausible) theorising, two comments are inescapable. Firstly, the indolence that ruined primitive communism would probably once again ruin communism, if re-established ; there would still be drones willing to live at the expense of others, *laborem fugientes* in the language of St. Thomas

[1] *De la Législation*, p. 54.
[2] *Ibid.*, p. 26.
[3] *Doutes*, p. 33.
[4] *De la Législation*, p. 76.

Aquinas. And secondly, it reveals an extraordinary confusion of thought and of argument to proclaim that communism is the only condition in which men may live virtuously and happily, and in the same breath explain that communism was abandoned because the ordinary citizen failed to play fairly by his fellows, or alternatively because the leaders of society were dishonest and given to nepotism. The Abbé, in spite of himself, is being forced back to acknowledge the reality of original sin.

That property is the source of ' tous les malheurs ' and of ' tous les maux ' hardly calls for particularisation, inasmuch as the argument is on familiar lines.[1] The moment property is established, inequality becomes inevitable, with the result that there are henceforward opposed interests, all the vices of wealth and all the vices of poverty, brutalisation of men's minds, corruption of civil manners, and much more.[2] Carrying the argument a stage further, the existence of property leads to war.[3] It is property that has introduced *l'oisiveté* and *la fainéantise,*[4] those pet aversions of Saint-Simon later; although oddly enough, as has been seen, it was this penchant to *l'oisiveté* that led to the establishment of property. In language closely resembling that used by Babeuf, the thought constantly recurs that what one has in excess is obtained at the cost of others suffering deficiency. More important from the point of view of the theory of property, it is contended that property finds no support in the laws of nature; its sanction is to be found solely in convention; and what convention has made, convention may unmake.

If it be argued, as for example ' Milord ' (representing commonsense) does in fact argue in *De la Législation*, that a ' stimulus ' is needed, and that, in short, ' on ne travaille pas pour les autres avec la même ardeur que pour soi,'[5] Mably, disguised on this occasion as the Swedish philosopher, has two answers. Firstly, even if less were produced, it would be better so. There are more important things than opulence. Adam Smith said as much, having his mind directed to the issue of national defence. For Mably (or the Swede) the thing that is more important than Abundance is Virtue. It is more advantageous for the human race to have *quelques vertus* than *beaucoup de fruits.*[6] It sounds like the echo of an unimpeachable copybook Latin tag. Moreover, to those who seek and attain unto simplicity, everything else is added. Adam Smith's ' defence,' for instance, comes in as a by-product of a life spent in spare leanness. With a curious innocence of mind he holds that such a society is safe from its enemies. If you have any doubt on the subject, he refers you to Plato and Socrates for reassurance; for is it not written that a poor army,

[1] *Droits et Devoirs*, pp. 378–379; *De la Législation*, p. 47.
[2] *Doutes*, p. 10. [3] *Ibid.* p. 14. [4] *Ibid.* p. 9.
[5] *De la Législation*, p. 79. [6] *Ibid.* p. 82.

if composed of happy citizens, is invincible, and will always be victorious over an army three times as numerous, which has the handicap of representing a rich State?[1] In the twentieth century the assurance even of Plato brings us no comfort on this point.

The second answer suggested by Mably on this question of stimulus —and he is abundantly right—is that avarice is not the only motive capable of moving the human heart. Unfortunately, he pins his faith to a motive which for his purpose would be but a broken reed. There are such things, he says, as 'distinctions'; and if society had in time devised an adequate system of distinctions, the whole evolution of property could have been nipped in the bud. This 'amour de la gloire et de la considération' obviously played a considerable part in Mably's ideas relating to the ordering of the universe. Milord's objection that a man works hardest when working for himself is met with the retort that he is in very deed, *véritablement*, working for himself, if the horizon is dotted with prospects of 'glory' and 'distinctions.' In a rather absurd phrase, what will a man not do to 'goûter le plaisir qui accompagne la considération'?[2]

The idea that the world may find its driving force in a Birthday Honours List (giving the King, if necessary 365 official birthdays in the year) occurs with pathetic frequency in the more Utopian forms of socialist literature, although perhaps few are so badly bitten with the notion as is Mably. Fourier doubtless is more extreme, but he is always in a class by himself. It is a foolish doctrine anywhere, but nowhere more foolish than in Mably. For in his scheme of things, he makes use of 'distinctions' to induce every one to work, so that, had matters been arranged properly, society need never have been driven to the recognition of property. But obviously, if any were wise or depraved enough to say that they preferred indolence to a ribbon (and there would be many such) they would have to be allowed to continue to lead idle lives, sponging on their neighbours; perhaps some who had at last attained the ribbon might burst into a blaze of *fainéantise* in order that they might without distraction savour the pleasure which accompanies consideration. Mably's world, in short, is one in which it is expected that work will be done by all, without intermission, in the hope of a distinction to come, or in gratitude for a distinction already received.

But indeed the idea that the normal motives of life can be replaced by the desire of the scholar to be created, let us say, a Companion of the Midnight Lamp, or by the ambition of the worker to become a Member (Fourth Class) of the Most Assiduous Order of the Indefatigable Beaver, is a delusion revealing a strange misreading of human psychology in these matters. A distinction is a distinction, only if it

[1] *De la Législation*, pp. 86–87.
[2] *Ibid.* pp. 77–82; *Doutes*, p. 9; *Droits et Devoirs*, p. 384.

distinguishes; and no commodity so precipitously loses all value, so rapidly comes to be shunned, as a distinction somewhat too generously shared with others. There is, moreover, a further point on which the Utopian resort to 'distinctions' and 'honours' as a substitute for more sordid incentives lamentably fails. Mably, since he at the moment is giving evidence, does not say how or by whom his distinctions are to be conferred: he is always vague when the point at issue calls for something more precise than a lugubrious shaking of the head. But it is assumed, and always is assumed, that there will be a universal and unquestioning belief that the fountain of honour has sprayed its refreshing waters on all the most deserving and on none but the most deserving. This naively innocent faith does not exist in the world we know, nor is it likely to exist in any earthly paradise that man may imagine. In the absence of such a faith, the shower of distinctions which Mably thinks ought to have saved the world from its selfishness might have precisely the contrary effect. An Honours List, while it is designedly an official commendation of those contained therein, is also inferentially, if not an official censure, at least a display of official frigid neutrality, of postponed approval with regard to those excluded. As Tertullian says, 'choice implies rejection.' It skilfully attains two ends simultaneously; it gives, or is supposed to give, pleasure to those included, if only by enabling them to contemplate the mortification of the less fortunate: no less emphatically it annoys, or may annoy, those who are excluded, and this annoyance is caused not by their exclusion, which might be borne with fortitude if not indifference, but by their having to witness the inclusion of others whom they deem less worthy. A general or a civil servant, kept waiting unduly in the queue for the Bath, may find his youthful ardour replaced by the sourness of hope deferred, and zeal may flag. Mably wants to confer honours on the shepherds whose flocks are most prolific (doubtless, the Order of the Fecund Ewe), the hunter who is best able to bear fatigue and the rigours of the seasons, and many more, including 'la femme la plus ocupée de ses devoirs domestiques.' Here indeed would be a nice apple of discord to toss lightly into the ranks of the W.R.I. and a copious cause of heart-burning among the excluded marginal women. This may appear a trivial, almost a puerile question, almost unworthy of mention; yet the search for non-material stimuli in the form of what Mably calls 'considération,' is so recurrent, that it deserves somewhere to be looked at rather more closely.

Having thus laid bare the evils of the past and the present, Mably might be expected to hold out some hope for the future. He is, however, almost unique in his pessimism: never was a diagnostician so gloomy in his prognosis. It is a recurrent note in his lamentations that our accumulated vices have made any return to a state of happiness impossible. In preaching equality, he makes it clear at the outset that in his view no human power could now restore it without causing greater disorders than those sought to be avoided; and a few pages later he adds that the evil to-day is too deeply rooted to allow any hope of a cure.[1] The barriers between us and the true order of nature are insurmountable.[2] How gladly would one return to the equality established by Lycurgus and sought after by Plato, but in this world of ours this equality can be but a chimera.[3] Moreover, the world is foolish and there is no use in trying. We have reached such a stage of corruption that 'l'extrême sagesse doit paroître l'extrême folie, et l'est en effet.'[4] The Swedish philosopher, who without injustice may in general be taken as the mouthpiece of Mably, declares that if he were to attempt to re-establish equality, he would most infallibly be taken for a fool.[5] The Apostle Paul was not so sensitive.

This is indeed the voice of Timorous, who, having had his vision, such as it was, of the Celestial City, turns back in his pilgrimage, because of the lions in the way, not caring to know whether they were sleeping or waking, or perhaps even chained. From Mably, in short, we may look for no solution, for our evils are 'sans remède.' The utmost he can suggest lies in the adoption of a few 'palliatives,' in order perhaps to soften and somewhat diminish our misfortunes. The laws should be fashioned so as to discourage avarice and ambition, the two primary vices which property and inequality engender. The substance of his suggestions is somewhat archaic, as is indeed everything in Mably. The State must set the example. It must have few requirements: expenditure and taxation must be kept down to the minimum.[6] As a slight contribution in this direction (and for other reasons) magistrates should be unpaid. The citizens should be induced to be content with a mediocre fortune, and to achieve this end riches should be rendered *inutiles.*[7] Most of all he recommends sumptuary laws, of wide range and universal application. Luxury must be abandoned, and in this thirst for primitive simplicity, the Arts also should go: 'je demande à quoi peut nous être bonne une académie de peinture?'[8] The law of inheritance and bequest should be modified to prevent accumulation of wealth: a single daughter would be forcibly given two adopted brothers, in order to prevent her from being corrupted by an excess of wealth. Commerce should as far as possible be forbidden: it is undertaken for reasons of cupidity, and against the interests of good government. A merchant is a dangerous person, in that he has no fatherland. Here, mixed up with physiocratic views, is a reminiscence of the mediaeval doctrine that a merchant can hardly

[1] *Doutes*, pp. 12, 19.
[2] *Ibid.* p. 36.
[3] *Droits et Dévoirs*, pp. 379–380.
[4] *Ibid.* p. 386.
[5] *De la Législation*, p. 97.
[6] *Ibid.* pp. 116–117.
[7] *Ibid.* p. 133.
[8] *Ibid.* p. 135.

be pleasing to God. But indeed Hosea had already said it: 'He is a merchant, the balances of deceit are in his hand: he loveth to oppress.' Such, more or less, are the stale pills which Mably offers to the patient whom he has already pronounced too far gone for recovery.

On his own meagre merits, Mably might be left undisturbed in the complete oblivion that has overtaken him; but such a test is not the only proper criterion in an attempt, however sketchy, to trace the development of ideas and of thought. In his own lifetime and during the succeeding generation, he was an influence of the first magnitude in stressing the idea of absolute equality—although, indeed, his communism is largely based on the more or less uniform capacity of the human stomach, as man 'leaves the hands of Nature,' to borrow one of his favourite expressions. To take one instance of his influence (if it be not an absurd conjunction of names), there can be little doubt that he is the connecting link between Plato and Babeuf. His very great contemporary fame is slightly incomprehensible, even admitting that in many ways—as, for example, in his rapt admiration of the noble savage—he is of his time. But though a passable writer, discoursing with reasonable competence and adequate book-learning on a vast range of subjects,[1] no one would now call him a good writer. He is an uninteresting pedestrian who in time covers the ground several times. Moreover, when we turn to the substance of Mably, it is difficult to resist the impression that, if not a sham (and no one ought to allege this), his socialism was an artificial, academic product, quite out of touch with the needs of his own, and still more of the next, generation. It is exclusively a product of Plato and Lycurgus. His dream is of a primitive community which has succeeded in banishing luxury and the arts, or has never had them; which takes its magistrates direct from the plough, and which looks to its poverty and its temperance as the most potent munitions of war against any possible external enemy. Nor does Mably even have the redeeming feature of feeling at one with the people; in his heart he feels something approaching contempt for his fellows. In short, Mably is, all the time, looking in the wrong direction—backward and not forward; and it is rather odd that his own generation should apparently have had no instinctive feeling of this disabling characteristic.

(*c*) MORELLY

It is now universally accepted that *Le Code de la Nature, ou Le Véritable Esprit de ses Loix de tout tems négligé ou méconnu*, which appeared anonymously in 1755, in the same year as Rousseau's

[1] Though one may perhaps have momentary reservations in the case of an author who refers to the English political parties as 'Wighs' and 'Thorys' (*De la Législation*, p. 220).

Discourse on Inequality was the work of Morelly; but Morelly remains, nevertheless, the most elusive of figures. For long the work was attributed to Diderot, and indeed so generally attributed that *Le Code* in fact appears in certain collected editions of Diderot's works. Such an attribution is, however, an insult to the memory of the great. It is for the expert in French literature to assess the evidence which has fathered this work on Morelly. To the outsider, the chief reason seems to be that *Le Code* contains in the early pages, and throughout, somewhat fulsome praise of a bad allegorical political poem, *La Basiliade*, published two years earlier; and as it seems to be agreed that no one but the author of *La Basiliade* could possibly praise *La Basiliade*, it follows that the author of *Le Code* was the author of *La Basiliade*, who was Morelly. Doubtless, this is not the only piece of evidence bearing on this point. Unfortunately this conclusion does not take us much further. Certain other very minor works swim into the picture, and there have been suggestions that there are two Morellys, a father and a son, sharing the honours between them. Perhaps in all this we should remember that fine flower of classical criticism, crystallised in the saying that 'the Iliad was not written by Homer, but by another man of the same name.' The only fact that clearly emerges is that nothing is known of Morelly. 'Morelly,' in short, is little more than a convenient abbreviation for 'the author of *Le Code de la Nature*.'

But whether *Le Code* was written by Morelly, or by his father, or his son, or by another man of the same name, the book itself remains a work of capital importance as an influence in the second half of the eighteenth century, and beyond. The *Code* is as nearly destitute of intrinsic merits as it is possible for any book to be, though it has its interests. Apart from those spiritually akin to Babeuf, the critics have been uniformly harsh in their attitude toward Morelly. Raynal, on its appearance, described it as possessing 'ni suite, ni méthode, ni vues'; another contemporary critic found 'ni principes, ni raison, ni lumières dans son livre.'[1] Much later, from an impartial distance, Janet pronounced Morelly's socialism as 'un socialisme sans lumières et sans culture,' and Morelly himself as 'un esprit vulgaire et de bas étage.'[2]

These criticisms are substantially justified. Morelly annoys—and in many ways. He is complacent, self-satisfied, and shallow; he dabbles in psychology and theology, indulging in doubtful disputations beyond his stunted depth; he is uniformly rather dreary. Moreover, putting aside as irrelevant (if one may rise to such heights of magnanimity) all these many occasions of irritation, Morelly has the further disability that he has not much to say that is in any way peculiar

[1] Edition of Edouard Dolleans. Introduction, pp. xix, xx.
[2] Janet: *Les Origines du Socialisme Contemporain*, p. 128.

to himself. He believes that man is fundamentally good, and not depraved ; he holds that the wickedness of man is occasioned by the society in which he lives and the corrupting institutions which surround him ; and that ultimately all these evils spring from the existence of property ; and he further seeks to persuade his readers that a better society, indeed a perfect society, would result from the abolition of property. All this is moderately common late eighteenth-century, left-wing doctrine, presented with no distinction. Where Morelly differs from anyone else is that he endeavours to codify the Code of Nature, and prints a ' Model of Legislation conforming to the intentions of Nature.' Natural law is spread all over the eighteenth century, but for obvious prudential reasons, it is usually left vaguely in the air, without a too precise definition of its contents. It is the merit, or at least the peculiarity, of Morelly, that he rushed in where Quesnay and many others had feared to tread, and laid down in a terrifying document the fundamental laws of a society that would seek to conform to the intentions of Nature.

We may pass over the compliments which at the outset the author of *Le Code* pays to the author of *La Basiliade*, a work which is supposed to clothe with poetic grace the truths about to be demonstrated in prose. Having discharged this pleasant duty, Morelly turns to the first point of his programme, the perverse and erroneous views of the political and moral philosophers. Morality ought to be as simple and as evident in its first axioms as mathematics, but it has become disfigured and clouded with prejudices. The fundamental error of the moralists is that they have assumed as their foundation the proposition that man is born vicious and evil (*vicieux et méchant*). It is, it will be observed, the repudiation of the Fall of Man and of the doctrine of Original Sin, which is so large a part of socialist teaching for the next three generations. It has not, he says, occurred to anyone (although in the fullness of time it will most emphatically occur to Fourier) that the problem is ' to find a situation in which it is almost impossible for man to be depraved or wicked.' [1]

The view of the philosopher is that even before Man is born, he carries within himself the baneful seeds of his depravity, urging him to seek his own good at the expense of all his kind.[2] This is self-interest (*amour propre*), and Morelly's attack on the philosophers is largely a white-washing of this self-love, and a demonstration that self-love ought to lead to sociability. For this self-love, transformed by the moralists into an hundred-headed hydra, is something entirely innocent ' in the order of Nature.' It is nothing more than a constant desire to preserve one's existence by means which are both easy and innocent, and which Providence has placed within the reach of all. But when human institutions have surrounded these innocent means

[1] Morelly: Dolleans' edition, p. 9. [2] *Ibid.* p. 10.

with insurmountable difficulties and much more, need it cause surprise that this self-love is transmuted into a multitude of vices ?[1] It is, however, from this 'triste Morale' of the philosophers, and not from Nature, that this ill-omened leaven derives.

The Supreme Wisdom, to which Morelly has at all times free access, intended, however, something entirely different. Its purpose was to make the human species an Intelligent Whole, which should arrange itself by a mechanism as simple as marvellous—indeed by a species of 'moral attraction,' another pointer in the direction of Fourier.[2] For out of self-love there springs, or ought to spring, a 'benevolent affection' for all that alleviates or helps our weakness. The desire to be happy may be fundamental, but self-love achieves nothing without assistance, and this impels us to the happy necessity of being benevolent. Crystallised in a sentence: 'Tu veux être heureux; sois bienfaisant.'[3] Benevolence is the path by which self-love realises itself.

Had we but followed the intentions of the Supreme Wisdom, the situation should have been an entirely happy one. Using in a contrary sense a metaphor to which Malthus was later to give an unenviable notoriety, Morelly assures us that

> the world is a table sufficiently furnished for all the guests, whose provisions belong in their entirety, sometimes to all because all are hungry, sometimes to some only because the others are satisfied: thus no one is absolutely the master, nor has the right to claim to be so.[4]

Nature has ingeniously contrived a number of devices whereby men are impelled, though perhaps not very effectively, towards unanimity and general concord. It has given us a sense of equality of conditions and of rights and of the necessity of labouring in common by showing us our 'parity' in feeling and in needs. By temporary variations in our needs, so that all are not equally affected at the same time (we are not all hungry together), it has warned us that we should sometimes renounce our rights for the advantage of others. By endowing men differently in strength, in industry and in ability, it has pointed the way to different employments. The pain and effort of satisfying our needs when acting alone, impress on our minds the necessity of looking for the assistance of others, and inspire us with an affection for all that helps us. Thus Morelly, revealing the inner workings of the divine plan, shows how the stage was set to urge man on to a comprehensive benevolence; and these urgings the politicians and the moralists should have seconded, instead of playing the part of 'maladroit mechanicians,' breaking the springs and thereby involving the dissolution of humanity. Morelly is rather proud of his view of society as an automatic machine, and it recurs.

[1] Morelly: Dolleans' edition, pp. 10–11.
[2] *Ibid.* p. 12.
[3] *Ibid.* pp. 60, 71.
[4] *Ibid.* p. 13.

The methods by which primitive legislators should have kept man in the straight path are not obscure. There is but one vice in the world, namely Avarice.[1] All other vices, how different soever they may present themselves to the human eye, ultimately resolve themselves into a desire to possess, *le désir d'avoir* ; and it therefore follows, with a devastatingly simple logic, that where there is no property, there can likewise be none of the pernicious consequences flowing from property. But our legislators, those pretended sages whom our imbecility admires, have broken the bonds of sociability in recognising property.[2] The law should have regulated, not property, but the use of property. Even now (apparently) if property is abolished, all will be well. If we are but delivered of this tyrant, as he tells us in a phrase of delicious and superfluous emphasis, it will be ' impossible de toute impossibilité ' that man should be guilty of crime, that he should be either a thief, an assassin, or a conqueror.[3] The legislators, however, missed the golden opportunity of basing society on the true intentions of Nature which, as will be seen presently, can be summarised in a few simple propositions. So far as concerns the application of these principles in practice to such matters as the direction of each to his appropriate employment and the assignment to each of the means of subsistence—all the tasks of the Ministry of Labour and of the Ministry of Food—this need cause no anxiety. Morelly belongs to that long and pathetic line that believes that the business of this world and the administration of government are matters which any child could compass in his less intelligent moments. All these questions, he says, merely amount to a simple matter of enumeration of things and of persons, a simple operation of calculation and combination and, consequently, ' susceptible d'un très-bel ordre.' Too often have socialist dreams of a Utopia been vitiated by the innocent faith that all business is ' merely a matter of accounting.'

One other point in Morelly's general theory is perhaps worth mentioning, as it serves to link him with anarchist thought of a later date. He will have nothing to do with the suggestion that men are by nature indolent, or in any way averse from labour. If men appear to be lazy, or to be addicted to an untimely folding of the hands together, this also is the result of prejudices, springing from the institutions by which we have been corrupted. We have fixed a permanent condition of repose on some whom we call prosperous, leaving to others the heat and burden of the day. In these circumstances, where idleness is the privilege of the fortunate, it is natural that the others should acquire an aversion, indeed a *dégout*, for work imposed upon them. That men are not naturally idle, may, however, be inferred from the zeal with which the rich seek ' le tumulte fatiguant des plaisirs pour se délivrer d'une oisiveté importune.' It is a wholly fallacious

[1] Morelly : Dolleans' edition, p. 15. [2] *Ibid.* p. 19. [3] *Ibid.* p. 65.

argument which in the fullness of time is called upon to bear a heavy burden.[1]

The peculiarity of Morelly, however, lies in the fact that in the fourth part of the *Code* he is so temerarious as to give a model of legislation which conforms with the intentions of Nature.[2] It is a curious document. Quite obviously the intentions of Nature are not what they are usually assumed to be ; moreover, Nature, which ought to confine herself to generalities, condescends to questions of detail which ought to be beneath her dignity. There are three fundamental and sacred laws, which are guaranteed by Morelly to cut the roots from the vices and evils of any society. These laws are buttressed by laws on specific subjects—distributive laws, agrarian laws, sumptuary laws, laws relating to the form of government, conjugal laws, penal laws and so on. These are not certified as fundamental and sacred ; and on certain matters they contain very detailed provisions, sometimes of a rather arbitrary nature. What Morelly does is to present, professedly as a code of laws—though no lawyer would recognise it as such —the picture of a communistic society which owes not a little to More's *Utopia*. The three fundamental and sacred laws are somewhat general in their character. The first prescribes that there shall be no private property, apart from the things of which a man is making actual use, whether for his needs, his pleasures or his daily work—a definition which already opens a whole corridor of serious doors. The second, in a rather curious phrase, requires that every citizen is to be an ' homme public,' maintained and employed at the expense of the public. The third imposes on every citizen the obligation to contribute to the public good according to his strength, his talents and his age.[3]

The Morellian commonwealth is in part an orthodox Utopia ; in part it has original features. However viewed, it would be a thoroughly unpleasant place of residence. The structure rests on families, tribes, cities and, if need be, provinces ; and there is a system of government by rotation which may represent an obeisance to the principle of equality, but which would certainly sacrifice the remnants of efficiency. As in Utopia, goods are accumulated in, and distributed from, public magazines. In the event of a shortage of ' provisions d'agrément,' there may be a suspension or restriction of supplies. Essential goods are, however, dealt with on a different basis : ' on prendra garde, avec soin, que ces accidens n'arrivent pas à l'egard de choses universellement nécessaires.' [4] That ought to be quite enough to put a stop to a bad harvest. Every citizen works in agriculture from the age of 20 to 25, which again brings an echo from *Utopia*. Boys and girls are sorted out at the age of five, and entrusted to a curious rota of fathers and

[1] Morelly : Dolleans' edition, p. 32.
[2] *Ibid.* pp. 85–109.
[3] *Ibid.* pp. 85–86.
[4] *Ibid.* p. 87.

mothers, who do duty consecutively for periods of five days. It does not seem a very effective system of education ; fortunately, education seems to end at the age of ten. At that age the children pass to the workshops: indeed, those who are bright may have acquired before then the rudiments of their destined trade. They are married off at the earliest possible moment, between the ages of fifteen and eighteen ; and all marriages take place together at the beginning of the year. Religious, metaphysical and philosophical doctrine is prescribed, and no departure tolerated. Children are not to have their minds 'imbued' with any 'fable, conte, ou fictions ridicules.'[1] The animosity of Utopians towards Red Riding Hood is deep-seated and ineradicable. There is an astonishing wealth of detailed provisions regarding divorce: Utopia apparently does not guarantee connubial felicity. One provision is so surprising that it deserves to be expiscated ; the children (both sexes) remain with the father in the event of a divorce, and the woman whom he has last married will alone be regarded as their mother ; none of those who have preceded her may take the title with regard to the children of the husband. This may be in conformity with the intentions of Nature, but one would like to know the sources of Morelly's information.

Lastly, these laws partake in part of the nature of the laws of the Persians and the Medes. The section dealing with government (foolish enough in itself) is, like the fundamental laws, to be reputed sacred and inviolable: 'they cannot be changed or abrogated by anyone soever.'[2] Morelly shows a ghoulish enjoyment in the prospect of punishing his offenders, though it is odd that in a world where it was to have been 'impossible de toute impossibilité' for man to err, there should still be a place for penal laws. He is not the first of whom it may be said that the latter end of his commonwealth forgets the beginning. These laws for the restraint of criminals are, however, 'aussi douces qu'efficaces.' Morelly's ideas of a 'douce' punishment are somewhat peculiar. There are two grades of offenders, those who have merited separation from society for a time, and those who have deserved to 'die civilly'—in other words to be separated perpetually from their fellows. In the least agreeable and most barren part of the country, Morelly contemplates the creation of a gloomy prison and a cemetery in close proximity. The prison with the heavy gratings is not, indeed, for those who would tamper with the laws. It is reserved for minor offenders, doing time—adulterers, those who speak disrespectfully of the Senators, and such small fry. Those who have deserved to die civilly, the would-be tamperers with the law, are accommodated *in* the cemetery, in spacious caverns with heavy iron bars, until they are not merely civilly dead, but dead in very deed. Thereafter the cavern becomes their tomb. It is an arrangement

[1] Morelly : Dolleans' edition, p. 104. [2] *Ibid.* p. 99.

which is at least ultimately economical in the matter of transport; and again one can but wonder at the intentions of Nature.

Doubtless few will dissent from the verdict of M. Janet that this is indeed 'un esprit vulgaire, et de bas étage,' and that his is a socialism without light and without culture. This, however, does not prevent him from having given light, albeit a murky light, to others. Morelly and Mably indeed go hand in hand for many years, the inspiration of the egalitarian side of the French Revolution, culminating in the mysterious conspiracy of Babeuf. Babeuf was right when he said that the author of *Le Code* was the leader of his conspiracy: that he happened to call him Diderot is irrelevant. What chiefly astonishes and offends us to-day is perhaps not so much Morelly's shallow pilferings from all ages and his total lack of comprehension and profundity in face of the problems with which he professes to grapple, as his effrontery in fathering on Nature the details of a constitution and a system of law of which (apart from hints from Plato and More) no one but he could be the begetter. History, unfortunately, demands a place even for foolish people, and Morelly cannot be ignored here, partly because of his relation to Babeuf; partly (though one says it with regret) because in certain respects he holds out a hand to Fourier.

(*d*) BABEUF

At the portals of what purports to be a history of thought, Babeuf—Gracchus Babeuf or François Noël Babeuf, according as one prefers his familiar adopted name or his forgotten baptismal name—should perhaps knock in vain; for there are those who have suggested that Babeuf was innocent of thought. Yet he has a place in history, and in some ways is a portent. Babeuf represents a combination of Mably and Morelly, transferred to the field of action. The pessimistic shrug of the shoulders with which Mably had acknowledged the futility of doing anything is replaced by a demoniacal subterranean energy, aiming at the destruction of all things. On the theoretical side, the doctrine is unalloyed Mably-Morelly, apart from such minor modifications and variations of emphasis as inevitably emerge when an accepted point of view is restated in the light of another environment. Babeuf had not enjoyed the ample surroundings which had enabled Mably to discourse frigidly of equality in classical dialogues. On the contrary, poverty had lurked incessantly by his doorway. It would probably be true to say that Babeuf was not without envy in his heart, envy of those who had been more kindly treated in the lottery of life. His appeal for a higher way of life is accordingly addressed to the lower instincts and passions of mankind. Babeuf is thus of interest as showing the logical continuation, downhill, of Mably and Morelly, when their gospel is accepted by one who is not beset by academic jitters, as was Mably. He is also of interest because, in the rage for destruction which finally consumed him and his sect, the Babouvists are a connecting link with nihilism and later destructive anarchism.

The stormy life and the tempestuous death of Babeuf are part of the history of the French Revolution. The barest bones, designed to ' place ' him, must suffice here. Born in 1764, he was already a provincial journalist, practising in Amiens on *Le Correspondent Picard,* before the Revolution sucked him into the Parisian vortex. He became a figure on the extreme left-wing, assumed the name of Caius Gracchus, and was ever afterwards known as Gracchus Babeuf. Also, without any authority apart from his own mere volition, he called himself the ' Tribune of the People,' and in the course of time published under this title a paper which periodically went underground. After the fall of Robespierre and under the reaction of 1795 (*la réaction thermidorienne*), Babeuf developed an extraordinary subterranean activity, which culminated in the notorious ' Conspiration.' The object of the conspiracy, engineered by the ' Secte des Egaux ' was to overthrow the existing government and to establish complete and ' real ' equality. The whole story of the conspiracy has about it a flavour of fantastic melodrama, and in view of its wide ramifications and extensive publicity, the existing government was rather obtuse not to have become alive to the danger sooner than it did. It may be that we of our generation have little experience of conspiracies of this nature ; yet, even allowing for our disability in this respect, it is difficult to resist the impression that the conspirators were melodramatically acting the part of plotters, and were greatly enjoying the experience. In time they established a ' directoire secret de salut public.' There is a curious document enacting that ' the people is in insurrection against tyranny,' preceded by four pages of clauses, each beginning with ' considérant que . . . ' for all the world as though they were the I.L.O. in full session.[1] It is not thus, one imagines, that conspiracies are usually run. At the last moment, the plot was betrayed by a traitor to the cause, Georges Grisel. The leaders were arrested, and a somewhat wearisome and protracted trial ensued. In the end, Babeuf and his chief supporter Darthe were condemned to death. Across the distance of years, it is rather surprising that in so far-reaching a conspiracy, justice was supposed to be satisfied with a mere two capital sentences. The final scene has an element of ghoulishness which happily is almost unique. True to the inspiration of the name ' Gracchus ' and the old Roman Stoic virtues which it suggested, Babeuf and Darthe endeavoured to fall on each other's swords after being condemned. Such a method of suicide obviously calls for a certain technique of its own, nor is suicide the kind of thing in which the necessary dexterity can be acquired by practice. The conspirators merely succeeded in

[1] Buonarotti : *Conspiration pour l'Egalite dite de Babeuf,* vol. 2, pp. 244–248.

grievously wounding each other, so that they bled profusely until their execution next day (24th February, 1797): it was what Buonarotti rightly calls ' une exécution sanglante.'

Even in the most summary account of Babeuf, this fellow-conspirator, Buonarotti, has an indefeasible right to be mentioned, for in a sense he supplies the epilogue. It is not clear why he escaped the fate of Babeuf, for, assuming guilt, he seems to have been as guilty as any. In his own words the Tribunal merely said to him and some others: ' Allez traîner une vie malheureuse loin de la patrie dans des climats brûlans et meurtriers,' [1] which may be accepted as an ornate paraphrase of a sentence of banishment. But before the end Buonarotti had given the martyrs a solemn pledge that he would one day write the full story of the conspiracy, and justify their memories. He kept his word, although not until after the lapse of some thirty years of vagabondage. His *Conspiration pour l'Egalité, dite de Babeuf* (1828), with as many ' pièces justicatives ' as time had spared, was until quite recent years the real source of our knowledge regarding Babeuf. Moreover, though it may not be a great book, it is a book of some interest as carrying still further the Mably-Morelly tradition.

A consideration of Babeuf raises a question of great historical interest, which in its time has been much discussed. How far was the French Revolution a movement inspired by socialist ideas in the ordinary acceptation of the phrase? The fullest answer in one sense has been given by M. Janet.[2] The lectures which lie at the base of M. Janet's book were delivered in 1872. Doubtless the acid test of what should be regarded as socialism in 1872 is not what would be accepted as appropriate to-day; doubtless also M. Janet was sufficiently near the generation of Sudre, Thonissen, and Reybaud, to have an instinctive feeling that socialism was of the devil. Yet, with these reservations, the conclusions of M. Janet are probably substantially correct. For Janet, socialism covers generally any doctrine which undermines the principle of private property; just as conversely (if it is conversely) the strongest weapon against socialism is private property. Now according to Janet, ' nowhere, at no time, and in no country, has the right of private property been more firmly claimed and more firmly guaranteed than by the Revolution.' [3] For the detailed argument the reader must consult Janet himself; in the brevity which is here imposed, it is sufficient to recall that the right of property was indeed viewed as one of the fundamental rights of man. In the Constitution of the French Republic decreed in the year 1793, it is expressly stated (Article 2) that the natural and imprescriptible rights of man are: ' l'égalité, la

[1] Buonarotti, vol. 2, p. 61.

[2] Janet: *Les Origines du Socialisme Contemporain.* See also Faguet, *Le Socialisme en 1907.*

[3] Janet: *op cit.*, pp. 1–3.

liberté, la sureté, la propriété'; and Article 16 defines the right of property as 'celui qui appartient à tout citoyen, de jouir et de disposer à son gré de ses biens, de ses revenus, du fruit de son travail et de son industrie.'[1] Much of Babeuf's revolutionary activity was directed to getting back to the Constitution of 1793, as a stepping-stone, but he never disguised the fact that its consecration of property was, in his eyes, a grave blot. Buonarotti quotes with approval the superior version of the Declaration of the Rights of Man, drafted by Robespierre, where property is defined as 'le droit qu'a chaque citoyen de jouir et de disposer à son gré de la portion de bien qui lui est garantie par la loi.' Those who attacked property were, according to Janet, a dissident minority, standing apart from the main stream of thought and action, which, while it doubtless interfered with property in various ways, never dreamed of questioning the fundamental right of property. Here then lies the significance of Babeuf; he was a protest against the Revolution stopping halfway in its task; in a world that spoke of Equality, he clamoured for 'real' equality, which (he held) could not be attained so long as property existed.

Even a brief summary of Babeuf runs the risk of being a tedious repetition, on a different plane, of a point of view encountered elsewhere. Yet though the substance does not differ materially from what may be found in those who inspired him, the flavour in Babeuf is different; and enough must be said to catch, if it be possible, something of this peculiar flavour. Apart from what he wrote for *Le Tribun du Peuple*, Babeuf was a very valiant correspondent. M. Maurice Dommanget has brought together in a volume of *Pages Choisies* as much as—indeed probably a great deal more than—anyone is likely to desire in the matter of Babeuf's writings. For that matter a very lengthy letter of July 28, 1795, together with No. 35 of *Le Tribun du Peuple*, are sufficient to give the clotted cream of Babeuf's views on things in general.[2]

The starting-point is inevitably the familiar contention that Nature has made all men equal in rights and needs. If there are inequalities, the law of society should act so as to redress the balance and maintain the equality designed by Nature; but in fact it has acted in precisely the opposite direction.[3] Babeuf is perhaps peculiar in the emphasis he lays on the fact that human prejudices have unjustly favoured certain occupations. Some are given 'une valeur d'opinion.'[4] It is a point on which he is almost inclined to nag, so that one almost suspects that the prosperity of some of his fellow-villagers had become an offence to him. In fact, all honest men are equal. Every one 'qui a des

[1] This constitution will be found among the *Pièces Justificatives;* Buonarotti, vol. 1, p. 65.

[2] Dommanget: *Pages Choisies de Babeuf*, pp. 207–221, 250–264.

[3] Dommanget, *e.g.* pp. 76, 237, 251. [4] *Ibid.* p. 124.

vertus ' honours his calling, and all should therefore enjoy ' une égale aisance.'[1] There is perhaps more originality—and up to a point more commendable originality—in his views on education. Babeuf has that pathetic faith in education, which is to be found only in those who have been denied it, and who have struggled to make good a self-confessed deficiency. It colours all his frequently expressed anxieties with regard to the future of his children. Yet to Babeuf, with his eyes intent on equality, the system of education is full of dangers. For inequality has one of its roots in the different education of rich and poor. In a phrase which has an arresting quality seldom found in Babeuf, he asserts that education has become ' a species of property.' Education, like other property, should therefore be something that all should share alike. There is a touch of the wild language later characteristic of the Secte des Egaux in Babeuf's exclamation that there should either be no education at all, or all should be able to have it equally. Consistently through life, he was an advocate of ' all or nothing.'[2]

Where there is inequality, there must be injustice; if one has superfluity, another must lack. For Babeuf, like his immediate predecessors, is extraordinarily well informed as to the intentions of Nature, and is able to define these intentions with the utmost precision. Nature, which is described as ' économe de ses dons,' produces only just approximately what is useful for all the beings it creates[3]; apparently, Nature takes a census, and quite apart from what may be done meanwhile by the beings it creates, it sends sufficient rations and no more, like a somewhat stingy Minister of Food. It follows that if one enjoys superfluity, drawn from this nicely calculated store, somewhere else there must be someone suffering a corresponding deficiency: ' ce qui manque au grand nombre existe dans le *trop*, dans le superflu du petit nombre.'[4] By a natural transition (even though Proudhon has not yet spoken the word) this becomes a species of theft. The deficit, where there is a deficit, springs from what others have stolen—' stolen legitimately, if you like, with the help of laws made by brigands.'[5] There is here sufficient groundwork for an extreme statement of the class warfare, and Babeuf expresses it in various picturesque phrases. There is perpetual war between the starvers and the starved, *les affameurs et lés affamés*; a war between rich and poor; a war between those who have nothing and those who have all.[6] Moreover, the doctrine of the class war is driven home by a liberal and oratorical appeal to the envy and the discontent of the unfortunate. Why should some have *la bonne table*, and others *le pain noir*?[7] How can you expect me, Babeuf, to ' temporiser,' to ' politiquer,' when I have not eaten for 48 hours; when, on rising in the morning, I do not know

[1] Dommanget, p. 79.
[2] *Ibid.* pp. 85–86.
[3] *Ibid.* p. 81.
[4] *Ibid.* p. 237.
[5] *Ibid.* p. 256.
[6] *Ibid.* pp. 186, 238.
[7] *Ibid.* p. 115.

whether it is my old breeches, my shirt, my shabby coat, or my frayed bed-cover that I shall have to sell ? [1]

In the eyes of Babeuf, as of Fourier later, everything is wrong ; and in the extremely significant letter of July 28, 1795 (or should we say, of the 10th thermidor of the Year III ?), addressed to Charles Germain, he comes nearer than elsewhere to a systematic indictment of the world in which we live.[2] Commerce exists, he says, for the purpose of pumping the sweat and blood of more or less everybody, in order to form lakes of gold for the benefit of the few ; it is a Fourieresque thought, down even to the confused picture which it evokes. The idea of exploitation is hinted at on lines familiar to a later generation. There is a conspiracy (complot) of the part against the whole : the procedure, in a rather cumbrous and lumbering phrase, is to contrive to set in motion a multitude of arms without allowing those who in fact move these arms to receive their destined fruit. Wealth flows to criminal speculators, who are aided and abetted by merchants, their *co-voleurs*—a pleasant word. The most essential workers get least : this, in a significant phrase, is ' la loi barbare dictée par les capitaux.' It is a world of uncertainty : we can never be sure that we or our offspring are secure against the danger of destitution. It is a thought which obsesses Babeuf, ever yearning for his children. He has already reached the characteristic note of the later ' Conspiration,' in avowing that the only course is to destroy everything. Had I but the magic fairy ring, he exclaims, ' je ferais la poussière du passé,' and simultaneously evoke from the earth the much-dreamed-of Société des Egaux. Here, as with the anarchists of the deed, what is desired is the annihilation of all things, trusting that out of the dust of destruction a fair city may arise. And buoyed by such a hope, how blithely would Babeuf bide the stour.

Putting it otherwise, the revolution, however nobly it may have been originally designed, has turned out a misfire, above all since 1793. So long as everything that is worthless has not been overthrown, we have not yet ' assez revolutionné pour le peuple.' So far as the people are concerned, there has been no revolution. The revolution must be continued until it becomes the revolution of the people. Indeed, the whole thing must be done over again : *la révolution est à réfaire.*[3] And in this, what is primarily necessary is a work of destruction.[4]

[1] Dommanget, p. 249. [2] *Ibid.* pp. 207–221. [3] *Ibid.* pp. 265–266.

[4] As the more important documents relating to the conspiracy may have been written by one or other of his fellow-conspirators, though inspired by Babeuf, it may be as well to give a brief passage from Babeuf writing in his own person, in one of his wilder and more tumultuous moods. This is from No. 35 of *Le Tribun du Peuple :*

' Répétons-le encore : Tous les maux sont à leur comble ; ils ne peuvent plus empirer ; ils ne peuvent se réparer que par un bouleversement total ! ! ! Que tout se confonde donc ! . . . que tous les élémens se brouillent, se mêlent et s'entrechoquent ! . . . que tout rentre dans le cahos, et que du cahos sorte un monde nouveau et régénéré ' (p. 264).

Before we glance at certain of the documents relating to the conspiracy, Buonarotti, in his capacity of literary and revolutionary executor, should perhaps be allowed to supplement Babeuf. Apart from the *pièces justificatives* which throw a flood of light on dark places, the chief interest of Buonarotti lies in the fact that a substantial part of the first volume is devoted to a systematic outline of the Babouvist heaven. Babeuf had been anything but systematic, and Buonarotti's re-editing of the ultimate aims of the conspirators, thirty years after the event, is a better statement than Babeuf could himself have produced. What, however, most impresses in reading Buonarotti is our nearness to Mably and Morelly. In this world of 'égalité sans mensonge,' the right to property is replaced by a right to an existence as happy as that enjoyed by anyone else [1]; although, obviously, a state that seeks to equalise so elusive a thing as happiness has some nice psychological problems in its path. It is a world of abundance to all, with, however, this caveat, that what cannot be 'communicated' to all, must be severely cut down. In effect, unless everyone is to have everything, no one is to have anything.[2] It is a world of simplicity, cutting out the arts and turning its back on foreign trade and the luxuries and dangers it brings with it [3]; a world where every citizen is a soldier, and where youth will be encamped on the frontier, but which nevertheless finds its most sure shield of defence in its simplicity and integrity [4]; a world where there are few laws, for laws are not required where there is equality. What laws, indeed, beyond the simplest, are needed among a people who are 'without property, and without the vices and crimes which it engenders, without commerce, without money, without taxes, without finances, without civil processes, and without poverty'? [5] It is a world where education is to be 'national, common and equal,' since political equality springs from equality in education.[6] Unfortunately, and it represents the debit side of much socialist Utopian speculation, it is also to be a world in which the individual will have no life of his own: 'La patrie s'empare de l'individu naissant pour ne le quitter qu'à la mort.' [7] In a world which has shed so many things that laws have become virtually unnecessary, it is odd that the State should continue as an octopus, against whose encirclements the grave alone provides a secure asylum.[8]

[1] Buonarotti, vol. 1, p. 208.
[2] *Ibid.* p. 210. [3] *Ibid.* p. 217. [4] *Ibid.* pp. 237–239.
[5] *Ibid.* p. 271. [6] *Ibid.* p. 280. [7] *Ibid.* p. 282.
[8] Reference to a minor specific point may perhaps illustrate the abiding influence of Morelly more vividly than a discussion at large. In a passage cited earlier in the text, Morelly, dealing with the complications of administration in the matter of distribution, says: 'Je dirai que tout cela auroit été une simple affaire de denombrement de *choses* et de *personnes*, une simple opération de calcul et de combinaison, et, par conséquent, susceptible d'un très-bel ordre' (Morelly, pp. 38–39). Buonarotti, dealing with the same question, says: 'De là nait dans l'administration d'une société fort étendue, une certaine complication qui embarrasse extrêmement ceux

Even a short account of Babeuf calls imperatively for some reference to the numerous proclamations and what-nots in which his conspiracy was shrouded. Never surely was a conspiracy so amply ' documented ': the plotters shed their ink as freely as they urged their followers to shed their blood ; and the result is a curious collection of manifestos, draft decrees, and instructions which may be found among Buonarotti's *pièces justificatives.* They are of interest in showing the path a successful Babouvism would have followed. The most notorious is the *Manifeste des Egaux*, said to be the work of Sylvain Maréchal. This is a fire-eating and loud-mouthed production : the unkind might even call it rant. A few sentences will suffice :

> Eh bien ! We claim henceforward to live and die equals, as we have been born equals. We demand real equality, or Death ; that is what we must have.
>
> And we will have this real equality, no matter at what price. Woe to those whom we meet, coming between it and us ! Woe to whomsoever offers resistance to so determined a desire.
>
> The French Revolution is only the fore-runner of another revolution, still greater, still more solemn, and which will be the last. . . .
>
> We must have this equality, not merely transcribed in the declaration of the rights of man and of the citizen : we must have it in our midst, under the roof of our houses. We consent to everything for its sake, to make *table rase*, so that we may cleave to it alone. Perish, if need be, all the arts, provided there remains to us real equality ! [1]

The various projects and fragments of projects, the body of decrees drawn up by the ' insurrectionary committee ' in preparation for ' the day,' furnish an interesting introduction into the technique of revolution, though perhaps the ultimate lesson lies in the revelation of what should be avoided. The curious ' Acte d'Insurrection,' which purports to enact a state of insurrection, provides in Article 12 that all opposition will be overcome on the spot, and that those who oppose will be exterminated. More humanely (Articles 13 and 14) it provides for a free distribution of victuals to the people, and conscripts the bakers to bake bread incessantly. Article 17 provides for the goods of the enemies being distributed among the defenders of the Fatherland.[2] Another projected decree enacts that poor citizens who are at the moment badly housed, will not return to their ordinary dwellings : the houses and the furniture of the former rich will be made available for their use.[3]

qui la considèrent superficiellement ; mais au fond tout ceci n'est qu'une affaire de simple calcul, susceptible de l'ordre le plus exact et de la marche la plus regulière' (Buonarotti, vol. 1, p. 214).

This, it will be observed, is not Babeuf speaking ; it is Buonarotti, writing in old age in 1828, recalling the discussions of the conspirators round about 1796, and he professes to be giving an account ' aussi fidèle que me le permettent le laps du temps et le faible et unique secours de ma mémoire.' Yet, almost textually he uses the words of Morelly, written in 1755. Putting aside the poets, not many authors receive such a compliment after 73 years.

[1] Buonarotti, vol. 2, pp. 131–132. [2] *Ibid.* pp. 251–252.

[3] *Ibid.* p. 284.

There is something refreshingly humorous in a conspiracy, of which the primary purpose is the abolition of property, drafting in advance an enactment legalising loot. After a lapse of thirty years the point had obviously begun to worry Buonarotti. It would be wrong, he says, to consider the promise of a large distribution of goods as contrary to the spirit of communism which was aimed at: *Le grand point était de réussir.* This surely is the disarming simplicity of old age.[1]

There is further a fragment of an economic decree which seems to foreshadow something in the nature of national workshops, and is of some mild interest in tracing the affiliations of Louis Blanc.[2] Of more general significance, however, is a project of a police decree dealing with 'étrangers,' which, to avoid the implications of the words 'stranger' and 'foreigner,' should perhaps be translated as 'outsiders.' Those who do nothing for the Fatherland, that is, those not engaged in certain specified useful occupations (and in fact not all these), are classed as 'outsiders,' to whom the Republic accords 'hospitality,'—which sounds quite honorific. In fact, their ultimate destination is one or other of the small islands off the French coast, converted into places of correction. These islands, moreover, are to be 'rendered inacessible.'[3] The hospitality accorded by the unborn Republic is, in short, the hospitality of the concentration camp. There may have been many reasons for the failure of the 'Conspiration, dite de Babeuf.' A perusal of Buonarotti leaves little doubt that one reason among others was that they all talked too much, and spent too much time elaborating draft edicts to come into force on the blessed day of revolution.

Enough—perhaps too much—of Babeuf for the narrow confines of this book. Weighed dispassionately, he may have had few gifts, apart from a certain inflammatory biliousness in his pen. In ordinary times he would have been one of the world's very small men, going to and coming from his appointed task, somewhere in Picardy. Do not let us condemn him in that he called himself Caius Gracchus; it was in accordance with the custom of the time. Less pardonable was his assumption of the title of 'Tribune of the People'; for to such an office or dignity no man may nominate himself. Let it be remembered that he was dreadfully in earnest. Nor let us be too censorious over his censorious rebukings of the actors at Amiens, at whose hands he was condemned 'à voir des Marquis et d'autres gens de cette espèce.' 'Moi republicain, moi homme libre, moi ami de l'égalité' could hardly be expected to sit in the pit unprotestingly under such an outrage.[4]

[1] Machiavelli, of course, had said it. In his short biography of Castruccio Castracani, he recalls that this embodiment of Machiavellian virtues 'diceva che la vittoria, non il modo della vittoria, ti arrecava gloria.' Always, *le grand point est de réussir.*

[2] Buonarotti, vol. 2, p. 305.

[3] *Ibid.* pp. 301–304.

[4] Dommanget, p. 135.

He was a *sans-culotte*, and took himself seriously. Moreover, taking himself seriously, he was at times rather inclined to think well of himself, though this may have been but the workings of the inferiority complex. One feels most kindly towards Babeuf when reading his intimate letters, through which there glows such a love of wife and children as would have won the approval of Robert Burns in his more official moments. His letters written from prison in the last days almost achieve real pathos, and might have succeeded in doing so had he been able to prune somewhat the sproutings of his egotism. But even on the night before his execution, a man should not comfort his wife by foretelling the satisfaction she will feel when men say of her husband: 'Il fut parfaitement vertueux.' [1]

Nevertheless, when all has been said in demonstration of the inherent insignificance and commonplaceness of Babeuf, he remains vastly more interesting than many who have been more generously endowed. He represents one end of a tradition, if traditions ever do end without being immediately reborn. It is instructive, even if it be not edifying, to witness the platonic dialogues of Mably debouching in the rather fatuous decrees of La République des Egaux, conceived but never born. Babeuf is also of interest because his wild rage of destruction, his willingness to smash the universe if frustrated, is, in its intensity, something new, and for anything similar we have to await the Russian nihilists. The significance of Babeuf then is that he represents the nodal point at which the academic egalitarianism of Mably becomes transformed into the ungovernable destructiveness of left-wing anarchism.

There is another respect in which Babeuf, if certainly not unique, is at least an example of a moderately rare phenomenon. He speaks somewhere rather slightingly of Rousseau as a dreamer, the suggestion being that Rousseau was a dealer in words who did nothing. It is true that revolutionary writers have not always been revolutionaries, nor even conspirators. Even Marx beyond the age of thirty may perhaps be described as a dreamer in this sense, sowing revolutionary seed, but to the ordinary eye a mere bourgeois, living on the fringes of debt and of Hampstead. Lenin is perhaps the great example of the theoretical revolutionary carrying his theories into practice. It is a far cry from the Russian Revolution to the Conspiration des Egaux; but, to put it no higher, Babeuf would have liked to resemble Lenin.

(*e*) FICHTE

Johann Gottlieb Fichte (1762–1814) has incontestable claims to admission to a history of socialism, though there may be some doubts as to the precise chapter to which he should be shepherded. In some

[1] Dommanget, p. 312.

respects he has kinship with later German developments, in so far as German thought has always shown a marked tendency in favour of a strong State and a strict authoritarian régime. On the other hand, he is essentially of the eighteenth century, and perhaps therefore he may be included here among writers who on the whole represent late eighteenth-century impulses. Fichte may not unfairly be described as a Utopian, in the sense that the book with which we are here concerned (*Der geschlossne Handelsstaat*) is calculated to elicit the snorts of the practically minded; he is a philosopher; being of the eighteenth century, he moves within the framework of the idea of a Social Contract—not indeed of one contract, but of a whole plethora of contracts, which are held together and guaranteed by the State. Even of the exiguous contents of the *Geschlossne Handelsstaat* there is much that may here be left aside. What concerns us is his view of the functions of the State; of the relation of the State to its members, and of the members of the State to each other. The purpose of the State, in rounded language, is said to be to give to each what is his; to confirm each in his possession, and thereafter to protect him therein.[1] It is the State alone which has power to turn an indeterminate crowd into a 'closed whole'; through it alone a right to property can be established. The distribution of functions (if one may borrow a later phrase) rests on a contract of all with all, and the underlying assumption on which the contract is based is that all should have approximately an equal share of the pleasures and amenities of life: they must *alle ungefähr gleich angenehm leben können*.[2]

Who, it may be asked, are the parties to this contract or contracts? We have, it may be, come to swallow the idea of a Social Contract, as presented by Hobbes, Locke or Rousseau, without too much protest against the absurdity of the whole business—perhaps because most of us encounter these contracts at an early and unquestioning stage of our initiation into political wisdom. Elsewhere, fictitious and notional contracts reek of artificiality, and tend to provoke expressions of impatient incredulity—nowhere more so than in the case of Fichte. His contract is in the first place between the *Produzenten* and the *Künstler*, the producers of the original materials and the artificers—and ultimately as there are all manner of artificers, the number of contracts is proportionately multiplied. The substance of the contract, in very

[1] '. . . es sei die Bestimmung des Staats, jedem erst das Seinige zu geben, ihn in sein Eigentum erst einzusetzen and sodann erst ihn dabei zu schützen' (p. 4, edition Gustav Fischer).

[2] P. 7. This phrase, with variations, occurs so frequently that it may be as well o reproduce it in its most careful presentation: 'Nach dieser Gleichheit ihres Rechts muss die Teilung gemacht werden, so, dass alle und jeder so angenehm leben können, als es möglich ist, wenn so viele Menschen, als ihrer vorhanden sind, in der vorhandenen Wirkungssphäre nebeneinander bestehen sollen, also, dass alle ungefähr gleich angenehm leben können' (p. 7).

simplified language, is that each shall do his job, and stick to his job, and not interfere with the other man's job, and inevitably, of course, that each shall *ebenso angenehm leben können* as the others. To these presently come the merchants, the *Kaufleute*, with further proliferation of contracts, and obviously it is also essential that the Kaufmann should *ebenso angenehm leben könne* as the original producer and the artificer. The basis of all these imaginary contracts is that all should be able to enjoy an equally agreeable life.[1]

It is time to introduce the State into this orgy of contracts; for in one sense the function of the State is to assure the observance of all the contracts which have thus been made.[2] The fact that the argument is phrased with reference to contracts which were never made and never could have been made is immaterial: what clearly emerges is a State with devastatingly extensive powers. In the first place, it must determine the number of those to be admitted to each calling, and must never allow any excess over the number deemed necessary. And in this task it must see to the provision of essentials before allowing for luxuries. There must be enough for all, before there are superfluities for some.[3] The State must have an absolute power to refuse anyone the right to exercise a calling. Also there must be proof of capacity; every candidate must satisfy the *Kunstverständige*, the knowers-of-the-job. The number of merchants is likewise fixed, and they are under an obligation to buy or sell on demand, like the Bank of England in the matter of gold under the Act of 1925.[4] The whole of production is to be carefully planned on the basis of requirements; and control of the machine is facilitated by the fact that merchants are guaranteed their customers and their sources of supply. There are to be *bestimmte Verkäufer* and *bestimmte Abkäufer*—registered customers, in the language of a war-tried generation.[5]

The State must also fix prices which indeed are to be unalterable for all time. Into Fichte's theory of value it is unnecessary to enter. It is not a promising avenue to take as the measure of the relative value of things, the time we can live on them respectively.[6] His theory of value is mixed up with his theory of money, which, even on points of detail, is suggestive of Knapp, without the inconvenience of Knapp's

[1] *Op. cit.* pp. 8–10.

[2] *Op. cit.* p. 13.

[3] One sentence is almost an echo of a phrase frequently heard in discussions on the Report on Social Services: 'Es sollen erst alle satt werden und fest wohnen, ehe einer seine Wohnung ziert, erst alle bequem und warm gekleidet sein, ehe einer sich prächtig kleidet' (p. 14).

[4] *Op. cit.* pp. 17–18.

[5] *Op. cit.* p. 19.

[6] 'Der Massstab des relatives Werts der Dinge gegeneinander wäre die Zeit, binnen welcher man von ihnen leben könnte' (p. 21). On the other hand, a generation which has industriously ransacked economic literature for anticipations of the Austrian Theory of Value might find one subsidiary clause rather startling in its clarity: he says, '. . . da der sich selbst überlassene Mensch das Produkt des andern gar nicht nach der Mühe, die jener darauf verwandt, sondern vielmehr nach dem Nutzen schätzt, den er selbst davon zu ziehen gedenkt' (p. 65).

barbarous language.[1] The State must have its own money, which must be no one else's money, and as the State can do what it likes in these matters, prices may be fixed without any variableness or shadow of turning.[2]

One last point may be noted in this regimented world. As is indicated by the title of his essay, *Der Geschlossne Handelsstaat*, Fichte aims at creating a self-contained world. No one is to be allowed to engage in foreign trade. If there must be foreign trade (and the possibility is not wholly excluded), then it should be regarded—like the making of war, of treaties and alliances—as something to be done by the State alone. Any arrangement whereby the citizen of one State is allowed to have direct dealings with the citizens of another State must in fact view them both as citizens of one State.[3] The thought is not very gracefully expressed, but the implication is clear. Economic intercourse can take place only between citizens of the same state, and indeed it implies common citizenship. The frontiers within which intercourse may take place should therefore be adjusted accordingly. It is, from a different angle, akin to the physiocratic idea, that the merchant is a danger because he belongs to two countries. If goods are required from abroad—and in fact the need of imports can be cut down to the vanishing point—then the State and the State alone should do it on the basis of barter: rather pathetically, Fichte contemplates such arrangements (when necessary) as enduring to eternity, *zu ewige Zeiten.*[4]

Fichte does not usually figure with any prominence in histories of socialism—and perhaps rightly so. The network of contracts on which he bases his view of society may be ignored as eighteenth-century convention, quite becoming in a son of the eighteenth century; much (with all respect to a great philosophical name) may be regarded as somewhat foolishly impracticable; he may be criticised for his vagueness (if such a word may be applied to a complete silence) on the important question of the machinery through which the State will discharge its high tasks. But on two points at least, he is extremely instructive for our purposes and reveals insight denied even to some of our own day.

In the first place, Fichte's idea is that of a State of unlimited competence whose primary purpose is to guarantee to all the requirements of a reasonable life. But he does not delude himself, as some of our own generation do, into the belief that a State can provide for everyone on these lines, and yet leave everyone free to do as he likes. The price of a guaranteed security lies in a sacrifice of freedom. In Fichte's

[1] It is, for instance, a characteristic Knappian point to regard acceptance *by* the State as the decisive determining feature of money. Fichte argues that the State has merely to declare 'dass er selbst nur in diesem Gelde und schlechthin mit keinem andern sich werde bezahlen lassen' (p. 41).

[2] *Op. cit.* p. 43. [3] *Op. cit.* p. 64. [4] *Op. cit.* p. 122.

vision, the citizen, if he does not become the slave of the State, at least lives subject to the constant direction and redirection of a National Service Officer. It is by *Gesetz und Zwang* alone—by law and compulsion—that the State may discharge its obligations.[1] In the concluding paragraphs, Fichte realises that the opposition to his visionary proposals will come from those who incessantly call aloud for freedom, free trade, freedom from supervision by the police, freedom from order and morality. To these people, he adds contemptuously, anything aiming at regularity and a firmly established uniform march of events, appears as an infringement of their natural freedom.[2] To authoritarians of all classes, liberalism has always been the arch-enemy. Socialism of the type outlined by Fichte is, on his own analysis, incompatible with freedom.

The other point of interest in Fichte is in the central conception of the 'closed State,' the enactment that none shall engage in foreign trade. This may be, and perhaps is, foolish, especially with some of Fichte's refinements; but at least it may be urged that it is at worst a foolish answer to a real difficulty, and this is always more stimulative to the advance of truth than a failure to realise that a difficulty exists. Foreign trade is for Fichte an upsetting element in the national balance sheet: it represents the roots of instability. A State cannot guarantee the undisturbed continuance of a foreign market; if, with its encouragement, its citizens embark in enterprises which may suddenly come to an end, how can it then, in the day of adversity, discharge its primary duty towards its citizens? The question of foreign trade has long been a stumbling-block in socialist speculation. For the present day, Fichte's difficulty may be put more pointedly. We are told, by an increasing multiplicity of voices, that outside planning there can be no salvation. But, in effect, says Fichte, forerunner of planners,[3] no one may plan who does not have under his control all the elements that enter into the plan. In this sense, foreign trade is most emphatically not subject to control. If our national plan assumes the export of so much coal to Poland and Italy, or the export of so much salted cod to South America, and so on indefinitely, and if these countries should suddenly decide otherwise, what then becomes of the plan? In substance, Fichte's contention was that only a self-contained unit can 'plan'; and in this sense he was abundantly right.

[1] *Op. cit.* p. 26.

[2] *Op. cit.* p. 129. 'Ihnen erscheint alles, was strange Regelmässigkeit und einen festgeordneten, durchaus gleichförmigen Gang der Dinge beabsichtigt, als eine Beeinträchtigung ihrer natürlichen Freiheit.'

[3] . . . 'indem ja die verstattete Produktion und Fabrikation nach dem möglichen Bedürfnisse schon in der Grundlage des Staats berechnet ist' (p. 19). What, it may be asked, is the value of a plan which assumes that we are to build an underground railway in Leningrad?

CHAPTER V

WILLIAM GODWIN

In the case of William Godwin (1756–1836), though indeed this is true of not a few of those we encounter in these pages, it requires resolution to keep biographical details within the prescribed minimum. For Godwin, to express it with restraint, was an unusual man—as also were Saint-Simon, Fourier and Owen ; and the eccentric and bizarre always have a psychological fascination for the great unenterprising bulk of humanity, whose humdrum visages conceal no hidden weakness or waywardness. Godwin appears here as the first logical and consistent exponent of anarchism. Nevertheless he was cradled in the strictest orthodox piety, and was for a stretch of years a parson and a preacher in a dissenting sect, until evil communications and his own natural bent turned him into a rebel in matters political and religious alike. His great work, *An Enquiry concerning Political Justice, and its Influence on General Virtue and Happiness* (to give it for once its full title), appearing in 1793, had an astounding success. There is a traditional tale that Pitt declined to suppress *Political Justice*, on the wholly unconvincing ground that a book published at three guineas could not possibly do much harm—forgetting that the thirsty multitude may buy even a three-guinea book by combining their contributions. For a number of years following his great success, Godwin was one of the most outstanding personalities and one of the most influential writers of his time. Unfortunately, having shot his bolt at the age of 37, he had the misfortune to continue alive until he was 80. It is the tragedy of Godwin's life to trace his descent through evil days, until he was utterly forgotten—' that which was Godwin '—a miserable literary hack and a rather disreputable bookseller, steering for bankruptcy and sponging on those who could be induced to lend to him. Yet, despite the rather shady, shabby and shoddy tale of his later years, Godwin occupies a central position in the intellectual life of his times. He was not merely the Father of Anarchism, he was the husband of Mary Wollstonecroft, the first and fiercest exponent of women's rights ; he was the father-in-law of Shelley ; he was, by reaction, the spiritual progenitor of Malthus. The first edition of the *Essay on Population*, indeed, declares on its title-page that it contains ' remarks on the speculations of Mr. Godwin.'

Two characteristics of the man, or perhaps two aspects of the same characteristic, should be borne in mind as explaining much in Godwin's exposition. In the first place, never was there anyone who was more entirely the embodiment of intellect and reason. There is in his life no evidence of warmth or passion, and throughout he was incapable of understanding any deviation from reason in others. It was on reason that he based his friendships, and to those who are interested in such matters nothing could be more illuminating than the story of his marriages and his projected marriages. The *Memoirs of Mary Wollstonecroft*, in which he has been unsympathetically accused of 'stripping the dead body of his wife,' provides perhaps the extreme example of this detachment from ordinary human sensibilities.

Secondly, it follows from this peculiarly intellectual bias that he was utterly destitute of common sense. When he turned to business and the affairs of this life, he could not but fail. The extreme views professed, the paradoxical propositions propounded are in all cases the perfectly logical conclusions to be drawn from the axioms and assumptions from which he sets out. But, visualising human beings merely as the vehicle of reason, he forgets the necessity and the virtue of compromising where frail men are concerned. Life in fact is not run by logic; and the man who in all things is logical—as Godwin was—who leaves no place for the forces of unreason, ends by being a fool.

For our present purpose it is sufficient to confine our attention to the *Enquiry concerning Political Justice*, of which the first edition, in two stupendous volumes, appeared in 1793. In the second edition (1798), Godwin on a number of points is less extreme, or, perhaps, more guarded. In this life, however, whatever the moralists say, we never can live down our first editions; and as it was by the first edition that Godwin became known and exercised his influence, the later, slightly modified version may at present be disregarded except for minor points of comparison.

Turning to the written word, we find on the threshold, and throughout as an all-pervading influence, two ideas, one of which is a gross exaggeration of any truth it may contain, and the other is almost certainly entirely erroneous. These two *Idées Mères* are, indeed, but the reflection of Godwin's own personality and, to a certain extent, at least, the first is common form in a good many of the writers with whom we are concerned about this time. These two dominant ideas relate, firstly, to the old problem of innate ideas, and, secondly, to the place of reason in the individual's life.

On the first point, it is of the essence of Godwin's position that we bring into this world no innate principles: 'we are neither virtuous nor vicious as we come into existence.[1] Men are wholly and exclusively fashioned by their environment and by the influences to which they are exposed. The reason why 'superficial observers' are led to

[1] P. 12. (References, unless otherwise indicated, are to the first edition. The pagination is consecutive in the two volumes; volume 1 runs from p. 1 to p. 378; and vol. 2 from p. 379 to p. 895.)

believe in innate ideas (and, inferentially, in natural differences among men) is that they do not realise how soon the 'seeds of error' may be sown, and consequently they mistake for 'innate' what is in fact due to the world which operates on us from the moment of our birth. In a dreadful picture, Godwin shows how by the end of the first week—indeed probably on the first day—most of us have already probably been corrupted by the world, as represented by our parents. He is referring to the infant's inarticulate cry for assistance:

> In this neutral and innocent circumstance, combined with the folly and imbecility of parents and nurses, we are presented with the first occasion of vice. Assistance is necessary, conducive to the existence, the health and the mental sanity of the infant. Empire in the infant over those who protect him is unnecessary. If we do not withhold our assistance precisely at the moment when it ceases to be requisite, if our compliance or our refusal be not in every case irrevocable, if we grant anything to impatience, importunity or obstinacy, from that moment we become parties in the intellectual murder of our offspring.[1]

It is an appalling and disturbing thought that the incompetent and distracted parent, not knowing when to say 'No' to a muling child that will not cease to mule, has already sown the seeds of vice in the next generation, and is indeed, in part, the (intellectual) murderer of his offspring. Thus early, in the first days, do the shades of the prison-house besmirch our first innocence.

The conclusion from this line of argument—and it is to be found in Owen, Bertrand Russell and elsewhere, is that there is no such thing as guilt or crime, and indeed no such thing as moral responsibility. If we are what we are by virtue of our environment, we are entirely justified in transferring to our environment the responsibility for our shortcomings. Our parents may quite properly be blamed (though they, poor things, could not help themselves), or the schools in which we are miseducated, or society which has frustrated us. Here in one sense is the depth of pessimism, in that we are all caught in the web of circumstance; but, on the other hand, there is a great hope. In proportion as environment can be improved, so will mankind rise. If the incidents which influence us could be 'divested of every improper tendency, vice would be extirpated from the world.'[2]

The other governing idea in Godwin is to be found in a pathetic belief that men are reasonable beings capable of being persuaded, that truth when revealed will be recognised as truth, and that men will act accordingly. There are no half-shades in Godwin's world: Truth opposes error, and right opposes wrong; and in each case an intellectual proof will not merely demonstrate which is which, but will carry conviction, expressing itself in action. In short, men cannot possibly act unreasonably, and reason can always demonstrate what is

[1] P. 17. [2] P. 18.

right. As with Socrates, it is an intellectual problem: 'All vice is nothing more than error and mistake reduced into practice, and adopted as the principle of our conduct.' [1] As this touching faith in the demonstrability of truth (and right behaviour) and its power to prevail is in some ways the foundation-stone in Godwin, two detached sentences may be cited as samples of many other similar expressions on this point:

> Truth may be presented . . . in such irresistible evidence . . . as ultimately to conquer the most obstinate prepossessions. . . . It is the property of truth to spread.[2]
>
> Show me in the clearest and most unambiguous manner that a certain mode of proceeding is most reasonable in itself or most conducive to my interest, and I shall infallibly pursue that mode, as long as the views you suggested to me continue present to my mind.[3]

There is here little realisation of the fact that this is a complex world in which truth is a precious ore seldom mined in a pure state, and in which the problem of action is too frequently not the simple choice between right and wrong, but a choice between a number of courses of varying degrees of objectionability.

Such is the general framework within which Godwin majestically unfolds his speculations. Man is neither good nor bad, except in so far as circumstances and environment have moulded him. He is, moreover, a reasonable being who, if he could be brought to listen to the voice of reason, would inevitably do right, since the problems of life are intellectual problems. A further enormous simplification is made by Godwin. The environment which influences man is made up of many elements: the geographical and climatic had, for instance, been emphasised by Montesquieu. But Godwin in effect thrust these aside. Man is a creature of reason, and the environment which effectively shapes him is the intellectual environment. In his own words, 'it inevitably follows that physical causes, though of some consequence in the history of man, sink into nothing, when compared with the great and inexpressible operations of reflection.'

These successive simplifications of the problem, with the glorification of the place and power of reason, lead to what is in some ways the central Godwinian conception, that of the 'perfectibility of man.' If man is a function of his environment, then an approach to the perfect environment will bring with it an approach to the perfect man. The doctrine has been frequently misunderstood or misrepresented, and at times Godwin's statements, being expressed with his own peculiar extravagance, have naturally stimulated the scoffers. But in his more guarded moments, he did not so much imply that man would attain perfection (whatever that may be), as that there could and should be continual

[1] P. 31. [2] P. 63. [3] Second edition, vol. 1, p. 46.

progress in the direction of perfection: and thus expressed, the doctrine is not in itself inherently absurd.

Godwin's problem, in its widest statement, is how, in the light of these principles, man may be regenerated. The weapons of regeneration are in fact three; but two of them are merely mentioned in order to be put aside, leaving the third as the theme of his two spacious volumes. Yet his brief comments on Literature and Education, the first two engines for advancing mankind, are of great interest, if not in clarifying the problem of the ascent of man, then at least in revealing the essential Godwin. With regard to Literature, he argues that there are innumerable opinions prevailing on any subject; 'yet of all these opinions only one can be true'—a characteristically Godwinian statement. It is the function of Literature to extirpate existing prejudices and mistakes. Truth, he says, is infallibly struck out by the collision of mind with mind. All this is rather naive in its assumption that Literature can never disseminate error, and that all argument ends in clarification and never in obfuscation. Equally naive is his contention that 'if in any science we discover one solitary truth, it cannot be overthrown.' Literature, however, is of no use for Godwin's purposes. 'The multitude'—he is writing in 1793—'cannot partake of its illuminations.'[1]

Education, an 'engine of unlimited power,' is also put aside for the present as ineffective, for a rather disconcerting reason: 'Where must the preceptor himself have been educated, who shall thus elevate his pupils above all the errors of mankind?'[2] In other words, the right education demands the right teacher, who can himself be 'right,' only if he himself has had the right education. How indeed shall mankind escape from this, the most perfect of all vicious circles?

There remains as the third instrument of regeneration what Godwin calls 'Political Justice,' a vague phrase unless supplied with an interpretation. It is defined at the outset as 'the adoption of any principle of morality or truth into the practice of a community.'[3] Political Justice, as so defined, is given a pre-eminent position, because it is universal in its operation. Other influences are intermittent, but the machinery of society (and in effect Political Justice merely means the right kind of political machinery) influences a man all his life. Moreover, in the second edition, Godwin argues that Political Justice must come first, before any attempt is made to improve man in any particular point. To aim at reform in a rotten society is futile; but if the right society can be achieved, individual reforms will come unsought:

> May it not be found, that the attempt to alter the morals of mankind singly and in detail is an erroneous and futile undertaking; and that it will then only be effectually and decisively performed, when, by regenerating their political institutions, we shall change their motives and produce a revolution in the influences that act upon them?[4]

[1] Pp. 20–22. [2] P. 25. [3] P. 19. [4] Second edition, p. 5.

And indeed, looking around, Godwin has no difficulty in proving on familiar lines that the shortcomings of man are due to the defective institutions of society, and their inevitable consequences. Thus robbery and fraud spring from the very nature of the society in which we live: ' If every man could with perfect facility obtain the necessaries of life . . . temptation would lose its power,' and in such a society ' guilt could hardly be known but by report.' [1] Prevailing poverty has, however, repercussions in many directions:

> The poor man will be induced to regard the state of society as a state of war, an unjust combination, not for protecting every man in his rights and securing to him the means of existence, but for engrossing all its advantages to a few favoured individuals, and reserving for the portion of the rest want, dependence and misery.[2]

Here is the class war, and in these circumstances the privileges of the rich operate as a ' bitter aggravation ' of the calamity of the poor. The rich also become insolent, and develop ' a temper overbearing, dictatorial and tyrannical.' The rich, moreover, are ' directly or indirectly the legislators of the State; and of consequence are perpetually reducing oppression into a system.' These evils are confirmed by the law, for ' legislation is in almost every country grossly the favourer of the rich against the poor,' and further ' the administration of law is not less iniquitous than the spirit in which it is framed.' Is it any wonder that the poor are ' stung with the furies of envy, resentment and despair ' ? [3] Such, so far as possible in his own words, is Godwin's analysis of the baneful effect of our present society on its members. It does not perhaps differ greatly from what may be found in many other quarters, being largely a blend of the class war and the class State. If there is perhaps a distinguishing note, it may be that Godwin lays more emphasis on the insolence of the rich.

As against this mountain of injustice, what does justice require of us? The answer is of an astonishing simplicity when stated in general terms, though doubtless not so easy of interpretation and practice as Godwin assumed. ' If justice have any meaning,' he observes, ' it is just that I should contribute everything in my power to the benefit of the whole.' [4] There is, as is well known, another maxim in these matters which has enjoyed a considerable circulation, to the effect that we should love our neighbour as ourselves. Godwin glances at this rival principle somewhat disparagingly, remarking that ' this maxim, though possessing considerable merit as a popular principle, is not modelled with the strictness of philosophical accuracy.' It overlooks the fact that my various neighbours and I may have very different values for society.

[1] Pp. 33–34. [2] P. 35. [3] Pp. 36–42. [4] P. 81.

Here we come to the essential core of Godwin. This principle of justice, defined as imposing on each the duty of contributing everything in his power to the benefit of the whole, combined with the infallibility of human reason in guiding our actions, explains all the Godwinian paradoxes which so offended his own and later ages. All the rest of Godwin is merely an unfolding, in their various applications, of these two principles, urged ruthlessly to their frigidly logical ultimate conclusions.

As a preliminary to accompanying Godwin on his tour of destruction, it may be as well to be clear on a fundamental point. Godwin, living in an age much attached to the rights of man, is emphatic that there never can be rights, but duties only. A ' right ' in its very essence implies a discretion to do or not to do ; a right may or may not be exercised ; it involves an option. But it is of the essence of Godwin's philosophy that the principle of justice should guide our every action, and that our reason will interpret to us what justice is. *That* we must do, and no other. To do anything else is injustice, and there can be no right to do injustice. We never do have an option. Every shilling that we possess has already ' received its destination from the dictates of justice.'[1] Justice commands us in everything, leaving nowhere the minutest crevice for choice or discretion.

> Not a talent do we possess, not a moment of time, not a shilling of property, for which we are not responsible at the tribunal of the public, which we are not obliged to pay into the general bank of common advantage. Of every one of these there is an employment which is best, and that best justice obliges us to select.[2]

There we have Duty, a very stern daughter of the voice of God. I can only have a discretion, i.e. rights, in matters of total indifference, as for example, whether I shall sit on the right or left side of the fire, whether I shall dine on beef to-day or to-morrow. Even this field within which we may choose is much smaller than might be imagined, since before an option can be allowed,

> it must be proved that my choice on one side or the other can in no possible way contribute to the benefit or injury of myself or of any other person in the world.[3]

The very essence of rights consists in their ' absolute nugatoriness and inutility.' It will be conceded that life on these high moral altitudes would be somewhat exhausting: we are invited to live on a plane where even the boarding of a passing tram is only permissible after a long period of stubborn questioning.

In the light of Godwinian justice, what should be our attitude to our friends, and to our kith and kin ? Godwin resuscitates for us the fatuous fable of Fénelon and the housemaid. They are trapped in

[1] P. 796. [2] P. 432. [3] P. 112.

a blazing Palace, on the point of sizzling in the flames. Only one can be saved. Which shall it be? Obviously, the Archbishop every time. Everyone who has stuck in the middle of *Télémaque* will admit that Fénelon is vastly more important to humanity than a whole registry of housemaids, and that even in time of war. But if the housemaid had been my wife or mother—awful thought, if I had myself been the housemaid? The answer remains the same: Fénelon still has it, because justice tells me that the life of Fénelon ought to be saved at the expense of my wife, my mother or even myself. 'What magic is there in the pronoun "my," to overturn the decisions of everlasting truth?' [1]

Let us advance from friendship to gratitude. In the case cited, should not gratitude to my mother (assuming she were involved) have urged me to drag her out and leave the Archbishop behind? By no means: 'gratitude is no part either of justice or virtue.' [2] As always, we must have justice, pure unadulterated justice. Gratitude means preferring some one on grounds other than his superior usefulness or worth, when justice would have dictated another course. Anyone who does from motives of gratitude what he would not otherwise have done is therefore acting unjustly. As Godwin expresses it elsewhere tersely and in a somewhat abbreviated form: 'Gratitude is a vice and not a virtue.' [3]

Sliding down the slippery slope, we come, on a very different plane from Machiavelli, to the Machiavellian problem of the obligation to observe engagements. Clearly on Godwinian principles there can be no virtue in keeping promises merely because they are promises. We must always and everywhere do justice; that is to say, we must do what at the moment we are satisfied most conduces to the general good. In deciding what is justice, a past promise is an irrelevant consideration; but Godwin had better express it in his own language:

> 'I have promised to do something just and right.' This certainly I ought to perform. Why? Not because I promised, but because justice prescribes it. 'I have promised to bestow a sum of money upon some good and respectable purpose. In the interval between the promise and my fulfilling it, a greater and nobler purpose offers itself, and calls with an imperious voice for my co-operation.' Which ought I to prefer? That which best deserves my preference. A promise can make no alteration in the case. I

[1] P. 83. [2] P. 84.

[3] P. 199. Readers of Mr. Tawney, *Religion and the Rise of Capitalism*, hardly need to be reminded how close Godwin stands to certain phases of Puritanism. Mr. Tawney quotes one Puritan divine as saying 'every penny which is laid out . . . must be done as by God's own appointment.' Further, 'it is an irrational act, and therefore not fit for a rational creature, to love any one farther than reason will allow us. . . . It very often taketh up men's minds so as to hinder their love to God.' Apart from the fact that 'love to God' is replaced by 'the dictates of Justice,' there is almost identity of language.

ought to be guided by the intrinsic merits of the objects, and not by any external and foreign consideration. No engagements of mine can change their intrinsic claims.[1]

The case against the binding nature of promises may be stated in two forms. Firstly, the man who intimates that when the time comes to decide in any matter, he will be guided by considerations other than those which at that future date will be present to his mind, is acting viciously.[2] Because he has committed one error, that is no reason why he should be guilty of a second. In the language of a later anarchist, grappling with the same problem: 'Because I was a fool yesterday, is that any reason why I should be a fool to-day?' A variant of this is emphasised in the second edition. We are (it is optimistically assumed) always learning. To bind ourselves now as to how we shall act in the future is to preclude ourselves from the use of the knowledge we may have gained in the interval.[3] Such (doubtless with other considerations) are the grounds for the sweeping assertion that promises are, absolutely considered, an evil.[4] In a delicious phrase, dealing with the political side of the question, Godwin reveals the depths of turpitude which may be plumbed by those who teach that promises should be kept: 'It is impossible,' he says, 'to imagine a principle of more injurious tendency, than that which shall teach me to disarm my future wisdom by my past folly.'[5]

If the taint of vice adheres to the giving and keeping of promises, what shall we make of marriage, which is supposed to rest on promises from which death alone normally offers release and an avenue of escape? Rather oddly, Godwin launches his frontal attack on marriage primarily because it demands co-operation. It is the true anarchist who proclaims that 'everything that is usually understood by the term co-operation, is in some degree an evil.'[6] To be dependent on the convenience of others is anathema to Godwin, and indeed it is probably true that the necessity of fitting in with others as part of a machine may very well conflict with the awful dictates of justice which, as we have seen, lay down *for me* how the last minute of my time must be spent. Godwin's argument may appear trivial, yet two short illustrations are revealing:

> Why should we have common meals? Am I obliged to be hungry at the same time that you are? Ought I to come at a certain hour, from the museum where I am working, the recess where I meditate, or the observatory where I remark the phenomena of nature, to a certain hall appropriated to the office of eating; instead of eating, as reason bids me, at the time and place most suited to my avocations?[7]

It is still worse when a man is also obliged to consult the convenience

[1] P. 151.
[2] P. 156.
[3] Second edition, vol. 1, p. 202.
[4] *Ibid.* vol. 1, p. 198.
[5] P. 163.
[6] P. 844.
[7] P. 842.

of others. If I be expected to eat or work in conjunction with my neighbour, it must either be at a time convenient to me, or to him, or to neither of us. We cannot be reduced to a clock-work uniformity.[1]

How to escape co-operation in an industrial world based on division of labour is, admittedly, something of a problem. It is perhaps somewhat aside from our path, but it is extremely illuminating to note Godwin's speculative hints as to the way of escape. May there not be such an improvement of machinery that the most extensive operations may yet some day be within the reach of one man, so that any one will be able to do anything (and apparently everything), as and when he chooses, without being dependent on others? In a homely illustration he visualises a plough being turned into a field to perform its office without the need of superintendence. There are hints of concerts given by a one-man orchestra in order to relieve the musicians from 'the miserable state of mechanism' which has already become a 'topic of mortification and ridicule.' It cannot, however, be said that Godwin squarely confronts the difficulties in the way.[2]

It is interesting on this point to note the very different grounds on which Rousseau and Godwin alike object to co-operation. Rousseau in effect holds that whenever two people come together, one will take advantage of the other. Godwin's objection to having breakfast with Mrs. Godwin is based on the probability that the workings of their respective digestive organs may not synchronise. On these lines, and on his first principles, it is easy to see why Godwin condemns marriage. Perhaps the argument may be grouped under three main headings. Firstly, marriage rests on promises which should never be given; we should never bind our freedom of action. Secondly, marriage involves co-operation, and co-operation must mean some degree of dependence of one on the other, which must again entail some disobedience to the dictates of one's own conscience in the matter of justice. Thirdly (and more cryptically), 'all attachments to individuals, except in proportion to their merits, are plainly unjust.' [3] We should, he adds, be the friends of man rather than of particular men: presumably, though there is a prejudice to the contrary, we should be the friends of woman rather than of particular women. Expressed in this summary form, Godwin's argument against marriage may seem a relatively tepid affair. In fact he reserves his most glowing eloquence for his denunciation of marriage as a system of fraud and as the most odious of all monopolies.[4]

[1] P. 844. [2] Pp. 845–846. [3] P. 848.

[4] It is dangerous to criticise marriage, and probably a large measure of the offence that Godwin caused in his day was attributable to his proposals for the abolition of marriage. The pages which deal with this question are so characteristic of Godwin, that if one were called upon to choose from the 900 pages of *Political Justice* one extract as illustrative of the full flavour of Godwin, one would select this. The whole cannot be quoted here, but the following snippets may be illuminating.

'It is absurd to expect that the inclinations and wishes of two human beings

So far we have disposed of friendship ; we have seen that gratitude is a vice ; that promises are an evil, and that marriage is a fraud. It remains to abolish the State, Law and Property.

When we turn to the question of government, two general conclusions follow from the Godwinian assumptions. The first is that all government is an evil: we are perpetually reminded that while society may be a blessing, government even in its best state is but a necessary evil, springing from our weaknesses.[1] Government should therefore be restricted to a minimum, and we should moreover aim at reducing the scope of government still further:

> Above all we should not forget, that government is an evil, an usurpation upon the private judgment and individual conscience of mankind ; and that, however we may be obliged to admit it as a necessary evil for the present, it behoves us, as the friends of reason and the human species, to admit as little of it as possible, and carefully to observe whether, in consequence of the gradual illumination of the human mind, that little may not hereafter be diminished.[2]

Further the individual can never shed his moral responsibility by sheltering behind the State. He remains subject to his own conscience ; the voice of conscience is addressed to him directly, and not mediately through the State:

> No man can transfer to another the keeping of the conscience and his judging of his duties. . . . No consent of ours can divest us of our moral capacity.[3]

should coincide through any long period of time. To oblige them to act and to live together, is to subject them to some inevitable portion of thwarting, bickering and unhappiness. . . . The supposition that I must have a companion for life, is the result of a complication of vices. It is the dictate of cowardice, and not of fortitude. It flows from the desire of being loved and esteemed for something that is not desert.

'But the evil of marriage as it is practised in European countries lies deeper than this. The habit is, for a thoughtless and romantic youth of each sex to come together, to see each other for a few times and under circumstances full of delusion, and then to vow to each other eternal attachment. What is the consequence of this ? In almost every instance they find themselves deceived. They are reduced to make the best of an irretrievable mistake. They are presented with the strongest imaginable temptation to become the dupes of falsehood. They are led to conceive it their wisest policy to shut their eyes upon realities, happy if by any perversion of intellect they can persuade themselves that they were right in their first crude opinion of their companion. The institution of marriage is a system of fraud ; and men who carefully mislead their judgments in the daily affair of their life, must always have a crippled judgment in every other concern. We ought to dismiss our mistake as soon as it is detected ; but we are taught to cherish it. We ought to be incessant in our search after virtue and worth ; but we are taught to check our inquiry, and shut our eyes upon the most attractive and admirable objects. Marriage is law, and the worst of all laws. . . . Add to this, that marriage is an affair of property, and the worst of all properties. So long as two human beings are forbidden by positive institution to follow the dictates of their own mind, prejudice is alive and vigorous. So long as I seek to engross one woman to myself, and to prohibit my neighbour from proving his superior desert and reaping the fruits of it, I am guilty of the most odious of all monopolies' (pp. 849–850).

[1] P. 79. [2] P. 380. [3] Pp. 148–149.

Putting this last point in somewhat different words, there is in Godwin's scheme of things no place for obedience; nor can there be, if on every occasion our own conscience, for each of us, is a sufficient and imperious commander, not to be disobeyed. The dictates of justice exhaust the field; when we have lived up to the fundamental Godwinian principle, 'what province is there left to the disposal of obedience?'[1] Indeed, expressed in the extreme form which Godwin always loved: 'The first lesson of virtue is, "Obey no man."'[2] The compliance we yield to a government is, or should be, of the same nature as the compliance we yield to a wild beast, which may force us to go whither we would not.[3] In short, obedience, when we disapprove, rests solely on *force majeure*.

The second general conclusion to be inferred from Godwinian assumptions is that, in so far as government is necessary, it is a purely intellectual problem to determine what the form of government should be. For the somewhat dubious reason that truth is single and uniform, 'there must in the nature of things be one best form of government, which all intellects, sufficiently roused from the slumber of savage ignorance, will be irresistibly incited to approve.'[4] Also, as becomes more explicit in the second edition, this best form of government will be suitable to all peoples: 'If one form of government makes one nation happy, why should it not equally contribute to the felicity of another?'[5]

Thus armed, it is an easy task to turn to the various accepted types of government, and show how utterly absurd each and all of them are. Godwin follows the traditional classification of types of government into Monarchy, Aristocracy and Democracy—the rule of one, of a few, of many—which by long descent derives from Aristotle. It makes the problem somewhat too facile. Governments, at least in the modern world, are not so neatly classifiable; and even in Godwin's time, the monarchies of Western Europe could hardly be regarded as conforming to the irresponsible and absolute rule of one. It is unnecessary to delay unduly over his exposure of the absurdities of monarchy or aristocracy. Bearing in mind that he is dealing with a copybook king and a copybook aristocracy, made to conform to an unreal definition, he declaims the obvious—though, be it added, with oratory and effect.

For in the imagined world in which Godwin visualises a notional Prince, that Prince is inevitably badly educated. Truth is a stranger to his ears; he never learns fortitude.[6] By his very position, every King is by unavoidable necessity the enemy of the human race.[7] The picture is as black, or blacker, when we turn to survey the corruption

[1] P. 169. [2] P. 430. [3] P. 171.
[4] P. 182. [5] Second edition, vol. 1, p. 242. [6] P. 383.
[7] P. 397.

of courts, and observe how the contamination extends downwards to the subjects of the King. To one of Godwin's appalling honesty and disconcerting love of the literal truth, the fundamental defect of monarchy is that it is founded on imposture.[1] Kings possess no intrinsic superiority over their subjects ; and the pretence that things are other than they are spreads falsehood through the whole of society. Nor is the situation any better if we turn to an elective monarchy,[2] a limited monarchy,[3] or a president with regal powers.[4] A limited monarchy merely brings new absurdities. The doctrine that the King can do no wrong inevitably annoys Godwin. It is not true ; and to the extent to which it is supposed to embody a constitutional principle, it reduces the 'miserable wretch' to being no more than a 'vacant and colourless mirror.' Remembering also the first lesson of virtue (which is 'Obey no man'), it will be realised how absurd, or rather how 'fraught with degradation and meanness' is the very name of subject. Can an honest man honestly acknowledge a superior—being 'subject,' as he is, only to the laws of justice ? But indeed it is almost enough to fall back on the celebrated dictum of Montesquieu (whom he misunderstands and mistranslates) to the effect that 'we must not expect under a monarchy to find the people virtuous.' [5]

Aristocracy, as a form of government, need not delay us, though to a certain extent it delayed Godwin.[6] Again he rather labours the obvious. The whole idea of heredity is absurd, an insult upon reason and justice. At considerable length he dilates in his own language on the fairly obvious truth that the peer and the mechanic are examples of the same biped. Again there is the curse of the opulent, and therefore enervating, education. Like monarchy, aristocracy is founded on

[1] P. 423. [2] P. 435. [3] P. 441. [4] P. 454.

[5] P. 442. It may be a digression, but it is perhaps worth observing that the words 'virtue' and 'virtuous' (in Montesquieu, *vertu* and *vertueux*) are obviously full of dangers. Cruden's Concordance informs us that the words *virtue* and *virtuous* or *virtuously* each occur four times only in the Scriptures. The most familiar phrase, which covers two of these instances in the Synoptic Gospels, is that 'Virtue had gone out of him.' Virtue in fact means capacity or strength. Lemuel's 'virtuous woman,' formerly held up as a model to countless generations in young ladies' seminaries, is primarily a hard-working, capable, efficient business woman: She worketh willingly with her hands ; she bringeth her food from afar ; she considereth a field and buyeth it ; her candle goeth not out by night ; she looketh well to the ways of her household, and eateth not the bread of idleness. In fact she is anything but a good woman in the worst sense of the term. In the light of this, Montesquieu's observation, like many other apparent profundities, turns out to be something of a platitude. He makes it clear that he is talking of 'political virtue' (may we substitute *political capacity* ?) ; and he says that in a monarchy, as indeed in any state where everything is managed from the top, you cannot expect the people, who are excluded from affairs, to show political capacity. In different language, it is a familiar point in J. S. Mill's argument for restricting the functions of government. But in Godwin, the quotation conveys, and is designed to convey, an entirely different implication. Lastly, and irrelevantly, in what sense may *articles of virtue* be described as virtuous articles ?

[6] P. 461.

falsehood; if anything, it operates more harshly than monarchy. It accentuates inequalities, as it accentuates the pursuit of wealth.

Even at the first encounter, it is probable that most readers will find a certain air of unreality about Godwin's denunciations of monarchy and aristocracy: anyone who knows anything about anything must feel that he is not getting to grips with his subject, and that he is tilting, for instance, not so much at monarchy as at his idea of what monarchy, on a theoretical definition, ought to be. But if his rhetoric does not illumine his subject, at least it throws light on Godwin himself; for his criticisms reveal a naive, impractical, intensely earnest and honest man, whose honesty is rooted in a horrible literalness. He has not learned to appreciate the conventions or the virtue of compromise; he has not learned that there are many things that are not worth troubling about, and that, if any one cares to say so, life is full of conventional lies which, even at the Day of Judgment, will, we trust, matter not at all. Honourable members need not necessarily be honourable, and a Serene Highness has, presumably, occasional lapses from the Heights of Serenity; we do not always meet with gladness those whom we say we are glad to meet. But to Godwin such trifles represented the poison of falsehood choking the integrity of the nation. The House of Lords makes his indignation almost incoherent; he never realises how humorous an institution the Peerage really is.

The optimistic may hope that democracy will present a more pleasing prospect. And in a sense it does. Doubtless there are dangers; for as the unwise outnumber the wise, democracy may be at the mercy of ignorance and folly. Yet despite this and other obvious perils, democracy is admitted to be 'greatly preferable' to other systems; and by speaking and acting the truth—though this is difficult on Godwinian standards—the dangers of democracy may be avoided. But any satisfaction that this conclusion may afford vanishes when we reflect on how National Assemblies in fact behave and conduct their affairs.

Firstly, they produce a fictitious unanimity. But let Godwin himself speak:

> In reality all matters that are brought before such an assembly are decided by a majority of votes, and the minority, after having exposed with all the power of eloquence and force of reasoning of which they are capable the injustice and folly of the measures adopted, are obliged in a certain sense to assist in carrying them into execution. Nothing can more directly contribute to the depravation of the human understanding and character. It inevitably renders mankind timid, dissembling and corrupt.[1]

Secondly, national councils (i.e. representative bodies) bring about an unnatural uniformity of opinion. Men tie themselves to a party; every one considers 'the effects which the opinions he avows will produce on his own success.'[2]

[1] P. 569. [2] P. 570.

Thirdly, there is the absurdity of terminating a discussion by a vote. Not merely does the speaker aim at a transitory effect rather than a permanent conviction, but there is the ludicrous spectacle of men 'weighing particles and adjusting commas.' And finally there is 'that intolerable insult upon all reason and justice, the deciding upon truth by the casting up of numbers.' [1]

It will be observed that we have here come to the essence of anarchism. The objection to democracy is that, being still a form of government, it is still a tyranny, in which the minority is bound against its will by the decision of the majority and compelled to do what it would not. Godwin, it will be noticed, very subtly insinuates that the measures imposed by the majority are characterised by 'injustice and folly': the minority in fact is right.

Democracy, indeed, only becomes tolerable if the National Assembly (the machinery of democracy) meets at very rare intervals and on special occasions only: 'In a country in which universal truth was already established there would be little need of a representative assembly.' [2] Either they should be elected only for extraordinary emergencies, or they should sit periodically, as for example, for one day in the year. Our purpose should be to 'annihilate the quackery of Government.' [3]

From this orgy of destruction, what positive suggestions emerge? Briefly, after enunciating certain impeccable principles of benevolence towards other nations, it is argued, firstly, that there is unnecessary complication of government, and secondly, that small territories, as units, are preferable. The only two legitimate purposes for which a government may exist are, on the usual *laissez faire* lines, (i) the suppression of injustice against individuals, and (ii) defence against external invasion. But the former of these merely calls for an area large enough to provide for the institution of a jury to deal with offences and questions regarding property.[4] In fact, on the basis of small areas, comparable to a parish, the world could govern itself without knowing it was doing so. Controversies would not arise between parishes; and so far as the criminal is concerned, he would be kept in check 'by the general inspection that is exercised by the members of a limited circle over the conduct of each other,' [5] somewhat after the manner of the Sick Visitors in the older Friendly Societies. If for any reason, at long intervals, an Assembly should be required, it will ultimately be sufficient to 'invite' the various parishes to co-operate for the common advantage.[6] 'Invitation' takes the place of command, and in the internal administration the same pleasant distinction holds good. When the whole species shall have become 'reasonable and virtuous,' the task of the jury will take a new form:

[1] Pp. 570–571. [2] P. 552. [3] Pp. 574–575.
[4] P. 564. [5] P. 565. [6] P. 576.

'It will then be sufficient for them to invite the offenders to forsake their errors.'[1] In a world of men full of Godwinian reason, what more could possibly be required? Thus government is reduced to a National Assembly which (if possible) never meets, a suggestion of a Parish Council, though in fact the 'general inspection' of the inhabitants does the trick, and juries who invite offenders to forsake their wicked ways. As, however, the whole argument tends to prove that there will be no offenders, the juries will perpetually wallow in a spate of white gloves. In all essentials government has been abolished.

Having abolished government and the State, it may seem somewhat otiose to make a special holocaust of the Law; yet there are reasons for holding a separate inquest on the Law, and demonstrating its monstrosities. In the first place, Law is not really urgently required, 'if a society be contented with the rules of justice.'[2] But apart from this, the whole conception of Law is open to numerous objections, of which three in particular may be specified, as revealing the Godwinian point of view.

Firstly, Law is endless, as it is incomprehensible. 'Edict is heaped upon edict, and volume upon volume.' In this welter, no action of any man is ever the same as any other: he would imply that no two murders (e.g.) are the same murder. But along comes the Law with its Procrustean bed and applies the same test to all. Hence it becomes necessary either to wrest the Law, or perpetually make new ones. Hence also arises the uncertainty of the Law: no one can foretell what the result of any action will be. It has become 'a labyrinth without end,' and 'a mass of contradictions that cannot be extricated.'[3]

Secondly, a consideration even more offensive to Godwin, Law pretends to foretell the future. It partakes of the nature of prophecy and of promises. It takes upon itself to say what men will do, and what will happen, forgetting that in the interval we may acquire additional knowledge; it tends to produce stagnation and permanence in place of unceasing perfectibility.[4]

Thirdly, and most fundamentally—a pervasive influence through all that Godwin wrote—is the fact that Law is restraint on people in whom the beginning of virtue is that they should obey no one.

In the light of these considerations, 'we cannot hesitate to conclude universally that law is an institution of the most pernicious tendency'; and it follows also that 'a lawyer can scarcely fail to be a dishonest man.' 'This,' adds Godwin magnanimously, 'is less a subject for censure than for regret.' Not only so, but in the 'perhaps altogether impossible' contingency of a perfectly honest lawyer being discovered, he would probably be a more pernicious member of society than the dishonest lawyer.[5]

[1] Pp. 577–578. [2] P. 766. [3] Pp. 766–769.
[4] Pp. 769–770. [5] Pp. 771–772.

Apart from these considerations, there are more profound reasons, stretching back to Greek philosophy, for questioning the expedience of Law. Right is something that transcends Law: Law cannot make anything right that was not right before:

> Men cannot do more than declare and interpret law; nor can there be an authority so paramount, as to have the prerogative of making that to be law, which abstract and immutable justice had not made to be law previously to that interposition.[1]

There is here something of the Physiocratic doctrine of the priority of *Loi Naturelle*; going further back, there are memories of Cicero, groping for a right superior to, and antecedent to, human law. Without in any way speaking disrespectfully of Natural Law, its obvious weakness as a guide to everyday life is that it is so singularly silent on the Isle of Wight bee disease, the muzzling of dogs, and the precise day in October on which the close time for trout should begin.

What is to take the place of Law? Again we are in a world of echoes from the past. The answer is that the true principle is to be found in 'reason exercising an uncontrolled jurisdiction upon the circumstances of the case.'[2] There ought to be men among us 'whose wisdom is equal to the wisdom of the Law,' and we should therefore leave the decision to the wisdom of unfettered men, doing what seems right at the moment. It is the view to which Plato tends in one of his dialogues.[3]

Of crimes, little need be said. There is no such thing as Free Will; as has already been noted, we are entirely the results of our environment: 'my propensities are the fruit of the impressions that have been made upon me.'[4] In one of those extravagant phrases beloved of Godwin, 'the assassin cannot help the murder he commits any more than the dagger.'[5] It follows that all ideas of guilt, of crime, of desert, of accountableness are out of place. No pot in the potter's hand was ever more helpless than Man, as Godwin sees him, held in the clutch of circumstance. We are villains by necessity and fools by heavenly compulsion. 'It is through the Lord that I fell away,' as an earlier shirker of moral responsibility expressed it, with a greater semblance

[1] P. 381. [2] P. 773.

[3] See *The Statesman*. How much of (this) Plato there is in Godwin, or how much of Godwin there is in Plato, may be very briefly indicated in the reproduction of three disconnected sentences. 'The best thing of all is not that the law should rule, but that a man should rule supposing him to have wisdom and royal power.' The reason is that 'Law does not perfectly comprehend what is noblest and most just for all and therefore cannot enforce what is best. The differences of men and actions, and the endless irregular movements of human things, do not admit of any universal and simple rule.' Consequently, law is 'like an obstinate and ignorant tyrant, who will not allow anything to be done contrary to his appointment, or any question to be asked—not even in sudden changes of circumstances, when something happens to be better than what he commanded for someone' (Jowett's *Plato*, vol. 4, pp. 496–497).

[4] P. 713. [5] P. 690.

of piety than would have been proper to the later Godwin. Moreover, we must remember that no two crimes were ever alike. Who can fathom the hidden impulses of the criminal, or measure the temptations by which he may have been beset? Robert Burns, in more enduring words, has said something to the same effect. On these matters, Godwin rather naively suggests that the criminal is probably better informed than the judge.[1] The logical conclusion of the Doctrine of Necessity in this extreme form is the abolition of the criminal law altogether. Godwin, as always—though indeed it is characteristic of most anarchist writers—has infinite faith in the power of Reason. As with Socrates, sin is ignorance. Demonstrate to the supposed criminal what is right, and he cannot help doing it: 'if they made him understand with how much reluctance they had been induced to employ the force of the society against him, if they presented truth to his mind with calmness, perspicuity and benevolence . . . his reformation would be almost infallible.'[2]

We reach the last stage in this long process of annihilation, when we come to property—though indeed the essential Godwinian doctrine with regard to property is already contained in the doctrine that under the dictates of justice, all that we have has already had its final destination determined, so that we may not enjoy the free disposal of so much as a penny, or of a moment of time. On this view, surveying that marginal penny in my pocket, to whom does it in fact belong? Obviously, to him to whom its possession is most beneficial:

> To whom does any article of property, suppose a loaf of bread, justly belong? To him who most wants it, or to whom the possession of it will be most beneficial. Here are six men famished with hunger, and the loaf is, absolutely considered, capable of satisfying the cravings of them all. Who is it that has a reasonable claim to benefit by the qualities with which this loaf is endowed? They are all brothers perhaps, and the law of primogeniture bestows it exclusively on the eldest. But does justice confirm this award? The laws of different countries dispose of property in a thousand different ways; but there can be but one way which is most conformable to reason.[3]

It follows also that when we give, we merely do what we ought to do, and can claim no merit for our action; in fact we are merely handing property to its rightful owner, or at least to some one with a greater claim to it than we possess. In all this matter we have deluded ourselves or been deluded, and have been taught 'to treat the practice of justice, not as a debt, which it ought to be considered, but as an affair of spontaneous generosity and bounty.'

> The consequence of this has been that the rich, when they bestowed the most slender pittance of their enormous wealth in acts of charity, as they

[1] Pp. 720–722. [2] P. 747. [3] Pp. 789–790.

were called, took merit to themselves for what they gave, instead of considering themselves as delinquents for what they withheld.[1]

Into the evils that result from the existence of property, the sense of dependence, the truckling spirit, the pride and the crimes which its presence or absence engenders, it is unnecessary to enter. Though rich in Godwinian phrases, the discussion adds little to the picture, as it adds little to what others have said.

Such for our purposes are the main points in Godwin. He is, it will be observed, the complete anarchist, and when, with his scythe of reason and justice, he has finished mowing in the field of human hypocrisy, singularly little is left standing. Also, of course, though he is a universal destroyer, the work of destruction is inspired by the highest of motives. Godwin was an impossibly good man, of impossibly high ideals; and he is in himself almost sufficient confirmation of the old saying that the anarchist is a man who is too good for this world. And it fits in with the picture, though at first sight it is somewhat astonishing, to note how singularly 'unrevolutionary' Godwin is. There is to be no rebellion, no revolution as ordinarily understood, no violence, no tyrannicide. In the matter of martyrdom, Godwin expresses the view that he would rather convince men by his arguments, than seduce them by his example. No doubt so would most martyrs; but the Godwinian elimination of emotion and of passion is noteworthy. Moreover, who knows what opportunities of usefulness might offer themselves in future, should life be prolonged?[2] There may have to be a certain amount of passive resistance; but otherwise Godwin shows infinite faith in the power of talk. 'Show people the truth,' is the beginning and end of Godwin's strategy. 'The phalanx of reason is invulnerable,'[3] but an appeal to force may have a dubious issue. What is required is an 'universal illumination.' If that can be achieved, 'not a sword will need to be drawn, not a finger to be lifted up.'[4] A much later generation dreamed of a revolution *à bras croisés*; Godwin's revolution was to be, if anything, more easily accomplished.

Or again, take that vexed question of the right or duty of tyrannicide, so much discussed throughout the ages. Godwin deals with the matter on the level of a cold intellectual logical syllogism: 'either the nation, whose tyrant you would destroy, is ripe for the assertion and maintenance of its liberty, or it is not.' In the former case, the tyrant should be deposed, 'with every appearance of publicity'; in

[1] P. 797. [2] P. 194.

[3] P. 203. Godwin's faith in the human response to 'demonstration' is infantile beyond words. It occurs everywhere. Take this at random: 'Ten pages that should contain an absolute demonstration of the true interests of mankind in society could not otherwise be prevented from changing the face of the globe, than by the literal destruction of the paper on which they were written' (p. 211).

[4] Pp. 222–223.

the latter case, it will do no good and may do much harm to remove, or attempt to remove, the tyrant, before in fact conditions are ready for his removal.[1] Everywhere, it is not martyrdom and tyrannicide and all that sort of thing that we require, but 'illumination.' Given light and still more light, given truth and still more demonstrations of the truth, and all problems solve themselves.

Even in the matter of property, Godwin is perhaps less revolutionary than appears at first sight. This is above all true if reference be made to the second edition, where Godwin, on certain points, assumes a garment of greater restraint. But even in the first edition it should be remembered that Godwin mingles his thoughts of the present with fantasies of the future, when men will labour but for half a day, and will nevertheless live abundantly, because they live simply. In such a world of superlative abundance and abnegation, the Godwinian principles in property will clearly be less difficult to apply. Moreover, it is fairly clear that Godwinian justice does not entitle anyone to walk off with my property, merely because he considers his needs greater than mine. It is for me to decide: it is on my conscience and judgment, and not on his, that the decision hinges. Admittedly, once my judgment has done its work and my conscience has spoken, I have no option. In a sense, Godwin does not deny property: all he does is to restrict infinitely the use the owner may make of his property. There is a rather ridiculous illustration which compresses Godwin's attitude into a grotesque sentence. If a man wants my table, I have apparently a choice of three answers. I may tell him to make one for himself (a course which would probably commend itself to most); if I happen to be more skilful in making tables, I may offer to make one for him; lastly, if his need is urgent and he says he must have the table now, I may invite him to sit down and compare (and discuss) the urgency of our respective needs, and thereafter let justice decide. It is assumed that I shall listen to the voice of justice without bias.[2]

It has been indicated that Godwin imperceptibly fades from his criticism into his Utopia. Putting it another way, he realises that before he can have his particular brave new world, men will have to be changed. In this same question of property, he is confronted with the objection that his vision is impracticable because of what, in a most charming phrase, he calls the 'allurements of sloth.' His answer is that before these things can be, we must first reach 'a state of great intellectual improvement'; 'the general mind must be highly cultivated.'[3] Without this preliminary exaltation, any attempt to realise his vision 'will be productive only of confusion,'—presumably the allurements of sloth will continue to allure. So also the objection that such a system as he outlines would lack permanence he counters

[1] P. 227. [2] P. 858. [3] P. 820.

by emphasising his presupposition that these changes will have been 'produced by the serious and deliberate conviction of the community at large.'[1] He postulates in effect the universal acceptance of the Godwinian idea of justice, and on this assumption the change will exhibit permanence, if men are permanently changed. In this world of reason, all passion spent, men will 'derive infinitely more pleasure from simplicity, frugality and truth, than from luxury, empire and fame'[2]; and will realise that 'the tendency of a cultivated and virtuous mind is to render us indifferent to the gratifications of sense.'[3]

In this chapter, Godwin has intentionally been accorded a somewhat fuller treatment than that to which he may be thought to be entitled on a strict assessment of his importance in the socialist tradition. If an apologia be required, it would be that Godwin sums up, as no one else does, the sum and substance of anarchism, and thus embodies in himself a whole tradition—a tradition, moreover, which has tended to be neglected by a generation which has laid (we hope) an undue emphasis on Marx. Godwin may be foolish; but he is always logically foolish. He may, as most of us do, make mistaken assumptions; but once these assumptions are granted, the torrent of his oratory flows on with admirable consistency to conclusions which, doubtless, may be rejected as contrary to every-day common sense, but which can never be condemned as fallacious within the framework of the general principles which have been postulated. In Godwin we find that the essence of anarchism lies in the supreme importance attached to the individual. Nothing must fetter him. His judgment—and by that we mean his judgment at any moment—is always right for him; and in the interest of the untrammelled liberty of the individual, we are called upon to abolish everything—the State, the law, the binding nature of all engagements. There is no contract which cannot be broken at will; no promise should impede his freedom to judge and act. Since co-operation links him with others, and may therefore impose restraint upon him, all co-operation is evil. Godwin, however, differs from later anarchistic egotists in this respect that while with him the individual is unfettered, this freedom is not given him for selfish ends. Godwin's individual may be free from all external restraint, but he is fettered, horribly fettered, to the task and duty of promoting the general good, so that in the end he becomes the slave of his conscience, which never in fact leaves him any choice of action, even in the most trifling affairs of life. But it is *his* conscience, *his* judgment that commands.

NOTE.

It is difficult for us to-day, a century and a half after the event, to appreciate the horror with which, on its appearance, Godwin's *Political Justice*

[1] P. 831. [2] P. 834. [3] P. 870.

was viewed by the respectable classes. But it is sometimes possible in unexpected ways to catch a whiff of the old righteous indignation. The 1793 edition, with its stately type and its gracious margin, offers ample opportunity for a running comment, if the reader is inclined to unburden his mind. In the copy in the Library of Edinburgh University, the original owner, whoever he may have been, has taken full advantage of the opportunity of addressing remonstrances to Mr. Godwin. It was the custom of the age. In places the abuse and the refutation flow on from page to page, and add materially to the enjoyment of perusal. It is only possible to give a few of the shorter and snappier of these pointed arrows:

Here you show your cloven hoof, Mr. Godwin (p. 30).

O you cold-hearted blackguard, this is what you have been working (? to) for so long, is it? (p. 425).

Well done, Mr. Godwin, that's worthy of yourself, you rascal! (p. 430).

Ah, you dog, you dare openly find fault with our nobility, you vile atheist and democrat! (p. 473).

O, you devil incarnate! (p. 515).

That's right, you devil, out with it at last! (p. 797).

But it's the dictate of the Bible, you wretch! (p. 849).

Godwin is also at times a 'consummate blackguard,' an 'unprincipled cunning rascal,' and an 'insufferable fool.' After all these years, it is but right that all this spluttering rage should be allowed to work its way to the daylight.

CHAPTER VI

SAINT-SIMON AND THE SAINT-SIMONIANS

(*a*) SAINT-SIMON

COUNT HENRI-CLAUDE DE ROUVROY DE SAINT-SIMON [1] is one of the great eccentrics of history, though indeed it may be that his eccentricity has been accentuated in the growth of legend and tradition. He was a man who deliberately, with something of the purposefulness of Faust, set himself to drain the cup of life to the dregs and to taste all experience. In consequence, having been all things and having touched all extremes, he emerges as a somewhat confusing bundle of contradictions and incoherences, with nevertheless one central purpose dominating all his life. Born in 1760, into one of the most ancient families of France, claiming descent from Charlemagne, Saint-Simon never ceased to be the grand seigneur, conscious of the great things expected of him ; although to describe him as the last gentleman and the first socialist, as has been done, is perhaps to use a phrase too devastating in its implications. ' Rise, M. le Comte, you have great things to do to-day ' : such, according to the legend, was the formula with which his valet was instructed to call him, when still a boy, to each new morning. It is at least true to the spirit of Saint-Simon, for ever panting after great things, and true to his love of doing things in the large spectacular manner. When but a lad he fought, and fought well, in the American War of Independence, returning with military rank disproportionate to his years. America left a permanent impression upon him. On the one hand, despite his creditable record, it turned him very decisively against the profession of arms. In his own words, he realised that his profession was not that of a soldier. It would be unjust to say that America made him a pacifist ; it certainly made him a man of peace. Further, America revealed itself to him as very visibly the representative of a new era, a country which had shed, or had never acquired, the trappings of feudalism, a country where all men worked and none were idle.

His colourful life can be but glanced at. Back in Europe, taking Mexico on the way (with projects for a Panama Canal), he abandoned the army and travelled to Spain and Holland. His consciousness of his mission grew upon him : ' Je devais beaucoup observer,' [2] as he said

[1] Is it necessary to say that our Saint-Simon is *not* the Saint-Simon who is known as the writer of historical memoirs ?

[2] Œuvres Choisies, vol. 2, p. 415. It may be convenient to note the most accessible sources for the student who desires to avoid the awful vortex of Saint-Simonian

later with much simplicity. The French Revolution found him renouncing his title, and becoming Citoyen Bonhomme; it also enabled him to speculate in Church lands and thereby acquire a considerable fortune—not for low ends as he was careful to explain, but as a means to the execution of great projects. The revolution also consigned him for about a year to prison, where Charlemagne, his great ancestor, appeared to him in a vision, and spoke comfortably to him.

At an age when, as he over-modestly says, his brain had lost its malleability, Saint-Simon took to serious study, but in the grand manner he required the most eminent savants to wait upon him. True to his declared intention to lead 'la vie la plus originale et la plus active possible'[1] he studied much more than his studies. Also he married; according to the legend, he entered on matrimony, stipulating for a three years' contract. A wife at the end of the banqueting table obviously laid a better foundation for an intensive study of mankind than could be hoped for from any arrangements resting on more transitory birds of passage. The story of the three years' contract may be a myth; but Saint-Simon, in his fragment of autobiography, says unashamedly: 'J'ai usé du mariage comme d'un moyen pour étudier les savans, chose qui me paraissait nécessaire pour l'éxecution de mon enterprise'[2]—a statement which is at least not inconsistent with the grotesque tradition. In any case, marriage as a device for studying society was not a success. Saint-Simon complained that his guests ate more than they talked, or at least more than their talk was worth; and he draws a pathetic picture of himself sitting silently in a corner, listening to twaddle and falling asleep. The Saint-Simonian home may have been a 'social centre'; but one year was enough, and at the end of this period divorce put an end to this phase of his education. Some natural tears he dropped, but wiped them soon; and went to call on Madame de Stael.

His visit to Madame de Stael is the peg on which more foolish legends have been hung. What is certain is that in the following year (1802), having reached the moderately mature age of 42, he published his first work, the *Letters from an Inhabitant of Geneva to his Contemporaries*. Having put pen to paper, Saint-Simon, with an increasing consciousness of a mission and with that passionate vehemence which

literature at large. There is a volume published in Paris in 1841, edited by Rodrigues, *Œuvres de Saint-Simon*, containing some of the more significant writings of Saint-Simon. A three-volume edition of Œuvres Choisies, published in Brussels in 1859, gives more than all that anyone can possibly desire. *Saint-Simon, sa Vie et ses Travaux*, by M. G. Hubbard, 1857, is the best early biography; the volume is mostly *Fragments Divers*. In our own day, M. Bouglé has published (1925) *L'Œuvre de Saint-Simon*, which is really a Saint-Simonian anthology. It has the merits and defects of a book consisting professedly of extracts. On Saint-Simon, the man, the last word has been said by Maxime Leroy: *La Vie Véritable du Comte Henri de Saint-Simon* (1925).

[1] *Vie de Saint-Simon, écrite par lui-même*, in Rodrigues, p. xxxiii.

[2] *Vie*, in Rodrigues, p. xxiii.

never deserted him, continued to write and to write incessantly, pouring out the most extraordinary series of pamphlets, catechisms, projects, plans of later books, plans of books that were never written—a disordered, turbulent flood of words. Gone were the spacious years of worldly splendour. His marriage had proved a somewhat too expensive finishing course. He sank into poverty, living and starving in a garret, earning a pittance as a clerk, supported in part by a former retainer. In his despair he attempted suicide, with but indifferent success. His last years were somewhat less uneasy. An unsuccessful prosecution for sedition at the age of 59 earned him a certain measure of publicity, which always has its uses. Before his death he attracted a certain number of disciples among whom for a time were Thierry and Comte. He died among friends, and his last words (or so nearly his last words as to make no difference) were a summary of his life: 'Souvenez-vous que pour faire quelque chose de grand, il faut être passionné.' The epilogue is strangely in tune with the prologue. As a boy, fifty years earlier, he had each day eagerly sprung from his bed, because great things were waiting to be done, and to be done that day. He died, impressing on his disciples that, in order to achieve great things, passion is that which is needful. Despite his chaotic and incoherent life, there is a strange unity about Saint-Simon. He was dominated by a passion for the achievement of great things.

Saint-Simon's writings are a confused jungle, partly because as a grand seigneur he somewhat despised the literary arts; and also in part because for him time was always urgent. He was always writing to catch the post: next week would be too late. He acknowledges his shortcomings with considerable naiveté and some condescension: 'I write because I have new things to say; I will present my ideas as they have been forged by my spirit. I will leave to professional writers the care of giving them polish. I write like a gentleman, like a descendant of the Counts of Vermandois, like an inheritor of the pen of the Duc de Saint-Simon '[1] Thus are the 'ecrivains de profession' put in their proper and subordinate places. But it is chiefly the urgency of things that explains Saint-Simon's turbulent disorder. There is no time for literary grace: he is compelled to give his ideas 'dans leur état de nudité native.'[2] He would have approved the spirit of Lord Keynes' advice to the economist of a later generation that he should cultivate a 'willingness to spill his ideas, to flick them at the world,' and the implied injunction 'to pluck the day, and fling pamphlets into the wind.' Never was a writer so assiduous as was Saint-Simon in flicking his ideas at the world, so free (in the words of an earlier enthusiast) from 'le soin vulgaire d'effacer ses contradictions.'[3]

[1] *Introduction aux Travaux Scientifiques du dix-neuvième Siècle*, Œuvres Choisies vol. 1, p. 60.

[2] *Travail sur la Gravitation Universelle*, Œuvres Choisies, vol. 2, p. 177.

[3] Introduction to Œuvres Choisies, p. xvi.

What were these so new things that Saint-Simon had to say? What, it may be asked, was all the hurry about? In one sense, the Saint-Simonian problem, if not the Saint-Simonian solution, can be put in a few words. He wrote, be it remembered, in the back-wash of the French Revolution, and in the years following the Napoleonic Wars. The world was confronting a new era; the eighteenth century, an age of criticism and destruction, had gone; it was to be the task of the new century to construct and rebuild. The feudal world had passed, giving way to an Industrial Age. Also the world, in this era of transition, when the old was dead and the new not yet born, had lost its guides. The teeming multitudes of Europe were as sheep without a shepherd—and sheep need a shepherd. The temporal power had gone; the spiritual power was no longer respected. Where in the new age—an industrial age with all the implications of an industrial age—are we to find a new temporal power and, even more important, a new spiritual power? This is the question that obsessed Saint-Simon; and for the salvation of the world an answer had to be found forthwith. Herein lies the strange unity of Saint-Simon. He may have given a different answer every time he flicked a pamphlet in the face of the world; but it was always the same question he was trying to answer.

Perhaps at the risk of some disproportion it may be permissible to look at his first book in somewhat greater detail than will be possible elsewhere. In its chaotic confusion, its grotesqueness of suggestion if taken literally, in its appeal to divine vision and illumination, this first publication, purporting to be letters from an inhabitant of Geneva, is pure Saint-Simon; not only so, it may with a little imagination be viewed as the whole of Saint-Simon, indicating in embryo the various directions along which subsequent pamphlets were to gush. The first letter, expounding the proposal, extends to a little over a page; there is a 'reply from a friend,' purporting to ask for more details, but in fact blowing off Saint-Simonian steam; then there are two more letters (which are not letters) in expansion of the project. Take as characteristic the opening of the first letter:

> I am no longer young; I have observed and reflected with much activity during the whole of my life, and your happiness has always been the object of my labours: I have conceived a project which, it appears to me, might be useful to you, and I am going to present it to you.
>
> Open a subscription before the tomb of Newton: subscribe all of you, indiscriminately, for the sum you wish.[1]

This, it will be agreed, is a somewhat brusque debut for a man of letters, entering into his kingdom at the age of forty-two. The

[1] *Lettres d'un Habitant de Genève,* Œuvres Choisies, vol. 1, p. 3. Also in Rodrigues and Hubbard.

proposal, in what he would have called its ' crude nudity,' is that by a system of universal subscriptions and universal election, there should be set apart three mathematicians, three physicists, three physiologists, three writers, three painters and three musicians. The men so elected are to accept no position or employment; they are to be free to make what use they will of their powers, and being thus consecrated and honoured, they will be able to render to humanity the greatest services of which they are capable.

Here, in the Council of Newton, there is, despite its fantastic appearance, a plea that spiritual leadership should be entrusted to the *savants*. These men are the torches, the *flambeaux* of humanity, and, as we are assured by another authority, it is of the essence of torches that they should be altruistic:

> Heaven doth with us as we with torches do,
> Not light them for themselves.

Nevertheless humanity does not reward its torches as it should. His battle-cry at this stage is, ' Down with the Alexanders; long live the Archimedes!'—' Plus d'honneur pour les Alexandre: vivent les Archimède!'[1] Much of the pamphlet is taken up with appeals to the intellectuals, to the landowners and to the people at large, giving reasons why they should each accept the scheme. The *savants* are most obviously and directly interested in the success of the subscription. The appeal to the proprietors is based on the fact that they have already lost the battle and that it is in their interest to adopt this measure in order to avoid greater evils. In his appeal to the people at large, Saint-Simon is (as perhaps always) the slightly condescending and benevolent aristocrat. Somewhat patronisingly, he suggests that they should show a becoming gratitude for what has been, or may be, done for them. They should remember that though the proprietors are inferior in numbers, yet they are superior in *lumières* (a word very dear to Saint-Simon), and that, for the general good, authority should be distributed according to *lumières*. Or take this, as the basis of an appeal to the man in the street to support the torches with his subscriptions:

> On Sundays, eloquence has charms for you; you find pleasure in reading a book well-written, in looking at beautiful pictures or lovely statues, or in listening to music capable of fixing your attention. In order to speak or write in a manner that may entertain you, to make a picture or statue which gives you great pleasure, one must work hard. Is it not just, my friends, that you should reward the artists who fill the intervals of your occupations with pleasures most fitted to develop your intelligence. . . . Subscribe all of you, my friends. . . .[2]

All this is rather condescending and even foolish, especially as, apparently, all the contributions are going as a free gift to the twenty-

[1] Œuvres Choisies, vol. 1, p. 12. [2] *Ibid.* vol. 1, pp. 29–30.

one chosen torches. The idea of popular election in this matter is doubtless somewhat disturbing, but Saint-Simon explains to his proletarian friends what he proposes to do, and counsels them to follow the same procedure: he will ask all his mathematical friends who are the three greatest living mathematicians, and he will be guided by their advice. It is at least an innocent mind that looks forward to a time when the conversation in the taverns of Wapping will range round the comparative merits of Einstein and Max Born as torches. There then, embedded in much that is curious, is Saint-Simon's first suggestion in this problem that so obsesses him. In his own words: 'the spiritual power in the hands of the *savants*; the temporal power in the hands of the proprietors; the power of nominating those called to fulfil the functions of leaders in the hands of everyone.' [1]

But beyond this, Saint-Simon branches out in this same pamphlet into other matters that bulk largely in the ample brood of sequels. In a vision in which God speaks to him, it is ordained that the Pope, the Cardinals, the Bishops and the priests will henceforth cease to speak in his name; and the reason is that God will always withdraw from the Ministers of his altars 'the power to speak in my name as soon as they shall have ceased to be more learned (*savants*) than the flock whom they would lead, and shall have allowed themselves to be dominated by the temporal power.' Accordingly, and it is God who is speaking in the vision, the religion of Newton is ordained: 'The Council of Newton will represent me on earth.' Speaking in large capitals, the Almighty declares that 'Women shall be allowed to subscribe: they may be elected.' [2] Detailed instructions are given as to the building of temples and mausolea, and one such instruction gives clear evidence of its divine origin. It is that none of the libraries attached to the temples of Newton shall ever contain more than five hundred volumes.[3]

The other side of Saint-Simon, that leading to socialism, is also present in embryo in these Geneva letters. Further on (and again large type underlines its significance) God declares that 'All men shall work'; and in his own comment, on waking up, Saint-Simon says:

[1] Saint-Simon, of course, has no copyright in all this torch-*lumière* business. It is not without some interest to note the parallelism between Saint-Simon's Council of Newton and Salomon's House in Bacon's *New Atlantis*: 'the noblest foundation as we think, that ever was upon the earth, and the lantern of this kingdom.' In *The New Atlantis*, the reader may encounter the 'merchants of light'; and the members of another subsection of Salomon's House are briefly designated 'Lamps': their function is 'to direct new experiments, of a higher light, more penetrating into Nature than the former.' It was left to a later and more saccharine age to mingle their light with sweetness.

[2] The tradition is that this sentence was included chiefly to propitiate Madame de Stael. It is said to be the only reference to women in the writings of Saint-Simon; which is perhaps odd, considering how largely the question of women bulked in the discussions of the later Saint-Simonian school.

[3] Œuvres Choisies, vol. 1, pp. 32–36.

The obligation is imposed on each one to give constantly to his personal forces a direction that is useful to humanity; the arms of the poor will continue to nourish the rich, but the rich receives the commandment to make his brain work, and if his brain is not fit to work, he will certainly be obliged to make his arms work; for Newton will assuredly not leave on this planet, one of the nearest to the sun, workers who are wilfully useless in the workshop.[1]

The *Letters from an Inhabitant of Geneva* have been surveyed in some detail, because they conveniently present a summary of the lines along which Saint-Simon wrote and speculated for the rest of his life. How far this nonsensical dream of a temple of Newton and of the popular election of 'torches' was seriously meant; how far the divine vision was merely a literary exercise, how far the bulk of the pamphlet is blague with a substratum of serious intention, would provide interesting questions for leisurely discussion. The important point is that here we have Saint-Simon groping to establish leadership in a world that does not recognise its leaders; we see him seeking to establish some form of intellectual aristocracy; we have his criticisms of all established religions on the ground that their priests are, by their ignorance in essential matters, no longer qualified to be leaders; and we already have his emphasis on the obligation resting on all to work for the common good, and an expression of that rage which filled him increasingly with the years, whenever he thought of the idlers—*les fainéants, les oisifs.*

The earlier disciples of Saint-Simon tended to represent him as having passed through a scientific, a political, a moral and a religious phase. This is a rather dangerous over-simplification; for though doubtless his main interest moved in something like the direction indicated, and though, despite much oscillation, his thoughts tended to crystallise on certain points, yet Saint-Simon was not the man to allow his 'phases' to be neatly partitioned and docketed. His ultimate aim throughout life was singularly unchanging; it was to reorganise, and indeed (remembering his passion for great things) it was nothing less than to reorganise all knowledge and all science, and all the applications of knowledge and science. The only object worthy of pursuit was to labour for the reorganisation of the system of *morale*, of the religious and of the political system[2]; elsewhere he speaks of the urgent and immediate task as being that of finding a solid foundation on which to reconstruct the scientific, the religious and political edi-

[1] Œuvres Choisies, vol. 1, p. 40.

[2] *Memoire sur la Science de l'Homme*, Œuvres Choisies, vol. 2, p. 10. It may be as well to note how complete is the task of reorganisation contemplated by Saint-Simon: 'aujourd'hui, le seul objet que puisse se proposer un penseur, est de travailler à la RÉORGANISATION du système de *morale*, du système *religieux*, du système *politique*, en un mot, du système des IDEÉS, sous quelque face qu'on les envisage.'

fice.[1] In his earlier stages, fresh from his academic coaches, it is naturally the reorganisation of scientific knowledge that is his consuming interest; only later did the social and political problem assert its insistence.

Saint-Simon was not a scientist; his recurrent speculations on the possibility of the beaver, as the most intelligent animal, ultimately replacing man is enough to classify him among the attractive amateurs. In any case what he has to say with regard to scientific method falls outside our immediate province. It has, however, an application to the matters with which we are concerned. He is never tired of repeating, with considerable variety of phraseology, that the eighteenth century had been critical, destructive, revolutionary; it was the task of the nineteenth century to be *organisatrice*, it was time to 'changer de route'; the discoveries now due to be made could only be achieved by abandoning the *a posteriori* for the *a priori* method.[2] Looking back to the fifteenth century, Saint-Simon also emphasised the continual decline of the theological principle compared with the physicist principle. A modern of the moderns, indeed a man to whom the future alone was of interest, Saint-Simon even in 1813 could say (somewhat prematurely perhaps) that whereas the test of education used to be whether a man 'possessed' the Greek and Latin authors, now the question was: 'Is he strong in the Mathematics?'[3] In this general reorganisation and affiliation of all sciences at which Saint-Simon aims, it is essential that all sciences should become positive sciences. The ultimate end then is to give to the 'science of man' a positive character, basing it on observation, and treating it by the methods employed in the physical sciences. For is not man, in a phrase to which he recurs, 'un petit univers'? Moreover this science of man, thus viewed, is to become the chief object of public education.[4]

All this, of course, is more or less Comte, who for a time was proud to sign himself 'Élève de Henri Saint-Simon.' The implications of this view are, however, far-reaching, with remote repercussions on Saint-Simon's doctrines regarding politics and government generally. For when politics becomes a positive science, those whose business it is to resolve political problems, if they know their physiology, will look on their difficulties—it comes with rather a shock—as being merely questions in hygiene.[5] Putting it in more general terms, in the new

[1] *Mémoire sur la Science de l'Homme*, p. 141.

[2] *Introduction aux Travaux Scientifiques du dix-neuvième Siècle*, Œuvres Choisies, vol 1, p. 164; *Travail sur la Gravitation Universelle*, Œuvres Choisies, vol. 2, p. 237.

[3] *Mémoire sur la Science de l'Homme*, Œuvres Choisies, vol. 2, p. 14.

[4] *Ibid.* vol. 2, p. 144.

[5] *Op. cit.* p. 23. It is true that this occurs in a lengthy statement professedly expressing the views of M. Burdin; but obviously, Saint-Simon is the author of M. Burdin's views, just as in the *Letters from Geneva* he is the author of the views expressed by the Almighty.

scheme of things, the questions raised will be eminently 'positives et jugeables,' and the decisions given will be the result of scientific demonstrations. Thus as an engineer is supposed to be able to give the answer to a question submitted to him, so will the expert politician, if qualified in his job and trained in the positive 'science of society' (the phrase is notable), be able to give the right answer; and inferentially, all expert politicians, being positive scientists, will give the same answer, which will be capable of scientific demonstration.[1]

Thus along one line we are led to government by the expert, without as yet knowing who the expert is. Indeed in a sense we are led to the elimination of government in the traditional and political sense of the word. Reaching forward in anticipation to the *Catéchisme Politique des Industriels* we find this line of argument leading to a favourite doctrine of Saint-Simon, that society is destined to pass from the *régime gouvernemental* to the *régime administratif*.'[2] This replacement of government by 'administration' may at first appear, and indeed it is, a somewhat delusive idea; yet it ought not to be unfamiliar to the present generation. It is surprising to note how frequently arguments are advanced that this or that subject should be 'taken out of politics.' Looked at rigorously, it is a somewhat pathetic admission that democracy or parliamentary government is not wholly fitted for its entire task. A generation ago it was a common argument throughout the world that the tariff should be 'taken out of politics'; in our own day an attempt was made to make the G.P.O. something not quite like an ordinary government office; in its early days the Unemployment Assistance Board (while it was still the U.A.B.) was in intention designed to be something apart from the Minister of Labour, and indeed from anyone else. The whole brood of half-way houses, the Central Electricity Board, the B.B.C., the London Passenger Transport Board, etc., are all attempts to take things 'out of politics.' Saint-Simon would have said that they represent the transition from government to administration; they have reached a stage where they are better run administratively, like any other business enterprise, even if in some ways they acknowledge a social responsibility. Saint-Simon is here the prophet of a certain type of Neo-Capitalism, freed from parliamentary criticism because parliamentary criticism is incompetent, yet working primarily for the common good.

Before leaving Saint-Simon's general views on science and knowledge, reference should be made to one further point which colours his outlook in various respects. It relates to his attitude to history and the writing of history. In his eyes, history is a science, and he com-

[1] *L'Organisateur*, Œuvres Choisies, vol. 2, p. 374; *De L'Industrie*, Hubbard, p. 157.

[2] *Catéchisme Politique des Industriels*, Rodrigues, p. 97.

plains that we have so far no histories written in such a way as to provide the means of inferring what will happen from what has happened.[1] This, with more excuse, was the view of Machiavelli. It is nevertheless a pestilential heresy, and hardly requires refutation. Just because men are unwise and curiously planned, it is never possible to foretell their behaviour, either individually or in the mass. It might, however, be argued that the Machiavellian view of history as the Prophet's Pocket-Guide to the Future ought to be true on Saint-Simonian principles. If, politics having become a positive science, the political expert can always show, with scientific demonstration attached, what is the only possible right answer in every case, this happy result must rest on the fact that human beings are no longer incalculable, but are as amenable to law as the elements hydrogen and nitrogen, assuming that these are still elements. In this case there would be no absurdity in assuming that history provided an unerring basis of prediction. It could then be said of History, as of Wisdom, that she knoweth things of old, and conjectureth aright what is to come. Saint-Simon is logical; his error lies in pressing too far the claims of the science of society to be a 'positive science.'

There is another historical heresy to which Saint-Simon succumbs. To discover an analogy between the life of the individual and the life of the race is a snare which has beguiled many. That the individual is born, is a child, in process of time—having passed through the seven ages of man—becomes toothless and decrepit, are obvious truths, quite apart from what Shakespeare may have said on the subject. That the human race should pass through corresponding stages is a hypothesis which seems to have fascinated not a few. Saint-Simon swallowed the view whole-heartedly, and pressed the analogies further than most. In the earliest of all our days, to eat is our sole joy and occupation; so with the earliest stages of civilisation of which we have knowledge. Grown somewhat older, the child plays with bricks: the Egyptians erected pyramids. Arrived at puberty, we cultivate the fine arts; at a certain stage we all write poetry, and give way, even if furtively, to music and painting. The Greeks represent this efflorescence of youth. Later we desire to employ our forces, and look upon others as rivals; and the Romans were conquering warriors.[2] It is, of course, all nonsense; but it is of some importance in studying Saint-Simon, because he had succeeded in persuading himself that humanity, when he wrote, was at an age corresponding to forty in the individual. As a further consequence the race was at the height of its

[1] *Introduction aux Travaux Scientifiques du dix-neuvième Siècle*, Œuvres Choisies, vol. 1, p. 196; *Travail sur la Gravitation Universelle*, Œuvres Choisies, vol. 2, p. 196.

[2] *Introduction aux Travaux Scientifiques du dix-neuvième Siècle*, Œuvres Choisies, vol. 1, p. 178; *Memoire sur la Science de l'Homme*, Œuvres Choisies, vol. 2, pp. 105–106.

powers, and also it possessed the maximum capacity for 'jouissances morales de tous les genres.' [1]

So far, we have been concerned with Saint-Simon's views on the methods and place of science, and the possibility of a positive science of society as the basis of the great reorganisation of all things which he viewed as his mission. It is time to go back and consider the progressive dissolution of society, as from the fifteenth century, which has made this great task of reconstruction imperative. For this state of affairs, Saint-Simon in diversified language assigns three reasons, which are doubtless interlocked. Firstly, from somewhere about the Reformation, Europe had lost her unity; secondly, the nobility, the temporal power, had lost its usefulness and significance; and thirdly, the same could be said of the clergy, the spiritual power. The old age, in fact, had passed away, leaving no leaders, no guides, no landmarks.

On the first of these points, Saint-Simon has much to say of Luther, who, in his writings, turns up in strange places. We shall presently confront Luther in greater detail as he appears in *Le Nouveau Christianisme*. For the present, it is sufficient to note that Saint-Simon invariably regards Luther as a disruptive force, as indeed he obviously was. Harmony prevailed from the ninth to the fifteenth century; the spiritual and the temporal powers were in happy equilibrium. Luther dissolved the European Federation; and in particular he broke the bonds which hitherto had linked England to the Continent, making the island insular and launching it on a path of its own.[2] On the second point, little need be said; from somewhere about the reign of Louis XI, an understanding between the Crown and Industry had deprived the nobility of their significance. They ceased to have any positive importance in the State. Louis XIV reduced them *à lui passer sa chemise et à le servir à table.*[3] And indeed what leadership can be expected of a Peerage whose primary purpose is to pass the Prince his purple pyjamas?

It is on the third point, the decay of the influence of the spiritual power, that Saint-Simon is most expansive, not to say reiterative, and most illuminating. In a sense the point had been put with sufficient clarity in the vision incorporated in the *Letters from Geneva*; briefly, whatever may have been the position in the past, the clergy were now no better—by which, of course, was meant that they had no more *lumières*—than the laity. They were, therefore, as God had declared in the Vision, no longer fitted to be his representatives—blind mouths,

[1] *Travail sur la Gravitation Universelle*, Œuvres Choisies, vol. 2, p. 236.

[2] *Introduction aux Travaux Scientifiques du dix-neuvième Siècle*, Œuvres Choisies, vol. 1, pp. 252–254; *Travail sur la Gravitation Universelle*, Œuvres Choisies, vol. 2, p. 198.

[3] *Catéchisme Politique des Industriels*, Rodrigues, pp. 18–27.

that scarce themselves know how to hold a sheep-hook, as Milton exclaimed in a gorgeous galaxy of mixed metaphor ; and—Saint-Simon would have added—lamentably ignorant of the Theory of the Steam Engine.

The authority of the clergy, of any clergy—their power to lead—thus depends on knowledge ; and Saint-Simon leaves no doubt as to the kind of knowledge that is requisite. In the golden age before the fifteenth century, when their authority was greatest, the clergy were leaders in the cultivation of the soil and in irrigation ; they applied themselves to mathematics and the physical sciences ; they established hospitals and were leaders in education. Roger Bacon was a monk: everybody who was anybody in the way of increasing *lumières* was a monk or a priest. In short, they engaged in ' useful works.' And they had their reward in influence and in authority and in other ways. Since then they have declined from their high estate, and the reason is that they no longer ' laboured in a direction useful to the progress of science.' [1] For the clergy to be useful it must be respected, and that it may be respected it must be not merely ' savant,' it must be ' le corps le plus savant.' [2] Failing in this respect, its power will pass into the hands of the physicists who surpass them in knowledge. Indeed in any age, leadership in science should be not merely the essential mark of the clergy ; it should be the quality that defines them : ' le clergé doit être le corps scientifique.' [3] If anything more emphatic is required, this may serve: ' Le pouvoir sacerdotal et la capacité scientifique sont identiques dans leur essence.' [4] The moment the clergy forfeit this qualification, they fall into disesteem, and are in the end replaced by ' la reunion des hommes les plus savants.' As against this statement of the Saint-Simonian ideal of what the clergy should be, they have in fact gradually sunk since the fifteenth century until to-day they have become ' partie de la classe la moins eclairée.' [5] Saint-Simon did not quote, though he might have done so, the dictum of the prophet to the effect that the priest's lips should keep knowledge.[6]

What, it may be asked, is the nature of this religion for which the Fellows of the Royal Society will act as Chief Priests ? Going deeper, who is the God whom they will serve ? Clearly, at any age, according to Saint-Simon, religion is merely the sum-total of scientific knowledge, presented, if that be possible, in a sacred form, as revealing the works

[1] *Introduction aux Travaux Scientifiques du dix-neuvième Siècle*, Œuvres Choisies, vol. 1, pp. 205–208.

[2] *Ibid.* p. 225.

[3] *Mémoire sur la Science de l'Homme*, Œuvres Choisies, vol. 2, p. 25.

[4] *Ibid.* p. 104.

[5] *Travail sur la Gravitation Universelle*, Œuvres Choisies, vol. 2, p. 247.

[6] On this aspect of Saint-Simon, compare Professor John Macmurray : ' The scientists are the " hermits " or " monks " of the modern world ' (*The Clue to History*, p. 190).

of God. Moreover, the progress of science has consisted in substituting one cause for many causes, and so far as the enlightened were concerned, this transition had now been completed.[1] There was one universal law, the Law of Gravity. It is curious to observe how the Law of Gravity fascinated the speculators of the time. Fourier, also, put the Law of Gravity in the centre of things, and endeavoured to be a second Newton, extending his law from the material to the spiritual world. For Saint-Simon the acceptance of one law, the Law of Gravity, was to be the foundation of all future philosophy. A new religion, shortly to appear, would also be based on the conception of the universality of one law. His own views, expressed more than once, were not wholly free from a certain suggestion of intellectual dishonesty: there should for a time be two distinct doctrines—Physicism for the instructed classes, and Deism for the ignorant.[2] It is, however, interesting to note how close to the heart of the future religion the Law of Gravity is placed. He does not exactly say that the Law of Gravity is God ; but he comes very near to it. The idea of gravitation, playing the rôle of a general absolute idea, is to replace the idea of God ; it is the immutable law by which God governs the universe. The binding link in the conceptions of the learned will in future be, not the idea of 'God,' but the idea of gravitation, considered as the Law of God.[3] Thus does the Law of Gravity just fall short of replacing God and the Ten Commandments.

For Saint-Simon, the urge to a new orientation of science, a new philosophy, a new religion could not be kept apart from the other aspect of the great problem of the age. Factory and foundry, forge and loom proclaimed that this was a new age, an industrial age in which France was assuming the similitude of a workshop, in which all men were jostling together, partners at the same bench. The industrial age, into which humanity had been projected, had two characteristics at least ; firstly, there must be perfect equality, though this, in the Saint-Simonian world, is interpreted as equality of opportunity ; and secondly, all privileges, in particular all privileges of birth, must be abolished. Perhaps there should be added (for it was never absent from Saint-Simon's mind) the further consideration that the world was now no place for idlers. This new world had, however, the wrong kind of government: there was a maladjustment between the government and the world it was supposed to govern. Surely it was an

[1] *Mémoire sur la Science de l'Homme*, Œuvres Choisies, vol. 2, pp. 123–129.

[2] *Introduction aux Travaux Scientifiques du dix-neuvième Siècle*, Œuvres Choisies, vol. 1, p. 214 ; *Mémoires sur la Science de l'Homme*, Œuvres Choisies, vol. 2, p. 41.

[3] *Travail sur la Gravitation Universelle*, Œuvres Choisies, vol. 2, pp. 219, 226, 238. The original is worth quoting for its precision: 'Ce n'est plus l'idée Dieu qui doit lier les conceptions des savants, c'est l'idée de la gravitation considerée comme loi de Dieu.'

offence to see the 'nation travaillante dirigée, et, qui pis est, gouvernée par la nation fainéante et incapable.' [1] In more general terms France presented the extraordinary spectacle of a country which was essentially industrial, and of which the government was nevertheless essentially feudal.[2]

This question obsessed Saint-Simon throughout his life, and in a plethora of pamphlets and catechisms he outlined a multitude of varying solutions, in very varying degrees of detail. He rung the changes on the *industriels*, the *artistes*, and the *savants*, now advancing, now degrading one or other of the possible claimants. It would be an interesting, though probably an unprofitable task, to plot through time the variations in the Saint-Simonian solution. Perhaps the most elaborate, certainly the most detailed, of his many solutions is that contained in the *Organisateur*, where the curious will find outlined a somewhat fearsome constitution, resting on three chambers, a *chambre d'invention*, a *chambre d'examen*, and a *chambre d'exécution*. The *chambre d'invention* is to comprise 200 engineers, 50 poets 'or other inventors in literature,' 25 painters, 15 sculptors or architects, and 10 musicians. Here indeed is Technocracy, and in a world panting for exploitation this solid phalanx of engineers will be able to circumvent the efforts of this medley collection of poets, musicians and others. Doubtless it will be easier to get 200 qualified engineers than 50 certificated poets. The *chambre d'examen* is less motley: it will be constituted by 100 biologists, 100 physicists and 100 mathematicians. The *chambre d'exécution* is to be drawn from all the branches of industry. After the lapse of more than a century, constitution-mongering on these lines can bring but a wan and faded smile to the lips of the reader.[3]

One interesting interlude in this long story of reshuffling the *industriels* and the *savants* is represented by what may be called his parliamentary phase. Round about the time of the fall of Napoleon, Saint-Simon became for a brief period an enthusiastic admirer of the British Parliamentary system, and a zealous advocate of its propagation throughout Europe.[4] In each country the old organisation is to be replaced by a Parliamentary government, recognising the supremacy of a general parliament placed above them. In its complete development there will be an international House of Lords, and indeed what he calls 'le roi du parlement européen,'—a post so ticklish to fill that Saint-Simon showed uncommon sense in postponing detailed discussion to a later work. Not the least interesting aspect of this curious

[1] *Lettres aux Jurés*, Œuvres Choisies, vol. 2, p. 414.

[2] *Catéchisme Politique des Industriels*, Rodrigues, p. 37.

[3] *Organisateur*, Hubbard, pp. 226–231.

[4] *De la Réorganisation de la Société Européenne* (October 1814), Œuvres Choisies, vol. 2, pp. 251 *et seq.*; *Opinion sur les Mesures à prendre contre la Coalition de 1815* (May 1815), Œuvres Choisies, vol. 2, pp. 335 *et seq.*

phase in Saint-Simon's pilgrimage is the zeal with which he pleads for a union of England and France, in order to avoid on both sides greater evils to come; it will not merely be a nucleus of the European parliament; this first step will inevitably impel other countries to link up with them.

This sudden enthusiasm for the machinery of Parliamentary government is, however, but a passing phase, induced by the urgency of political occurrences. It has been said above that Saint-Simon shuffles and re-shuffles his *industriels*, his *savants* and his *artistes* in varying combinations. While this is true, it is not wholly true, or at least is not the whole truth. Increasingly, as he grew older, Saint-Simon laid greater emphasis on one of the possible candidates for authority in the new age. In an industrial age, the important class was clearly *les industriels*; and it was therefore the *industriels* who should be in control. Over long stretches, the writings of Saint-Simon resolve themselves into a most extravagant hymn of praise in honour of *les industriels*, the men who do things and get things done. No organ of the opposition ever clamoured more insistently for a 'business government.' Open Saint-Simon's later works anywhere, and the chances are that you will be within a few pages of some reinforcement of this, his dearest theme. The intelligent reader may wish to know who is an *industriel*; for, left in the vague, he is as much clouded in ambiguity as his frequent companion in the pages of Saint-Simon, *le savant*. In the first question and answer of the *Catéchisme Politique des Industriels* Saint-Simon gave a lengthy and comprehensive definition which must here suffer abridgement. An industrial, we are told, is one who labours to produce, or place within the reach of the members of society, one or several means of satisfying their needs or their physical tastes. Thus a farmer who sows corn or raises stock is an *industriel*. A wheelwright, a farrier, a locksmith are all *industriels*; a manufacturer of shoes, of hats, of cloth is an *industriel*. A merchant, a carter, a sailor on a merchant vessel are all *industriels*. Industrials fall into three great classes: agriculturalists, manufacturers and merchants. Thus Saint-Simon, almost trembling on the brink of an attempted definition of productive labour.[1]

For Saint-Simon's views on the ineffable merits and the supreme importance of the industrial class, and its consequent sole competence to govern, reference may be made to three publications, ignoring many illuminating comments elsewhere. In his *Vues sur la Propriété et la Législation* (1818), the motto already sounds the appropriate note: 'tout *par* l'industrie; tout *pour* elle.' In the Preface the reader is told among other things that 'the industrial class is the sole useful class'; and further that all laws and administrative measures must be judged

[1] *Catéchisme Politique des Industriels*, Rodrigues, pp. 1–2.

by one test only, namely whether they are useful or harmful to industry.[1] In the course of the argument he claims that industry ' s'est emparée de tout '—it has laid its hands on everything.[2] It has taken over even war; and with a singularly modern note, he points out that in modern warfare (1818), the armies have been reduced to a subordinate position. They merely apply the products of industry; and, apart from complete incapacity on the part of the generals, the army which is best looked after by industry will win. In summing up at the end of these *Vues*, he expresses himself thus, with much more to the same effect:

> The only class in society whose ambition and political courage we should like to see increased, the only one in which this ambition could be useful and in which this courage is necessary, is, in general, the class of the industrials; for their particular interests are in perfect harmony with the common interest, by the mere force of circumstances. It is because we realise this truth that we have zealously embraced the cause of the industrials, looking upon them as the true centre and hearth-stone of civilisation.[3]

A considerable extrinsic interest attaches to the *Parabole de Saint-Simon* [4] (1819), which, it was suggested, instigated a murder, and which certainly led to a prosecution, happily unsuccessful. It also had as sequelæ a series of letters to the jury, providing them with gratuitous instruction in Saint-Simonian principles. In its form it is one of the most peculiar and fantastic of Saint-Simon's writings. It is but a diminutive opusculum, extending to a mere five pages in Hubbard's edition. ' We suppose,' he begins with characteristic abruptness— ' we suppose that France suddenly loses her fifty leading physicists, her fifty leading chemists, her fifty leading physiologists, her fifty leading mathematicians, her fifty leading . . .' After a time he pauses for a semi-colon and a breath, and resumes a new paragraph: ' her fifty leading mechanics, her fifty leading engineers civil and military, her fifty leading . . .' In due course there is another semi-colon, and the next paragraph opens with ' the fifty leading bankers . . . ' The eye of the reader skims down the lines and over the page, on which every fifth or sixth word is ' cinquante,' until finally he finds refuge in the peaceful haven of a full stop. There they are, the three thousand leading ' savans, artistes et artisans de France.' The result of their loss? These men are the most useful to their country; France would become a body without a soul in the moment of their disappearance. It would require at least a generation to repair the disaster.

Let us pass, says Saint-Simon, to another supposition—and the

[1] *Vues sur la Propriété et la Législation*, Rodrigues, p. 243.
[2] *Ibid.* p. 335; also Hubbard, p. 194.
[3] *Ibid.* p. 360; also Hubbard, p. 206.
[4] Conveniently, either in Rodrigues, Second Part, pp. 71–80, or Hubbard, pp. 221–225.

heart of the reader sinks within him. Now, however, he assumes the loss of a few individuals, or of large battalions in place of the niggling instalments of fifties, so that the tale of destruction is compressed. Suppose that instead of losing all these leaders in the arts and the sciences, France were to lose Mr the Brother of the King, the duc de Berry, and a few odd specified Duchesses ; all the officers of the Crown and Ministers of State, all Cardinals, Archbishops, Bishops and such like ; all judges and the ten thousand wealthiest proprietors among those ' who live nobly '—thirty thousand in all.

Such a thinning of the ranks of *Who's Who* would certainly grieve the French people, ' parce qu'ils sont bons.' The loss would, however, be a purely sentimental one ; there would result no evil to the State. There are quite a number of Frenchmen capable of discharging the functions of the brother of the King ; there are no lack of soldiers as good as our field-marshals. There are barristers quite willing to take the place of our judges, curés ready to step into the shoes of the bishops. To this odd *Parabole* Saint-Simon adds a few comments, marked by a certain bitterness to which he is ordinarily a stranger. These thirty thousand men are not merely neutral ; they are positively injurious to the progress of the sciences and the arts, which is alone what matters. They are injurious in perpetuating an outworn way of looking at things ; they are injurious in depriving the true leaders of society of their rightful place ; they are injurious in using their means in the wrong way and in diverting the resources of the nation into wrong channels. The present state of society is the world upside down—*le monde renversé*. The final words are almost like an echo of the concluding paragraph of Rousseau's *Discourse on Inequality*. Everywhere, says Saint-Simon, the incompetent are put in charge of the competent ; the most immoral are called to fashion the citizens in virtue ; the great criminals are appointed to punish the shortcomings of the petty delinquents. Saint-Simon was seldom so inflammatory: it was unfortunate that one of the thirty thousand, whom he had specified by name, the duc de Berry, should have been assassinated within three months of the appearance of the *Parabole*.

The third of the writings of Saint-Simon to which it is proposed to refer on this question of the world upside down, as evidenced in the lack of respect paid to the industrial class, is the *Catéchisme Politique des Industriels*. A catechism is, on the whole, an unsatisfactory vehicle for propaganda, partly because of a certain infantile atmosphere which almost inevitably pervades the discussion, and partly because the Questioner and the Instructor always seem to be in undesired collusion. Certainly Saint-Simon's questioner invariably asks the right question, and indeed from time to time provides most useful summaries of what he has been told. The purpose of the Catechism is to prove the superiority of the industrial class over all others ; to show why they have hitherto failed to attain the position due to their merits; to sow in their hearts the seeds of discontent, and to show the means whereby they may gain their rightful rank and influence. It is a discussion overflowing with history and comparative politics. After defining what is an industrial in terms already summarised, the Catechism proceeds:

> Q. What rank should the industrials occupy in society?
> A. The industrial class should occupy the first rank, because it is the most important of all; because it can do without the others, and none of the others can do without it; because it exists by its own forces, by its personal labours. The other classes ought to work for it, because they are its creatures, and because it maintains their existence; in a word, everything being done by industry, everything should be done for it. (*Tout se faisant par l'industrie, tout doit se faire pour elle.*)
> Q. What rank do the industrials occupy in society?
> A. The industrial class, in the present social organisation, is constituted the last of all. The social order still accords more consideration to secondary works and even to idleness than to the most important labours and those of the most urgent usefulness.[1]

A little later, though still in the early stages of the Catechism, we are given a summary statement of the reasons which make the industrial class fitted to govern:

> The reason is simple: the political inclination of the vast majority of society is to be governed as cheaply as possible; to be governed as little as possible; to be governed by the most capable men, and in a manner which will completely assure public tranquillity. Now the only means of satisfying, in these various respects, the desires of the majority, consists in entrusting to the most important industrials the task of directing the public fortune; for the most important industrials are most interested in the maintenance of tranquillity; they are most interested in economy in public expenditure; they are most interested in restricting arbitrary power; lastly, of all members of society, it is they who have given proof of the greatest capacity in positive administration, the success which they have achieved in their various enterprises having given evidence of their capacity in this respect.[2]

That the industrials alone are interested in economy, that they alone have given proof of capacity, that they least of all desire to meddle for the sake of meddling—these reasons for the supremacy of the industrial class are the constant theme of Saint-Simon's reiterations; but above all, merely because this is an industrial age, it is a *chose monstrueuse* that the direction of affairs should be elsewhere than in the hands of the industrials.[3] The industrials have hitherto been denied their rightful place, because they have not been conscious of the superiority of their class. They have shown excessive prudence and insufficient firmness: they have, in other words, been too busy with their own affairs. Also they have themselves desired to rise, to become barons, or to marry

[1] *Catéchisme Politique des Industriels,* Rodrigues, pp. 2–3.
[2] *Ibid.* pp. 6–7. [3] *Ibid.* p. 46.

their daughters into the aristocracy—anxious, in a fine phrase, to associate themselves with the *débris de la féodalité*. But now the industrialists must ally themselves with the Monarchy against the nobility. There must be formed the *parti industriel*; the Industrial Monarchy will be established, with the King proud of being the 'first industrialist.'[1]

In this future industrial state, two questions arise which are of considerable significance, alike in the later Saint-Simon and in the Saint-Simonian school after his death. The first relates to the end and functions of government; the second to the place of property in the scheme of things. A few words on each may complete this side of the picture.

It is one of the complaints of Saint-Simon that the purpose of the association of citizens, making up the nation, has never been adequately defined.[2] In the simile of two caravans, which at one time enjoyed a certain celebrity, he contrasted the position of one in which the instruction to the conductors was, 'Take us to the place where it will be best for us to go,' and the other in which the conductors were told, 'You know the way to Mecca; take us there.'[3] In the first, the conductors are everything; the caravan counts for nothing. In the second, the conductors are mere guides, discharging subordinate and controllable functions. In the same way, although clearly the analogy must not be examined too curiously, it is not enough to say that government should be in the interests of the governed and for their well-being. Such a statement is too vague and requires content. As made more precise by Saint-Simon, the sole and permanent object of the social organisation is to apply, for the satisfaction of the needs of man, all the knowledge acquired in the sciences and the fine arts, and in the arts and crafts, and to propagate, increase and perfect this body of knowledge as far as possible.[4] Here is a utilitarian government in the strictest sense; and in his later years this conception of the State came more easily to Saint-Simon, because he entertained the agreeable belief that the last shot had been fired at Waterloo, and that henceforward there would be but the rivalries of peace. In practice, however, throughout his many schemes of government, it is curious to note how consistently Saint-Simon conceived the task of government as being primarily that of preparing a *projet de travaux*, a plan of public works, partly to provide employment, but more fundamentally because this represents the task of civilisation and of the industrial age.[5] Later

[1] *Catéchisme Politique des Industriels*, Rodrigues, pp. 64, 122, 151.

[2] *Suite à la Brochure: Des Bourbons et des Stuarts*, Œuvres Choisies, vol. 2, p. 439.

[3] *Organisateur*, Hubbard, pp. 231–233.

[4] *Organisateur*, Œuvres Choisies, vol. 2, pp. 366, 370.

[5] *E.g. Des Bourbons et des Stuarts*, Œuvres Choisies, vol. 2, p. 438.

this was to become the 'exploitation of the globe by association.' In that fantastic outline of a super-European Parliament, to which reference has already been made, the primary function of this new creature was to carry out enterprises of general usefulness for the society of Europe, linking the Danube and the Rhine, the Rhine and the Baltic, peopling the globe with the European race and breaking the world in for the use of Europe. In short, however he might define it, for Saint-Simon the primary function of government was the preparation of projects of public works—preferably of a grandiose character.

The general question of the legitimacy of property and the limits of its use was destined to become a crucial point in the transition from Saint-Simon to the Saint-Simonians. Saint-Simon's position, to say the least, is hesitant and ambiguous and invited criticism. Probably it was an issue on which the descendant of Charlemagne had difficulty in coming to terms with the ancestor of a long line of socialists. Nowhere does he suggest any definitive restriction on property or on the use of property. The legislature, he says in one place, must assure the free exercise of property.[1] In his *Vues sur la Propriété et la Législation*, while he does not suggest changes in property rights, he gets as far as suggesting the possibility and the legitimacy of such changes. He remarks (and in Saint-Simon it is somewhat surprising) that the law which constitutes the form of government is less important, and less influential on the happiness of nations, than the law defining the exercise of property. Property is the real foundation of the social edifice. The right of property must therefore be founded in such a manner as to be most favourable to the increase of wealth.[2] From the fact that this law is fundamental, it must not, however, be assumed that it cannot be modified. As the point subsequently becomes of primary importance in the Saint-Simonian tradition, the crucial sentence of the Master may be quoted :

> It is therefore evident that in every country, the fundamental law is that which establishes property and the provisions necessary to secure that it is respected ; but from the fact that this law is fundamental, it does not follow that it cannot be modified. What is necessary is a law which establishes the right of property—not a law which establishes it in such and such a manner. It is on the conservation of the right of property that the existence of society depends ; but not on the conservation of the law which originally consecrated that right.[3]

Further, the individual right of property can be founded only on the

[1] *Introduction aux Travaux Scientifiques*, Œuvres Choisies, vol. 1, p. 221.

[2] *Vues sur la Propriété et la Législation*, Rodrigues, pp. 257–259 ; also Hubbard, pp. 161–162.

[3] *Ibid.* p. 265 ; Hubbard, p. 165.

general utility which springs from the exercise of this right, and this utility may vary from time to time.

This amounts to saying that the institution of property must justify itself on public grounds; but such a conclusion has all the vagueness which characterised the caravan travelling to an unknown destination. When he ought to say something more precise, Saint-Simon is as uncommunicative as a Parliamentary Under Secretary left stranded by his chief. In one place he says that the moralist ought to urge public opinion to punish the idle proprietor by depriving him of all 'consideration.'[1] Elsewhere, approaching the question from the positive rather than the negative side, he says that property ought to be so constituted as to stimulate the proprietor to make it as productive as possible.[2] Towards this laudable end, Saint-Simon contributed as best he might by invariably holding up the idler to contempt; at the thought of *les oisifs* and *les fainéants*, he gives way to ungovernable rage. A *rentier* who does nothing is a burden on society, even if he be an alms-giver.[3] 'Rentiers,' he exclaims, 'classe encore plus sotte et plus méprisable, qui cherche dans la vie des jouissances obtenues sans travail.'[4] For Saint-Simon the first law of morality and the first law of religion was that 'Man must work.'[5] The teaching of Saint-Simon on property may then, not unjustly, be summarised as implying that property was not, at least for the present, to be disturbed; but that, secondly, under the pressure of public opinion, the owner of wealth must be made to feel that he has responsibilities and that he must not, in any case, shelter behind his wealth in order to enjoy a life of ease. Whether this is a logical or satisfactory position need not be debated; it is not, however, substantially different from the views of St. Thomas Aquinas, on the one hand, or of Charles Kingsley, representing the Christian socialists, on the other.

In the foregoing pages, all reference to Saint-Simon's last work, *Nouveau Christianisme*, has been rigorously and intentionally avoided. The early commentators and biographers, such as they were, seem to be agreed (perhaps not with complete justification) that this dialogue stands apart from the rest of his writings, and that it is here that he comes nearest to that socialism of which he is one of the many reputed fathers. In a sense, *Nouveau Christianisme* is a fragment, designed to be completed in two further dialogues; but even had he lived, Saint-Simon having been Saint-Simon, there is no guarantee that they would have been written.

Though in fact Saint-Simon continues to embroider the old themes

[1] *Introduction aux Travaux Scientifiques*, Œuvres Choisies, vol. 1, p. 221.
[2] *Vues sur la Propriété*, etc., Rodrigues, p. 248.
[3] *Introduction aux Travaux Scientifiques*, Œuvres Choisies, vol. 1, p. 221.
[4] *Mémoire sur la Science de l'Homme*, Œuvres Choisies, vol. 2, p. 46.
[5] *Introduction aux Travaux Scientifiques*, Œuvres Choisies, vol. 1, p. 220.

in this, his last work, and though, in many respects, he continues to repeat what he has already repeated, there is undeniably an indefinable quality about *Nouveau Christianisme* which explains the position of honour frequently assigned to it. In the socialist tradition it has been the most influential of his writings. It is the least marred by Saint-Simonian eccentricities. Though in form a dialogue between a *Conservateur* and a *Novateur*, the Conservateur agreeably fades away, so that the reader forgets his presence. Here also Saint-Simon, in his zeal for humanity, seems somewhat to have shed the patronising airs which elsewhere cling to the grand seigneur.

Throughout his life Saint-Simon had preached the need for a new religion. In the *Travail sur la Gravitation Universelle*, he had already said that the Christian religion, after rendering great services, had fulfilled its missions and completed its usefulness.[1] Is it possible to restate the essence of Christianity, in accordance with the needs of the new industrial age? Such, briefly, is the theme of Saint-Simon's last testament. In approaching this question, probably as a concession to the Conservateur, Saint-Simon (who may be identified with the Novateur) admits that what God personally has said cannot be perfected or restated; but this must be distinguished from what the clergy said in his name. This constitutes a science capable of improvement like any other science.[2] If the human element (what the clergy have said) is abstracted, there remains but one principle representing the divine element in Christianity. It is the injunction that men should behave to each other as brothers. This and this alone is the essence of Christianity, and Saint-Simon deduces from it, in more lengthy phraseology which recurs like a *Leitmotiv*, the essential doctrine of the New Christianity. It is that men

> should organise their society in the manner most advantageous to the largest number; they should propose, as the end to be aimed at in all their works and in all their actions, to ameliorate as promptly and as completely as possible the moral and physical existence of the most numerous class.[3]

La class la plus nombreuse—this swarming multitude! Hitherto, they have been crowded at the back of the stage; from time to time they have been heard 'off.' Is this the first time they have been thrust into the spotlight, and their condition and well-being made the primary, indeed the sole, end of every political and social institution, and of all political and social activity? For this also, be it observed, should be the end of religion—of all religion and of any religion [4]: 'Religion should direct society towards the great aim of the most rapid amelioration of the lot of the poorest class.'

[1] Œuvres Choisies, vol. 2, p. 188.

[2] *Nouveau Christianisme*, Rodrigues, Part 2, p. 94. Also in Hubbard, and in Œuvres Choisies, vol. 3. The references are to Rodrigues.

[3] *Ibid.* p. 95.

[4] *Ibid.* p. 104.

Such is the sum and substance of *Nouveau Christianisme* ; but in the remainder, which is largely a criticism of Roman Catholicism and of Protestantism, there is much that throws light on Saint-Simon. The Catholic religion, he argues, is but a Christian heresy. The clergy (his old theme) should be capable of directing their flocks in works designed to increase their *bien-être*: they obviously are not. They should preach the possibility of 'amelioration'—that blessed word: they simply do not have the necessary 'connaissances.' The ecclesiastical estates are badly administered ; and much more.[1]

He is more interesting in his criticisms of Protestantism, above all as embodied in Luther. Luther made quite a number of mistakes. Saint-Simon gives a lengthy speech which Luther ought to have addressed to the Pope, initiating him into the cream of Saint-Simonian ideas. Luther should have said that the theory of Christianity had been sufficiently perfected: it was now time to turn to application. True Christianity should make men happy not merely in Heaven, but here on this earth. He should also have told the Pope—though it would have been something of an anachronism if he had—that Christianity no longer recognised the right of one man to command another, and that Royalty was an institution designed to prevent the rich and the powerful from oppressing the poor. He should also have urged on a very astonished Pope the importance of a large plan of public works, making it clear that the only way of gaining eternal life was by labouring to increase the well-being of the human race.[2]

A further criticism of Luther is also of interest in revealing Saint-Simon. It is that Luther reduced religion to preaching. In doing so, *il a prosaïqué*, he reduced to prose the body of Christian sentiments.[3] The poet ought to support the preacher ; the musician, the painter, the sculptor should surround him: but all this side of life Luther banished from the temple. And lastly, in this incomplete summary, Luther erred in regarding Christianity as perfect in its origin, and as having deteriorated ever since. He urged his followers to study Christianity as expounded in the books written when it was founded, above all in the Bible ; just as well might a chemist or a mathematician claim that their sciences would be best studied in the earliest known works on the subject. As a consequence of this odd error on the part of Luther, there are even now Bible Societies, distributing millions of copies of the Bible among the public ! [4]

Doubtless from the point of view of theology and religion, *Nouveau Christianisme* cannot be regarded as a weighty contribution. It may be doubted whether what it preaches is a religion at all. It is a gospel of material betterment, of increased power over nature directed to the increase of human happiness, and of happiness here and now, and not

[1] *Nouveau Christianisme*, Rodrigues, Part 2, pp. 108–110.
[2] *Ibid.* pp. 138–146. [3] *Ibid.* p. 154. [4] *Ibid.* p. 164.

merely in some shadowy future existence. Perhaps its significance does not even lie in its proclamation of universal brotherhood—doubtless a noble sentiment, but apt to be swamped in foam and froth. If all the world is my brother, Proudhon remarked later, then I have no brother. But that the whole machinery of society and of the State exists in order to care for *la classe la plus nombreuse et la plus pauvre*—*there* was an idea worth launching on the world.[1]

It is now possible to assess the legacy of Saint-Simon when he died in 1825, and to consider his position in the socialist succession. He began, as has been seen, very largely as a critic of scientific method, looking forward to the development of a positive science of society. In this respect he is a forerunner of Comte. He was concerned with the creation of a spiritual power and of a new religion fitted to the needs of the new industrial age. In emphasising the characteristics of this new age, he was led to extol the virtues of the industrial classes, and became the prophet of big business, even if of big business with a sense of social responsibility. In all this, there is little of socialism as ordinarily understood ; and it may be forcibly suggested that Saint-Simon's claims to be one of the fathers of socialism rest on very slender evidence of paternity. Even on a generous interpretation of the essentials of socialism, the distinctly socialistic elements in Saint-Simon are minimal. He saw that in this new world there must be perfect equality, in the sense of equality of opportunity ; or, putting it from another angle, that all privileges must be abolished. Also he saw that in this new world there would be no room for the idler, though he never faced up to the question of how the congenital idler can be made to work. In his last book, he asserted the claims of the masses—the most numerous and the poorest class—to be the particular care of the State ; and whatever other functions government might have, he was never in doubt that it had to provide work and education. On property, that thorniest of questions in socialist theory, he spoke with an uncertain voice : it was to be respected, but the owner had to be educated, or compelled by public opinion, to use his wealth for the public good. Beyond these few points, it is difficult to squeeze another drop even of the most diluted socialism out of Saint-Simon.

How then does it happen that he is invariably classed among the founders of socialism ? The answer probably is that in some ways he began to live after his death. The Saint-Simonians, whose history represents one of the most fantastic tales of human freakishness, took

[1] Lavoisier, whose genius as a chemist has overshadowed his distinction as an economist, had already come near to the same point of view : 'Le but de toute institution sociale est de rendre le plus heureux qu'il est possible, tous ceux qui vivent sous les lois. Le bonheur ne doit pas être réservé à un petit nombre d'hommes, il appartient à tous. Ce n'est point un privilège exclusif qu'il faut disputer ; c'est un droit commun qu'il faut partager, et la félicité publique est une source dans laquelle chacun a le droit de puiser la sienne.'

over part of his theories, and by certain apparently slight but far-reaching modifications in his doctrine, linked Saint-Simon to the main line of socialist development. But the Saint-Simonian school is sufficiently apart from Saint-Simon to merit the compliment of a separate sub-section.[1]

(*b*) THE SAINT-SIMONIANS

Let no one flatter himself that he is dead, merely because he has been buried. Scarcely had the curtain fallen on the tempestuous life of Saint-Simon, when it was rung up again on what may, without harshness, be called the fantastic farce of the Saint-Simonian Church. Saint-Simon had had but little influence and but few faithful followers in his lifetime. Thierry and Comte, sufficiently distinguished disciples for anyone, had moved elsewhere. There is a significant admission in the introduction to the *Doctrine de Saint-Simon*, to the effect that Saint-Simon had left 'un très-petit nombre d'élèves,' and that his doctrine had been studied scientifically by 'très-peu de personnes.' The true heir to Saint-Simon, the follower nearest to him in the last few years and at his death, was Olinde Rodrigues; and with filial piety he sought to bring together a company of disciples to carry on the master's work. The history of the Saint-Simonian movement becomes forthwith a whirl of lectures, conferences, newspapers, with a surprisingly large influx of recruits. Rodrigues was soon displaced in the leadership by Enfantin and Bazard. It was probably Bazard who supplied the brains and the ideas, while Enfantin gave the movement its bizarre elements. With the increase of disciples there emerged a sacred college of apostles. By this time there was professedly a Saint-Simonian religion and a Saint-Simonian Church, with six departmental churches throughout France. With true missionary zeal the Church carried its gospel abroad. The curious burrower in libraries may find pamphlets revealing that the chief of the Saint-Simonian religion in England in 1833 was a certain Fontana, and that the preacher of the movement was called Prati. The names hardly suggest that the new religion had had time to attract the indigenous elements.[2]

[1] The few sentences with which Emile Faguet opens his study of Saint-Simon provide so just a characterisation of Saint-Simon, and are so admirable an example of Faguet's unfailing felicity that they may be quoted here: 'Saint-Simon est un rare exemple d'incohérence dans la vie, d'incohérence dans le caractère, d'incohérence dans les idées de détail, et de fixité dans l'idée maîtresse.

—Autrement dit, c'est un fou.

—Très exactement, beaucoup plus nettement que Rousseau lui-même; mais c'est un fou très intelligent, comme il arrive.'

[2] For the incredible tale of the Saint-Simonian movement—incredible apart from the fact that it appears to have happened—the reader may refer to A. J. Booth: *Saint-Simon and Saint-Simonism* (1871); and in much greater detail, Sébastien Charléty: *Histoire du Saint-Simonisme, 1825–1864*. Some idea of the far-reaching repercussions of the movement may be gathered from E. M. Butler: *The Saint-Simonian Religion in Germany*.

The roots of the Saint-Simonian religion may not unnaturally be found in Saint-Simon. One of the best known passages in Saint-Simon is that in which he chides the imagination of the poets for placing the age of gold in the cradle of the human race—in the Garden of Eden, in the symbolism of the Old Testament: 'The age of gold of the human race is not behind us; it lies ahead of us; it consists in the perfection of the social order. Our fathers have not seen it; our children will arrive there one day; it is for us to mark the path.'[1] This amounts to a repudiation of the doctrine of the fall of man and of all its implications. We have always been rising; we are rising now; we shall continue to rise. This is the Law of Progress. Infuse with this the spirit of *The New Christianity*, and it may be deduced that the true religion consists in working for the betterment of men here and now. Science is holy, and industry is holy; for these are the instruments of human betterment.[2] This, in so far as it is a religion, is a secular religion in which the emphasis is laid on work and service in the interests of the general welfare of humanity.

One other point follows from the repudiation of the doctrine of the Fall. If man has not fallen, there is no angry God to be appeased; and there is accordingly no particular reason why we should not find happiness, perhaps even pleasure, in life. The problem of the dualism of spirit and flesh had been much in Saint-Simon's mind; in his followers, in the Saint-Simonian religion, this line of development led to one of their most famous catchwords. They believed in 'the rehabilitation of the flesh'; the flesh should be no longer mortified and crucified, but should have its claims recognised. And indeed why should we labour for the happiness of mankind, if mankind are not prepared to be happy?

It was, however, over the question of women that the Saint-Simonian Church, like so many other gallant adventures, finally came to grief. Apart from the statement in the *Letters from Geneva*, that women were to be allowed to contribute to the support of the Council of Newton, Saint-Simon had been extraordinarily discreet on the question of women, at least in his writings. Moreover, if one wishes to be pedantically precise, it may be recalled that this particular statement was made by the Deity and not by Saint-Simon. His followers, however, showed less discretion; and presently the question of women became the chief bone of contention in the infant Church. They proclaimed, as one of their leading principles, the 'emancipation of woman.' Now there may be much to be said for the 'rehabilitation of the flesh'; there doubtless always has been, and always will be, much to be said for the 'emancipation of woman.' But, given the infinite possibility of human misunderstanding, they are principles

[1] *De la Réorganisation de la Société Européenne*, Œuvres Choisies, vol. 2, p. 328.
[2] *Doctrine de Saint-Simon, Exposition, Première Année*, p. 70.

which, if only for prudential reasons, ought not to be brought into too close contiguity, especially by an Enfantin.

It is difficult at this distance of time to decide whether Enfantin was a complete charlatan or a sincere but temporarily unbalanced religious enthusiast. It was perhaps permissible to glorify Saint-Simon; after all, he was not merely dead, but he was the presumed founder of the presumed religion. Even so, it seems to be going rather far to assign him 'un rang plus élevé que le fils de Dieu,[1] or to summarise history tersely in the statement that 'Moïse a promis aux hommes la fraternité universelle; Jésus-Christ l'a préparée; Saint-Simon la réalise.'[2]

But Enfantin, being still alive, was in a different case; yet he encouraged in his followers an extravagance of language which far exceeds the bounds of the ludicrous. Fortunately, he retained just enough sense to assure them that he was not God. His influence over his disciples was unlimited and somewhat uncanny. He dressed them in absurd garments of varying shades of blue to denote different grades in the hierarchy, and devised a wonderful symbolic waistcoat, which no one could put on or off without the assistance of one of his fellows, thereby impressing the useful lesson of our mutual dependence on each other. The same lesson had been taught in *The Wealth of Nations* on less picturesque lines. He led his followers into monastic retreat, where, to the disgust of their abandoned wives, they vied with each other in the length of beard they could produce during their period of celibacy. In short, the Saint-Simonian Church under Enfantin became a pantomime, one of the gratuitous entertainments of Paris, almost the song of the drunkards.

In addition to proclaiming the emancipation of women, Enfantin also discovered that the social unit in future was to be, not man, or woman, but man plus woman—a discovery with curious theological repercussions. Whether his teaching on woman and marriage was or was not immoral, is neither here nor there. What is important is that it was generally assumed to be so; and Bazard, the most intelligent of the Saint-Simonians, shared this view. His withdrawal from the Church on this issue led to the great schism. It also led to his ceremonial chair being vacated; for Bazard and Enfantin, as the leaders, had hitherto enjoyed no ordinary chairs. The chair continued to be left vacant; for if Enfantin was *Le Père*, clearly the other chair should be reserved for *La Mère*—but where was she? If we are to pursue our emancipation of women to a logical conclusion, it is clear that God must manifest himself in a female as well as in a male form.

[1] *Doctrine de Saint-Simon, Première Année*. Preliminary letter, p. 59.

[2] *Ibid.* p. 70. It is interesting, even if of no importance, that precisely the same phrase appeared on German picture post-cards round about 1933 with reference to the greatness and the unity of Germany, the ascending stages being marked by Frederick the Great, Bismarck and Hitler.

Indeed, if one is not careful—and the Saint-Simonians were not—the next question that comes up for discussion is that of the sex of God, who obviously ought not to show any partiality in these matters by being one or the other. The vacant chair thus remained as the symbol of the female Messiah who would one day come, and without whose help Enfantin felt his efficiency impaired. In the end Enfantin was prosecuted, along with certain of his followers, partly for teaching immoral doctrine and partly for convening illegal meetings. The trial was a supremely successful show, and even to-day it is possible to read a few pages at a time (here and there) of the volume in which the Saint-Simonians embalmed, for the instruction of posterity, a verbatim report of the proceedings. Enfantin and two others were condemned to a year's imprisonment and a fine of 100 francs. The movement never really recovered from this blow. Meanwhile, the bulk of his followers, having satisfied themselves in some way that the female Messiah was to be found on the banks of the Nile, proceeded to Egypt in order to summon her to fill the vacant chair. They did not find her; but they stayed on to help in the construction of dams. Not the least amazing feature of this fantastic story is that, after the Saint-Simonian Church as an organisation had faded out, almost without exception the leading Saint-Simonians, including Enfantin himself, moved into what Marshall would have called 'the ordinary business of life.' There they succeeded in showing that their youthful eccentricities in no way debarred them from distinguishing themselves in this competitive world. Indeed most of them were amazingly, almost disgustingly, successful. Above all in banking, in engineering and in railway administration, France in the next generation owed an enormous debt to the scattered remnants of the Saint-Simonian Church.

That a successful banker or railway magnate may in his youth have sought for the female Messiah on the banks of the Nile is a startling thought, doubtless calculated to provoke edifying commentaries on the unsearchableness of Man. This curious tale has, however, been glanced at with a different object in view. Saint-Simon and his enormous influence can be understood only if we appreciate the nature of the Saint-Simonian school, which just fell short of transforming their neglected master into a god, and which, though mixing much tinsel, if not dross, with their efforts, nevertheless succeeded in making Saint-Simon one of the great influences of the nineteenth century.

For us the essential point to disentangle is the process whereby the Saint-Simonians transformed the rather tepid, hesitant and attenuated socialism of their Master into a socialism which in places is as aggressive as that of Marx or Proudhon. Let no one seek to master Saint-Simonian literature. The Saint-Simonians were a numerous company of men, and of young men at that, who talked and preached incessantly, and who seem to have printed all that they said. Anyone who allows himself to be sucked into this whirlpool will never emerge again. Fortunately, the essentials of the Saint-Simonian school and of its modification of Saint-Simon can be obtained conveniently in the so-called *Doctrine de Saint-Simon: Exposition, Première Année* (1829). This dates from the period of expansion of the Saint-Simonian school when life, as in the days of the early Fabians, was a long vista of uninterrupted conferences, across which the female Messiah had not yet cast her baleful shadow.

In the first place, the *Doctrine* is somewhat more specific than Saint-Simon had been with regard to the direction in which humanity is marching; or if this statement may seem to do injustice to Saint-Simon, a man ever looking to the future, we may say that his followers sought to give precision and currency to Saint-Simon's ideas by the reiterated use of certain catchwords—the secret of all successful propaganda. The past had represented the 'exploitation of man by man,' as in war and otherwise; this is to be replaced by the harmonious action of man *on* nature. Humanity is gravitating to 'universal association.' This universal association, moreover, is to be given a 'pacific direction.' The love of the works of peace has already succeeded 'the ardour of combat.' [1] Under the influence of Christianity, the activity of mankind has been directed to the 'exploitation of the globe.' [2] With a rather pathetic optimism, it is asserted that the contrast between the past and the future, already described as the contrast between the exploitation of man by man and the exploitation of nature by man, may also be summed up still more briefly as the contrast between war and peace.[3] Even the character of our wars is changing: there are no longer wars of destruction and pillage, nor even for territorial possessions.[4] Such was the confiding and innocent faith of 1829. There then we have one of the most familiar catch-phrases of the Saint-Simonians: the human race is to become one—united in the 'exploitation of the globe by association.'

Meanwhile, how are we equipped for this great task of exploitation? The Saint-Simonians would have answered: 'Very badly.' They agreed with Saint-Simon that each science works on its own; and even if there be academies, 'nulle grande vue n'harmonise leurs travaux.' [5] But indeed what is wrong everywhere is precisely that there is 'nulle grande vue.' Saint-Simon had been apt to grovel before big business and industry, as the only homes of efficiency and competence; his followers, turning to industry, found that here also there was evidence of disorder. Here also everything was turned over to the uncertain chances of *lumières individuelles*. Once more it is a

[1] *Doctrine*, pp. 108–110, p. 144. [2] *Ibid.* p. 157. [3] *Ibid.* p. 162. [4] *Ibid.* p. 174. [5] *Ibid.* p. 83.

world of isolated efforts, in which, as often as not, management falls into incompetent hands.[1] This is the result of *laissez faire*, which assumes—quite fallaciously—that personal interest will always be in harmony with the general interest. *Laissez faire* means that a few happy people triumph—but at the cost of the complete ruin of countless victims. If we are to have the best use of property and of the machinery of production, these must be entrusted to the most competent hands—*aux mains les plus habiles*. But what in fact happens? The accident of birth distributes resources blindly, and if the proprietor is incompetent, or elects to be an *oisif*, there is no remedy.[2]

We have reached the crux of the School's modification of the teaching of the Master. Things cannot be right, so long as the mere chance of birth, operating through the law of inheritance, distributes resources blindly throughout society. In such a world there can be no equality of opportunity, which is the only equality that matters: the competitors do not start fair. For though the Saint-Simonians have conceded that the exploitation of man by man is the mark of the past, in contrast with the association of all men which will prevail in the future, it must not be imagined that exploitation has ceased. It remains—and here the Saint-Simonians stretch out a hand to the Marxians—in the relationship of master and wage-earner, the last transformation that the system of slavery has undergone. The worker is indeed the descendant of the serf. The transaction between master and servant is not a free one. The worker, whose daily sustenance depends on the previous day's work, may exist only on conditions imposed upon him by a small group whom the law has invested with a monopoly of wealth, and to whom it has given the power, even while living in idleness, to dispose of the instruments of production. Consequently the worker is exploited materially, intellectually and morally. Only one revolution remains to be accomplished—that, namely, which will put an end to this exploitation, completely and in all its forms.[3] This is the language of Marx, rather than of the aristocratic Saint-Simon.

The remedy lies in a revision of our ideas regarding property. For even if property be regarded as the basis of the political order, the law regulating property is, nevertheless, subject to modification.[4] Property, inasmuch as it enables some men to live in idleness, must be changed. It has become—and it is Proudhon speaking out of due season—'the privilege of imposing a levy on the labour of others,' *le privilége de lever une prime sur le travail d'autrui*.[5] The obvious solution is of astonishing simplicity, though its repercussions are far-reaching. The evil springs from the fact that by inheritance wealth is handed on within the family.[6] It is therefore only necessary to

[1] *Doctrine*, pp. 88–89.
[2] *Ibid.* pp. 91–92.
[3] *Ibid.* pp, 174–177.
[4] *Ibid.* p. 179.
[5] *Ibid.* p. 182.
[6] *Ibid.* p. 179.

abolish inheritance and transfer to the State, ' devenu Association des travailleurs,' the right of succession. It is carefully explained that this does not mean community of goods ; nor does it mean equality. It does mean that the privileges of birth will at last be completely extirpated, and that henceforth capacity and work will be the sole titles to wealth.[1]

It will be seen how the Saint-Simonians, by an apparently slight alteration of the Saint-Simonian structure, have given the whole of the Master's doctrine an entirely revolutionary significance. Saint-Simon had asserted that equality was to be the mark of the new industrial age: he was right. In consequence, he proclaimed the abolition of all privileges: he did well. But on the question of property and the greatest of all privileges which is to be found in inheritance, the trumpet had given forth a very uncertain sound. In essence, the Saint-Simonian contribution was to insist that this privilege too must go: indeed, they made it the cardinal point of their programme.

The State, even if it is disguised as the ' Association des travailleurs,' thus becomes every man's heir ; and, assuming that the State rises to its task, this universal heir will be committed to a complete scheme of State socialism. For obviously, in the course of little over a generation, it will own everything—or as near everything as makes no difference. In the vision of the Saint-Simonian school there was to be here a social institution which would be the depository of all the instruments of production, which would preside over that part of the exploitation of the globe which fell within its province, and which would direct production. In short, it would be possible to organise industry, and obtain that *grande vue* which was the dream of Saint-Simon and his disciples alike.[2]

Enough has been said in the foregoing pages to indicate the nature of the influence exercised by Saint-Simon, directly and through his school. He was the forerunner of Comte and of positivism ; he was the apostle of big business combined with equal opportunity ; at times almost a forerunner of ' technocracy ' ; a believer in a business government, preferably with government replaced by administration—in that rather cryptic phrase. By their modest addition, the Saint-Simonians took a short cut to a complete system of State socialism. On one point, however, in order to avoid any misapprehension, a further word may be allowed. While insisting on equality of opportunity, the whole Saint-Simonian school set its countenance rigidly against any suggestion of equality in fact—the ' real ' equality desired by Babeuf. Indeed, they almost boasted of their belief in the natural inequality of men ; and (with some justification) regarded this as the basis of association, and as an indispensable condition of the social

[1] *Doctrine*, p. 187. [2] *Ibid.* p. 193.

order.[1] It is, they would have said, precisely because men are unequal and unlike that you can dovetail them together. So also, they repudiated suggestions of equality of reward. Men were, in their familiar formula, to be placed according to their capacity, and rewarded according to their works. Indeed the idea of a hierarchy is almost too dear to the hearts of the Saint-Simonians. In the new State, become the universal heir, the social fund is to be exploited not merely by association, but *hiérarchiquement*—which somehow sounds a barbarous word. In looking to the future, what the Saint-Simonians hope to attain is 'Order,' which is expanded to mean 'la hiérarchie la plus unitaire, la plus ferme.'[2] We seem to be trembling on the brink of the totalitarian State. Moreover, our uneasy feeling is somewhat accentuated by the writer of the introduction to the *Doctrine de Saint-Simon* who, in a passage aiming at eloquence, exclaims: 'Partisans de *l'égalité* ! Saint-Simon vous dit que les hommes sont *inégaux*. . . . Défenseurs de la *Liberté* ! Saint-Simon vous dit que vous aurez des *chefs*'; and he goes on to add that those whom he is addressing may have desired in the past to get rid of detested masters, nevertheless they never said, 'plus de guides pour l'humanité ! plus de grands hommes !'[3] Saint-Simon, groping for spiritual leadership, for torches and *lumières*; the Saint-Simonians, demanding of the future the 'most unitary hierarchy'; Carlyle, in search of the hero and extolling hero-worship—what is all this but the *Führerprinzip* of latter days ? Perhaps we have grown rather tired of the *Führerprinzip* and of all its works, and of the 'qualities of leadership' which the aspiring young are sometimes expected to reveal in the course of an oral examination. For the trouble about the *Führerprinzip* is that while it postulates a Leader, it equally postulates that all the rest shall be prepared to be led or misled as the case may be, and that they will with lamblike simplicity walk up any garden path they may be invited to enter. And there is this further evil consequence that the cult of leadership may be, and is, invoked to relieve the flock from all moral responsibility for what they may have done in too faithfully treading, in simplicity or in cowardice, in the Leader's footsteps. 'As for these sheep, what have they done ?' The question derives from the Psalmist David in one of his less ecstatic moments; but with variation in intonation and application, it recurs throughout history whenever the *Führerprinzip* has succeeded in landing its victims in a mess. Enough, however, at this stage to note

[1] The most illuminating statement on this point is contained in the letter addressed by Enfantin and Bazard to the President of the Chamber of Deputies, October 1, 1830. See note at end of chapter.

[2] *Doctrine*, p. 218.

[3] The sentence which follows is extremely illuminating regarding the outlook of the Saint-Simonians generally: 'Vous n'avez pas voulu comprimer les cœurs, courber les intelligences, écraser les forces, sous le joug pesant, sous l'absurde niveau de l'ÉGALITÉ (*ibid.* pp. 55–56). So much for Babeuf.

that, on one side, Saint-Simon and the Saint-Simonians alike, in their love of order, of hierarchy and of leadership, are at the roots of the tradition that blossoms in the full enunciation of the *Führerprinzip*.

NOTE.

One of the most important documents in Saint-Simonian literature is the letter which Enfantin and Bazard addressed jointly to the President of the Chamber of Deputies on 1st October, 1830. In a debate in the Chamber reference had been made to the Saint-Simonians, attributing to them advocacy of community of goods and the enunciation of immoral doctrines on the question of women. The letter, which is obviously the work of Bazard, contains one of the most concise statements of what the Saint-Simonians regarded as their essential tenets, and an extract from this document may be a useful addition to the foregoing chapter.

'Le système de la communauté des biens s'entend universellement du partage *égal* entre tous les membres de la Société, soit du fonds lui-même de la production, soit des fruits du travail de tous.

'Les Saint-Simoniens repoussent ce partage égal de la propriété, qui constituerait à leurs yeux une violence plus grande, une injustice plus révoltante que le partage inégal qui s'est effectué primitivement par la force des armes, par la conquête :

'Car ils croient a l'INÉGALITÉ *naturelle* des hommes, et regardent cette inégalité comme la base même de l'association, comme la condition indispensable de l'ORDRE social.

'Ils repoussent le système de la communauté des biens ; car cette communauté serait une violation manifeste de la première de toutes les lois morales qu'ils ont reçu mission d'enseigner, et qui veut qu'à l'avenir *chacun soit placé selon sa capacité, et rétribué selon ses œuvres.*

'Mais en vertu de cette loi, ils demandent l'abolition de tous les priviléges de la naissance *sans exception*, et par conséquent la destruction de l'HÉRITAGE, le plus grand de tous ces priviléges, celui qui les comprend tous aujourd'hui, et dont l'effet est de laisser au *hasard* la répartition des avantages sociaux, parmi le petit nombre de ceux qui peuvent y pretendre, et de condamner la classe la plus nombreuse à la *dépravation*, à l'*ignorance*, à la *misère.*

'Ils demandent que tous les instrumens du travail, les terres et les capitaux, qui forment aujourd'hui le fonds morcelé des propriétés particulières, soient réunis en un fonds social, et que ce fonds soit exploité par *association* et HIÉRARCHIQUEMENT, de manière à ce que la tâche de chacun soit l'expression de sa *capacité*, et sa richesse le mesure de ses *œuvres.*

'Les Saint-Simoniens ne viennent porter atteinte à la constitution de la propriété qu'en tant qu'elle consacre, pour quelques uns, le privilége impie de l'OISIVETÉ, c'est-à-dire celui de vivre du travail d'autrui ; qu'en tant qu'elle abandonne au *hasard de la naissance* le classement social des individus.'

CHAPTER VII

CHARLES FOURIER

CHARLES FOURIER occupies a singular position among the fathers of socialism ; indeed, viewed from any angle, he is a unique and enigmatical phenomenon. He was born in Besançon in 1772, the son of a linen-draper in reasonably easy circumstances. On leaving school, he travelled for a time, somewhat extensively, for various firms, visiting Belgium, Germany and Holland. On his father's death, he inherited sufficient to enable him to start business in Lyons. In the troubles of 1793, Lyons, revolting against the Convention, was bombarded. Fourier narrowly escaped being shot, and he did lose his entire fortune. Thereafter for two years he served, an unwilling soldier, in the army. During the remainder of his life, nothing happened to Fourier, not even marriage. He travelled for various firms ; he was a clerk ; he served commerce intermittently, but always on the lowest rung of the ladder. On the strength of an exiguous legacy, at times he did nothing ; and he wrote a number of extraordinary books in which he said the same things over and over again. He floated about between modest private hotels and furnished apartments, and in this depressing environment he died in 1837, being then 65 years of age.

Such is the outline. Yet two reasonably authenticated incidents deserve mention for their influence on the development of his mind. When a boy in his father's shop—indeed at the age of five, it is said—he received correction from his father for revealing to a customer some petty trick in the retail business ; and the infant Fourier, realising that commerce was built on deceit, swore, like the infant Hannibal, that he would destroy the great enemy, which in this case was commerce. He complained that he was taught to tell the truth in church, and to tell lies in his father's shop. References to this 'Hannibal oath' occur throughout the literature of Fourier. Later, having attained man's estate and being at Marseilles, it was his duty to assist at dead of night in discharging into the harbour a cargo of rice, which the owners had allowed to spoil in expectation of a rise in price. Fourier, observing the stealthy destruction of what had once been food, and thinking of the hungry men sleeping uneasily all around, realised anew the shortcomings of civilisation and of commerce alike, and found occasion to renew his 'Hannibal oath.' Fourier did not succeed in destroying commerce ; on the contrary, he spent a large part of his life as one of the least of its bondsmen. But the two legends are none the less significant.

As to the man himself, Fourier is almost the perfect example of

G*

furtive insignificance. Indeed he is worse than that. His was the insignificance, the timidity, the absurdity which inevitably provoke a smile even in recollection. An apostle of chaotic liberty, he nevertheless had a mania for orderliness, and was never happy unless things could be docketed and arranged in series. Even when he gained disciples, he never could be prevailed upon to speak, and throughout life had a great gift of silence. Old maidish in his habits, he had two passions, one for cats and the other for flowers. Perhaps music should be added as a third: he never could resist the impulse to march behind the band. Only very moderately educated in his youth, he belongs to the race of authors who have no desire to know what others have thought or said. Despite his modesty, he has accordingly no hesitation in proclaiming himself the first person for two thousand years to illumine the world's darkness. In a phrase which should give comfort to all, Emile Faguet has said of him that he has the disadvantages of ignorance which are great, and the advantages of ignorance which are enormous. 'Moi seul' and 'moi le premier' are recurrent motives in the writings of this unheroic commercial traveller who was cast for the part of Timorous rather than of Great-Heart. Take, as an example at random, one resonant blast of his goose-quill;

> Moi seul j'aurai confondu vingt siècles d'imbécillité politique; et c'est à moi seul que les générations présentes et futures devront l'initiative de leur immense bonheur. Avant moi l'humanité a perdu plusieurs mille ans à lutter follement contre la nature; moi le premier . . .

and so on, rising to one of his few recurrent tags: 'Exegi monumentum aere perennius.' [1]

Fourier, moreover, has a childish, rather than a childlike, faith in God and the goodness of God. Indeed, in some respects, Fourier's 'theology,' to give it a somewhat pretentious name, provides the foundation-stone of all his theories, and will require to be noticed in somewhat greater detail presently. Lastly, and it is the point which distinguishes him from the rest of mankind, Fourier was blessed or cursed with a most riotous and unpruned imagination, so unrestrained indeed that it is doubtful how far he could have passed any of the ordinary tests of sanity. There is nothing which his disordered imagination cannot vividly conceive, either at the foundation of the world or in the days of Harmony yet to be realised, and he writes it all

[1] Œuvres Complètes, vol. 1, p. 285. The so-called Œuvres Complètes of Fourier extend to six large volumes. Vol. 1 comprises the *Théorie des Quatre Mouvemens*; vols. 2–5 are given up comprehensively to the *Théorie de l'Unité Universelle*, some of which was originally published under another title; vol. 6 contains *Le Nouveau Monde Industriel et Sociétaire*. The Œuvres Complètes (published between 1841 and 1845) are, however, anything but complete. Apart from some substantial works, there are quite a number of other volumes drawn from his manuscripts and articles. The most important omission from the Complete Works, and the only one to which it will be necessary to refer here, is *La Fausse Industrie*. Unless otherwise indicated, references are to the six volumes of the Complete Works.

down in the minutest detail, with the calm assurance of a perpetual private secretary to Providence from whom nothing has been concealed. It would perhaps be unjust to suggest that no writer, living or dead, has ever produced a larger volume of outrageous nonsense than has Fourier. A much subtler diagnosis is required. In him the form is always much more grotesque than the substance; but undeniably he clothes all he has to say in a fantasy and an imagery which are so charged with the ludicrous that Fourier is scarcely to be read without, intermittently, loud guffaws of uproarious and irreverent laughter. Moreover, everything about Fourier is bizarre. A reader not accustomed to such things may be surprised to find a 'Postface' at the end of a volume, or to be confronted with an 'extroduction,' a 'postienne' or a 'citerlogue.' The diatonic scale turns up in unexpected places; there are strange symbols, K's, X's, and Y's, now lying on their back, now standing upside down. In at least one case (*La Fausse Industrie*), the pagination would defy an army of detectives to unravel. Fourier may at times be a hilarious farce: at times he is also an impenetrable mystification. Let no one, approaching Fourier, imagine that he is taking up a volume marked by the decorum, the austerity and the conventionality of John Stuart Mill.

Before attempting to give a more or less orderly account of that chaos that is Charles Fourier, it may be permissible to state briefly wherein lies his significance, and what is his place in the unfolding of socialist doctrine. Stated somewhat summarily, the importance of Fourier lies in the fact that, like Saint-Simon, he is a link, and a very interesting link, between the eighteenth and the nineteenth centuries. They are indeed very different links, though they have this in common, that these two fathers of socialism are not in essence particularly socialistic; they are disfigured by strangely conservative features which do not appear in the child. They both cling to property; they are alike devotees of inequality. The essence of Fourier is that, as he looked round the world, he saw that everything was wrong, not merely a few things here and there, but the whole scheme of things. It was in a sense civilisation itself that was wrong—civilisation with all its attendant conventions and consequences. In this respect he is an echo, perhaps a caricaturing echo, of that greater voice from the eighteenth century, of Jean Jacques Rousseau, who also found that somehow the human race had taken the wrong turning. And if both found that our civilisation was a poor thing, a whited sepulchre, there is this to be said for the insignificant Fourier, as against his mightier predecessor, that he was at least constructive. Rousseau is after all little more than a wail of despair, an ineffective wringing of hands. But Fourier knew, with the utmost precision and definiteness he knew, what he wanted and what had to be done, and how in short the world could be put right in the brief space of two years. It is only necessary to abandon Morality, that evil legacy of civilisation, and to listen to our natural impulses, and we should straightway overcome all the trickery, the deceits, the hypocrisy, the divided interests, the parasitism which is what civilisation is. We shall in fact have established Harmony, and Harmony is the co-operation of men who sing at their work. Nothing could be simpler. It only requires a capitalist, and not even a very big one, to give the thing a start, and the rest is as easy as falling off a house.

In a sense Fourier's religion provides the starting-point of all his observations and of all his criticisms. It pervades all his thoughts, and it will constantly recur in almost every paragraph of this chapter; for this reason it may be as well to seek at the outset the dominant *idées mères* of Fourier on this subject. The old truth that man created God in his own image, that 'thou thoughtest I was altogether such an one as thyself,' is nowhere more startingly illustrated than in the case of Fourier. That God is good, that God has done well in all that he has done, that he has done nothing without a meaning and a purpose, sum up in general terms the essence of Fourier's religion; but with the acute logic of a somewhat unbalanced mind, he pushes this body of doctrine to conclusions which are much less orthodox than are usually drawn from these premises. He is severe on those who 'half believe' in God.[1] Belief in the goodness of God implies belief in the goodness of all that God has done; it is therefore inconsistent with a belief that a good God could make man with evil impulses and passions against which men have to wage incessant war. This, which is the line of the moralist and the theologian, is to establish war between God and man; indeed it is to set God at war with himself. We should seek for the laws of God in the impulses that come from God[2]; he foresaw, for example, that we should wish to eat three times a day. Those who write facetiously about 'la galanterie et la gourmandise' are ignorant of the importance which God attaches to our pleasures; for it is by 'Attraction'—by pleasure—and not by constraint, that God governs the universe. It is thus that he governs planets and insects; it is thus that he intended to govern Man.

Moreover, in creating this unhappy world of ours, God was not engaged, as Burns would have put it, in trying out his 'prentice hand.' He has created milliards of globes before ours, and has thus acquired vast experience 'pendant l'Eternité passée.'[3] Elsewhere, even more patronisingly, he explains that God has had ample time to learn by experience in creating men in milliards of other worlds. In short, he knew what he was doing when he made men as they are; and instead of correcting the work of God, we should endeavour to find out how he meant his works to be used.[4]

[1] Vol. 1, p. 29.
[2] *Fausse Industrie*, p. G. 8.
[3] Vol. 3, pp. 112–114.
[4] Vol. 3, p. 272.

And, primarily, God's intentions were that we should enjoy ourselves. Not only so, it would be an insult to God to expect him to provide merely mediocre pleasures.[1] To ask merely for our daily bread—*le misérable pain*, says Fourier, who never could abide bread—is to misconceive the magnanimity of God. In a phrase which comes with a certain shock by reason of its reversal of Christian ideas,[2] 'Dieu nous doit beaucoup, puisqu'il peut beaucoup'; he owes us infinite happiness in this life and in the life to come. It is God who is *our* debtor. He hath made us, and not we ourselves; in fact (though Fourier does not stress the point) we were not consulted. He gave us a yearning for happiness; and as (by definition) his power is infinite, he owes us happiness pressed down and running over, a perpetual and unconditional pouring out of a blessing from the windows of heaven, so that there shall not be room enough to receive it.

Fourier, as has been hinted above, presents his criticisms of life and his social theories in a fantastic and indeed grotesque framework. It would be easy, by appropriate selections, to present him as a figure of farce and low comedy; but it would probably be equally wrong, again by appropriately different selections, to present him as a sober-minded and austere critic, adding his ponderous brick of thought to the construction of the socialist edifice. Many writers in their references to Fourier give the reader no hint, or but the merest hint, that Fourier was most emphatically not as other men: indeed in some respects he is a unique phenomenon in the world's literature. This designedly tactful drawing of a veil over Fourier's peculiarities is mistaken, if only because it gives a wrong and one-sided view of the man he was. After all, there is nothing to be ashamed of in being slightly deranged. For all we know, it may be the condition of the bulk of humanity: it all depends on the standards we choose to apply. But in the case of Fourier, there is this further most decisive reason against suppressing any acknowledgment of his eccentricities that his sanity and his apparent deviations from normal sanity are strangely intermingled. Indeed his whole criticism of civilisation to a certain extent postulates as a background his fantastic cosmogony and his views regarding the stages through which humanity must pass.

With this semi-apology for an apparent departure from accustomed austerity, we may endeavour to illustrate some of the more unexpected ideas which may surprise a reader embarking, unwarned, upon the turbulent waters of Fourier. Most intimately interwoven with the essence of his thought are his theories regarding the Cosmos. This

[1] Vol. 1, p. 272.

[2] For example, very emphatically and characteristically, in Karl Barth: 'The creation is under a debt of gratitude to God' (*The Knowledge of God and the Service of God*, p. 38). Even viewed exclusively as a theological problem, the answer obviously should depend, in part, on how we are predestined to spend eternity.

world has been granted a life of 80,000 years ; there are 40,000 of ascending vibrations and 40,000 of descending vibrations. The arithmetic may seem weak, since there is also a period of 8,000 years of complete happiness, the *Apogée du Bonheur*.[1] Doubtless this minor discrepancy is covered by Fourier's general reservation that everything he says is subject to an exception of an eighth or a ninth. In all there are 32 periods, 16 in the upward and 16 in the downward ladder. We are at present in the fifth of the first eight stages, having passed through what Fourier calls the *Sectes Confuses*, *Sauvagerie*, *Patriarchat* and *Barbarie*. Ahead of us lies *Garantisme*, a stage in which human rights will be effectively guaranteed to us ; at times, however, it is rather suggested that we may by-pass Garantisme. These eight stages take up 5,000 years, and we shall then find ourselves in Harmony—indeed more and more delirious grades of Harmony, for 35,000 years. Thereafter for 8,000 years we shall have that lofty table-land of perfect bliss, after which the world will go downhill again through precisely the same stages in the inverse order ; and at the end, if any of us are left, we shall be transported to another planet.

It is when we approach Harmony that things will begin to hum. A Northern Crown (after the manner of Saturn's rings) will encircle the Pole, shedding a beneficent aromatic dew on the earth. The sea will cease to be briny, and, greatest of delights, will be transformed into lemonade, for which unsatisfying beverage Fourier seems to have had a marked partiality. Six moons of a new and superior quality will replace our present inefficient satellite. A new race of animals will emerge. In place of the lion, there will be the anti-lion, all that a lion is not, docile and serviceable ; there will be anti-wolves and anti-bears, and a whole race of really nice beasts. If things are only taken in hand at once, telescoping various stages, the anti-bug may be looked for in 1829, along with the anti-rat. This is indeed good news for ' le beau Paris, si richement meublé de punaises,' of which incidentally there are 42 varieties.[2] Our argosies, knitting land to land, will be drawn by anti-whales. After these marvels, it is perhaps rather a disappointment to know that we shall then live only 144 years, of which, however, 120 will be spent in the active exercise of love.[3]

It is perhaps a corollary to this lively interest in the history of the globe that Fourier is also so much concerned with the stars and the planets, which in so many ways influence our lives now and hereafter.

[1] Vol. 1, p. 50. The reader who has the option should read the first volume in the original edition of 1808 when it appeared anonymously as *Théorie des Quatre Mouvemens et des Destinées Générales*, and was professedly published in Leipzig, for the sufficient reason that it had, of course, no connection with Leipzig. In particular, the Chart showing the various phases of cosmic history is a wonderful thing to gaze at in the ' Leipzig ' edition, whereas in the Complete Works it is merely a cnart.

[1] Vol. 6, pp. 448–449. [3] Vol. 3, p. 322.

The stars and planets are animated beings like ourselves, only perhaps more so. They also have their passions, and from their passions spring other stars and planets, but also plants and animals. The planets seem to be androgynous, like plants self-contained for purposes of reproduction; but they also have intercourse with other planets. Unless Fourier is more confused than usual, the Aurora Borealis merely betokens that the Earth is holding out lonely hands of love to Venus. Fourier tabulates at considerable length the various animals and plants we owe to Jupiter, the Sun, Venus and so on. The death of Phoebe (otherwise known as the Moon) plays a large part in this astronomical fantasy. Phoebe, whom he rather rudely calls a *cadavre blafard*, died of a putrid fever, contracted from the Earth fifty years before the Flood: it was indeed the death of Phoebe that caused the Flood. The absence of her contribution to the last creation caused some strange omissions in the animals and plants we ought to have had. In particular, the world has been the poorer by the absence of a very special gooseberry, of which it was robbed by the untimely decease of Phoebe. The discriminating reader will have begun to discern dimly how the anti-lion and the anti-bug are to be generated: another creation, under more favourable conditions and therefore consisting predominantly of good beasts, is pending, and will mark the transition to Harmony.[1]

Fourier's concern for human happiness is not limited to what happens in this transitory life. He believes not merely in immortality; he believes also in metempsychosis. We shall return again and again, and keep on returning; and that is one reason why we should be so intensely interested in what is going to happen. It is important that this should be a world worth returning to. On all this, Fourier is as extensively and as exactly informed as he is regarding the death of Phoebe. He knows exactly how long we shall be away, when and how we shall return. He knows how what we do now influences the lives of those waiting to come back, and again it is all told with a wealth of ludicrous detail which may not be so exciting as his account of the passionate drama of the love affairs of the planets, but is equally full of information which, as the reviewers say, is not readily available elsewhere.

Enough perhaps of the fantastic side of Fourier; yet perhaps so much is necessary, firstly because these extravagances may not be dismissed as idle weeds that grow in the sustaining corn; they are, as has been suggested above, an integral part of Fourier; and secondly, because it is as well that the reader should know in advance that there

[1] Fourier's astronomy (if this is astronomy) is, like everything else he concerns himself with, scattered throughout all his works, but it will be found in a peculiarly clotted and concentrated form in a note in vol. 4 of the Complete Works, pp, 241–268. Probably nowhere else in literature is it possible to point to so much that is surprising, compacted in the space of 28 pages.

are moments of wild surprise in the perusal of our author.[1] Yet it will be conceded that a writer with pretensions to seriousness who buries his message under such a superstructure of airy imaginings, imposes upon himself a very considerable handicap. Discarding, so far as one may, these outpourings of an unduly exuberant imagination, is it possible to detach the essentials of Fourier, and restate them, as they might have been stated by John Stuart Mill ?

In rationalising Fourier, one may, in the first place, distinguish between a critical and destructive exposition of what is, and a constructive part designed to produce a happier world. On the former aspect —and to a large extent it explains the significance and the influence of Fourier—there never has been a more acute, a more uncompromising and unsparing critic of civilisation ; his criticism is doubtless expressed with a Fourieresque exaggeration and bizarrerie, yet there are few honest men who can read Fourier without being made at times slightly uncomfortable, just as the virtuous may be disconcerted by the innocent prattling of a child. To borrow the words of Polonius, referring to another case where the question of sanity has been much debated, Fourier's barbs have a happiness that often madness hits on, which reason and sanity could not so prosperously be delivered of.

As Fourier sees this world, it is not a question of things here and there being wrong: it is the whole scheme of things that stands condemned. In civilisation, every human relationship is warped by deceit, intrigue and falsehood. Repeatedly and rather plaintively, with the hurt cry of a disillusioned child, he laments that virtue and truth, which ought to lead to prosperity and wealth, in fact lead merely to poverty and disgrace. Virtue is less lucrative than vice ; in this world you will get nowhere if you rely on *la Vérité*. If you want to succeed, you must swindle your way to success. *La fourberie au plus haut degré* [2]—there you find the chief mark of civilisation. The least desirable elements always come out on the top ; honesty and integrity merely provide a short-cut to failure.

Is it necessary to say anything with regard to marriage, that bulwark of civilisation ? Perhaps it would be wiser to refer the curious reader to the pages of Fourier for enlightenment. On this school of hypocrisy and deceit, Godwin's views are tepid and insipid compared to those of Fourier, who, at any moment, in contrast to the mediaeval ' quinze

[1] While there is almost nothing that the reader may not find in Fourier, he should perhaps be warned that he will *not* find one pleasing fiction frequently attributed to him. It was for long currently believed that he had foretold that men would in the happy future be equipped with long tails with an eye on the tip. It would doubtless be a useful endowment for a harassed housewife, tidying an untidy cupboard ; but the fiction seems to spring from malicious satire rather than from the authentic text of Fourier.

[2] Vol. 1, p. 128.

joies de mariage,' will provide the reader with a complete ' Gamme des disgrâces de l'état conjugal.'[1] Fundamentally, what is wrong here is that ' la fidélité perpétuelle en amour est contraire à la nature humaine'; and an institution resting on a wholly contrary false assumption must necessarily engender hypocrisy and falsehood. Fourier, holding the views he did, showed wisdom in dying a bachelor.

But to get back to safer ground and the items of the indictment against civilisation, it is further to be observed that civilisation rests on the mutual enmity of each against all, so that each indeed is forced by his own interests to desire the misfortunes of all the rest. In short, we each make our living out of the mishaps that befall our neighbours. On this characteristic point, it may, however, be as well to quote the words of Fourier:

> Every person engaged in an industry is at war with the mass, and malevolent toward it from personal interest. A physician wishes his fellow citizens good, genuine cases of fevers, and an attorney good lawsuits in every family. An architect has need of a good conflagration which should reduce a quarter of the city to ashes, and a glazier desires a good hailstorm which should break all the panes of glass. A tailor, a shoemaker, wishes the public to use only poorly-dyed stuffs and shoes made of bad leather, so that a triple amount may be consumed—for the benefit of trade; that is their refrain. A court of justice regards it as opportune that France continues to commit a hundred and twenty thousand crimes and actionable offences, that number being necessary to maintain the criminal courts. It is thus that in civilised industry every individual is in intentional war against the mass.[2]

In civilisation, however, we are not only natural enemies of each other; if we be candid, we will admit that most of us are parasites. Take four men at random, and probably three are doing useless work that would not need to be done in a sane world. We set four children to look after five cows; and even so the grain is nibbled. Fourier, with his usual gusto, gives an appalling list of twelve classes of parasites, and few there be who escape his net. There are first of all three classes of domestic parasites which in all conscience are sufficiently sweeping. There are three-fourths of the women in the cities, and a half of the women in the country; there are likewise three-fourths of the children, condemned as entirely useless in the towns and of negligible use in the country; there are three-fourths of household domestics. Passing to social parasites, at one sweep there are the armies of the land and sea; there are the legions of administration (now known as the hordes of civil servants); half the manufactures are in effect

[1] Vol. 4, p. 69.

[2] Vol. 6, pp. 33–34 (as translated in *Selections from the Works of Fourier*, Social Science Series). After the manner of Fourier, the same passage occurs elsewhere (vol. 2, Part II, pp. 38–39), with some variations in the examples of our divided interests: the soldier wishes for a good war, in order to secure promotion by the slaughter of half his comrades; the parson wishes ' de bon morts,' *i.e.* funerals at 1000 francs a head; the wine-merchant wishes ' bonnes grêles sur les vendanges et bonnes gelées sur les bourgeons.'

useless; nine-tenths of merchants no better. And so we advance through absenteeism, the devotees of St. Monday, a most ruinous saint who is fêted fifty-two days in the year, and workers who lean on their spades to see a cat pass, ending with what he calls the seceders, a miscellaneous collection of sharpers, vagrants and beggars—now more politely called the unsocial elements.[1]

Moreover, whatever we do, we do inefficiently. Everywhere civilisation is marked by *gaspillages*. The root evil on this side is our industrial incoherence. Industry, in his favourite word, is *morcelée*; it ought to be *combinée*. When Fourier, with a lordly sweep, consigns three-fourths of all women to a status of uselessness, he is not in any way denying the worth of women, or underestimating their afflictions. Anything but: Fourier is in fact almost the first, as he is certainly the most valiant, defender of Women's Cause. But he is maddened by the sight of 300 women, in 300 little houses, lighting 300 little fires, and cooking 300 little dinners in 300 little pots for 300 little men returning from their work; when three or four women, with the help of one large pot and one large fire, could produce better results. Possibly, as he says, three families could not be associated successfully; but 300 could. His illustrations, it is true, chiefly concern domestic arrangements and agriculture; he has little to say of industry, which indeed he habitually regarded with a certain repugnance. On the main point, however, he is clear: it takes 40 civilised people to do the work of five Harmonians, because of our absurd addiction to small units, because we refuse to associate.

If such be the views of Fourier with regard to the harmless necessary housewife, he cannot, in view of his youthful Hannibal oath, be expected to be tolerant of commerce. He quotes with approval the saying of St. Chrysostom that a merchant cannot be agreeable to God: 'accordingly merchants are excluded from the Kingdom of Heaven, although the elect of all other professions are admitted, even a lawyer in the case of Saint-Ives.' In a sense commerce represents in an extreme form the vices which mark civilisation; but apart from this general ground, it is condemned by Fourier in the main for two reasons which, however, intermingle. In the first place, commerce is the natural home of deceit and falsehood. What is commerce, he asks? The answer is: 'C'est le mensonge avec tout son attirail, banqueroute, agiotage, usure et fourberies de toute espèce.' [2] Commerce, in a state of complete liberty, is a sewer of infamy, a *cloaque d'infamies*. It is a sphere of life from which truth is banished. In antiquity merchants were called little thieves, but they are no longer 'des petits voleurs.' [3] In one of his marvellous synoptic tables, Fourier arranges the crimes of commerce under 36 headings, over which the leisurely reader may

[1] Vol. 4, pp. 173–179. [2] Vol. 1, p. 339.
[3] Vol. 3, p. 199–202.

ponder awestruck.[1] Moreover, the misdeeds of commerce operate in the direction of a universal worsening of the conditions of life:

> One would have augured a reform of this sink of corruption, of this inept mechanism, which, by the concurrence of sixty malevolent characteristics,—makes industry a trap for the nations, and aggravates at once their wretchedness and their depravity. It is maintained that people are not more deceitful than they were formerly; nevertheless one could, half a century ago, obtain at a reasonable rate goods of a durable colour, and natural foods; to-day adulteration, knavery, prevail everywhere. The cultivator has become as great a defrauder as the merchant used to be. Dairy products, oils, wines, brandy, sugar, coffee, flour, everything is shamelessly debased. The masses can no longer procure natural foods; only slow poisons are sold them, such progress has the spirit of commerce made even in the smallest villages.[2]

This, though it savours somewhat of the folly of saying that the former times were better than these, against which we have been officially warned, is sufficiently clear. Commerce, leading to cut-throat competition and to *la manie d'écraser*, is a provocation to all the vices. Moreover, the frauds and other crimes of commerce are contagious.[3]

The second line of criticism is that commerce has usurped a place in society to which it is not entitled. Commerce should be subordinate; freedom of commerce should be subject to restrictions according to the needs of the social body.[4] On the contrary, the merchant has become an industrial pirate, living at the expense of the manufacturer and producer, whose servant he ought to be. Indeed, the mercantile power tends to pass beyond this and to keep the governments themselves in tutelage.[5] Perhaps, however, enough has been said to indicate the nature of Fourier's criticism of civilisation. We are all natural enemies, prospering on, and praying for, each other's misfortunes; most of us are parasites. Even those of us who do anything, do it badly. In different ways, marriage and commerce are fruitful nurseries of all the vices of hypocrisy and deceit. Civilisation, in short, is an endless morass of mess, inefficiency, swindling and lying—a sewer in which every human relationship is poisoned and warped.

Such is the diagnosis; and it will be conceded that if Fourier is even, as the saying is, substantially correct, it would be as well to seek for a remedy. As it happens, the remedy is of an astonishing simplicity. It is to put your trust in God and not in men, least of all in philosophers and theologians; it is to believe with childish simplicity in the goodness of God, and abolish the evil thing we call Morality. We are confronted once more, it will be observed, with Fourier's

[1] Vol. 3, p. 219.
[2] Vol. 6, p. 43 (as translated in *Selections from the Works of Fourier*).
[3] Vol. 1, p. 377; *Fausse Industrie*, pp. 535–536.
[4] Vol. 1, p. 359.
[5] Vol. 3, pp. 204, 217.

religion, from which indeed Fourier himself seldom escapes for more than a few pages, and of which something has already been said in anticipation. Not always without producing an absurd effect, Fourier likes to compare himself with Newton—sometimes, indeed, to Newton's disadvantage. Newton discovered the Law of Attraction; but, be it added, he confined himself to the useless side which ministers to mere curiosity. For in what way are we advantaged if we do know the weight of each of the planets?[1] Fourier regarded himself as the Newton of the spiritual and moral world. The great Law of Attraction governs the planets: so also God, the Governor of the Universe, governs men by attraction. Men may rely on compulsion and restraint; but not God. If he had meant to constrain us, he would have created a race of giants with the object of bullying us. He has, on the contrary, elected to give us attraction and repulsion impelling us in various directions, and he has distributed these in such proportions as are adequate for the achievement of his designs. This 'attraction' is, in the hands of God, a magic ring, transforming into pleasures functions which are in themselves repugnant. What could be more repugnant than the care of an infant—puking and muling, and worse? But God transforms this *soin si déplaisant* into a pleasure by giving the mother *attraction passionnée pour ces travaux immondes*.[2] This also explains the somewhat cryptic statement inscribed on Fourier's tombstone as a convenient summary of his gospel: 'Les Attractions sont proportionelles aux Destinées.' God, the great economist, distributes attractions just in the amount required to enable (and compel) us to fulfil our destined task.

There then, in Fourier's own view, is his great discovery, placing him, if anything, slightly above Newton. The Law of Attraction is manifested in the play of the human passions, by which we are impelled in one direction or another. All that is required is that we should respond to these promptings, that we should in fact obey this law of passional attraction. Humanity has lost two thousand years, because it has been on a false scent, blinded and misled by philosophers. Fourier has very decided opinions about philosophers. They are sophists, a more hateful race of men, if that be possible, even than merchants. For it is under their malign influence that men have plagued themselves with ideas of morality and of duties. If God be good, and if he implanted these passions in our hearts, he meant us to follow these passions. He does not despise the works of his hands. Humanity has been taught that these passions are things of evil, to be fought against and subdued. But this is a delusion. Fourier's premises will not allow him to admit that God could spoil his own work and be at enmity with himself.

[1] Vol. 6, p. 156.
[2] Vol. 3, p. 246.

Would that your Causer, ere knoll your knell
For this riot of passion, might deign to tell
Why, since It made you
Good in the germ,
It sent a worm,
To madden Its handiwork, when It might well
Not have assayed you.

Thus Thomas Hardy, facing the same problem, as he contemplates the portrait of a woman about to be hanged—speaking, Fourier would say, like a sophist in his assumption that God could mar what he had made, and that he could lay snares and gins for his creatures.[1] There is no passion that does not come from God, and there is therefore not one, not a single one—and Fourier's voice seems to rise—which is not good. It is neither God nor the passions that are evil; if in civilisation our passions are baneful, it is the environment that makes them so, and it is therefore men's environment and not men's passions that must be altered. And that for Fourier is indeed the whole problem. Assuming that men's passions are good, and this assumption is forced on us by their divine origin, how are we to modify men's environment so that these passions may, all and without exception, have free play? How can we arrange things so that Nero, following his passions, will be as useful a citizen as Marcus Aurelius?

Before this, it ought perhaps to have been hinted that the word 'passion' in its Fourieresque context may be ambiguous and misleading. It may be due to these philosophers and sophists whom Fourier could not abide, but indubitably 'passion' conveys the impression of something peculiarly purple in hue, an avenue at the end of which looms a *crime passionel.* In Fourier the 'passions' are little more than the various ways in which pleasure may be experienced or heightened; or putting it in other words, which Fourier would have said amount to the same thing, they are the various channels whereby God exercises attraction. Inevitably, much of Fourier's attention is devoted to an analysis of these human passions, and in fact vast tracts of incomprehensibility are devoted to this subject. There are in all twelve 'passions'—or avenues along which we are lured to pleasure at the promptings of God; fortunately it is only with three, perhaps primarily only with two, that we are here concerned in this restricted study of Fourier. There are, firstly, the five passions corresponding to the five senses of taste, smell, hearing, sight and touch. These, among other things, account for the pleasures of gluttony and the opera, which occupy an altogether peculiar position in Fourier's scheme of things. Then there are, further, four passions of the soul, arising from men's need of sympathy and sociability;

[1] Like the hero of one of Hauptmann's novels, Fourier would have found the petition, 'Lead us not into temptation,' rather curious in its implications.

and these are represented by friendship, ambition, love and family affection. Of these it is significant that friendship and ambition are classified as 'major,' whereas love and 'le famillisme' appear subordinately as minor. As distinguished from the passions of the senses, which are concerned with 'luxe,' these four passions lead to the formation of groups. Then above these, there are three distributive or governing passions which, though perhaps not immediately comprehensible, lie at the core of Fourierism. To these three passions he gives the names of *la Papillonne*, *la Cabaliste* and *la Composite*. What are these so mysterious passions to which we are subject, and which are so important that they govern all the rest?

Firstly, be it observed that these distributive passions are wholly misunderstood in the civilised order, where, as they only lead to confusion and disaster, they are regarded as vices. The first of them, the Papillonne, represents man's love of variety and change: it is the butterfly in the heart of each of us. If God had meant us to spend fifteen hours a day in stupefying work, he would have given us a taste for monotony, an abhorrence of variety.[1] On the contrary he has placed a whispering butterfly close to our ear. God did not make man for monotony, any more than for monogamy. Fourier would have held that man is not made for mono-anything. Whatever we may be doing, we are presently hankering after something else. An hour and a half of any occupation is about as much as any of us can stand, without falling a victim to the roving eye and the wandering thought. There then is the Papillonne, the butterfly passion. Man is so made (and is so made deliberately and intentionally by God) that he desires, and his nature demands, constant change, not merely in work, but in all things. Who are we that we should stifle the voice of the butterfly, the prophet of God?

Secondly among the governing passions is *La Cabaliste*, which denotes men's love of intrigue and emulation, the passion that makes men take sides and work for their side. It is, we are told, a favourite passion among women: 'elles aiment à l'excès l'intrigue.'[2] This is by no means a denigration: it merely proves their pre-eminent fitness for the new social order. Also in all deliberative assemblies, men tend to become pronounced Cabalists: having prayed that unity and concord may prevail, they at once rush into the lobbies in order to 'cabaler et intriguer de plus belle.' Fourier quotes the Almighty in reply to those who would have no rivalry among men:

> The Deity mocks at them when they address a stupid prayer to him to make them all brothers, all united in opinion, according to the wish of Plato and Seneca. God answers them: 'Milliards of years ago I created the passions such as the unity of the universe demanded; I am not going to change them to please the philosophers of an imperceptible globule, which must continue,

[1] Vol. 4, p. 409.

[2] Vol. 4, p. 405.

like all the others, subject to the twelve passions, and particularly to the tenth, the Cabalist.'[1]

This may be a somewhat unnecessarily crushing and undeserved retort to Plato and Seneca, who meant well and who are not accustomed to being called the philosophers of an imperceptible globule. Yet Fourier is right. A world in which every one agreed would be of a heart-rending insipidity. It is, moreover, curious how Fourier is justified in strange places. Schools, which by nature have no 'houses,' have taken to the creation of fictional and notional houses, in order to stimulate the tumult and the shouting on sports day; in so doing, they are paying a distant tribute to Fourier. During the execution of the Soviet Five Years Plan, the frequent challenge of one factory to another in the matter of the time required to do a job would have been hailed by Fourier as a notable example of the Cabalist in action.

Of the Composite, 'the most beautiful of the twelve passions,'[2] little need be said. We are told that it is incompatible with civilised labour, and for this reason it may be found somewhat elusive by those who have not advanced beyond civilisation. It is described as the blind enthusiasm which springs from the combination of two kinds of pleasure, a pleasure of the sense and a pleasure of the soul. It is perhaps possible to realise dimly what the Composite passion is, if we reflect how little pleasure there is in sharing a bottle with a surly man; how, even in the most delightful conversation, there is a sense of something lacking until our host ventures to ask the question for which we have been waiting. Pleasures are more than proportionately heightened by the addition of pleasures of a different character; and this is the doing of the Composite passion. In the words of a knowledgable authority: 'A concert of musick in a banquet of wine is as a signet of carbuncle set in gold.' Fortunately, a comprehension of Fourier does not call for an exact appreciation of what precisely the Composite passion is.

So far we have been concerned with Fourier's analysis of this present evil world, his views on the nature of God and the psychological make-up of man, which in all things embodies the intentions of God. It remains to consider the constructive side of Fourier. How are we to transform the society we know into Harmony, where those we now call evil men will become virtuous citizens, precisely because they will then be able to satisfy those God-given instincts which now are so charged with evil consequences? Harmony will be a world where men will be governed by passional attraction, urging them in constantly changing directions, a world where monotony will be unknown, in which also men will be governed by the Cabalist passion, inciting them to rivalry and intrigue.

[1] Vol. 4, p. 407. [2] Vol. 4, p. 408.

It is here that we come to what, if not the most characteristic, is at least the most celebrated of Fourier's contributions to speculation. Even if little else of Fourier's is remembered, it is at least generally known that he devised in imagination the Phalanx, that associative self-contained unit of co-operative workers on which Harmony will be built. 'Theory'—though do not ask too curiously in what way—indicates that to start a Phalanx, 1,620 people will be required, or approximately 1,800 to allow for a margin; it is also desirable to find a pleasant situation, a valley with a broad river and fertile land, set in something of the mystery and the charm of forests. After all, we are raising the curtain on Fairyland, and some latitude may be allowed the dreamer. The Phalanx is to be self-supporting, although in a world of phalanxes, different units would necessarily specialise in different directions.

It would, however, be an error to assume that the Phalanx is a communistic body. It most emphatically is not. In certain respects this father of socialism is incorrigibly conservative in sentiment. It is true that all the members of the Phalanx live in one building, called the Phalanstère, a very sumptuous building with dining-halls, dancing-halls, pleasing colonnades and much more than West-end luxury can devise. But the Phalanstère does not destroy the individuality of those who dwell there. Anyone who chooses and who cares to pay extra may have his meals in his own room in preference to the larger dining-room. There are at least three tariffs, so that it is possible to dine cheaply or expensively; there are luxurious rooms and rooms which the race of landladies would call moderate. In fact there are wealthy and not-so-astonishingly wealthy Harmonians. There are, of course, no poor Harmonians: compared to anyone in civilisation, the eyes of the poorest Harmonian bulge out with fatness. According to his substance, each pays his money and takes his choice. In short, the Phalanstère is a conglomeration of service-flats to suit all purses. It is perhaps anticipating what may come later, and indeed discretion should perhaps suggest the omission of further discussion, but it may be mentioned that life in the Phalanstère is enormously simplified by the fact that all—fathers and mothers alike—are privileged to lead a bachelor existence.

It may be as well to emphasise on the threshold of the Phalanx, how pronouncedly inegalitarian Fourier is, how far removed he is from any attack on property as such. They accuse me of attacking property! he says with indignation—'moi, inventeur du bouclier de la propriété.'[1] He constantly emphasises that the *régime sociétaire* is incompatible with equality: it calls for contrasts.[2] The Phalanx must therefore be composed of 'gens très-inégaux en fortunes'[3]; in fact it is the extreme inequality prevailing in Harmony that makes the wheels go round.

[1] *Fausse Industrie*, p. F. 7. [2] Vol. 3, p. 4. [3] Vol. 5, p. 511.

In short, Harmony is a place where ' toute égalité est poison politique.'[1] Clearly there is not much of the leveller about Fourier.[2]

When we turn to the internal organisation of the Phalanx, the first question to be considered is the eternal problem of work. In this life, as we know it, for most of humanity work is something that is loathsome and repugnant. This is indeed part of Fourier's indictment of civilisation. In one of those strangely penetrating flashes which periodically stab through the Fourieresque phantasmagoria, he observes that ' Morality ordains that we should love our work ; let it then know how to make work lovable.'[3] It is a just and profound observation. In Fourier's scheme of things, work is to be made attractive: *le travail attrayant*, indeed, becomes one of the watchwords of the school, and in a sense is accepted as a legacy in the anarchist tradition, which holds that men will do something rather than be completely idle, and that therefore the world's work may be accomplished by people fleeing from the boredom of standing with folded arms.

The secret of making work attractive is found by having appropriate regard to the passions, and in particular to the Papillonne and the Cabaliste. People should work at what attracts them, and no one should work at anything for more than an hour or an hour-and-a-half, or at the outside two hours. A spirit of rivalry and emulation should be infused into all labour, and accordingly the workers should be associated in series and groups in active but friendly competition. In a passage which is marked by an unaccustomed degree of orderliness, Fourier in one place enumerates seven essential conditions on which the attractiveness of societary work will depend. The first has a peculiarly modern ring about it. It is that every worker is to be a partner, remunerated by dividends and not by a salary. Here it is possible to see the Guild Socialist horror of wage-slavery. The third embodies the principle of short sessions, two hours being the utmost limit of human enthusiasm in any direction. The fourth, suggested by the Cabaliste, is that work should be carried on by companies of friends, spontaneously united and stimulated by active rivalries. The

[1] Vol. 6, p. 115.

[2] Scores of quotations could be produced to show that Fourier held the idea of equality in complete abhorrence. The point ought not to require further emphasising but for the fact that Mr. Shaw invites his Intelligent Woman to read, among much more, ' the speculations of Saint-Simon, the Communism of Fourier,' etc., and adds that ' if they do not mean equality of income they mean nothing that will save civilisation.' How even Mr. Shaw, even in instructing his Intelligent Woman, could give utterance to such a perverse judgment, is difficult to understand. Presumably he did not brush up his Fourier—nor his Saint-Simon—before meeting his pupil, who, though intelligent, was singularly ignorant, or at least Mr. Shaw constantly addresses her as if she were—which again, of course, may not prove anything one way or the other. For a comparable example of unblemished and impeccable inaccuracy, we must go to Mr. Bertrand Russell, in whose eyes Saint-Simon was essentially a mediaevalist who disliked industrialism and the modern world (*Freedom and Organisation*, p. 207). The things they *do* say !

[3] Vol. 2, p. 147.

sixth requires that division of labour (as Fourier understood it) should be carried to the last possible point, in order to give to everyone his appropriate opening. Underlying all these is the 'pivotal' condition of the guarantee of a minimum sufficient to free everyone from anxiety.[1]

These principles may give a sufficient indication of the nature of the industrial organisation in Harmony. Work is carried on by groups united by a common interest and inspired by passion for their work. The groups are united together in series, and the principle of division of labour (always remembering that the phrase has here a rather special significance) is carried to the utmost degree possible in each group. Thus you may have competing groups devoted to the cultivation of white hyacinths, blue hyacinths and red hyacinths, the whole of these groups forming the series of hyacinth growers. There is an inordinate amount of discussion in Fourier regarding the proper grading of the groups. Inside the series there is the ascending and descending wing, as well as the centre, and these require to be carefully balanced. Normally the two wings will compete against the centre. There is one pleasant picture of 32 groups of pear-growers, ranging from the *bâtardes dures* to the *bâtardes molles*, through all degrees of hardness and softness, and showing how their rivalries may be stimulated. And indeed, with a little ingenuity, there need be no limit. Soft-pear growers compete against hard-pear growers; pear-growers compete against apple-growers; women pear-growers compete against men pear-growers. And each group has its banner under which it marches out to its task. It will be observed that when Fourier speaks of division of labour, his mind is not moving in the grooves of Adam Smith. It will also be apparent that when we pass the portals of the Phalanx, we move as in Fairyland, and our earthly cares do not extend beyond blue hyacinths and soft pears. It should be added that each worker joins as many groups as he wishes, normally from 30 to 50. In whatever directions his tastes lie, he will be able to work an occasional hour with the appropriate group.

It has already been remarked above that Fourier is no egalitarian. It is not merely that he regards inequality as something designed by God, and as a healthy influence in the life of Harmony; in other ways he is throughout extremely tender in his treatment of Capital. There is indeed something which would be slightly repulsive, if it were not wholly grotesque, in his attempts to wheedle Capital into acceptance of his scheme. He looked for a capitalist to launch his first Phalanx, and he kept a list of 4,000 'candidates,' who might be persuaded to save humanity. Before these he dangled the whole gamut of hereditary sceptres. For the merest paltry sum anyone might have been Emperor, Calif, King, Duke or anything else. But apart from such adventitious rewards, Capital will be generously treated in Harmony. It is un-

[1] Vol. 3, p. 15.

necessary to say that the economies of association and the zeal of enthusiastic workers spurred on by the Cabalist passion will result in a world bursting with prosperity. This surplus Fourier proposed to divide in the ratio of four-twelfths to Capital, five-twelfths to Labour and three-twelfths to Talent, a proportion which, giving less than a half to Labour, need certainly alarm no capitalist. It is here that we encounter one of the most characteristic ideas of Fourier. Prosperity will be so outrageous in the Phalanx that there is no reason why all should not be capitalists. To encourage this desirable end, he adopts a childish device whereby the rate of interest will vary inversely with the number of shares held in the Phalanx. The poor Harmonian (if a contradiction in terms may be permitted) will be able to look for a 30 per cent. or even a 40 per cent. return. The object of this is to convert him 'd'emblée à l'esprit de propriété et de conservation, d'où naissent les bonnes mœurs,' [1] a horribly bourgeois sentiment. The medium Harmonian will get a modest 15 per cent. The wealthy Harmonian will have to put up with a beggarly 5 per cent. Thus there is no one in Harmony who need be without a share. Looking round him, he may say with complacency: 'My library; my dining-hall; my fields' [2]—just as the worker in the South Metropolitan Gas Company may say: 'My gas tanks, my railway trucks, my directors.'

But indeed Fourier goes much deeper than this. To all talk about the class struggle and about class consciousness, his answer is simple. It is, in effect, to confound the classes. If the trumpet give an uncertain sound, who shall prepare himself to the battle? As a result there will be no battle. This ultimately is one reason why each one attaches himself to some thirty or more groups. In Harmony, each one will certainly be a capitalist. He may have shown talent (either in supervision or in invention) in the merino group or the street-paving group. In addition he may be entitled to remuneration as a worker in two dozen other groups. Under these circumstances he ceases to be exclusively a capitalist, a manager or a wage-earner. Each man becomes a microcosm, and such conflicting interests as might emerge are harmoniously resolved in the breasts of each. All realise in fact that if they push their interest too far in one direction, they will only damage themselves in another. There will be no conflicts, since each one will know that what he loses on the swings he will make up on the roundabouts.

The reward given to each series does not depend on the product of its work, but is professedly based on the necessity and usefulness of its task, and inversely on the agreeableness of the occupation. The application of this general principle reflects Fourier's own tastes. The cultivation of fruit ranks low, because no place is so delectable as an

[1] *Fausse Industrie*, p. Z. 7.
[2] *E.g.* vol. 2, p. 199, and, of course, elsewhere.

orchard. The opera, oddly enough to those who do not know Fourier, ranks first in the order of necessity. It has been indicated that a 'pivotal' condition of labour being made attractive is that a minimum be guaranteed. Fourier never fails to underline that society owes the individual a living, whether he earns it or not. In places, this takes the moderate form of a guarantee of work in health, and of assistance, a social minimum in case of infirmity; and indeed he speaks of an extension of assurance as one way of escaping from civilisation into the next state, *le régime garantiste*.[1] But elsewhere the guaranteed minimum rather suggests what in another quarter has been called the vagabond's wage. The reason for the minimum is of some interest. It is that civilisation has deprived us of certain rights which primitive man enjoyed—the chase, fishing, 'gathering' and pasturage.[2] In another place he gives a more lengthy list of rights, with a pleasing addition in the form of *l'insouciance*, of which civilisation most certainly has deprived us.[3] For these losses we are due compensation. Fourier, who is always precise, tells us exactly what the minimum should be:

> Board at tables of the third class, five meals a day;
>
> A decent suit, and uniforms for work and for 'parade,' as well as all the instruments for husbandry and manufacture;
>
> Individual lodgings, consisting of a room with a *cabinet*, and admission to the public halls, to fêtes of the third class, and to plays in third-class *loges*.[4]

Work then is to be done under the influence of attraction. . What is to happen in the case of work that is positively and of necessity disagreeable and even repulsive? It is a question on which there has been much discussion, sometimes rather puerile, in socialist literature. Fourier's solution is so characteristic, and in a sense so logical on his premises, that it deserves to be mentioned, even at the risk of straying into the field of education and the upbringing of the youth. The problem, expressed crudely, is that of scavenging in an ideal world where all follow their natural bent in competing in the cultivation of white and blue hyacinths. Applying Fourier's doctrine of passions, it is possible to get the solution at the first guess. Who are those among us who positively enjoy being dirty? Is not Fourier right in saying that at a certain age most boys and some girls are *vrais maniaques de saleté*, little devils for dirt, to translate freely. Parents daily reproach their offspring for what they foolishly regard as their unnatural dislike of cleanliness. They forget that all our passions are good, and given us for a purpose. Children have their defects; but this love of dirt is socially their salvation; they are in fact 'passionately attracted' to the work of scavenging, and this work is therefore entrusted to them, grouped together in the corporation known as 'Little Hordes.' But Fourier is here too Fourieresque to escape quotation:

[1] Vol. 4, pp. 276–278.
[2] Vol. 3, p. 179.
[3] *Fausse Industrie*, p. 490.
[4] Vol. 4, p. 445.

The madness for dirt which prevails among children is merely an uncultivated germ, like wild fruit; it must be refined by applying to it the two forces of the religious unitary spirit, and of corporative honour. Supported by these two motives, repugnant occupations will become games, having indirect composite attraction. . . .

For long I made the mistake of censuring this odd peculiarity in children, and of trying to make it disappear in the mechanism of the 'passionate series'; that was to act like a Titan, wishing to change the work of God. I achieved no success until I decided to speculate in accordance with attraction, and to make use of the inclinations of childhood, as they have been created by Nature. . . .

. . . There is nothing, therefore, left for children to do but to take over the field of unclean work,—charity of high statesmanship, since it saves from contempt the last industrial classes, and in consequence the intermediate classes also.[1]

These Little Hordes 'are always on foot at 3 o'clock in the morning, even in the depth of winter, attending to the animals, working in the slaughter-houses.' The Little Hordes also repair the highways, turn out in any emergency, kill reptiles and vipers, and do all the other things Boy Scouts dream of doing.

There are two large questions on which Fourier has much to say, but as they lie somewhat off our main path, a brief notice may be sufficient. The first relates to education in general, and the second is the large question of the place of women in society, with the allied problems of marriage and feminism. The civilised child Fourier holds in complete detestation, and the tone of his voice, when he refers to them, suggests that he must have suffered at their hands: a man of somewhat eccentric habits, who talks loudly to himself as he walks the streets, frequently does. Children move him to a bitterness of irony which is unusual in Fourier. He speaks of 'la société des tendres enfants hurlant, brisant, souillant, etc.,'[2] and of 'le doux plaisir d'entendre un marmot hurler jour et nuit.'[3] With an admirable right-and-left, he refers to 'les tendres enfants, si dignes de leurs vertueux pères, *petits vandales, bien dignes de grands vandales*.'[4] In short, they are a 'race demoniaque,' little anti-Christs.[4]

This is the product of civilisation, where we make the mistake of beginning education too late. The child is kept inactive until the age of six or seven, and then turned on to theory, whereas it has been for many years before that striving to express itself actively. The instincts of early childhood are to rummage, to make a noise and to imitate

[1] Vol. 5, pp. 158–162. Extracts, however, do not do justice to Fourier's arguments that this madness for dirt, *la manie de saleté*, is a part of the divine mechanism of attraction, and that here, as always, the Creator 'a donc bien fait tout ce qu'il a fait.' The whole passage should be read by discriminating readers.

[2] Vol. 4, p. 540.

[3] Vol. 5, p. 57.

[4] Vol. 5, p. 102.

[5] Vol. 5, pp. 42, 53.

(*singerie*),[1] and these elementary instincts should be used to find out in what directions a child's tastes lie. From the age of two children will therefore be taken about by their nurses to places where people are working, and there will everywhere be small hammers and small tools so that the instinct to imitate will make even very young children useful workers before, with us, education begins at all.[2] At the age of 25 months, they will be proudly shelling peas, increasing the dividends payable to shareholders in the Phalanx. The great defect in our system is that one method is applied to all. In Harmony, relying on the imitative instinct and a child's readiness to learn from those a few months older, education will pursue a different course for each child, who will quite naturally reveal in what direction 'passionate attraction' draws him. And for further education, the two great instruments are cookery, to cultivate the active sense of taste and smell, and the opera, to cultivate the passive ones of sight and hearing. 'Children and cats,' as he tells us, 'would be for ever nosing about the kitchen, if they were not chased away. As for the magic of the opera and of Fairyland made visible, there is nothing more captivating for a child.' [3]

Fourier would not be Fourier if he did not arrange his children into Nourissons (up to 15 months), Poupons (from 16 months to 33 months) and Bambins (from 34 to 54 months). Indeed there are subdivisions, for are there not Pouponnains, who are *doucereux* in disposition ; Pouponnards, who are *mutins* ; and Pouponnâtres, who are *démoniaques* ? [4] Of the later stages we have already met the 'Little Hordes,' whose duty it is to clean the streets and kill the reptiles. But these are the 'bad' children, who are passionately attracted to personal uncleanliness, that is to say, two-thirds of all boys and one-third of all girls. On the other hand, two-thirds of the girls and one-third of the boys are drawn in the direction of personal cleanliness and neatness. These are incorporated in the 'Little Bands,' who are the gentle element in life, and form the necessary counterpart to the Little Hordes. They give examples in good manners ; they design costumes for ceremonials ; they correct their parents' bad pronunciation—the little prigs. They look after the pigeons and the flowers.[5]

It is when we come to the next stage in the development of the young that Fourier caused most embarrassment to his followers, and indeed

[1] Vol. 6, p. 181. [2] Vol. 6, p. 173, etc.

[3] Vol. 5, p. 76. It is interesting to note how much (probably unconscious) Fourierism there is in Dr. Enid Charles's proposals regarding education in *The Menace of Under-population*: 'In a rational system of education a child would begin by learning to perform all the manual operations carried out by the adults round him' (p. 221). She goes on to consider the advantageous results which would follow 'if the child becomes a producer soon after birth.' The phrases might be, in substance, direct transcripts from Fourier.

[4] Vol. 5, pp. 55, 57–58. [5] Vol. 5, pp. 178, etc.

caused not a little embarrassment to himself. Despite distinctions and subtleties there is nothing remotely resembling marriage in Harmony, and at a certain stage the education of the young prepares him for what is to follow. Women at a certain age may select one of three grades of what we should call infidelity in these matters, enrolling themselves in the appropriate *Corporation amoureuse* ; but as they may vary their option at any time, they might as well opt forthwith for the corporation that gives the greatest liberty. Even in the most binding union there is nothing wrong with inconstancy, provided it is a matter of reciprocal agreement ; indeed short ' truces ' (an unhappy word) for a few days will not be regarded as inconstancy, provided they are registered in the Chancellory of the Court of Love.[1] Such ' truces ' are frequent, above all when there are ceremonial visits to the Phalanx : presumably something must be allowed in the sacred name of hospitality. Fourier was careful to explain that this transition to a state of completely free love would not take place until the third generation of Harmony, and further that it would be effected only with the unanimous consent of all concerned. As if this were not sufficient safeguard, he indicated that in the interval God would doubtless give a new revelation and expressly authorise the new code. After all, as he contrives to hint, the God of the Book of Genesis can scarcely be regarded as a bigoted advocate of monogamy. Finally, as he points out, the customs he advocates are those in force in the planet Herschel.

Waiving Jehovah and the planet Herschel, who on this question may not cut much ice, the interesting fact is that here again, as in Plato and Campanella and so many others, we have socialist thought passing condemnation on the family ; and it is interesting to note what in this case are the underlying reasons. The first takes us straight back to Plato. It is that marriage and the family, inasmuch as they create special interests, are anti-social and prevent a man from doing his duties by his fellows. It is more or less the view of the Apostle Paul, with whom otherwise Fourier has little affinity : ' He that is married careth for the things that are of the world, how he may please his wife.' Marriage, says Fourier, binds two people in a league against all that surrounds them, and makes them indifferent to public misfortunes ; the highest praise that can be given to anyone is to say that marriage has not changed him.[2] When a man marries, it is a notice of dismissal to all his friends (and perhaps there is here a pathetic fragment of autobiography).[3] In a hundred families there are a hundred egotists : not one is a citizen. Each considers himself justified in any swindle because he is working for his wife and children. Plato himself

[1] Vol. 5, p. 468 ; *Fausse Industrie*, pp. 585, 586.
[2] Vol. 1, pp. 211–212.
[3] Vol. 4, p. 118.

could not have expressed more forcibly the danger of worldly entanglements.[1]

The other motive that urges Fourier to abolish the family and establish the reign of free love is, rather oddly, his championship of women. There has never been a more zealous, if perhaps injudicious, defender of women than Fourier. No one has emphasised so strongly that in civilisation woman is 'made for slavery,' and that, given a chance, she is fit for better things.[2] Of eight queens who have reigned 'libres et sans époux,' seven have reigned with glory; of eight kings, seven are usually accounted as duds. No one has more emphatically stated that the position assigned to woman is the acid test of any society.[3] Women then must receive a larger freedom. The first and most fundamental wrong done to woman lies in the quiet assumption that all women were meant to be housekeepers. At most Nature has made only one woman in eight a *ménagère*.[4] The result is that seven-eighths of women are misfits, in a perpetual state of irritation which affects the remaining eighth. So far are women from being naturally domesticated that not one woman in a hundred at the age of 30 knows how to set a fire.[5] Women in fact were not intended for marriage.[6] It is a recurrent thought in Fourier that God has given us our passions and instincts, not with reference to the 5,000 years of misery through which we are now passing, but to fit us for the 70,000 years of bliss that await us; and the ratio of one natural *ménagère* in eight indicates what proportion will be required domestically in these happier days. The situation might of course have been met by altering the 'passions' of women, as we draw near to Harmony; but apparently it is easier for God to create an anti-whale than to alter the disposition of a

[1] The tradition of antagonism to the family shows strange persistence. Take, *e.g.* Professor Laski, in a passage where the argument may be confused, but the intention is clear:

'I suspect, indeed, that it is not accident that both the teaching of Jesus and the doctrine of the *Communist Manifesto* are at one in their emphasis upon the danger of the family which, in an acquisitive society, acts as a barrier between men and women, instead of a link which binds them together. For it is the central faith, alike of the Gospels and of Socialism, that there is neither Jew nor Greek, neither bond nor free; but where the claim of son upon parents, or brother upon brother, is set in terms of the view that proximity of relationship means that one's property is proportionately available to one's kin also, the family becomes the nurse of avarice and narrowness, a hindrance, rather than a help, to fraternity in the commonwealth' (*Faith, Reason and Civilisation*, p. 97).

While the family gets all the knocks in this matter, it may be observed that there is a potential conflict with the ultimate socialist ideal, wherever there is, in the pedantic words of Godwin, any preference among our fellows, not based on 'reasons which equally appeal to all understandings.' The anti-social consequences of such irrational preferences are admirably depicted by Zorobabel in his hymn in praise of women: 'A man taketh his sword, and goeth his way to rob and to steal, to sail upon the sea and upon rivers; and looketh upon a lion, and goeth in the darkness; and when he hath stolen, spoiled and robbed, he bringeth it to his love.'

[2] *Fausse Industrie*, p. T. 8.

[3] Vol. 1, pp. 195–196.

[4] Vol. 4, p. 154.

[5] Vol. 5, p. 120.

[6] Vol. 1, p. 170.

woman. Those women whom civilisation looks upon as vicious, because undomesticated, will find their place in Harmony; and that they may have freedom, domesticity is replaced by an unending succession of fleeting lovers, and any incidental children are entrusted to groups and series of nurses. It is a chastening reflection: with a great sum obtained they this freedom.

Perhaps we may take a last glance round the Phalanx before passing through the turnstile into the light of common day. In the construction of his Utopia, Fourier reveals himself as a man rent by two entirely contradictory and inconsistent passions. On the one hand it is a world of license, not to say licentiousness, of liberty in excess, of pleasure pursued to a point where the discussion becomes almost nauseating. His is a heaven, securely based on copulation and cookery. The joy of eating is almost converted into the central point in the machinery of God's providence. There are five meals a day, and these of such extent and quality as beggar all description. If the finest roast fowl from the table of the first gourmand of France were offered to the Harmonians, the official ' tasters ' would overwhelm it with such a flood of criticism that a black ribbon of disgrace would be attached to the banner of the poulterers.[1] But Fourier is not content with pleasures coming as single spies: he will have what he calls a *parcours* of pleasures, seven or eight pleasures piled on each other, and—believe it or not—the rich Harmonian has two or three such *parcours* each day.[2]

On the other hand there is in Fourier the instinct of the subordinate clerk, the orderly book-keeper, and this requires that everything in

[1] Vol. 1, p. 245.

[2] If the envious reader seeks enlightenment as to what exactly is a *parcours*, he may first of all study Fourier's own definition:

' Le parcours est l'amalgame d'une masse de plaisirs goûtés successivement dans une courte séance, enchaînés avec art dans un même local, se rehaussant l'un par l'autre, se succédant a des instants si rapprochés qu'on ne fasse que glisser sur chacun, y donner seulement quelques minutes, à peine un quart d'heure à chaque jouissance ' (vol. 4, p. 188).

Secondly, and perhaps with greater advantage, he may study a *parcours* in concrete form, and observe a crowded hour of glorious life, as experienced by Dorval, who in the course of sixty minutes experienced eight major pleasures: (1) and (2)—a double pleasure of the senses and the soul, and therefore counting as two—he succeeds with a woman to whom he has been making advances; (3) she hands him the commission of a lucrative post she has obtained for him; (4) they pass to the salon, where he meets a dear friend whom he had thought dead; (5) presently there enters a great man, a Buffon, a Corneille, whom Dorval had wished to meet; (6) an exquisite dinner, at which (7) Dorval finds himself next to an influential personage who engages to help him; and lastly (8) in the course of the repast he receives a message that he has won a law-suit. It happens, just like that, in Harmony. And apparently, even with three *parcours* a day, the springs of happiness continue to well, though doubtless the constituent elements vary. Presumably the man who lost the law-suit was not having his *parcours* just then.

Substantially the same *parcours* figures in vol. 6, pp. 348–349, with Léandre as the happy man.

the Phalanx should be docketed and tabulated, that everything should march like clockwork. In every one of the 2,985,984 phalanxes which will ultimately cover the globe, matters will move according to plan, with something of the rigidity of the military parade-ground. Punctuality in everything is the rule in Harmony—*tout à minute fixe et sans attendre qui que ce soit.*[1] Each day begins with a hymn and with fanfares, and with banners flying the groups and the series march off to their appointed tasks. And how comely it is and how reviving to observe how colourful a life we may lead, when once we have cast aside the sophists and the philosophers, and the nightmare of morality! The *Bandes Roses*, arriving from Persia, are followed by the *Bandes Lilas* from Japan, displaying their prowess against all comers in drama and in poetry[2]; there are pleasant reunions of the true friends of the turnip and of the equally true friends of the onion; there are perpetual meetings in the afternoon in the orchards, charged with intrigue and rivalry; and everyone is as agreeable and charming as the charming and agreeable people whom somehow we seem to meet only when we are on holiday.

The peculiarity of Fourier is that his terrible imagination compels him to see every general proposition in concrete form in the lives of individuals directly affected. Thus the arrangements in Harmony are always discussed by reference to events in the lives of Harmonians who, somewhat incongruously, usually bear classical names. Perhaps it would be truer to say that Fourier himself lived in Harmony as a way of escape from his drab life. The spacious Phalanstère was a refuge from his cramped lodgings; the five meals a day (and such meals!) reflected his bare table; the women who might be loved, and loved so excessively, in Harmony were all his landlady was not. Yet this curious habit of giving concrete shape to his argument is largely responsible for the aroma of absurdity which is never long absent from Fourier. For even when he is making a good point, the incident by which it is illustrated is frequently not far from buffoonery. Thus, to illustrate how happy is the father of undowered daughters in Harmony compared with one similarly placed in civilisation, he gives a full length biography of each of the six daughters of Damon—and rather scandalous biographies they are.[3] So with Lunarius, who had a passion for eating spiders, but who nevertheless thereby fulfilled the intentions of the Almighty,[4] and with countless other burlesque figures who pass through his pages, the effect is rather to delight the scoffer than to edify the humble.[5]

[1] Vol. 4, p. 372.
[2] Vol. 1, p. 233.
[3] *Fausse Industrie*, p. 577 *et seq.*
[4] Vol. 5, p. 347.
[5] Perhaps the most sustained and unrestrained flight of Fourier's imagination is found in his account of the great battle of the *Pâtés*, fought out by contending armies (of cooks, of course) near Babylon, with sixty empires participating, and reported on from day to day in the *Bulletin de Babylone*, and ending with the syn-

What is there of substance and of permanence to be derived from this strange farrago of mixed feeding? More perhaps than might be imagined, for Fourier, pruned of his exuberant excesses, has been a strangely abiding influence, above all in France. Following for once Fourier's excellent habit of enumeration, let us indicate some points in his legacy. In the first place, there has never been a more acute critic of the lack of organisation and the waste resulting from unrestrained individualism. Then, secondly, his influence has been very great in the development of the co-operative movement. The elimination of waste by co-operation has its greatest exponent in Fourier. It is perhaps not irrelevant to observe that in London, Paris, New York, and indeed all great cities, people are drifting to that hotel life which at least represents an approach to some of the aspects of the Phalanstère. It may be that the home will go down increasingly before the service flat. Thirdly, it is to Fourier's credit that he saw deep into the meaning of the conflicts of Labour and Capital, and in substance what he says on the desirability of confusion of the classes still merits our attention. The South Metropolitan Gas Company, with its harmonious history, is in its way a monument to Fourier. Then, fourthly, viewed in essence and apart from its embroideries, the Phalanx itself embodies a certain ideal. Fourier was no enemy of Capital, but he certainly detested industrialism. He was in fact an advocate of a 'Back-to-the-land' policy, and moreover, back-to-the-land with an emphasis on market gardening and fruit, with the population living in something that we should now call Garden Cities. Fifthly, we must allow him an abiding influence, above all on the anarchists, in connection with his doctrine of 'attractive labour'; his emphasis on the autonomy of the Phalanx also ranges him with those opposed to centralisation.

Such was Fourier, a strange mixture of a child and of one hovering perilously near the thin line which divides sanity from insanity, with all the directness of a child and the strange intuitions of a madman. He is a figure never far removed from absurdity. Yet when we have finished smiling, it is a strangely pathetic, wistful, lonely figure that our unheroic hero presents. There are few things more moving in human biography than the ageing of Fourier. He had persuaded himself that a capitalist with lavish hands would come to him, and provide the means for the regeneration of the world. And like the timid, deferential gentleman that he was, he had made it known that he would be at home daily at a certain hour, in order that his expected patron might not be inconvenienced. For would it not be a terrible thing if the opportunity of saving the world should be thrown away by such a mischance as Fourier's absence when the benefactor of humanity

chronised popping of the corks of 300,000 bottles of sparkling wine. Next year's contest: a battle of *Omelettes soufflées* (vol. 5, pp. 352 *et seq.*).

arrived? So, for the last years of his life, whatever else might happen, Fourier was punctually at his post when the clocks chimed the appointed hour, waiting, attentively listening—doubtless each day, a new hope; each day, a fresh disappointment. And then one morning he was found dead in the little furnished room which he occupied, kneeling by the bedside. A greater than the unknown capitalist had called, and Fourier had slipped out of life as furtively as he had passed through it.

CHAPTER VIII

ROBERT OWEN

AMONG that queer bunch of visionary and Utopian socialists, to whom in some undefined proportion is usually ascribed the paternity of socialism, Robert Owen (1771–1858) presents some strange contrasts to his nearest bed-fellows. Saint-Simon had been an aristocrat, always conscious of the fact. Fourier, if we look at his drab life in the cold light of dawn, had been at best an unsuccessful commercial traveller. Godwin, to go further back, was obviously, in the world's estimation, destined to be a confused and bankrupt bookseller. Louis Blanc (coming further down than the fathers) was a journalist, graduating to an uneasy position in an uneasy government, as a prelude to a prolonged exile. It used to be a common reproach that one or other of many Cabinet Ministers, while aspiring to control the destiny of an empire, would have been incompetent to run a whelk-stall—though the special appropriateness of this particular entrepreneurial venture for purposes of comparison and contrast was never wholly clear. But the implied criticism, so far as it was justified, might certainly have been applied to the earlier socialists: they criticised the management of the world, but they themselves had 'done nothing' and had shown no marked ability, either in managing their own or other people's affairs. Robert Owen, up to a point, is a bird of entirely different plumage. True, he spent his last years in a rather undefined state of dependence; but so long as he cared for making money, he showed that he could do the trick. In the great years of his uprising, he made it clear that he could beat the magnates of the Industrial Revolution at their own game; if success in business and the accumulation of capital was to be the acid test of managing a whelk-stall, Robert Owen could give abundant evidence of his competence. Indeed, had his life stopped at the right moment (for this purpose) he might have been the ideal copy-book boy for innumerable volumes on Self-Help and Industry: 'Seest thou a man diligent in his business? He shall stand before kings.' If, in fact, Owen threw aside his supreme qualification for inclusion in the works of Samuel Smiles, it was an act of voluntary abdication, in pursuit of another vision.

As a matter of literal fact, Robert Owen did, on one momentous occasion, stand, or at least bow, before the Queen, on the presentation of Lord Melbourne—dressed up like a monkey, as he complained. Owen was then (1839) of doubtful respectability, and loyal hearts (in particular as represented by the delightfully named 'Society for

Peaceably Repressing Infidelity') were moved to concern and alarm for the safety of their young and uncontaminated sovereign. Doubtless, however, the wisdom of Solomon should not be taken over literally; and in its broad interpretation, there is here another obvious contrast between Owen and the other founders. At the height of his influence and powers, Owen knew everyone; he was indeed a European figure. Saint-Simon had unquestionably his aristocratic connections, but somehow he rather gives the impression of a decayed gentleman, who has put much aside. Godwin at one time had an immense reputation, but it was essentially literary. Fourier knew no one, apart from his landladies and their cats, and latterly a few disciples as uninfluential as himself. But Owen, among the early socialists, is a portent: a man who has made money, and to whom at one time all doors were open.

One other preliminary consideration arises. Few figures in the history of socialism represent, as does Owen, the combination of theory and practice; and it follows that even in what is designed to be, as exclusively as may be, a history of thought and doctrine, the biography of Owen asserts itself. In a sense his life was his socialism, and even if he had refrained from writing the whole of his lengthy series of books and pamphlets (and much more), he would still have been a remarkable figure in the history of socialism. Owen, once he yielded to the vice, never stopped writing, and he never ceased 'trying' and projecting; and in the fabric of his life, his writings and his strivings are inextricably interwoven.

It may, however, be possible even in the case of Owen to confine the biographical details within bounds. Owen was born in 1771 in Newtown, Montgomery, where his father had a combined business of sadler, ironmonger and postmaster. If Owen plunged young into life, it is not to be assumed that he was driven by poverty; it was merely the custom of the age and of his people. He seems to have acquired all that his school could teach him by the time he had reached seven, and thereafter for two years he was promoted to be an 'usher'—two lost years, he regrets, 'except,' he adds, 'that I thus early acquired the habit of teaching others what I knew.' In view of the subsequent seventy-five years of didactic activity, this salvage from the wreck of these two years has an ominous and foreboding sound. At nine he was by way of being a shop assistant in his native town, and at ten he journeyed to London, and soon afterwards was employed at Stamford with a linen-draper bearing the improbable name of McGuffog. In spite of his labours, he was able to read much, confusedly, at Stamford. After some years, he was back in London, in a shop at Ludgate Hill, where he was grotesquely overworked; and so to Manchester, where his meteoric career began. By the age of 19, he had become manager to Drinkwater, cotton-mill owners in Manchester, with (having regard to the year, 1790, and his age) the almost princely salary of £300 a year. In due course, after various moves onwards and upwards—ever the conscientious, hard-working young man—there came in 1797 the purchase on behalf of himself and his partners of the New Lanark establishment from Dale (and subsequently, as becomes a business romance, his marriage to Miss Dale), and so finally in 1800 he came into his own kingdom, and in his own characteristic words, 'entered upon the government of New Lanark.'

To a very large extent, Robert Owen is New Lanark, and New Lanark has little significance apart from Robert Owen. Here, also, his glory is unsullied; in everything else in the life of Owen there is frustration and failure, however greatly he may have designed; and indeed, as the years advance, there is too frequently a touch of the grotesque which is even more fatal than failure. But in New Lanark he wrought a miracle, not merely unaided, but in the face of obstacles over and above those inherent in the task. There were difficult partners, shying at philanthropy, and there were consequently business reshufflings. He was distrusted as an alien by the jealous Scot. He would have us believe that many of his flock knew only Gaelic [1]; even in 1800, it was an unusual accomplishment among pauper children drafted from Edinburgh; perhaps their Scots accent was such that to Owen, a Welshman, it might just as well have been Gaelic. But despite friction with his partners and sullenness from his workers, at least in the early stages, Owen persevered until the face of New Lanark was entirely transformed. Doubtless Owen would have said that all this was a witness to the truth and the efficacy of the theories on which he acted. We shall presently survey his writings so far as they bear on this period; for the present it may be a sufficiently accurate first approximation to regard Owen as of the school of Godwin in these matters. The doctrine he sought to apply in New Lanark was the familiar theory of human irresponsibility, Godwin's 'Necessity,' the view that men are good or evil according to their environment, and that therefore an improved environment, resting on improved education, provides the path to all progress. It is, however, fairly clear that what wrought the miracle was Owen's personality, and not abstract devotion to the theory of 'Necessity.' Indeed, it might plausibly be argued that a thoroughgoing belief throughout a community that no one was responsible for anything might lead to the most deplorable results. If, the more I wallow in sin, the more eager do my fellow-men become to express their sympathy with me because of the malady from which I suffer, and to find excuses for me in the notorious deficiencies of my parents, it may be that I, enjoying sympathy, may qualify for still larger doses. It may be doubted whether even a sermon-tasting Scottish community

[1] *The Revolution in Mind and Practice*, etc., p. 11.

would be reformed by listening to Owen preaching his favourite sermon; but there is nothing absurd in believing that they may have been saved, and perhaps awed, by his personality, his zeal, and his obvious sincerity in all the works of his hands.

New Lanark, when Owen assumed the government, was probably more degraded than most similar places at the time of the Industrial Revolution. To a considerable extent it had been recruited in Dale's time by child-labour drafted from the workhouses of Edinburgh and Glasgow at an incredibly early age. The adult population seems to have consisted largely of thieves, drunkards and blackguards. Systematically, Owen proceeded to turn this citadel of vice into a model village. He turned off the supply of over-juvenile juveniles, and as education was in his theory the centre of all things, he began his great work with infant schools. On this side of his activities Owen was not merely a pioneer, but he held views which entitle him to a place in the history and theory of education. That singing and dancing should occupy so large a place in the scheme of things was an innovation in this environment. Meanwhile, perhaps somewhat dictatorially and undoubtedly somewhat patriarchally, Owen continued the work of reformation. A tolerable standard of cleanliness was attained without too much effort. Drunkenness was a more difficult failing to eliminate; but even here, by controlling the public-houses, Owen got what he wanted. Scarcely any aspect of welfare known to us to-day was neglected by Owen in these years, culminating in the 'Institution for the Formation of Character,' the opening of which on January 1, 1816, was the occasion of one of Owen's most characteristic speeches. This institution was in fact meant to be a centre of communal life. During all these years, the fame of New Lanark spread, and increasingly it became a place of pilgrimage, visited by princes, prelates and potentates and by all and sundry who departed saying that the half had not been told. Looking back, towards the end of his life, Owen described the inhabitants of New Lanark as having been 'literally a self-employing, self-supporting, self-educating, and self-governing population.'[1] This is perhaps New Lanark seen, not wholly justly, through a shimmer of years; for Owen always was, and never could be anything but, the benevolent autocrat. Yet, whether self-governed or more probably Owen-governed, it remains indisputable that out of the dross and grime of the Industrial Revolution, he made a fair community where little girls were taught to sing and dance, and where, as he boasts, there was not 'one legal punishment inflicted upon any one of these people during that period.' One may not inappropriately borrow the words used by Disraeli in describing another village which obviously drew its inspiration from New Lanark; 'The men were well clad; the women had a blooming cheek;

[1] *Revolution in Mind and Practice*, p. 29.

drunkenness was unknown; while the moral condition of the softer sex was proportionately elevated.'[1] This was the first stage of Owen's life, during which he was pre-eminently the successful and model employer, in all matters of welfare more than a century before his time.

In the second phase of his life, Owen was primarily a dreamer of dreams and a seer of visions. The two parts of his life, although in a sense well-defined, inevitably overlap to a considerable extent. It is probable that almost from the outset Owen looked on New Lanark as a model on which the whole world was later to be fashioned. Along with fairly orthodox activities directed to a limitation of the hours of labour, he began increasingly fairly early in the New Lanark days, to advocate the establishment of communistic settlements, his famous 'parallelograms.' Much of later Owenite history is occupied with the attempt to establish such 'villages of co-operation.' Though he did not finally and formally sever his connection with New Lanark until a considerable number of years later, the turning-point in Owen's life was probably the public meeting which he addressed in London on August 21, 1817, when he went out of his way to make a frontal attack on 'the errors—gross errors—that have been combined with the fundamental notions of every religion that has hitherto been taught to man.'[2] Later he was assumed to have made a similar frontal attack on the whole institution of marriage, although on one view he might have been interpreted as having merely demanded easier conditions of divorce. But the effect of his supposedly infidel and immoral views was to deprive Owen increasingly during the remainder of his life of that very large measure of public, and indeed distinguished, support which he had enjoyed when he was primarily the model employer. Of his experiments in communism, the most famous was that of New Harmony in Indiana, which he acquired from the Rappites in 1824. Others were at Tytherly in Hampshire, and at Orbiston near Glasgow. All of these, sooner rather than later, fell into a decline and expired for reasons which will be found analysed in the biographies of Owen. New Harmony is also notable because it devoured a large part of the wealth previously accumulated by Owen, so that his later years were spent in comparative poverty. Apart from these communistic experiments, which were in a sense the fulfilment of certain of his New Lanark writings, Owen, back in Europe and finally severed from business, gave himself up to such projects as the 'Grand National Consolidated Trades Union' and the 'National Equitable Labour Exchange,' a marvellous store or bank, whose object it was to eliminate money in the ordinary sense. And so on to advanced old age Owen continued campaigning, never ceasing to proclaim the faith that was in him, though fewer listened, never desisting from writing, though fewer read and

[1] *Sybil.* [2] Selection of Owen's works in Everyman series, p. 216.

of these perhaps some read with a smile, ever scattering his seed in many fields, yet reaping no visible harvest.

Before turning to such of Owen's writings as it may be necessary to take down from the bookshelf, it may be well to supplement the foregoing bald biographical details by looking at the man himself. For again it is more important than it is with many of those who stray through this book that we should ask what manner of man this Robert Owen was. Admittedly, he is something of an enigma. Mr. Podmore, greatly daring, ventured to suggest that he 'was not, by the modern standard, a good man of business.'[1] Certainly, over large tracts of his life, especially in the second phase, he showed precious little business or common sense. Yet on the crude test of 'getting there,' Owen advanced from being a miscellaneous message-boy to wealth, influence and controlling power in what, for such a transformation, was a remarkably short period of time. Probably the secret of business success was as much of a mystery in the days of the Industrial Revolution as in later times; but if business ability is proved by being successful at business; then it is difficult to deny that Owen, at least in his younger days, had this ability.

On this point there may have been something of a break in Owen's life; having made money in the first phase, he proceeded to show, in more senses than one, that he did not know the meaning of money. But in all other respects, Owen's life is of a singularly uniform texture. His dominating characteristic—one that may become rather nauseating if expressed too frequently—was without doubt the love of his fellow-men. Yet though Owen's presentation of benevolence may at times grate, he was unquestionably sincere; he was indeed aflame with a passionate love of humanity. With this it must be admitted that he never lived down the education he gave himself. In his early youth he read too much, and he read too much without guidance; as a consequence he read with more zeal than profit. An autobiography put together by an octogenarian may not be the safest authority on the intellectual development of the writer as a child ; but if we are to believe Owen's *Life*, his views on all essential matters were 'set' by the time he was twelve. He had already discovered the 'errors' in all religions; he had already realised that he was but the creature of the influences to which he was subjected. As he went through life, Owen showed himself utterly incapable of shedding an old idea or of acquiring a new one. There is a devastating remark by Harriet Martineau to the effect that 'Robert Owen is not the man to think differently of a book for having read it.'

The consequences were somewhat disturbing, both on his own contemporaries and on all who have come after. He imagined he was

[1] Frank Podmore: *Robert Owen*, p. 644.

a pioneer when in fact he was but playing amateurishly with problems which have engaged the mind of man since the beginning of time. He became more and more dogmatic, the complete egotist, underrating all others, indeed assuming the ignorance of all others as a first axiom. Behind all he wrote, and doubtless behind all he spoke, could be heard the words: 'I'm not arguing with you: I'm telling you.' As a result he became the greatest bore of his generation, seizing every occasion to pour out interminably his theories on the formation of character. Yet his personality was such that he was greatly loved by those who knew him; we of subsequent generations, who may not see his countenance, can clutch at nothing to relieve our boredom. Owen is tolerable to anyone who confines himself to what he wrote up to 1821; but beyond that he kept on writing and writing and writing, saying the same thing over and over again, for ever returning to the same point of departure,

> Like a homing pigeon, never by doubt diverted.

When we turn to his writings, it is, as has been indicated, almost absurdly true that the reader can get all that he needs or requires in a very small sample of the whole. The essays which are comprised in *A New View of Society* and the so-called *Report to the County of Lanark* are almost in themselves sufficient; even within this limited compound Owen says all the essential things much oftener than once.[1] Owen's point of departure is essentially the same as that of Godwin, although from this common central core he subsequently branches in different directions, above all in his applications. Almost the whole of Owen is comprised in one proposition which, with significantly little change, he continued to repeat throughout the years. That proposition is that our characters are made for us, and that accordingly we are in no way responsible for what we are. Owen considered that he had discovered a new science, which he called 'the science of the influence of circumstances,' though in fact the development of the science never got much beyond the frequent reiteration of the fundamental proposition.

As concise a statement as any is that contained in the Third Essay (of *A New View of Society*), where it takes this form with all the added emphasis of italicised type:

> Every day will make it more and more evident that the character of man is, without a single exception, always formed for him; that it may be, and is, chiefly, created by his predecessors; that they give him, or may give him, his ideas and habits, which are the powers that govern and direct his conduct.

[1] It is unwise to read too widely in Owen. All any reader need wish to have is contained in the admirable selection made by Mr. G. D. H. Cole for the Everyman series, under the title, *A New View of Society, and other writings by Robert Owen*. The reader goes outside this at his peril. References given, unless otherwise stated, are to this edition.

Man, therefore, never did, nor is it possible he ever can, form his own character.[1]

This is the error which the human race must in some way formally renounce, and Owen resorts to what is, for him, considerable violence of language in denouncing this evil legacy. It is 'a fundamental error of the highest possible magnitude'; it is 'the true and sole origin of evil'; it has been 'the Evil Genius of the world.' Rising to further heights, the notion that individuals form their own character becomes 'this hydra of human calamity, this immolator of every principle of rationality, this monster.'[2] Almost a generation later, the principle of Good is 'the knowledge that man is formed, without his consent, by nature and society'; while the principle of Evil is 'the supposition that man forms himself.'[3]

It follows, on Godwinian lines, that since our character is made for us, character may be moulded by changing the environment, but Owen differs from Godwin in the emphasis he lays on the mathematical precision with which any desired result can be obtained in this great human laboratory:

> Any general character, from the best to the worst, from the most ignorant to the most enlightened, may be given to any community, even to the world at large, by the application of the proper means; which means are to a great extent at the command and under the control of those who have influence in the affairs of men.[4]

Further it will become

> evident to the understanding, that by far the greater part of the misery with which man is encircled *may* be easily dissipated and removed; and that with mathematical precision he *may* be surrounded with those circumstances which must gradually increase his happiness.[5]

This explains the importance of education in Owen's scheme of things; for there is literally nothing that education cannot do. Godwin, it will be remembered, shied at education as a possible regenerator, not because of his lack of faith in the power of education, but because of the impossibility of finding the right preceptors in a world where all school preceptors are fettered by their old school ties. But Owen has no such qualms, and education may produce the perfect community:

[1] *A New View of Society*, Third Essay (Everyman), p. 45.

[2] *Ibid.* Fourth Essay, p. 65.

[3] *Revolution in Mind and Practice*, p. 1.

[4] *A New View of Society*, First Essay (Everyman), p. 20. The Owenite idea was, of course, in the air. As Mrs. B. (an admirable reflector of the *Zeitgeist*) said to Caroline in 1816: 'Youth and innocence may be moulded into any form you chuse to give them' (Mrs. Marcet, *Conversations on Political Economy*, p. 159). Youth we may define, even if arbitrarily. But who is innocent? According to Godwin, as we have seen, the innocence of childhood is already sullied in the first seven days of life.

[5] *Ibid.* p. 20.

On the experience of a life devoted to the subject, I hesitate not to say, that the members of any community may by degrees be trained to live *without idleness, without poverty, without crime, and without punishment*; for each of these is the effect of error in the various systems prevalent throughout the world. *They are all necessary consequences of ignorance.*[1]

The plasticity, especially of the young, is a point to which Owen frequently recurs:

Human nature, save the minute differences which are ever found in all the compounds of the creation, is one and the same in all; it is without exception universally plastic.[2]

As a result of this plasticity and the mathematical precision with which the educational manipulator can work, 'the rising generations may become in character, without any individual exceptions, whatever men can now desire them to be, that is not contrary to human nature.' [3]

With Owen it follows also that ignorance, vice and misery are more or less different words for the same thing, and that (as in Socrates and Godwin) knowledge and virtue are identified. It is not merely that, in general terms, ignorance is the sole obstacle in the way of realising a world without crime and without poverty; but that in some mysterious way (which flies in the face of most mundane experience) happiness is in proportion to knowledge:

When the knowledge he receives is true and unmixed with error, although it be limited, if the community in which he lives possesses the same kind and degree of knowledge, he will enjoy happiness in proportion to the extent of that knowledge. On the contrary, when the opinions which he receives are erroneous . . . his misery will be in proportion to the extent of those erroneous opinions.[4]

Again, as in Godwin, truth has but to be seen to be embraced: it imposes itself:

Let truth unaccompanied with error be placed before them; give them time to examine it and to see that it is in unison with all previously ascertained truths; and conviction and acknowledgment of it will follow of course.[5]

Such is the philosophical framework of all Owen's thoughts, and it is already adequately presented in *A New View of Society*, although in the foregoing summary a few supporting phrases have been borrowed from elsewhere. It will be noticed how close in all this he stands to Godwin. Men have their characters formed for them; no one can *will* his beliefs. No one is responsible for anything. Consequently the whole idea of punishment is out of place. Owen frequently com-

[1] *A New View of Society*, Second Essay, p. 37.
[2] *Ibid.* Fourth Essay, p. 72.
[3] *Report to the County of Lanark* (Everyman), p. 279.
[4] *A New View of Society*, Third Essay, p. 55.
[5] *Ibid.* Second Essay, p. 24.

plains that Society makes men criminals and then punishes them for their crimes. Also there is no conceivable foundation for private displeasure or public enmity; hence also 'the irrationality of being angry with an individual for possessing qualities which he had not the means of preventing.'[1] This high standard of refraining from all anger, Owen endeavoured to realise, and with considerable success.

Into all these questions of Providence, Foreknowledge, Will and Fate, heaven forbid that we should enter. With the discussion of such problems, it will be remembered, the fallen angels beguiled the tedium of their waiting hours, 'and found no end in wandering mazes lost'; and to such higher intellects of more ampler leisure such issues may be left. It may merely be observed that the argument for improved environment does not require for its support the extreme view regarding the formation of man's character postulated by Owen. The wonderful works at New Lanark might have been founded on common sense, and not on the curious hybrid between metaphysics and theology which, in Owen's imagination, supplied the driving power.

Education, as has been noted, is to be the great engine of transformation. Apart from noting that Owen has a healthy distrust of bookish learning, and that his object is to make children rational creatures and not mere receptacles of decanted knowledge, skilled in knowing all the answers, his educational theories may be left to the educational expert.[2] But again, although this represents unquestionably one of the brightest sides of Owen, he frequently mars his argument by grotesque overstatements, and by the exuberant and buoyant expectations with which he regards the coming world. By the application of his system, he says, there will be produced characters which even in youth will 'greatly surpass the wise and learned of the present and preceding times.'[3] The adoption of his plans 'will show the boasted acquirements of Greece, of Rome, and of all antiquity, to be the mere weakness of mental infancy.'[4] And if these rosy prospects may be thought to be lacking in precision, there is nothing vague about his bold undertaking on behalf of the child properly trained on Owenite lines: 'Before he is twelve years old he may with ease be trained to acquire a correct view of the outline of all the knowledge which men have yet attained.'[5]

[1] *A New View of Society*, Second Essay, p. 23.

[2] One point of general interest may, however, be extracted. The boys of Owen's future settlements are to wear kilts, or, in more dignified language, 'a dress somewhat resembling the Roman and Highland garb.' 'The Romans and Highlanders of Scotland,' he says, 'appear to be the only two nations who adopted a national dress on account of its utility, without, however, neglecting to render it highly becoming and ornamental.' But it may be doubted whether Owen really understood the inner mechanism of the kilt (*Report to the County of Lanark*, pp. 277–278).

[3] *A New View of Society*, Third Essay, p. 49.

[4] *Ibid.* Fourth Essay, p. 80.

[5] *Report to the County of Lanark*, p. 284.

Of remedial measures apart from education, Owen (at the stage of *A New View of Society*) suggests an overhauling of our legislation with a view to ' withdrawing ' (by which presumably he means ' repealing ') those laws which rest on the erroneous doctrine that man is responsible for the formation of his own character. It would be a curious question to enquire how far such an instruction to the Parliamentary draftsman might not result in the repeal of all existing legislation, and the diligent research student could possibly unearth passages in the later Owen indicating that he would not be averse from such a solution. But what he has in fact primarily in mind, as ripe for 'withdrawal,' are the laws which train the population to every kind of crime, those which encourage ' the consumption of ardent spirits,' those which legalise and sanction gin-shops and pot-houses, gambling and lotteries. To these, which are legitimate and orthodox fields of reform, Owen adds among the laws which should be withdrawn the rather cryptic phrase, ' those of punishment.' [1] Contrary to his usual practice, he does not dwell on this ; but the implication clearly is that all penalties of any kind should be abolished.

Alongside education and the repeal of laws inspired by the ' erroneous principle,' there is a third proposal in which Owen is a century in advance of his times. He suggests the need of a thorough-going system of labour statistics as a preliminary to the State providing work for the unemployed. The information is to be supplied ' by the clergy, justices of the peace, or other more competent persons,' [2] —the ' other more competent person ' being a distant foreshadowing and adumbration of the Ministry of Labour official. His suggested questionnaire is reasonably concise and to the point. The return should cover : (i) the average price of manual labour in each district ; (ii) the number dependent on their labour (or the parish) for support, who are at the time unemployed, but are yet able to labour, *i.e.* the number available ; (iii) the number partially employed, and the extent of their partial employment ; (iv) a statement in respect of each of their former employments, and the ' best conjectures ' as to the kind and quantity of work each may be supposed capable of performing. This ' best conjecture ' seems to bring Owen agreeably into direct relationship with the manager of the present-day Employment Exchange, who also on many occasions is still reduced to his ' best conjectures.' And Owen adds to his discussion :

> It would, perhaps, prove an interesting calculation, and useful to Government, to estimate how much its finances would be improved by giving proper employment to a million of its subjects, rather than by supporting that million in ignorance, idleness and crime . . .[3]

[1] *A New View of Society*, Fourth Essay, p. 66.
[2] *Ibid.* Fourth Essay, p. 83.
[3] *Ibid.* p. 85.

a question which, with appropriate modifications, some have still the temerity to ask.

So far we have been concerned with those aspects of Owen's teaching that spring more or less directly from his views on Man and the formation of Man's character. Perhaps those parts of his argument which rest on general humanitarian considerations, rather than on logic-chopping discussions on Man's will, make a stronger appeal to our generation, if only because here Owen is more universally human. Here indeed Owen rises to real eloquence—if indeed the eloquence be his; for there is a vague tradition that Owen, who became an increasingly barbarous writer as he advanced in years, had the prudence to have his earlier writings, or some of them, revised by Francis Place. When he pleads for justice to the oppressed, above all when he upholds the cause of the little children, he touches a chord which still vibrates; and he is, perhaps curiously, no less effective because in the earlier days his argument is reinforced by the consideration that it pays to be kind. The most famous of these passages—unfortunately too long for unabridged quotation here—is in the *Address to the Superintendents of Manufactories, etc.*, originally prefixed to the Third Essay in *A New View*. Here he contrasts the care given to the animate and that given to the inanimate machines:

> Many of you have long experienced in your manufacturing operations the advantages of substantial, well-contrived, and well-executed machinery.
>
> Experience has also shown you the difference of the results between mechanism which is neat, clean, well-arranged, and always in a high state of repair; and that which is allowed to be dirty, in disorder, without the means of preventing unnecessary friction, and which therefore becomes, and works, much out of repair. . . .
>
> If, then, due care as to the state of your inanimate machines can produce such beneficial results, what may not be expected if you devote equal attention to your vital machines, which are far more wonderfully constructed?
>
> When you shall acquire a right knowledge of these, of their curious mechanism, of their self-adjusting powers; when the proper main-spring shall be applied to their varied movements,—you will become conscious of their real value, and you will readily be induced to turn your thoughts more frequently from your inanimate to your living machines; you will discover that the latter may be easily trained and directed to procure a large increase of pecuniary gain, while you may also derive from them high and substantial gratification. . . .
>
> . . . And when in these transactions you estimate time by minutes, and the money expended for the chance of increased gain by fractions, will you not afford some of your attention to consider whether a portion of your time and capital would not be more advantageously applied to improve your living machines? From experience which cannot deceive me, I venture to assure you, that your time and money so applied, if directed by a true knowledge of the subject, would return you, not five, ten, or fifteen per cent. for your capital so expended, but often fifty, and in many cases a hundred per cent.[1]

[1] *A New View of Society* (Everyman), pp. 8–9.

This somewhat lengthy quotation may perhaps be forgiven, because it shows Owen at his best, both in substance and in manner of expression, combining the sweetness of reason with the wisdom of serpents, reconciling philanthropy with fifteen per cent. When he deals with the evils of child labour in the *Address to the British Master Manufacturers*, there is just a suggestion of righteous indignation in the voice of Owen, although indignation was alien alike to his temperament and his principles. Pleading that no child should be employed under the age of twelve, he argues (as in the passage already quoted) that the child who is put to work at too early an age is an ' inferior instrument ':

> I think an intelligent slave master would not, on the sole principle of pecuniary gain, employ his young slaves even ten hours of the day at so early an age. And we know that judicious farmers will not prematurely put their young beasts of burden to work; and that when they do put them to work it is with great moderation at first, and, we must remember too, in a healthy atmosphere. But children from seven to eight years of age are employed with young persons and women of all ages, for fourteen or fifteen hours per day in many of our manufactures, carried on in buildings in which the atmosphere is by no means the most favourable to human life.[1]

In his appeal to his fellow-manufacturers, another and more modern note creeps in. It is a plea for a policy of high wages on the ground of the importance of maintaining the purchasing-power of the population at large. No evil, he says, ought to be more dreaded by master-manufacturers than low wages of labour. By virtue of their numbers, the workers must always be the greatest consumers of all articles. High wages and general prosperity go together. Moreover, in the manufacturers' interest, the worker should not merely be well paid; he ought to have the time and the instruction necessary to make him a judicious purchaser.[2]

While Owen's starting-point in this matter is thus an appeal, as from one employer to another, to do the right thing in their own interest, he not unnaturally arrives at a condemnation of the ' system ' and to the familiar analysis of the evils of individualism, which is more in line with the socialist tradition. So far as the worker is concerned, the position has been brought to ' a point of real oppression.' ' The employer regards the employed as mere instruments of gain.'[3] So also he speaks of the ' blind avarice of commerce.' More in line with the exploitation theories Owen refers to the inventions of the Industrial Revolution as having ' created an aggregate of wealth, and placed it in the hands of a few, who, by its aid, continue to absorb the wealth produced by the industry of the many.'[4] As a consequence, ' the mass

[1] *To the British Master Manufacturers* (Everyman), p. 142.
[2] *Ibid.* pp. 143–144.
[3] *Observations on the Effect of the Manufacturing System* (Everyman), p. 121.
[4] *Report to the County of Lanark* (Everyman), p. 258.

of the population are become mere slaves to the ignorance and caprice of those monopolists.' Much later Owen was to speak of 'the money-making, health-and-happiness-destroying factories of our country'[1]; it is clear that even when he was part of the machine he looked at it dispassionately from the outside.

From this it is an easy transition to consider Owen's criticisms of individualism, although in fact the question arises more prominently in connection with his communistic proposals which will be noted presently. In the earlier writings, to which in fairness to Owen reference alone should be made, the most clear statement occurs in a passage in the *Report to the County of Lanark* in commendation of the principle of co-operation. Here, after having condemned the present arrangement of society as 'the most anti-social, impolitic, and irrational that can be devised,' he continues:

> From this principle of individual interest have arisen all the divisions of mankind, the endless errors and mischiefs of class, sect, party, and of national antipathies, creating the angry and malevolent passions, and all the crimes and misery with which the human race have hitherto been afflicted.
>
> In short, if there be one closet doctrine more contrary to truth than another, it is the notion that individual interest, as that term is now understood, is a more advantageous principle on which to found the social system, for the benefit of all, or of any, than the principle of union and mutual co-operation.[2]

There is in its implications an even more extreme passage in one of the London speeches of 1817—the notorious speech of August 21—where in contrasting life under what he calls the 'cottage system' as against complete co-operation, he paints a somewhat grotesquely glowing picture of what happens when all men have all things in common, so that even widowhood would not be the awful thing it now is. Even if a dear one dies 'they have consolation in the certain knowledge that . . . they have many, many others remaining.' 'As far as the eye can reach or imagination extend' there are thousands and thousands ready and willing to offer aid and consolation. As another poet has it:

> Seid umschlungen, Millionen!
> Diesen Kuss der ganzen Welt!

But indeed, when love of humanity becomes so diffused, it is in danger of becoming sloppy; and the *Kuss der ganzen Welt* may afford little real consolation in bereavement. As against this dream-world, where thousands and thousands are prepared to stand by, in the contrary condition:

> All are individualised, cold and forbidding; each being compelled to take an hundred-fold more care of himself than would be otherwise neces-

[1] *Manifesto of Robert Owen.*

[2] *Report to the County of Lanark* (Everyman), p. 269.

sary; because the ignorance of society has placed him in direct opposition to the thousands around him.[1]

Later in life Owen came to denounce private property with a full-blooded vigour which may be equalled, but is certainly not excelled, elsewhere: 'Private property is one of the great demoralising and repulsive powers, arising from the laws of men, and is the cause of innumerable crimes and gross injustice. . . . It is strongly calculated to make man look upon his fellow man as his enemy, and to create general suspicions of the motives and actions of strangers, and even of neighbours. . . . The evils of private property tend in all directions.'[2] But down these many alleys it is unnecessary to follow Owen.

We have listened to Owen giving most excellent advice to his fellow-manufacturers. Not unnaturally, Owen being Owen, counsel is also freely imparted to the other side. It is, however, less excellent advice, having regard to the frailty of man, and it derives its interest almost exclusively from the light which it throws on Owen and the curious workings of his mind. It is found at its best in *An Address to the Working Classes*, dated March 29, 1819. He assures the workers that 'the time is at hand'—but unfortunately there is one formidable obstacle. All uncharitableness and anger must be laid aside; in other words, the working classes must rise to a full appreciation of the Owenite doctrine that no one is responsible for what they are, and that therefore there can be no rational ground for anger, even against their greatest oppressors and their most bitter enemies. Owen presents his favourite sermon in tabloid form for the rumination of the workers:

> An endless multiplicity of circumstances, over which you had not the smallest control, placed you where you are, and as you are. In the same manner, others of your fellow-men have been formed by circumstances, equally uncontrollable by them, to become your enemies and grievous oppressors. In strict justice they are no more to be blamed for these results than you are; nor you than they; and, splendid as their exterior may be, this state of matters often causes them to suffer even more poignantly than you.[3]

If the workers show any desire violently to dispossess the rich of their power, emoluments and privileges, 'the contention between the rich and the poor will never have an end.' Owen indeed seeks to impose on the working classes a kind of Credo, an adherence to the only faith, as a necessary condition of the day being at hand:

> Are you then prepared to look upon all your fellow-creatures, in power and out of power, rich and poor, learned and unlearned, good and bad, as beings formed solely by the circumstances of their birth, and who have been

[1] *Address of 21st August*, 1817 (Everyman), p. 215.
[2] *Revolution in Mind and Practice*, p. 111.
[3] *An Address to the Working Classes* (Everyman), p. 149.

made as they are, whatever they may be, from causes which exclude the possibility of the smallest control on their parts in the formation of those faculties and qualities they may happen to possess? If you cannot see and comprehend this truth, then is the time not yet come for your deliverance from the depths of mental darkness and physical misery.[1]

This line of argument is rendered possible because we are on the eve of a period when the poor will be able to relieve themselves of their poverty without infringing on the possessions of the rich. In future, 'the least gifted member of society will experience a larger share of continued and permanent happiness than has hitherto fallen to the lot of the most fortunate.' Besides, as is indeed obvious on Godwin's principles, the rich are not really such a bad lot. We have seen that frequently they suffer more poignantly than the poor: they 'call for our pity, not blame.' As if all that were not enough, Owen gives his own personal guarantee that the rich are not without their claim to a possible share of the world's decency:

> It must be satisfactory to you to learn that I have had the most evident proofs from many individuals, high in these classes, that they have now a real desire to improve your condition.[2]

One wonders how the 'working classes' reacted to this curiously maddening mixture of naiveté, condescension, philosophical generalities, and sheer obtuseness. At least it helps one to understand the saying that in conversation with Owen 'you could not put him in a passion nor keep yourself out of one.' [3]

In endeavouring to present a general picture of Owen's system of thought, a certain number of citations have already been given, which in their context will be found to have relation to his proposals for the establishment of communistic settlements, or villages of co-operation—'Owen's parallelograms,' as they were familiarly called with

[1] *An Address to the Working Classes* (Everyman), pp. 150–151.

[2] *Ibid.* p. 153.

[3] Owen's unsolicited testimonial to the well-meaningness of his fellow-employers may advantageously be compared with a somewhat similar utterance of Charles Kingsley later (1854), as representing the Christian Socialists: 'There is no doubt that the classes possessing property have been facing, since 1848, all social questions with an average of honesty, earnestness and good feeling which has no parallel since the days of the Tudors, and that hundreds and thousands of "gentlemen and ladies" in Great Britain now are saying, "Show what we ought to do to be just to the workmen, and we will do it, whatsoever it costs." They may not be always correct (though they generally are so) in their conceptions of what ought to be done; but their purpose is good and righteous; and those who hold it are daily increasing in number. The love of justice and mercy toward the handicraftsman is spreading rapidly as it never did before in any nation upon earth; and if any man still represents the holders of property, as a class, as the enemies of those whom they employ, desiring their slavery and their ignorance, I believe that he is a liar and a child of the devil, and that he is at his father's old work, slandering and dividing between man and man' (Preface addressed to the Working Men of Great Britain prefixed to *Alton Locke*).

an intended touch of ridicule. There is little doubt that Owen from the outset regarded New Lanark as an experiment to be applied later to the whole nation, and indeed in the days of his more grandiose dreams, to the world at large. As early as the second essay in *A New View* he had asked what there was to prevent such a system from being immediately adopted into national practice.[1] The argument for his increasingly communistic settlements is first elaborated in the *Report to the Committee for the Relief of the Manufacturing Poor* (1817), and it occupies a central position in the *Report to the County of Lanark* (1820). Later, of course, it is the staple of all his writings.

In its first appearance, Owen's 'Plan' was devised as a remedy against unemployment. He had already postulated in *A New View of Society* that it was a primary duty of every government that cared for its subjects 'to provide perpetual employment of real national utility, in which all who apply may be immediately occupied.'[2] The acknowledgment of such a duty was more than ever urgent in the circumstances of the times, of which Owen gives a penetrating analysis. The Industrial Revolution had, he argued, brought with it greatly increased productive power. In the result, 'individual interest . . . found mechanism to be a cheaper agency than manual labour'; workers were accordingly dismissed, and 'labour in consequence rapidly fell in value.'[3] It was this fall in the value of labour which, Owen contended, had to be remedied and for which his Plan was devised. If value is thus to be restored to manual labour, it can be done only by employment on the land, and accordingly what is aimed at is the creation of 'limited communities of individuals, on the principle of united labour and expenditure, having their basis in agriculture, and in which all should have mutual and common interests.'[4] Elsewhere, in the Lanark Report, he speaks of the great error that has been committed 'in separating the worker from his food.'[5] The worker therefore is to go back to the land, but not wholly to the land; the habitations of Owen's vision are described as 'combined agricultural and manufacturing villages.[6]

Such settlements are to be financed by the State in one way or another. The minimum number in each will be 300, 'men, women and children in their natural proportions,' with a maximum of 2,000; but somewhere between 800 and 1200 is indicated as the optimum.[7] The inhabitants will live in large buildings arranged in a parallelogram,

[1] *A New View of Society*, Second Essay, p. 36.
[2] *Ibid.*, Fourth Essay, p. 86.
[3] *Report to the Committee for the Relief of the Manufacturing Poor*, p. 157; *Address of 21st August*, 1817, p. 211.
[4] *A Catechism of the New View of Society* (Everyman), pp. 175, 180.
[5] *Report to the County of Lanark*, p. 266.
[6] *Catechism of New View*, p. 180.
[7] *Report to the County of Lanark*, Part III: Details of the Plan, p. 264.

and the apportionment of the various wings to their respective uses is amply detailed by Owen. Pleasing pictorial representations of these may be unearthed by diligent students in the literature of the period. They are obviously first cousins of the Phalanstère, although Fourier, on whom Owen acted as a perpetual irritant, never admitted kinship. Of the success of such villages of co-operation Owen never entertained any doubt. He held that with the increased power of production, it was possible 'to saturate the world with wealth'[1]; but owing to our mismanagement—and here he strikes a modern note—'in the midst of the most ample means to create wealth, all are in poverty, or in imminent danger from the effects of poverty upon others.'[2]

As additional aids to prosperity, Owen has two further recommendations. The first is that we should abandon the plough and return to the spade.[3] It may be doubted whether Owen knew very much about either the spade or the plough; but that, of course, is no reason why he should not dilate at very considerable length on the superiority of the spade as an agricultural instrument. With the spade, Great Britain and Ireland could support in high comfort a population greatly exceeding one hundred millions; whereas, relying on the plough, it was already supposed to be greatly overpopulated. Owen's passion for the spade is perhaps best viewed as merely an additional resonant bee in his teeming bonnet; but of course it may be linked up with a semi-conscious realisation that if ever his villages of co-operation were realised, having regard to their population and the area assigned to them, their agriculture would probably of necessity have to take the form of market gardening.

The other aid to prosperity is concerned with more fundamental problems, being nothing less than a suggestion for a new standard of value, which is necessary, if we are, in a pleasing phrase, 'to let prosperity loose on the country.'[4] Owen, it is to be feared, was not a currency expert—who is?—and a perusal of his arguments may produce in the mind of the reader a pale reflection of that confusion in which Owen groped. On the side of theory his observations have some interest, inasmuch as they show Owen stretching forth a hand—a somewhat shaky hand—towards Marx; on the practical and historical side, they have some significance as supplying the basis on which that later fiasco, the National Equitable Labour Exchange, was based.

Expressed broadly, Owen's position here is tolerably clear. It is 'that the natural standard of value is, in principle, human labour, or the combined manual and mental powers of men called into action.'[5] Obviously, the difficulty under any circumstances of applying a labour

[1] *Report to the County of Lanark*, p. 247.
[2] *Ibid.* p. 270.
[3] *Ibid.* p. 259.
[4] *Ibid.* p. 248.
[5] *Ibid.* p. 250.

standard will be considerably accentuated by lumping manual and mental powers together. It would be an invidious task to check up on the amount of effort (and experience) the spring poet puts into a love song. In order to make labour the standard of value, it will be necessary, says Owen, to ascertain the amount of it in all articles to be bought or sold.[1] All articles thereafter are to be exchanged at what he calls their 'prime cost.' The awkward fact, as was made manifest in the experience of the National Equitable Labour Exchange, is that there can never be any guarantee that people at large will be willing to exchange at the rates so determined, assuming indeed that it is possible to determine such rates at all. Almost inevitably a notional number of hours comes to be assigned as that necessary for the commodity's production, and in arriving at a decision in this matter, the calculator consciously or unconsciously bases himself on what is happening in the open market, where the despised money prices prevail. Owen, although he fails to make his proposals clear, at least remained faithful to the view that money, as we know it, is an evil. Much later he declared that until we should have disabused our minds of this insane money-mystery, it was impossible that the world could be other than a great lunatic asylum.[2] At this later stage a paper money resting on the credit of the British Empire appears to represent his aspirations.[3]

Thus launched, preferably with the aid of the spade and a new standard of value, the villages of co-operation will propagate until all the world is shaped in their similitude. It is the usual naively pathetic vision which has sustained so many dreamers, again rather reminiscent of Fourier's faith in the triumphant spread of the Phalanstère, but perhaps still more in line with Louis Blanc's confidence that competition would be driven out by competition, so that the beaten capitalist would come creeping into the workshop. Not merely will society permit these new establishments to supersede other forms of enterprise, since these latter are 'wretchedly degrading'[4]; a more cogent argument is that the parish poor, for whom in the first place these projects were devised, will under the new arrangements become the envy of the rich and the indolent.[5] Here indeed is an inverted principle of 'greater eligibility.' No wonder that Owen could say that the utmost bounds of his ambition was to become an undistinguished member of one of these happy villages[6]; or that he could claim with his usual buoyancy that 'to resist the introduction of this plan, in any part of the world, will *now* be as vain and useless, as for

[1] *Report to the County of Lanark*, p. 262.
[2] *Revolution in Mind and Practice*, p. 35.
[3] *Ibid.* p. 53.
[4] *Catechism of the New View* (Everyman), p. 181.
[5] *Further Development of the Plan*, etc. (Everyman), pp. 231–232.
[6] *Address of 14th August*, 1817 (Everyman), p. 201.

man by his puny efforts to endeavour to preclude from the earth the vivifying rays of the sun.[1]

Owen is commendably vague as to how his parallelograms are to be run; but it is perhaps of the essence of dreams that they achieve their effect by the vividness of the general impression rather than by consistency of operative detail. The villages, townships, or whatever they may be called, are to be governed by Committees of all the members of a certain seniority. But in the last analysis, they will run themselves, so that in a sense we come back to Godwin once more: 'In a short time the ease with which these associations will proceed in all their operations will be such as to render the business of governing a mere recreation.'[2] Later in life, as his dreams became still more exuberant, Owen was to make the surprising discovery that each township was to become 'the immediate agent of God, to carry into execution the laws of the Universal Creating Power'[3]; and on this basis he exercised his fancy and ingenuity in strange flights of constitution-mongering. But there was one current bogy in particular which Owen would in no wise allow to becloud his vision of a world gone parallelogram. This was the suggestion that the Malthusian devil of over-population might lurk in ambush on the path towards his earthly paradise. Owen will not have Malthus at any price. In an observation which may not indeed go to the root of the matter, but at least goes some distance in that direction, he remarks that Malthus 'has not told us how much more food an intelligent and industrious people will create from the same soil, than will be produced by one ignorant and ill-governed.'[4] Even if one may not accept his suggestion that the ratio is as one to infinity (meaning, of course, as infinity to one), this remains a just observation, and more to the point than his general argument that 'each individual brings into the world with him the means . . . sufficient to enable him to produce food equal to more than ten times his consumption.'[5] His attitude is stated more explicitly in one of his later writings, where in effect his answer is that the question cannot arise until the whole surface of the globe is studded with parallelograms; if that time ever does arise, the population of the world (having been for long indoctrinated with Owenism) will be 'highly good, intelligent and rational,' and they will know far better what to do than this present most irrational generation. But to worry about these questions at the present moment, when the earth is comparatively a waste and a forest, is 'one of the thousand insanities with which the present generation is afflicted.[6] Thus, like the burden

[1] *Further Development of the Plan*, etc., p. 232.
[2] *Report to the County of Lanark*, p. 287.
[3] *Revolution in Mind and Practice*, p. 72.
[4] *A New View of Society*, Fourth Essay, p. 85.
[5] *Catechism of the New View* (Everyman), pp. 181–182.
[6] *Revolution in Mind and Practice*, p. 122.

of the National Debt, in old-fashioned Financial Science, the responsibility is waltzed on to a future generation ; but the underlying assumption which justifies this postponement is that the village of co-operation will march relentlessly across the sands of the Sahara, through the dark swamps of the upper Amazon, and across the lonely high places of Tibet.

Perhaps it is not expedient, within the allotted framework, to carry further the presentation of Robert Owen. His views on marriage are outside our province, and are only of slight interest because here is still one further point in which he approaches somewhat to Godwin. His views on religion are of some significance because of the reasons underlying his comprehensive antagonism towards all the orthodoxies of the world ; it was that all known religions were guilty of the fundamental error involved in holding that a man may be held responsible for the formation of his character, and trafficked in rewards and punishments accordingly. They were therefore guilty of what, in Owen's eyes, was the greatest of all heresies ; they were tied to the 'principle of evil.' On a larger canvas it would be interesting to illustrate Owen's dislike of political action and agitation, and indeed his distrust of the political machine generally. Though the second part of his life was a succession of fiascos, ending in the shoals and shallows of a very peculiar type of spiritualism, there is nevertheless force in the contention that in countless ways he was one of the most pervading influences in the later nineteenth century, and that, in current jargon, his was a seminal mind. Yet the ordinary man turns back to the miracle of New Lanark, as the crowning achievement of Owen, who, in the darkest days of the Industrial Revolution, showed, even if in undemocratic ways and building on strange principles, what love could do to regenerate a fallen community. And even if the second part of his life was barren of achievement, so far as the world's coarse thumb and finger could assess, Owen's life is memorable, if not unique, in presenting us with a man who achieved wealth and success, and yet, counting these as dross, cast them aside to gain for his fellow-men a greater salvation : 'Blessed is the rich that is found without blemish, and hath not gone after gold. Who is he ? and we will call him blessed ; for wonderful things hath he done among his people.'

CHAPTER IX

LOUIS BLANC

UNLIKE most of those whom we encounter in these pages, Louis Blanc (1813–1882), in addition to occupying a very distinct corner in the development of socialist thought, was also for a time an active and practising politician, having been a member of the provisional government after the Revolution of 1848. This incursion into the limelight was followed by a prolonged period of exile in England, from which he did not return to France until 1870, when he again appeared on the political stage, without, however, getting anywhere in particular. His intromissions with public affairs do not concern us here, and we are accordingly spared the problem of disentangling the connection, if any, between the fiasco of the National Workshops of 1848 and the proposals bearing on the same issue which are of the very essence of Blanc's writings. But, if one may judge from the printed word, it is difficult to imagine anyone less fitted than was Louis Blanc for the trials, the tribulations and the responsibilities of a politician's existence.

On the other hand he had very great gifts as a journalist, and was indeed a supremely successful journalist at a surprisingly early age. He was also professedly a historian, waging war against the Bourgeoisie throughout the ages, and laying up for posterity numerous volumes which at this distance of time posterity, at least in this country, very wisely refuses to read.[1] For the present generation, and for all who come hereafter, he is the author of one book, *L'Organisation du Travail*, which originally appeared in substance in *La Revue du Progrès Social*, in 1839. It is a short book, even when expanded with replies to critics which were added in subsequent editions. And of subsequent editions there were many, for in this work Louis Blanc contrived to write a best-seller.

[1] Henri Baudrillart's comments on Blanc as a historian are so pleasingly acid, that they deserve not to be wholly forgotten : ' L'auteur a beaucoup lu, non pas sans doute comme lit un historien impartial, mais comme lit un avocat donc la thème est fait d'avance. . . . Plusieurs de ces récits rapellent la manière dont Tacite, qu'il semble vouloir imiter et avec lequel je ne le compare pas, dépeint la revolte des légions de Pannonie et de Germanie. Sa concision piquante se plait aux portraits et y réussit. Je parle de l'effet et non de la justesse' (Baudrillart: *Publicistes Modernes*, 1863, p. 305). The reader who feels that it may be unjust to Blanc to judge him solely by *L'Organisation du Travail*, as is now almost universally done, may read the first (of the twelve !) volumes of the *Histoire de la Révolution Française*. This volume is devoted to the history of Europe viewed as a preparation for the French Revolution. All history is regarded as the record of the conflict and interreactions of three principles, Authority, Individualism and Fraternity. The Bourgeoisie is identified with individualism. The whole volume is a rather curious example of carrying current antipathies and nomenclature into the narration of the past.

Nor is it difficult to understand the success which attended *L'Organisation du Travail.* There is a persuasiveness and a glitter about it, which could scarcely fail to turn the heads of those to whom it was addressed. Yet the qualities which made it so effective on its appearance now perhaps make us feel that it has worn rather thin. Never was there a writer given to so violent exaggeration. Few have cultivated so gaudy and flamboyant a style, or been so familiar with the rhetorical question which expects no answer. His pages are cluttered up with marks of exclamation and of interrogation. There are immeasurably far too many *Quoi's*, and *Eh quoi's*, and *Mais quoi's.* The result is a heady beverage which may appear great stuff to a reader in a moment of exaltation, but somehow it sounds rather differently when read in the cold light of dawn. In short, Louis Blanc has neither moderation, nor restraint, nor sense of proportion, and such merits as he possesses seem, on a second reading, to be contaminated with the meretricious and the cheap.

The significance of Louis Blanc lies in the fact that in a sense he represents the transition from Utopian socialism to what, for convenience, may be termed proletarian socialism. We have left behind the wild imaginings of Fourier, the revelations of Saint-Simon and the parallelograms of Owen. For Louis Blanc claims to have a sense of reality, and he would like to be regarded as moderate. 'To prepare for the future without breaking violently with the past,' as he once described his purpose, is an excellent ideal. Doubtless, with Fourier and Owen, he is an 'associationist,' but the form of association at which he aims has a more modern flavour; nor is it expected that some generous millionaire will by his touch heal and renew this putrescent world.

For, among much that is nebulous, Louis Blanc sees with extreme clarity just exactly whence our salvation must come: Our safety cometh from the State. Blanc may or may not have been original in this, but at least no one before had so clearly taught that the State, with which we are familiar here and now, such as it is, must be used to establish a new social order. Social and political reform are intertwined; if the former is the aim and object, the latter is the means. For it is not enough to decide, according to the rules of reason, justice and humanity, where you want to get to in this matter of the organisation of labour. You must be in a position to give effect to the principles decided upon. Power is needed; and power is ultimately a matter of laws, tribunals and soldiers—in a word, the State. In a somewhat famous sentence he adds the warning that if you do not make use of the State as an instrument, you will encounter it as an obstacle. Moreover, the magnitude of the task of emancipating the proletarians is such that all the power of the State is needed. What is required is that they should be given the necessary tools of production ; and here precisely is the function of the government. In a definition, more arresting than just, ' the State is, or ought to be, the Banker of the Poor.' [1]

Thus the State must intervene ; there is indeed no other authority to whom appeal can be made. Authority is invoked, it should be observed, in the name of Liberty itself ; for Liberty, in the world as seen by Blanc, is but an affair of theoretical rights which cannot be enforced. There can be no liberty where an ' immense weakness ' confronts an ' immense strength '. The State must make these rights a reality, and for this purpose it must be a strong State, since there are those who in their weakness need its protection.[2]

But though a strong State is needed now, it is significant that Blanc regards this as a temporary necessity. When there is no longer an inferior class, no longer any downtrodden, there will no longer be the same need of a strong and active government. At the first blush this is curiously suggestive of the ' withering-away ' of the State, as contemplated later by Marx and Engels ; but of course the reason for the ' withering-away ' is diametrically opposed in the two cases. For Marx-Engels, the State is the expression of the dominant class, and when there are no longer classes, there can clearly be no dominant class (and equally no class to be exploited), and therefore there can no longer be a State, if the Marxian conception of the State is true. In Louis Blanc's vision, on the other hand, the State is potentially and in design a beneficent agency as the protector of the downtrodden ; but when the weak and defenceless are no longer defenceless and weak, though the State may continue to exist, it will no longer require the giant's strength needed to make it an adequate protector.

Such is the framework as set out in the Introduction ; and though Morelly may have pointed in the same direction, and though it is possible to find in the noble confusion of Saint-Simon's mind, suggestions of the beneficent State, Louis Blanc may claim credit for having brought socialism into everyday politics, and made it a matter of the ballot-box. Also, for what it is worth, he may be given some credit for realising that the State, whether we like it or not, is there, occupying the ground ; and for the rather Fabian argument, that it is better to make use of it than to force it into the opposing camp. There is one other point of interest relating to the framework, as it emerges in the introduction. In intention and profession, at least, Louis Blanc is remote from the class struggle and its implications. In some editions, the opening sentence is an appeal to the rich, since the cause of the poor is their cause also. It is on this note that the Introduction ends, and though the passage is marred by an unusually heavy dose of Blanc's

[1] P. 14 (for convenience, references to Sir John Marriott's edition).
[2] P. 17.

tinsel rhetoric, the intention is clearly to express in moving language the solidarity and the community of interest that link all classes, and to unite the efforts of all in the work of emancipation. If, as has sometimes been suggested, Louis Blanc represents the swing of socialism to the left, it is significant that he thus so completely disowns the doctrine of the class struggle which was later to become the core of scientific socialism.

Much of the success of Louis Blanc as a propagandist is due to the simplicity of his diagnosis. Like Mr. Blatchford in his more robust days, he avoids unnecessary and confusing complications. There is a certain measure of truth in the criticism which suggests that ' in Louis Blanc's creed whatever is, is wrong.' And the reason for the wrongness of everything is to be found in the existence of competition. In a sense Louis Blanc was so successful because he set himself too easy a task. Nothing is easier than to show how monstrously unjust is this world, unless perhaps it is to prove how grotesque and baneful may be the effects of competition. Neither youth nor inexperience need deter anyone from enlarging on either of these themes. And in fact Louis Blanc, with his congenital tendency to exaggeration, his exuberant rhetoric, his unfettered loquacity and mais-quoisity, does it remarkably well. He avoids the initial tactical mistake, into which so many fall, of suggesting that some have a good time at the expense of others. In fact, this is a thoroughly bad world for everybody, for rich and poor alike, and no one is really interested in the maintenance of the existing social order. How unhappy are the happy, could you but see into their hearts. For every poor man who grows pale from hunger, there is a rich man who turns pale from fear. Competition may be a system which exterminates the ordinary people; but likewise it impoverishes and ruins the Bourgeoisie. All are interested in putting an end to the existing system: here also is solidarity.

In the eyes of Louis Blanc, contemplating a world inhabited by proletarians with nothing but their labour to offer in the market-place, the fundamental right is the *droit au travail.* Indeed, with his incessant preaching of the *droit au travail*, he was probably the spiritual father and begetter of the Revolution of 1848. In considering the effect of competition on the worker, the crucial question is whether it can assure him work. And here in a much quoted and characteristic passage is Louis Blanc on what competition does for the worker:

What is competition, relative to the workers? It is work put up to auction. An entrepreneur has need of a worker: three present themselves. . . . How much for your work? . . . Three francs: I have a wife and children. . . . Good. And you? . . . Two and a half francs: I have no children, but I have a wife. . . . Marvellous. And you? . . . Two francs are enough for me: I am alone. . . . You get the job. The transaction is ended: the bargain is concluded. What will become of the two proletarians who are excluded? It is to be hoped that they will allow themselves to die of hunger. But suppose they become thieves? Have no fear; we have policemen. And murderers? We have the hangman. As for the most fortunate of the three, his triumph is only provisional. If there should come along a fourth worker sufficiently sturdy to fast every other day, wages will slide down to the bottom: there will be a new pariah, a new recruit for the convict-prison, perhaps![1]

It is to be hoped that this picturesque and dramatic passage sounds better in French than it does in halting English. The view here expressed by Louis Blanc is, of course, merely an extremely rigid statement of the so-called Iron Law of Wages, frequently, but wrongly, fathered on Ricardo. It is easy, and it is true, to say in the case of Marx and many before his time, that they did not foresee the effects of the Trade Union movement in this sphere. Probably Marx, breathing the fetid air of the British Museum, reading round about 1860 the Blue Books of 1810, was at least a generation, if not two, behind the times in which he lived. But the comforting reflection that Trade Unions have probably to a large extent equalised bargaining power, and nullified the foolishly-so-called Iron Law of Wages, should not blind us to the fact that probably at the time when this principle was first enunciated by Turgot (if Turgot it was), it was probably a fairly accurate statement of what happened. For, left to themselves in an eighteenth-century 'state of nature,' there is no employer who would not prefer to pay a low wage rather than a high, if given an assurance of equal efficiency in every respect between the employees. This is indeed all that is implied in the original statement of Turgot, who, needless to say, is less dramatic than Blanc. In any case, Louis Blanc is satisfied that under competition a continuous fall in wages is necessarily a general, and in no way an exceptional, phenomenon.

This fall in wages means poverty, and poverty means crime. Blanc proves the extent of crime by producing appropriate statistics, and he illustrates the enormity of crime by revolting reports from the Police Courts. This is of interest only because it is implicitly part of Blanc's case that *all* crime is due to poverty, and that therefore at one remove all crime is due to competition. Like nearly all the earlier socialists (in this very different from later schools), he showed a touching solicitude for the reputation of the Almighty in this matter. He dare not claim that men are born necessarily perverse, 'for fear of blaspheming God.' Rather would he believe that the work of God is good and holy: 'Let us not be impious merely in order that we may absolve ourselves from the charge of having spoiled it.'[2] He then refers to certain unnamed 'great philosophers' who have thrown doubts on man's free will: in any case it can hardly exist for the poor who suffer from 'la tyrannie des choses,' which claims as its victims all who are in need

[1] P. 30. [2] Pp. 47–48.

of nourishment, clothing or shelter. There is a good deal of fine confusion in this medley of philosophy and theology, but Blanc's argument is meaningless, unless it means that all crimes can be attributed to our defective social organisation as embodied in the prevalence of competition.

For all this evil Louis Blanc naturally claims that there can be only one remedy, that, namely, devised by Louis Blanc—in other words, a 'saine organisation du travail.'[1] His rather disgruntled frame of mind, his instinctive abhorrence of all moderation despite contrary professions, are well seen in his attitude towards the proposals of other well-meaning reformers. Take, for example, the whole question of savings and the establishment of Savings Banks as a means of raising the worker. Had Blanc been content to say that it is rather futile to expect savings from a worker, living under the harsh dispensation of the Iron Law of Wages, he would merely have been expressing the reasonably defensible. But, remembering that whatever is, is wrong, Louis Blanc must still be talking. What are these Caisses d'Epargne anyhow? Their deposits are only in part the fruit of honest labour. They are blind receivers of illicit profits: they receive—indeed after encouraging them—all who present themselves, 'from the servant who has robbed his master to the courtesan who has sold her beauty.'[2] This throws a startling light on the activities of Savings Banks; and Savings Bank Managers, who have read their Louis Blanc, realising that increased deposits in all probability reflect increased embezzlement and prostitution, would accordingly do well to moderate their annual speeches of self-congratulation.[3]

But apart from this lurid sidelight, Blanc argues that under present conditions, the practice of saving is a vice rather than a virtue. Firstly, it attaches the worker too securely to the existing order from fear of losing his savings—an argument that springs from the sentiment that has prompted the long-continued opposition of Trade Unions towards

[1] P. 57. [2] P. 58.

[3] It may be irrelevant, but it is not without interest to note that Savings Banks in their early days had a somewhat rough passage at the hands of socialist criticisms and suspicions. Almost contemporaneously with Louis Blanc's outrageous comments, a somewhat minor Scots poet, Alexander Rodger, wrote a quite diverting satire entitled, *Shaving Banks; or, Matthew's Call to the Worthless, to come and be shaved o' their siller*:

For we've established SHAVING BANKS,
For shaving o' the lower ranks,
For which we claim the gratefu' thanks,
Withouten flattery,
Of you, wha are but useless blanks
In life's great lottery.

But Rodger, though more amusing, lacked the bright ideas of Louis Blanc. For him the Shaving Bank was merely a device for the swindling of the poor, and the better observance of the Iron Law of Wages. As a mere Scot, it would not occur to him to bring in 'la courtisane qui a vendu sa beauté.'

profit-sharing schemes. Nor is it an argument that can be lightly dismissed as wholly without substance. The worker who has shares in the enterprise in which he works, who has, in one form or another, given his savings into the custody of the government, has undeniably, for good or for evil or more probably for both, given hostages to fortune. It is part of that process of ' bourgeoisification,' later to be so lamented as the grave of revolutionary impulses. Yet it is an argument which requires careful statement, if only because in unskilful hands it tends to become a plea that the worker should be kept unhappy, in order that he may continue to be discontented and revolutionary.

But going beyond this, saving, in an individualistic world, is merely another symptom of selfishness and depravity: he who saves for his old age merely demonstrates how little faith he puts in the goodness of his fellow-men. Blanc here states so clearly what others have hinted at, that he may be allowed to speak for himself:

> In itself, thrift is an excellent thing: it would be merely puerile and foolish affectation to deny it. But,—and it should be carefully noted,—when combined with individualism, thrift engenders egotism; it competes with alms-giving; it imperceptibly dries up in the best natures the sources of charity; it replaces by a greedy satisfaction the holy poetry of benevolence. Combined with association, on the other hand, thrift acquires a respectable character, a sacred importance. To save only for one's self is to manifest an act of distrust with regard to one's fellows and with regard to the future; but to save for others at the same time as for one's self, *ce serait pratiquer la grande prudence, ce serait donner à la sagesse les proportions du dévouement.*[1]

This last phrase is best left in the original, because though it may have meant something to Louis Blanc, it is difficult to say what it can mean to anyone else, and mistranslation is accordingly almost inevitable.

But to go still deeper into the depths, poverty, springing from competition, brings with it ultimately the dissolution of the family and all the horrors of infanticide, *enfants trouvés*, child labour and much more —a ' homicidal regime which compels fathers to exploit their own children.'[2] But would factory legislation, by limiting the hours of juvenile employment, afford any protection? The parents have no desire for such legislation, for the simple reason that they cannot afford it: to keep the house going, the wages of child labour is necessary, and thus competition is preparing for the future (it sounds even more horrible in French) *une génération décrépite, estropiée, gangrenée, pourrie.*[3] Lastly, there is education, also advocated by some as a weapon of regeneration. Louis Blanc quotes with approval the view that where you open a factory, you may as well close the school.[4] Once again, the worker cannot afford it: if he is called upon to decide between the school and the factory, he cannot for a moment be in

[1] Pp. 59–60. [2] Pp. 61, 67. [3] Pp. 67–68. [4] P. 69.

doubt. For the factory has one decisive pull in its favour; 'in the school, the child is taught; in the factory, he is paid.'[1] It is here significant as between Louis Blanc and Owen, at whom in all this he is tilting, that Blanc makes the calm continental assumption that beneficent legislation, even if passed, will be broken, whereas Owen proceeds on the humdrum Anglo-Saxon assumption that we are a law-abiding nation, and that Factory Acts and Education Acts will be administered, even if parents are tepid.

Such are the baneful effects of competition on the worker; but it is no less a cause of ruin for the Bourgeoisie. In a florid passage, Louis Blanc shows the evil effects of 'cheapness,' which is supposed to sum up the benefits of competition. If, however, cheapness profits the consumer, it does so at the cost of bringing ruinous anarchy among the producers.[2] And indeed Louis Blanc elsewhere, in what is almost a parody of himself, proves, on the same lines as applied to workers, how destructive competition is likewise to the employer, how 'where one man stands erect, another has been killed.' 'You are going into business: Good: but where will you get your customers?'—'I will take those of my neighbour.'—'Then your neighbour will die.'—'What can I do about it? If it had not been he, it would have been I.' Thus in bright chatty conversation, he drives home the point.

Thus is the malady laid bare: competition, ruining all alike, transforms the whole of industry into a battlefield strewn with dead bodies. And the simple diagnosis points to a simple remedy. It is merely necessary to eliminate competition, and this task must be taken in hand by the State, having regard to the pre-eminent rôle which Blanc in his introduction has already assigned to the State. The Government, being viewed as 'the supreme regulator of production,' should raise a loan and with this should create what are here called *ateliers nationaux* (social workshops) in the most important branches of industry.[3] The State, as the founder of the workshops, will draw up the necessary statutes. To these workshops will be summoned all workers who can offer 'guarantees of morality'—whatever that may be. Wages would be equal, though on this point Blanc oscillates somewhat, being restrained by the consideration that at the outset the false and anti-social education from which the world has hitherto suffered will offer an obstacle to the immediate realisation of the ultimate ideal. During the first year the government would run the show, at least to the extent of 'regulating the hierarchy of functions'; but after a year's tutelage, the workers having meanwhile had time to 'appreciate each other,' the workshops will be run by popular election among the workers—in short, democracy in industry.[4] To complete the picture of the internal arrangements of the workshops, the net profits are to be divided annually into three portions, the first to be divided equally

[1] P. 70. [2] Pp. 76–77. [3] P. 102. [4] P. 103.

among the members of the association; the second to be devoted to the support of the aged and infirm, and also to help other industries suffering from 'crises,' since here mutual aid is seemly; and the third to be set apart for the provision of tools for those who wish to join the association, with a view to the indefinite extension of the system. Moreover, while at the outset each worker will have freedom to dispose of his wages as may seem good, yet the manifest advantages of a life in common will soon conduct them from an association in work to a fuller voluntary association in the satisfaction of their needs and pleasures.[1] In short, the social or national workshop will tend to develop into a communistic cell.

It is, however, in the relationship existing between these 'workshops,' launched by the State, and the remaining individualistic sector of enterprise that Blanc is most interesting. The State, in taking action, resorts to the weapon of competition in order to secure the disappearance of competition: despite the scriptural warning, it purposes to make use of Beelzebub in order to drive out Beelzebub. The capitalists, if they so wish, will be allowed to enter, and will be guaranteed interest on the capital they bring with them; but otherwise, except in so far as they work, there will be nothing for them. In effect, the individual employers may retire into private life as debenture holders—probably, from Blanc's point of view, had he thought more about it, a weak point in the scheme. If, however, the representatives of private enterprise should elect to continue the struggle, then there would soon be made manifest the pleasing spectacle of competition serving the high end of extirpating competition. For, after a short struggle, private enterprise would be defeated. It could not stand up against a system enjoying all the economies resulting from a communal life, where 'all the workers, without exception, are interested in producing quickly and well.'[2] Here indeed would be a competition very different from that with which we are now familiar—a competition designed only to attain the pacific absorption of the individual private workshops in the social workshops. And the outcome would be the happiest imaginable: from all quarters, workers and capitalists would flock (*accourir*) to the national workshop.

Beyond this, there would later on inevitably be further ramifications. In any given industry, the various workshops could not be allowed to compete against each other: there would therefore be for each industry *un atelier central*, to which all the others would be subsidiary and supplementary. In short, in more modern or more ancient phraseology (which so often come to the same thing) the industry would be transformed into the semblance of a self-governing guild. Inevitably, also, there looms up the further stage of establishing some kind of solidarity between the various industries: and from this lofty

[1] P. 104. [2] P. 105.

peak in the Delectable Mountains, we can surely descry from afar the ways of pleasantness of Guild Socialism.[1]

Agriculture has always presented a difficult problem in socialist theory. Blanc endeavours to deal with it along the lines of his proposals for industry. Collateral successions are to be abolished, and declared communal property. In this way each commune would acquire a domain which would be inalienable and which would presumably be extended, until in time all the available land vested in the commune. Cultivation would be on a large scale, and as the principles of the *ateliers sociaux* would apply, the net result would appear to be a joint exploitation of the lands of the commune by the available agricultural population.[2]

Perhaps we have followed Louis Blanc as far as is profitable in an enterprise of this magnitude. In summary, it may be said that his diagnosis was too simple, and that the remedy prescribed reveals the same defect. To attribute all the maladies of this world to competition shows a singular lack of knowledge of the profundities of the human heart and of the many sources from which evil may spring. His remedy is ultimately a strong State in which all property and all enterprise shall vest. Louis Blanc of course denied this, but his feverish denials carry little conviction. In later editions of *Organisation du Travail* he reprinted criticisms and reviews of his work together with his triumphant replies to his critics. This procedure has the merit of doubling the length of a rather short book, but it cannot be said that it adds materially to the substance of the original statement. One point of interest, does, however, emerge. In these pages, Louis Blanc shows himself almost abnormally sensitive with regard to any suggestion that his view of the State resembles that of Saint-Simon (or should it be that of the Saint-Simonians ?). In rebutting the charge that he contemplates a devouring State, he is at pains to show how limited are the powers he in fact assigns to the Government. His view is that the State is to be the *regulator* of industry: it is not itself to be the entrepreneur. There is to be a mere administrative intervention in the first year. He adds with that naive innocence of the world of business which not unnaturally distinguished Socialism in its irresponsible days: *la machine une fois montée, elle marcherait d'elle-même.* Unfortunately, there are few things in this life which, even when mounted, march of themselves. As against the Saint-Simonian purpose of transforming the State into ' le pape de l'industrie,' in his solution the State merely provides a code of legislation.[3] Elsewhere he endeavours to escape the taint of what is assumed to be the Saint-Simonian State by remarking that whereas Saint-Simonianism had thought in terms of *L'Etat propriétaire,* he, Louis Blanc, had spoken in terms of *la Société propriétaire.*[4] But in fact the difference, especially on Louis Blanc's assump-

[1] Pp. 108–110. [2] P. 115. [3] Pp. 148–149, 165. [4] P. 191.

tions, is not so *énorme* as he would gladly believe. Before the critics had wounded him with their suggestions of his indebtedness to Saint-Simon, he had called upon the State to ' put itself resolutely at the head of Industry.' [1] There is a convenient, if inconsequent, German proverb which observes that ' whoever says A, says B ' : and even if Louis Blanc flatters himself that he would confine the State's intervention to the first year, he would in time have discovered that he had begotten an omnicompetent and omnivorous State.

Louis Blanc's Utopia (for such it is) has also this feature in common with other Utopias that he asks, alas, too much of human nature, forgetful of the Mr. Hyde who is attached to every Dr. Jekyll. It is the everlasting dilemma, the vicious circle of all Utopias, that they are caught between two irreconcilable propositions, firstly, that to inhabit Utopia, man must have a higher moral stature than he now possesses: and secondly, that the only way to attain to this higher moral stature is to have lived for some time, indeed to have been brought up in Utopia, away from the perverse social institutions of this world which are the sole cause of our depravity. Louis Blanc was not wholly consistent in his pronouncements on the problem of distribution. At first he had allowed wages to be graded according to the ' hierarchy of functions,' but this was merely a concession to the false and anti-social education which has corrupted us. Later he moved towards equality of reward ; but also, as the highest ideal, he advocated remuneration according to needs. He realises the need of a ' stimulus '—the question that had also troubled William Thompson whom we shall meet presently. He clings, however, to the view, contrary to all evidence and probability, that the mere fact that the worker will share in the prosperity produced will induce him to labour with zeal and intensity. There is here still personal interest, but as all are in the same boat it is purified and becomes ' an encouragement to fraternity.' [2] He never faces up to the obvious consideration that this ' personal interest ' becomes painfully exiguous, when the fruit of a single worker's zeal is shared with a large number of his fellows, and in fact becomes almost precisely nothing at all in an atmosphere of national guilds such as, in effect, Blanc contemplated. This ' personal interest,' however it may be purified, must indeed be supplemented by a noble sense of duty in the heart of every worker—one of the first fruits of living in the new Utopia. Doubtless there must be a stimulus ; but, he asks with many others, must the reward be a material one, measured in terms of wealth ? Positions of authority, it is suggested, are not among the things in which one ought to traffic. By cutting out the emphasis on material reward, authority would be made more worthy of respect and less a subject of envy ; such a course would cut out the greedy mediocrity and limit authority to those who

[1] P. 111. [2] P. 138.

have a call. In a phrase of the kind beloved by Blanc, this would transform obedience into an act of gratitude. In the final statement of Louis Blanc's ideal, a man's needs are the indication given by God of what Society owes him ; his abilities, on the other hand, are equally a God-given indication of what he owes society. The legitimate empire of superior ability should be confirmed not by the extent of the tribute levied on society, but by the magnitude of the services rendered to society.[1] Here is a standard of conduct which may well bring a blush to the hardened forehead of even the most self-righteous among us. In the last resort Louis Blanc's society is to work through a universal dissemination of the principle of *Noblesse oblige*, by the glow that comes from the consciousness of work well done, and by an overflowing gratitude welling up in every heart towards those who are so self-sacrificing as to shoulder the responsibilities of life. It is magnificent ; but it is not for this world. *Noblesse oblige*, on this standard, begins to fray at the edges for most of us as we approach the pensionable age. These inhabitants of the national workshops who thus harbour such elevated sentiments on waking up in their Utopia have shed nearly all the qualities of frail and sinful men as we know them. The point would not be worth elaborating but for the fact, so characteristic of a great deal of socialism on the more Utopian side, that, as has been observed in an earlier chapter, it makes its task easy by creating a new unfallen man to walk, transfigured, the golden streets of the New Jerusalem.

By a curious irony, Louis Blanc, more than most reformers, was brought within measurable distance of being given an opportunity of realising his dreams. For, as has been said, after the Revolution of 1848, he was one of the leading members of the Provisional Government, and perhaps that government is now most enduringly remembered by the extraordinary fiasco attending its policy of establishing national workshops. Louis Blanc's reputation naturally did not escape all the retrospective slinging of mud which this gigantic failure occasioned. But it seems probable that he cannot be held directly responsible for a scheme which ended so disastrously, and which, as he protested, was not in accordance with his idea of things. If, however, he was not directly responsible for the scandal of the *ateliers nationaux*, he can hardly escape a certain mediate responsibility. Louis Blanc's incessant preaching of the 'right to work' was an important ingredient in the ferment which produced 1848, and the national workshops represented the attempt of the government to redeem the pledges which Blanc was supposed to have given. It is a complicated story, and those who wish to assess the rights and wrongs of the issue must look elsewhere for the evidence.

[1] Pp. 141–142.

CHAPTER X

P. J. PROUDHON

Of all the writers whose works have gone to the fashioning of socialism, none occupies so peculiar and ambiguous a position as Pierre-Joseph Proudhon ; none has been so perpetually a cause of exasperation and annoyance to the commentators and the critics, who quite obviously have, for the most part, never quite known what to make of him. Doubtless, here as elsewhere, the early years helped to make the man, and may in part (though not wholly) explain the enigma of Proudhon's psychological make-up. Born in 1809 at Besançon (Fourier's town) he experienced in his early days the bitterness of extreme poverty, and the shame that poverty may bring to a sensitive temperament. Though his father worked in the town, the tradition and the background of the family tied them to the land. The memories of the days when he herded cattle in the fields around Besançon remained with Proudhon, and in odd ways helped, until the end of his life, to make him a peasant at heart. Arrived at years to take up something more than casual employment, Proudhon became a printer's compositor. It was both a fortunate and an unfortunate choice—fortunate, in that the sensitive cowherd had been a bookish lad, so that his new work lay in the line of one of his interests ; unfortunate, in that it gave him the opportunity of reading all the books set up in the establishment. Proudhon, in fact, never lived down the surfeit of theology which he imbibed at this period, as an incidental by-product of his daily activity. He became, and he remained through life, a man of vast, if somewhat undigested, erudition, which he was never at any pains to conceal. It has been the custom to decry Proudhon, as one who too easily got beyond his depths ; yet it is only fair to acknowledge that the four volumes of *De la Justice dans la Révolution et dans l'Eglise* probably contain more miscellaneous and abstruse learning than is likely to be encountered in any other book of comparable size, apart from an encyclopaedia. The award of a scholarship by the Academy of Besançon enabled Proudhon to read and study more systematically, and the publication of *Qu'est-ce que la Propriété ?* made him known and, indeed, what is no less desirable, perhaps even notorious. Thereafter his life was a prolonged campaign of pamphleteering, if the term may be used with reference to such substantial works as Proudhon normally produced, varied by a slight and unsuccessful incursion into active politics as a member of the Constituent Assembly in 1848. He had his share of persecutions and his periods of imprisonment, but as imprisonment was not allowed to interfere with his writing, it was more or less an unnoticed incident in his life. Also at times it appeared inexpedient to live in France; but again, a writer, with the pen of a ready writer, may write as readily in Brussels as in Paris or Besançon. He wrote to the end, and indeed he left a very considerable number of volumes to be published posthumously. But he left no school; and Proudhon, detesting 'sects,' would probably have preferred it so.

For indeed it is in the loneliness of Proudhon that we find his most arresting characteristic; it is scarcely a figure of speech to say that he went through life in a minority of one. It is probably in any case impossible to understand Proudhon; but there can certainly be no beginning of an understanding until the springs of his loneliness are laid bare. One governing consideration has already been indicated. Proudhon was, in his very bones, of the people. In applying to the Academy of Besançon for the award of his scholarship, he had expressed the intention of devoting his studies to the improvement of the physical, the moral, and the intellectual condition 'de la classe la plus nombreuse et la plus pauvre.'[1] The words are a literal transcription from Saint-Simon's last testament. Much later he was proud to boast that he had enjoyed the rare advantage of being born of the people and of remaining one of the people.[2] In this, of course, he was not unique. There are, however, two points which should be borne in mind in assessing the influence of Proudhon's origin. The first is that up to the point now reached, nearly all those who, in the socialist sense, had spoken for the people, had nevertheless not been of the people. The second modifying consideration is that, mingled with Proudhon's somewhat too acute consciousness of his plebeian origin, there are memories of a world which had not been overkind to him in the early days of his schoolboy poverty. Proudhon was therefore sent into the world conscious that he was different from others, and prepared to be antagonistic to others.

Moreover, Proudhon was temperamentally destructive and critical. His instinct was to attack everything and everybody. Towards the end of his life, he showed a considerable degree of sensitiveness with regard to the charge that his contribution had been purely negative, and he produced an impressive list of his positive contributions to thought.[3] But the record is against him. *Nier, toujours nier*, he had proudly proclaimed to be his principle of procedure, and as early as *What is Property?* he had boasted that he had taken an oath to be faithful to his work of demolition, and that he would continue to

[1] Preface to *Qu'est-ce que la Propriété?* p. v (1841 edition).

[2] *De la Justice* (1868 edition), vol. 1, p. 103: 'J'ai eu le rare avantage, si c'en est un, de naître peuple, d'apprendre ce qui a fait le peuple tel qu'il est aujourd'hui, et de rester peuple.'

[3] *Théorie de la Propriété*, pp. 215–216.

pursue truth *à travers les ruines et les décombres.*[1] If not exactly in the Mephistophelian sense, his was essentially a *Geist der stets verneint.* Moreover, Proudhon, more than most writers, periodically expressed a phobia of the commonplace ; the fact that a view is commonly held, or held by a considerable number of his fellow-men is for him sufficient reason for holding it to be not merely erroneous but absurd. His choice is invariably for a daring paradox in preference to a hackneyed truth. Further, if the paradox appears to be one that is likely to shock, it becomes still more desirable, as more calculated to arrest attention.[2]

The result is that Proudhon throughout life rushed about like an infuriated bull, tossing all his fellow-socialists aloft on his indignant horns. Even in his own lifetime, the critics found amusement in collecting choice posies of Proudhon's abuse of all other socialists and all other schools of socialism. Louis Blanc is the ' declared enemy of Liberty ' [3] ; Cabet is abused with a refreshing persistence which never flags. There is something invigorating in a supposedly leading socialist who declares roundly that ' le socialisme n'est rien, n'a jamais rien été, ne sera jamais rien,' [4] or who asks impatiently whether his correspondent has ever found in socialism *autre chose que de la vanité et de la bêtise.*[5] More devastating is an exclamation addressed to the communists, which somehow sounds almost unduly grotesque if translated into English : ' Loin de moi, communistes ! votre présence m'est une puanteur, et votre vue me dégoûte.' [6] Rousseau, a respected name if not a respectable character, becomes the ' Genevese charlatan.' [7] Indeed Proudhon washes his hands of everybody : ' Comme homme de réalisation et de progrès, je répudie de toutes mes forces le socialisme, vide d'idées, impuissant, immoral, propre seulement à faire des dupes et des escrocs.' [8]

[1] *Qu'est-ce que la Propriété?* p. 270.

[2] The character of Proudhon has been most admirably portrayed in anticipation by Molière :

> Et ne faut-il pas bien que monsieur contredise,
> À la commune voix veut-on qu'il se reduise,
> Et qu'il ne fasse pas éclater en tous lieux
> L'esprit contrariant qu'il a reçu des cieux ?
> Le sentiment d'autrui n'est jamais pour lui plaire ;
> Il prend toujours en main l'opinion contraire ;
> Et penserait paraître un homme de commun,
> Si l'on voyait qu'il fût de l'avis de quelqu'un.
> L'honneur de contredire a pour lui tant de charmes,
> Qu'il prend, contre lui-même, assez souvent les armes,
> Et ses vrais sentimens sont combattus par lui,
> Aussitôt qu'il les voit dans la bouche d'autrui.
>
> (*Le Misanthrope*, ii. 5.)

[3] *Les Confessions d'un Révolutionnaire* (1851 edition), p. 88.

[4] *Systèmes des Contradictions Economiques* (1846 edition), vol. 2, p. 364.

[5] *Contradictions Economiques*, vol. 2, p. 379. [6] *Ibid.* p. 355.

[7] *General Idea of the Revolution in the Nineteenth Century* (English translation), p. 120.

[8] *Contradictions Economiques*, vol. 2, p. 396. The whole passage recalls the ' flytings ' of early Scots literature.

All this is very confusing to those who like their specimens of humanity to be neatly docketed. The confusion is rendered worse by Proudhon's incurable tendency to violent language and to extravagant utterances which he did not mean, or did not wholly mean, or did not mean without qualification. For long Proudhon was generally known exclusively in virtue of two statements, firstly, that 'La propriété, c'est le vol'—that property is theft—which throughout his life served as his signature-tune; and secondly that 'Dieu, c'est le mal'—that God is the principle of evil. But in fact, as we shall see presently, Proudhon did not in the least believe that property was theft: indeed he spent a large part of his life proclaiming the virtues of property and preaching the universalisation of property. A more scrupulous Proudhon would have said, not that property is theft, but that under certain circumstances property *may* enable its owner to acquire an income in ways of which he, Proudhon, disapproved. But such a statement would clearly have been useless as a signature-tune. Nor did Proudhon really believe that God is the principle of evil. He found much currently accepted theological doctrine obscure, not to say incomprehensible, and he was in no way attracted to the God whom certain of his neighbours professed to serve. But again in probably neither of these respects was he unique.

Proudhon's natural impulse to 'demolition,' his thirsty joy in attacking and refuting any statement made by anyone, would probably in any case have made it a difficult task to reduce him to a formula. Unfortunately, Proudhon, falling under the influence of Hegel, exalted his besetting weakness into a fundamental principle which he elected to follow in the development of his thought. It is highly probable, as Marx suggests, that Proudhon did not understand Hegel—but in such a matter who is justified in throwing the first stone? Proudhon confesses that the Hegelian dialectic intoxicated him—*la dialectique m'enivrait*[1]—and the symptoms of his intoxication are manifest everywhere, but particularly in the *Contradictions Economiques*. Periodically, Proudhon gives elementary lessons for babes in Hegelian principles, and rather scolds the world for not being properly initiated. In practice, the great principle that the thesis should give way to the antithesis, and that both should be reconciled in the synthesis, does not quite work out that way in Proudhon. He appears to have flattered himself that he was conforming to Hegelian principles if he argued on both sides of a question. His devotion to antinomies is revealed in the extreme intellectual delight which he experienced in showing that 'Yes' and 'No' were alike equally absurd answers to any given question. But the peculiarity of Proudhon is that, despite professions and intentions, he never really gets to a synthesis. The 950 pages (approximately) of the *Contradictions Economiques* are devoted, in

[1] *Les Confessions d'un Révolutionnaire*, p. 147.

the name of Hegel, to a mutual destruction of the arguments, for and against, on most of the subjects of current human interest. Emile Faguet has admirably shown what a snare a supposed devotion to Hegel may be to a mind of Proudhon's type. If he is trapped in a glaring contradiction, he has but to say: 'Ah, but I was then expounding the thesis, whereas now I am in the anti-thesis.' If presently he says something which is consistent with neither of the contradictory doctrines to which he has already pinned his faith, he has but to say: 'And this, my friends, is by way of being the synthesis.' As interpreted by Proudhon, Hegelianism was not merely a licence, it was an injunction to be self-contradictory. Thus in the matter of property, Proudhon's utterances cover the whole gamut of possible views on the subject; yet he never admitted inconsistency or contradiction. On the contrary, in putting forward one extreme view, he boasted of the glory due to him for having expressed the entirely contrary view. Later, the intoxication occasioned by Hegel wore off. In one of his posthumous works, Proudhon acknowledges that the thesis and the antithesis are not in fact resolved; the problem is not that of their fusion, *qui serait la mort*, but of their equilibrium.[1] This somewhat tardy abjuration of Hegel, however, came too late to prevent a lifetime devoted to ransacking the world for contradictions.

All these influences help to explain why this 'enfant terrible du socialisme,' to adopt a phrase from Malon, has been somewhat gingerly treated by the critics. He fits in nowhere. On the first encounter, and indeed much later, he appears to be a mass of extravagant, irresponsible and contradictory contentions leading nowhere. It also explains why there is such considerable diversity in the various presentations of Proudhon. According to taste, and by judicious selection of citations, Proudhon may be made to appear as the embodiment of revolutionary destructiveness or the essence of die-hard individualism. A writer who is so elusive and so Protean has only himself to blame if in the end the world finds the task of attempting comprehension disproportionate to the reward.

Yet Proudhon, in the anarchist and syndicalist tradition, has been an influence, and indeed one of the greatest. It is therefore not permissible, as was rather the tendency a generation ago, to thrust him aside as a negligible purveyor of cheap catch-phrases, much as the apparent chaos of his writings might tempt one to pursue such a course. Moreover there is, fundamentally, much more consistency than may at first sight appear. If he be pruned of his exaggerations, his violences, and his paradoxes; if (not so easy a task) allowance is made for the element of negation, and of the negation of the negation which a misconstrued Hegelianism imposed upon him, there are certain

[1] *Théorie de la Propriété*, pp. 52, 206.

cardinal points on which Proudhon remained immovable and invariable. Doubtless a summary of the essential Proudhon should conclude, and not precede, any attempted exposition of his 'doctrine'; but in view of the difficulty which Proudhon has presented to the humble seeker for understanding for almost a century, it may be permissible in the present chapter, even at the risk of repetition, to reverse the logical procedure. A brief statement of the points on which Proudhon was relatively invariable may provide a guide through the Proudhonian jungle, a framework into which his contradictory statements may fit with a minimum appearance of contradiction.

The fundamental conception in Proudhon—the *idée mère*, to use that convenient phrase—is that of justice. He has his own definition of justice, but for the present it is unnecessary to come to closer grips with this most elusive of virtues. That justice should be done is the supreme test in all things, and lengthy stretches in Proudhon resolve themselves into hymns in praise of justice. It is because property may give rise to an unjust source of income that property is theft: it is because property, if rightly used and justly distributed, need not do so, that Proudhon is enabled to maintain simultaneously that property is liberty and the salvation of society. It is in 'justice' that we must seek the overriding consideration. In practice, putting aside Proudhon's definition, justice is throughout very largely interchangeable with 'equality'; and we may therefore say that justice, interpreted as equivalent to equality, is the first of the constant elements in Proudhon's waywardness.

Secondly, Proudhon is consistent in his extreme individualism, which manifests itself in an incessant feud against all kinds of authority. The two most obvious authorities, issuing commands to the individual, are the State and the Church; and, accordingly, Proudhon is consistently anarchist and anti-clerical. But more intelligent than most, he has sufficient insight to realise that most of the forms of socialism then in vogue are in their way as authoritarian as the most authoritarian and arbitrary State, and that the tyranny of socialism may be as oppressive to the individual as the tyranny of the State under which we now groan. This explains the unending feud he carried on against 'communists,' and in particular against Louis Blanc and Cabet, who represented the types of authoritarian socialism which were especially repugnant to him. Justice, interpreted as equality, and freedom from restraint, represented by the extremest individualistic liberty, are then the two principles which commanded Proudhon's unwavering loyalty. Perhaps just here is a further explanation of the confusion which swamps Proudhon. For in spite of the tradition of the French Revolution which harnessed Freedom and Equality along with Fraternity, it may be doubted whether Proudhon's two ideals, as he interpreted them, are in fact reconcilable. If we are to have real equality, we must be coerced into it by the State or by some other authority; if, on the other hand, we are to have unrestrained, unfettered, untrammelled liberty, then among other things we must be left free to be unequal. It is a dilemma which in fact Proudhon never solved, and in a sense it pursued him into many fields of controversy.

Probably a systematic statement of Proudhon's theories ought not to begin with a consideration of his views on Property, but should rather approach this subject as a particular illustration of his more general doctrines regarding Justice. As, however, such a systematic statement of the chaos that is Proudhon is in any case impossible, there is a certain advantage in beginning where Proudhon in effect began, especially as the subject of Property, cutting across all other conceivable topics, runs throughout the whole of Proudhon's writings from his earliest work of real significance to the posthumous volume which was designed as a full and complete statement of his views on this question. Let it be premised that although Proudhon does not expressly say so, it is primarily property in land that he has in mind, as is perhaps fitting in one who remained at heart a peasant. It was the opening paragraph of *Qu'est-ce que la Propriété ?* that made Proudhon. In this somewhat too notorious passage, he remarks that if, in reply to the question: *What is Slavery ?* he were to answer in a word *C'est l'assassinat*, he would at once be understood. Why then can he have no hope of being understood if, in reply to the question: *What is Property ?* he replies with equal truth that *Property is theft*, although this is but the previous proposition expressed in different words ? [1] There then is the proposition, *La Propriété, c'est le vol !* which for the vast majority of Proudhon's contemporaries and for most of the world ever since was the essential and, indeed, almost the sole contribution of Proudhon to the advancement of thought. Unfortunately it was not even original, and critics were not slow to point out that identical words had been used by Brissot, and Emile Faguet quite properly cites similar expressions in Saint-Simon and Morelly, adding characteristically that the thought 'a toujours été dans le cœur de ceux qui ne possèdent pas.' But Proudhon remained bombastically and childishly proud of his great discovery, even while advancing views regarding property which were entirely inconsistent with his primary title to glory:

> The definition of Property (he exclaims) is mine, and my whole ambition is to prove that I have understood its meaning and its scope. *La Propriété, c'est le vol !* Not in a thousand years is utterance given twice to such a saying as this. I have no possession in the world other than this definition of Property; but I hold it more precious than the millions of the Rothschilds, and I venture to say that it will be the most considerable event of the government of Louis Philippe.[2]

[1] *Qu'est-ce que la Propriété?* pp. 1–2.
[2] *Contradictions Economiques*, vol. 2, p. 328.

As to the unworthy suggestion that this, his most precious possession, was also a theft—from Brissot or another—Proudhon can but shrug his shoulders somewhat cavalierly. Brissot, he observes, did not understand the meaning of his own words[1]: and with even more indignation he challenges his accusers to prove that Brissot knew what he was saying![2] Thus might one find excuses for plagiarising the Apocalypse by calling on the prosecution to prove that St. John understood what he had written.

The essence of Proudhon's first attack on Property is extremely simple, though inevitably (the author being the man he was) the argument overflows its banks in contrary directions. But in essence, had Proudhon been compelled to summarise his argument in six pages, he would have said that the customary expositions of the right of property are inadequate. In the main (and again it should be recalled that he is consciously or unconsciously thinking of land) the basis of property is ordinarily found either in the right of first occupancy or in the so-called 'Labour Right,' with which we are familiar in Locke and Mill—the right of the producer to what he has himself produced. So far as occupancy is concerned, it is argued that there can be no right created against later comers or later generations: 'si les premiers occupants ont tout occupé, qu'est-ce que les derniers venus occuperont?'[3] Going back to Cicero's rather foolish analogy drawn from seats in a theatre, to Grotius and others, the utmost that can be conceded is that all have an equal right to what is necessary for their maintenance. Thus the argument in favour of property (so far as permissible) leads to an argument for equality, which is the negation of property.[4]

Nor (according to Proudhon) can labour give a right to property, along the lines of Locke's argument. According to Locke, the worker 'mixes his labour' with the gifts of nature, and what results is his, as a kind of extension of his personality; but clearly this argument assumes that the gifts of nature are not yet appropriated. In a world where all things are appropriated, the lone labourer has nothing wherewith to mix his labour. If a worker assiduously mingles his labour with the waters of the Tweed, and elicits a salmon, so far from the salmon being his property, he will (unless fortunate) be prosecuted for poaching, since, in what used to pass for a witticism in Scotland, 'the Earth is the Laird's, and the fullness thereof.'

Indeed anyone whose duty it is to expound to the young the more or less commonly accepted 'bases of private property' must confess,

[1] *Théorie de la Propriété*, p. 211.

[2] This is a typical Proudhonian attitude. Fourier was 'ce reveur que personne jusqu'à ce jour ne me semble avoir compris' (*De la Création de l'Ordre dans l'Humanité*, p. 85). Needless to say, Adam Smith did not grasp the significance of what he said about Division of Labour (*ibid.* p. 300).

[3] *Qu'est-ce que la Propriété?* p. 63. [4] *Ibid.* p. 33.

if he be honest, that he approaches the subject with a somewhat apologetic air. The generally accepted ' bases of private property ' comprise a curious medley of juridical, moral and economic considerations, and give but a dusty answer, if they give an answer at all, to the fundamental question of why private property exists. Indeed—no uncommon occurrence in life—they tend to give an answer to the wrong question. Assuming that it has been decided that private property shall be allowed to exist, then it is permissible to say that property may be founded on labour, or contract, or prescription, or on any other ground that may be deemed valid. But to the deeper question of why property should exist at all, these various considerations are not relevant. To any one brought up in Icaria or any other Utopia, who should challenge the right of private property *in toto*, it is obviously no answer to plead the right of prescription, and to say in effect: ' I am justified in owning this, because it has been mine for a long time.' To the profounder question which centres in the justification of private property as such, it is probable that there is no satisfactory theoretical answer; and this is, in a sense, the sum and substance of Proudhon's dissertation. All that the sensible man can do (and it is what Proudhon does elsewhere, when he is sensible) is to fall back on Aristotle, and plead that private property is justified because it is in accordance with human nature and satisfies a natural human instinct.

As in the case of the argument for property based on occupation, Proudhon contends that the labour basis, in so far as permissible, also tends to equality. In most of his discussion on this point, he is more obscure than usual, but the main point advanced in support of his position here is that wealth is produced socially: the greater the number of workers, the smaller is the task assigned to each, so that natural inequality in men's endowments is neutralised in an expanding society.[1] A wholly different argument is that the higher capacities which on orthodox (and Saint-Simonian) theory call for higher remuneration, are made possible only when society has sufficiently enlarged itself to allow the creation of such superior posts. It is, he would seem to argue, the queue at the cinema door that makes the film star, who would languish if restricted to the population of St. Kilda or Tristan da Cunha. Thus it is society, and not the individual, which creates the more responsible position.[2] The familiar fact of mutual interdependence makes the work of production a common and joint effort. In a phrase which deserves to be pondered, he speaks of the worker as being, with regard to society, a debtor who necessarily dies insolvent.[3] None of us ever can meet our obligations to our fellows. Largely, therefore, because no one can claim merit, and because the work of no one can be isolated, the development of society is towards equality.

[1] *Qu'est-ce que la Propriété?* p. 130. [2] *Ibid.* p. 146. [3] *Ibid.* p. 158.

In the course of his diffuse argument on this question, Proudhon throws out an idea, of which, if one may borrow his own reference to Brissot, he does not appear to have realised the full significance: at least he does not return to it, as he does to most ideas dear to his heart. It is, however, of some interest as containing the germ of a theory of exploitation different from that which Marx was later to place on the centre of the stage. He argues that the worker, even after he has received his wages, has a natural right of property over the thing he has produced. This is so because the worker is necessarily underpaid. While the employer pays so many days' wages in respect of the effort of each worker, nothing is paid in respect of 'cette force immense qui résulte de l'union et de l'harmonie des travailleurs.' There is an additional productivity arising from union, and this 'force collective' goes unremunerated. This explains, in a phrase used by Proudhon but more familiar elsewhere, the 'exploitation de l'homme par l'homme.' [1]

To return more closely to the central question of property, we have seen that 'Property is theft'; yet it is obvious, even at the moment of its utterance, that this portentous formula, as has been well expressed by Suranyi-Ungar, has a somewhat *hohlen Klang*, a hollow sound; that it is but an *inhaltsloses Kampfgeschrei*. For even in this first and most extreme pamphlet, it is not really property that Proudhon condemns; it is what, with a curious affectation of learning, he calls the *droit d'aubaine* inherent in property—that quality which enables the owner to exact a revenue from others. In an illuminating phrase in his posthumous *Théorie de la Propriété* Proudhon explains that by property he means the sum total of the abuses that may spring from property.[2] It is a curious procedure to define an institution as the abuses which may be associated with that institution; yet this is what Proudhon does when disporting in that field of dialectic in which Property is theft.

The right of *aubaine* may, of course, take different forms: rent in respect of land or houses, interest on investments, gains and profits—in short, all possible revenues deriving from possession, all the possible devices whereby 'le propriétaire moissonne et ne laboure pas, récolte et ne cultive pas, consomme et ne produit pas, jouit et n'exerce rien.' [3] Here we come to the crux of Proudhon on this question of property. It is this *droit d'aubaine* that constitutes the right of theft, *le droit de vol* [4]; if property can be purified by the infusion of his beloved justice, so that it no longer enables the owner to exact a revenue, so that the elements 'hostile to sociability' are eliminated,[5] then indeed property

[1] *Qu'est-ce que la Propriété?* pp. 117–125, especially p. 121.
[2] *Théorie de la Propriété*, p. 17.
[3] *Qu'est-ce que la Propriété?* pp. 163–164.
[4] *Ibid.* p. 189. [5] *Ibid.* pp. 280–281.

will no longer be anathema. At this stage Proudhon flatters himself that he has done the trick when he replaces property by possession, so that the privileges of ownership will be restricted to the usufruct.

Proudhon ends *Qu'est-ce que la Propriété?* with a characteristic boast that as a result of his tract, 'Property is vanquished; it will never again raise its head.'[1] To learn how blessed and beneficial, how essential and eternal a thing property is, one must turn to the *Contradictions Economiques* and the posthumous *Théorie de la Propriété*. The *Système des Contradictions Economiques, ou Philosophie de la Misère*, to give it its full title for once, is a somewhat maddening book, and Karl Marx is not the only one who has been maddened beyond endurance by its 960 ample pages. Fortunately there are now few who expose themselves to the risk. It represents a spurious Hegelianism run mad. There are doubtless considerable stretches where interest revives; somewhat oddly, one of the most effective passages is that devoted to a destructive criticism of orthodox socialism. Yet the effect of the whole is asphyxiating. In design, Proudhon aims at discussing such things as Value, Division of Labour, Machinery, Competition, Monopoly, and much more, showing in each case how that which is good and necessary leads to that which is evil and deplorable. Division of labour, for example, is a condition of progress; but as the arts progress, there is retrogression of the artisan. 'Comment un principe dont le développement est visiblement utile, peut-il être en même temps funeste?'[2] This question, as it happens, has specific reference to competition, but in fact it governs the whole of the two bulky volumes. It is, of course, designed to be the Hegelian thesis and antithesis, but Proudhon is singularly ineffective in getting anywhere near a synthesis. The scheme of this, his most pretentious work, does in fact, however, provide an elastic framework within which he may argue on both sides of any given question.

In the main, however, on the question now before us, the weight of the argument in the *Contradictions Economiques* is not merely on the legitimacy of property, but indeed on the necessity of its universalisation. In the opening pages he introduces the new theme by admitting that the renting or hiring of land (*le loyer*), as indeed of money or any other object of value, is a spontaneous and universal fact, 'qui a sa source au plus profond de notre nature,' and which by its development becomes one of the most potent springs of organisation.[3] Now he depicts the fatal consequences which would follow the abolition of property: 'With the destruction of property, society would fall into a disorganisation without end.'[4] He identifies property with the family, which, for Proudhon, the strictest of all puritans, is the most sacred of

[1] *Qu'est-ce que la Propriété?* p. 309.
[2] *Contradictions Economiques*, vol. 1, p. 187.
[3] *Ibid.* vol. 1, p. 16. [4] *Ibid.* vol. 2, p. 235.

all institutions: 'La famille et la propriété marchent de front, appuyées l'une sur l'autre.' The aim of the legislator is, not to abolish, but to realise for everyone three things which are intertwined: *le mariage, la famille, la propriété.* Moreover, in the interests of the family, there must be inheritance; for without inheritance there can be neither husbands nor wives, neither ancestors nor descendants. There *must* be inheritance, 'parce que la famille ne doit jamais périr.'[1] Here it is Proudhon, the patriarch, the incurable individualist, who is speaking. Even if, with every desire to render Proudhon comprehensible, the ideas of property and possession are kept apart, it is difficult to see how 'possession,' to which inheritance in this patriarchal sense has been added, differs from property in the ordinary sense.

In the posthumous *Théorie de la Propriété* we make further progress in discovering how property, purged by justice—that is to say, deprived of its power to exact a revenue from others—becomes not merely defensible, but praiseworthy. And indeed we are provided with a wholly new, and highly curious, theory in defence of property; and, odd as it may appear in the light of all that has gone before, a reason for preferring 'property' to the more anæmic 'possession' originally commended for our acceptance. The impulse to this new theory of property is to be found in the horror with which Proudhon, as an extreme individualist and anarchist, regarded any State or any authority. Accordingly he now argues that the justification of property is to be found, not in its origins but in its 'ends.'[2] The State being what it is, it is necessary to create a counterpoise, to balance its power. The only possible and adequate counterpoise for this purpose is in fact to be found in property. Property has always been the most redoubtable enemy and the most perfidious ally of the prevailing power, and that is why every Government and every Church distrusts property. Property is the greatest revolutionary force in existence, and the only one that can be opposed to that mysterious thing which Proudhon calls 'le pouvoir.' The formidable power of the State can be balanced only by uniting the power of the proprietors, and thus may liberty be guaranteed. Nor can this miraculous effect be produced by 'possession' in the Proudhonian sense: for possession, implying thereby usufruct as apart from absolute ownership, is itself dependent on the State, and instead of opposing the State, it will come to its aid.[3] Property is thus a liberating influence,[4] and indeed it has always been so regarded in the liberal tradition. Much of this may not appear to be a very convincing defence of property, especially if it be remembered that Proudhon, when approving property, thinks in terms of small and preferably

[1] *Contradictions Economiques*, vol. 2, pp. 253–258.
[2] *Théorie de la Propriété*, p. 128.
[3] *Ibid.* Mostly from pp. 135–138.
[4] *Ibid.* p. 150.

peasant proprietors; but it is not without interest in revealing the flexibility and the versatility of Proudhon's mind.

For the rest, the *Théorie de la Propriété* tends to become a panegyric of property, it being always understood that property is now purged and purified of the unjust *droit d'aubaine*, and the equally offensive *jus abutendi* of the Roman lawyers. If marriage were the right to abuse one's wife, would it, he pertinently asks, be a respectable institution?[1] But assuming that property is divested of such unsocial accretions, it emerges free of reproach, and no praise is too high for it. It is by virtue of property that the ego, which is 'individuel, insocial, avare, envieux, jaloux, plein d'orgueil et de mauvaise foi,' ceases to possess all these undesirable characteristics, and is transformed into something higher.[2] Thus in what is perhaps the most crucial sentence on this subject, 'Property which is in its origin a principle vicious in itself and anti-social, is destined to become, precisely through its generalisation, the pivot and the mainspring of the whole system.'[3] 'Property,' he exclaims elsewhere, 'must never perish; it must remain in the heart of man as a perpetual stimulant to labour.'[4] Indeed, Proudhon ends by regarding himself as the saviour of property: 'Odd, that after waging war against property for fifteen years, I am perhaps destined to save it from the inexpert hands of its defenders.'[5] Finally, for those who share Proudhon's delight in a concatenation of adjectives, property appears as 'libérale, fédérative, décentralisatrice, républicaine, égalitaire, progressive, justicière'—all of these being in the Proudhonian sense adjectives of commendation.[6] Such is the end of the journey which began with the loud trumpeting of the identity of property and theft, and the triumphant proclamation that property would never again raise its head.

At the risk of a somewhat disproportioned account of Proudhon's writings as a whole, his views on property have been examined in some detail in the foregoing paragraphs, for two reasons. Firstly it may give some idea of the chaos (perhaps more apparent than real), of the inconsistencies and contradictions in which he chose to cloud all that he had to say. We have seen how he damns and praises property in the same breath; and while asserting that property will be the salvation of society, he boasts of the glory due to him for having discovered that property is theft. In fact, as has been indicated, property at times means for Proudhon 'property,' and at times it means the 'abuses of property.' If, sacrificing literary grace, he had called them P_1 and P_2, his argument might have been clearer and his conclusions less apparently contradictory. The second reason for dealing in some detail

[1] *Théorie de la Propriété*, p. 203. [2] *Ibid.* p. 167. [3] *Ibid.* p. 208.

[4] *Le Droit au Travail* (1850 edition), p. 49. The words which follow are almost equally significant: 'comme l'antagoniste dont l'absence ferait tomber le travail dans l'inertie et la mort.'

[5] *De le Justice*, vol. 1, p. 236. [6] *Théorie de la Propriété*, p. 208.

with Proudhon's views on property is that, though he may have been more influential elsewhere, it was this subject that made him known, and for long it was on this that his fame (or his notoriety) rested. Not much of Proudhon's writings has passed into general knowledge, and for this Proudhon is himself largely to blame; but the first thing that is known of him (even if frequently it is also the last) is that he fathered (or step-fathered) the great phrase that property is theft. It has therefore seemed excusable to examine what in fact he did say.

Property, it has been seen, will become sacred, if it is purged and infused with justice. It is time to consider how this purging process can be effected. Broadly, the remedy obviously lies in extirpating the *droit d'aubaine*, the power to extract a revenue from others which property confers on its owner. In a characteristic phrase, property in land deprived of its rent will be 'cured of its leprosy'[1]; and the same applies to other types of ownership. Justice must be introduced; and on one view, the whole of Proudhon is a groping after justice and an attempt to apply it—as he conceives it—to all human relationships. Whether justice in the abstract is an ideal which can be attained is extremely doubtful. It is perhaps even open to question whether we know what we mean when we speak of justice; or whether (Plato's *Republic* notwithstanding) any of us could define justice without using terms which are even more elusive and ambiguous. Doubtless, it may be possible to give a limited and circumscribed definition of justice which would bring it within the field of human pursuit; but justice in the large eludes us.[2]

Proudhon, of course, has his own definition of justice; but as used by him throughout his endless writings, the word overflows all definitions, and becomes the living God. *La Justice est le Dieu suprême, elle est le Dieu vivant.*[3] When he compels himself to be more specific, justice, putting it somewhat colloquially, may be summed up as involving respect for human dignity in our neighbours as well as in ourselves.[4] His complete definition may be given: Justice is 'the respect, spontaneously felt and reciprocally guaranteed, of human dignity, in whatsoever person and in whatsoever circumstance it may be compromised, and to whatsoever risk its defence may expose us.'[5]

[1] *General Idea of the Revolution* (English translation), p. 211.

[2] On 'Justice' as an ultimate standard, see concluding chapter, pp. 493–4.

[3] *De la Justice*, vol. 1, p. 43.

[4] *Ibid.* p. 216.

[5] *Ibid.* p. 224. 'Justice' is so much the whole of Proudhon, and the definition of this *Idée princesse*, as he poetically calls it, is so artificial that the original may be given: 'c'est le respect, spontanément éprouvé et réciproquement garanti, de la dignité humaine, en quelque personne et dans quelque circonstance qu'elle se trouve compromise, et à quelque risque que nous expose sa défense.'

It is perhaps somewhat outside our territory, but it may be worth noting that when Proudhon endeavours to adhere to his definition, he tends to interpret it as an injunction to behave as other people expect us to behave, or as they would like us to behave. Whatever the moralists may say, this is a poor guide through life. There

The first and most obvious application of justice, however it may be defined, is in the elimination of the *droit d'aubaine*, where interest represents the heaviest burden resting on labour.[1] The reduction of the rate of interest to approximately zero accordingly became to a surprising extent the panacea which, with unusual consistency, Proudhon throughout his life advanced as a cure for the world's ills. It is rather odd how frequently writers who are blessed with an enviable ignorance of the mysteries of money, turn to a monetary solution of the perplexities of this life. The organisation of a Bank which would give free credit, or at least credit at a minimal rate to cover office expenses, was of all projects the dearest to Proudhon's heart, and indeed considerable steps were taken to bring it into existence. What Proudhon says with regard to the organisation of credit and indeed on money generally, somewhat resembles the twenty-third chapter of the Book of Ezekiel, wherein the prophet discourses of the whoredoms of Aholah and Aholibah. While it is possible to apprehend generally what is the theme of discussion, few readers could conscientiously say that they grasp the course of the argument.

Although Proudhon flatters himself that 'les hommes du métier' will easily comprehend his train of thought,[2] fortunately only the connoisseur in museum-pieces need trouble about the details of his Bank. As expressed in general terms by Proudhon, the underlying idea is that the workers should mutually guarantee each other in respect of both work and a market, and that for this purpose they should accept as money their mutual obligations.[3] The workers require credit, but credit is just precisely what the State cannot give. The State possesses nothing but debts and bayonets.[4] In a phrase which doubtless delighted the author, the State, eternally unproductive,

is an illuminating and highly curious passage in *De la Justice*, vol. 3, pp. 166–167, in which he explains that slavery, war, usury, polygamy, continence and theft are things of naught; they are but accidents. Justice alone matters, that is to say, respecting others as we would wish to be respected if we were in their place. He cites a primitive oriental world of polygamy and concubines, in which the woman, accepting her inferiority, makes no complaint on the subject, and is proud only of her high purchase price. What is justice in these circumstances? It is that the man should treat his wives and concubines, as he would wish to be treated by his owner, if he were a concubine; and justice for the concubine is that she should conduct herself towards her 'chef,' as she would like her concubines to conduct themselves, if she were the supreme overlord. All this tends to be rather confused, especially in the gender of the pronouns, and it might require a considerable effort of imagination on the part of the concubine; but it would seem to indicate that if in this happy society, the 'chef' liked his concubines to enjoy a whipping every morning, then (as an act of justice, and in order to pay him that respect which they would like paid to themselves if, etc., etc.), they should endeavour to find as much enjoyment as possible in the performance of the rite. In the words of a forgotten insured person, 'If this is justice, I am no judge.'

[1] *De la Capacité Politique des Classes Ouvrières* (edition 1868), p. 122.

[2] *Organisation du Crédit et de la Circulation*, p. 119.

[3] *Les Confessions d'un Révolutionnaire* (1852 edition), p. 13.

[4] *Banque d'Échange*, p. 219.

is not the prince of credit, but 'le type du discrédit.' [1] The workers must therefore provide their own credit; they will do so by rendering each other mutual support. Credit can be organised, putting into practice the principle that products exchange against products. Credit must be given so large a basis that no demand can exhaust it. To do this, the sovereignty of money must be destroyed, and to this end every product of labour must become current money. Under the domination of the money system as we know it, credit is unilateral; with a system of reciprocity, credit will be bilateral. In more technical language, Proudhon claims that his proposal is merely a generalisation of 'la lettre de change.' [2] To the Bank erected for the purpose, the would-be borrower will present himself with the title of his property; the Bank will give him coupons to the value of two-thirds or three-quarters of his property, and the coupons will henceforth be money.[3] The emission of this new paper can never be excessive, provided it takes place only against 'bonnes valeurs de commerce' and according to the demand for discount.[4] Thus by providing gratuitous credit in this simple way, Proudhon imagined that, applying the principle of 'Mutualism,' he had overcome that loathly dragon, *le droit d'aubaine*.[5]

Proudhon's Bank, designed to provide free credit, has been cited as an example of what he called indifferently 'Mutualité' or 'Mutualisme.' This *Système mutuelliste* to which Proudhon looked forward as providing a better world is in its widest definition a society which holds together its members by promising and assuring 'service pour service, valeur pour valeur, crédit pour crédit, garantie pour garantie.' [6] Mutualism is in fact Proudhon's particular brand of socialism, and is doubtless best considered as part of the general question of his views on government.

It is doubtless on this side, on the question of government, that Proudhon has been most influential, though indeed not most notorious: here also he was probably most consistent. As a starting-point, it should be noted that fundamentally he was an outrageously extreme

[1] *Contradictions Economiques*, vol. 2, p. 126.
[2] *Organisation du Crédit*, especially pp. 90, 112, 114.
[3] *Banque d'Échange*, p. 218.
[4] *Organisation du Crédit*, p. 117.
[5] This is admittedly a very inadequate account of all that Proudhon wrote on the subject of gratuitous credit and the means to attain it. But for our present purpose this is perhaps immaterial. All that really matters is the quite extraordinary importance Proudhon attached to getting rid of interest; the puerilities by which this end was to be attained have little significance or subsequent importance. Any reader who wishes to be further befuddled may refer to three pamphlets, *Organisation du Crédit et de la Circulation*, *Banque d'Échange* and *Banque du Peuple*, which, in the older editions of Proudhon, were published together in the volume bearing the title *Solution du Problème Social*. The subject is dealt with incidentally in many other places: it was one of the more active bees in Proudhon's bonnet.
[6] *De la Capacité Politique des Classes Ouvrières*, p. 77.

individualist. There are a number of pages in the *Contradictions Economiques* in praise of competition in which the orthodox views of the ultra-classical school of English Political Economy are expressed with a disgusting nudity and crudity. Man, he tells us, emerges from his indolence only when need disquiets him; the surest way of extinguishing his genius is to deliver him from all anxiety, and transfer to the State the responsibility of his inertia. A man may love his fellow to the point of dying for him, but not to the point of working for him. Again, the only encouragement to work is to be found in profit. Men are so constituted that 'dès que leur bien particulier les sollicite, ils désertent le bien général.'[1] All this might be the voice of McCulloch in one of his graver lapses into orthodoxy. Nor is this merely a comment on the weaknesses of others from which, after the manner of writers, he claims to be personally free. In scoffing at the 'fraternity' of the socialists and their schemes of distribution, he exclaims: 'I intend to be rewarded in the measure of my work: otherwise, I stop working.'[2] Elsewhere his comment on the problem of the small shopkeeper is remarkable in a prophet of equality: 'Au plus diligent et au plus probe la faveur des chalands.'[3] What more could James Mill desire?

This extreme individualism carries Proudhon further, and makes him the first conscious advocate of what, with a curious affectation in the matter of hyphens, he calls an-archy; for an anarchist is merely the limiting case of a liberal individualist whose commonsense has become infinitesimal. Incessantly and perpetually, in season and out of season, he protests against all that government stands for: 'We do not admit the government of man by man any more than the exploitation of man by man.'[4] With a more personal and rebellious note, he exclaims: 'Whoever lays his hands on me to govern me is a usurper and a tyrant; and I declare him my enemy.'[5] He speaks consistently of the State as of something he would not touch with a barge-pole: 'I have never asked the State to do anything,' and again 'I want no State even for a servant.'[6] The same attitude is observed with regard to laws: 'If there must be legislation (I wish) to be my own legislator.'[7] Even more emphatic is this complete renunciation of the Law and all its doings: 'In so far as I have not wanted the law, in so far as I have not consented to it, voted for it, signed it, I am under no obligation to it; it has no existence.'[8] He protests, like an exponent of the theory of multiple sovereignty, against 'cette funeste théorie de la

[1] *Contradictions Economiques* (with much more to the same effect), vol. 1, pp. 189–200.
[2] *Ibid.* vol. 1, p. 248.
[3] *De la Capacité Politique des Classes Ouvrières*, p. 137.
[4] *Les Confessions d'un Révolutionnaire* (1851 edition), p. 12.
[5] *Ibid.* p. 31.
[6] *Ibid.* p. 239.
[7] *General Idea of the Revolution*, p. 146.
[8] *Ibid.* p. 258.

compétence de l'État.' [1] The State becomes a monster: it is 'that fictitious being, without intelligence, without passion, without morality, that we call the State.' [2] To be governed—but it requires the best part of a page to present briefly and concisely the degradation of being governed. It is among other things (for this is merely a selection):

> to be kept in sight, inspected, spied upon, directed, law-driven, numbered, enrolled, taxed, indoctrinated, preached at, controlled, estimated, valued, censured, commanded by creatures who have neither the right, nor the wisdom nor the virtue to do so . . . enrolled, stamped, measured, numbered, assessed, licensed, authorised, admonished, forbidden, reformed, corrected, punished . . . repressed, fined, despised, harassed, tracked, abused, clubbed, disarmed, choked, imprisoned, judged, condemned, shot, deported, sacrificed, sold, betrayed; and to crown all, mocked, ridiculed, outraged, dishonoured.[3]

Any one harbouring such views is of necessity an anarchist, believing that the State is void of virtue. In particular, however, the State is worse than useless for any kind of revolutionary activity. That Louis Blanc failed to realise this, and sought to make use of the State as his tool, explains the contempt which colours all Proudhon's references to Blanc. His emphasis on this point again takes us to the roots of syndicalism. You cannot by Satan cast out Satan, and you cannot by the State effect a revolution. He has much to say about revolutions *par en haut*, and revolutions *par en bas* [4]; but any revolutionary activity is repugnant to the State which in its very essence is counter-revolutionary. Every revolution, to be efficacious, must be spontaneous: it must spring, not from the head of the powers-that-be, but from the entrails of the people.[5] The root-cause of his lively criticism of his contemporary socialists is his contention that they did not realise this; they worshipped power and thirsted for authority. Authority has its seat in the family and nowhere else, and Louis Blanc's mistake was to transfer and apply to the State what was true only of the individual and the family.[6]

Nor is this antagonism to the State confined solely to States which are ordinarily regarded as of the authoritarian and repressive type. The idea of nationality, of the sovereignty of the people, of democracy, and of association were in Proudhon's day much in evidence, and were hailed as the angels of freedom and of progress. Perhaps just for this reason they left Proudhon frigid, or provoked him to the congenial task of destruction. In the matter of nationality, the two outstanding cases of his time were presented by Poland and Italy. On each Proudhon went his own wayward way, looking on the unification of Italy, for

[1] *Les Confessions d'un Révolutionnaire*, p. 99.
[2] *General Idea of the Revolution*, p. 208.
[3] *Ibid.*, at greater length, p. 294.
[4] *Les Confessions d'un Révolutionnaire*, p. 34. [5] *Ibid.* p. 79.
[6] *Contradictions Economiques*, vol. 1, pp. 282, 362.

reasons to be noted presently, as a mistake. No one has more effectively laid bare the elusiveness of the 'people,' for whom sovereignty is claimed. It is sometimes said, he observes, that the people rose as a single man: and he goes on to ask, 'pense-t-il aussi comme un seul homme? réfléchit-il? raisonne-t-il? conclut-il? a-t-il de la mémoire, de l'imagination, des idées?' These and many more searching questions await an answer: if they cannot be answered, then 'your respect for the sovereignty of the people is but an absurd fetichism.'[1] It is but a fiction, a myth.[2]

On democracy and the machinery of democracy, Proudhon also pours forth his contempt, coming rather close to certain modern schools of thought who would claim that all representation is bound to be misrepresentation. In a somewhat startling phrase he asserts that government is by divine right (as he would probably admit it to be in the case of a father of a family), or it is nothing: democratic government is but a contradiction. Is the ballot, he asks, more trustworthy than tradition or heredity?[3] In any case, what do numbers prove? By adding together votes, you can never arrive at any general thought.[4] The greatest men may not be able to find a solution; yet ten million citizens, 'feebly minded,' can infallibly solve the problem of the revolution![5] Nor can there be any legitimate representation of the people; all electoral systems are merely 'des mécaniques à mensonge'; the deputy never represents more than one idea, one interest; all the rest are pitilessly excluded.[6] Half the electors plus one may decide the election; in which case half the electors minus one are for ever unrepresented or misrepresented. It has again been a familiar line of argument in these latter days; it suffices to prove to Proudhon that democracy is a *Chimère*.[7]

With regard to association, Proudhon is not wholly condemnatory, but his attitude is, if anything, on the icy side of tepid. Acknowledging that he distrusts fraternity, he finds in 'association in general' more evil than good. Here, as elsewhere, his antagonism springs from his distrust of Utopias and fine words. Association is for him merely a dogma. It is neither a directing principle nor an industrial force: there is nothing in it which makes the worker stronger or quicker, reduces the cost of production, or achieves any measurable end.[8] In its essence, association is sterile and indeed injurious, since it places fetters on the liberty of the worker: 'Never, except in spite of himself, and because he cannot do otherwise, does man associate.'[9] This

[1] *Solution du Problème social*, pp. 42–43.
[2] *Théorie du mouvement constitutionel*, p. 199.
[3] *General Idea of the Revolution*, pp. 138, 148.
[4] *Solution du Problème social*, p. 62.
[5] *General Idea of the Revolution*, p. 144.
[6] *Solution du Problème social*, pp. 50, 54.
[7] *Ibid.* p. 66.
[8] *General Idea of the Revolution*, p. 79.
[9] *Ibid.* p. 83.

again is a curious reflection of a world in which there are no trade unions, no need for trade unions, and no appreciation of trade unions. This is well illustrated by the case in which Proudhon does admit association, and which he introduces as if it were exceptional. There are, he realises, 'certain industries, which require the combined employment of a large number of workers, a vast array of machines and hands,' and much more. Where there is great division of labour and a considerable collective force, association among the workers imposes itself of necessity; and every such industry is 'destined to become a society or company of workers.'[1] That Proudhon should have laid the emphasis where he did, placing the field of non-association before the field of association, shows how much he moved in thought in the village and in the world of small industry. Yet with regard to these 'certain industries' his vision was that of the Guild of recent thought: 'A railroad, a mine, a factory, a ship, are to the workers who use them what a hive is to the bees, at once their tool and their home, their country, their territory, their property.'[2] In the main, however, his criticism of association is that of the confirmed individualist. Either association is compulsory, or it is voluntary. If compulsory, then it is merely slavery; if voluntary, what guarantee can there be that the members will work according to their capacity, or that the association will reward them according to their needs?[3]

In the light of this antagonism to all government and to all the machinery of government, and indeed of his dislike of anything that brings men together, Proudhon could not fail to be an anarchist. Government must disappear, and indeed anarchy is approaching daily. 'La liberté, toujours la liberté, rien que la liberté, et pas de gouvernementalisme'—there, he exclaims, is the whole revolutionary catechism.[4] What, in Proudhon's vision, is to take the place of the detested governmental machine? Two ideas, which are in a way interlocked, provide the clues to Proudhon's anarchy. The first is mutuality or mutualism which has already been mentioned in connection with gratuitous credit; the second is the development and extension of a system of free contracts. The *système mutuelliste* is in some ways so much the whole substance of Proudhon on the constructive side, that it may be as well to give one of the more lucid definitions of what it implies. Under mutuality:

la société, doit être considerée, non comme une hiérarchie de fonctions et de facultés, mais comme un système d'équilibrations entre forces libres,

[1] *General Idea of the Revolution*, pp. 215–216.
[2] *Ibid.* p. 216. See also *De la Capacité politique des Classes Ouvrières*, p. 135.
[3] *Ibid.* p. 97.
[4] *Les Confessions d'un Révolutionnaire*, p. 236. Also *Qu'est-ce que la Propriété?* p. 301.

dans lequel chacune est assurée de jouir des mêmes droits à la condition de remplir les mêmes devoirs, d'obtenir les mêmes avantages en échange des mêmes services, système par conséquent essentiellement égalitaire et libéral, qui exclut toute acception de fortunes, de rang et de classes.[1]

With this system of reciprocal rights and duties, it is necessary to consider the important part assigned by Proudhon to contract. Outside the family, there is no place for authority [2]; contract is accordingly the only moral bond which free and equal beings can accept. Moreover, while Proudhon claimed that he was in no way a consenting party to law, he acknowledged that he was of necessity a consenting party to any contract into which he might enter. A system of contract must therefore replace a system of laws; and as contracts necessarily imply that they are made between equals, such a system will furnish the blessed trinity of Liberty, Equality and Freedom, with Order thrown in. The contract, he claims, solves all problems.[3] Thus in the end there will be no void caused by dissolving, submerging and suppressing the whole governmental machine: industrial organisation will take the place of government, and in place of laws there will be contracts.

Let no one raise foolishly commonsense objections that Proudhon's anarchy, or any other anarchy, would not 'work.' To ask what would happen if . . . is merely to reveal ignorance of the conventions and of the rules of the game. There is, however, this to be said for Proudhon's anarchy, that even if a world wallowing in contracts, with no power to enforce them, is something of a nightmare, the spirit of Proudhon's anarchy suggests certain halfway houses which are by no means so repugnant to experience. For at the root of all Proudhon's political theories the one constant element is hatred of the dominating centralised authority; the one remedy is decentralisation and still more decentralisation, and this is quite a practical policy, provided one stops short of making every man his own lawgiver. Mutuality on the political and international plane becomes federalism,[4] and Proudhon is the prophet of federalism. The twentieth century, he prophesies, will open the era of federations [5]; and even if events have not so far fulfilled his prophecy, the idea is certainly in the air. The advantage of federalism in Proudhon's eyes is that it tends to diminish power by breaking it up. His opposition to the national movement in Italy in so far as it tended to lead to unification, was caused by the view he took that Italy (as it then was) was specially created for a federal constitution. In any case, the fewer centralised states the better. Every centralised State is by its very nature annexationist, but 'une

[1] *De la Capacité politique des Classes Ouvrières*, p. 69.
[2] *General Idea of the Revolution*, p, 171.
[3] *Ibid.* pp. 205, 173.
[4] *De la Capacité Politique des Classes Ouvrières*, p. 144.
[5] *Du Principe Fédératif*, p. 78.

confédération demeure sans force pour la conquête,' just as it discourages the effervescence of the masses.[1]

One other aspect of Proudhon's federalism plays a considerable part in history. He represents, for reasons already given, the claims of the local authority against the central State. The question of municipal liberties is, he says somewhat extravagantly, the whole of federation.[2] In practice this, of course, means, in Proudhon's environment, the claims of the Commune, for which he claims sovereignty as against the State. A highly significant passage may be cited in an abridged form, as it gives the whole of Proudhon on this point, and is not without importance in connection with subsequent political theory:

> La commune est par essence, comme l'homme, comme la famille, comme toute individualité et toute collectivité intelligente, morale et libre, un être souverain. En cette qualité la commune a le droit de se gouverner elle-même, de s'administrer, de s'imposer des taxes, de disposer de ses propriétés et de ses revenus. . . . La commune, en conséquence, prend des arrêtés, rend des ordonnances: qui empêche qu'elle aille jusqu'à se donner des lois ?[3]

It is on this quasi-political side that Proudhon becomes a figure of importance in the development of thought. The conception of federalism passed to Bakunin; and as embodied in Bakunin, became a rock of offence to Marx and the seed of dissension in the First International. The Paris Commune was inspired by Proudhonian ideas. Later, his doctrines lie at the root of much that became syndicalism: the social theories behind Guild Socialism are Proudhonian in essence. The eclipse of the old doctrine of sovereignty in our time could appeal to his writings for justification. He showed, none more clearly, how unrepresentative a representative system may be, and in the bubbling cauldron of political speculation this too has been an ingredient in later times. Proudhon stands by the side of all who support the London County Council against the Ministry of Health; the Borough of Wandsworth against the London County Council; the ward committee against the Borough of Wandsworth; the Trade Union Branch against the Trade Union Executive Committee; the Presbytery against the General Assembly; the Kirk Session against the Presbytery; and whether they know it or not, all these dissidents are in his debt.

In dealing with a writer so diffuse and contradictory as Proudhon, who moreover aims at discussing every aspect of everything, any attempt to grasp the essentials in a few pages is bound to lead to the exclusion of much that may be of interest in itself or might claim a place in a full-length study, but which is less essential when Proudhon

[1] *Du Principe Fédératif*, pp. 61, 71.
[2] *De la Capacité Politique des Classes Ouvrières*, p. 226.
[3] *Ibid.* p. 230.

is viewed as a link in a chain. Nevertheless, a slight reference to a few points which have been by-passed in the foregoing pages may be of service in completing the picture.

The first and most obvious question is that of value, that miry pit in which, as it happens, Proudhon flounders more than most. Justice, the chief characteristic of the *Système Mutuelliste*, will limp unless value is determined.[1] On the main point, he is in the Marxian line, orthodox and unsurprising. It is labour that determines value, and for this purpose labour is to be measured by time.[2] But this is complicated by a curious idea that value has in some way to be *constituée*.[3] This, so far, has been done only for gold or silver. As the saying is cryptic, it may be given in his own words, so that each may interpret it according to his will and capacity: 'Or, ce que nul n'a remarqué, c'est que de toutes les marchandises, l'or et l'argent sont les premières dont la valeur soit arrivée a sa constitution.'[4] On the general principle, justice requires that every product shall exchange for another product which shall have cost the same sum of effort and expense.[5] This is comprehensible or at least familiar, even if practical difficulties leap to the eyes. Proudhon, however, in effect, suggests an elaborate system of price control. There is virtue in the *prix fixe*; and very naively he says that *la vente à prix fixe* is more dignified than *la vente à marchandage*; indeed if we all sold at *prix fixe*, we should have Mutuality.[6] But who in a Proudhonian world is to fix prices remains a mystery. If authority, then we continue to groan under governmental tyranny; if the 'law of supply and demand,' then we are still in the jungle of injustice.

Something has already been said about equality, which in Proudhon's earliest tract had figured as a necessary condition of liberty.[7] Equality is in general for Proudhon the manifestation of justice. Yet he is here curiously rent between an abstract and somewhat intellectual love of equality and his individualistic instincts to let the best shop-keeper get the largest number of customers. But in his egalitarian moments he tries to persuade himself against his better judgment, and by curious arguments, that men are in fact equal, and that equality is the law of nature. The progress of society, he holds, tends to make all alike and is leading us to an equivalence of talents and knowledge.[8] The man of genius is merely a man of good constitution who has had the opportunity of working, thinking and analysing, whereas the dull dog is merely one who has killed his intelligence by his inertia.[9] This is somewhat to over-simplify the problems of psychology. Greatly daring, he goes beyond this and argues that equality is the law of Nature.

[1] *Contradictions Economiques*, vol. 1, p. 51.
[2] *Ibid.* p. 60. [3] *Ibid.* p. 64. [4] *Ibid.* p. 69.
[5] *De la Capacité Politique des Classes Ouvrières*, p. 92. [6] *Ibid.* p. 83.
[7] *Célébration du Dimanche*, p. 42.
[8] *Contradictions Economiques*, vol. 1, p. 93. [9] *Ibid.* p. 138.

The number of days in the year is constant; the years are equal; the revolutions of the moon, if slightly variable, return to equality. The amount of rain in the year is sensibly constant. Equality governs the oceans where flux and reflux march with the regularity of a pendulum. Leaf is equal to leaf; flower to flower. Inequality comes not from the essence of things, but from the 'milieu.'[1] Never surely was there such a fantastic argument for the equality of man.

Perhaps, and still more oddly, the desire that man should be equal explains Proudhon's paradoxical appearance as an apologist of war. In one of his most perverse books, *La Guerre et la Paix*, Proudhon reveals himself, for the greater part of its 800 pages, as an enthusiastic defender of 'le droit de la force.' War is represented as a religious revelation, a revelation of the ideal; it is even—most perverse of all, and in Proudhon of all people—a revelation of Justice. Doubtless before he has exhausted the subject, it is indicated that war, like religion, is something that mankind has outgrown, and indeed that war 'a tenu sa dernière assise' in the events leading to 1815.[2] But the effect of the whole volume is to convey the impression of a Prussian enthusiasm for war as such. Fundamentally, however, as Emile Faguet has indicated, war is commended because it is, or is supposed to be, a leveller, and equality can be attained by eliminating the weak as well as by more humanitarian methods. This too is his attitude to inferior races; for, despite his devotion to equality, he admits that such exist. There are 'races mal nées ou abâtardies,' races whose inferiority will be only more clearly demonstrated by any attempt to educate them. But the remedy here is that they will be absorbed, 'et finiront par s'éteindre.' 'L'EGALITE OU LA MORT!' he exclaims in capital letters, 'such is the law of the revolution.' It is an echo of Babeuf, but with a new significance; for now we are to attain equality by snuffing out those who are inferior.[3]

There is, however, a limit to the egalitarianism of Proudhon, and it is highly significant. All the earlier Utopian socialists had been feminists proclaiming the equality of woman, seeking to remedy her manifold wrongs. Proudhon is the great exception. He does not like woman. She is 'impudique et provocatrice par nature'[4]—an observation which somehow suggests kinship with some of the more pointed *ex parte* statements in the Book of Ecclesiasticus. He would have approved, though he could not have devised in its terseness, that somewhat whimsical simile, according to which 'from garments cometh a moth, and from women wickedness,' so that woman's depravity is seen to be but the spontaneous and effortless flowering of her personality. In all his utterances on this question, one suspects in Proudhon (as in Fourier) a complex deriving from unrevealed early

[1] *De la Justice*, vol. 1, pp. 301–302.
[2] *La Guerre et la Paix*, vol. 2, p. 346.
[3] *De la Justice*, vol. 1, pp. 304–305.
[4] *Théorie de la Propriété*, p. 163.

experience. He writes habitually like an adolescent who has not recovered from the outrage of having been seduced, or like a Joseph fleeing from a danger too great to be challenged. For Proudhon woman is essentially inferior, a creature to be kept in her place (which is by the fireside), one who finds her expression only through a father, a husband, a brother or a lover. He observes, just in passing, that the day on which his wife is given a vote will be the day of his divorce [1]; and for once one feels that here is a thesis to which there can be no anti-thesis. When contrasted with Thompson, Fourier, Godwin and many others, this complete denial of women's rights is curious—or perhaps it may not be so curious. To no one did the sacredness of the home and the family mean so much; to no one was any suggestion of scortatory love [2] so nauseating and repugnant (it was this that had made the communists a *puanteur*); no one was ever of a more ferocious and uncompromising chastity than was Proudhon. Communism might be all very well for prostitutes and nuns, but it was not for the mothers of families.[3] The home, for Proudhon, was everything, the one cell in society where authority prevailed, and within that home everything must be subject to the 'master.' It is the morality of the austere and puritanical peasant.[4]

Lastly, in this brief catalogue of references to points lying somewhat off the main path, Proudhon was of course anti-religious, or at least (if one wishes to be fastidious in the use of language) he was anti-clerical and anti-Christian. Did he not coin the phrase: 'Dieu, c'est

[1] *Théorie du Mouvement Constitutionnel*, p. 188.

[2] For this pleasing expression acknowledgments are due to Fontana and Prati, leaders of the Saint-Simonian Church in England.

[3] *Contradictions Economiques*, vol. 2, p. 357.

[4] The question of feminism is fortunately somewhat off our path; but Proudhon is so intransigent on this question that a footnote may be pardoned. No one has ever, in modern times, declared more categorically and uncompromisingly that woman is in all respects an inferior animal. 'L'être complet . . . c'est le mâle. La femme est un diminutif d'homme' (*De la Justice*, vol. 4, p. 134). She is a kind of mean term between man and the rest of the lower creation: 'une sorte de moyen terme entre lui et le reste du regne animal' (vol. 4, p. 135). As to the function of woman in the scheme of things, Proudhon shares the Napoleonic view: 'En elle-même, je parle toujours du physique, la femme n'a pas de raison d'être: c'est un instrument de reproduction' (*ibid.*) Her inferiority is marked in every field. So far as physical strength is concerned, she is to man in the ratio of 2 : 3. *Dura lex, sed lex*, if that is any consolation. In intelligence, she is also in the same ratio. Her *valeur physique et intellectuelle* is accordingly to that of man in the ratio of 4 : 9. But that is not the end of the story. In morality, the situation is no better; we are still haunted by the 2 : 3 ratio. 'Par sa nature, la femme est dans un état de démoralisation constante.' The final result of the calculation is that the *Valeur totale* of men to women is in the ratio of $\frac{3}{2} \times \frac{3}{2} \times \frac{3}{2}$, or 27 : 8. Plausible as the proposition may appear, it seems to call for a more rigorous proof than Proudhon offers. The feminist will find, scattered throughout the last volume of *De la Justice*, a wealth of chastening quotations from the Christian Fathers and other well-informed authorities. Proudhon would have agreed with the eighteenth-century melodramatic villain, who declaimed to the descending curtain:

He seldom errs,
Who thinks the worst he can of womankind.

le mal'? And indeed those who search will find even more astonishing observations. That enormous book, *De la Justice dans la Révolution et dans l'Eglise*, is indeed merely a lengthy over-grown anti-clerical tract, the theme of which is that Justice is to be found with the Revolution and not with the Church. A very considerable section of that early essay in destruction, *De la Création de l'Ordre dans l'Humanité* is devoted to proving the hostility of religion to science and progress, and to the establishment of the simple proposition that 'l'homme est destiné à vivre sans religion.'[1] We are not concerned with Proudhon's theology (if such it may be called), but it is interesting to note the varying impulse to the anti-religious attitude of so many of the early socialists, apart from amiable optimists like Fourier. Godwin's irreligion was based on the fact that all religions, and especially Christianity, taught obedience and submission, whereas the first lesson of morality is to learn to disobey: the only command should in effect come from one's own conscience. Owen's quarrel with religion was that all religions had failed to grasp 'the science of circumstances'; they held that men were responsible for what they were, whereas our characters are made for us. Proudhon, on the other hand, was anti-clerical, because (as he saw it) the Church stood for injustice, both in the large sense and in the more restricted sense of his own definition. For what justice is there—though he did not so express it—in the doctrine of Predestination or the Shorter Catechism of the Westminster Divines? Starting from Proudhon's peculiar definition of justice, that it means respect for human dignity in one's self and others, the impulse to anti-clericalism is even stronger. For the Church in Proudhon's eyes is chiefly concerned in teaching us to despise ourselves: we are full of wounds and bruises and putrifying sores, and our righteousness is as filthy rags. The first principle of Christianity—to quote Proudhon rather than Isaiah—is 'la condemnation du moi humain, le mépris de la personne, le viol de la conscience'; its fundamental assumption is that the natural state of man is a state of sin.[2] And this, according to Proudhon, is to strike at the roots of justice. We are here, though with a very different driving force, nearer to Saint-Simon, who, in substance if not in terms, dissented from the doctrine of original sin and all its implications, for the very simple reason that, unlike St. Paul, he did not regard himself or his fellows as sinners in any remarkable or outstanding degree.

So perforce we must leave Proudhon, the most difficult and the most elusive of all the great figures in the history of socialism. Glaring and confusing as are the apparent contradictions in his writings, they are not greater or more astonishing than the contradictions in the man

[1] *De la Création de l'Ordre dans l'Humanité*, p. 63.
[2] *De la Justice*, vol. 1, p. 199.

himself. He was a writer of infinite violence when armed with a fountain-pen or its mid-nineteenth-century equivalent; but the bitterness and the gall were in the fountain-pen and not in his heart. In himself he was the simplest and least offensive of men, just and upright, austere and incorruptible—if it were not for the pain it would have caused him, one might even have added that he lived a god-fearing life. The most moving pages in Proudhon—pages of real eloquence—are those in which he recalls his early days as a cowherd beside the Doubs.[1] He was always at heart a peasant, and he had all the virtues and some of the limitations of the best type of peasantry. Had fate been kind to him, it would have made him a patriarch, with patient and placid cows and a very placid and patient wife—sweet Stay-at-Home, sweet Love-one-Place—surrounded by his children's grandchildren, running to do his bidding. For what Proudhon desired was a village of individualistic peasant owners, free from the offensiveness of wealth, a wife who could always be found in the kitchen, and—'that the tooth of usury be grinded that it bite not too much'—an agreeable bank granting loans at $\frac{1}{8}$ per cent. Reybaud speaks of Owen as a combination in which Abraham is greatly astonished to find himself in contact with Babeuf. The picture is even truer of Proudhon.

[1] *De la Justice*, vol. 2, p. 208.

CHAPTER XI

EARLY ENGLISH SOCIALISM

IN the present chapter some consideration is given to certain representatives of a group of English writers who, though individually not of great importance or reputation, are nevertheless not without interest and significance, when viewed as a company. We have become more aware than were our predecessors half a century ago that the essential elements of the Marxian way of thinking may be found expounded with much lucidity, though without the Marxian trimmings, in certain writers, some of whom were almost unknown in their own day, and who have only been rescued from oblivion at a much later date. For our present purpose, and pending a closer examination in the next chapter, we may regard the essence of Marx as consisting of a doctrine of exploitation, of 'unpaid labour,' arising from the fact that a worker who may be able to support himself by labouring for a certain number of hours, is nevertheless compelled, as a result of the sale of his labour-power, to work for a longer period, so that the proceeds of these unremunerated hours fall into the lap of the capitalist. It should be observed that if strict regard were had to chronology, these writers ought to have been presented at an earlier stage of this history; but as the interest which they evoke derives very largely from the extent to which they anticipate scientific socialism, it has been thought expedient to keep them waiting until we are on the threshold of Marx.

THE AGRARIANS

On the way to the English pre-Marxian socialists, it may, however, be as well to glance at certain representatives of agrarian socialism, who taught the doctrine of theft and spoliation as applied to land. For this purpose it may be sufficient to cite Spence and Ogilvie.

(*a*) SPENCE

Thomas Spence (1750–1814) is in himself rather a poor creature of little capacity and less gifts; but, oddly, he became a symbol and played a certain part in history. At the age of 25, Spence, who was a school-teacher, delivered, to the Philosophical Society of Newcastle-on-Tyne, a lecture on *The Real Rights of Man*, 'for printing of which,' as he boasts, 'the Society did the Author the honour to expel him.' The parents of his scholars seem to have conferred upon him a somewhat similar honour. It is not much of a lecture, but it carried Spence through life, and it has been printed more frequently than its exiguous merits justify. The rest of his life was devoted to political agitation of various kinds. He formed a sect, the 'Spenceans,' and framed a constitution for the 'Spencean Commonwealth.' He was sent to prison when, passing beyond philosophic dissertations on natural law, he exhorted his hearers to scalp the landed proprietors. Among his various journalistic adventures he edited for a short time a periodical with the pleasing title, *Pigs' Meat, or Lessons for the Swinish Multitude*: he was, however, seldom so inspired. But though he may claim the honour of having been made the subject of a biography, his ideas, such as they were, are all contained in the few pages of the Newcastle lecture which launched him on his career.[1]

The essence of the lecture is an appeal to natural law, under which all have an equal property in the land: in the language of a more recent generation, 'God gave the land to the people.' Nor can this right be bartered away, for succeeding generations are also interested, and in this matter ancestors have no right to deprive their posterity of their due inheritance. Consequently, it follows that at any given time the land belongs to the living inhabitants of any country. In fact, however, the land has been claimed by a few, without whose permission others may not live. The first landholders were usurpers and tyrants, and all who have come after have owned by virtue of inheritance or purchase from the original usurpers. The landowner may in law oblige every living creature to remove off his property, and if they acted in concert, and took their property into their hands, 'all the rest of mankind might go to heaven if they would, for there would be no place found for them here.'[2]

Spence's remedy is that the inhabitants of each parish should meet and take over their long-lost rights. The land being thus vested in the parish or corporation, the rent would be paid into the parish treasury, and used for all manner of laudable ends, instead of being applied 'to support and spread luxury, pride and all manner of vice.'[3] Beyond this, Spence moves away into a world of Godwinian anarchy in which the central government fades away, and we are left with a world of parish councils, who contrive to do very little, for the excellent reason that there is very little for them to do. 'Government does not meddle in every trifle,'[4] having the good sense to leave most things to the inactivity of the parish councils. Moreover, there will be no taxes apart from the rents that flow into the parish treasuries; for with a central government that has abdicated or been emasculated, expenditure will be wondrously cut down: there will be no custom-house men, no collectors, no army, no pensioners, 'nor such like ruination vermin

[1] Spence and Ogilvie may both be found in *The Pioneers of Land Reform* (Bohn's Popular Library). References are to this edition.

[2] Spence, pp. 6–9. [3] *Ibid.* p. 12. [4] *Ibid.* p. 12.

to maintain.'[1] Civil servants have had many hard things said about them, but this is as unkind as any. The end of Spence is thus a world of Godwinian parish councils, maintained by the rent of the land which has been vested in the parish.

(*b*) OGILVIE

Of entirely different calibre is William Ogilvie (1736–1819), a Professor in King's College, Aberdeen, who in addition to professing humanity, also professed a practical interest in agriculture. His *Essay on the Right of Property in Land* appeared in 1782, and as befits professorial dignity, it would appear to have been his sole contribution to current controversy. As he indicated on the title-page of his work, Ogilvie also is interested in the Law of Nature, and its bearing on this issue. The earth, he holds, was given to man 'in common occupancy'[2]; but from this general right, no one can derive a title to more than an equal share of the soil of the country.[3] This title to an equal share is, moreover, indefeasible; it is a birthright which cannot be renounced. It is antecedent to municipal laws and cannot be abolished by them. It is the duty therefore of the State to reserve for its citizens the opportunity of entering upon this birthright, should they so desire.[4]

It is odd that Ogilvie, with others of the same tendency, groping after the teaching of Natural Law in these matters, should so invariably have interpreted the 'Law of Nature' as applying within the frontiers of a State to the inhabitants of that State; for there is here a glaring and obvious fallacy. It is always somewhat risky to endeavour to codify too precisely the contents of Natural Law, or to pry too curiously into the mind of the Creator, forgetful of the words of a high authority in these matters that 'verily, thou art a God that hidest thyself.' Even if, in the careful language of Locke, 'God gave the earth in common to all men,' it does not follow that he gave the soil of England to the English, or the soil of France to the French; and indeed, looking over the history of the last two thousand years, it is extremely probable that he did not. From the basic principle that 'God gave the earth in common to all men,' Ogilvie may not properly infer that any one of us is entitled to the 46-millionth part (approximately) of the soil of Great Britain (with possible modifications in respect of Northern Ireland); on the contrary, my lawful claims would be to the appropriate aliquot part of the surface of the whole world, and the like claim would be vested in every inhabitant of China, Peru and Liechtenstein.

Reverting to Ogilvie, the difficulty with which he is confronted springs from his realisation that, interwoven with the right we each

[1] Spence, p. 15.
[2] Ogilvie (same edition), p. 35.
[3] *Ibid.* p. 36.
[4] *Ibid.* p. 38.

have to hold our proportionate share of the soil, is the other right, based on labour in respect of improvements effected.[1] For he is too much of a practical agriculturalist to be willing to forget this. To combine these two possibly conflicting principles should be the object of all agrarian laws.[2] In his endeavour to disentangle what is due to a cultivator who is in possession of more than his appropriate fraction and who has effected improvements in all the land which he occupies, Ogilvie divides the purchase price of land into three portions. There is, firstly, the original value of the soil (the bloodless elusive ghost which hereafter Ricardo is destined to pursue); there is, secondly, the value of the improvements due to the proprietor or his predecessors; and, thirdly, there is the 'contingent or improvable value,' by which is meant the value it may yet receive from cultivation—a hypothetical potential increase. Any landowner is entitled to all three portions in respect of the land that may be assigned to him as his due share; but in respect of his excess holding beyond his quota, he is entitled only to the second portion; to the original and to the contingent value of his excess holding he can have no claim.[3] It is a pleasing academic solution, but would be a maddening problem to submit for the determination of a chartered accountant in any particular case.

Not merely does Natural Law call, so far is is practicable, for a settlement of the population on the soil, but such a course is also manifestly in the public interest. Ogilvie could scarcely be of his time without being a Utilitarian, believing that the end of the State is the increase of public happiness; as a Professor of Humanity, he could scarcely fail to identify happiness with virtue; as a part-time agriculturalist, he knew that the cultivators of the soil were the most virtuous of men. There is indeed a pronounced physiocratic strain in Ogilvie, who believed that labour devoted to agriculture increased public wealth more than if applied in any other direction. He is indeed somewhat depreciatory with regard to the importance of manufactures and commerce. 'That nation,' he observes, 'is greatly deceived and misled which bestows any encouragement on manufactures for exportation or for any purpose but the necessary internal supply'—at least, until agriculture has reached its fullest development.[4]

If a multiplication of workers on the land would thus be advantageous in every direction, so contrariwise the 'exorbitant right of property in land' brings with it many pernicious consequences. It is in his discussion of this aspect of the question that Ogilvie qualifies for admission to a section leading to the forerunners of Marx. Owing to this engrossing of land by a few men 'the happiness of mankind has been for ages more invaded and restrained, than by all the tyranny of kings, the imposture of priests, and the chicane of lawyers, taken to-

[1] Ogilvie (same edition), p. 41.
[2] *Ibid.* p. 42.
[3] *Ibid.* pp. 43, 44.
[4] *Ibid.* pp. 52–53.

gether, though these are supposed to be the greatest evils that afflict the societies of human kind.' [1] 'By exacting exorbitant rents,' he adds, 'they exercise a most pernicious usury, and deprive industry that is actually exerted of its due reward.' [2] It is a monopoly tending to the starvation of the population at large no less than would a monopoly of bakers, so that in the end, as he observes alliteratively, 'the race becomes dwarfish, debilitated and deformed.' [3] While the landlords object to the taxes imposed by the State, and clamour against pensions, they should remember that 'their own large incomes are indeed pensions, and salaries of sinecure offices.' 'Whoever,' he adds, generalising, 'enjoys any revenue not proportioned to such industry or exertion of his own, or of his ancestors, is a freebooter, who has found means to cheat or to rob the public, and more especially the indigent of that district in which he lives.' Moreover, the hereditary revenue of the landholder increases without any effort of his: 'It is a premium given to idleness.' [4]

This is the voice of a Boanerges, rather than of a Professor of Humanity. It will be observed that rent—or at least exorbitant rent—is attacked because it deprives industry of its due reward; and it is further implied that revenues should be proportional to industry or exertion—although indeed in the crucial passage he is prepared to allow our ancestors to work for us. But when Ogilvie turns from denunciatory analysis to practical proposals, his roaring becomes as innocuous as the cooing of the amorous turtle-dove. Indeed, in the light of his talk about freebooters, Ogilvie may well have been astonished at his own moderation. For what it all comes to is that every citizen of the age of twenty-one may claim a holding of not more than forty acres, to be assigned in perpetuity for residence and cultivation. Into the details and possible modifications of the scheme it is unnecessary to enter; but the holding is not to be had free. There is to be a rent, even if a fair rent, payable to the landlord, and also a temporary rent payable to the former tenant. Also, even if it is tucked away in a footnote, the claimant must show that he is a man of some substance. It is significant also of Ogilvie's gentleness in practice that among the lands which may not be taken for this purpose is 'the farm or park belonging to the lord of the manor,' that is to say, the freebooter's own special farm. More astonishing is the suggestion that the new holder of land should 'pay to the lord of the manor certain aids and services of a feudal nature, so regulated as to produce that degree of connection and dependence which may be expedient for preserving order and subordination in the country without danger of giving rise to oppression and abuse.' Thus, despite the vehemence of his denunciations, when it comes to practice, Ogilvie produces no more than a modest measure

[1] Ogilvie (same edition), p. 59.
[2] *Ibid.* p. 60.
[3] *Ibid.* p. 63.
[4] *Ibid.* pp. 67–69.

for the encouragement of small holdings, encumbered by conditions that are extremely discouraging.[1]

Perhaps not in themselves of great importance, yet significant as showing how utterly remote Ogilvie fundamentally was from any proletarian or democratic instincts are certain observations he makes on the problem of how these changes may be brought about. His suggestion is that the reform might be effected by a conquering monarch at the head of his victorious army; and he goes so far as to suggest that the attainment of such a reform ' might even in the eye of reason and philosophy almost justify the ambitious desire of conquest in the breast of a heroic prince.'[2] Also ' princes sitting on disputed thrones ' might use the scheme as a bribe to render their seat more easy.[3] It is the figure of Frederick the Great that he has here in mind. It is rather odd to look to the generous disposition of a heroic Hitler or a triumphant Tamberlaine for the achievement of agrarian reform.

Such are Spence and Ogilvie, representatives of the tradition of agrarian socialism; they may not have much in common with the pre-Marxians, but at least in respect of one kind of property—land—they popularised the ideas of theft, robbery and spoliation.

THE PRE-MARXIANS

The English pre-Marxians, meaning thereby those writers who arrived at what is substantially the Marxian theory of exploitation and of surplus value—not infrequently, like Marx, building on Ricardo—are, for our purpose, five in number. They are Charles Hall (? 1745–? 1825), William Thompson (1785–1833), Thomas Hodgskin (1783–1869), J. F. Bray (?–?) and John Gray (1799–? 1850). It is impossible, and probably undesirable, to consider these Marxian forerunners in any detail, but enough should be said of each to give the flavour of the group.

(c) CHARLES HALL

Charles Hall inevitably comes first in the bunch of early anticipators of Karl Marx, partly because the date of his birth so decrees; and partly because his attitude of mind and the solutions which he advocates demand that he should be placed as near as possible to the agrarians who have just been noticed. Little is known of him except that he was a physician, and obviously a ' good physician,' in the West Country; he had a large family, and he died in a debtor's prison—not because he was insolvent, but because he refused to come out. He did not in fact acknowledge the debt in dispute; and, like a man of high principle,

[1] Ogilvie. The complete scheme is embodied in fifteen articles, pp. 139–148.
[2] *Ibid.* pp. 82–83.
[3] *Ibid.* p. 110.

he refused to purchase his liberty by acquiescing in the demands of injustice.

He was a good physician, and he wrote as a good physician. To those who would ask why a doctor, a mere doctor, should consider himself competent to write on such matters, he replies, and with justice, that no one is so well qualified as a doctor to write about the conditions of the people:

> He is admitted into the dwellings of all ranks of people, and into the innermost parts of them: he sees them by their fire-side, at their tables, and in their beds: he sees them at work, and at their recreations: he sees them in health, in sickness, and in the article of death: he is frequently made acquainted with their hopes, and their fears, their successes and their disappointments, as these have often a relation to their diseases; and, possessing their confidence, they frequently also unbosom themselves to him on matters not connected with the state of their healths.[1]

Such is the proud boast of the family doctor, and it is well founded. The physician, always assuming that he is a good physician, has unique opportunities of getting to know his fellow-men. In the case of Hall, this quality colours his whole discussion. Somehow he conveys in fuller measure than any other writer in the socialist tradition, the impression that he has lived very near to suffering humanity.

Hall's one book bears the title, *The Effects of Civilisation on the People in European States*, and his thesis is a simple one. It is that however much civilisation, and with it the concomitants of civilisation, may have been of advantage to a privileged minority, it has depressed and rendered miserable the bulk of humanity. In every respect, and however matters may be viewed, the poor in civilised countries are uniformly taken advantage of, and get nothing out of the assumed progress of humanity. In a book wholly concerned with the effects of civilisation, it is well to ask at the outset what in fact the author means by 'civilisation.' Hall is ready with a precise definition: civilisation 'consists in the study and knowledge of the sciences, and in the production and enjoyment of the conveniences, the elegancies, and luxuries of life'[2]—but, as the argument proceeds to make clear, these conveniences, elegancies and luxuries are not for the poor. They are reserved for the privileged.

The outstanding feature of society as seen by Hall in the daily pursuit of his calling lies in the division between the rich and the poor. The poor are not merely neglected: they are the forgotten men. Politicians and statesmen may be interested in instituting enquiries into other aspects of the life of the nation, but when it comes to

> the state and condition of the great mass of the people: how are they fed; how they are clothed; what kind of houses they live in; how they are

[1] *The Effects of Civilisation*, etc., pp. iii–iv.

[2] *Ibid.* p. 1.

supplied with fuel; how they are instructed; in short, what advantages, corporeal, mental, and even spiritual, they enjoy or are deprived of,

no one (he is writing in 1805) is so curious as to ask. It is the miserable state of the poor that Hall places in the forefront. Most fundamentally, 'the poor are not in fact furnished with the requisite quantity of the necessaries of life.'[1] Their employment in manufactures is injurious to their health; their minds are necessarily uncultivated; their moral and spiritual instruction is neglected.

When we turn to consider Hall's analysis of the causes and consequences of this prevailing poverty of the poor, we are at once confronted with a bias which affects the whole discussion. Hall is profoundly antagonistic to trade and manufactures; in an almost physiocratic sense, he regards agriculture as natural. If it be asked why there is scarcity, he does not tarry for an answer. It is that 'a sufficient number of hands are not employed on the land.'[2] Hall is quite clear that no sane man would ever voluntarily abandon the land for any other occupation: 'it was never through choice that manufactures were entered into by any people.'[3] He gives a somewhat gloomy, but not too gloomy account (having regard to the date, 1805) of the horrors of manufactures. Despite their variety, they are all

carried on within doors, in confined rooms, shutting out the pleasant objects of nature, frequently within frames like cages, in offensive atmospheres, generally rendered more nauseous by the effluvia of the subject worked on, always by that of the bodies and filthy clothes of the workmen; their postures bent, doubled, and every way distorted.[4]

Despite the repulsive nature of manufactures, however, the wealth of the rich 'draws off the labour from the cultivation of the land' by a kind of compulsion,'[5] and directs it above all to what Hall calls 'refined manufactures,' created exclusively for the enjoyment of the rich. The compulsion so exercised is indeed summarised in a formula: the rich in effect say:

If you will labour for me in such and such a way, I will give you out of those things such as you stand in need of; but unless you will do these things which I require of you, you shall have none of them.[6]

There is thus no voluntary labour contract, but rather a state of coercion which derives its sanction from the wealth of the rich, and which leaves the poor no choice.'[7] This indeed, in a notable definition, is the essence of wealth. 'Wealth,' says Hall, 'is the possession of that which gives power over, and commands the labour of man: it is, therefore, power; and into that, and that only, ultimately resolvable.'[8] Nor is this a

[1] *The Effects of Civilisation*, etc., p. 4. [2] *Ibid.* p. 37.
[3] *Ibid.* p. 41. [4] *Ibid.* pp. 40–41. [5] *Ibid.* p. 43.
[6] *Ibid.* p. 44. [7] *Ibid.* p. 72. [8] *Ibid.* p. 48.

mere metaphor or simile. The power of the rich is as strong and effective as that of the most absolute monarch that ever lived:

> To condemn so many to the mines; to confine such numbers to such nauseous, irksome, unwholesome, destructive employments, is more than equal to any kingly power on earth.[1]

The fact that wealth means power vested in one to order the lives of others means likewise that there is a complete opposition of interests between the two classes. Wealth is an advantage to the possessor, precisely because, and only to the extent to which, it is a disadvantage to the non-possessor. What the possessor has, the non-possessor is deprived of: 'The situation of the rich and the poor, like the algebraic terms *plus* and *minus*, are in direct opposition to, and destructive of each other.'[2] There is here no suggestion of 'economic harmonies'; indeed the foundations of the doctrine of the class war could not be more clearly expounded.

But wealth is not merely power over the labour of others; it is, in Hall's analysis, power at large, in a sense which points to the Marxian doctrine of the class State. In civilised states, he tells us, the wealthy part 'have in their hands all power: the legislative, the executive, and judiciary, in all their branches, viz. ecclesiastical, magisterial, martial, etc.'[3] As a consequence the rich form an aristocracy, in which the effective power is lodged: 'It is wealth universally that puts power into the hands of those that have it.'[4]

We have seen the poor labouring for the rich under the coercion of 'absolute necessity.' Hall makes a laudable effort to estimate what portion of the proceeds of the labour of the people at large is appropriated by the rich, and how much is left for their own use. The calculation is probably not above reproach, and indeed the statistical material of the time was hardly such as to justify the attempt being made. What is more significant than the conclusion at which he arrived is the fact that he endeavoured to express the problem in concrete terms, and that in doing so, he came very near to the Marxian formula for surplus value. After presenting his estimate, he says:

> If this statement is true, eight-tenths of the people consume only one-eighth of the produce of their labour: hence one day in eight, or one hour in a day, is all the time the poor man is allowed to work for himself, his wife and his children. All the other days, or all the other hours of the day, he works for other people.[5]

One other Marxian dogma which is stated with remarkable precision is that of the Increasing Degradation of the Working Classes. It follows almost automatically from the view that the rich and the

[1] *The Effects of Civilisation*, etc., p. 49.
[2] *Ibid.* pp. 66–67.
[3] *Ibid.* p. 74.
[4] *Ibid.* p. 75.
[5] *Ibid.* p. 118.

poor are in the relation of *plus* and *minus*, combined with the uncontested fact (in 1805) that the rich are growing richer. Increase of the wealth and the power of the few must therefore mean 'an increase of poverty in the people, as it subjects them to new and additional demands for the produce of their labour.'[1] As a consequence, it is argued that the poor are becoming every day poorer and poorer in most States. Further, this increasing misery or degradation (not that Hall uses the expression) is occasioned in the two ways which are indicated later in *The Communist Manifesto*. It is 'brought about not only by those, already in a state of subjection, being placed in a state of still greater subjection; but also because more people are reduced to that state.'[2] This is almost an anticipatory glimpse of the process whereby the lower strata of the middle class, the small tradespeople, and many more 'sink gradually into the proletariat.'[3] It should perhaps be added that on this point Hall almost goes beyond Marx, for he holds that there is no limit to the extent to which this increasing Marxian misery may be carried. There are no bounds, he asserts, to the quantity of labour that the rich may have the power of claiming from the people, and it follows likewise that there are no bounds to the 'diminution of the necessaries of life that remain to the poor for their own use.'[4]

Before looking at Hall from a somewhat wider point of view, one last connecting link with the later Marx-Lenin tradition may be noted. Hall is emphatic that wars, if not exclusively, are yet predominantly, attributable to what a subsequent generation has come to call the Capitalistic System. 'The objects of all wars,' he says, 'whether near or distant, are to increase trade, or to extend territory'; they are occasioned, in a rather odd phrase, by 'the ambition or irritability of the rich.'[5] Wars are caused by the wealthy, and their object is an increase of wealth. To this he adds, as a further comment, that the education of the children of the rich tends in the same direction; the jargon had not then been invented, but he implies that they are educated to think imperially.[6]

[1] *The Effects of Civilisation*, etc., p. 94. [2] *Ibid.* p. 95.

[3] *The Communist Manifesto*.

[4] *The Effects of Civilisation*, p. 96. Hall, making use of the 'Sic vos non vobis' theme, comes near to suggesting certain very familiar lines of Shelley. Shelley indeed had considerable kinship with the group now under consideration:

> The seed ye sow, another reaps;
> The wealth ye find, another keeps;
> The robes ye weave, another wears;
> The arms ye forge, another bears.
>
> Sow seed,—but let no tyrant reap;
> Find wealth,—let no impostor heap;
> Weave robes,—let not the idle wear;
> Forge arms,—in your defence to bear.

[5] *Ibid.* p. 171. [6] *Ibid.* p. 172.

So far we have in the main been concerned with those aspects of Hall which would arrest the attention of a Marxian student, reading backwards. In fairness to Hall, however, one ought to have regard to the general framework in which these Marxian sentiments find expression. In essence, it may be said that Hall is primarily an agrarian with a quite peculiarly strong antipathy against manufactures and trade, pushed indeed at times almost to the verge of paradox. The inequality which Hall analyses has, in his view, its distant source in the original appropriation of land and its distribution among a few.[1] This is clearly in conflict with the design of the Almighty, which was that the land should belong to the people, and that the people should never be divorced from the land:

> It is evident, therefore, that the Creator intended the land for the use of the creatures he has put on it. Consequently, that no creature ought to be cut off from the possession of some part or other of the earth, and that in such quantity as to furnish him with the necessaries of life.[2]

It is a recurrent thought in Hall that the impotence of the poor springs from the fact that they are thus cut off from the possession of some part of the earth. 'If every person had an allotment of land,' he says in one place, 'the labour of the people would remain free, and under their own direction.'[3] Such an arrangement would, in more modern phraseology, restore equality of bargaining power; the poor would no longer be under that 'absolute necessity' which now subjects them to the will of others.

As against agriculture (at least of the peasant-proprietor type) which stimulates men to industriousness and restores to them their freedom, trade and manufactures exist exclusively for the rich, and are merely additional means of exploitation. Take, for example, trade. The essence of trade is to send out of the country what the poor, the great mass of mankind, have occasion for, and to bring back 'what is consumed almost wholly by a small part of these nations, viz. *the rich*.'[4] Very few imported goods, he argues, come down to the use of the poor. The rich are thus enabled to consume in a short time the work of many people: or, if the phrase be preferred, it enables them 'to commit greater waste than it would otherwise be in their power to do.'[5] This is almost the voice of Veblen, analysing the phenomenon of 'conspicuous waste.' Nor will Hall have anything to do with the antiquated argument that the expenditure of the rich is 'good for,' and gives employment to, the poor. Very tersely he observes that 'the rich are employed in the consumption, not in the production of things.'[6] Moreover (and it is an echo of scholasticism) all trade is a species of exploitation. These articles which are the subject of trade are all the

[1] *The Effects of Civilisation*, p. 133.
[2] *Ibid.* p. 107.
[3] *Ibid.* pp. 68–69.
[4] *Ibid.* p. 83.
[5] *Ibid.* pp. 84–85.
[6] *Ibid.* p. 103.

products of labourers, manufacturers [1] and others, 'from whom they are obtained for less than their full value: a profit otherwise could not be made on them.' [2] Thus the traders also subsist on 'the fruits of the labour of the poor.' Nor is the position more favourable if we turn to 'manufactures' in the more modern sense of the word. It is true that Hall distinguishes between manufactures 'of the grosser kind,' that is to say, of articles in general use, and those manufactures which are 'more refined' [3]; and he is certainly more indulgent and tender to the former. But the impulse given by the rich is all in the direction of 'refined manufactures' [4] which the poor produce, but may never enjoy. Indeed, with a touch of paradox, Hall claims that extensive manufactures are both a cause and a sign of poverty in a nation, the argument resting on the contention that none but the poor and the destitute would ever consent to engage in industry:

> The great quantities of manufactured goods suppose a great number of manufacturers,[5] who, if they were not poor, would not submit to the employments that produce them.[6]

The remedies which Hall suggests spring from his general views of what constitutes a healthy society, rather than from the Marxian elements with which he spices his discussion. In his description of what is required in the 'happiest state,' where activity and rest are held in harmonious balance, he postulates two governing principles. The first is that each man should labour so much only as is necessary for his family; and the second is that each should enjoy the whole fruits of his labours.[7] They are alike principles which tend to give a somewhat elusive answer when it is sought to apply them to specific instances. It is unnecessary to consider in any detail Hall's more detailed proposals. He would abolish primogeniture.[8] Refined manufactures—the particular object of his detestation—he would either entirely prohibit by law, or alternatively he would burden them with such taxation as would effectively limit their production.[9] Taxation, indeed, should be imposed on none but the rich. Lastly, he proposes a scheme of extreme agrarian reform, whereby land would be vested in the State, and distributed among the entire population, remaining inalienable but subject to periodic redistribution.[10] He dreams wistfully of the Mosaic Law, of the year of Jubile, and of Sparta. In an odd way, since the two men are entirely different, there is nevertheless in the final result a certain kinship with Mably. Hall also would lead us back to a simpler life, to a world which has forsworn luxuries

[1] 'Manufacturers,' as understood in 1805, *i.e.* people who make things with their own hands.
[2] *The Effects of Civilisation*, p. 70. [3] *Ibid.* p. 38. [4] *Ibid.* p. 45.
[5] Again in the eighteenth-century sense. [6] *Ibid.* p. 144.
[7] *Ibid.* p. 261. [8] *Ibid.* p. 216. [9] *Ibid.* p. 218.
[10] *Ibid.* p. 277.

and 'refined manufactures,' where everyone, in the secure possession of a few acres, will live happily even if plainly, tyrannised by none, content with nine bean rows and a hive for the honey-bee. It is easy enough to criticise Hall: he doubtless lacked a rigorous economic discipline. Even in his time it may be doubted whether foreign trade could be discussed on the simple assumption that we exported the necessities of the poor and imported the luxuries of the rich. It may be doubted whether he is quite right in his interpretation of human psychology, whether in fact the comparative allurements of agriculture and manufactures, so far as concerns vast numbers of the population, are quite in accordance with his interpretation. Nevertheless, *The Effects of Civilisation* is a book with a peculiarly persuasive quality. The argument marches in an orderly manner; the case for the oppressed is all the more cogent, because it is stated with admirable restraint; behind the lines there is very obviously a large-hearted man. Of all the English anticipators of Marx, Hall is the one whose greater acquaintance one would most ardently desire. A day with Hall visiting his patients would have been a day well spent.

(*d*) WILLIAM THOMPSON

William Thompson, according to Foxwell, 'deserves to be regarded as chief of the English Socialist School'; Menger refers to him as 'the most eminent founder of scientific socialism.'[1] Yet most readers who turn to his chief work, known for short as *An Inquiry into the Principles of the Distribution of Wealth* (1824),[2] will doubtless experience a numbing sense of disappointment. A man of ample leisure, he devoted his leisure to the leisurely exposition of his views. In his style, he is something of a hangover from the eighteenth century, and he moves unhurriedly through his 600 closely printed pages, saying what he has to say at inordinate length (and not infrequently saying it oftener than once); unveiling the obvious with dignity and decorum, taking delight in expanding a sentence into a paragraph, a paragraph into a page. 'Why demonstrate what no one disputes?' he asks on one occasion, and the reader is startled into momentary attention by this psychic example of thought-reading stretching across the ages. Thompson has great merits; but he torpedoes himself by his unconquerable dreariness and prolixity. Even though for some reason he was reprinted in a third edition (abridged) as late as 1869, it is a fairly safe

[1] Menger: *The Right to the Whole Produce of Labour*, with introduction by H. S. Foxwell (1899). It was this volume that brought belated recognition to the members of this group.

[2] After the manner of the age, the title was, of course, considerably longer. It should be: *An Inquiry into the Principles of the Distribution of Wealth most conducive to Human Happiness; applied to the newly proposed system of the Voluntary Equality of Wealth.*

assumption that never hereafter will anyone read all, or most, of Thompson unless goaded on by a misplaced sense of duty.

Thompson adopts as his starting-point an extreme and repulsive form of Utilitarianism. 'The greatest possible quantity of human happiness,' 'the greatest happiness of the greatest number,' 'the happiness of the community,' and 'the happiness of the whole,' are expressions which he considers may be indifferently used.[1] It is for the ethical expert to follow Thompson into this field, but the innocent non-ethical outsider may be allowed a certain scepticism regarding the perfect interchangeability of these phrases. In any case, he comes down in the end in favour of accepting as the criterion 'the greatest quantity of happiness, wherever it may be found to alight.' If one human being could prove that he was so fashioned as to be endowed with an indefinitely greater capacity for happiness than the rest of his fellow-men, then wealth and all the other means of happiness ought to be 'applied' to him.[2] Consistently with this, if out of ten men, the slavery of nine and the superlative happiness of the tenth were to represent together a higher sum-total of human happiness than that attainable by any other possible arrangement, then this distribution should be adopted.[3] Here indeed is a glad gospel for those who attach importance to their capacity for enjoyment.

But indeed, although Thompson commits himself to these startling theoretical possibilities, he does not in practice allow things to work out so favourably for the expert in pleasures. For he tells us on the next page that 'all sane individuals are capable of equal enjoyment from equal portions of the objects of wealth.'[4] This proposition is not only extremely doubtful in itself, but it also raises the awkward question of the position of one who is not sane. Should we all sacrifice ourselves to enhance the ecstasy of an unusually potentially cheerful idiot? But again, it is hardly claimed that this basic proposition is in fact true; it is rather that any contrary proposition would be incapable of proof: 'to us therefore such inequalities of capabilities of enjoyment *do not exist*, because they are by us inappreciable; . . . they can no more than the galvanic fluid be seized and measured.'[5] In other words, the calculus of happiness does not enable us to calculate. These are deep and troubled waters; but so much had to be said to show how whole-heartedly Thompson believed that the increase of the sum-total of human happiness should be the end of all human endeavour; and inasmuch as wealth is produced to create happiness, that distribution of wealth is best which yields 'the greatest possible quantity of happiness to those, the society or community, that produce it.'[6]

[1] *Inquiry into the Principles of the Distribution of Wealth*, pp. 1–2.
[2] *Ibid.* p. 19. [3] *Ibid.* p. 20. [4] *Ibid.* p. 21.
[5] *Ibid.* p. 22. [6] *Ibid.* p. 19.

What then is the nature of this wealth, which is to be so distributed as to maximise human happiness? It is noteworthy that Thompson, like others of his school, defines wealth in such wise that the definition already contains implicitly the distant end which he hopes to prove. Wealth is defined as 'that portion of the physical materials or means of enjoyment which is afforded by the labor and knowledge of man turning to use the animate or inanimate materials or productions of nature.'[1] Not merely is it true to say that 'without labor there is no wealth'; but likewise 'Labor is the *sole* parent of wealth.'[2] Petty had allowed wealth to have a father and mother; Thompson assigns to wealth a parthenogenetic origin. Neither rarity, nor beauty, nor the pleasure to be derived from it; neither necessity nor utility can make an object wealth. Wealth springs from labour alone—always assuming that desire is present.[3] Without suggesting any dishonest intent (for Thompson was the most honourable of men) it should be obvious that if the definition selected gives in advance an assurance that labour is the *sole* parent of wealth, this ought to be a considerable aid towards proving that wealth may be attributed entirely to labour.

We reach the central point in Thompson's thought, if we reflect that wealth is produced by labour, and that accordingly labour requires a stimulus to induce it to maintain the maximum of production. Is it, consistently with justice, possible to find such a stimulus? Or is there an everlasting conflict between the claims of justice and the claims of efficiency? It is a difficulty that Thompson never solved, perhaps for the adequately excellent reason that it is insoluble. It is, moreover, a difficulty which lies, an ineluctable stumbling-block, at the threshold of many socialist systems. If we attain justice, assuming that we know what justice is, do we run a fair chance of drying up the world's production? Putting it otherwise, if we concede as just the workers' 'right to the whole produce of labour,' may we not be opening the door to the horridest inequality, of all things the most unjust? How far are certain of the ideals of socialism indistinguishable from the extremest and most selfish individualism? In the last analysis—putting it in ethical terms—may we not each individually be acting with extreme selfishness in insisting that we receive the tribute of our just rights?

The dilemma is a familiar one and has often been urged by bourgeois economists; but it has never been more clearly stated than by Thompson. The inferences which he draws from the utilitarian theory impel him to regard equality as the ultimate expression of justice; but the necessity of finding a 'stimulus' simultaneously impels him to give the worker the whole fruits of his labour: for is not labour the sole

[1] *Inquiry into the Principles of the Distribution of Wealth*. p. 6.
[2] *Ibid*. pp. 6–7.
[3] *Ibid*. p. 17.

parent of wealth, and accordingly is not the acknowledgment of this claim not merely another form of justice, but also the most cogent encouragement the worker can receive? For clearly the strongest possible stimulus is to be found in giving to the worker what Thompson calls 'security.'[1] 'Security,' as he is well aware, is here used in rather a special sense. In fact, he distinguishes in this matter between genuine and false or spurious security.[2] Genuine security, as he understands it, means 'the exclusive possession by every man of all the advantages of his labour'—in other words, the right of each worker to the whole produce of his individual labour; moreover, without security in this sense, 'labour would not be called forth.' False or spurious security, on the other hand, is something designed 'to soothe the imaginary alarms of the rich, protecting mere possession, however acquired.' But clearly, in so far as equality is attained, it will in general be at the expense of 'security,' in Thompson's sense of the word, and therefore will stultify the workers' stimulus to production. The application of equality would accordingly in such cases destroy the source of supply. Moreover, in an unexpectedly frank phrase, Thompson acknowledges that 'non-production is a greater evil than inequality of distribution'[3]; likewise he acknowledges that the individual producers, unable to fight down the old Adam, would never consent that what they had produced for their own purposes and enjoyment should be taken from them and distributed to increase the happiness of others.[4] Thus we see Thompson, confronted with the familiar difficulty that a theoretically more equitable system of distribution may get you no further, if its effect is to dry up the flow of production; or, to put it otherwise, we observe him torn between two conflicting ideals of justice, endeavouring to attain a basis of reconciliation.

Thompson's solution is not very satisfactory, and obviously he did not find it so. His general principle is that 'wherever equality does not lessen production, it should be the sole object pursued. Wherever it decreases really useful production . . . it saps its own existence, and should cease.'[5] In amplifying his argument, he postulates, after the manner of the theoretical economist, a hypothetical world where the necessary goods are produced independent of human effort, but only in quantities sufficient to give a limited supply. In these imaginary circumstances, an entire equality of distribution is the only equitable rule.[6] But as soon as we turn to a world where these

[1] *Inquiry into the Principles of the Distribution of Wealth.* pp. 35, 584.
[2] *Ibid.* pp. 145–147, 584.
[3] *Ibid.* p. 381.
[4] *Ibid.* p. 583.
[5] *Ibid.* p. 91.
[6] Among the goods which he supposed to be thus produced without labour are hats, and in dilating on the monstrosity of some being hatless in a world where others are multiple-hatted, he uses a phrase which curiously illustrates changing valuations: 'There are no limits to the consequential evils that may arise to the health, independent of the daily disreputableness and discomfort, of those who are compelled to do without hats' (p. 92).

same goods are produced by labour, a new law of distribution must be introduced, since 'every one sees that the blessings of equality cannot in this case be obtained without injury . . . to those whose exclusive labor has been employed in the production of the articles in question.' [1] The new law must seek to give the worker Thompsonian security, to which absolute equality must be sacrificed. But the resulting inequality, so far as it is regarded as permissible, must be reduced to a minimum. To the two fundamental principles that labour shall be free and voluntary, and that labour shall have 'security' as here understood, he now adds, as a step to the realisation of his compromise, a third condition, namely, that all exchanges, which inevitably arise in a world of division of labour, shall likewise be free and voluntary. It is in his discussion of this third principle that Thompson comes into the full stream of pre-Marxian thought. For in the past, and in the world as he saw it, there have been no 'voluntary exchanges.' The sole consideration has been 'to enrich the dominant party, at the expense of the greater number of the community, of the productive laborers, seizing the products of their labor by force.[2]' Force, in fact, has been universally prevalent: only in the United States of America (though Bray, now waiting to testify, might have taught him otherwise) have exchanges been voluntary. The whole tribe of 'bounties, protections, apprenticeships, guilds, corporations, monopolies,' and much more, all alike invade the sacred principle of security, and the no less sacred principle of equality, 'which should never be departed from but in obedience to security,' thus depriving the worker of his due.[3]

Among these deductions or 'defalcations' abstracted from what would otherwise be the reward of the worker, rent and profit naturally call for special consideration.[4] It is significant that Thompson does not entirely wipe the capitalist out of the picture, as perhaps on the logic of his assumptions he ought. 'Doubtless,' he says, referring to capital products, 'the laborer must pay for the use of these, when so unfortunate as not himself to possess them.' [5] All these deductions, whether called profits, or taxes, or theft, discourage production.[6] Moreover these capital goods are entirely attributable to the worker, and without the worker they are useless: ''Twas labor that gave to all these their value as wealth, before they came into the hands of the mechanic; and by his additional labor alone can their value be still further increased.' [7] Nevertheless, despite his use of such unambiguous words as 'defalcation' and 'theft,' the only question raised by Thompson in confronting the problem of the relation of the worker to the

[1] *Inquiry into the Principles of the Distribution of Wealth*. p. 94.
[2] *Ibid.* p. 99.
[3] *Ibid.* pp. 103, 143.
[4] *Ibid.* pp. 164–165.
[5] *Ibid.* p. 167.
[6] *Ibid.* p. 165.
[7] *Ibid.* p. 166.

employer relates to the amount payable for the use of capital goods: 'the question is how much of the products of his labor ought to be subtracted for their use.' [1]

Here then is the central problem: what should the worker pay for the hire of capital? And here he suggests, perhaps in rather misleading phraseology, what he called 'two measures of the value of this use,' according as the problem is viewed by the worker or the employer, respectively.[2] From the point of view of the worker, the contribution would be, briefly, the cost of replacement of the capital over the period of its depreciation and exhaustion, together with compensation to the owner to enable him to live 'in equal comfort with the more actively employed productive laborers.' The capitalist, on the other hand, looks for the additional value produced by labour in consequence of the use of machinery: 'the whole of such surplus value to be enjoyed by the capitalist for his superior intelligence and skill in accumulating and advancing to the laborers his capital or the use of it.' The 'surplus value' here spoken of by Thompson is not quite the same as the more notorious 'surplus value' of a later date; nevertheless the first, even if perhaps fortuitous, collocation of these two words on page 167 of Thompson's work almost deserves to rank as an event in socialist literature.

We thus arrive at Thompson's analysis of exploitation. In one place he states that the constant effort of the whole machinery of society has been 'to deceive and induce, to terrify and compel, the productive laborer to work for the *smallest possible portion* of the produce of his own labor.' [3] This, of course, is merely crude and unrefined Ricardo, as later distilled into Marx. In the passage in which he alights on the phrase 'surplus value' the test is somewhat different. Here it is rather that the labourer shall be allowed to enjoy what he formerly enjoyed: 'Before the invention of machinery . . . what was the amount of produce which the unaided powers of the laborer produced? Whatever that was, let him still enjoy'—along with the comfort of working with better tools.[4] On the other hand, all the additional wealth due to the use of machinery goes to the capitalist, 'as a reward for and stimulus to his superior intelligence in the fabrication or acquisition' of the necessary buildings and machinery. While the worker's position thus remains stationary, the total fruits of progress fall to existing wealth. On the basis of the employers' interpretation of what is due (and this is what is operative), it is inevitable that there should be vast accumulations of wealth in the hands of those who possess, at the expense of the less fortunate; and Thompson, in a glowing passage, which is singularly suggestive of the more

[1] *Inquiry into the Principles of the Distribution of Wealth*, p. 167.
[2] *Ibid.* p. 167.
[3] *Ibid.* p. 36.
[4] *Ibid.* pp. 168–169.

prophetic pages in Marx, denounces the greed and the rapacity of the capitalist.[1]

Perplexed by the insoluble problem of reconciling the conflicting claims of equality with those of the worker's right to his product (' security '), Thompson turned more and more to what he called ' voluntary equality in the distribution of wealth.' By this phrase, in effect, he meant co-operation along Owenite lines, and the concluding part of his *Distribution of Wealth* and the later pamphlet, *Labor Rewarded,* tend to be expositions of the co-operative gospel. *Labor Rewarded,* it may be noted, professes in the first edition to be written by ' One of the Idle Classes.' [2] In this later work he realises, more clearly than before, the impracticable selfishness implicit in the socialist ideal, if interpreted to mean that each worker should be individually assured of the entire product of his labour. ' Were every active laborer strictly to consume himself the whole produce of his labor, what would be the consequences ? The aged would starve. The very young would starve. Many women in producing and rearing children would starve.' In fact, though he does not carry the argument so far, if all the farmers all over the world consumed all that they produce, the bulk of the world would starve. Thompson's difficulty has merely to be stated in order to indicate that what each produces is in fact inde-

[1] The influence of the early English socialists on Marx has been so much discussed that the reproduction of an unusually Marxian paragraph from Thompson may be enlightening :

' If, on the contrary, the measure of the capitalists prevails, what is the consequence ? Whetted by the stimulus of the gratification of unbounded desires, of superiority without assignable limit to the destitution around him, the desire of accumulation supersedes with the capitalist even the love of enjoyment. To inequality of wealth there is no bound : it becomes the ruling passion : the distinction which it confers, the envy which it excites, urge men on to acquire it by any means : talents, virtue are sacrificed to it. Every expedient which force and cunning can use to appropriate the fruits of other men's labor, and with this view to turn the mass of mankind into ignorant contented drudges, is erected into a custom or a law. A universal and always vigilant conspiracy of capitalists, of necessity the most intelligent, exists everywhere, because founded on a universally existing interest, to cause the laborers to toil for the lowest possible, and to wrest as much as possible of the products of their labor to swell the accumulations and expenditure of capitalists. Yet such is the rage of these men for distinction, for expenditure as an instrument of distinction rather than of any direct enjoyment, that the products of the labor of thousands are swallowed up for no other end than to gratify such unsubstantial desires. What accumulated wealth there is in such a community, is gathered into the hands of a few ; and as well from its bulk as from its contrast with the surrounding poverty, it strikes every eye. The productive laborers stript of all capital, of tools, houses, and materials to make their labor productive, toil from want, from the necessity of existence, their remuneration being kept at the lowest compatible with the existence of industrious habits. . . . The extremes of luxury and magnificence prevail. The evils of inequality are pushed to the utmost. The desire of accumulation reigns unbounded: production is stimulated chiefly by want ' (pp. 170–171).

[2] The full title is : *Labor Rewarded. The Claims of Labor and Capital Conciliated : or, How to Secure to Labor the Whole Products of its Exertions. By One of the Idle Classes.*

terminate. The conclusion that he draws, however, is merely that 'a necessity for mutual co-operation, for the mutual insurance of numbers, to a certain extent, immediately presents itself.' [1] Into his plea for co-operation it is not possible to enter here. But *Labor Rewarded*, though not adding much to its ponderous predecessor, has its interests. As the title may suggest, it is written in partial criticism of Hodgskin's *Labour Defended*; and, odd as it may appear, it is written as a mild plea on behalf of the capitalist against the harshness of Hodgskin. For Hodgskin would have entirely cut off all supplies from those living on interest and profit. That they ought not to fare better than other people Thompson readily admits: 'but that they are not entitled to any share of the national produce will perhaps be conceded by few.' [2] On the other hand, he protests against the 'preposterous claims of mental laborers to an exorbitant portion,' such as he imagines he detects in Hodgskin. Why should he 'shove capitalists out of the field of competition altogether,' merely in order that 'he himself and his associates may step into their vacant places.' [3] It would, Thompson says, be a sorry exchange if the productive classes were to pamper 'a new host of conceited swaggerers . . . instead of the old stupid herd of capitalists.' [4] Thompson, of course, was a landlord and a capitalist; Hodgskin looked upon himself as an intellectual. But, apart from this interchange of courtesies, which is of some slight entertainment-value in illustrating how hard it is, even for an enlightened altruistic utilitarian, to suppress the whisperings of self, Thompson is surprisingly sound in pointing out how difficult it is to eliminate the capitalist. From free exchanges (a principle dear to his heart) there springs the possibility of accumulation; from accumulation there springs the capitalist *in posse*: 'you cannot abridge the exchanges and consequent accumulations of the capitalist without at the same time abridging all barter.' [5] And no less searching is the question, springing from his love of unlimited freedom in all exchanges and contracts: 'Why not permit the laborer to exchange for the use of a house, a horse, a machine, as well as for its possession?' [6]

Enough has perhaps been said to indicate the core of Thompson's criticisms, his perplexities and hesitations. But though they may not have much relevance to his place in the development of socialist doctrines, there are two passages which linger in the memory, revealing the man. The first is in the section dealing with the evils of competition, and for a moment the reader feels transported to the extravagant world of Fourier, whom it would be pleasing to think that Thompson had read. In words which come very closely to those used in one of Fourier's immortal libels, Thompson tells us:

[1] *Labor Rewarded*, p. 13. [2] *Ibid.* p. 2. [3] *Ibid.* p. 3.
[4] *Ibid.* p. 6. [5] *Ibid.* p. 16. [6] *Ibid.* p. 17.

In medicine, it is the interest of the physician to cure diseases, but to cure them as slowly and with as much profit as the competition of other medical men will permit. It is the interest of all medical men that diseases should exist and prevail, or their trade would be decreased ten or one hundred fold.

This criticism, of course, *mutatis mutandis*, applies to the whole world, and is so applied by Fourier, and indeed by Thompson, who finds everywhere a conflict between competition and benevolence. But having pointed to the doctor's natural tendency to cure disease as slowly as possible, carefully nursing a good illness, fearful lest it may be terminated by an untimely recovery, Thompson proceeds to add an illuminating comment:

Hence the almost universal inattention, nursed by the interests of physicians, to regimen, to the *preservation of health*, by attention to food, air, moisture, cleanliness, and all other circumstances influencing it.[1]

That Thompson should thus, in 1824, so seize on the essentials of preventive medicine, italicising the crucial words, places him in the heart of one of our current controversies.

The other incidentally interesting point shows him in line with Bray in rebelling against the tyranny of parents. All parents, he finds, have a 'tremendously despotic power' over the minds and the bodies of their offspring; and this power, which is inseparable from the system of individual competition, is 'liable to enormous abuses.' Accordingly, this part of parental power, tending to evil purposes, should be 'lopped off,' leaving only that part that can be turned to 'purposes of beneficence'—doubtless the equivalent of Bray's caressings of parental love. The same idea, of course, occurs in Fourier. On the whole, the best authorities seem to agree that there is much to be said in favour of the abolition—or the 'lopping off'—of parents.

(*e*) THOMAS HODGSKIN

Among the English forerunners of Marx, it is Thomas Hodgskin (1787–1869) who gives most clearly the impression of intellectual eminence and distinction, and who leaves most acutely a feeling that here was one designed for greatness which, owing to the misfits of time and of life, was never attained. An officer in the Navy, his lively sensitiveness to injustice impelled him to publish in 1813 *An Essay on Naval Discipline*, which naturally resulted in the enforced abandonment of his profession. In 1815 he went abroad in order to observe the world and its ways, and for three years he wandered about France and Italy, but above all Germany, doing most of his travels on foot. After his return, he published in 1820 two very weighty volumes of *Travels in the North of Germany*, in which innocent *Reisebilder* are

[1] *Distribution of Wealth*, p. 371.

interlarded with anarchistic and revolutionary digressions, doubtless to the amazement and perturbation of many of his readers. As one of his contemporaries complained, the information which the author conveyed was 'interspersed with remarks, not in the best taste or indicating the soundest judgment and principles.' In 1825, he wrote the short pamphlet which gives him his place in history, *Labour Defended against the Claims of Capital.* Meanwhile he had become active in the establishment of the London Mechanics' Institution, where he delivered lectures which subsequently developed into *Popular Political Economy* (1827), where 'popular,' as Hodgskin himself points out, does not mean 'amusing,' but rather that the subject is approached from the point of view of the people. Somewhat later he published a volume in the form of letters addressed to Lord Brougham on *The Natural and Artificial Rights of Property Contrasted*; and thereafter in the lugubrious and pathetic phrase of M. Halévy—sombre as an epitaph—Hodgskin 'disparaît, après 1832, dans l'obscurité du journalisme anonyme.' [1]

Somewhat curiously, perhaps, the fundamental element in Hodgskin is a blend of Adam Smith and Godwin. He has the liberal distrust of the State, which in the anarchist becomes an obsession ; and never by any chance does he shed his individualism. His very extensive book of travel is now chiefly of interest because of his reactions to the spectacle of 'the much governed countries of Germany,' [2] and he eagerly seizes every opportunity of underlining the evils of government interference. Thus one typical comment is that 'we may conclude that the real business of men, what promotes their prosperity, is always better done by themselves than by any few separate and distinct individuals, acting as a government in the name of the whole.' [3] This sentiment may indeed rise to a full confession of anarchist faith as in the following disturbing conclusion to a general chapter on the government of Hanover:

> When it is remarked, that the prosperity of every nation is in an inverse proportion to the power and to the interference of its government, we may be almost tempted to believe the common opinion, that governments are necessary and beneficial, is one of those general prejudices which men have inherited from an ignorant and barbarous age, and which more extensive knowledge and greater civilisation will shew to be an error full of evil.[4]

Elsewhere he throws doubts on the utility of legislative assemblies generally, pointing out that 'the whole of European legislation, in

[1] Elie Halévy: *Thomas Hodgskin* (1903), p. 142. It is rather extraordinary, and not wholly creditable to us, that we should be indebted to a Frenchman for the only biography of Hodgskin ; it is even more extraordinary that we should have to rely for our knowledge of a large part of Hodgskin on such extracts from his unpublished papers as M. Halévy has elected to translate into French.

[2] *Travels in the North of Germany*, vol. 1, p. 210.

[3] *Ibid.* vol. 1, p. 292.

[4] *Ibid.* vol. 1, p. 417.

so far as the production of wealth is concerned, is, and has long been, a violation of all those natural laws by which wealth is produced.'[1] Nature, he reminds us, in a phrase reminiscent of the Physiocrats, has already made laws for the conduct of individuals and of nations, and further legislative assemblies would but increase the evils of too much government. Indeed he supports the extreme anarchist view that the existence of a penal law defeats its own end: it puts evil thoughts into our minds, and perversely we are beguiled into doing something which otherwise would never have entered into our heads to do: 'when men are told they must not do any certain action under the penalty of being hung, they are immediately persuaded that it will be a great advantage to them to do it, provided they can escape detection.'[2] The ultimate ideal, in short, is to get away from the House of Commons and other similar institutions, looking forward to a time when the human race 'will lose the idle reverence with which it now worships some individuals, and submit itself only to reason as its natural lord and sovereign.'[3] In the unpublished correspondence with Place, and in his later writings which M. Halévy has piously retrieved in part from the tomb of anonymous journalism in which they were interred, there are even more extreme statements of his leanings to anarchism. It is, however, clear from what Hodgskin published under his own name, that the framework of his thought was fundamentally anarchistic.

No less interesting is it to note the sanity and the tolerance of Hodgskin in unexpected places. On the whole anarchists are somewhat innocent of the ways of the world which they condemn; but this criticism cannot be levelled against Hodgskin. His observations with regard to Trade in his *Popular Political Economy* are singularly appreciative. Retail dealers are 'indispensable agents,' and he sniffs at Mr. Owen, who imagines that in his co-operative parallelograms he can do without this useful race of men.[4] When he turns to the wholesale trader, his dissertation resolves itself into a hymn in praise of trade and of the blessedness of free trade, which Adam Smith himself could not have bettered.[5] Moreover his defence of this race of men is on familiar lines. 'They take to their business with no such high object in view; they are led to it by an instinctive view of their own interest.' But, while labouring for themselves they are useful to others. Their motives may be selfish, but the consequences of their proceedings are none the less beneficial.[6] This is not merely the shadow of Adam Smith's invisible hand: it is the hand itself. Moreover, bankers—a much abused tribe—'are still very important, and have long been very useful labourers.'[7] Even here Hodgskin's *laissez faire* principles

[1] *Travels in the North of Germany*, vol. 1, p. 467. [2] *Ibid.* vol. 2, p. 180.
[3] *Ibid.* vol. 2, p. 205. [4] *Popular Political Economy*, p. 150.
[5] *Ibid.* pp. 168–170. [6] *Ibid.* p. 149. [7] *Ibid.* p. 206.

do not desert him: 'Banking, let us never forget . . . is altogether a private business, and no more needs to be regulated by meddling statesmen, than the business of paper-making.' [1]

One further example of surprising orthodoxy may be cited. Although Hodgskin has much to say of money-price and natural-price, his discussion leads to no revolutionary proposals. Indeed, his conclusion is that the price system is not merely the index to the wants of society; it is even 'the finger of Heaven, indicating to all men how they may employ their time and talents most profitably for themselves, and most beneficially for the whole society.' [2] Even an orthodox economist of these days, brought up on Tales from the Viennese Woods, may well be forgiven if his faith falters when invited to identify the price-system with the finger of Heaven.

This extreme individualism, overflowing into anarchy, might, of itself, place Hodgskin in the line that runs from Godwin to Bakunin, and beyond. Within this framework, it is necessary to seek for those elements that make him a forerunner of Marx. Here the essential point in Hodgskin is to be found in the supreme importance which he attaches to labour in the scheme of things, and to his development of ideas which, on this point, he can claim to derive from Smith and Ricardo. For Hodgskin, labour is everything. In what is doubtless a rhetorical hyperbole, he tells us that 'Labour, enlightened, well-directed labour, converts the sterile rock into a fertile field; and it is no exaggeration to say that it gathers bread from the salt wave.' [3] In other words, his purpose is to eliminate land and capital, the other so-called factors of production, or alternatively reduce them to labour.[4] Land does not create wealth, any more than rain or sunshine; and in a lengthy letter to Place, quoted by M. Halévy, he subjects the whole of the Ricardian analysis of Rent to a destructive criticism which is far from ineffective.[5] Apart from human labour, there are, he argues, no original and indestructible qualities of the soil, and wages on the land are determined by the fact that the soil of Europe was formerly cultivated by slaves, and by memories of the remuneration formerly given to slaves.[6] That the days of slavery and of bondsmen cast their shadows over the present is an idea that frequently recurs in Hodgskin's writings.

In the small pamphlet, *Labour Defended against the Claims of Capital*, [7] Hodgskin is chiefly concerned with the elimination of Capital as an agent of production, relying on an analysis of the teaching of economists on the question. First of all, what is this circulating capital, on which, according to McCulloch and the elder Mill, the

[1] *Popular Political Economy*, p. 218. [2] *Ibid.* p. 235.
[3] *Ibid.* p. 16. [4] *Ibid.* p. 19.
[5] Halévy: *Thomas Hodgskin*, pp. 54–72. [6] *Ibid.* pp. 59–60.
[7] References are to the 1922 reissue by the Labour Publishing Company.

worker is dependent while he is working?[1] Clearly, no capitalist possesses stores of commodities which he advances to his workers. Those things which the worker requires are produced as operations advance. Bread, for example, is baked daily; the capitalist does not start off with a store of bread which will see the job through. No worker depends on a previously prepared stock, for no such stock exists.[2] What he does depend on is the 'co-existing labour' of other workers. In short,

> all classes of men carry on their daily toils in the full confidence that while each is engaged in his particular occupation some others will prepare whatever he requires, both for his immediate and future consumption and use.[3]

Turning to fixed capital, it is not merely that the necessary instruments and tools are nothing more than the products of labour: more emphatically the argument rests on the fact that in themselves these are but 'inert, decaying and dead matter,' unless they are 'guided, directed and applied by skilful hands.'[4] In short, 'fixed capital does not derive its utility from previous, but present labour; and does not bring its owner a profit because it has been stored up, but because it is a means of obtaining a command over labour.'[5] Thus capital becomes 'a sort of cabalistic word'[6]; 'it is a miserable delusion to call capital something saved.'

With this emphasis on the supremacy of labour, implicit in the Ricardian theory of value, Hodgskin is able likewise to appeal to the Ricardian teaching on wages. Waiving reservations and refinements, in the gloomy Ricardian world wages are naturally such as will enable the labourers, one with another, to subsist, and perpetuate their race, without either increase or diminution. 'Such,' comments Hodgskin in confirmation, 'is all which the nature of profit or interest on capital will allow them to receive, and such has ever been their reward.'[7] Thus while the benefits of division of labour should naturally belong to the labourers, 'all the produce of increasing skill and knowledge, falls into the power of the rapacious landlord, the usurious capitalist, and the profligate dependents on, and profligate supporters of, profligate governments.'[8] Capital, the universal middleman, is in a position to exact, and its demands are without bounds.

There are three points of general interest in which Hodgskin is more enlightened than some other members of this group. The first relates to the vexed question of the right of the worker to what he has himself produced. At times Hodgskin, perhaps incautiously, uses language in this matter which tends to a somewhat revolting and

[1] *Labour Defended*, p. 38.
[2] *Ibid.* p. 44.
[3] *Ibid.* p. 51.
[4] *Ibid.* p. 53.
[5] *Ibid.* p. 55.
[6] *Ibid.* p. 60.
[7] *Ibid.* p. 81.
[8] *Popular Political Economy*, pp. 120–121.

selfish individualism[1]; but in his guarded moments, as in *Labour Defended*, he realises that in a complex world, resting on division of labour, it is impossible to speak of anyone producing anything, since everything becomes a joint venture: 'there is no longer anything which we can call the natural reward of individual labour.' There is nothing the worker can seize and say: 'this is my product, this will I keep to myself.'[2] This is a just observation, and it is a consideration which torpedoes much socialist argument, including also some of Hodgskin's own most effective passages. Nor is it easy to devise a solution. Hodgskin's own suggestion is futile to the point of fatuity. It is that the question be left to be settled by 'the unfettered judgments of the labourers themselves,' but when the meaning of labour is extended, as Hodgskin is willing to extend it, this assuredly offers no broad highway to the paradise of industrial peace. The second point of some interest is that Hodgskin finds it expedient to enter a mild protest against the tendency to restrict 'labour' to manual labour. Mental skill is as important as muscular exertion, and accordingly Hodgskin, writing anonymously as a 'Labourer,' reinforces his *nom-de-plume* by cautioning his fellow-labourers 'not to limit the term labour to the operations of the hands.'[3]

And thirdly, Hodgskin is extraordinarily clear as to the distinction between the capitalist and the undertaker, whose functions are frequently merged in one person. 'Masters,' he says emphatically, 'are labourers as well as their journeymen,' and in so far as they are labourers, their interests are identical with those of their men. It is as capitalists that they appear as middlemen and oppressors, and for correct reasoning it is necessary to divide that part of the master which makes him a labourer from that other part in virtue of which he is a capitalist and an oppressor.[4] The wages of the master have been 'blended' with the profits of the capitalist,[5] and though doubtless their labours have been remunerated too highly, it is clear that Hodgskin has no objection to 'wages of management' as such. Indeed, he rather casts a fly over the noses of the employers by suggesting that in the event of the profit of the capitalist being diminished, 'the masters, as skilled labourers, will share in the increased rewards of industry.'[6]

Hodgskin's pre-eminent service is thus in pushing towards their

[1] *E.g.*: 'From this fact we may learn that men are only improvident in proportion as their wants are supplied by other persons, and that the simple means of making the race frugal, is to supply the wants of no man, and to leave every man the produce of his own labour (*Travels in the North of Germany*, vol. 2, p. 86).

'The object in labouring is to supply the individual's wants. Nature gave him his faculties and powers for this purpose; for this purpose only, and not for the purpose of supplying the wants of other men whom she equally endowed' (*Popular Political Economy*, p. 51).

[2] *Labour Defended*, p. 85. [3] *Ibid.* p. 87. [4] *Ibid.* pp. 90–91.

[5] *Ibid.* p. 89. [6] *Ibid.* p. 90.

final conclusions the implications of classical political economy, above all as represented by the Ricardian theories of value and wages; and his criticism is accompanied by a generous sentiment of indignation which at times rises to eloquence, as in a notable passage towards the end of *Labour Defended*:

> I am certain, however, that till the triumph of labour be complete; till productive industry alone be opulent, and till idleness alone be poor, till the admirable maxim that 'he who sows shall reap' be solidly established; till the right of property shall be founded on principles of justice, and not on those of slavery; till *man* shall be held more in honour than the clod he treads on, or the machine he guides—there cannot, and there ought not to be either peace on earth or goodwill amongst men.[1]

Yet, after a full diet of Hodgskin, most readers will feel a certain sense of disappointment that so little is said as to the path to be followed to realise his dreams. Hodgskin is in no way hostile to property. Property, he assures us, is the result of natural laws, and indeed he speaks of the 'sacredness of the present right of property'—although, it is true, this sacredness is chiefly emphasised against 'the aggressions and violations of government.'[2] But property, to be justified, must be based on individual industry: the ideal is that 'labour shall be opulent and idleness have nothing.'[3] But although in the passage from *Labour Defended* cited above, Hodgskin recognises the difficulty, under modern conditions, of saying what any one produces, nevertheless in general he continues to think in terms of an individual worker producing something which will be irrevocably his, to the exclusion of all others. Property, indeed, is defined as a man's right 'to appropriate whatever he creates by his own labour.' He is, however, somewhat vague as to his ultimate ends, as to how these aims may be attained, as to how, if attained, they may be preserved, unless serious limitations are imposed on that right of property which he regards as essential. In short the stubborn individualism, not to say anarchism, which lies at the foundation of Hodgskin's thoughts exercises throughout a somewhat paralysing influence on his aspirations to socialism.

(*f*) J. F. BRAY

Of J. F. Bray, the author of *Labour's Wrongs and Labour's Remedy* (1839), very little is known beyond the fact that his name appears on the title-page of this book. Of all the pre-Marxian writers, he is perhaps in places the most Marxian. Though at times not wholly guiltless of a certain repetitiveness, he nevertheless writes with fire in the essential passages, so that even after more than a century he holds the attention more than most of his contemporaries. His background is not markedly

[1] *Labour Defended*, pp. 104–105.
[2] *Popular Political Economy*, p. 237.
[3] *Travels in the North of Germany*, vol. 1, p. 302.

dissimilar from that of other members of the group, and may be described as a blend of Owen and Godwin. More specifically, he is frankly utilitarian. Like others of his age, he can claim insight into the mind of the Almighty and is zealous for the reputation of his Creator. 'To assert that, amidst a universe of joy, man alone is born to sorrow and to trouble, is to commit a foul libel upon the Almighty and perfect disposer of all things!'[1] 'The Creator,' as he elsewhere observes, 'intended all creatures to be happy'[2]; if a man is now unhappy, it is because he exists in an unnatural state. Further, he is at one with Owen and Godwin in his extreme belief that men are made by their environment, and that by the application of the appropriate environment they can be made into anything. Character, whether good or bad, is but a factitious quality acquired by man. The European and the Ethiopian, different as they may be, could be made to change characters and opinions by effecting an exchange of the influences to which they have been respectively exposed.[3] 'Circumstances,' that blessed word that fascinated Owen, 'furnish the seed of good or ill, and man is but as the soil in which they grow.'[4] Lastly, Bray is a most thorough-going pessimist with regard to things as they are: 'it is certain that a worse system than the present one can by no possibility be devised.'[5] The voice of pessimism could not be more emphatic.

If men, despite the intention of the Creator, are thus, and ever have been unhappy, what is the secret enemy, 'the Great Enemy,' that has thus frustrated the scheme of things?[6] With a great cloud of other witnesses, Bray points to the 'institution of property as it now exists'; later, and perhaps not wholly consistently, he follows Rousseau in declaring that 'all the wrongs and the woes which man has ever committed or endured, may be traced to the assumption of a right in the soil, by certain individuals and classes, to the exclusion of other individuals and classes.'[7] The secret enemy is thus to be found in the existence of property, especially in land, and in the fact that whereas man was meant to live 'in communion,' there is division between employers and employed, between idlers and workers. Also this is not a question of Government: Bray glances at the conditions of republican America, and witnessing there the extremes of inequality, he is content to shrug his shoulders.[8]

In seeking to refashion the world it is necessary to go to the root of the matter and to adhere to first principles, and Bray takes pride in doing so. Of such first principles, he enunciates four which, he claims, are 'promulgated in the great book of Nature.' The first

[1] *Labour's Wrongs and Labour's Remedy* (London School of Economics Reprint), p. 10.
[2] *Ibid.* p. 40. [3] *Ibid.* p. 113. [4] *Ibid.* p. 115.
[5] *Ibid.* p. 123. [6] *Ibid.* p. 17. [7] *Ibid.* p. 34.
[8] *Ibid.* pp. 19–22.

is that all men are alike; their nature and their wants are the same. Secondly, with reasons annexed, every human being ought to labour. Thirdly, since men are alike, their rights must be equal, and consequently the earth, from which all draw their sustenance, must be the common property of all its inhabitants. To these he adds, fourthly, on a somewhat different plane, that equality of labour ought to receive equality of reward.[1] As against these first principles, instituted by the Creator for the guidance and welfare of man, we are confronted with a world in which property in land has led by degrees to what in effect is property in man, in which all laws are tyrannical and all known governments are irresponsible.[2]

Proceeding, Bray calls the exponents of Political Economy to the witness-box; for it is a favourite sport of the time to cross-examine these hostile witnesses, and extort from them damaging admissions, thus 'fighting them upon their own ground and with their own weapons.'[3] The economists, who are here a somewhat shadowy race, have laid down three conditions for the production of wealth: firstly, that there shall be labour; secondly, that there shall be accumulations of former labour, known as capital; and thirdly, that there shall be exchanges.[4]

How in the eyes of Bray, looking around him, are these conditions observed? With regard to the first, it is argued that the injunction to labour applies to society as a whole; it is a general law to which there are no reservations. Somewhat absurdly, we are told that 'the ban—"THOU SHALT LABOUR"—rests alike on all created beings. To this great law, from the minutest animalcule in a drop of water, to the most stupendous whale which dives beneath the waves of the ocean, there are naturally, and there should be artificially, no exceptions.' The ban can only be avoided by one man at the expense of another; if some escape labour, the burden rests heavier elsewhere. Moreover, although with less felicity of expression, he anticipates Browning's observation that all service ranks the same with God. Inequality of value in labour is no reason for inequality of reward. Convenience and justice alike are on the side of equality of reward, provided there has been equal application of labour. We are all 'links,' and in effect one job is not more important than another. If the inventor wants more than the man who works his invention, he can rely on 'the tribute of our admiration.' Such in outline is Bray's argument, in which, as might be pointed out in a junior debating society, the condition that 'there shall be labour' is surreptitiously changed in mid-stream to the divine injunction, 'Thou shalt labour,' addressed alike to the minutest animalcule and the most stupendous whale.[5]

With regard to the second of the conditions fathered on the 'econo-

[1] *Labour's Wrongs and Labour's Remedy*, pp. 28–30. [2] *Ibid.* pp. 34–36.
[3] *Ibid.* p. 41. [4] *Ibid.* p. 42. [5] *Ibid.* pp. 42–45.

mists,' that of the necessary 'accumulations,' Bray endeavours to eliminate the individual from the picture, and to make wealth a national inheritance and its continuance a national responsibility. Our 'accumulations' come from preceding generations, and we 'merely hold them as it were in trust, for the benefit of ourselves and our successors'[1] It is our duty to hand on these accumulations with an appropriate increase: but it is vain to ask the 'productive classes,' as Bray almost invariably calls them, to accumulate, since the existing accumulations 'which have been handed down for the benefit of the present generation as a whole,' have been appropriated and are enjoyed exclusively by particular individuals and classes. It will be observed that, without expressly saying so, Bray makes the nation, or the State, the universal heir on the demise of each of its citizens: all inherited wealth belongs to the community. It is an approach to the view, if not of Saint-Simon, at least of the Saint-Simonians.[2]

It is with regard to the third condition, namely, that there shall be exchanges, that Bray is most effective and most obviously the begetter of Marxian thought. An exchange takes place between two parties, each of whom gives to the other something which he desires less than that which he receives in exchange.[3] The example to which he devotes his entire attention is the pre-eminently Marxian one of the labour contract between the worker and the employer. In a system of exchange, it is necessary that the parties should be not merely mutually benefited, but also equally benefited. 'Equal values should always exchange for equal values'—a dark saying which postulates that we know what value is. Exchange should therefore be 'equal': it is Bray's thesis that in this imperfect world all exchanges are 'unequal exchanges,' and it is in the curse of unequal exchanges that we must look for the root of all our troubles. For what happens now is that the worker gives the capitalist the labour of a whole year in exchange for the value of only half a year[4]; he gives the employer six days' labour for an equivalent worth only four or five days' labour.[5] Indeed it is an understatement to say that we are here dealing with unequal exchanges: strictly speaking, there is no exchange whatever. For the capitalist gives nothing. He gives no labour, for he is innocent of work; he clearly gives no capital, for by definition a capitalist is incessantly growing more and more wealthy. What really happens is that 'the capitalists and proprietors do no more than give the working man, for his labour of one week, a part of the wealth which they obtained from him the week before!' He gives the worker nothing for something. The whole transaction is thus, in the words of Bray, a palpable deception, a mere farce, a barefaced though legalised robbery.[6] All this is of the

[1] *Labour's Wrongs and Labour's Remedy*, pp. 46–47. [2] *Ibid.* p. 47.
[3] *Ibid.* p. 47. [4] *Ibid.* p. 48. [5] *Ibid.* p. 56.
[6] *Ibid.* pp. 49–50.

essence of Marx, and it is perhaps not wholly insular pride that makes one feel that in some ways it is rather better done than in Marx. Nor does Bray fall behind in his purple passages, as when he declares that 'this wealth has all been derived from the bones and sinews of the working classes during successive ages, and it has been taken from them by the fraudulent and slavery-creating system of unequal exchanges.'[1] It is also due to the unseen magic of these unequal exchanges that Capital and Labour have become two separate and antagonistic powers; and that the wealth and supremacy of one class is based upon the poverty and degradation of the other.[2] It is only an extension of the same argument that, in the matter of taxation, the whole burden rests on the workers, since the capitalists, inasmuch as they give no aid in production, have nothing of their own with which to pay taxes. Likewise, of course, the establishment of equal exchanges would compel the idler to work.[3]

To meet such a situation, a complete change of system is necessary. Bray devotes considerable space to proving what he calls the 'Inutility' of the remedies ordinarily advanced. All suggestions fail because they aim at effects, leaving causes sacred and untouched[4]: but what else is to be expected from 'shallow-pated drivellers'? Political remedies are useless; so likewise are the efforts of Trade Unions. In an illuminating phrase, these aim merely at 'the *partial* amelioration of the condition of the working class *as a working class*.'[5] In other words, Trade Unions would leave the employer-employed nexus intact. Emigration, then a popular remedy, would under existing conditions merely alter the scene of the workers' injustices. As to the form of society which should replace that in which mankind now suffers, Bray is clear that 'community of possessions is in every respect the most perfect form of society which man can institute,'[6] and the phrase is almost an echo of Plato. Unfortunately, it demands a 'corresponding degree of excellence' of those who would enter this earthly paradise. Bray is clear-sighted here on a point where many visionaries have been blind. He realises that past communistic experiments have often failed because those who entered 'were taken almost promiscuously from the world at large, and they carried with them their old feelings, prejudices and habits.'[7] There is a certain danger in filling the streets of the New Jerusalem with the damaged goods of this world, tainted by 'the foul and loathsome selfishness which now more or less accompanies every action, clings to every thought, and pollutes every aspiration.'[8] Consequently, those who seek to introduce the new system must be possessed of sufficient capital to tide over the period of man's

[1] *Labour's Wrongs and Labour's Remedy*, p. 57.
[2] *Ibid.* pp. 60–61.
[3] *Ibid.* p. 74.
[4] *Ibid.* p. 98.
[5] *Ibid.* p. 100.
[6] *Ibid.* p. 133.
[7] *Ibid.* p. 130.
[8] *Ibid.* p. 133.

regeneration, or alternatively we must be content for the present with a half-way house.[1]

To the elaboration of such an 'intermediate resting-place,' which he describes elsewhere as 'fitted to take society as it is, and to prepare the way for other and better changes,'[2] Bray devotes considerable attention; but on this point it is perhaps unnecessary to follow him in any detail here. He was obviously impressed by the progress and efficiency of Joint Stock Companies, and he had the insight to realise that 'these companies are usurping, in all directions, the places and occupations hitherto confined to individual capitalists and traders.'[3] He is accordingly inspired to propose that there should be a 'joint-stock modification of society.'[4] Each trade is to establish within itself the germs of a future company. In the end, society will be 'as it were, one great joint-stock company, composed of an indefinite number of smaller companies, all labouring, producing and exchanging with each other on terms of the most perfect equality'[5]; and, of course, the individual employers and capitalists will be superseded. Bray's account, especially on the side of finance (where he is invariably weak) is not wholly clear; but the end result, so far as it is possible to visualise it, would appear to yield a society which would be something like a cross between the projects of Robert Owen and Louis Blanc.

There is, however, one point in this 'joint-stock system' which is of more than topical interest. Bray is one of the earliest and most extreme advocates of Family Endowment, and would end the dependence of wives on their husbands and of children on their parents. 'The maintenance and education of children by their parents is,' he declares, 'a glaring defect in every social system in which the practice prevails.' Every child should be looked upon as the child of society, and parents should have 'no offices to perform but the caressings of parental love.'[6] Bray is entirely silent as to the machinery, financial and otherwise, required to realise his scheme of family endowment; but as an instalment towards the complete 'community' which is his ultimate aim, the disappearance of the family is almost inevitably imposed upon him.

From the point of view of persuasive propaganda, Bray is probably the most effective of the English pre-Marxians. Perhaps on a second, and still more on subsequent perusals, the reader may have an uneasy feeling that not infrequently he contrives to smuggle the thesis to be proved in amongst the definitions and the postulates from which he starts out. But, of course, he is not unique in this respect. Indeed, it is perhaps the essence of successful propaganda.

[1] *Labour's Wrongs and Labour's Remedy*, p. 134.
[2] *Ibid.* p. 194.
[3] *Ibid.* p. 155.
[4] *Ibid.* p. 161.
[5] *Ibid.* pp. 170–172.
[6] *Ibid.* pp. 165–166.

(g) JOHN GRAY

John Gray is one of the liveliest of the early English anticipators of Marx; but his greater liveliness has not prevented him from becoming, like some other members of the group, a somewhat shadowy figure. He is said to have been of Scottish extraction, to have worked in London in his younger days and to have returned to Scotland later, where, contrary to the views of Dr. Johnson, greater prosperity awaited him. After the manner of mankind, he would seem to have become less revolutionary with advancing years. Here we are concerned with his earlier days as represented by his *Lecture on Human Happiness,* which, published in 1825, when Marx was seven years old, provides in many ways a somewhat remarkable anticipation of certain of the cornerstones of the Marxian edifice.

Gray's starting-point is in some ways reminiscent of Adam Smith, who placed Division of Labour in Chapter 1 of Book I, and founded it on a peculiar 'propensity to truck.' According to Gray it is a 'propensity to exchange labour for labour' that enables men to leave the lower creation behind.[1] It is through barter, and not through the defects of government, that the possibility of tyrannising was introduced into the world; it is on barter and barter alone that society is founded; on barter and barter alone that all institutions rest. This starting-point is cunningly chosen in order to emphasise later the importance of just exchanges. Further, Gray, as becomes his times, is undilutedly utilitarian: happiness is 'the end and object of every human pursuit.'[2] Nor will he be fobbed off with the soothing consolation that happiness consists in the pursuit and not in the possession of the object desired. With the voice of common sense, Gray makes it clear that when he pursues, he means to get there; that while he is prepared to travel joyfully, he also means to arrive.

> Which of us, when overtaken with hunger or thirst, ever found more pleasure in the pursuit than in the enjoyment of food? Which of us, if by chance exposed to the inclemencies of the weather, drenched with rain, or frozen with cold, ever experienced more pleasure in the search of a fireside than in the enjoyment of it?[3]

To the importance of barter as the basis of civil society, to the utilitarian assumption that happiness is alone what matters, it is necessary, in order to complete Gray's fundamental assumptions, to add the distinction between productive and unproductive labour—that evil legacy of the Physiocrats. Every necessary, convenience or comfort of life comes from labour. Various types of labour are indicated, and all who do not fall within this classification are unproductive and useless members of society, and are (in the largest capitals) a 'DIRECT

[1] *Lecture on Human Happiness* (London School of Economics Reprint), p. 5.
[2] *Ibid.* p. 13. [3] *Ibid.* p. 13.

L

TAX' on the productive classes.[1] Moreover, Gray's idea of productive labour is extremely narrow. As he says elsewhere, with all the added emphasis of italics, '*they only* are productive members of society who apply *their own hands* either to the cultivation of the earth itself, or to the preparing and appropriating the produce of the earth to the uses of life' [2]; beyond this, he makes a somewhat grudging concession in the case of merchants, manufacturers and others (' mere distributors of wealth ') who are ' useful only in a *sufficient* number.'

With these guides to our footsteps, let us see what society, as we know it, looks like. Gray's general view, disclosed in a passing observation, is that it is wonderful that ' the existing arrangements of society drive comparatively so few men mad.' [3] He had been much impressed, as were all his generation, by Colquhoun's *General View of Society*, which purported to show, for 1812, how the New Property in Great Britain and Ireland, arising from various sources, was distributed among the various classes of the community.[4] On the restricted de-

[1] *Lecture on Human Happiness*, p. 15.

[2] *Ibid.* p. 69.

[3] *Ibid.* p. 28.

[4] The title of Patrick Colquhoun's book is *A Treatise on the Wealth, Power and Resources of the British Empire*, and it is the fourth chapter of this quite impressive work that flits through early English Socialist literature. This chapter makes a quite laudable attempt to estimate the income of various classes, and there is attached to it a Table (No. 4) which is called *An Attempt to Exhibit a General View of Society* (pp. 124–125). Needless to say, the discussion and the table alike are somewhat amateurish, giving at best very approximate guesses in respect of ill-defined categories. The contemporary references to Colquhoun, in Gray and elsewhere, may, however, give a wrong impression to a reader who is unable to unearth and carry to a place of security Colquhoun's massive treatise.

It is not, as might be inferred from Gray, a remote ancestor of Fabian Tract No. 5, *Facts for Socialists*. Colquhoun is beset by Adam Smith's definition of productive labour, and thinks in terms of ' vendible commodities.' His own estimate (p. 109) is that on this definition one-fifth part of the whole community are unproductive labourers, and that they secure one-third of the new property created annually. But he hastens to warn his readers that the unproductive labourer, on Adam Smith's definition, may be a very useful person: ' with a few exceptions . . . they eminently tend to promote, invigorate, and render more productive the labour of the creating classes.' Indeed (p. 105), he somewhat too zealously goes out of his way to prove (with few exceptions) the great usefulness of everybody. Gray, taking Colquhoun's table and adding to it, makes his own estimate of the useless and the useful, on a purely arbitrary basis which reflects his own prejudices. It is a significant testimony to his prudence that while temporal and spiritual peers and all other ' gentry ' are 100 per cent. useless, no impious voice of criticism is raised against even the remoter branches of the Royal Family, who are classed as 100 per cent. useful. Eminent clergymen are 100 per cent. useless; lesser clergymen are 100 per cent. useful. The whole profession of law, from judges down to ' clerks, etc.,' are useless. The theatrical profession (rather oddly) leaves the inquisition without a stain on its honour, being found 100 per cent. useful. Again, rather oddly, the class of lunatics produces none who are useless. In most cases, there is merely an arbitrary cutting down to a half or a third, the residue (with their families) being ' useless.'

Where Colquhoun may quite legitimately irritate—if, after reading Owen, one is so weak as to feel irritation against anyone—is in his doctrine of the usefulness of Poverty in a State, resting on the distinction between poverty and indigence. Every State, he says, is supported by the poverty of the community (p. 110); and the reasoning is almost grotesquely simple. Riches are the offspring of labour;

finition of 'productive labour' to which Gray adheres, his conclusion, on the figures given by him, is that the productive classes fall considerably short of half the total population, and that they receive only about a fifth of what they produce.[1] Gray is most interesting and at times most spicy in the comments which he adds on the fifty-one categories into which, building on Colquhoun, he divides the population, and which indeed he annotates *seriatim*. Thus in sweeping aside that comprehensive group labelled 'Nobility, Gentry, Knights, Esquires, Ladies and Gentlemen,' he adds, very much in the manner of Owen, the extenuating plea, that 'it has been the misfortune, not the fault, of the higher classes, to be born under an unjust system.'[2] On his modest proposal for the abolition of every kind of lawyer 'without a single exception,' Gray speaks with the authentic voice of Godwin. Like many others, he seems to be under the curious impression that all law is criminal law, and that all lawyers spend all their waking hours in trafficking with crime and criminals. The argument for abolishing lawyers is that punishment, so far from preventing crime, has an invariable tendency to increase it. The magnitude of crime keeps pace with the magnitude of punishment. 'Invariable kindness' is the only effective prescription. We must exhibit to the understanding, without anger, the effects which bad actions produce in society. It is gratifying to know that this mode of treatment can never fail to produce the desired effect—although, admittedly, it must be persevered in.[3] Could Godwin himself have put it more clearly?

In his comment on the group of 'Shopkeepers and Tradesmen retailing goods,' Gray achieves an effect of extravavagant fantasy which is more in line with Fourier. The number of these, he remarks with sobriety, is 'limited not to those who are *really required* to transact the business of a town in a rational and proper manner, but to those who can *get a living* in it.' As for the race of shopkeepers themselves, he says with a fine irony:

> Certain it is that these men are not unproductive, for never, upon the face of the earth, was there anything half so productive of deception and falsehood, folly and extravagance, slavery of the corporeal, and prostitution of the intellectual faculties of man, as the present system of retail trade. . . . A fourth or fifth part of their time is expended in decorating their shop windows, that is, in spoiling goods, and at least half of it in waiting about for their customers or doing nothing useful.[4]

Somewhat in the same spirit, and on this same question of retail trade, there is a passage elsewhere to the effect that false representation

and labour can result only from a state of poverty! But below poverty lies indigence, and by 'well-timed props,' the poor must be prevented from lapsing into indigence, at which point they become a burden to others. They must (in a very fine phrase) 'be again restored to their former rank of independent poverty' (p. 113).

[1] *Lecture on Human Happiness*, p. 20.
[2] *Ibid.* p. 22.
[3] *Ibid.* p. 24.
[4] *Ibid.* pp. 26–27.

is the inevitable end of competition. Equal capitals, with equal skill and industry, will command goods at equal prices; and consequently, there follows a never-ceasing competition in which each strives to make his goods appear cheaper than his neighbour's. Truth is of no use here, and it follows that falsehood must be resorted to:

> What says experience? There is not one advertisement in one hundred, which appears in the public prints, relating to the prices of goods in retail shops, but what is untrue. Let any man deny this, who knows anything of business. The printers of newspapers ought to place all advertisements from retail shops, under the head of '*Falsehoods, misrepresentations, etc.*' Can general sincerity exist in such a state of society as this? [1]

Without venturing on an assessment of the justice of Gray's final conclusion, it will be observed that the underlying postulate is that there exists everywhere 'equal industry and skill'—in other words, he assumes the existence of that uniformity of man which so frequently emerges in the socialist tradition.

In this analysis of society, what are we to make of the 'independent classes'? Remembering the primary assumption that everything comes from labour, then these independent classes are of all men the most dependent. They are indeed doubly dependent: they are dependent on the industry of their fellow-creatures, and they are dependent on the injustice which enables them to command it. The first point is proved by an obvious train of reasoning:

> They are dependent upon the baker for their bread, and upon the butcher for their meat. They are dependent upon the bricklayer for their houses, and upon the upholsterer for the furnishing of them. They are dependent upon the tailor and upon the dressmaker for their clothes; and upon their valets and maids to put them on. If there is a name which, better than any other, will describe this class of men, it is the word DEPENDENTS.[2]

If it be argued in rebuttal that they live on their property, then Gray replies, almost in the words of Marx, that 'Labour is the sole foundation of property, and that, in fact, all property is nothing more than accumulated labour.' [3] If the defence further is that they give an equivalent in money for what they consume, then it may be answered that the money is not theirs to give. It springs from Rent and Interest, which have no foundation in justice, and therefore the independent classes are solely dependent upon injustice for their daily bread. To us in these days there again appears to be undue emphasis on rent and interest, which are not the sole, nor, in our times, the main sources of excessive gains. Whatever breeds millionaires nowadays, it is certainly neither rent nor interest in any exact sense. So far as rent is concerned, in Gray's view it rests solely on the 'power and custom of obtaining it.' [4] Interest is merely another method of obtaining labour without giving

[1] *Lecture on Human Happiness*, p. 43.
[2] *Ibid.* p. 34.
[3] *Ibid.* p. 34.
[4] *Ibid.* p. 36.

an equivalent for it. In a rather ridiculous illustration, he imagines a manufacturer of hats, accumulating 10,000 hats valued at 20*s*. each. He turns these into money, and after living well for a lifetime, he still has intact the equivalent of his 10,000 hats. 'Can the bee do this? Can the ant do this?' he pertinently asks.[1] It is like a burlesque inversion of a music-hall song of a generation ago, which, after reciting the accomplishments of a hen, asked with equal relevance: 'Could Lloyd George do it?' As St. Paul observed, there are diversities of gifts.

As against this type of spoliation, 'all just contracts have for their foundation equal quantities of labour.' This, of course, is drawn from Ricardo unalloyed, slurring all the points of difficulty; but it is in line with Gray's starting-point that society is based on barter, and that it is by the door of barter—unjust barter—that tyranny enters into the world.

In contrast with the sorry state of the world as we see it, what, Gray asks, would be the position if the 'useful labourer' were allowed to 'keep for his own use the property he creates'?[2] For this is the only reform required: and it will be observed that it has the strict individualistic tendencies of all rigorous announcements of the right of each to his entire produce. To take only one suggestive point in passing, this right of each to his whole produce without impairment, is clearly inconsistent with any form of Poor Law or public assistance, otherwise than on a voluntary basis. Logically, indeed, it may be doubted whether it can be reconciled with any system of taxation, other than that which might be imposed by a State ridden by the extremest *laissez faire* doctrine. The result of such a reform, in Gray's opinion, would however be to produce a state of universal opulence for all, at the cost of but a few hours' daily work; for Gray, like most of the group, is a convinced adherent of the 'poverty-in-the-midst-of-the-possibility-of-plenty' idea. He refers to the most important truth ever submitted to the mind of man, which is that, while poverty prevails,

> those very inhabitants, aided by the great mechanic power of which they are possessed, are capable of creating, by their own labour, all those necessaries and comforts of life to an almost unlimited extent, certainly to an extent amply sufficient to supply the wants of every member of their respective communities.[3]

In analysing why society falls short of its potentialities in this respect, Gray in part discloses points of view with which we are, now at least, familiar; in part also he dwells in darkness. Fundamentally, he endeavours to show that at present Capital is brought into competition with Capital, instead of being brought to act in conjunction with it. This is a clear pointer in the direction of the replacement of com-

[1] *Lecture on Human Happiness*, p. 38.
[2] *Ibid.* p. 57.
[3] *Ibid.* p. 60.

petition by co-operation. There are, it is argued, two natural limits to the production of wealth, to be found, firstly, in the exhaustion of our productive powers, or, secondly, in the satisfaction of our needs. But we have created a third, and unnatural, limit to production, as represented by Competition.[1]

This third limitation of production springs fundamentally from the fact that, as things are at present, production is determined by, and is dependent upon, demand. The question is never that of ascertaining how much is required to satisfy the needs of mankind; but rather, how much can be disposed of at a profit. What is produced has no regard to the satisfaction of our wants or the extent of our powers of production; it is determined solely by a calculation as to how much the market can absorb and still yield a profit.[2] It is unnecessary to observe that this argument is one of the corner-stones of Guild Socialism of a later generation, crystallised in the familiar phrase that production, as we know it, is for profit and not for use.

So far, we are on easy and familiar ground. If, however, production is limited by demand, the next stage in the argument is to enquire what it is that limits demand. Demand is nothing more than the aggregate quantity of wealth which 'the labour, the services, and the property' of the whole community will command.[3] But this, in each case, according to Gray, is kept down to a minimum by the influence of competition. So far as concerns wages, the argument is obvious, and in the circumstances of the time sufficiently cogent. It is a straightforward invocation of Ricardian and Marxian ideas. The competition of the unemployed, 'candidates for employment,' has the effect of 'keeping down the quantity obtained by the mass, to that portion which is *just sufficient* to support bodily strength and to continue their race.'[4] But Gray is not content with an Iron Law of Wages: he will have an Iron Law operative throughout the whole of society, manifesting itself in an Iron Law of Profit, and an Iron Law of Interest, and so on. Thus profits are cut down to a minimum by competition, each being compelled by competition to sell as near as may be to cost price; and the same, *mutatis mutandis*, applied to the rent of houses and the interest on money. These conclusions lead to a general principle:

> That, therefore, the income of EVERY INDIVIDUAL, *and consequently of the* WHOLE COMMUNITY, except only those persons who have fixed money incomes, is LIMITED BY COMPETITION, and that each obtains the LEAST that his labour, his services, or the use of his property CAN POSSIBLY BE OBTAINED FOR.[5]

This analysis, be it said with all respect, is not merely confused; it defeats the end of Gray's argument, if it does not border on the absurd. The exploitation of the worker under a Ricardian-Lassallean Iron Law

[1] *Lecture on Human Happiness*, pp. 60–61. [2] *Ibid.* p. 62.
[3] *Ibid.* p. 62. [4] *Ibid.* p. 63. [5] *Ibid.* p. 65.

is a sufficiently comprehensible concept; but the exploitation, where it exists, is to the advantage of the other party to the transaction. Here we are asked to view (sympathetically) the landlord and the capitalist being ground down to the lowest rent or the lowest rate of interest he can possibly accept (as doubtless he may be under the inexorable law of Austrian economics where the margin dominates the situation); but a society which is characterised by exploitation must manifest exploiters and exploitees. Gray's world is one consisting entirely of exploitees—apart from those who are in receipt of fixed money incomes. Even these, it may be observed incidentally, will doubtless have their incomes fixed as low as possible: in a world where the Iron Law of Wages is stalking about seeking whom it may devour, even an Education Authority, in fixing the wages of its teachers, will obey its stern behests.

The final result of this unnatural restraint on production is more clearly stated than the argument on which it rests. It is that the inhabitants of this country are now 'in possession of powers by which they can create wealth without any known limits, and yet one-half of them are in a state of actual poverty.' [1]

Perhaps Gray tails off in cogency towards the end of his argument. His diagnosis—which is broadly that of an insufficiency of purchasing power everywhere—would seem to point to a monetary solution; and indeed it was the question of money with which Gray concerned himself in his later years. At the stage of the *Lecture on Human Happiness* he is content to say that competition, the unnatural barrier which forces poverty upon us, must be abolished. But apart from giving an assurance that it could be abolished at any time, without the slightest difficulty, it cannot be said that he is very helpful to any crusader who would seek to follow in his footsteps. No doubt he appends articles of agreement for the formation of a community on principles of mutual co-operation, which seem to foreshadow a cross between Owen and Fourier. Those who are interested in the affiliation of ideas will note with interest how much of Fourier there is in the seventeenth of these articles, which lays down that every species of co-operative exertion is to be rendered *attractive* to the members; and that one way of engendering attraction is 'by the facility and variety of occupations, no one occupation continuing, except by choice, for more than two or three successive hours.' [2] Fourier's butterfly, while demurring to the monstrous and inordinate length of these 'sessions,' would have conceded that Gray was on the right lines.

Such is John Gray, and though he may not have completed the journey to the Finland Station, his place as an exponent of Marxism at a time when Marx was still playing marbles, or should have been playing marbles, in the streets of Trier, is sufficiently remarkable.

[1] *Lecture on Human Happiness*, p. 66. [2] *Ibid.* Appendix, p. 10.

He taught that property was but accumulated labour ; he taught the doctrine of exploitation, indeed of robbery and of spoliation ; he taught that the competition of the unemployed (later to be enrolled as the Industrial Reserve Army) pressed down wages until they were merely sufficient to enable the workers to continue their race. If something more specifically Marxian in phraseology is required, let it be recalled that Gray explained the poverty of the poor by the fact that there are ' persons who buy their labour from them at one price, and sell it at another.'

CHAPTER XII

SCIENTIFIC SOCIALISM

(*a*) MARX AND ENGELS

DURING the last generation Marx has occasioned such a devastating torrent of exposition, criticism, deification and denigration, that here, if anywhere, one might be justified in waving the still curious reader to the ample and accessible literature, pressed down and running over, which may so easily be found elsewhere on the subject. Yet though this inordinate flood of books, and of books upon books, might well afford any prudent man complete justification for refusing to write one further book on Marx, it can hardly be invoked as an adequate plea for silence where, as here, we are concerned with successive phases of socialist thought and with their mutual inter-reactions. Accordingly, much as a sensitive typewriter may rebel against being called upon to perform so hackneyed a task, it is necessary that we should seek to reproduce sufficient of the essential core of Marx to understand his place in the succession. Unfortunately, on any line of approach, it is a rather large and intractable core, with numerous facets.

We are not here concerned with Marx's biography, except in so far as it is related to, or helps to explain, his doctrine. He was born in 1818 in Trier, and like most of the theorists of socialism he belonged to what he himself would have called the Bourgeoisie. He was of Jewish descent, but his family had undergone a recent conversion to Christianity. It has been ingeniously suggested that, in an anti-semitic environment, the converted Jew suffers doubly. He is treated as a Jew, without having the moral support and consolation of knowing that he is one of God's chosen people. Marx married, as the Victorians would have said, 'above him.' His wife, Jenny von Westphalen, was of a family with distinctly superior connections, a fact of which rather oddly (or perhaps not so oddly) Marx seems to have been rather proud. From his entrance upon the world until 1848 he lived the life of a professional revolutionary, with no rest for the sole of his foot. From 1848 until 1883 he was a political exile, living, but for minor interludes, in London. The year 1848 represents a landmark in Marx's life: he remained curiously a man of 1848. The conditions under which he did his work in London, above all in the earlier years, make it something of a miracle that he ever did any work at all. The real hero, or martyr, of the Marx household was his wife: but it is unwise of a revolutionary to marry a Jenny von Westphalen and take her to Dean Street. She seems to have been something of a saint;

but even a saint may be pardoned for becoming neurotic if she happens to be married to a Karl Marx. No one so qualified as she to claim for herself the familiar hymn: 'Nobody knows the trouble I've seen.' In a world full of the glorification of Marx, somewhat scant justice has been done to his suffering wife.

Further, Marx was throughout his London life increasingly dependent in a sense and to an extent which would have been entirely repugnant to any ordinary man, and which in his innermost soul must have been repugnant even to him, successful as he may have been in concealing it. It was Friedrich Engels (1820–1895) who kept the Marx household going, and without his unstinted and inexhaustible generosity it would probably have foundered quite early in the days of London exile. All these circumstances in his life naturally tended to undermine Marx's self-respect and confidence, and to produce in him an almost complete example of the manifestations of the Inferiority Complex. He was suspicious of everyone; he quarrelled sooner or later with everyone—Engels alone excepted; he was arrogant and self-assertive; for all who did not acknowledge his superiority, he had the supremest contempt. In his heart there was envy and bitterness and hatred; for the world at large he had neither tolerance nor love.

Engels, who has been mentioned as the material saviour of the Marx household, was, however, much more than that. The collaboration of Marx and Engels is surely something that is unique in literary history. Many of the most significant Marxian productions—including *The Communist Manifesto*, 'the best thing Marx ever wrote'—were in fact written jointly. It was Engels who edited (and some would suggest that he rather more than edited) the second and third volumes of *Capital* after Marx's death. For almost forty years there was scarcely a thought of Marx which was not also a thought of Engels. He was the one friend whose friendship for Marx endured, though indeed it was sorely tried on one occasion. That it did endure was due solely to Engels' extraordinary willingness to play second fiddle and to subordinate himself in all things. He tied himself to an uncongenial occupation (which, strictly speaking, it ought to have been against their joint-conscience for him to accept) entirely in order to gain the means which enabled Marx to frequent the British Museum as a full-timer. There have been many instances in history where a man has sacrificed everything for a woman, and doubtless just as many where a woman has sacrificed everything for a man. It is not easy to find a parallel to the case of Engels who, for the sake of a common cause, gave his whole life in order that another, with no claims of blood or relationship upon him, should be exempted from the necessity of earning his own livelihood. Despite his own very considerable independent work, Engels has until recently stood somewhat overmuch in the shadow of Marx. The 'Marx-Engels-Lenin Institute' in

Moscow has, by its title, at last done tardy justice to Engels' place in the scheme of things.

Marx was the founder of 'Scientific Socialism,' as opposed to 'Utopian Socialism.' The distinction, of which Marx and Engels were very conscious, may call for a preliminary word of explanation. The 'Utopians' were pre-eminently Saint-Simon, Fourier and Owen. In *The Communist Manifesto*, the reproach directed against them is that they had no knowledge of the Proletariat as such; they made their appeal to the whole of society, by preference to the ruling classes; they dreamed fantastic pictures of a new society, and even sought to create 'duodecimo editions of the New Jerusalem.' To the Utopians, socialism was the expression of absolute truth.[1] They appealed to morality; whereas, 'from a scientific standpoint, this appeal to morality and justice does not help us an inch further.'[2] The Utopians constructed the outlines of a new society out of their own heads,[3] and looked round, like Fourier, for a capitalist to 'launch' it. In other words, they did not have a philosophy of history. The function of scientific socialism was to reveal socialism as 'a necessary product of historical development.' Given a knowledge of the laws according to which human history unrolls itself, the scientific socialist could show, with a wealth of obstetrical metaphor for which they manifested a marked partiality (invoking wombs, midwives and umbilical cords),[4] that the existing capitalistic society could not fail to give birth to a socialist order. The appeal to morality and justice, the vision and the dream, were replaced by an understanding and acceptance of historical development.

Many commentators have stressed the view that Marx can in no respect lay claim to 'originality.' It may be true; it is certainly immaterial. It may not be so in the world of science and scientific discovery; but in the realm of thought, there are few ideas which, with a little ingenuity, cannot be shown to have had a long ante-natal history, or perhaps to be but the restatement of something suggested out of due season to an earlier generation. In the words of a musical critic, dealing with the somewhat analogous question of musical plagiarism, 'it is not the tune that matters, but what you do with the tune.'[5] In the same way, it is doubtless true that the component parts of Marxian thought can be traced to a multitude of sources. He collected his bricks from many masons' yards; but he used them to construct a building which was very much according to his own design.

[1] Engels: *Anti-Dühring*, p. 25. [2] *Ibid.* p. 168. [3] *Ibid.* p. 292.

[4] Not always without producing rather grotesque effects. Thus the official biography of Lenin tells us (p. 35) that 'Lenin discerned the processes that were going on in the womb of capitalist society.' Not even Socrates, who has some claims to be the originator of this long line of metaphor, regarded himself as so skilful a midwife.

[5] Mr. Fox Strangways, in a private letter.

The sources of Marx may be glanced at, even if in the space available here the glance may be little more than an enumeration. Firstly, there was Hegel, who dominated his earlier years ; for Marx belonged to a generation when Hegelianism was as fashionable as Fabianism in the late 'nineties. From Hegel he learned the principle of development by contrast and by conflict. Every state, condition or proposition calls forth its negation, which in turn provokes the negation of the negation, which contains in itself the original positive and the subsequent negation. Every thesis reacts to its anti-thesis, which leads to the synthesis, combining both thesis and anti-thesis. Hegel had yoked his apparatus to the car of idealism. It was Feuerbach who made Marx a 'materialist,' but though Marx abandoned Hegel's idealism, he continued throughout life to think in terms of the Hegelian dialectic, and to find particular pleasure in anything that might seem to exemplify the negation of the negation. Hegelianism is the kind of thing that ought to be left to Hegelians who presumably know the secret of Hegel. In less expert hands, as in those of Proudhon, it seems to the illiterate and ignorant outsider to become a mere toy which enables every swing of every pendulum to be regarded as the embodiment of a great philosophical principle.[1] Enough here to note that it was from Hegel that Marx learned that development, the unfolding of events, results from the conflicts of opposites, leading to a synthesis on a new plane.[2]

From the earlier French socialists, with whom he had contacts during the period of his residence in Paris, it is probable that Marx derived the phrase, if not precisely his conception, of the 'class war.' For indeed, the idea of the class war, if one so chooses, goes back to a famous phrase in Plato's *Republic* ; but before Marx, the 'class war' (expressed or implied) had been conceived rather in terms of the conflict of interests between rich and poor. Neither Marx nor Engels was interested in the poor as such ; like a good deal of modern social legislation, they tended to restrict their interest to 'employed persons' ; and the class war, from being the conflict between rich and poor, became the war between employer and employed—which is not by any means necessarily the same war. On the economic side, the affiliation and sources of Marx are clear beyond all shadow of dubiety.

[1] The examples of the 'negation of the negation' given by Engels (*Anti-Dühring*, pp. 151–159) may be sound Hegelianism, but otherwise they appear rather silly. A seed of barley falls into the ground and germinates : negation of the seed. In the autumn it produces more grains of barley : negation of the negation. A butterfly comes from an egg : negation of the egg. After many transformations, the butterfly mates and dies : negation of the negation. Negate a, and you get $-a$; negate $-a$ (this time by multiplying by $-a$), and the result is a^2 : negation of the negation, in which both a and $-a$ are firmly embedded, since the square of each is a^2. Hegel is surely something more than this.

[2] Marx's summary of Hegelianism is not without entertainment value, especially so, perhaps, if left in the French of *La Misère de la Philosophie* : 'Le oui devenant non, le non devenant oui, le oui devenant à la fois oui et non, le non devenant à la fois non et oui, les contraires se balancent, se neutralisent, se paralysent.'

He is merely the continuator of classical English Political Economy. To the outward eye of the unsophisticated man, the Marxian theory of value is no more than Ricardo transcribed, doubtless supported by a proof which Ricardo surely would have disdained. It is necessary to state this identity with extreme circumspection, for in truth (as we shall see presently) no one quite knows what Marx meant by value, and consequently no one can say with assurance what the Marxian theory of value involves. But as a first approximation, and keeping in mind the possibility that Marx may have meant something quite different from what he appeared to say, it remains true that on all this question of value, Marx *is* substantially Ricardo. Lastly, the conception of surplus value, as has been seen in the foregoing chapter, was familiar to Gray, Hodgskin and the other members of the rediscovered group of early English socialists, and was expressed by them with the utmost precision, though again doubtless without the Marxian trimmings.

Such a survey of the Marxian system as the scope of this chapter allows may conveniently be brought under four headings, though it is of the essence of Marx's genius that the various parts of the completed structure are most intricately and ingeniously interwoven. There is, firstly, a background, a view of history—a ' philosophy of history,' in the ordinary phrase—which is embodied in what has acquired the rather misleading title of the ' Materialist Conception of History.' This again is manifested in a perpetually recurring and never-ending class struggle in which the negation of the negation leads to ever new negations. Secondly, there is the economic analysis, which represents the central core in the system so far as Marx endeavours to be *rein wissenschaftlich*. This is concerned with the exposition of a theory of value, and is applied to lay bare the secrets and the procedure of capitalist exploitation. There is, thirdly, a body of prophecy, designed to show the future development of the capitalistic system and its ultimate destination. Lastly, there is a view of the State, with some shadowed hints as to the technique of revolution and the far-off haven when we shall have outgrown the need of the machinery of the State. Each of these aspects of Marxism may be briefly surveyed.

The Materialist Conception of History is not too happy in its baptismal name: Mr. Cole has suggested as an improvement the ' Realist Conception of History,' but, having noted its inadequacy, it may be convenient to adhere to the familiar phrase. Adam Smith says somewhere that ' the understandings of the greater part of men are necessarily formed by their ordinary employments.'[1] In their context, these words may not have a pronounced Marxian flavour ; but when unscrupulously detached, they represent a fair first approximation to

[1] *The Wealth of Nations*, Book V, chap. 1.

the Materialist Conception of History. In their enunciation of this view of the unrolling of events, Marx and Engels were concerned to repudiate the 'idealist' view of history, that men are what they are by virtue of ideal influences, that they are fashioned by their religion, their laws, their literature and their art. The relationship, they would hold, is the other way round. In what was supposed to be an epigrammatic summary of the theory, 'it is not religion that makes men, but men who make their religion.' In an innocuous and generalised summary given by Engels, the essence of the theory is 'to trace political events back to the effects of what are, in the last resort, economic causes.'[1] The economic factor, above all the manner in which men earn their daily bread, provides the dynamic factor in history, in the light of which everything else—the structure of society, religion, law and art—must find their explanation.

Rather oddly, in the matter of what some have regarded as the most characteristic and original feature of the Marxian system, there is nowhere, either in Marx or Engels, an adequate or systematic account of the Materialist Conception of History, and of its implications. It is scattered about in odd pages and paragraphs, and probably the clearest expressions are to be found in Engels rather than in Marx. What has come to be regarded as the most significant and completest statement is contained in the Preface to Marx's *Critique of Political Economy*. There is a frequently quoted passage in one of Engels' later introductions to *The Communist Manifesto*. Strange as it may appear, one of the best known 'sources' for the Marxian theory is in a speech delivered by Engels at the graveside of Marx. There is at least one significant passage in *The Eighteenth Brumaire*; the theory is scattered pretty liberally up and down *German Ideology*; the anthologist of the Materialist Conception will find some quite useful quotations in *Anti-Dühring*; and lastly (or lastly to be noted here), it is a frequent and recurrent theme in the correspondence of Marx and Engels.

In view of the considerable controversy which the Materialist Conception of History has occasioned, and of the sparseness and diffusion of the authoritative sources, there may be advantage in assembling a few of the more significant sentences in which Marx and Engels themselves declared their faith. Take, first of all, a short extract from the clearest of Marx's statements:

> In the social production of their means of existence men enter into definite necessary relations which are independent of their will, productive relationships which correspond to a definite stage of development of their material productive forces. The aggregate of these productive relationships constitutes the economic structure of society, the real basis on which a juridical and political superstructure arises, and to which definite forms of social

[1] Preface to *The Class Struggles in France*, p. 10.

consciousness correspond. The mode of production of the material means of existence conditions the whole process of social, political and intellectual life. It is not the consciousness of men that determines their existence, but, on the contrary, it is their social existence that determines their consciousness. (Preface to *Critique of Political Economy*).

From *The Eighteenth Brumaire of Louis Bonaparte*:

Upon the different forms of property, upon the social conditions of existence, as foundation, there is built a superstructure of diversified and characteristic sentiments, illusions, habits of thought, and outlooks on life in general. The class as a whole creates and shapes them out of its material foundation, and out of the corresponding social relationships.[1]

From *The German Ideology*, out of a considerable number of possible quotations, a few sentences may be selected:

By producing their means of subsistence men are indirectly producing their actual material life. . . . What they are, therefore, coincides with their production, both with *what* they produce and with *how* they produce. The nature of individuals thus depends on the material conditions determining their production.[2]

We do not set out from what men say, imagine, conceive, nor from men as narrated, thought of, imagined, conceived, in order to arrive at men in the flesh. We set out from real, active men, and on the basis of their real life-process we demonstrate the development of the ideological reflexes and echoes of this life-process. . . . Morality, religion, metaphysics, all the rest of ideology and their corresponding forms of consciousness, thus no longer retain the semblance of independence. They have no history, no development; but men, developing their material production and their material intercourse, alter, along with this their real existence, their thinking and the products of their thinking. Life is not determined by consciousness, but consciousness by life.[3]

From the same work a mangled sentence may be taken explaining that their view of history was to start out from the simple material production of life:

and so, from this starting point, to explain the whole mass of different theoretical products and forms of consciousness, religion, philosophy, ethics, etc., etc., and trace their origins and growths.[4]

A statement of some interest derives from *The Poverty of Philosophy*:

Social relations are closely bound up with productive forces. In acquiring new productive forces, men change their mode of production; and in changing their mode of production, in changing the way of earning their living, they change all their social relations. The hand-mill gives you society with the feudal lord; the steam-mill, society with the industrial capitalist.[5]

[1] *Eighteenth Brumaire*, p. 55.

[2] *The German Ideology*, p. 7.

[3] *Ibid.* pp. 14–15.

[4] *Ibid.* p. 28.

[5] *The Poverty of Philosophy* (edition published by Martin Lawrence), p. 92. The concluding sentence is frequently quoted in German literature as a convenient and easily remembered summary of the whole theory: 'Die Handmühle ergibt eine Gesellschaft mit Feudalherren; die Dampfmühle eine Gesellschaft mit industriellen Kapitalisten.'

Two snippets may be given from Engels, speaking alone, in order that he may make his special contribution to this anthology. The first is from *Anti-Dühring*:

> The materialist conception of history starts from the principle that production, and with production the exchange of its products, is the basis of every social order; that in every society which has appeared in history the distribution of the products, and with it the division of society into classes or estates, is determined by what is produced and how it is produced, and how the product is exchanged. According to this conception, the ultimate causes of all social changes and political revolutions are to be sought, not in the minds of men, in their increasing insight into eternal truth and justice, but in changes in the mode of production and exchange; they are to be sought not in the *philosophy* but in the *economics* of the period concerned.[1]

The second is from the speech at the graveside of Marx. Engels then said that Marx had

> discovered the law of evolution in human history; he discovered the simple fact, hitherto concealed by an overgrowth of ideology, that mankind must first of all eat and drink, have shelter and clothing, before it can pursue politics, science, religion, art, etc.; and that therefore the production of the immediate material means of subsistence and consequently the degree of economic development attained by a given people or during a given epoch, form the foundation upon which the state institutions, the legal conceptions, the art and even the religious ideas of the people concerned have been evolved, and in the light of which these things must therefore be explained, instead of *vice versa* as had hitherto been the case.[2]

Lastly, though it is strictly outside the scope of this chapter, yet nevertheless is interesting as illustrative of a tradition, two sentences from Lenin may be given:

> People always were and always will be the stupid victims of deceit and self-deceit in politics until they learn to discover the *interests* of some class behind all moral, religious, political and social phrases, declarations and promises.[3]
>
> By disclosing that all ideas and all the various tendencies, without exception, have their *roots* in the condition of the material forces of production, Marxism pointed the way to an all-embracing and comprehensive study of the process of rise, development, and decline of social-economic formations.[4]

Intentionally and of design, we have courted the danger of wearying the reader with this short selection of somewhat ponderous pronouncements. The Materialist Conception of History tends to be discussed somewhat in the air. It is not always made clear just how far the theory was carried by Marx and Engels, who frequently dealt with the question in an *obiter dictum*, or in an incidental aside. Accordingly it seemed expedient to reproduce textually a few of the more precise statements of the principle, so that it might be presented in the authentic

[1] *Anti-Dühring*, p. 294.

[2] Prefixed to most editions of *The Communist Manifesto*; also Marx: *Selected Works*, vol. 1, p. 16.

[3] Lenin: *The Teachings of Karl Marx*, p. 11. [4] *Ibid.* p. 24.

voice of the authors, rather than in a summary or commentary which might be suspected of distortion. The general contention, as laid down in the earlier statements, is, however, clear. It is the economic factor—so it is argued—above all, as that is embodied in the conditions of production, that ultimately determines all things. It governs the structure of the society in which men live. It fashions their religion ; it determines their laws ; it shapes their literature and their art. The spiritual is determined by the material ; things are in the saddle and ride mankind. It is a view which, despite disclaimers, tends to a doctrine of fatalism.[1]

Inextricably bound up with the Materialist Conception of History, at least in its Marxian presentation, is the theory of the Class Struggle. The Materialist Conception of History, indeed, expresses itself in and through an everlasting struggle between classes. The *Communist Manifesto* puts this in the forefront : ' The history of all hitherto existing society is the history of class struggles.' The *Manifesto* proceeds to record the opposition of freeman and slave, patrician and plebeian, baron and serf, guildmaster and journeyman, leaping somewhat too lightly through the centuries. There is no history, apart from the record of class struggles ; and presumably what is left of history when the class struggle is decanted is but the record of insignificant trivialities. The phase of the class struggle (reached in 1848) was revealed in the opposition of interests between the Proletariat and the Bourgeoisie. The theory of the class struggle, as found in Marx, is, of course, merely a somewhat mechanical application of the Hegelian formula. Hegelianism requires that the negation, having asserted itself, should proceed to struggle with its opposite and rise to a higher synthesis, the negation of the negation ; and accordingly, classes must toe the line and behave accordingly, whether they like it or not. It is, however, by no means obvious—as is implicit in Marxism—why the struggle pending in 1848 between Capitalism and the Proletariat should conduct us to the final synthesis and the disappearance of all classes, leading, as Mr. Bertrand Russell notes with horror, to a state of Byzantine immobility.

One aspect of this continuous class struggle, though perhaps it has not received much notice from the commentators, is nevertheless curious and significant. The later editions of *The Communist Manifesto* have

[1] The author of *The Interest of Scotland* (1700), offers an interesting, if provocative, example of the operation of the Materialist Conception of History in one of its aspects. He is discussing the venerable question of the differences between the Englishman and the Scot. ' Although the Nobility and Gentry of both Kingdoms are the same in Humor, and Conduct of Living ; yet there is a great Disparity between the Common People, both as to Humor and Constitution of Body, by reason of their different way of Feeding. The *English* is Self-conceited, Lovers of their Belly, and daring ; Whilst the *Scots* are patient, sober in Diet, and hath something of a Timorous Civility.' Happily the justice of this judgment need not be considered ; but obviously ' der Mensch ist was er isst.'

a correcting footnote to the famous opening sentence, pointing out that, to be exact, the proposition that all history is the history of class struggles should be restricted to 'recorded history.' For Engels, as he grew older, fell under the influence of theories explaining the origin of society; and he became satisfied that there had been an early golden age, when there was neither property nor a State. *The Origin of the Family*, in large stretches, is a glorification of this lost paradise, in contrast with later unhappier times. These questions had better be left to the expert, in whose number it may be doubted whether Engels had claims to be included. It is, however, always of interest to note where, in the view of our authorities, the human race took the wrong turning. In this case, the evil thing was the introduction of division of labour, so near and so dear to the heart of Adam Smith. Division of labour and private property are, we are told, identical expressions. Division of labour implies unequal distribution both of labour and of its products.[1] A more emphatic indication of the far-off source of the class war in division of labour may be found in this passage:

> The division of labour implies from the outset the division of the *conditions of labour*, of tools and materials, and thus the splitting up of accumulated capital among different owners, and thus, also, the division between capital and labour, and the different forms of property itself.[2]

Primitive society (the so-called 'gentile constitution,' in Engels' phraseology) was shattered by division of labour and the consequent cleavage of society into classes.[3] That the principle of division of labour lies at the root of all class struggles also provides the theme for the concluding section of *Anti-Dühring*, where, as we shall see later, Engels (with Marx's approval) draws, quite logically, a pretty picture of a Utopia where division of labour, like some other things, will have withered away.[4] In attempting an assessment of the social philosophy of Marx and Engels, it is perhaps necessary to distinguish between the earlier and more rigid statements of the Materialist Conception of History, and what it tended to become later under criticism. For beyond a doubt it was watered down with the years. In one of his later letters addressed to J. Bloch (September 21, 1890), Engels goes far towards emptying the doctrine of its characteristic content, and acknowledges that Marx and he were partly to blame if the younger generation (or some of them) had laid more stress on the economic side than was due.

If, however, we take the Materialist Conception of History, in its earlier forms, stimulating as it may be in providing a canon of interpretation, it is obvious that it falls short at many points. History cannot be explained solely in terms of the economic factor, because the other

[1] *The German Ideology*, pp. 21–22; see also pp. 8–9.

[2] *Ibid.* p. 65.

[3] Engels: *The Origin of the Family*, p. 193.

[4] Engels: *Anti-Dühring*, p. 309.

factors, however they may have originated, do in fact attain to an independent existence. Religion and patriotism, a country's laws and traditions, certainly develop into primary forces, imperiously dictating in defiance of economic considerations.

The most obvious difficulty of the Materialist Conception of History, at least in its less guarded statements, is seen in its helplessness when confronted with the problem of mind, and of the influence of mind on mind. Doubtless great men are conditioned by their environment, but they are certainly not produced by their environment; we all reflect our times. It is easy enough to persuade ourselves that any of the leaders of humanity could have appeared only when he did appear. It is absurd to assume that any great man was *bound* to appear at the appropriate juncture. When he was old enough to know better, Engels, in a letter of January 25, 1894, more or less champions this extraordinary view. That Napoleon, 'just that particular Corsican,' appeared and did what he did, was an accident, but if just that particular Corsican had failed to turn up, 'another would have filled the place'—apparently with equal efficiency. 'The man has always been found as soon as he became necessary.' Presumably the man is also found as soon as he is unnecessary, of whom there are many at large in the world in these latter days. Engels can hardly have thought of the curious theological implications of the view that we all have somewhere our deputy ready to do our work when we are put out of action. It is indeed by no means overwhelmingly obvious that if Hegel and Marx had died in their infancy, the Hegelian philosophy would have been produced by someone called Schmidt to give a flavour to the three volumes of *Capital*, written by some one called Meyer: on the whole, the chances are against it.

Indeed, it may be doubted whether one can eliminate from history the possibility of mighty repercussions, springing from trivial and non-economic causes. There have been some who have suspended the world's destiny from the classical shapeliness of Cleopatra's nose. If Shakespeare is right, she was probably not the woman to allow a mere broken nose, had such befallen her, to stand between her and the fulfilment of her destiny. Without, however, invoking such a far-fetched and hackneyed example, it might be interesting to speculate on the consequences to this country of the virginity of Queen Elizabeth. Had she married and had issue, there would clearly have been no union of the Crowns in 1603; and, the opportunity missed, who knows when it might have recurred? Perhaps 'ultimately' it might have been all the same; but for some centuries many things in these islands might have been entirely different.

In the Marxian statement, the class struggle is so intimately a part of the Materialist Conception of History, that anything tending to undermine faith in the general doctrine must also weaken the plausibility of the view that the eternal ineluctable class struggle provides the whole content of history. The class war, however, is so much the entire substance of syndicalism later, that it may be wise to listen to the syndicalists before coming to a conclusion in the matter.[1] Two things only need be said here. The first is that, quite obviously, it is absurd to seek to show that there must be an economic occasion to every conflict in history. Perhaps ultimately the moral factor is a more potent divider of men than is the economic; men consciously engage in conflict, in defiance of the dictates of their economic interests. Mr. Penty, to whom the Guild Socialist movement owed so much in its early development, expressed the point unambiguously: 'it is the moral issue,' he observed, 'that finally divides men.'[2] Wars based on religion or national feeling play a considerable part in the unrolling of events. Religion and patriotism, as has been seen, are real forces, much as Marx and Engels may deplore them as superfluous luxuries, in process of atrophy. It is significant of their short-sightedness in certain respects that they could, as far back as *The German Ideology*, declare that big industry in all countries had created a class 'with which nationality is already dead.'[3]

The other preliminary point to be noted at this stage is that where the sentiment of the class war does exist to-day, it is very largely attributable to the teaching of Marx himself. The contrast between rich and poor goes back to Plato and the Book of Ecclesiasticus, and doubtless beyond. Marx's peculiar contribution was to discover that in the relationship of employer and employed, there were such seeds of antagonism that the whole of society, so long as there were employers and employed, could be nothing but a perpetual warfare between these two classes. Mr. Bertrand Russell's conclusion was that Marx by his teaching created the class war which he had prophesied[4]; and M. Gonnard, somewhat too ingeniously, finds in this a demonstration of the falsity of the central Marxian thesis, since the class struggle is thus due to an ideological cause, namely, 'l'idée de la lutte de classes: De sorte que là où Marx semble avoir raison—il a tort.'[5] This, if not exactly convincing, is at least subtle.

The Materialist Conception of History has thus, in the general Marxian presentation, provided us with the key to the understanding of the world's history: the doctrine of the class war shows us the mechanics of the theory. In the everlasting unfolding of the class war, in which the under-dog becomes the top-dog, only to beget a new under-dog, called for short the negation of the negation, we have

[1] For a more general discussion, see the concluding chapter, pp. 499–504.
[2] Penty: *Post-Industrialism*, p. 94.
[3] *The German Ideology*, p. 57.
[4] Bertrand Russell: *Freedom and Organisation*, p. 249.
[5] Gonnard: *Histoire des Doctrines Economiques*, vol. 3, p. 124.

reached (1848) the stage where the position of the Bourgeoisie, of the Capitalist, is challenged by the rising Proletariat. It becomes necessary, therefore, to consider the hidden springs of this antagonism, and to reveal how the worker is inevitably exploited by his employer. This leads to the Marxian theory of value, with its corollary or adjunct, the doctrine of surplus value, which most Marxians regard as more important than its parent doctrine.

Here we reach the core of Marx, and here Marx becomes *rein wissenschaftlich*. Also, because he becomes *rein wissenschaftlich*, he places his demonstration of the theory of value in the opening sections of the first volume of *Capital*: ‘ die schwerst verständliche nicht nur, sondern auch die schwächste,’ not only the most difficult to understand, but also the weakest, as a sympathetic critic has very justly observed.[1] The discussion of the Marxian theory of value offers such a well-trampled field, and the perusal of Marx in his more characteristically Marxian moments is so emphatically as the climbing up a sandy way to the feet of the aged, that few readers will look for, and none will find here, a systematic survey of the salient features of Volume I of *Capital*, with digressive glances at later volumes. It should be sufficient to say just enough to recall what everyone is supposed to know, and to provide a basis for the few comments which it may be necessary to make here. Unfortunately, while there is little doubt as to what Marx said—for the printed word is there to testify—there seems to be increasing doubt among his intelligent followers as to whether Marx quite succeeded in saying what he meant, since it seems fairly obvious that he cannot have meant what he said. The present generation has profited from one excellent volume bearing the title *What Marx Really Meant*, but there is still room for another on *What Marx Really Meant, Actually*. For the present, in summarising, we shall proceed on the assumption that in general Marx meant what he said ; or, in other words, we shall meanwhile stifle those doubts as to the meaning of Volume I of *Capital* which naturally became vocal a generation later with the publication of Volume III.

With (it is hoped) no greater inaccuracy than is perhaps inevitable in a condensed summary for revision purposes, it may be said that in its broad shape the Marxian theory of value is merely the Ricardian theory, transplanted and in some ways made more rigid. The opening pages, with a courage that Ricardo lacked, attempted a rigorous proof, ultimately resting on the contention (or assumption) that ‘ commodities ’ are exclusively the products of labour, and that labour is (after the exclusion of other possibilities) the only element common to two commodities whose exchange is in question. Accordingly, the equation, expressing the ratio of exchange, tells us that labour, the common element, is present in equal quantities in the commodities

[1] Wilbrandt: *Karl Marx*, p. 98.

exchanged. The proof, as such, is a mere burlesque, and involves such crude disregard for the ordinary laws of reasoning that, if indeed it were seriously intended, it affords striking evidence of that complete absence of self-criticism which in some ways distinguished Marx. 'Sie sieht aus wie ein Beweis—ist aber keiner,' says Wilbrandt with much restraint: 'It looks like a proof, but in fact is none.'[1] In pursuance of this train of reasoning, we must, however, cease to think of labour as being the labour of a joiner or a mason; we must train ourselves to think in terms of that elusive abstraction, the element in labour which is common to all labour, or 'human labour in the abstract' whatever that may be. One further reservation is necessary at this stage: labour may be inefficient or unskilful, and a bungling worker, by expending more of his bungling labour or by working with primitive tools, clearly does not thereby increase the value of his product. The labour that determines value is therefore the labour that is socially necessary in the conditions of production of the time.

But, apart from the question of normal efficiency, it may further be said that all labour is not effective. It is possible to labour and produce nothing that anybody wants. In such a case, the labour does not count as labour, whatever else it may count as. So, also, more labour than is socially necessary may be devoted to the production of a commodity, so that a glut arises. In that case, the labour is not to be counted as labour to the full extent. In short, though of course Marx does not so express it, labour is to be graded up or down until the right answer is obtained. Another example of manipulation occurs in the problem of how to deal with skilled labour; for skilled labour, in the Marxian world, is merely simple labour intensified or multiplied. The reduction of one to the other is made by a process which goes on behind the backs of the workers; but again the solution is quite clearly a glaring example of reasoning in a circle. If you want to find the appropriate multiplier which will put the work of a skilled engineer and a charwoman on an equality, you can only consult the market and find out what happens there. In order (apparently) to explain the situation in the market, you get from the market the multiplier which, when appropriately used, will give a satisfactory explanation of the behaviour of the market. Subject to these rather far-reaching embroideries, the value of a commodity is nothing more than the labour embodied in it.

But this Labour Theory of Value is for Marx but a stepping-stone towards unveiling the secret of capitalistic accumulation, of the exploitation to which the worker is subjected. This is made clear in the doctrine of surplus value, which is by way of being a pendent to the theory of value. Accumulation and exploitation are possible because there happens to be on the market for sale a commodity possessing quite peculiar properties. This is 'labour-power,' which on the Marxian

[1] Wilbrandt: *Karl Marx*, p. 100.

view is quite distinct from labour. Labour-power, not labour, is the commodity which the capitalist purchases. Now labour-power also has its value. Ricardo has taught us, as he has taught Marx, what that is. The natural price to pay for labour is that which enables the worker to subsist and continue his race ; in fact, it is the cost of production of labour. This is the value quite properly paid for labour-power ; but when labour-power is used, it gives off more value than it cost. The worker may make enough for his maintenance (his necessary wage) in six hours ; but he has sold himself with his labour-power, and he may be made to work ten or twelve hours each day. The difference (in this case, the work of four or six hours) represents the exploitation of the worker ; it is unpaid labour appropriated by the capitalist.

It will be observed that the whole of the surplus value is derived from labour. Indeed, on the theory, as initially stated, it would appear to be derived from the individual worker ; each individual worker would appear to be robbed by his own particular employer. This view is, however, modified by later elaborations of the analysis. That the surplus value comes from labour, and from labour alone, is reinforced by a distinction which is fundamental to the Marxian analysis. Capital is differentiated by Marx into constant and variable capital, corresponding broadly to the distinction between machinery and wages. But machinery yields no surplus value. It is of the essence of a machine that, in being used up, it transfers its value, neither more nor less, to the product. Whatever be thought of the validity of the argument, it has at least the advantage that it thrusts on labour the whole burden of providing surplus value. It should be noted for its significance later that industries will vary from each other according to their ' organic composition ' ; the ratio of constant to variable capital, low in some industries, will be high elsewhere.

Capital exists in order that surplus value may be created, and that it may be created more abundantly. There are two obvious ways of achieving this end. There is the possibility of prolonging the working-day (supplemented by reduction of meal-hours) ; there is equally the possibility of reducing the number of hours during which the worker must necessarily labour in order to secure his own maintenance. If, by further introduction of machinery or by improved technical processes, it is made possible for the worker to earn his subsistence in four hours instead of six, two additional hours will have been made available for the production of surplus value. Surplus value may further be increased by roping in the wives and the children ; for the theory of the so-called Iron Law of Wages (whether as in Ricardo or in Lassalle) postulates that the family wage should be no more than sufficient for the maintenance of the family. Theoretically, therefore, the long-run result of employing the wives and the children is that their services are got for nothing, to the greater increase of surplus value.

Along these lines, then, capital seeks to satisfy its insatiable lust for increased surplus value. But here we encounter the first of the two snares which, quite apart from many other besetting difficulties, in the end brought the Marxian system, on this side at least, to irremediable confusion. The capitalist, thirsting for surplus value, introduces more and more machinery, in order thereby to cut down the time required for the worker's maintenance and so increase the number of hours available for the production of surplus value. But, as we have seen, constant capital yields no surplus value, which can be derived only from variable capital. There is something whimsical in the suggestion that, in order to increase surplus value, the capitalist thus cuts down that part of capital which yields surplus value, replacing it by that part of capital which can yield none. The contradiction is glaring, and Marx's explanation will resolve it only for those who can humbly say: *Credo quia impossibile.* Marx, according to Engels, was well versed in mathematics, though he never got the length of understanding the meaning and the limitations of an average. Nevertheless, he found an average a very present help in time of trouble.[1] It is unnecessary here to go into detail in the matter of the explanation offered. Briefly, it would seem to be that the surplus value is averaged out and distributed among the employers; and though doubtless the introduction of machinery reduces the amount of surplus value, nevertheless the employer who takes this course secures for himself a bigger whack of what is going.

The other 'inherent contradiction' has proved even more fatal to the solidity of the Marxian structure, and has proved the fruitful mother of a whole literature devoted to the alleged inconsistency between the first and the third Volumes of *Capital.* The difficulty here arises from Marx's assertion, imposed upon him by his propagandist tendencies, that all surplus value springs from labour alone, combined with the other fact stressed by him that the 'organic composition' (the ratio of constant to variable capital) varies enormously from one industry to another. From these two propositions, it *should* follow that an industry with a high percentage of variable capital should enjoy a higher rate of profit than one in which labour occupies a less important place. It obviously is not so. The capitalist looks for a more or less uniform rate of profit in all enterprises; he does not expect, and he certainly does not get, an abnormally high rate of profit in industries where there is much labour to be exploited, nor an abnormally low rate where machinery has stepped in to do the bulk of the work. The difficulty is frankly faced in Volume I of *Capital*; but the solution (though it appears in the Marx-Engels correspondence) was

[1] Mr. Joseph (*The Labour Theory of Value in Karl Marx, e.g.* pp. 39, 66, 73) has shown clearly how utterly confused Marx became when he began to play about with averages.

not given to the public until the appearance of the third volume, twenty-seven years later. The text of the explanation will be found by the enquiring reader in the ninth chapter of that volume; but for a comprehension of what is contained in this statement, he must rely on an inner illumination. Mr. Postgate's statement on the subject is admirable: surplus value, he says, 'is shared out over the whole capitalist class, by a very complicated and esoteric process, which cannot be explained here'[1]—nor anywhere else, he might almost have added, had he wished to make his delphic utterance somewhat less delphic. It would be well if Mr. Postgate's reticent example were followed by all subsequent Marxian commentators, as it shall certainly be followed here.

The one fact that does emerge from Marx's tangled attempt to reconcile the uniform rate of profit with his original labour theory of value is that commodities are now said to exchange at their 'prices of production,' which is equivalent to their cost-price plus the average profit—not at their 'value.' Indeed, it is only by the merest accident that commodities will exchange at their value; apart from a contingency which is so remote as to be negligible, commodities will exchange above or below their 'values,' the extent to which some sell above their 'values' being balanced by the corresponding extent to which others sell below their 'values.' And here, if the reader has not already done so, he may well pull himself together and ask what indeed is this thing that Marx calls value. For it would not occur to one reader in a thousand, coming to *Capital* with a virgin mind and a candid spirit, that in the first volume Marx was doing anything other than searching for an explanation of value which would tell us in what ratio commodities would exchange against each other, and that the Law of Value which he reached was in fact meant to explain prices. In the third volume we have clearly stated a distinction between prices and value, and we are told that commodities never (or so nearly never as to make no difference) exchange at their value, but at a price which is above or below their value. No wonder that the publication of the third volume called for a process of mental readjustment.

The mess in fact cannot be tidied up; nor is it worth while composing an Apology for Chaos. The labour theory of value is, however, so much the core of Marxism, viewed as a system with claims to be *rein wissenschaftlich* that a few general observations may perhaps be tolerated. In the first place, it is universally acknowledged that Marx's Theory of Value is that part of the system which has frayed most, and most irretrievably, with the passage of time. Having discussed the problem of value for well over two thousand years, it is probable that the human race will continue the discussion, so long as they retain the power of reason and of speech; and also (despite J. S. Mill) it is

[1] R. W. Postgate: *Karl Marx*, p. 78.

extremely improbable that they will ever be able to say that this ghost is effectively laid. But at least it can be said with some assurance that the type of theory which Marx took over from Ricardo is for ever dead beyond hope of resurrection. We have learned from the Austrians that value cannot be explained as a summation of past costs; value looks to the future and to use in the future. No doubt the Austrian way of thinking is also beginning to show threadbare patches; and the indications are that the next generation will manipulate 'scales of preference,' and slide along 'curves of indifference.' But nothing can ever bring back the way of thinking in which the Marxian theory of value is rooted; it was indeed part of Marx's misfortune that he should adopt for his purpose a theory already moribund.

A second consideration that cannot fail to bring an increasing sense of discomfort to a balanced reader of Marx and of orthodox Marxian literature alike is that so frequently words in ordinary use are employed with a special connotation, the reader generally being left to sense the difference. For Marx, the individual worker and the individual employer have no real existence except in so far as they represent the class to which they belong. He argues in terms of an abstract worker and an abstract employer, each of them as anæmic as that other Victorian ghost, the economic man. Nowhere is there any suggestion that work and management are alike human functions, that business may be a ticklish affair, in which money may be lost as well as made. In Marx's world, at least in the earlier phases of the exposition, an employer just cannot help making money: all he has to do is to employ workers, and if he doubles the number of his workers, he will double the flow of surplus value. And in the same way all workers are alike and interchangeable. Sometimes the essential ideas of a school are most clearly seen in the exposition of orthodox and uninspired disciples, if only because they are less intelligent and more unguarded. Kautsky somewhere accepts the view that any five adult farm labourers will do as much as any other five.[1] The argument, of course, holds not merely of farm labourers. Just as the employers automatically decant surplus value in proportion to the number of workers employed, so workers also, as indistinguishable as a flock of sheep, automatically give off surplus value. There is no skill, no management, no competence anywhere.

The most glaring and pervasive distortion of an everyday term is of course with regard to 'Capital' itself, the most crucial word in the whole discussion. In Marx, as indeed throughout Marxian literature, capital has a meaning to which the whole world, outside Marxian colleges, is a complete stranger. For Marx, it is not every one who owns wealth who is a capitalist; nor is he necessarily a capitalist who, possessing the means of production, uses these to accumulate gain.

[1] Kautsky: *Economic Doctrines of Karl Marx*, p. 125.

A capitalist is one who, being himself idle, lives entirely on surplus value extracted from workers in his employment. If, by one of the devices familiar in the pages of Hans Andersen and Grimm, an industrious apprentice could invent a machine capable of doing all the work of Lancashire, then if only he could work it himself, he might corner the cotton of the world and hold humanity to ransom, but he would apparently leave the Marxian court with clean hands, so far as surplus value is concerned. The beginning of evil is in a contract of employment. The point could be illustrated from Marx himself, but again it may be more instructive to see it in the broad stream of the Marxian tradition. Thus the faithful Kautsky, before he became Kautsky the Renegade, defines capital as 'value that breeds surplus-value.'[1] Even more illuminating is Kautsky in a later passage drawn from the same source:

> The employer of wage workers only becomes a capitalist when the mass of surplus-value created by them is large enough to assure him a comfortable income and to increase his wealth, without his being obliged to put his own shoulder to the wheel.[2]

Mr. Emile Burns expresses the same view when he remarks that

> Property (whatever the physical form) only becomes capital in the economic sense when it is used to produce surplus value; that is, when it is used to employ workers, who in the course of producing things also produce surplus value.[3]

So also with regard to smaller people, who are to be allowed to escape the damnation of being capitalists:

> It does not make any difference whether in fact he employs one or two men; the point is that he works, and must work, because he cannot live on the labour of the few men he is able to employ.[4]

The implications here are curious: if surplus value is a species of theft, apparently it becomes reprehensible only if enough is taken to put the robber at his ease; if he is obliged to eke out his plunder by doing some work of his own, he escapes condemnation, apparently under the happy dispensation of *de minimis*. For the present, however, we are concerned with the fact that in the Marxian tradition, capital is not capital unless it enables the owner to live entirely on surplus value, and unless in fact he does live in idleness on his surplus value.[5]

One last point is of interest in visualising the Marxian world which is governed by the Marxian Law of Value. It is a world in which all workers are engaged in the manufacture of 'commodities'—'vendible commodities,' to use the offending phrase in which Adam Smith sought

[1] Kautsky: *Economic Doctrines of Karl Marx*, p. 54. [2] *Ibid.* p. 124.
[3] Emile Burns: *What is Marxism?* p. 21. [4] *Ibid.* p. 62.
[5] In this phase of the Marxian tradition, the almost proverbial clergyman's widow, with an income of £150 derived from industrial shares, is more typically a capitalist than Lord Nuffield or Lord Melchett.

the test of ' productive labour.' Now it is a long time since all labour was embodied in ' vendible commodities,' and for good or evil we are moving to a position in which ' services ' bulk more and more largely in what labour does. It is indeed a mark of advancing society. Mr. Colin Clark has familiarised us with the increasing importance of tertiary, as against primary and secondary industry. Heaven forbid that anyone to-day should entangle himself in the old quagmire which concerns itself with the distinction between productive and unproductive labour; but obviously the armies of administration (of all kinds), of transport, of entertainment—to go no further—do not fit in with a Marxian world where the production of commodities with a view to sale exhausts the whole content of economic life. It would be difficult, for instance, for the Musicians' Union to express their grievances and claims within the framework of Marxian ideology.

The Marxian world, in short, is a wholly abstract, artificial and unreal construction, entirely distinct from that in which any of us have pursued our economic activities. Doubtless, in all sciences, it is a common procedure to make simplifying assumptions, and from the original hypothesis to make a gradual approach to reality—even if some of us may refuse to contemplate a world where ' the only consumable good is a single species of economic cake.' The Marxian world is just as unreal as this example drawn from unimpeachable economic orthodoxy. The objection to the Marxian assumptions is not that they are assumptions, not that they represent a departure from reality; but that their author never makes it clear that they are abstractions. Marx writes throughout as if he were concerned with reality: he never warns his readers that, as a first step and in order to simplify his reasoning, he is meanwhile arguing on certain not wholly real assumptions and hypotheses. The reader never knows at any moment whether he is concerned with abstraction or reality; and it is fairly clear that Marx himself neither knew nor cared. Indeed it took the world at large almost two generations to realise that just here perhaps lies the greatest obstacle to a comprehension of Marx.

For indeed it becomes ever increasingly clear that the real issue on this, the central element of Marxian doctrine, is not whether he succeeded in ' establishing his case,' but rather, what was the case he was trying to establish. The unanswerable, if not very satisfactory, reply to such criticisms of Marx as are contained, for instance, in the classical exposition of Böhm-Bawerk, or more recently in that by Mr. H. W. B. Joseph, is that while the critic may be very successfully directing his artillery against something that Marx (quite obviously) said, in fact (whether he said it or not) Marx meant something entirely different. This retort is indeed almost a matter of course from the Marxian side. Thus Dr. Lindsay—and in this respect he is not unique—admits that ' no one can read and master these refutations without agreeing that they are unanswerable on the assumption that they describe correctly the question that Marx was trying to answer and Marx's answer to it.'[1] Instead of repeating these misdirected criticisms, it may be more instructive to interrogate a few of the more intelligent admirers of Marx, and ascertain, if possible, what they make of it all; in particular, arising out of the 'apparent discrepancy' between the first and third Volume (to use the discreet phraseology of Whitehall), what they think Marx meant by the labour theory of value; and, to particularise still further, what they think he meant by 'value.' In view of the space already squandered on Marx, only a few witnesses may be cited.

Because he is rather in line with the argument developed in the preceding paragraphs, Croce may be taken first. He points out that it is far from easy to understand the exact *nature* of the investigation which Marx carried out. And he adds (which is not wholly surprising) that 'it does not appear that the author himself always realised fully the peculiar character of his investigation.'[2] *Capital*, we are told, is an abstract investigation, concerned with 'an ideal and formal society, deduced from certain hypotheses, which could indeed never have occurred as actual facts in the course of history.'[3] It would be difficult to express more emphatically the view that *Capital* has as much relation to actuality as would be possessed by a discussion of the application of the Pareto line to the Kingdom of Heaven. Lastly, not to linger too long with Croce, it may be instructive to note the test he applied in assessing the Marxian theory of value. He asked himself, he says: 'Under what conditions and assumptions is Marx's theory *thinkable*?' It is Croce who italicises the last word.

Loria is perhaps scarcely a serious critic; yet, as the writer who has excelled all others in the extravagance of his eulogies of *Capital*, he ought to be heard. For him *Capital* 'is a masterpiece wherein all is great, all alike incomparable and wonderful'—and much more. Yet to Loria the third Volume of *Capital* was a death-blow to the system, and the consciousness that it would prove to be so explains Marx's failure to complete *Capital* in his lifetime: 'Need we wonder that his hand trembled, that his spirit quailed, before the inexorable act of destruction?'[4] This is somewhat too melodramatic; Marx's failure to complete *Capital* is indeed something of a problem, but it is more likely that the explanation was rooted in his liver. For the present purpose, however, we are concerned to note that the third volume forces Loria to the view that Marx's 'fundamental economic theory is essentially vitiated and sophisticated, and that he is himself responsible for reducing it to hopeless absurdity.'[5]

[1] Lindsay: *Karl Marx's Capital*, p. 55.
[2] Croce: *Historical Materialism and the Economics of Karl Marx*, p. 48.
[3] *Ibid.* p. 50.
[4] Loria: *Karl Marx*, p. 78.
[5] *Ibid.* pp. 83–84.

Let us cast the net somewhat wider. Professor Wilbrandt, in his very sensitive appreciation of Karl Marx, offers us two points which are of some interest towards an appreciation of what Marx's admirers think that Marx really meant. The first is a rather naive admission that the first Volume (1867) was bound to be misunderstood, until such time as the third appeared.[1] In the course of these twenty-seven years Marx himself died, and as there are some who would place on Engels a not inconsiderable share of the responsibility for the third Volume, it might be a matter for consideration whether Marx himself ever had an opportunity of understanding Volume I—which, of course, is more or less what Croce says. In fact, however, it was not the publication of the third Volume which made possible a comprehension of the first: it would be truer to say that the publication of the third Volume imposed, post-haste, a revision of the orthodox interpretation of the first Volume, if a show of consistency was to be maintained.

The other significant contribution made by Wilbrandt towards a comprehension of Marx is, at the first blush, rather surprising. In opposition to the view that *Capital* represents an analysis of the workings of an abstract capitalism, not of any particular capitalistic State, but of a State which corresponds to the concept of pure capitalism as ideally conceived, Wilbrandt would have us believe that Marx, in writing the first volume, had in mind pre-capitalistic mediaeval conditions; and in this consideration alone do we find justification for Marx.[2] It is not the usual view; but it has at least this in common with the totally opposed conception, that it makes it clear that whatever Marx may have been talking about, it was certainly not this world that we know here and now.

We are not without guides in our own country. On the whole, probably Dr. Lindsay sheds as much darkness as light on the questions he illumines. He has learned from Croce that the capitalism which Marx is analysing does not exist, since no society is completely capitalistic. He outlines a possible view, and adds: 'If this is really the kernel of Marx's doctrine . . .,' but somehow there is no assurance in his voice that it is.[3] He realises that if Marx is to escape the charge of being an incapable bungler, it must be allowed that he is talking of economic value in two senses, 'firstly, in the sense of price, and secondly in a peculiar sense of his own.'[4] But we are still left very much in the dark as to the nature of that peculiarly Marxian value, which flits back from the third Volume to illumine the dark places in the first

[1] Wilbrandt: *Karl Marx*, p. 96. 'Aber der erste Band, dem erst nach Jahrzehnten die anderen folgten, gab so wenig Fingerzeige für das richtige Verständnis, dass er missverstanden werden musste, solange man den dritten Band nicht hatte.'

[2] *Ibid.* pp. 100, 106.

[3] Introduction to Croce: *Historical Materialism and the Economics of Karl Marx*, p. xx.

[4] *Ibid.* p. xviii.

Volume of *Capital*—that value described by Loria as a ' fantastical or transcendental value ' which neither possessed nor could possess any relationship to facts.[1] Dr. Lindsay at least realises that some definition of the elusive ' value ' is required, and he suggests that ' intrinsic exchange value is for Marx the value which a commodity would have in a properly organised society where labour was performing its proper function.' [2] Apart from legitimate doubts as to where such a view could be founded in Marx, it will be observed that we are very properly left to guess for ourselves what is a properly organised society, and when labour is performing its proper function—two very sizable hares to start in one sentence.

It is to Mr. Cole that we owe the alluring and confident title: *What Marx Really Meant*. On the immediate question, he argues—and rightly, if regard is to be had to the third Volume—that the Marxian theory of value is somewhat unique in not being a theory of prices; indeed, as he adds, it is doubtful whether in the end it has any point of contact at all with prices.[3] As to the elusive Marxian ' value,' we are told that in Marx's writings, ' value ' came to mean what commodities were really worth in consequence of the amounts of labour incorporated in them, as something quite distinct from the prices which they actually fetched, or tended to fetch, in the market.' [4] But the identity of value and embodied labour was surely something that Marx thought he had *proved* (and which therefore required proof) in the opening pages of *Capital*. It is true that Croce also says that Marx *assumed* the equivalence of value and labour. If the identity of value and labour is a matter of definition and assumption, then at least we know the meaning Marx attaches to ' value ' ; but in that case the pretended proof in the opening chapter is mere eye-wash; since one states, but does not prove, definitions. Also in that case it is to be feared that the whole of *Capital*, resting on an arbitrary definition which implies the conclusion to be reached, is an example of wandering vainly in a circle, even more glaring than the most critical critics had thought possible. If, on the other hand, the identity of value and labour is a matter of proof and not of definition, we are still left to grope for the meaning Marx attaches to ' value.'

The theory to which Mr. Cole guides us is that ' the Marxian theory of value is a theory, not of prices, but of the social distribution of the resources of production.' [5] If we must read into Marx something that is not very obviously there, if (as with Croce) our approach is to be determined by asking under what conditions and assumptions Marx's theory is ' thinkable,' then this is as good a theory as any other: in

[1] Loria: *Marx*, p. 77.
[2] Lindsay: *Karl Marx's Capital*, p. 71.
[3] Cole: *What Marx Really Meant*, p. 207.
[4] *Ibid.* p. 211. [5] *Ibid.* p. 221.

fact it is better than most. The difficulty which Mr. Cole quite obviously and naturally feels is that in the course of all these thousands of pages, Marx himself said so little in support of what Marx really meant. 'Why,' Mr. Cole asks, 'why does Marx, in the first Volume of *Das Kapital*, so often speak as if commodities did tend to sell at their values, whereas such a view is plainly inconsistent with his case, and he makes it abundantly clear later on in his book that they do not?'[1] It is to be hoped that there is a better answer than Mr. Cole suggests. If throughout Volume I Marx speaks quite generally as if commodities tended to sell at their values, the plain man would suggest that it was probably because this idea was most frequently in Marx's mind. Marx was almost criminally careless in neglecting to define his terms, and the natural result of such carelessness is that words jostle about in the mind, each trailing half a dozen potential meanings, with consequent confusion of thought. With just a touch of scorn, Croce speaks of Marx as having 'despised and neglected all such preliminary and exact explanations as might have made his task plain.'[2] It is significant, in connection with Mr. Cole's question, that Engels, playing the part of official interpreter, also speaks as if the opening chapters of *Capital* provided a guide to the price-tickets in Bond Street. *Anti-Dühring* is for the most part a most dreadful book—fit only to be one of six books given to Hitler on a desert island—yet it has its uses as an official summary of Marxism as then understood. It is instructive to ponder what Engels implies when he speaks of 'the law of value of modern bourgeois economics, according to which the value of a commodity is measured by the socially necessary labour embodied in it.'[3]

We shall presently, in a subsequent chapter, hear Sorel at some length on Marx and the essence of Marx; but perhaps he may be allowed a somewhat premature appearance on the issue now before us. Sorel is quite obviously flummoxed by the difficulty which must confront all intelligent Marxians: seeing that Marx so clearly cannot have meant what he said, why on earth did he so signally fail to say what he meant? Having reduced the most of Marx to 'mythical images' in the Sorelian sense, the objection that apparently Marx did not himself realise that he was a purveyor of myths is met in a rather beautiful and ingenuous phrase: 'C'est qu'il était fort passionné et que, maintes fois, la passion l'a empêché de reconnaître des réalités très claires.'[4]

Other witnesses must be allowed an even shorter time in which to testify. There is Mr. Beer, who in all this part of Marx finds political

[1] Cole: *What Marx Really Meant*, p. 228.
[2] Croce, *op. cit.* p. 49.
[3] Engels: *Anti-Dühring*, p. 119.
[4] Sorel: *La Décomposition du Marxisme*, pp. 58–59.

and social slogans rather than economic truths.[1] The question of what Marx really meant is here disposed of somewhat too unblushingly. Marx, it is suggested, gives us slogans; he gives us Sorelian myths; and when you come to slogans and myths, the question of meaning, the question of truth fades into the background. It does not greatly matter what Marx meant, or indeed whether he meant anything: he produced half a dozen excellent battle cries. With more 'spirituality,' but substantially on the same lines, Mrs. Joan Robinson recalls an observation of Voltaire to the effect that it is possible to kill a flock of sheep by witchcraft, provided they are simultaneously given a sufficiency of arsenic. The sheep, it is suggested, are the complacent apologists of capitalism: for the rest 'Marx's penetrating insight and bitter hatred of oppression supply the arsenic, while the labour theory of value provides the incantations.'[2]

This anthology, drawn from the friends and admirers of Marx, becomes tedious; but the cloud of witnesses may yield a profitable lesson, not so easily to be learned otherwise. To witness Böhm-Bawerk or Mr. Joseph carving up Marx is but a pedestrian pleasure; for these are but pedestrian writers, who are so pedestrian as to clutch at the plain meaning of words, not realising that what Marx really meant has no necessary connection with what Marx undeniably said. To witness Marx surrounded by his friends is, however, a joy of an entirely different order. For it is fairly clear that none of them really knows what Marx really meant; they are even in considerable doubt as to what he was talking about; there are hints that Marx himself did not know what he was doing. In particular, there is no one to tell us what Marx thought he meant by 'value.' And indeed, what all these conjectures reveal is somewhat astounding, and, one would like to think, unique. *Capital* is, in one sense, a three-volume treatise, expounding a theory of value and its manifold applications. Yet Marx never condescends to say what he means by 'value,' which accordingly is what anyone cares to make it as he follows the unfolding scroll from 1867 to 1894. Nor does anyone know to what world all this applies. Is it to the world in which Marx wrote? Or to an abstract, 'pure,' capitalist world existing ideally in the imagination, and nowhere else? Or (odd as the suggestion may appear) was Marx (probably unconsciously) thinking in terms of mediaeval conditions? No one knows. Are we concerned with *Wissenschaft*, slogans, myths, or incantations? Marx, it has been said, was a prophet—albeit a prophet whose ambitions lay in another direction—and perhaps this suggestion provides the best approach. One does not apply to Jeremiah and Ezekiel the tests to which less inspired men are subjected. Perhaps the mistake the world and most of the critics have made is

[1] Beer: *The Life and Teaching of Karl Marx*, p. 129.
[2] Joan Robinson: *An Essay on Marxian Economics*, p. 27.

just that they have not sufficiently regarded Marx as a prophet—a man above logic, uttering cryptic and incomprehensible words, which every man may interpret as he chooses.' [1]

No apology need be made for attaching the foregoing somewhat general discussion to the consideration of the Marxian Theory of Value and of surplus value. For these, thin as they may have worn, are the core of Marxism as a 'system.' Engels indeed finds in the Materialist Conception of History and in the doctrine of surplus value the whole of Marx and the whole of socialism. The remaining parts of Marx must be dealt with much more summarily. Firstly, there are the various 'prophecies,' the indications of the path capitalism would follow until the birth of the new order. We left the capitalist grasping in every direction for increased surplus value—rather short-sightedly introducing machinery with this end in view. Various results follow. There is thus created the Industrial Reserve Army, a force maintained to do the bidding of capitalism when occasion arises. With this there is necessarily the disappearance of all the middle classes, thrust down into the proletariat, sunk in ever-increasing misery and degradation. There is the Law—or Principle, or Prophecy or whatever it may be called—of the Concentration of Capital: ever fewer and bigger capitalists at one end with an increasing mass of misery at the other, until finally the expropriators are expropriated, and a new order begins. That the spoilers will one day be despoiled is, of course, in a sense, the common substance of all prophecy: in the words of an earlier Hebrew seer, the far-off day is one in which it can be said that 'the extortioner is at an end, the spoiler ceaseth, the oppressors are consumed out of the land.'

It was the dilatoriness of the world in fulfilling the Marxian prophecies that later led to 'Revisionism.' Probably Marx is on strongest grounds as a specific prophet in regard to the Industrial Reserve Army. No doubt the modern problem of mass unemployment does not quite fit into the Marxian framework of prophecy: like a thorough-going pessimist, Marx looked forward to an uninterrupted process of continual pejoration. Yet, without doubt, unemployment, by whatever name it is called, is the greatest sore in our present social structure,

[1] Perhaps one does not naturally turn to the novels of Vicki Baum for guidance in these matters; nevertheless the narrator in *Marion Alive* obviously speaks from experience:

'The writings of Karl Marx were given to me like a sort of Bible, to learn the fundamentals of socialism from them. Like the Scriptures, they were deeply absorbing in stretches and absolutely barren in others. Like the Scriptures, they contained much intentional or unintentional darkness. Like the Scriptures, they contradicted themselves and, as with the Bible, it was a hopeless undertaking ever to get through reading it all' (p. 135).

Apart from the suggestion that it is a hopeless undertaking to read the Scriptures, this judgment is not so far out.

and it is at our peril that we fail to find a remedy. In the matter of the concentration of capital, a half-hearted claim may be advanced on behalf of Marx. Concentration there clearly has been; but it has been primarily concentration of management. It is doubtful whether there has been any significant concentration of possession; and in any case, there has been simultaneously considerable diffusion of wealth. The small owner, cherishing a tendency to a 'bourgeois' frame of mind, abounds. On the disappearance of the middle classes, the prophecies of Marx have been entirely wide of the mark. Society has, with admirable stubbornness, refused to segregate itself into two extreme camps.

The doctrine of the increasing degradation and misery of the working classes is of some interest in Marxian exegesis, because apparently it is susceptible of four, if not five, different interpretations. Not every dogma is so considerate of tender consciences. As enunciated in *The Communist Manifesto*—whatever arguments may subsequently have been advanced to the contrary—it is clear that we are concerned with literal and absolutely increasing misery:

> The modern worker, on the contrary, instead of rising with the progress of industry, sinks ever deeper beneath the social conditions of his own class. The labourer becomes the pauper, and pauperism increases even more rapidly than population and wealth.[1]

Looking round, after consulting our grandparents, it is quite obvious that the poor have not become poorer since 1848; there has not been 'increasing misery.' With one way of dodging the whole question, we are already familiar. 'When Marx talked of increasing misery,' we are told by one authority, 'he was talking of what would be the outcome of unmodified capitalism.' Now capitalism, it is argued, has never existed by itself, and accordingly the historical facts can neither confirm nor refute the accuracy of Marx's diagnosis. He was merely concerned with the 'logical effect of a hypothetical capitalism on wages.' This, of course, is merely to transfer Marx to the fairyland of hypothetical capitalism in which no one else is specially interested.[2] But, apart from the literal interpretation, which alone fits *The Communist Manifesto* (and Engels), and Dr. Lindsay's escape to unreality, there remains a choice of three other possible interpretations. Firstly, the increasing misery may be 'relative' and not absolute. The working classes may possibly have improved their position, but not in proportion to the increased wealth of the community as a whole. This doctrine has kinship with Rodbertus's 'Diminishing Wage Share.' If the rate of progress made by the working classes is less favourable than that made by their more fortunate betters, then relatively (so it

[1] *Manifesto of the Communist Party*.
[2] Lindsay: *Karl Marx's Capital*, p. 25.

might be argued) their position may be said to be one of increasing misery. It is doubtful whether even this case can be established, especially in the light of the level of taxation we now enjoy. Secondly, there is the psychological explanation of 'misery,' which Muckle, for instance, considers the only defensible interpretation.[1] On this view, quite irrespective of wages, and whether they be high or low, capitalism imposes degradation, springing from dependence and subjection. In the Gotha programme, the psychological theory alone appears:

> In present-day society, the instruments of labour are the monopoly of the capitalist class; the resulting dependence of the working class is the cause of misery and servitude in all its forms.[2]

Later, in Guild Socialism, this appears as the 'beastliness' of the wage system and of wage-slavery; the mere fact of receiving wages makes men increasingly and acutely unhappy.

But there is still a further interpretation of the doctrine of 'increasing misery,' which may perhaps be described as the theory of 'delayed action.' This theory to a certain extent holds out a hand towards Lenin. It will be found expounded in the pages of Mr. Cole. Marx, he holds, foresaw the advent of the age of economic imperialism.[3] It is only as the era of wars of colonial conquest and of imperial rivalries is reached, that the capitalist system turns

> by an inherent tendency which it cannot escape, into a fetter upon the effective use of the available resources. At this stage, but not until this stage has been reached, Marx holds that the capitalist system involves, by virtue of its essential nature, a fall in the working-class standard of life.[4]

Putting it otherwise, so long as capitalism continued to be a developing system, a rise in working-class standards would be possible; but with capitalism in difficulties, the situation would be otherwise, and working-class standards would be forced down. 'This interpretation alone,' says Mr. Cole, 'is consistent both with what Marx said and with the subsequent evolution of capitalism.'[5] It is not every prophet whose prophecies are so indulgently reinterpreted in the light of subsequent evolution. According to Mr. Cole, the change-over took place in this country in the first decade of the twentieth century; in actual fact, it is fairly clear that Marx, writing in 1848 (however he may have modified his views later), was satisfied that capitalism was already in extreme difficulties, and that the axe had been laid to the root of the tree. The doctrine of increasing misery (of immiserization, to use Professor Schumpeter's convenient but barbarous translation) has doubtless played a larger part in continental controversy than with us;

[1] Muckle: *Die grossen Sozialisten*, vol. 2, p. 116.
[2] In *The Critique of the Gotha Programme*, p. 7.
[3] Cole: *What Marx Really Meant*, p. 57.
[4] *Ibid.* p. 59. [5] *Ibid.* pp. 112–113.

it is, however, of some interest here as illustrating the latitude of interpretation consistent with orthodoxy. You may side-track the whole doctrine to an abstract capitalism that never was on land or sea ; or you may declare yourself an adherent of the literal, the relative, the psychological, or the ' delayed-action ' school of thought.

In the foregoing pages, little has been said, except by way of implication, regarding the Marxian view of the State, the nature of the coming revolution, or of what may be thereafter. On the nature of the State, there are innumerable passages in Marx and Engels alike, enabling the position to be stated with precision and clarity. On the other hand, on the inevitable revolution, still more on the structure of society and the working of the machine thereafter, Marx is extremely reticent ; and reliance must therefore be placed on gleanings from relatively few passages which have in consequence received an eminence which in themselves they hardly merit.

The Marxian view of the State, as it now exists, is, in a sense, a corollary of the Materialist Conception of History. The State is ' nothing more than the form of organisation which the bourgeois necessarily adopt both for internal and external purposes, for the mutual guarantee of their property and interests.' [1] The words may vary, but the idea remains constant : the State is a class organisation, representing the interests and reflecting the ideas of the dominant class. Marx's description of the July Monarchy in France may have specific reference to one State, but the general conception is common to all : it was ' nothing other than a joint stock company for the exploitation of French national wealth, the dividends of which were divided among ministers, Chambers, 140,000 voters and their adherents.' [2] Moreover, being the expression of the dominance of a class, and therefore part of the machinery of the class struggle, the essence of State power lies in its ' purely repressive character.' More tersely, if we may invite Engels to his customary rôle of singing in unison : ' The State is nothing more than a machine for the oppression of one class by another.' [3] With the reiterated assertion that the State is a class organisation, it is scarcely too much to say that the political philosophy of Marx begins and ends.

In turning to the future, Marx was designedly vague. The expropriators are in due course to be expropriated ; but by what process this will be accomplished, just precisely what will be the situation on the morrow of the revolution, are questions to which Marx gives no limpid answers ; nor does he regard it as his function to give detailed prescriptions in such matters. Yet on one point he is clear. When

[1] *The German Ideology*, p. 59.
[2] *The Class Struggles in France*, p. 36.
[3] Introduction to *Civil War in France*, p. 19.

the expropriators are expropriated, there will still for a time be need of a State, even if not of the old State machine which is contaminated in too many respects by virtue of its old associations. The French Commune served Marx and Engels alike as an interesting object-lesson in the technique of revolution, and it is interesting to note Engels' words (written in 1891): 'The Commune was compelled to recognise from the outset that the working class, once come to power, could not carry on business with the old State machine.' [1] Doubtless the ultimate purpose of the revolution will be the abolition of all classes, but this end will not be attained forthwith. The new organisation—State, call it what you will—will still be a class organisation, but now the dominant class whose interests it will represent will be the proletariat. The *locus classicus* for this is contained in the *Critique of the Gotha Programme*:

> Between capitalist and communist society lies the period of the revolutionary transformation of the one into the other. There corresponds to this also a political transition period in which the State can be nothing but *the revolutionary dictatorship of the proletariat.*[2]

This is the somewhat too famous and too frequently misunderstood 'Dictatorship of the Proletariat.' The present State with all its class machinery will be replaced by a State which will be no less a class organisation, making no claims to comprehensiveness or to impartiality. The difference between the present bourgeois State and the 'Dictatorship of the Proletariat' is that the State we know aims at the maintenance of class distinctions and its own permanence, resting on these distinctions; whereas the 'Dictatorship of the Proletariat,' by aiming at the abolition of all classes, prepares the way for its own extinction.

For in this matter the Engels-Marx theory is beautifully logical, as a theory, however badly it may fit the facts of future revolutions. For if the State, by its very essence, is the expression of the interests of a class, it follows that with the total, final and irrevocable abolition of classes, the State must also disappear. The abolition of classes implies the abolition of the State; and in a society where there are no classes, there can be no State. Unfortunately, the passages in which this view is most clearly expressed derive from Engels rather than from Marx—not that it matters in the case of these twin souls. The most familiar is a passage from *Anti-Dühring*, from which a few sentences must almost inevitably be quoted, if only because of the celebrity of the culminating phrase.

> When ultimately it (the State) becomes really representative of society as a whole, it makes itself superfluous. As soon as there is no longer any

[1] Introduction to *Civil War in France*, p. 17.
[2] *Critique of the Gotha Programme*, p. 28.

class of society to be held in subjection . . . there is nothing more to be repressed which would make a special repressive force, a State, necessary, The first act in which the State really comes forward as the representative of society as a whole . . . is at the same time its last independent act as a State. The interference of the State power in social relations becomes superfluous in one sphere after another, and then ceases of itself. The government of persons is replaced by the administration of things and the direction of the processes of production. The State is not ' abolished,' *it withers away.*[1]

No less emphatic, but perhaps even more contemptuous, is a somewhat less well-known passage from *The Origin of the Family*:

We are now rapidly approaching a stage in the development of production at which the existence of these classes has not only ceased to be a necessity, but becomes a positive hindrance to production. They will fall as inevitably as they once arose. The State inevitably falls with them. The society which organises production anew on the basis of free and equal association of the producers will put the whole State machinery where it will then belong —into the museum of antiquities, next the spinning wheel and the bronze axe.[2]

Such is the ' withering away of the State,' the culminating far-distant point to which Marxian politics tends.[3] Saint-Simon also, it will be recalled, played with this same idea of replacing government by administration ; yet it is the merest will-o'-the-wisp. It is not so easy to ' take things out of politics.' Even when matters have been reduced to a state of ' Byzantine immobility,' it is possible for men to wrangle over ' administration '—indeed it is impossible that they should not do so. Easy enough to say that we shall take the Unemployment Assistance Board out of politics and run it as a business show without a Minister to speak of ; but that does not prevent the most violent storms from raging in Parliament and in the country, as soon as the unfortunate Board formulates its first Means Test. But the interesting—indeed the rather fascinating—point is that we are here back in a state

[1] *Anti-Dühring*, pp. 308–309.

[2] Engels: *Origin of the Family*, p. 198.

[3] Some interest attaches to a passage in Fichte in which, writing in 1794, he lays down in all its essentials the doctrine of the withering-away of the State. It will be found in the lecture bearing the title *Über die Bestimmung des Menschen in der Gesellschaft*, which is the second of the *Vorlesungen über die Bestimmung des Gelehrten.* He is here concerned with the distinction between Society and the State. The State is merely a means to an end, and like all human institutions which are merely means to an end, it tends to bring about its own destruction: ' Es ist der Zweck aller Regierung, die Regierung überflüssig zu machen.' He hastens to add that this event is not imminent ; indeed myriads of years, if not myriads of myriads of years, may be necessary. But as a theoretical proposition there lies ahead of us a time ' wo alle Staatsverbindungen überflüssig seyn werden.' That time will come when reason, in place of strength and cunning, will be universally recognised as the supreme judge. This does not mean that in this remote period, after these myriads of myriads of years, men will no longer err, and by their errors injure their fellow-men ; but it does mean that in that remote future any chance criminals will be of the type known to Godwin and Bertrand Russell, that they will in fact be open to conviction, and on being convinced of their error, they will forthwith reform (Fichte's *Sämmtliche Werke* (1845 edition), vol. 6, pp. 306–307).

of Godwinian anarchy, with 'free associations of producers' jostling each other in the void.

One glimpse of the future, indeed, takes us straight into a Fourieresque Utopia. It will be recalled that the remote beginnings of separation into classes are attributed in Marxian theory to division of labour. The Marxians, in their curious way, are nothing if not logical, according to their lights. Just as the State, on the Marxian definition, must 'wither away' when classes are no more; so also, if division of labour is the ultimate cause of the existence of classes, it too must be for ever scotched to prevent the re-emergence of classes. In a communist world, everyone must do everything. This antipathy to division of labour appears in *Capital*; more specifically, and at greater length, it gives a rosy glow to the concluding pages of *Anti-Dühring*. The former division of labour, it is said, must disappear. Productive labour in the new golden age will become a means to the emancipation of men

> by giving each individual the opportunity to develop and exercise all his faculties, physical and mental, in all directions; in which, therefore, productive labour will become a pleasure instead of a burden.[1]

That each individual should have the opportunity of developing *all* his faculties, physical *and* mental, in *all* directions, is a dream which will cheer the vision only of the simple-minded, oblivious of the restrictions imposed by the narrow limits of human life. For life is a series of acts of choice, and each choice is at the same time a renunciation and an act of abdication.

> Something unborn within me dies
> With each new day;
> And every night before me lies
> A straiter way.

Even the inhabitant of Engels' future fairyland will have to decide sooner or later whether he wishes to be Archbishop of Canterbury or First Sea Lord, whether he should seek to excel as a violinist or as a pugilist, whether he should elect to know all about Chinese literature or about the hidden pages in the life of the mackerel. The passage in *The German Ideology* is even more diverting in revealing the ultimate confusion which would prevail in a world which sets out to realise the ideals of Marxian confusion:

> In communist society, where nobody has one exclusive sphere of activity but each can become accomplished in any branch he wishes, society regulates the general production and thus makes it possible for me to do one thing to-day and another to-morrow, to hunt in the morning, fish in the afternoon, rear cattle in the evening, criticize after dinner, just as I have a mind, without ever becoming hunter, fisherman, shepherd or critic.[2]

A short week-end on a farm might have convinced Marx that the cattle themselves might have some objection to being reared in this

[1] *Anti-Dühring*, p. 322.

[2] *The German Ideology*, p. 22.

casual manner, in the evening. On the more general issue it is odd that what is usually regarded as the most authoritarian school of socialism should thus culminate in anarchy; that the writers who were most openly contemptuous of Utopias should lead us to a Utopia to which even Fourier could scarcely add any finishing touches.

That this chapter has assumed more ample dimensions than was designed may perhaps be excused on the ground of the central position which Marx occupies in determining the later development of socialism, and the quite unique influence which he has exercised on thought and on the march of events. Yet Marx remains an abiding and inscrutable riddle. His system has worn thin to the point of being threadbare; his most devoted followers show little compunction in throwing most of him overboard, provided they can make a pretence of hanging on to something of the Marxian legacy. Probably the most significant and enduring portion of Marx is contained in the Materialist Conception of History; for here there is something which (especially if restated sensibly as by Mr. Cole) does at least provide an interesting technique in historical interpretation. It is unfortunate that with it he linked up the doctrine of the class struggle, which has had a narrowing and sterilising effect on the subsequent development of socialism. Next to this, the most significant portion of Marx to-day is probably to be found in that aspect which links up with Lenin, as in the 'Dictatorship of the Proletariat' and the technique of revolution. This is not a question of *Wissenschaft*; but at least we here see Marx as a power and an influence. On the other hand, the whole theory of value (so far as comprehensible) is dead beyond the power of recovery, and none so poor as do it reverence; and with it, the doctrine of surplus-value must also go, for it is in essence an inference from the theory of value. There is nothing so silly as the fairly common affectation that, though the theory of value may be sacrificed as bad economics and as unessential, the doctrine of surplus-value nevertheless may be left intact. It did not require a Karl Marx to come from Trier to the British Museum to prove to us that the poor have, more often than not, had a rough deal in history. If this is what is meant by retaining the doctrine of surplus-value, it clearly does not require 'scientific' proof; moreover this is not what the doctrine of surplus-value teaches us. Its essence lies in the contention that whenever one person is employed and paid wages by another, he is necessarily defrauded—a proposition not so easily swallowed. So likewise, the 'specific' prophecies for the most part have refused to be fulfilled, as indeed is sufficiently evidenced by the development of Revisionism which was provoked into existence by the failure of the world to follow the lines forecast in Marxian prophecy. On the whole, then, little of Marx is left; and what does endure is not strictly of the essence of the Marxian system.

One other point is of some interest. It has been seen that the best authorities seem to be agreed that Marx was concerned with the study of an abstract world, which never has existed or could exist, of a 'hypothetical capitalism,' in Dr. Lindsay's phrase. Now if this is so, the success of Marx rests on his having been completely misunderstood. We have seen Professor Wilbrandt underline the same point from a different angle. There was, in his view, no possibility of understanding the first Volume of *Capital* (1867) until the appearance of the third in 1894. Yet in these years the bases of Marx's influence were laid. It is difficult to recall any other similar case where a book has been influential largely because it has been misunderstood.

Nor can it reasonably be said that Marx's influence rests on his captivating style. Parts of Volume I of *Capital* have a certain quality of fire; but in the main he is a villainous writer, and he is no better in German than in English. Anyone who doubts may try his teeth in the first fifteen pages of *Capital.* Or take such a sentence as this; 'The relation of the productive forces to the form of intercourse is the relation of the form of intercourse to the occupation or activity of the individuals.' This is not a specially bad sentence; indeed there are far worse sentences in the page that precedes and that which follows; but, being longer, they are not so apt for quotation. But can anyone say that a dog's breakfast of sentences like that quoted is the stuff to fire the proletariat to action?

Nor was Marx, on the record of his life, the kind of man who would be expected to make an appeal to the workers of the world. It may be doubted whether he met or knew any honest-to-God British or German workers, or would have known how to deal with them, or speak to them, if he had. His natural associates were intellectual revolutionary exiles and international intriguers—a very different type of person from the worker to whom he thought he was appealing. Nor indeed can it be said that Marx had any real knowledge of the world he was so active in analysing. He did not, with a curious eye and a question on his lips, haunt places where men work. Doubtless he knew a vast deal, but it was derived from blue-books, already fading history when he read them. Wilbrandt has an unintentionally illuminating phrase on this matter. Speaking of the relationship of Marx and Engels, he says: *Engels ist sein Auge für die Wirklichkeit*—it was Engels who was his 'eye for reality.'[1] It is said in high commendation of Engels: in fact it reveals the nakedness of Marx. For Reality is precisely the thing that none of us can see through the eyes of another. Marx spent much of his life chewing his intellectual cud, with his back firmly planted towards the window.

Yet despite his prosy and interminable dullness, despite the confusions and inherent contradictions of his theories, despite his manifold defects in temperament and disposition, rendering him the least fitted

[1] Wilbrandt: *Karl Marx*, p. 14.

of men to be a hero of the people, the indubitable fact remains that Marx has proved the most influential figure of the nineteenth century. Perhaps some approach to an explanation of this mystery may be found in the fact that the Marxian tradition and influence has developed along two very different lines. In this country at least, Marx has tended to become in the main the cult of a somewhat anæmic intelligentsia who, like Marx himself, prefer to see reality through the eyes of another. In this rarefied atmosphere, it is possible to discuss which of five possible interpretations should be placed on the doctrine of 'increasing misery'; or just how a theory devised for a hypothetical capitalism may be applied to a capitalism which is not so hypothetical. But beyond this, there are those who believe in Marx without having read him—perhaps who believe in Marx just because they have not read him. It is probably a safe surmise that to-day the third Volume of *Capital* is even less read than that single chapter which has conferred immortality on the prophet Obadiah, and when read, is read with as little comprehension. Just as, according to some and to judge from their practice, a good Christian need not read his Bible, so a good Marxian does not need to read his Marx: he *knows* it is there. Thus, for the great body of the faithful, Marx has become the inspired author of a body of Sorelian myths, which sum up, and fit in with, their general view of life, which clarify and illumine their daily strivings, which rationalise and crystallise their instincts. And these people, quite rightly, are not concerned with the metaphysical refinements of a theory of value. They accept the fact of 'exploitation' which has been proved by Marx, whom the doubter can read if he can and if he so chooses—by Marx who had read so many books that the list of his references runs to pages and pages of close type. Moreover 'increasing misery' means 'increasing misery,' neither more nor less; and in a world where we all feel so much less fortunate than we think we ought to be, it is comforting to be told that we are right, and to know who is responsible for our unhappiness. This is what Marx did, and here lies the secret of his influence. To consider whether Marx was 'right' or 'wrong'; to dredge Volumes I and III of *Capital* for inconsistencies or logical flaws, to 'refute' the Marxian system is, in the last resort, sheer waste of time; for when we consort with Marx we are no longer in the world of reason or logic. He saw visions—clear visions of the passing of all things, much more nebulous visions of how all things may be made new. And his visions, or some of them, awoke a responsive chord in the hearts of many men. Perhaps the last word may be allowed to Professor Wilbrandt: 'Das ganze System ist Darstellung, nicht Beweis.'[1] The Marxian system, if we may translate not over accurately, is pictorial representation, not proof. He gives us a vision; and visions soar above logic.

[1] Wilbrandt: *Karl Marx*, p. 128.

Note on Value.

Without allowing one's self to be beguiled into the awful morass of the Theory of Value, this at least may be said in partial illumination of Marx's later desire to differentiate between Value and Price. No one who has ever seen behind the scenes of a Price Regulation Committee will ever again lecture with a light heart on the Marshallian, or any other theory of Value. Prices to-day are to a large extent fixed somewhat arbitrarily within a moderately wide range. The theoretical reason for this is that most commodities are virtually joint products, inasmuch as no industrial unit produces one article only, or one line only of a given article. This means that 'cost of production' tends to be indeterminate. There are always common costs, 'overheads,' the distribution of which is largely a matter of policy. If a firm wishes to push a line, it will relieve it of most of its share of overhead costs; if elsewhere the 'traffic' will bear more, it will be called upon to bear more than its share. In addition, the retail end may add on a flat rate of 33·33 per cent. or 50 per cent., irrespective of the specific cost of marketing the commodity in question, thereafter smoothing out the answer to the nearest convenient round figure, which may be 2*s.* 11¾*d.* With this, there is the whole problem of price-differences, determined in part by tradition, and in part by what the public wants and expects. In selling a cheap, a medium and a superior line of any commodity, the spacing is more or less rigidly determined in advance; and the public which is prepared to go beyond 1*s.* 11*d.* may be suspicious if the next price is less than 3*s.* 1½*d.*, or whatever it may be. Also there are certain prices on which there rests a kind of taboo. It would be interesting to speculate on the economic implications of the cryptic aphorism that '11*s.* 11*d.* isn't a price.' If 11*s.* 11*d.* isn't a price, what on earth is it? Does it fail to qualify as a price, because 11*s.* 11*d.* looks silly on a price ticket, especially if the symbol for a shilling is inclined at the same angle as the various '1's'? Or is it because 'Eleven, eleven' may be confusing to the ear as doubtless 'Seven, double seven, double seven' may be to a telephonist? On the other hand, 9*s.* 9*d.* seems to be a price. The realisation that prices contain an arbitrary element may well provoke the curious enquirer into groping for a 'Value' which is not thus subject to caprice. But at least terms should be defined; and in seeking for truth one should not wander in a circle.

(*b*) LASSALLE

Marx has become, for later generations, so exclusively and sufficiently the exponent of scientific socialism—especially if 'Marx' be taken as a convenient abbreviation for the Marx-Engels partnership—that any embroidery in the way of pendents might almost be regarded as unnecessary. Yet there are two other names which may not in justice be passed over altogether in silence, even if, in the field of theory and thought, they add but little that is specifically their own to the Marxian edifice. There is, in the first place, Ferdinand Lassalle (1825–1864), somewhat younger than Marx, a man who perhaps figures more prominently in the history of the socialist movement than in the history of socialist theory; and there is, secondly, Johann Karl Rodbertus (1805–1875), Marx's senior, pre-eminently a Fabian thinker who, shunning the busy hum of men, philosophised in retirement, and who, as some would have it at one time, was one of the writers whose ideas Marx appropriated.

Ignoring strict chronology, Lassalle may be glanced at first, in deference to his greater place in history.[1] Many of the writers caught in the net of this volume are somewhat enigmatic figures; none, at least in some respects, is more enigmatic than Lassalle—whether he be a fascinating enigma, as George Meredith apparently found him,[2] or a somewhat repulsive and repugnant enigma, depends to a large extent on the biographer whose guidance is, for the time being, accepted. George Brandes, writing sympathetically, finds in him a caged eagle, a tragedy of greatness, marred by 'an impure deposit of pride and haughtiness.'[3] On the other hand, anyone reading the extraordinary biography by Mr. Arno Schirokauer is left, despite its apparent panegyric intentions, with the impression that in Lassalle we have surely plumbed the deepest depths of human offensiveness. It is fairly clear that everything that Lassalle did or wrote dripped with vanity and conceit. He was a showman, a fop and a dandy; at times legitimate doubts arise as to his sincerity; his private letters are frequently nauseating. On the other hand, the meretricious tinsel which somehow adheres to Lassalle throughout Schirokauer's biography just fails to fit in with the obvious learning, scholarship and industry manifested in the authorship of *Das System der Erworbenen Rechte*, which, with its 900 pages of meat, is the kind of professorial work which is not lightly displaced from its appointed station on the shelves of the Law Library. Nor does the final tragedy of his death in a more than usually foolish and unnecessary duel, with all the attendant circumstances, fit in with the part he essayed to play as a Tribune of the People, or for that matter with the authorship of the *Acquired Rights*. And this the German workers felt quite distinctly, even if dumbly, after his death. Labour leaders do not get killed in silly duels—least of all where the occasion of the duel is a daughter of the Philistines. The fundamental doubt remains whether Lassalle throughout may not have been merely a skilful actor in the melodrama of life.

Nevertheless, though there may be doubts as to what Lassalle in his innermost core really was, there can be no dubiety as to what he did. He carried the gospel of Marx (and of others) to those for whom it was designed. He made socialism a political movement; to him was due the creation of the General Union of German Workers (the *Allgemeine Deutsche Arbeiterverein*). No honest workman in his senses will ever profess to enjoy the Marxian subtleties and subter-

[1] His name was really Lassal. As a very young man he went to Paris Lassal, and came back Lassalle. It is somehow characteristic and symptomatic.

[2] *The Tragic Comedians* is undisguisedly the story of Lassalle, idealised and transfigured.

[3] Brandes: *Ferdinand Lassalle*, p. 222.

fuges of the opening chapters of *Capital*; Marxism in itself is an indigestible by-product of a sedentary life spent in the British Museum. Lassalle was the missionary, the interpreter, the populariser, endowed with the gift of tongues and inflammatory rhetoric, an admirable Aaron to Marx's Moses. Large tracts of Marx are calculated to extinguish any fire: Lassalle was nothing but fire, and in the last two years of his life he was a whirlwind, an ascending tornado, leading up to the final climax or anti-climax. And at least he had his reward. He may now have tended to fade into the background with the passage of years, when to all but a few the shortcomings of the 'Fortschrittspartei' are no longer of vital interest; for it is the fate of the politician to sink into insignificance when his peculiar problems are forgotten. But at the time of his death he was a giant and a flaming symbol, compared to Marx. He became a legend, the theme of folk-song, one of the great dead who would come again to deliver his people.[1]

We are here concerned, at the most, with the briefest possible statement of Lassalle's position, indicating, so far as may be, the points on which his contribution diverges from that of Marx. Summarised in a sentence, with the injustice which such an extreme summary always entails, Lassalle's position may be said to be based theoretically on a straightforward Marxian foundation; but he differs from Marx with regard to the programme of action for the immediate future. Here, despite his denials, he draws his inspiration from Louis Blanc, and as a necessary consequence he further differs fundamentally from Marx in his conception of what the State is, and of what can be done by and through the State.

Of the very considerable spate of publications that distinguished the concluding stormy years of Lassalle's agitation—there were twenty in twenty-seven months!—probably the three most significant will yield sufficient for our purpose. There is, firstly, the *Arbeiter-Programm*, a speech delivered on April 12, 1862, outlining a general philosophy and a general programme for the Workers' Movement. There is, secondly, the *Offenes Antwortschreiben*, a statement of Lassalle's views, written on request, clarifying the relationship of the Workers' Party to other parties (above all, to the Fortschrittspartei) in the political configuration of the time. There is, thirdly, the so-called *Herr Bastiat-Schulze von Delitzsch*, which, according to Bernstein, is Lassalle's chief work in the social-economic field. Schulze-Delitzsch was at the time an eminent member of the Liberal Party, posing as something of an economist and a philanthropist, given to the gospel of Self-Help and Savings Banks. His views largely reflected the

[1] *E.g.*:

Zu Breslau ein Kirchhof,
Ein Todter im Grab;
Dort schlummert der Eine,
Der Schwerter uns gab.

orthodox middle-class complacency of Bastiat. Lassalle took it upon himself to deflate Schulze-Delitzsch ; but the moderately extensive pamphlet in which he does so can hardly be said to be pleasant reading. He quotes, almost *in extenso*, a recent publication by Schulze, and for 250 pages he pours upon his antagonist a flood of vituperative contempt, treating him as the world's greatest nit-wit, and, if one may borrow a picturesque, if perhaps unjustifiable, phrase from Sir Thomas Urquhart, railing at him like a tripe-seller's wife.

We are here concerned with those aspects of Lassalle which do not fall neatly inside the Marxian hold-all, and to a certain extent with those elements of Marxism to which Lassalle gave a special emphasis, implanting them in the popular mind by popularising a phrase which has endured. It is of the essence of ' Scientific Socialism,' which seeks to prove that the coming of socialism is part of the ineluctable march of events, that it must be based on a philosophy of history. Lassalle's ' philosophy of history,' if the dignified phrase be permissible, is simple and pervasive. He views all history as divided into three periods by the revolutions of 1789 and 1848. In a sweeping generalisation, he holds that revolutions can never be *made* ; all that can be done is to give legal recognition and effect to a revolution that has already taken place in the actual relationships existing in a society. In short, a revolution is an acknowledgement and endorsement of what has already taken place.[1]

On this view, the French Revolution of 1789 chronicled the fact that the nobility, whose power rested on the possession of land, had been reduced to a position of complete insignificance, and had become dependent on the Bourgeoisie.[2] It gave the *tiers état* in law the position it had already acquired in fact.[3] But this third estate did not really represent the cause of the whole of humanity.[4] What emerged was a Bourgeoisie, with a claim to privilege resting on property qualification. *Kapitalbesitz* had now become the determinant of political power, in place of land.[5] The French Revolution had doubtless declared Labour to be free, but it had endowed the worker with no *Kapital.* He was *rechtlich frei und faktisch mittellos*—free in the eyes of the law, but in fact without means, compelled to sell life itself for the means of life.[6] The year 1789 had displaced the Nobility, resting on land, in favour of the Bourgeoisie, resting on ' capital-possession ' ; the year 1848, displacing the Bourgeoisie, was destined to usher in the era of humanity, securely planted on universal suffrage—of all which, more hereafter. Thus does Lassalle divide the history of humanity into two eternities, separated by a brief interval of fifty-nine years.

[1] *Arbeiter-Programm*, p. 32. (In the Reclam edition, No. 6048.)
[2] *Ibid.* p. 23.
[3] *Ibid.* pp. 36–37.
[4] *Ibid.* p. 39.
[5] *Ibid.* p. 47.
[6] *Herr Bastiat-Schulze von Delitzsch*, pp. 105–106.

Though Lassalle was writing and speaking in 1862–63—well after the revolution of 1848—his analysis would indicate that the new era had not so far enjoyed a very effective dawn. In the main, though perhaps more picturesquely and with greater propaganda skill, the core of his proof of exploitation coincides with that given by Marx. The worker always pays; he is always the loser. First of all, there bulks largely in Lassalle's mind a point which had not then attracted the attention it was to receive later: the relative merits and consequences of direct and indirect taxation. In the nature of things, indirect taxation rests preponderatingly on the poorer classes; in more modern language, it is regressive. But, in the world known to Lassalle, the bulk of the State's income was derived from indirect taxation, mostly paid by the poor; political power, on the other hand, under the property qualification, was based on direct taxation, which contributed little. This elaborate system of indirect taxation was the device—Lassalle called it the 'institution'—whereby the Bourgeoisie contrived that large capital should continue to enjoy immunity from the burden of taxation.[1]

The central proof of exploitation is pure Marx, without the Marxian complications and involutions, and therefore more comprehensible and more convincing: in short, it is more in line with the early English anticipators of Marxism. The worker receives bare subsistence (*Lebensnotdurft*); the entrepreneur takes the rest.[2] But if it would involve vain repetition to state the substance of Lassalle's views at greater length, three incidental points arising out of the manner of his statement should be noted. In the first place, Lassalle invented, or at least he gets the credit of having invented, the phrase which describes the alleged tendency of wages to subsistence-level as the 'Iron Law of Wages.' It is an old doctrine, to be found in the pages of Turgot in a more classic and precise form than that which Ricardo gave to it. Strictly speaking, Lassalle called it 'das eherne Gesetz,' which is a 'brazen law,' rather than an iron law: in any case, being metallic, it does not greatly matter. A maniac for accuracy might indeed point out that what he most frequently called it was 'das eherne und grausame Gesetz,' which somehow sounds even more horrible. In a way, this baptismal effort was, in the field of letters, Lassalle's crowning achievement. The Iron (or the Brazen) Law of Wages was an idea with immense propaganda possibilities which Lassalle exploited to the uttermost. The paternity of the phrase, indeed, has a fair chance of being, in the long run, Lassalle's most abiding title to fame.

The second point to note is that Lassalle's statement of the 'Iron Law' has its roots intertwined with a primitive and crude Malthusian-

[1] *Arbeiter-Programm*, pp. 50–51.
[2] *Offenes Antwortschreiben* (Buchhandlung Vorwärts edition), p. 39.

ism. Indeed, the Iron Law of Wages, to be made plausible, demands that any temporary aberration of the wage-level above the subsistence line will be at once neutralised by a devastating torrent of children. This in fact is Lassalle's position: if the worker receives enough for his subsistence, he will automatically produce the next generation for the employer's behoof.[1]

The third point arising from Lassalle's use of the Iron Law has reference to his relationship to Ricardo. It had been rather an affectation of the scientific socialists and their early English predecessors to claim that they were attacking the orthodox economists with their own weapons: and it has long been a commonplace (perhaps originally intended as a paradox) to look upon Marx and his fellows as the last of the classical school. Lassalle himself states the position with admirable clarity. Ricardo, he says, had carried 'bürgerliche Oekonomie' (may we say the classical school?) to its highest point, where the only possible further development was to transform it into 'Sozial-Oekonomie': 'Socialism' (if one may thus freely translate *Sozial-Oekonomie*) is nothing other than a fight against Ricardo, but it is at the same time a fight which is just as much an immanent continuation of his doctrine. The point is well and justly made.[2]

A somewhat different (perhaps even inconsistent) source of exploitation brings Lassalle more closely into touch with Proudhon. He attaches a quite extraordinary importance to the principle of division of labour, and draws from it conclusions which reach far in various directions. It is, among other things, one of the impulses to exploitation. He argues, dubiously, that it is only under division of labour that labour can produce any surplus above subsistence level.[3] It doubtless depends on what is meant by 'division of labour,' which admittedly is patient of many interpretations. He argues further, and much more indefensibly, that division of labour is the source of all wealth—'die Theiling der Arbeit ist die Quelle aller Reichthümer.' What the capitalist does is to appropriate the advantages of division of labour and the ever-increasing productivity that springs from it.[4]

The principle of division of labour is further used by Lassalle to develop an idea very dear to his heart; order, he held, prevailed in production, whereas in distribution we are confronted with chaos. It

[1] See, e.g. *Bastiat-Schulze von Delitzsch*, p. 44. The point is put more bluntly elsewhere; for example, it is argued that if the worker is given 'die übliche Nothdurft—seien Sie unbesorgt, den Jungen wird er sich schon erzeugen, wenn auch nicht gerade um des Unternehmers willen!' (*ibid.* p. 195).

[2] Lassalle's words are worth quoting: 'Er (Ricardo) hat die bürgerliche Oekonomie bis zu ihrem Gipfel entwickelt, d.h. bis hart zu dem Abgrund, wo ihr vermöge ihrer eignen theoretischen Entwicklung selbst nichts mehr übrig bleibt, als umzuschlagen und Sozial-Oekonomie zu werden. Die Soziale-Oekonomie ist nichts als ein Kampf gegen Ricardo, ein Kampf, der eben so sehr eine immanente Fortbildung seiner Lehre ist (*Bastiat-Schulze von Delitzsch*, pp. 156–157).

[3] *Ibid.* p. 110.

[4] *Ibid.* pp. 210–213.

is of the essence of division of labour (it is indeed a text-book commonplace) that it means a more complicated pattern; it means an extended chain between the producer and the consumer. There may have been a time when men, in Marxian language, produced 'use-values'—living on the work of their own hands. Now no one produces anything that is even sellable, or on which he can live.[1] And it is indeed true that the wretch who makes the eighteenth part of a pin, can neither sell the eighteenth part of a pin, nor feed it to his wife. With the lengthening chain to the consumer at the world's end, we are all liable to be upset by what happens anywhere. Consequently, in opposition to liberal complacency regarding man's 'responsibility' for his actions, Lassalle replies in a phrase which pleased him, that in the economic sphere to-day each man is made responsible precisely for what he has *not* done.[2] In all this, we are subject to chance, and where chance prevails the freedom of the individual no longer exists.[3] There is also a further contrast which also leads to an epigram: as against the traditional theory (as in Locke) which speaks of the 'labour basis' of private property, and founds property in the right of the labourer to what he has himself produced, we are living in an age in which everyone aids in the production of 'exchange-values' designed to pass into circulation, and in which therefore everyone can call that 'his' which in fact he has not produced. In a rather famous and untranslatable phrase: 'Das Eigenthum ist Fremdthum geworden'[4]; which, though it has sometimes been thought to be a free appropriation from Proudhon, in fact represents a different line of approach.

Combining these various lines of thought, it is possible to descry dimly on what grounds Lassalle, with something of the guile of the later Fabians, was able to suggest that we were already, even if unconsciously, living in a semi-socialised world. For the mere existence of division of labour binds us together; it implies work carried on in union; it is a bond linking society together with a view to production.[5] In production there is therefore order, the order of the workshop, the order that springs from union for a common end. But not so with distribution. The deep inner contradiction in our organisation is that we have *Gemeinsamkeit* in production, and *Individualismus* in distribution.[6] We are accordingly living in a state of 'anarchic socialism.'[7] Something of the order, of the *Gemeinsamkeit*, that prevails in production must be introduced elsewhere, so that our socialism may cease to be one-sided. Lassalle, it must be admitted, is here less plausible than the Fabians.

[1] *Bastiat-Schulze von Delitzsch*, pp. 107–108. [2] *Ibid.* p. 37.
[3] *Ibid.* p. 41. [4] *Ibid.* p. 215.
[5] *Ibid.* pp. 114, 217. Labour to-day is described, if one can get one's tongue round it, as 'eine streng in einander eingreifende gemeinschaftliche Vereinigung Vieler zur Hervorbringung desselben Produkts' (*ibid.* p. 57).
[6] *Ibid.* p. 57. [7] *Ibid.* p. 216.

It is when Lassalle turns to the question of immediate remedies that he diverges sharply from Marx and Rodbertus. We have already seen that the French Revolution, while giving the worker an empty freedom, nevertheless refrained from giving him any capital; and he therefore remained helpless, forced to sell himself, when face to face with the entrepreneur. What must be done is to convert, or degrade capital into what it should be, to wit, a lifeless instrument in the service of labour.[1] A large part of the *Offenes Antwortschreiben* is devoted to revealing the inadequacy of the Schulzian proposals, which appealed to the principles of responsibility, of self-help and other kindred virtues. But Lassalle, heavily armed with the Iron Law of Wages—*das eherne und grausame Gesetz*—knows the answer which effectively crushes all these rose-tinted proposals for reform. Nothing is done to raise the general level. Savings Banks, for example, may help a few, and even these not effectively: the final result is merely to prolong the death-struggle. Consumers' Co-operative Societies are in the same case. For in the background there is always the *eherne und grausame Gesetz*, so that if, exceptionally and against all probability, it were possible to raise the general condition of the workers under the banner of Self-help, immediately and automatically the 'Iron Law' would depress their wages by precisely the amount by which their position had speciously been bettered.[2] Along these lines, the Iron Law, as visualised and applied by Lassalle, is seen to be an insurmountable barrier blocking all aspirations towards benevolent amelioration.

Yet, if the worker is to be saved, the Iron Law must be circumvented. The solution in its phraseology is somewhat suggestive of Fourier; in its substance, it is, as near as may be, straightforward Louis Blanc. The workers—or rather the *Arbeiterstand*, the workers as a class—must become their own 'undertakers.' The principle of association doubtless does provide the path to salvation, but it must find its application and extension in the field of production, in *fabrikmässige Grossproduktion.* Industry is therefore to be transformed by the creation of productive associations—guilds, ateliers, or whatever they may have been called at different eras—with ownership and control vesting in the workers. In this way, and the phrase sets many chords vibrating, the distinction between wages and profits (between *Arbeitslohn* and *Unternehmergewinn*) disappears, as indeed does the conception of wages itself. Labour will receive as its reward the produce of labour, the *Arbeitsertrag*.[3]

The final solution, as has been indicated, so closely resembles that proposed by Louis Blanc that, in the pleasing German phrase, it would

[1] 'das Kapital wieder zum todten, dienenden Arbeitsinstrument zu degradiren' (*ibid.* p. 217).

[2] *Offenes Antwortschreiben*, p. 44.

[3] *Ibid.* pp. 45–46.

scarcely be 'rewarding' to pursue it in further detail. Lassalle protested vigorously against being identified with the 'ateliers nationaux' of unhappy memory. Perhaps rightly: for it is at least an open question how far Louis Blanc was himself identified with, or responsible for, the 'ateliers nationaux,' or how far they reflected his ideas. Yet no one who reads Louis Blanc and Lassalle together can have any doubt that their proposals, as embodied in the printed word, are substantially identical: if there are minor differences, they are of an order of magnitude which at this distance of time makes the issue one of purely antiquarian and specialist interest.

Of greater importance than the ultimate view of a world of co-operative workshops is the question relating to the manner of their establishment. For here Lassalle, in discussing ways and means, adds as a kind of pendent his theory of the State. It is perhaps the most significant feature in Lassalle, as it is the least Marxian. Obviously the workers cannot, of themselves, effect the transition; for this, they must look to the State, whose business and task it is to further the great cause of free association among the workers, and whose 'most sacred duty' it is to provide the necessary means.[1] This is indeed a very different State from that which flits furtively in the background of Marx and Engels, and which ultimately colours the stream leading to syndicalism, where the State is regarded as of necessity a tyrannous class organisation, of which the best that can be hoped is that some day it will be smashed and that later, when there are no more classes, its successor will itself wither away. What then is the State in Lassalle's eyes? Addressing the German workers, he tells them that the State belongs to them and to the needy classes, and that they and their association *are* the State. The State is 'die grosse Organisation, die grosse Assoziation der arbeitenden Klassen.'[2]

Here is a very positive and active State, bubbling over with benevolent subsidies; and Lassalle consciously contrasts it, in a passage which is almost classic, with the contrary 'bourgeois' view of the State, which is that the purpose of the State consists, solely and exclusively, in the protection of the personal freedom of the individual, and of his property. This is indeed the *laissez faire* idea of the State which tended (as in von Humboldt) to limit the State's functions to protection in the narrowest sense. In a phrase which has endured, Lassalle characterised this conception as a *Nachtwächteridee*, viewing the State as a night-watchman, solely concerned in preventing theft

[1] *Offenes Antwortschreiben*, p. 46.

[2] *Ibid.* pp. 53, 57. Lassalle's words may be quoted as a striking contrast to the main Marxian tradition: 'Ihnen also, meine Herren, den notleidenden Klassen, gehört der Staat, nicht uns, den höheren Ständen, denn aus Ihnen besteht er! Was ist der Staat? frage ich, und Sie ersehen jetzt aus wenigen Zahlen handgreiflicher als aus dicken Büchern die Antwort: Ihre, der ärmeren Klassen, grosse Assoziation—das ist der Staat!' (p. 53).

and burglary; and he adds significantly that, in this liberal view, if there were no longer any thieves or robbers, then the State would become a superfluity.[1] Thus, the far-off consummation devoutly desired by the anarchist, the syndicalist, and the later communist is spoken of by Lassalle in the confident tone of one who produces an unanswerable *reductio ad absurdum*.

So far from wishing to reduce the State's function to a minimum, or looking forward with equanimity to the process of its withering away, Lassalle sees in it, now and hereafter, an abiding engine for the moral uplift and regeneration of mankind. He becomes almost lyrical in his praises of the State. In the *Arbeiter-Programm*, the State exists to develop the freedom of mankind; it is the union of individuals into a spiritual whole; its purpose is to enable the individual to attain heights which he could never have reached by his own unaided efforts.[2] In the *Offenes Antwortschreiben* he is, if possible, even more emphatic. There he argues that it is the task and the purpose of the State to facilitate and bring about the cultural progress of mankind; and he adds in words of almost excessive emphasis: 'Dies ist sein Beruf. Dazu existiert er; hat immer dazu gedient und dienen müssen.'[3] This is more in line with that worship of the State as something divine which, Marx and his school apart, runs through so much of German thought.

All very well for Lassalle to assure his hearers that *they* are the State; but are they? Has he not himself described them as the 'disinherited'? All very well to say that it is the State's most sacred duty to launch a thousand ships in the form of productive associations; but was the Prussian State of 1862 likely to rise to its most sacred duty? This brings us to a last point which indeed is the first plank in Lassalle's immediate political programme. The State will only rise to the height of its duty when it represents the whole of the people; and therefore the immediate objective must be the attainment of universal suffrage.[4] When the workers have obtained this, all other things will be added unto them. But this is the first essential condition, and this explains the foundations of Lassalle's policy, which was that the workers should form a political party, distinct from and apart from all others, and that this party should concentrate on the attainment of the suffrage as the first step to the enjoyment of the 'helping hand' of the State. In the light of subsequent disillusionments and later criticisms, it is rather pathetic to note the touching faith which Lassalle displayed in the efficacy of the ballot-box. It is rather assumed that the attainment of universal suffrage and the official opening of the New Jerusalem will more or less synchronise, with the least imaginable time-lag.

[1] *Arbeiter-Programm*, p. 65.
[2] *Ibid.* pp. 66–67.
[3] *Offenes Antwortschreiben*, p. 48.
[4] *Ibid.* pp. 31, 58.

Such is Lassalle: so far as theory is concerned, largely a purveyor and populariser of Marxian doctrine, though it should be remembered that, in the nature of things, he was denied the opportunity of reading *Capital*, and therefore had to draw his sustenance from the earlier writings of Marx. Above all he concentrated on ' exploitation,' in so far as that has its roots in the ' Iron Law '—a phrase to which, with great propagandist skill, he gave enduring currency.[1] But he was latterly a politician even more than a theorist of socialism; and as such he deviates from orthodox Marxism in his faith in the State, in his view of the uses to which the State can be put, and of the help which the State can afford—once the elected body, by a system of universal suffrage, has been made a true reflection of the people at large. If he is not, as he has sometimes been called, the first State Socialist—that title should rather go to Louis Blanc—he is probably the first who was prepared to be a Labour Prime Minister; nor would he have disdained an Earldom on his retirement.

In the foregoing brief summary of Lassalle's views, it has been assumed that he meant what he said. Perhaps it is immaterial whether he did or did not. Yet, to revert to a point touched upon at the outset, in reading Lassalle and of Lassalle, one is haunted by the gnawing doubt whether he was in fact moved by any consideration other than a passion for the limelight and the furtherance of his own glittering career. There are traditional (and doubtless apocryphal) tales of bright young things with their eyes on Parliament, realising that they might get in each other's way in the race for the Premiership if they adhered to the same Party, and accordingly resolving the difficulty by leaving it to the toss of a coin to determine which should go Liberal and which Conservative. It would take too long, and in any case would be outside the scope of this discussion to consider just precisely what incidents and phrases, perhaps of no great importance in themselves, give rise to the suspicion that Lassalle in the same way

[1] It is significant and symptomatic that Lassalle largely survives on the strength of two imaginative and effective phrases, and one short passage of ironical sarcasm. The two phrases which serve as Lassalle's lifebuoy down the waves of the years are, of course, the ' Iron Law ' and the comparison of the bourgeois State to a ' night-watchman.' The ironical passage is that in which he makes merry over the conception of interest as the ' reward of abstinence,' with special reference to the House of Rothschild as a supreme example of the rewards that go to ascetic and, if possible, total abstinence. As it is one of those passages which somehow are generally known about, without being known, and as it affords an example of Lassalle's effective but not too scrupulous tinsel, it may perhaps be reproduced in the compressed type of a footnote:

'Der Kapitalprofit ist der 'Entbehrungslohn'! Glückliches Wort, unbezahlbares Wort. Die europäischen Millionäre Asketen, indische Büsser, Säulenheilige, welche auf Einem Bein auf einer Säule stehen, mit weit vorgebogenem Arm und Oberleib und blassen Mienen einen Teller in's Volk streckend, um den Lohn ihrer Entbehrungen einzusammeln! In ihrer Mitte und hoch über all seine Mitbüsser und Entbehrer das Haus Rothschild! Das ist der Zustand der Gesellschaft! Wie ich denselben nur so verkennen konnte!' (*Bastiat-Schulze*, p. 121).

might very well have argued with equal dexterity and declaimed with equal eloquence in any other cause, if glory and applause had beckoned elsewhere. Nor need we in this matter be unduly affected by the *obiter dicta* of Marx, generously scattered throughout his correspondence, on the subject of Lassalle's shortcomings. Lassalle had been both generous and helpful to Marx; he was a very dangerous potential rival—both excellent reasons for Marx's increasing contempt and hatred. Lassalle's luxurious, sybaritic and apolaustic private life; the fantastic publicity of the Countess Hatzfeld affair; the noise and the fury of political agitation; the opening moves in the political chess-game with Bismarck; the final folly of his death in a duel—all this is much more the raw material of a spectacular 120-minute film than a page from real life; and from a film hero one does not necessarily ask for translucent sincerity. The indubitable historical fact is that it was Lassalle, whatever his qualities and vanities, who created the German Workers' Movement as a political force.

(*c*) RODBERTUS

Johann Karl Rodbertus (1805–1875), who here appears third among the exponents of scientific socialism, might claim, if only on chronological grounds, the right to the highest seat. At one time, indeed, his delirious followers claimed for him a place in the German firmament comparable to that ordinarily assigned to Goethe, and feuds as to the extent to which Marx plagiarised Rodbertus periodically illumine an otherwise dull page. It may be an unworthy suspicion, but it is difficult, two (or three) generations after the event, to resist the impression that the quite obviously unjustifiable adulation of Rodbertus has its hidden springs in a desire to play down Marx by those to whom Marx was antipathetic. While this may have been a highly natural impulse, the results are not always happy. When one overhears the worshippers of Rodbertus speaking of *Unser Denker*, almost is one persuaded to be a Marxian.

But if in Germany Rodbertus was for a time a philosopher almost grotesquely overrated (by some), he has exercised no influence and has never excited more than the most tepid interest in this country. Even the gallant, if somewhat uninspired, attempt of the late Sir Edward Gonner to present *The Social Philosophy of Rodbertus* to the English-speaking world made little impression on the general indifference. Rodbertus has remained little more than a name which the navigator of the Marxian wastes periodically encounters on the fringes of his explorations.

While therefore he may not be ignored, nevertheless in this country and for this generation, he receives adequate attention if, despite his priority in time, he is treated somewhat summarily as a supplementary note to Marx. The man himself, in his aloofness from the battle, in his leisured air of well-being, provides an interesting contrast to Marx and Lassalle alike. He was a lawyer, practising—but not for too long—in the State service. While still young, he bought the estate of Jagetzow in Pomerania, and was consequently known as Rodbertus-Jagetzow. He played some part in local politics, and indeed was for a few weeks, in 1848, Minister of Education. Thereafter he was the cultured country squire, dividing his time between the management of his estate and speculations on what was wrong with the world, and how, given a few centuries, it could be put right. In the peace of his Rittergut, he was able to view things from afar.

Rodbertus, in his general theoretical position, is not far removed from Marx; though indeed the same is true of the early English pre-Marxian socialists. In other words, he is largely engaged in pushing Ricardian conclusions a stage further to serve ends of which Ricardo never dreamed. There is a good deal of justification for calling him the ' Ricardo of Economic Socialism '—a phrase coined by Wagner.[1] But though Rodbertus and Marx are not far apart in the main as theoretical analysts of the world and of ' Capital,' there is nevertheless a considerable difference in the atmosphere. Rodbertus is interested in the ' Social Problem ' and its solution. He would have said that his life was devoted *Zur Beleuchtung der Sozialen Frage*—to quote the title of his most significant book—to the illumination of the social problem. And if anyone asks what he understood by the ' social problem,' the answer here is singularly precise, and perhaps somewhat limited. Expressly in his own words, the social problem consists, and consists exclusively, in *Pauperismus* and *Handelskrisen*—in the prevalent increasing poverty and in commercial crises.[2] Rodbertus throughout is concerned, directly or indirectly, with these two questions and with these two questions alone. It is indeed his unquestioned merit that no one previously had placed what we should now call the Trade Cycle so completely and so emphatically in the centre of things, as in large measure the source of the world's maladies.

The dominant factor in Rodbertus' economic theorising is to be found in his unquestioning acceptance of the Ricardian Law of Wages, in the sense in which it was also understood by Lassalle. Whether or not this was a faithful interpretation is immaterial. Wages, he asserts, have never, or for any length of time, been above the necessary subsistence level.[3] He uses the same adjective as does Lassalle: it is the *grausame Gesetz*, whereby wages gravitate to the level of bare necessities.[4] To arrive, almost prematurely, at the central and most

[1] Introduction to *Zur Beleuchtung der Sozialen Frage*, Theil II, p. xxv.

[2] *Erster Brief an Von Kirchmann.*

[3] *Zur Beleuchtung der Sozialen Frage*, Theil I, Zweiter Brief, p. 51.

[4] *Offener Brief an das Comité des Deutschen Arbeitervereins zu Leipzig*, reprinted as Appendix to Kozak, *Rodbertus-Jagetzow's Socialökonomische Ansichten*, p. 339.

characteristic idea in Rodbertus' presentation, we must combine this statement of the Iron Law of Wages in its most brazen form with the undoubted fact that wealth is increasing, that we are living in an age of ever-increasing abundance. If wages are depressed to subsistence level (with, if possible, a tendency downwards), while the sum total of wealth is simultaneously increasing, it follows naturally and ineluctably that that part of the national dividend that is devoted to wages must represent a diminishing share of the nation's income. Thus we arrive at the Law of the Diminishing Wage Share. The amount of wages need not decline absolutely; with an increase in the number of workers, the total wage-bill would presumably rise. But the proportion which it bears to the total will, as things are, go on falling. Wages, the reward of the 'labouring classes,' will be a perpetually shrinking share of the nation's wealth.[1]

It is this Law of the Diminishing Wage-Share which, for Rodbertus, sheds a light on most dark places. It is the operation of this law which must be abrogated, if the world is to be healed. Though slightly off our main path, it may be noted that it furnishes, to Rodbertus' satisfaction, an explanation of commercial crises. The trade cycle (to use later terminology) rests on the fact that purchasing power and productivity do not keep in step. Rather is it true that the purchasing power of the largest part of society diminishes in proportion to increased productivity. Consequently, society finds itself producing use-values which are no longer market-values, although need, so far as concerns most of the population, is still unsatisfied.[2] Waiving the phraseology of Rodbertus, which has here a somewhat Marxian aroma, the explanation of the trade cycle here offered is that periodically maladjustments arise, because of a comparative failure of purchasing power on the part of a large part of the population. It is extremely doubtful whether the 'diminishing wage-share' can logically be called upon to bear the burden thus placed upon it; but the theory has obvious kinship with various later lines of thought.

But though the 'Commercial Crisis' is almost half the picture in Rodbertus' presentation, its significance lies chiefly in the fact that it periodically accentuates the poverty and the misery already prevalent. Let us look somewhat more closely at these 'labouring classes,' and see their position in the scheme of things. First of all—a general consideration—all commodities are, for Rodbertus, the product of labour and of labour only: putting it otherwise, all wealth is the

[1] The Law of the Diminishing Wage Share is so recurrent and so fundamental in Rodbertus, that one of his more precise statements may be given: 'Die Vertheilung des Nationalprodukts nach den "natürlichen" Gesetzen des Tauschverkehrs bringt es mit sich, dass bei steigender Produktivität der Arbeit, der Lohn der Arbeiter ein immer kleinerer Antheil am Produkt wird' (*Zur Beleuchtung der Sozialen Frage*, Theil I, p. 47). Elsewhere he uses the phrase: 'eine immer kleinere Quote des Nationalprodukts' (Vorwort to *Erster Brief an von Kirchmann*).

[2] *Zur Beleuchtung der Sozialen Frage*, Theil I, p. 50.

creation of labour. Yet the labourers do not receive what they produce, nor on the basis of what they produce. Nor let anyone say that they are paid 'out of capital,' as the later Wages Fund Theory would have us believe. They are paid out of what they produce. Capital is merely 'vorgethane Arbeit'—labour previously accomplished, requiring present labour to make it effective. There are only two kinds of income. There is, firstly, rent, which Rodbertus uses comprehensively to cover the revenue derived from the ownership of land and of capital alike. It is, in either case, an income derived by virtue of possession and without labour; and rent can arise only when society has advanced so far that labour produces more than it requires, and when there are arrangements and institutions which deprive the labourer of his surplus and enable it to be transferred to others. Apart from rent (comprehensively used to cover all unearned incomes) there are wages, which in effect are what is left over after all deductions have been made.[1]

We have witnessed the operation of the Iron Law (though the copyright in the phrase belongs to Lassalle). If we grope for the 'sanctions' behind the Iron Law, we find that ultimately it derives its force from the fact that land and capital have become vested in individuals as their private possessions. The owners, confronting workers with empty hands, are thus enabled to allow them to work only on conditions; and the conditions imposed (if things are left to themselves) are naturally that the worker, in return for permission to live, shall surrender a portion, and ultimately the whole, of his surplus produce.[2] The ultimate cause of poverty and instability, working back through the diminishing wage-share and the Iron Law of Wages, is thus found in the private ownership of land and the means of production. Here is the seat of the world's malady.

But indeed the position of the working classes is even worse than this analysis discloses. Not only does the 'natural' wage exclude the worker from any share in his own mounting productivity, but simultaneously the burden of taxation imposed on him tends to increase until proportionately he has become the most heavily taxed of all, while at the same time he shares least in the benefits of State expenditure.[3] These are indeed, in Rodbertus' own words, *Berge von Unrecht* —mountains of injustice. He might have quoted his favourite Shakespeare. What are the working classes but camels, who have their provand only for bearing burdens?

All this is the result of leaving things to 'natural' laws, and, assuming that the analysis is correct, Rodbertus is abundantly right

[1] Most of this is drawn from the *Zweiter Brief an von Kirchmann.*
[2] *Dritter Brief an von Kirchmann.*
[3] *Zur Beleuchtung der Sozialen Frage,* Theil II, p. 20.

in suggesting that these ' natural ' laws should be replaced by ' rational ' laws; in place of what is *natürlich*, we ought to establish what is *vernünftig*. It is an emphatic voice of protest against *laissez faire* and all its ways. On the side of social philosophy, as distinct from economic analysis, it is the most distinctive and abiding note in Rodbertus. The dominance of the private owner subjects the world to caprice, whereas we should be guided by reason and foresight. It is to the State that we must look for unbiased judgment and for decisions in the common interest of all: it is to the State that we must look in future for the conduct of enterprise. The worship of the State (using the words in no metaphorical sense) is a well-defined tradition in German thought, and to Rodbertus the State is divine. States pursue *nur göttliche Ziele*. Politics is the *höchste und königlichste Kunst*; and States themselves are *die edelste Bildungen die es auf der Erde giebt*,[1] These phrases are best left in the original; they are so alien to our way of thinking that any attempted translation might convey a suggestion of burlesque, or even of mockery, not present in Rodbertus' words. He belonged to the generation of Germans who quoted Shakespeare, seeking by preference their inspiration in less familiar passages; it is not without significance that he places in the forefront the words of Ulysses in *Troilus and Cressida*:

> There is a mystery—with whom relation
> Durst never meddle—in the soul of state;
> Which hath an operation more divine
> Than breath or pen can give expressure to.

In one passage of fundamental importance, Rodbertus outlines his views of the nature of the State and of its responsibilities for its own development. States, he says, are organisms, living organisms, and therefore subject to perpetual development. Moreover, they lead a *selbstschöpferisches Leben*; they are self-creative, and it is their task to prescribe the line of their own development, and to devise such organs as may be necessary for the fulfilment of their own destiny.[2] The passage, which has a certain eloquence has also a certain nebulousness; but it is clear that, in Rodbertus' view, States prescribe their own path down the course of history, that it is their task and their chief labour to devise laws and measures which will keep them in the right way, as equally to avoid laws and measures which will lead them astray. Here at least is a vision of purpose, of design, of continuity. With the aid of such a State, consciously pursuing an end determined by itself, we may hope to bring things more into conformity with reason, or at least—for Rodbertus is no optimist—we may prevent things from getting worse. But, on the threshold, it is as well to clear away certain

[1] *Zur Beleuchtung der Sozialen Frage*, Theil II, pp. 64–66.
[2] *Ibid.* pp. 58–60.

possible deluding suggestions. We have seen that the root-trouble lies in the present ownership of land and capital, which has as a consequence that the workers with weak bargaining power—if indeed they have any at all—are compelled to sell their labour at bare subsistence rates. It is, however, no solution to suggest that land or capital, or indeed the product of labour itself, should belong to the worker. As in Lassalle, the principle of division of labour plays a quite large part in the theorisings of Rodbertus. It is division of labour that gives unity to society; but also it is division of labour that makes private property possible and renders exploitation inevitable. With the utmost emphasis, accordingly, Rodbertus declares (somewhat flamboyantly) that so long as division of labour pours out over society the cornucopia of its inestimable treasures, *neither* land, *nor* labour, *nor* the product of labour may be allowed to belong to the worker.[1] In short, under division of labour it is impossible to say what anyone produces: production is a social process.

Further, the 'right to the whole produce of labour' is a delusion because of deductions which must be made. All commodities are, as has been seen, the products of labour, and only labour entering directly into production has to be taken into account. In his first main statements, Rodbertus rather tends to side-track all work other than manual work. This does not, however, mean that there are not other activities, essential to the continuance of the Commonwealth, which need to be maintained. There is the doctor; there is the judge; there are the instruments of administration. Before the workers' share is determined, there must be an appropriate deduction to meet these essential claims. Subject to these reservations, rewards should be based on work done; just as, in a rational society, value, if not determined by labour, would at least be based on labour, so that in exchange equivalent sacrifices on the two sides would be involved.

Rodbertus has a tolerably precise view of the future—the very remote future—to which we are tending. It will be the complete example of State Socialism, where the State is divine, and where, at least by inference, the State authorities are perfectly wise and the rest of the population perfectly docile, so that they are under no temptation to question the State's perfect wisdom. The *Leitung*, the administration, of all things would be in the hands of the State, and all income would rest on work done and services rendered. With regard to the more immediate future, Rodbertus' vision is more clouded. Let us not delude ourselves. The world is not yet ready for socialism—will not be ready for socialism for another five hundred years. It is not for our time. The free will of society is not yet strong enough to do without the compulsion to work; there are hints that we still need the *Geissel der Noth*, the scourge of need, to impel us onwards. In

[1] *Zur Beleuchtung der Sozialen Frage, Dritter Brief*, pp. 82–85.

short our moral strength is not yet great enough ; we have not yet ended our journey in the wilderness. Moreover, the owners of capital and land—but perhaps especially the owners of land, since Rodbertus was a landowner—discharge certain functions which the State is not yet ready to take over. Consequently, possession must not for the present be disturbed. Present conditions may represent ' mountains of injustice ' ; but as we are insufficiently developed morally, we must just lump it for a few centuries longer.[1] The inevitability of Mr. Sidney Webb's gradualness was as nothing compared to the gradualness of Rodbertus' inevitability.

Meanwhile measures should be taken to prevent a further deterioration, or perhaps even to effect an improvement. It is significant for Rodbertus' outlook that he turns to the throne for effective leadership. A socialist monarchy, or a monarchy preparing the path to socialism is his ideal.[2] Except on one point, his ameliorative measures are statements of ends, rather than of means to ends. Rent (in his sense) should be restricted ; the Law of the Diminishing Wage-share must be counteracted—indeed, wages must rise. The workers' demand for *mehr Besitz*, a larger share of what is going, must be satisfied [3] ; and with the increased productivity which will spring from better organisation, it will be possible to meet this claim without in any way curtailing (meantime) what others receive. The workers must be protected against the uncertainties of the trade cycle ; and taxation, now pressing on the worker with unjustifiable weight, must be reformed.

The one point on which (perhaps unfortunately) Rodbertus aimed at a more specific remedy was his suggestion for the prescription of a normal working day. This, with the Law of the Diminishing Wage-share, is what has remained most closely associated with the name of Rodbertus. Perhaps at the first blush the phrase is slightly misleading. Rodbertus was not concerned with anything so commonplace as a mere restriction of hours. Rather he aimed at the definition (inevitably to be done by tbe State) of a unit of work constituting for each occupation the normal working day. There should be a definite performance in normal time. This would open the way to equitable exchanges ; it would assure the worker a share in increased productivity ; and it would also make it possible to dispense with money. The State would in effect define for all industries what should be regarded as equivalent amounts of output, and workers would be paid accordingly with certificates testifying the amount of normal days' work accomplished. These would then be exchangeable for other

[1] Conclusion of *Dritter Brief*, *Zur Beleuchtung der Sozialen Frage*, pp. 221–222. Also *Zweiter Brief*, p. 28.

[2] ' Es ist dies deshalb von Bedeutung, weil, sobald ein ernstes Vorgehen beabsichtigt wird, es nur von Vortheil sein kann, wenn das Königthum als Schöpfer und Führer der Reform erscheint ' (*Sendschreiben an den Arbeitercongress*, etc.).

[3] *Die Forderungen der arbeitenden Klassen.*

commodities representing the same amount of normal working days. The central authority would doubtless have to be incessantly engaged in redefining the unit of work: they would also have to assume responsibility for the issue of the necessary paper money, and they would have to devise a *Magazinirungsystem*,—surely an unnecessarily barbarous word—a system of depots where goods could be deposited for exchange.[1] One seems to feel the near presence of Robert Owen. Apart from the incessant necessary task of tinkering with the appropriate units, the proposal gapes with difficulties. Among other things it is based on the fallacious Marxian assumption that all labour results in commodities. Where there is no measurable product, the task of defining the unit for the day's work is insoluble. Well might Adler say that Rodbertus' theory of labour-money conceals in itself a veritable nest of errors—*ein wahres Nest von Irrtümern.*[2] He picks out ten 'grave defects'; but this by no means leaves the nest empty.

Such, much too briefly, is *unser Denker*—an interesting figure who, if he was at one time unduly exalted, is perhaps now in danger of being unduly neglected. Without doubt, for what it is worth, he had a certain priority over Marx: he had certainly considerable influence on Lassalle and on the more academic socialists of Germany. In so far as concerns the substance of his teaching, it is obvious that a world intent on explaining away Marx, can scarcely be expected to be kinder to Rodbertus. In some respects, indeed, there is a certain similarity in the attitude adopted by their admirers. Adolf Wagner may be regarded as having been the High Priest of the cult of Rodbertus. Writing as far back as 1885, he defined his attitude to his master. The majority of Rodbertus' theoretical doctrines, he says somewhat bluntly, are false: in particular—and he proceeds to enumerate—his theory of value, his theory of rent and capital-formation, of population, of crises, his monetary and banking theories, *und anderes mehr.* It is a curious position. Apparently, according to his chief admirer, little that Rodbertus said is defensible or tenable, yet he remains a *bahnbrechende Denker* and an abiding inspiration. As we have seen, it is not so different in the case of Marx, where the efforts of his disciples have been increasingly devoted to showing that though each individual Marxian theory may have to be tossed to the critical wolves, yet the structure as a whole and the Marxian spirit remain above criticism. Otherwise Rodbertus is perhaps a somewhat ineffective philosopher. Never was there so complete a Fabian; never was there a socialist so conservative in his fundamental instincts. Somewhat ostentatiously, he shunned the dust and the heat and the turmoil.[3] Partly

[1] *Die Forderungen der arbeitenden Klassen.*

[2] Adler: *Rodbertus, der Begründer des wissenschaftlichen Sozialismus*, p. 83.

[3] 'Da ich kein Agitator bin und sein will, sondern nur nach wissenschaftlicher Wahrheit trachte' (*Zur Beleuchtung der Sozialen Frage*, Theil II, p. 19).

he was a pessimist; partly he was timorous. What could be more pessimistic than his firm conviction that the school can avail nothing against the grime and the need of the homes from which the children come?[1] What could be more pessimistic than his belief that we are morally still some centuries behind the standard which socialism demands? And fear too was in his heart. In the peace of his Rittergut, he was haunted by the thought that society might be producing a race of barbarians in soul and in spirit; that there might yet be new waves of barbarian invasions, coming from within society itself—rude men who preferred to lay waste the seats of civilisation rather than endure its miseries longer.[2] One thinks of Mably who also wrung his hands; one thinks of von Thünen who also, in his country retreat, brooded over the miseries of his less fortunate fellows. Rodbertus was pre-eminently a man of culture—probably of too much culture. His writings reveal a sensitiveness and a sympathy which are entirely lacking in the more metallic purple patches of Marx and Lassalle. In the end it is difficult not to feel kindly towards him—an earnest, sincere and just man, slightly fearful, made vaguely uncomfortable by the roughness of men who were nevertheless his fellows, and trying to forgive in advance those hordes of wronged barbarians who, in their frustration, might one day invade Jagetzow and trample his Shakespeare under foot.

[1] 'Der Schmutz und die Noth werden ewig zu nichte machen, was der Unterricht der Schulen bewirken will' (*Die Forderungen der arbeitenden Klassen*).

[2] *Erster Brief an von Kirchmann*; also *Die Forderungen der arbeitenden Klassen.*

CHAPTER XIII

THE ANARCHIST TRADITION

(*a*) BAKUNIN

MR. E. H. CARR, in his wholly admirable biography of Michael Bakunin, has presented a very living and very human picture of the most influential force in modern anarchism, and those who desire an intimate insight into the curious and contradictory elements which went to the making of this enigmatic figure may safely be referred to Mr. Carr. Equally, Mr. Gerald Brenan, in disentangling *The Spanish Labyrinth*, has unfolded the quite extraordinary influence which Bakunin has exercised in countries remote from Premukhino where he began his troubled and tempestuous life. Though it may be difficult to come by his writings (such as they are) we in this generation have little excuse for being ignorant about him.[1]

Bakunin was born to become a legend. Rising above his aristocratic traditions, he became a revolutionary by profession, associating himself with anything that might be termed an insurrection or revolt, and ultimately developing an insensate rage for destruction. Years of imprisonment and years of exile in Siberia (where, however, like Lenin, he does not appear to have been particularly unhappy) left him, after his escape to Western Europe by way of America, a great, bearded, toothless giant, returning like a spectre from the past to uphold the cause of anarchism and federalism against the authority of Marx. He remained a chaotic figure—chaotic in his life, chaotic in his thought, chaotic in his writings—thoroughly unpractical and destitute of common sense, as becomes an anarchist, yet with something about him of a likeable but rather spoiled child, mingling the real with the imaginary and playing at make-believe conspiracies, with all the paraphernalia of codes and cyphers designed to be used in communication with possibly non-existent correspondents.

Bakunin's place and influence in history are, in a sense, much more significant than his place in thought. There is justice in the criticism that, in his case, a pose takes the place of an argument. His writings are incoherent, and despite all his affectations of activity they are but scattered fragments. Nowhere is there a consecutive exposition of his views as a whole; and a grudging commentator might further suggest that even the substance of what he says is largely derived from his predecessors in the anarchist tradition. For the essence of Bakunin

[1] For those who have access to it, there is also a tolerable biographical notice prefixed to the second of the six volumes of Bakunin's published works.

is to a considerable extent a restatement of Proudhon by one bred in a Russian environment, with perhaps more distant memories of Godwin, though probably these are not so much the result of any Godwinian influence, direct or indirect, as the natural outcome of the anarchist way of looking at things. On the other hand, Bakunin, whatever his claims as a thinker and a theorist—and they are probably small—has nevertheless continued to play a considerable part in the unfolding of events. Much of the history of the First International was coloured by the feud between Marx and Bakunin, and it was indeed because of this clash of personality that the First International was ultimately extinguished. Even more significant is the fact that, so far as anarchism has been a distinct movement in more recent times, it is primarily to Bakunin that it has looked for inspiration, even if perhaps it be the inspiration derived from a legendary figure. In a chapter designed to illustrate the anarchist tradition subsequent to Proudhon, Bakunin must therefore be assigned the first place.

So far as Bakunin's analysis of existing society is concerned, it cannot be said that he differs materially from what is the core of the Marxian position. It is a world of exploitation, of class antagonism, with the State and the machinery of the State merely the property of one of these classes. As opposed to *les classes politiques* (which a conjectural footnote suggests should probably read *les classes privilégiées*) are *les classes ouvrières*, the disinherited, deprived of capital, of land and of education. Between these is a yawning gulf which may not be bridged.[1] Labour is thus the slave, the bondsman, of capital and of property. The civilisation of the few is based on the forced labour and the relative barbarism of the many.[2] It is not merely that some live at the expense of others[3]; but in bourgeois society, as we know it, every individual is necessarily impelled to be an exploiter of others.[4] In one place he defines property and capital as the power and the right to live on the labour of others, to exploit the labour of others who, possessing neither property nor capital, are compelled to sell their productive forces.[5] Moreover, throughout history, the State has always been the patrimony of some privileged class interested in its existence; indeed, for the safety of the State it is essential that there be some privileged class which is thus interested in its existence.[6]

This, however, is not of the essence of Bakunin. He may resent exploitation, but it is only in so far as exploitation is but a phase of

[1] *Fédéralisme, Socialisme et Antithéologisme,* Œuvres, vol. 1, p. 24.
[2] *Ibid.* pp. 26, 30.
[3] *Lettres aux Internationaux du Jura,* Œuvres, vol. 1, p. 255.
[4] *Dieu et l'État,* Œuvres, vol. 1, p. 314.
[5] Appendix to *L'Empire Knouto-Germanique et la Révolution Sociale,* Œuvres, vol. 3, p. 191.
[6] *Lettres aux Internationaux du Jura,* Œuvres, vol. 1, p. 226.

a much larger evil. What moves Bakunin is tyranny, and by tyranny he means any infringement of liberty. 'La Liberté, toujours la Liberté, rien que la Liberté,' had been the motto of his teacher Proudhon; and Bakunin equalled, if it was hardly possible for him to surpass, the uncompromising attitude of his master in this respect. It was his grievance against the earlier socialists that—Proudhon apart—they had been inspired by a passion for *réglementation*.[1] Liberty, he held, was indivisible. Cut off the minutest fraction, and the whole is gone; 'All my liberty is concentrated just precisely in that part, however small it may be, which you cut off.'[2] And the conclusion is pleasingly illustrated by reference to the wife of Blue Beard, who, being forbidden to enter one room, had no liberty whatever. Doubtless recalling Godwin's maxim that the first principle of morality is to disobey, she just had to enter the forbidden room as 'un acte nécessaire de sa liberté.' So, turning from very profane to sacred history, the same is true of the sin of Adam and Eve. The one prohibition imposed by the Almighty was 'un acte d'affreux despotisme.' Had they obeyed, the whole human race would have remained plunged in the most humiliating slavery: their disobedience was the first act of human liberty. Our first parents are to be commended because they underlined the two distinguishing features of man: 'la faculté de penser et le besoin de se révolter.'[3] The point is of some interest in connection with Bakunin's general political views to which we shall come presently: any command is an outrage to be resented and the only possible reply is disobedience—on principle.

The core of Bakunin thus consists in the repudiation of all authority, and—if rebellion means disobedience—rebellion against any authority claiming power of command, which by definition involves a restriction, and therefore complete annihilation of liberty. But indeed there are only two authorities which thus claim the submission and the obedience of man. There is God, and there is the State, who find themselves yoked together on the title-page of Bakunin's best-known pamphlet.[4] When God and the State are repudiated and overthrown, there will be no one to issue commands, and man will enter on a blessed era of Proudhonian liberty.

The revolt against God (or the idea of God) and the rebellion against the State—his atheism and his anarchism—may, in a sense, be regarded as the two phases of Bakunin's gospel of disobedience; but it would be truer to say that in his mind the two tyrants melt into one. As Sir Thomas Browne observed long ago, atheism can hardly exist; Bacon, pretty much to the same effect, held that the great

1 *Fédéralisme, Socialisme et Antithéologisme*, Œuvres, vol. 1, p. 39.
2 *Ibid.* p. 144.
3 *L'Empire Knouto-Germanique et la Révolution Sociale*, Œuvres, vol. 3, p. 19.
4 Not that the title of this fragment was chosen by Bakunin.

atheists are indeed hypocrites. In the case of Bakunin, it is not always clear whether he is frothing against God, or against man's imaginings of God; whether he is seeking to unseat a God who is, or chiding men for their folly in inventing a God who is not. This, happily, is not a history of atheism, and this phase of Bakunin might have been entirely ignored, but for the fact that it is inextricably intermingled with his political views and serves to illumine his anarchism.

In Bakunin's views, anarchism and atheism are almost interchangeable terms, though at times perhaps his atheism should rather be described as anti-clericalism. The revolution is, he says, bound to be atheistical; and the reason he gives is the rather surprising one that experience and logic alike show that one superior in heaven is sufficient to create thousands of superiors on earth.[1] Putting it otherwise, the idea of a superior being, even in the remoteness of heaven, must be extirpated, in order that there may be no encouragement to the idea of superiority on earth. Moreover, the Church (embodying the idea of religion and of God) and the State owe their origin to the same causes. They are alike instruments for the enslavement of the mass of humanity by the few. In a picturesque phrase, the State is the younger brother—*le frère cadet*—of the Church; and therefore the attack must be made on both together. And indeed, the close relationship of Church and State in Russia may explain a good deal, not merely in Bakunin, but in more recent history.

For the rest, Bakunin's atheism need be glanced at only in so far as it presents a precise analogy with his anarchism. The governing consideration is that the existence of an acknowledged superior anywhere implies and encourages subjection and slavery elsewhere. In what is meant to be an epigrammatic summary:

> Dieu est, donc l'homme est esclave,
> L'homme est intelligent, juste, libre—donc Dieu n'existe pas.[2]

With this is combined the essentially Proudhonian idea that inasmuch as religion teaches dependence and subjection, it undermines the dignity of man. A Christian, whatever else he may be—and he may be a prophet, a saint, a priest, a king and much more—cannot be a *man*, because, having no respect for human dignity in himself, he cannot respect it in others.[3] The essence of all religions lies in the *dénigrement* of humanity for the greater glory of what is divine.[4] Moreover, by curious reasoning which the enquirer may find in *God and*

[1] *Fédéralisme, Socialisme et Antithéologisme*, Œuvres, vol. 1, p. 89.

[2] *Ibid.* p. 64. The presumed dilemma recurs in substantially the same words in *L'Empire Knouto-Germanique et la Révolution Sociale* (Œuvres, vol. 3, pp. 43–44), with an added defiance to ' qui que ce soit ' to find a way of escape.

[3] *Dieu et l'État*, Œuvres, vol. 1, p. 280.

[4] *L'Empire Knouto-Germanique et la Révolution Sociale : Seconde livraison*, Œuvres, vol. 3, p. 62.

the State, the ideas of God and of immortality are fatal to love among men. They lead to complete egotism: protestantism in particular is a religious *sauve qui peut*.[1] Religion is necessarily anti-social; for the idea of God excludes everything else. To the religious man, his relation to God is the one thing that matters. Consequently he has morally no need of his fellows.[2] Nor is love possible except among equals. What is called the love between God and man, in view of their inequality, implies the despotism of the one and the slavery of the other. The only way in which God could emancipate man would be for him to abdicate.[3] All very well for Bakunin to suggest the abdication of the Almighty; but to whom should the abdication be addressed? and what would happen to Bakunin and the rest of us on the abdication of God, in whom we live and move and have our being? It is doubtless a profound metaphysical question, but Bakunin seems to have hit on the one thing that the Almighty cannot do. To Voltaire's famous phrase that if there had been no God, it would have been necessary for man to invent one, he retorts that 'si Dieu existait réellement, il faudrait le faire disparaître.'[4] What between the suggested abdication of God and Bakunin's readiness to make the Almighty disappear, we move in a strange world.[5]

This digression into a somewhat alien field may be excused in that it helps to an understanding of Bakunin, and facilitates the next stage of our journey. For his attitude to the State is merely, *mutatis mutandis*, the reflection of his attitude to God. If there is perhaps greater violence in his denunciation of the State, that is merely because the State is a more obviously immediate and ever-present tyrant. But the State also, in its very essence, issues commands, and thereby invades and destroys liberty, that choicest treasure. With surprisingly little variety of language, he repeats that the State is the negation of all liberty, that it is the sum of the negations of the liberties of all

[1] *Dieu et l'État*, Œuvres, vol. 1, p. 304.

[2] *Ibid.* p. 316. His fellows may indeed be an obstacle to the attainment of God. There is a hard saying, not wholly to be explained away as an example of oriental hyperbole, that 'if any man come to me, and hate not his father, and mother, and wife and children, and brethren, and his sisters . . . he cannot be my disciple.' Mr. Tawney, in summing up and commenting on the teaching of Luther, uses the significant words: 'the soul is isolated from the society of men, that it may enter into communion with its Maker' (*Religion and the Rise of Capitalism*, chapter II, (ii)).

[3] *Ibid.* pp. 317–318.

[4] *L'Empire Knouto-Germanique et la Révolution Sociale*, Œuvres, vol. 3, p. 48.

[5] Bakunin's theology is somewhat too often on the level of the blasphemings of the village atheist; *e.g.* 'Dieu est précisément une absurdité' (*Dieu et l'État*, Œuvres, vol. 1, p. 269). God is also 'L'absurdité par excellence' (*ibid.* p. 310). Even so, it is possible that Bakunin is insufficiently read in Divinity Faculties: it might be a useful college exercise to require theological students to write a reasoned refutation of the relevant passages of *Dieu et l'État* and of *L'Empire Knouto-Germanique*.

individuals, and much more.[1] It comes as a welcome change of phraseology to find, in a rather lumbering metaphor, that the State is an immense cemetery, in which all the manifestations of individual and local life, all that makes up 'society,' comes to be sacrificed, to die and to be interred.[2] The State has further this evil property in common with the Church that it assumes that all men are *foncièrement mauvais*.[3] It is almost a commonplace of religion to assume that every man from his youth is given to evil; the State in no way lags behind its elder brother in holding that men are incapable of looking after themselves, and that they need to be governed and punished. To cull, almost at random, a few more flowers for this anthology, it may be noted that crime is a necessary condition of the existence of the State; it is, rather oddly, its exclusive monopoly.[4] The State implies domination, and all domination implies the existence of masses who are dominated.[5] It is the guarantor of all exploiters, a device in which the minority plays the part of the hammer and the majority that of the anvil.[6] Perhaps, however, the most arresting and illuminating characterisation of the State is to be found in the culminating sentences of a long denunciatory passage in *God and the State*. Because of its peculiar flavour, it should preferably be left in French:

> L'État c'est l'autorité, c'est la force, c'est l'ostentation et l'infatuation de la force. Il ne s'insinue pas, il ne cherche pas à convertir: et toutes les fois qu'il s'en mêle, il le fait de très mauvaise grâce; car sa nature, ce n'est point de persuader, mais de s'imposer, de forcer. . . . Alors même qu'il commande le bien, il le dessert et le gâte, précisément parce qu'il le commande, et que tout commandement provoque et suscite les révoltes légitimes de la liberté; et parce que le bien, du moment qu'il est commandé . . . devient le mal. La liberté, la moralité et la dignité humaine de l'homme consiste précisément en ceci, qu'il fait le bien, non parce qu'il lui est commandé, mais parce qu'il le conçoit, qu'il le veut et qu'il l'aime.[7]

Even when the State commands what is good, the good thereby becomes evil, and the State's action excites 'legitimate revolts.' It is elsewhere said to be a 'legitimate sentiment' that arouses every man to rebellion against any measures imposed upon him, even if liberty itself is the ultimate object.[8] We are back, it will be observed, with the wife of Blue Beard, standing before the forbidden door. A mere command

[1] *E.g. Fédéralisme, Socialisme et Antithéologisme*, Œuvres, vol. 1, pp. 12, 143; *Lettres aux Internationaux du Jura*, vol. 1, p. 227; and almost throughout the six volumes.

[2] *Lettres aux Internationaux du Jura*, Œuvres, vol. 1, p. 225.

[3] *Fédéralisme, Socialisme et Antithéologisme*, Œuvres, vol. 1, p. 160; *Lettres aux Internationaux du Jura*, Œuvres, vol. 1, p. 224.

[4] *Les Ours de Berne et l'Ours de Saint Petersbourg*, Œuvres, vol. 2, p. 24.

[5] *L'Empire Knouto-Germanique et la Révolution Sociale*, Œuvres, vol. 2, p. 326.

[6] *Trois Conférences faites aux ouvriers du Val de Saint Imier*, Œuvres, vol. 5, p. 312.

[7] *Dieu et l'État*, Œuvres, vol. 1, p. 288.

[8] *Lettres à un français sur la crise actuelle*, Œuvres, vol. 2, p. 95.

spoils everything; the duty of disobedience overrides every other consideration—including what might otherwise have been our own desires in the matter.

All this leads inevitably to the repudiation of any and every body that claims to exercise any measure of control, to the rejection of any proposed organisation which involves the establishment of a regulating authority of any kind whatever.[1] From all these many iniquities and blemishes of the State, from the fact that it is in all regards a flagrant violation of humanity, entangling mankind in slavery, and much more, inadequately sampled in the foregoing illustrations, Bakunin infers the 'absolute necessity of the destruction of States'[2]; and in a significant phrase he extends his definition of Revolution, which means war, to cover the destruction of men *and of things*.[3] Destruction becomes an end in itself.

That way lies madness, a wild dream of 'amorphism,' of the universal destruction of all social institutions; and in Nihilism, which represents the development of this rage for destruction, we do in fact find a froth of words which could spring only from a mind where reason has been unseated. In the literature which centres round Bakunin, a quite prominent place has been assigned to the *Revolutionary Catechism*, a document in cipher produced at the trial of Netchaïeff in 1871.[4] It is probable that Bakunin was in fact the author of this document; this at least is the view of Mr. Carr, and his authority should be good enough for most. With this should be taken the Programme of the *Alliance de la Démocratie Socialiste*,[5] a body which was the peculiar creature of Bakunin. In these documents, anarchism, so far from being as in Godwin something like a hang-over from the Garden of Eden, becomes a propaganda of assassination, of universal destruction, of the necessity of ruthlessly and brutally so proceeding that not one stone shall be left standing on another. Chaos and old night are to come again, without overmuch thought of what is to follow chaos. Even if Bakunin may not have been the author of the *Revolutionary Catechism*, he certainly inspired and approved it. It is more plausible, but again a poor defence, to suggest that Bakunin, especially in his old age, liked to play the Bogy-man, until even he himself was impressed.[6]

[1] 'L'établissement d'une autorité réglémentaire de quelque nature que ce fût. *Fédéralisme, Socialisme et Antithéologisme*, Œuvres, vol. 1, p. 56.

[2] *Fédéralisme, Socialisme et Antithéologisme*, Œuvres, vol. 1, pp. 155–157.

[3] *Les Ours de Berne et l'Ours de Saint Petersbourg*, Œuvres, vol. 2, p. 20.

[4] See, *e.g.* Laveleye: *Le Socialisme Contemporain*, p. 237; Rae, *Contemporary Socialism*, p. 275.

[5] Laveleye: *op. cit.* pp. 229, 234.

[6] A very few sentences from these two documents may illustrate the shady underworld to which one side of Bakunin leads.

From the *Revolutionary Catechism*: 'The revolutionist is a man under a vow. He ought to have no personal interests, no business, no sentiments, no property. He ought to occupy himself entirely with one exclusive interest, with one thought

Let us resist the allurements which draw us towards amorphism and chaos, and the contemplation of Bakunin vigorously sweeping with the besom of destruction, and ask whether it is possible to find in him hints of a not-impossible world. Probably the answer we should get to such an enquiry is that, though all States may crumble and perish, nevertheless society may remain ; and it is society and not the State that is the important thing, just as it is society that provides the natural home of man. Beyond this, the answer is found in ' Federalism,' a word admittedly capable of more than one interpretation, but in the anarchist tradition largely implying the spontaneous and voluntary formation of associations. With these pointers, it may help to note how Bakunin in his more sober moments regarded the problem to be solved. He is sufficiently under the influence of Proudhon to define socialism as consisting of justice—most deceitful of words.[1] Justice, needless to say, is not the justice of Roman Law, nor the justice of the Churches, but is the justice which is founded on the *conscience* of man, in its French sense. Even on this definition justice remains somewhat nebulous ; but in Bakunin's view, the problem of justice may be reduced to fairly concrete terms. What is necessary is

> to organise society in such a manner that every individual man or woman, coming into life, should find approximately equal means for the development of his different faculties and for their utilisation by his work ; to organise a society which, making the exploitation of one by another for ever impossible, should allow each one to participate in the enjoyment of social riches (which are never in fact produced by anything but labour) only to the extent to which he will have directly contributed to the production of this wealth by his own labour.[2]

and one passion : the Revolution. . . . He has only one aim, one science : destruction. For that and nothing but that he studies mechanics, physics, chemistry and medicine. He observes with the same object, the men, the characters, the positions and all the conditions of the social order. He despises and hates existing morality. For him everything is moral that favours the triumph of the Revolution. Everything is immoral and criminal that hinders it. . . . Between him and society there is war to the death, incessant, irreconcilable. . . . He must make a list of those who are condemned to death, and expedite their sentence according to the order of their relative iniquities ' (Rae, *op. cit.* p. 275).

From the programme of the *Alliance* : ' The association of international brothers desires the universal revolution, social, philosophic, economic and political at the same time, in order that of the existing order of things, founded on property, on exploitation, on the principle of authority, whether religious or metaphysic, whether *bourgeoisement doctrinaire* or even *jacobinement révolutionnaire*, there shall not rest one stone upon another, at first in the whole of Europe, and later in the rest of the world. To the cry of " Peace to the Workers ! " " Freedom for the Oppressed ! " and of " Death to the tyrants, the exploiters, and guardians of every kind ! " we wish to destroy all States and all Churches, with all their institutions and their laws, *religieuses, politiques, juridiques, financières, policières, universitaires, économiques, et sociales* ' (Laveleye, *op. cit.* p. 234).

These few sentences may provide a sufficient glimpse into comprehensive Amorphism.

[1] *Fédéralisme, Socialisme et Antithéologisme*, Œuvres, vol. 1, p. 54.

[2] *Ibid.* p. 55.

In such a world each will be *le fils de ses œuvres*, and no more; it is a programme which, without pausing to consider how far it is realisable, brings Bakunin very close to the individualistic ideal of the Right-to-the-Whole-Product School in its most literal interpretation.

The environment in which justice, as so interpreted, will be realised, is that of federalism. In one place, Bakunin is surprisingly precise in the matter of federalism, outlining under quite a considerable number of headings the principles on which the United States of Europe may be established.[1] The 'salutary principle of federalism' is opposed to the centralisation and the omnipotence of the State,[2] and a first condition of the United States of Europe is that these States shall be very different from any State we now know. Centralised States may not be admitted; and the only basis of the future organisation of the world is the 'free federation of the individuals in the communes, of the communes in the provinces, of the provinces in the nations, and finally of these nations in the United States, first of all of Europe, and later of the whole world.'[3] At the first blush, this presents the appearance of a somewhat grandiose hierarchical structure; but later governing principles reveal that this sky-scraper, stretching from the individual to the United States of the World, is held together by no steel framework. For it is made clear that every nation, every province, every commune is to enjoy complete autonomy; and that there must be at all times the right of free union and free secession at every stage of the ladder.[4] This is indeed described as the first and most important of political rights: 'no perpetual obligation can be accepted'—nor for that matter, can any obligation, however evanescent. It is difficult to visualise these 'United States of the World,' which is clearly a misnomer as applied to a system in which everything is in perpetual flux; where there are no bonds; and where commune, province, and nation may secede and reaffiliate at less than two minutes' notice.

Along a somewhat different line it might be argued that Bakunin, when he aims at being constructive, almost falls into that tradition which would aim at the replacement of politics by 'administration.' In one place he argues that everything that partakes of the nature of political power must be abolished—for many reasons already cited; but once abolished 'it must be replaced by the organisation of productive forces and economic services.'[5] Elsewhere in the same tract he defines the ultimate aim as 'the transformation of the political federation into a national and international economic federation.'[6] This may be nebulous, but it is not intentional 'amorphism.' As

[1] *Fédéralisme, Socialisme et Antithéologisme*, Œuvres, vol. 1, pp. 14 *et seq.*
[2] *Ibid.* p. 12. [3] *Ibid.* pp. 16–17. [4] *Ibid.* p. 18.
[5] *Les Ours de Berne et l'Ours de Saint Petersbourg*, Œuvres, vol. 2, p. 39.
[6] *Ibid.* p. 57.

has been suggested elsewhere, however, the idea of maintaining economic administration (under whatever name) as something distinct from politics leads nowhere.

In any case there is clearly in all this no political structure; nor is there meant to be. It is of the essence of the anarchist vision that there should be, to fall back on Proudhon's formula, 'no governmentalism.' But there is society which is all that man needs, and which somehow will manage things without the alternating shackles and guidance of Whitehall. Not only so, but it is somewhat surprising to note how necessary, in Bakunin's view, society is for man. Society does not limit man's liberty; it is on the contrary society that creates his liberty.[1] It is the basis of his quite effective criticism of the whole conception of the Social Contract that this fiction recognises only isolated individuals and the resulting State, and forgets all about society, which is the 'natural mode of existence of people living together'[2] quite apart from any contract. Liberty is to be sought, not at the beginning of history, before a contract was devised; it is rather the end to which man moves. The complete emancipation of each individual is the supreme end of history.[3] It is only in society that man becomes man, and Bakunin comes as near as may be to quoting Aristotle. Likewise, so far is it from being true that the liberty of another is an infringement and a curtailment of my liberty, that in fact I can enjoy freedom only if all others are equally free. These are noble sentiments which admirably illustrate the idealist side of anarchism.

One last point before we leave Bakunin. We have seen the State marked for destruction; we have seen society survive. Society is natural and inevitable. In that future world when governmentalism will have passed away, men will still be restrained, and may need restraint. He will be restrained by society without, however, any infringement or curtailment of liberty. Bakunin distinguishes between the official, and therefore tyrannical, authority of the State, and the non-official and entirely natural action of society on each of its members. He comes very near to realising that this authority may be as tyrannical as that exercised by the State. The action of society is acknowledged to be more insinuating, more imperceptible, but perhaps for that reason none the less powerful. It operates through customs, habits, prejudices, traditions. Bakunin indeed speaks of 'la tyrannie sociale, souvent écrasante et funeste'[4] And to rebel against this (and rebellion is the primary duty of every anarchist) is as difficult as to rebel against Nature.[5] The pressure of society on the individual is,

[1] *Dieu et l'État*, Œuvres, vol. 1, p. 275.

[2] *Fédéralisme, Socialisme, et Antithéologisme*, Œuvres, vol. 1, p. 141; *Dieu et l'État*, Œuvres, vol. 1, p. 266.

[3] *Dieu et l'État*, Œuvres, vol. 1, p. 277.

[4] *Ibid.* p. 284.

[5] *Ibid.* p. 286.

as he says, immense.[1] Most men are happy only if they are faithfully following tradition and routine.

The position thus disclosed is somewhat curious. When the State with its armoury of laws has ceased to tyrannise, when we are past this tyrant's stroke, we are to be guided gently by public opinion and the silent pressure of our fellows. But in fact public opinion is a restraining influence only in small communities; and quite consistently anarchists always, professedly or by implication, dream of a world of village communities, where everyone has under his eyes and is actively interested in the occurrences in his neighbours' back-garden. Our neighbours' censure may count for a good deal in Hogsnorton; it counts for nothing, or next to nothing, in Wandsworth and Lewisham. And the further qualm which cannot be laid is this: where the circumstances are such that public opinion might be an effective substitute for a law-giver, it may reach a height of tyranny than which nothing more damnable can be imagined. Bakunin himself has said it: it may be a *tyrannie écrasante et funeste*. Anyone who has lingered with Kafka in the village that lay under *The Castle* will recall with horror one episode revealing how bitter may be the tyranny of proud and self-righteous tongues—a tyranny all the more terrible, because it is a vague, undefined tyranny. There is much to be said for what an earlier political philosopher called 'a known law.'

All of which suggests that Bakunin, in delivering the human race from a visible tyrant, may be subjecting him to a still more grievous tyranny.

(*b*) KROPOTKIN

Prince Kropotkin (1842–1921) is probably the most representative, as he is certainly the most attractive and engaging, of the modern anarchists. Nurtured in the highest court circles of what was once St. Petersburg, he moved inexorably to an exile spent, like most exiles, within our hospitable shores—largely at Harrow, and later at Brighton, if one may be geographically precise. Unfolding events made it possible for him, before he died, to exchange Brighton for the U.S.S.R.

The charm of Kropotkin lies in his inoffensiveness. Not for him the mouth-foaming of Bakunin; the violence, tinged with insanity, of the Nihilists. No one illustrates more admirably that strain in anarchism which makes it, in certain manifestations, a doctrine meet for vegetarians. Not indeed that Kropotkin shrinks from the idea of revolution; on the contrary, it occupies the centre of his thoughts. But, to revive a half-forgotten phrase, it is pre-eminently a *frische, fröhliche* revolution to which he looks forward, an urbane and humane

[1] *Dieu et l'État*, Œuvres, vol. 1, p. 295.

transition, in which no heads will be broken, neither will the red cock crow on any man's roof. With his benevolent beard billowing in the breezes of Brighton, he was deservedly the most beloved of political exiles.

The significance of Kropotkin is that, unlike most anarchist writers, who are anarchic in their presentation, he gives a reasonably systematic statement of the faith that is in him. He may not be able to make the impracticable appear practicable; but at least he reveals himself as a seductive guide along the primrose path to revolution. In substance, Kropotkin bears evidence of the continuing influence of Proudhon, with remoter memories of Godwin; while in the other direction he serves as a pointer towards syndicalism, though indeed syndicalism in its prime was a contemporary manifestation of Kropotkin's later active years.

What Kropotkin has in common with others may be touched on lightly. The fundamental fact is exploitation; the world is rich but the workers are poor. It is an old story, never better expressed than by a very early aphorist and poet;

> The rich hath great labour in gathering riches together: and when he resteth, he is filled with his delicates.
>
> The poor laboureth in his poor estate; and when he leaveth off, he is still needy.

The abiding poverty of the poor arises because the essential things have been appropriated by the few. So far we are on a broad road. Kropotkin is by no means unique in emphasising that production is a comprehensively joint process; but he certainly lays a quite unusual emphasis on this view, which indeed he makes the corner-stone of his reasoning. Just as, in the *soi-disant* science of finance, there is a somewhat heretical theory that all taxation ends in a general diffusion throughout society, so Kropotkin comes near to outlining a general diffusion theory of production. Everything is done by everybody; and nobody can be said to do anything unaided. There is not a thought, not an invention which is not common property.[1] In virtue of the past, production is a 'social fact.' The instruments of production are part of the common heritage of the race; no one can work without the assistance of all manner of other people, dead and alive. How then can we assess the share of each in the wealth which all have contributed to produce.[2] In a phrase more picturesque than usual, he declares Paris to be the fruit of eighteen centuries of toil, the work of fifty generations of the whole French nation.[3] How then can anyone appropriate the meanest building in such a city without committing a flagrant injustice? If the means of production are the collective work

[1] *The Conquest of Bread*, p. 7 (Chapman and Hall, cheap edition).
[2] *Ibid.* p. 33. [3] *Ibid.* p. 103.

of humanity, the product ought to be the collective property of the race. Everything belongs to all; equally, all belongs to everyone.

It follows from this that the wage-system stands condemned, and must be abolished; for it is of the essence of the wage-system that it consecrates individual ownership, differentiating between *meum* and *tuum*. Further, it assumes that it is possible to evaluate the work of each individual. It is one of the cardinal errors of the collectivists that they seek to maintain the wage-system. To proclaim the principle of 'To each according to his deeds' is but to perpetuate injustice, since the measurement of each man's deeds is for ever impossible.[1] So likewise the 'right to work' is but a delusion. What we must proclaim is the 'right to live'; needs (and their satisfaction) must be given precedence over duties. Society must share the means of existence.[2]

What about the State, to which (assuming it is properly used) the orthodox collectivist pins his hopes as potentially a bulwark against the exploiting tendencies of the selfish minority? Kropotkin's answer (or one of his answers) is that the State is the arch-offender and prime mover in facilitating and instigating the exploitation of man by man. The State, in a phrase more suggestive of prejudice than of calm ratiocination, is defined as:

> a society of mutual insurance between the landlord, the military commander, the judge, the priest, and later on the capitalist, in order to support each other's authority over the people, and for exploiting the poverty of the masses and getting rich themselves.[3]

This is pre-eminently the class organisation of the Marxians. Quite consistently also, Kropotkin disowns the argument that we are suffering from an 'anarchy of production' made possible by the remissness of a *laissez faire* State. His answer is that there never has been a *laissez faire* State; it has always been consciously on the side of the capitalists and monopolists and has never given the worker the liberty of opposing that exploitation. In fact, now and always, it is the State's 'push' that has provided the first foundation of all capitalist fortunes.[4] Just as private ownership must go, so also must the State, the organ and prime accomplice of the exploiters. For a proper comprehension of the anti-State theories of Kropotkin, it should, however, be recalled that he regards the State as something relatively recent in the history of modern European civilisation. The State, he holds, is a form of society, which has developed only since the sixteenth century.[5] It might be argued, therefore, that it is not the State as such that he attacked but the modern State (*quaere*, since the time of Bodin and Machiavelli). '*Real* historians,' he remarks, with the unpleasant innuendo of italics,

[1] *The Conquest of Bread*, p. 227.
[2] *Ibid.* pp. 28–29, 230–231.
[3] *Modern Science and Anarchism*, p. 81.
[4] *Ibid.* pp. 82–83.
[5] *Ibid.* p. 80; *The State, its historic rôle*, p. 10.

'know that the State was reconstituted only upon the ruins of the mediaeval free cities.' The question had better be left to *real* historians.

These then are the two objectives; and with a pathetic optimistic faith, Kropotkin contrives to persuade himself that the tide in the affairs of men is flowing strongly towards the double goal of communism and anarchy. Here we encounter some of the more significant ideas of Kropotkin. Perhaps he is on somewhat firmer ground when he infers a drift to communism than in arguing for a drift to anarchy, where he is not on firm ground at all. But even so, the weight of his conclusions in the matter of communism is a somewhat grievous burden to be borne by the few frail examples which he cites. Broadly, he argues that the communistic principle is being established 'in the thousand developments of modern life'[1]; though in fact the number of instances given falls lamentably short of this conveniently rotund figure. There are bridges on which tolls used to be paid; now you may cross and recross unchallenged. The water from the bath-room tap is yours without stint (assuming that the water-rate is paid); if there is a shortage, there may indeed be an appeal to be content with immersion in a five-inch bath, but your individual requirement will not be measured. (Strictly speaking, this is doubtfully true of large-scale consumers, but to note this is perhaps to niggle unduly.) Museums, libraries (provided by the municipality) may be enjoyed by the consumer to the point of exhaustion. A zone ticket on the railway, where available, enables the holder, if he chooses, to spend his days and nights in a railway carriage, within the frontiers of his zone. In all these cases, argues Kropotkin, the principle is 'Take what you need,' and he would have us believe that there is a general tendency not to measure individual consumption. Admittedly, the examples given by Kropotkin are somewhat tenuous; and for the most part they rely on the existence of an authority armed with very considerable powers, which ought to be abhorrent to an anarchist. Water does not flow from the bath-room tap in response to the antics of a water-diviner.

Kropotkin, writing to-day and speaking in terms of possibilities rather than manifest tendencies, might have put the point more strongly. For a generation has arisen which has learned that a society may exist in which money is impotent, unless waited upon by a train of attendant coupons. Moreover, the coupons, if not the money, are distributed to all gratuitously and (apart from special needs) in equal quantities. It would be interesting, even if unprofitable, to speculate on the inferences which Kropotkin might have drawn from a rationed world: for undoubtedly, a system of rationing which extends effectively to all the obvious essentials of life is a one-sided approach to communism,

[1] *The Conquest of Bread*, p. 35.

even if something more is required to make it more than a mere approach. Kropotkin, however, is probably right here in emphasising a possibility which is illustrated by the development of the Social Services. The future may very well reveal a State providing more and more 'services,' and making them available, either free of charge, or as required in return for a fixed charge. It is a short step from free meals to children to free meals to workers. It is not a very long step from a policy of heavy subsidies to secure cheap bread to a policy of somewhat heavier subsidies in order to provide gratuitous bread. The difference between municipal houses let at an uneconomic rent and at no rent at all is largely one of degree. It is not beyond the wit of man to imagine a State which will provide Post Office facilities free, placing the whole burden on the long-suffering tax-payer, assuming that he still survives. This is the real point in Kropotkin's argument, and it relates to one of the most significant features of our times. We are living in an age when all manner of commodities and all manner of services are being made more widely available, by a policy of subsidies, aids, subventions and what-nots. Free education leads quite logically to free text-books and free meals. Free medical attention quite logically to free medicines, and, without much ingenuity, one might argue, to free bread and free milk. We have subsidised our agriculture, and we have subsidised our coal. We live in a subsidised age. Whether a universally subsidised and subsidising society is also a communistic society is perhaps a problem to be discussed by undergraduates and fallen angels. On the immediate issue raised by Kropotkin it may, however, be observed that the type of communism which would be exemplified by the free distribution of bread would, to most people, be quite inconceivable apart from a strong State, blessed with a strong Chancellor of the Exchequer, a strong Ministry of Transport and a strong Ministry of Food.

Kropotkin's argument that we are experiencing a drift towards anarchism cannot even claim the merit of inviting a plausible and more tenable restatement. There is beyond a certain point, he argues, a tendency to shake off the yoke of authority and to aim at a system founded more or less on the principles of individual liberty.[1] More surprising is his extreme claim that 'everywhere the State is abdicating and abandoning its holy functions to private individuals.'[2] This 'tendency of the human race . . . to reduce government interference to zero'[3] is not just exactly the most obvious feature of the age in which we live, nor for that matter of the period in which Kropotkin wrote. The argument, so far as it is an argument, has kinship with one of the many facets of Guild Socialism later. It invokes the enormous multiplication, the 'prodigious development' of all manner of voluntary associations,

[1] *The Conquest of Bread*, p. 40.
[2] *Ibid.* p. 188. [3] *Ibid.* p. 41.

linking together people who have common interests or who desire to attain a common end. There are learned societies; there are Trade Unions; there are even the *Kegelbrüder*[1]—the Brothers of the Nine-Pins. There is the English Life-Boat Association; there is the Red Cross. Not only so, but some of these are international in their operation. Railway Unions, quite independently of the States involved, make and keep international agreements among themselves regarding matters where their interests impinge. In Kropotkin's view, the functions of government are passing from the State to these 'human groupings which form themselves freely.' Over a large part of the field we are thus bound together by free agreement; and an indefinite extension of these spontaneous groups will in the end relieve us from the incubus of the State. The world's work will be done by free associations, self-generated for the purpose.

Perhaps we may ignore these excellent fellows, the *Kegelbrüder*—the Brothers of the Nine-Pins—as only a very minor symptom or symbol. On the main issue, this vast multiplicity of voluntary organisations is an undeniable fact; but it is almost the reverse of the truth to regard voluntary associations as possible inheritors of the functions of the State. In the examples that are relevant to the question of the State's activity, the real sequence of events is that the voluntary organisation does the pioneering. When it has convinced the public conscience that it exists for a laudable end, the State takes it over, generally on the plea that voluntary effort may mean overlapping, and that in any case it may have difficulty in 'covering the ground.' The State has been a great generaliser and universaliser of private and voluntary effort. The voluntary hospital—*patet omnibus*—preceded and pointed the way to the Municipal and State Hospital; the Manchester Unity of Oddfellows (and many more) laid the basis of the Health Insurance Scheme; the Trade Unions aimed at a minimum wage long before the Trade Board Acts; it was late in the day, and after much disinterested labour, that the State began to take an interest in Boys' Clubs and Playing Fields. The list might be indefinitely extended. Enough has been said to suggest that voluntary associations, in our time at least, do not relieve the State of its functions: rather do they, if they are of the right kind, prepare the way for further extensions of State activity.

Despite the world's drift to anarchy, a revolution is nevertheless necessary, according to Kropotkin, in order to give effect to the expropriation of 'everything that enables any man to appropriate the produce of others' toil'[2]—also, of course, in order to realise the 'right to live.' In *The Conquest of Bread*, Kropotkin gives a somewhat detailed and extremely naive account of his revolution, which with its pleasant air of insouciance has a good deal in common with the General

[1] *Mutual Aid* (cheap edition), p. 208. [2] *The Conquest of Bread*, p. 57.

Strike, which some of the syndicalists proposed to combine with a picnic in the Bois de Vincennes. The communalisation of bread, dwellings and clothes comes first.[1] It is to be a spontaneous movement; groups are to spring up in every street to ascertain the available supplies, and supervise their distribution. To embark on a revolution, relying on 'groups springing up,' unfortunately fails to contemplate the possibility that more than one group may spring up. There may indeed spring up a plethora of groups, whose chance encounters, as they pursue their lawful affairs, may lead to friction in strange places. But in Kropotkin's world, everything is done by talk, and everyone is not merely agreeable, but reasonable—qualities not always conspicuous in the heat of revolution. Also, as with the syndicalists, there must not be undue preparation:

> In any case, a system which springs up spontaneously, under stress of immediate need, will be infinitely preferable to anything invented between four walls by hide-bound theorists sitting in any number of committees.[2]
>
> Man will accomplish greater things, and accomplish them better and by simpler methods than those dictated to him beforehand.[3]

This is the anarchist equivalent of the optimism which assures us that it will be all right on the night. Later, we shall find in the syndicalists that unreadiness becomes one of the chiefest of virtues, as indeed it was, in a certain sense, with the early Christians.

The account of that phase of the revolution which is concerned with the transfer of houses has become a classic example of the guilelessness of the anarchist, knowing not the world nor the things of the world. After the appropriate groups of volunteers have sprung up and done their scheduling, they convene *all* the inhabitants to meet at a convenient place to carry through the redistribution:

> Then, without waiting for anyone's leave, those citizens will probably go and find their comrades who were living in miserable garrets and hovels and will say to them simply: 'It is a real Revolution this time, comrades, and no mistake about it. Come to such a place this evening; all the neighbourhood will be there; we are going to redistribute the dwelling-houses. If you are tired of your slum-garret, come and choose one of the flats of five rooms that are to be disposed of, and when you have once moved in you shall stay, never fear. The people are up in arms, and he who would venture to evict you will have to answer to them.'[4]

> A solemn council forthwith to be held
> At Pandemonium,

says Milton; but it would be a feeble affair, compared to the great night when all the inhabitants of Battersea, Lambeth, Stockwell and parts of Wandsworth assemble in Battersea Park to talk over a little bit of business in the matter of houses. It is a curious carrying

[1] *The Conquest of Bread*, p. 64.
[2] *Ibid.* p. 80.
[3] *Ibid.* p. 107.
[4] *Ibid.* p. 108.

forward of memories of the Russian Mir to circumstances where, to put it no higher, another technique is required.

It is unnecessary to follow further the Songs of Innocence and Inexperience which provide the themes of Kropotkin's revolution. It is of more interest to visualise, if possible, the structure of society when anarchism of the Kropotkin type prevails. In essence this has already been indicated in connection with Kropotkin's argument that we are moving towards anarchism through the transference of the State's functions to numberless voluntary organisations.[1] Indeed, the chief aim of anarchism is represented as being that of awakening the constructive powers of the masses.[2] Here the kinship of anarchism to the liberal tradition is sufficiently manifest: the doctrine that the 'masses' should do things for themselves would have earned the cordial approval of John Stuart Mill. Thus, with a shrinking and shrivelling of the State, and with a sprouting of associations and of federations of associations, of communes and of federations of communes, all free to be born or die at will; to unite, affiliate or part company; all living in amity together, we reach the anarchist paradise.[3] This free functioning of free associations does not require, and indeed cannot make use of anything corresponding to representative government, which is the political form appropriate to capitalist rule. What is wanted (and the words are significant) is something 'more popular, more decentralised, and nearer to the folkmote of self-government.'[4] Just as Kropotkin does not, apparently, greatly object to the State as it was before the sixteenth century, so he does not object to the rudimentary folk-mote. Like Godwin, he is probably prepared to tolerate the Parish Council.

The conception of law is so closely linked up with that of the State that a glance at Kropotkin's attitude to law in general may be permissible. Obviously, an anarchist who tosses the State overboard must also be prepared to get rid of all law, leaving at most agreements voluntarily accepted and observed. Various reasons may, however, be advanced for discarding law, just as there may be various ways of getting rid of the undesired excrescence. Broadly, two ideas dominate what Kropotkin says on the subject. The first in effect is that law

[1] *Modern Science and Anarchism*, pp. 66–67.

[2] *Ibid.* p. 68.

[3] It may be convenient to reproduce Kropotkin's own definition, as given in one passage where he is obviously aiming at precision of language: 'The Anarchists conceive a society in which all the mutual relations of its members are regulated, not by laws, not by authorities, whether self-imposed or elected, but by mutual agreements between the members of that society, and by a sum of social customs and habits—not petrified by law, routine, or superstition, but continually developing and continually readjusted, in accordance with the ever-growing requirements of a free life, stimulated by the progress of science, invention, and the steady growth of higher ideals' (*Modern Science and Anarchism*, p. 45).

[4] *Modern Science and Anarchism*, p. 84.

is unnecessary. The idea of 'Mutual Aid'[1] plays a large part in Kropotkin's equipment; he held that the law of mutual aid was more important than the law of mutual struggle. The moral sense of mankind is, he argues, merely a further evolution of the instinct of mutual aid; and this provides a force 'infinitely more powerful than the orders of any religion or any law-makers.'[2] Waiving the terminology of his theory of mutual aid, this presumably means that the instinct of benevolence is sufficient to keep man straight without the command of law.

The second line of attack on law is designed to show that in essence it is a superfluity into which there has been injected something that is pernicious. The central core of law is represented by a body of usages and customs. Law merely confirms existing customs and crystallises them.[3] In an extreme statement, which even a casual glance at any statute-book is sufficient to refute, it is held that 'Laws can only *follow* the accomplished facts.'[4] So far law is merely the sum-total of 'certain habits and customs already recognised as useful.' But into this there is injected a pernicious infusion: the law-maker surreptitiously introduces something new 'which is entirely to the advantage of the military and governing minorities.'[5] A body of good traditions and habits is presumably unexceptionable; but 'law' should not be reduced to writing. It becomes a device whereby the past fetters the future. In a phrase which might be, and perhaps is confusedly, a quotation from Godwin: 'It is impossible to legislate for the future.'[6]

Perhaps enough has been said to indicate the chief features of Kropotkin's anarchism. He would, in short, revive a more populous Garden of Eden, teeming with guileless and guiltless men, nourishing themselves with the produce of glass-frames. For the rest, he is rather faithful to some of the elements which Fourier presented to the anarchist tradition. Work, of course, will be attractive and light—four or five hours a day, ceasing altogether in the middle or upper 'forties.[7] There will likewise be the possibility of varying it according to taste: not in vain did Fourier's butterfly flit from flower to flower.[8] All this inevitably demands the elimination of Fourier's parasites: think of 'how many, in the so-called civilised nations, produce nothing, how many work at harmful trades . . . and lastly, how many are only useless middlemen.'[9] Fourier had expressed this very true thought more fantastically, and therefore more memorably; More had said it with greater eloquence; Saint-Simon had said it in one

[1] *Mutual Aid* is probably the most significant of Kropotkin's books, although less important for our immediate purpose.
[2] *Modern Science and Anarchism*, p. 21.
[3] *Ibid.* p. 35.
[4] *Ibid.* p. 68.
[5] *Ibid.* pp. 72–73, 35.
[6] *Ibid.* p. 87.
[7] *The Conquest of Bread*, p. 130.
[8] *Ibid.* p. 137.
[9] *Ibid.* pp. 130–131.

brief all-comprehensive sentence that barked at the reader in capital letters. Lastly, that awful vision of eight million women, spending two or three hours at eight million fires, preparing eight million roasts —though the pen may be the pen of Kropotkin, surely the thought is the thought of Fourier. And contemplating from afar the chaotic, confused and redundant activity of these eight million women, perhaps the last thought left is this: how anarchic indeed will be our way of life, until we have the sense to adopt anarchism!

(c) BERTRAND RUSSELL

After *un ci-devant noble* (for thus does Bakunin describe himself), after a Russian Prince—an English Earl: for, when we come to the anarchists, we move in high society. There might conceivably be some argument as to whether Mr. Bertrand Russell (if we may continue to extend to him his more familiar designation) should properly appear in this section. He does not, it is true, recommend that we should forthwith 'go anarchist.' Indeed in the volume which is of most interest for our purpose, *Roads to Freedom*, considerable fragments of the State and of law are still left at the end to cumber the ground. But pure anarchism, though at present unattainable, is stated to be the ultimate ideal to which society should continually approximate; that it is at present unattainable is due to the imperfections of man which may gradually be overcome.[1] His final recommendation is of a system 'not far removed from that advocated by Kropotkin, but rendered more practicable by the adoption of the main principles of Guild Socialism'[2]—that is to say, a cross between pure anarchism and that system of socialism which has gone furthest in eliminating the State. This, it is true, was written in 1918, when Guild Socialism was still a coming force. In any case, whatever label, if any, may properly be attached to Mr. Russell, he has the mind of an anarchist and he pleads their cause. Indeed, on certain points he is extremely illuminating as to the essence of anarchism: he accordingly provides a welcome supplement to Bakunin and Kropotkin.

The primary impulse to Mr. Russell's social and political philosophy is doubtless to be found in his detestation of authority. He is a rebel; if he does not, like Godwin, regard disobedience as the first of virtues, at least he looks upon obedience as something incompatible with the fine flower of liberty. This explains his antagonism to the State as we know it. It is of the essence of the State 'that it is the repository of the collective force of its citizens.'[3] It exacts blind obedience. The excessive power of the State, it is argued, is 'one of the chief causes of misery in the modern world.'[4] Without going into other

[1] *Roads to Freedom*, *e.g.* pp. 12–13.
[2] *Ibid.* p. 192.
[3] *Principles of Social Reconstruction*, p. 45.
[4] *Ibid.* p. 65.

lines of argument, it may be noted here that one of the reasons why the State is so harmful is to be found in ' its vastness and the resulting sense of individual helplessness.' The machine is so large that, even in a democracy, the bulk of mankind are ' dwarfed by knowledge of their own impotence.' [1] The point is a familiar one in all current criticisms of the working of our democratic system. The puny elector in a constituency of 30,000 voters, called upon to choose between three unknown candidates dumped upon him by the Party organisations, may well be excused if from fatalism he drifts to indifference.

The same approach explains Mr. Russell's antagonism to State socialism. This ' road to freedom ' would still leave us moving in a world of authority, with the State as universal employer, and the individual worker still dwarfed.[2] Moreover, Mr. Russell is an author, a philosopher and a scientist, with sympathetic kinship with the arts, and the authoritarianism of the authoritarian socialist State fills him with horror. Art, we are told, springs from ' a wild and anarchic side of human nature ' [3]; the artist and the bureaucrat are for ever in antagonism. That the artist in his impulses should be fettered by authority, and should be required to create in accordance with the provisions of Statutory Rules and Orders is a ' nightmare ': ' In such a world all that makes life tolerable to the lover of beauty would perish.' Here perhaps we touch rock-bottom in Mr. Russell's political philosophy. What matters most in man is his artistic and creative impulses, which are essentially ' wild and anarchic.' Whatever authority may be necessary, it must at least be kept within such bounds as will leave this ' wild and anarchic side ' free play. Put more briefly and with much elision: Man in his essential and distinguishing features is by nature an anarchist.

On the economic side, the difference for Mr. Russell between anarchism and socialism is that orthodox socialism, hard-heartedly following St. Paul, would seem to exact at least a willingness to work as a condition of maintenance, whereas anarchism is more generous.[4] Indeed, the two essential features of anarchism in this interpretation are, firstly, that there should be provided to everyone, free of conditions, ' as much of all the ordinary commodities as he or she may care to consume ' (rarer commodities being divided equally); and secondly, and inferentially, that on no one should there rest any obligation to work. At this point the ordinary reader, whose vision has been beclouded by the mists of this present sinful world, may consider that we now enter a veritable fairy-land or Garden of Eden. For it is of the essence of anarchist theory that all work is or may be a pleasure; and that, if it is not, it is the mess we have made of things, the environment in which men work and the conditions under which they work,

[1] *Principles of Social Reconstruction*, pp. 59–61. [2] *Ibid.* p. 137.
[3] *Roads to Freedom*, p. 177. [4] *Ibid.* p. 105.

that prevent labour from being a perpetual fountain of joy. It was 'le travail attrayant' that was to make Fourier's Phalanx hum like a hive of singing masons. The question may appear trivial, but it is far from being so, involving as it does the profound problem of the nature of work and the thorny conundrum whether the sordid race of economists are justified in regarding it as a 'disutility.' Taking anarchistic literature in the bulk, and for the moment allowing Mr. Bertrand Russell to fall into a discreet background, there are two considerations on which this rosy view is based. Firstly, it has been argued, and the point may be conceded, that the dividing line between an activity that is work and one that is pleasure is at times mighty tenuous and fine. The mountaineer and his guide are to all intents and purposes going through the same motions, but one is supposed to be enjoying himself, and the other is working under a contract of (or for) service. The outward indifferent eye can see little distinction between a professional football-player, working hard to earn an honest living, and the amateur who perhaps sweats and grunts even more unrestrainedly on Saturday afternoon for the greater glory of Nether Muckridge; the activity of a racing motorist does not differ so greatly from that of some taxi-drivers; the pleasure of a holiday in the country, especially in war-time, is greatly increased if, within suitable limits, one is allowed to share the toil of the swinked hedger. Surveying these and a thousand other examples that might be cited, the innocent-minded asks why, if plutocrats pay vast sums to be allowed for a season to scramble o'er moor and fen, o'er crag and torrent, in pursuit of elusive and invisible deer—why indeed should not the shepherd in Inverness-shire be the happiest of men, since all these pleasures are his, every day in all the years, with the added satisfaction of at least being able to see the sheep?

The second prop of optimism is this: even admitting for the moment that work is unpleasant, there is by common consent a lower depth that is even more unpleasant. The unhappiest of men, at any rate after the first few days, is he who is condemned to do nothing and is effectively prevented from doing anything. And the proof is that the moment anyone is put in a position to do nothing, he at once proceeds to do something: he will keep bees, or collect firewood, or give his hours to the theory and the practice of the bagpipes. Unless for those who are utterly senile, some kind of activity is essential. Combining these two undeniable verities, the anarchist theory of work emerges. Hardly any kind of work is wholly unattractive under certain conditions. Man is a restless, fidgety animal that must be doing something. It follows that if people at large are exempted from the obligation of doing anything, they will, in order to escape the weariness and the lassitude of their unoccupied hours, forthwith throw themselves on anything requiring to be done; and so the problem is solved. The world's work will be accomplished by people in full flight from the boredom of idleness.

One need not be very old in order to detect at what point the premises are unequal to the burden of the conclusion. On the first point, it is true that there is hardly any occupation which it would not be pleasant, or at least interesting, to engage in once: a day in the mines as a stripper, or a trip on a trawler, perhaps even as far as Bear Island, would be an ' experience '—perhaps even a memorable experience. But it is of the essence of work—perhaps indeed it approaches to a definition of work—that it is an activity which must be continued, even after the novelty, the interest and the excitement have evaporated; and as we know things now, and probably to a large extent under any system of industrial organisation, it must go on, for it is given to few to play about from one trade or profession to another. The deck-hand on the trawler, having returned from Bear Island, must forthwith return to Bear Island—which is much less amusing. A dentist remains a dentist; an architect an architect. They may envy each other; but they cannot have a pleasant holiday by changing jobs for a month. The shepherd looking down the long years, sees an unending vista of sheep, bearing a marked family resemblance to each other. The burden of his life is that the sheep go on, and he cannot get away from them. An undergraduate with remarkable psychological insight has looked deep into the soul of a professor:

> Year after year I deliver the same lectures
> To fifteen crescents of stupid faces.
> God, how I hate their faces.
> They seem to get more stupid every year.[1]

They don't really; and viewed dispassionately, they don't even seem to; but even here, work is a ' disutility,' because it goes on and on, and must go on, beyond the point where, but for a sense of duty or the necessity of earning a living, the worker would gladly desist, or turn to something else—if it were available, which it seldom is.

One further point may appear too trivial for mention, but its consideration is obviously essential in connection with the anarchist view of work as seen in Godwin, and in Fourier, so far as certain elements of Fourierism are germane to the anarchist tradition. So long as we live in a society which has advanced in any degree beyond a state of primitive disintegration towards a condition of mutual interdependence, it is essential that we should be able to rely on each other. Expressed more sordidly and prosaically, this means that everyone must fulfil his contract, and in a sense make himself the slave of a time-table. We must know that the train will leave King's Cross at 10 A.M.; we must be able to rely on the engine-driver being there; we must have an assurance that he will see the job through.

[1] The name of the poet deserves to be perpetuated: Hugh Bankhead.

He may not, sixty miles from London, hand over the train to one of the passengers, merely because, with Delius, he has just heard the first cuckoo of the spring, because the meadows are bespangled with orchids, the ditches a gleam of golden king-cups, and all nature summons him to partner the dining-car attendant in a round of golf on an adjacent course. It is almost an insult to the compositor to ask him to set in type an observation so fatuously obvious; yet it is almost necessary, in view of the quiet assumption of so many of the philosophical anarchists that the world can be run without binding agreements, by people acting on the spur of the moment at the prompting of the Butterfly or, as in Kropotkin's revolution, by 'groups springing up.' For most people, the vision of the future is an indefinite continuation of the same *kind* of work; few people can effectively change the nature of their occupation beyond the age of thirty, if so late. So also, in the short period, for most people work represents the punctilious discharge of a duty at a definite place and at a predetermined hour. We bind ourselves to our fellowmen; and he who is bound cannot enjoy anarchic freedom.

The other limb in the anarchist argument is equally limp. Doubtless those who are so placed that they need not work, do in fact forthwith proceed to find 'occupation'; and they may indeed find extremely useful occupation. They may serve the State and their fellow-men by spending their nights walking the division-lobby of the House of Commons. More usefully, perhaps, they may help to administer the affairs of their county, their city, or their parish. And, as all anarchists emphasise without ceasing, there are all manner of voluntary bodies with which they may become associated, ranging from some of the highest importance down to the Society for the Promotion of Laudable Ends. This indicates the obvious weakness of this side of the anarchist argument. Work done by those who, being idle, are impelled by their conscience to be useful, may be work without which society could not stand; but it tends to be conspicuous; it tends to be honorific; it is by preference concerned with 'administration' and 'organisation' (equally blessed words). It does not put meal into the bin, or coal into the scuttle, or bring water from the tap. Life in a mine, where the only concession to the Butterfly is an alternation between Day Shift, Back Shift and Night Shift, is not in itself sufficiently attractive to overcome the 'allurements of Sloth.'

These observations, being designed to rebut the excessive rosiness of the anarchist view, may suggest a pessimism that is equally unjustified. An honest heart-searching will probably convince most people that the prospect of work (or at least, the thought of the *same* work in the future) is much more disconcerting than work itself. Work is not in itself disagreeable; most of it is, at worst, neutral, tending to the agreeable or pleasurable, especially where work is combined with the opportunity of human contacts. The question of the psychology of man's attitude to his work is, however, a vast problem which must be avoided here. It is sufficient for our purpose to note that work is not, and never can be, perpetually *attrayant*. The interesting question is why the thought of returning to work is so frequently loathsome and repugnant, while the actual resumption of work need not be in any way unpleasant. Probably the man who on Sunday shrinks from Monday's task does so because he then contrasts it with all the much more pleasurable things he might do; whereas on Monday, being occupied, he has no time for such day-dreams. Perhaps the nearest approach to the truth is to be found in the view attributed to the inhabitants of the City of the Sun, that all work is a discipline. It is a medicine, without which our life would be lacking in health.

In the foregoing discussion we have wandered somewhat from Mr. Russell to the general question of the anarchist view of labour. Mr. Russell is sufficiently realistic to concede that 'some necessary work must always remain disagreeable.' [1] He cites as examples the work of an agricultural labourer, a type of activity which many generations considered as alone compatible with human dignity, the work of a coal miner, and that of a stoker on an Atlantic liner. Under the influence of Guild Socialist affiliations, he believes that with the help of economic self-government, 'something of the artist's joy in creation' might inspire nearly all work. In this way, through the magic of self-governing associations, nine-tenths of the world's work could be made preferable to idleness, even in the eyes of men guaranteed a livelihood whether they worked or not. For the remaining tenth—the Atlantic stokers and their kin—the inducement of additional reward would be needed.[2]

The conclusion that Mr. Russell draws from the arguments in favour of anarchism are commendably cautious; it is that they are 'sufficient to make it seem *possible* that the plan might succeed, but not sufficient to make it so probable that it would be wise to try it.' [3] For the present, therefore, because of the attaching doubt, we are to be spared the undiluted blessings of anarchism; but Mr. Russell, seeking to find a halfway house between anarchism which has the advantage as regards liberty, and socialism which is more effective in the matter of inducements to work, presents a curious scheme which would present some nice administrative problems to the Ministry of Food in the future anarchic-socialist State, unless indeed they could be solved by the simple procedure of 'groups springing up' to see to it.

Under this scheme, the population falls into four grades, so far as concerns distribution and rewards. In the first place, the anarchist principle is observed in that there is to be a 'certain small income,

[1] *Roads to Freedom*, p. 112. [2] *Ibid.* p. 114. [3] *Ibid.* p. 115.

sufficient for necessaries,' payable to all irrespective of work or of willingness to work, payable therefore to the conscientious objector to work. This is later given the pleasing designation of the 'vagabond's wage,' and with a slight variation in terms is defined as 'sufficient for existence but not for luxury.'[1] In later discussions which scarcely concern us here, Mr. Russell tends to assume that the chief beneficiaries under the provision of the vagabond's wage will be artists who desire to give their whole time to their art, and others of the same breed who would gladly cultivate poetry and painting on pea-soup and potatoes. In fact, he scarcely seems to realise that the vagabond's wage, the reward of indolence, might attract predominantly a very different type of person.

Somewhere above this, there is to be a higher level of wages—how much higher is not and cannot be specified, since it depends on the productivity of the community—payable to all who are willing to engage in useful work, whether or not work can be found for them. Since all service ranks the same with the anarchists, as with God, there is no need to differentiate here between skilled and unskilled. This will in fact be the normal wage for all members of the community who profess to prefer useful work to a life of vagabondage, and it will be equal for all. But two variations are in fact suggested. There may be some who would like to cultivate the arts—but not as full-timers. Not for them the comparative rigours of a vagabond's life, receiving sufficient for existence but not for luxury. 'A little luxury and a little art,' is not an unreasonable motto; in fact, vagabonds and Bohemians are not temperamentally given to asceticism. We must therefore provide an intermediate rate of remuneration for the man whom we may call the semi-vagabond, who is willing to work for half the normal hours in order the more luxuriously to pursue art in the other half of his life. Lastly, there is the man who is prepared to be a stoker on the transatlantic liner and the few others on whom even economic self-government cannot confer the artist's joy in creation. These clearly must receive something more than the normal in order to overcome their natural aversion from disagreeable work. What all this means in concrete terms is of course not disclosed; but we may perhaps get some visual picture of what is involved if we imagine the vagabond receiving bones and stock; the semi-vagabond, dubious sausages and rabbits; the ordinary willing worker, beef and mutton; and the transatlantic stoker, salmon, grouse and fur coats.[2] This is Mr. Russell's suggestion of a practicable method of combining the advantages of anarchism and socialism.

Mr. Russell, it has been said, is not the complete anarchist; he realises that the State, if only in an attenuated form, is still necessary. This concession is very significantly linked up with the fact that Mr.

[1] *Roads to Freedom*, p. 179. [2] *Ibid.* pp. 118–120.

Russell is one of the few socialists who do not believe in the fundamental goodness of all men, or attribute all our evil instincts to our present evil environment. He usefully reminds us that our bad impulses are not wholly due to a bad social system.[1] He is here at one with the fundamental doctrines of Christianity:

> The faith that launched point-blank her dart
> At the head of a lie—taught Original Sin,
> The Corruption of Man's Heart.

There were wars, he tells us, before there was capitalism; wars, indeed, to some extent grow out of ordinary human nature. Man, in his view, is naturally competitive, acquisitive and pugnacious.[2] Respect for the liberty of others is not a natural impulse.[3] The general impression left by a perusal of Mr. Russell's writings is that he looks upon man as a bossing, bullying, blustering, interfering kind of animal, never content to leave his fellows alone: and perhaps he is right. 'People,' he says rather pathetically, 'who find a pleasure in ordering others about (and this includes most of the energetic people in the world) will not like anarchism, where every man can do as he pleases.'[4]

We cannot therefore count on crimes ceasing, merely on the ground that the proclamation of Utopia will undo the effects of the Fall of Man. There will be opportunities of theft—indeed copious opportunities, for the vagabond, not content with his meagre ration, may by direct action seek to achieve a more equitable and generous distribution. There will be crimes of violence. Utopia will not put an end to jealousy, the injured lover's hell; and we may therefore expect the usual crop of *crimes passionels*. Lastly, there may be subversive activities. There may be some—presumably those who find pleasure in ordering others about—who do not appreciate an anarchist regime, and they might be tempted to raise a private army, with sinister ends in view; which things could not be tolerated.[5] For all these reasons, to prevent violence, disorder and crime, something like a State is required.[6] It is, however, a curious commentary on the whole question that this nearest possible approximation to a condition of anarchy which seeks to abolish the State, is compelled to maintain in existence the remnants of a State, in order to prevent the State from being re-established.

In all this, there is something curiously reminiscent of mediaeval theology. The State, it will be recalled, was not a part of original natural law. Like the acceptance of private property, it was something added to natural law by human agreement, to meet the sinful state of man resulting from the Fall. The State was needed to restrain man's sinful impulses; and but for the frailty of man, there would be

[1] *Roads to Freedom*, p. 122.
[2] *Ibid.* p. 152; *Principles of Social Reconstruction*, p. 11.
[3] *Roads to Freedom*, p. 121.
[4] *The Prospects of Industrial Civilization*, p. 147.
[5] *Roads to Freedom*, pp. 127–130.
[6] *Ibid.* p. 144.

no need of the State. But, needless to say, Mr. Russell does not view sin with Miltonic eyes; rather is he the reincarnation of Godwin. In the forefront he places the contention that 'the whole conception of guilt or sin should be utterly swept away'[1]; and with it, naturally, the cognate idea of punishment. Crimes of violence are to be dealt with by a scientific psychological treatment, 'designed to elicit more beneficial impulses.'[2] Crimes, springing from supposed self-interest, are to be dealt with, apparently, by an appeal to reason. In a most delectable phrase, such an one

> ought to be made to feel that self-interest itself, when it is fully understood, can be better served by a life which is useful to the community than by one which is harmful. For this purpose, it is chiefly necessary to widen his outlook and increase the scope of his desires.[3]

Crime, in short (so-called), is to be treated no less tenderly than an infectious disease. Nor has Mr. Russell any doubts as to the efficacy of the cure: 'By the method of individual curative treatment, it will generally be possible to secure that a man's first offence shall also be his last.'[4] This is to reveal a faith in the power of reason for which there is no foundation, and a knowledge of human nature as touchingly inadequate as that of Godwin. When the vagabond steals the semi-vagabond's rabbits, it is to be pointed out to him that if he really wishes rabbits, he can get them by being useful to the community (an idea which, presumably, never occurred to him before), and we are further to increase the scope of his desires. There may just be a danger that when the scope of his desires has been sufficiently enlarged, he may proceed to steal the stoker's grouse.

Yet if, because of men's imperfections, we may not forthwith attain to anarchism, it is to that distant port that the ship of State should meanwhile direct its course, ridding itself of its ballast and its junk as it proceeds on its way. Government and law will be reduced to a minimum.[5] The transformation will be effected along familiar anarchistic lines. Autonomy will be granted to Churches and to industries, and indeed to any groups which have important common interests, not shared by the rest of the community[6]; and generally 'the positive purposes of the State . . . ought as far as possible to be carried out, not by the State itself, but by independent organisations.'[7] In a more carefully pondered phrase, we should aim at 'the increasing devolution of positive political initiative to bodies formed voluntarily for specific purposes.'[8] And under the stress of this process of devolution, what will become of the State, that stubborn reality? It will not wholly evaporate, but will become something like a federal authority or court of arbitration. But do not, please, ask who will enforce the

[1] *Roads to Freedom*, p. 133. [2] *Ibid.* p. 134. [3] *Ibid.* pp. 134–135.
[4] *Ibid.* p. 198. [5] *Ibid.* p. 197. [6] *Ibid.* p. 200.
[7] *The Prospects of Industrial Civilization*, p. 72. [8] *Ibid.* p. 75.

arbitration award. If this is not anarchism, the answer may be that it is a world which has the advantage of combining all the difficulties and impossibilities of Kropotkin, of Syndicalism and of Guild Socialism.

(*d*) CONCLUSIONS ON ANARCHISM

We have in earlier chapters seen the anarchism of Godwin and of Proudhon; and in the present have more briefly surveyed three more modern representatives of the school. We shall not meet the anarchists again, except in so far as anarchism is one of the ingredients of syndicalism. In concluding this chapter, it may be well to underline a few points which have not been discussed, or have only been touched upon incidentally, in the foregoing pages.

The fundamental trouble with the anarchist is that, though he may be highly intelligent, he has no sense. It follows that a fruitful discussion of anarchism is almost an impossibility. If they do not realise that they have set their nest among the stars, no word of man will persuade them that their thoughts are moving in a world unreal and unrealisable. Anarchists are a race of highly intelligent and imaginative children, who nevertheless can scarcely be trusted to look after themselves outside the nursery pen.

With regard to anarchism itself, one should perhaps distinguish between individualist anarchism, which is merely egotism run mad, the philosophy of the superman, and anarchist communism, which at least recognises the existence and the claims of other 'egos.' So also we are scarcely concerned with the conception of anarchism which, it is to be feared, is securely rooted in the popular mind, where, since the days of nihilism, an anarchist is a bomb-thrower, possessed with a rage of destruction. The expression of this phase of anarchism—to which Bakunin was not a stranger—can be but a frothing at the mouth, leaving no room for thought or social theory: it is 'bitter to a degree than seems scarcely sane,' [1] as Mr. Russell himself has it. For our purposes, anarchism is a philosophical theory of society and the State, which, though it may talk of revolution, has nevertheless affinities with pacifism.

So viewed, the central point in anarchism is not so much a passion for equality or justice as a horror of any kind of authority, any kind of command, any kind of restraint. It follows—the point may be noted without further discussion—that anarchism is almost necessarily atheistic, always bearing in mind Sir Thomas Browne's dictum, already cited, regarding the virtual impossibility of effective atheism. For God is the supreme authority, the ultimate law-giver of the Universe. Accordingly, in the more outspoken anarchists (Proudhon and

[1] *Roads to Freedom*, p. 66.

Bakunin, for example), God and the State are linked together as the twin manifestations of tyranny over man.

The second general point is that anarchists are bound to assume, explicitly or implicitly, that man is more or less flawless, and wholly reasonable. It is not always an easy task living with our fellows under any circumstances. A society where all restraint is removed, where each does what is right in his own eyes, insistently demands that all passion be spent, and that human benevolence and mutual tolerance should reach heights hitherto undreamed of. On somewhat similar grounds, anarchists have been universally impelled towards a preference for small groups. From Godwin downwards, the public opinion of the group is invoked as a restraining influence in place of law; but it is only in small groups that the averted glances of our neighbours can be effective in this way. Anarchism indeed only begins to be thinkable in a world of small, isolated, primitive communities, where reason has been enthroned, and where each man has crucified his own flesh.

With regard to that part of anarchist ideals which relates to an adequate distribution of essential goods to all, quite apart from any question of work done or of obligation to work, two points may be suggested. In the first place, it ought to be obvious that such a minimum dividend to all, though it may be part of anarchist theory, could never administratively be part of anarchist practice. Kropotkin cites, as a portent, the case of water supplied free to all to the utmost limits of requirements (apart, of course, from the payment of a water rate); Mr. Bertrand Russell adopts the illustration with approval. But a moment's reflection should satisfy anyone that the supply of water to all and sundry demands not merely the exercise of governmental authority (central or local, or both), but the development of administrative machinery of quite considerable complexity. Water mains are embedded in compulsory powers, in coercions and prohibitions. It is quite possible that Society may in time considerably extend the 'free list.' It is a development which the State socialist of the Fabian type may quite legitimately contemplate: but not the anarchist, so long as he remains within the disabling conditions of anarchism, since the development is one which would demand not merely a strong State, but an extremely efficient State.

The other point with regard to the 'free distribution' ideal may perhaps come rather close to current political controversy; but as it is germane to a consideration of anarchist philosophy, it should at least be glanced at here. The anarchist frequently says that even if a certain proportion of the population preferred to live in idleness, it would not greatly matter, or would not matter at all. And indeed if we accept the anarchist doctrine that work is a pleasure, then assuredly no great harm would be done in leaving work to those who enjoy it;

the idler might indeed be represented as a benefactor who by his unselfish abnegation increases the sum of the enjoyment of others. Yet to those who look on labour as a burden, and ultimately as a weariness, the situation will appear in a somewhat different light. For however it may be disguised, the conscientious objector to work, for whom the anarchist scheme of things is prepared to make provision, is a sponger and a sorner, living idly on the sweat of his fellows. To-day, however, beyond all doubt, the tide is flowing in the direction of a more tender attitude towards the idler ; and it may be interesting to speculate as to the underlying reason. It may be suggested that fundamentally it is not unconnected with the increasing complexity of the industrial machine. In the preceding chapters we have repeatedly heard witnesses, with varying degrees of emphasis, point out that under a far-reaching system of division of labour it is impossible to say what anyone produces. Kropotkin, who figures in this chapter, is an extreme example. In his eyes, production is a social process in which, more or less, everybody does everything, aided indeed by all previous generations ; and on the reverse side, in which no one specifically can be said to produce anything. There is too much mutual aid to make any calculation possible. When production becomes thus impersonal, the connecting link between the personal effort of any individual and the final result is lost sight of, and may indeed be forgotten. It is a text-book commonplace that division of labour may undermine the sense of responsibility. In such an atmosphere it is fairly obvious that the sight of one who eats, yet refuses to work, will give less offence than in an age and a society where the intimate relationship between individual effort and the final result is not merely recognised, but is accepted as one of the fundamental assumptions of life. And the force of this consideration will perhaps be more fully realised if we invoke the point of view prevalent where it is still impossible to conceal the original relationship between effort and result. The farming and the fishing communities are, almost proverbially, the most individualistic sections of the community ; and the reason is not far to seek. They are nearer the foundations and the realities of life. 'I went by the field of the slothful, and by the vineyard of the man void of understanding,' remarked Solomon ; and what he observed was strikingly in accordance with individualistic philosophy. A community of peasant proprietors would not lightly accept the proposition that they should supply all the needs of one in their midst who was idle 'through refusal of suitable employment,' because they know that, in their line of life, to the slothful Want cometh as an armed man. The same is true of the fisherman. No doubt there may be occasional miraculous draughts of fishes ; but over a season, the catch of fish is fairly proportionate to the competence, the industry and the carefulness of the skipper. It is the skipper who knows the fishing grounds and the unseen floor of the sea as he knows the back of his own hand ; who knows the winds and the tides and is weather-wise; who is willing to go out when others find a plausible excuse for staying at home; who knows how to be tender with his gear and his tackle—this is the happy fisher, this is he, whose boat comes in heavy with its load when others may return half-empty. And this explains why fishermen in the past, and in so many areas to-day, have turned resolutely away from co-operation, even in matters where co-operation would be beneficial. For where the relation between effort and result is immediate and obvious, co-operation to the self-reliant so easily appears to be a device whereby the slothful and the incompetent may take advantage of the industrious.

On the other hand, with increasing complexity of society, with the population at large increasingly remote from the producers of the actual commodities which would form the constituent elements of the vagabond's wage, the more marked will be the tendency to assume that the wealth of the world just happens to be there, awaiting distribution, without the previous necessity of labour on the part of anyone. A war periodically may, temporarily and partially but not very effectively, open our eyes. Modern society, largely because it is urban, does not know enough and does not think enough about what lies behind the satisfaction of its needs. The Kropotkin theory (expressed crudely) that everybody helps everybody to do everything is in practice easily re-interpreted as implying that all we need just comes to be there, in the shop windows or below the counter, without individual effort on the part of anyone.

In this impersonal atmosphere, proposals that the vagabond who refuses to work should nevertheless be a welcome guest at the common table do not shock as they would have done in less sophisticated times, when we all lived nearer to the tail of the plough and possessed the knowledge that such proximity brings. The conclusion is that this particular aspect of anarchism—the consecration of *The Right to be Lazy*, to fall back on the title of an older pamphlet—can be made plausible only in a somewhat artificial and top-heavy society whose complexity has obscured the foundations on which it stands.[1]

[1] Mr. Bertrand Russell's vagabond, with his vagabond's wage, was perhaps rather a figure of comedy when he first emerged; but since then, his sinister figure has appeared in unexpected places. Taking the *Report on Social Insurance and Allied Services* (Cmd. 6404), if the reader follows the history of the man disqualified for normal benefit, he will find his ultimate fate in paragraph 371. Here it is proposed that National Assistance sufficient to meet needs adequately up to subsistence level should be extended to, among others, 'men disqualified for unconditional unemployment benefit *through refusal of suitable employment*.' Here, undisguised though in less picturesque language, is Mr. Russell's vagabond, who is here accorded a new status and official recognition, and is assured in advance that even if he consistently and constantly refuses work (and suitable work at that), he will nevertheless have all his needs supplied. Now it is one thing to say that in what purports to be a civilised State, even a conscientious objector to work should not be left to die in a ditch, when he makes his presence manifest; it is quite another thing to put in the shop window an announcement that all who refuse work will be adequately cared for. The inclusion of this element drawn from the anarchist tradition is something of a blot on an otherwise well-intentioned report.

CHAPTER XIV

EVOLUTIONARY SOCIALISM

(*a*) FABIANISM

FABIANISM in Great Britain occupies—with, however, one significant difference—a place which in some respects corresponds to that assigned on the Continent to Bernstein, who will be noted at the close of this section. Bernstein essentially represents a conscious reaction against Marx, a plea for evolutionary as against revolutionary socialism, for patient reform and construction against the violence and the impatience of the Master. But although in substance the Fabians may have kinship with the point of view of Bernstein, there was in their case little or no Marx to react against. For it was true in the 'eighties, as it is true to-day, that—intellectuals apart—Marx has never struck deep root in this country. The dominant influences here are to be found in distant memories of the Chartists, in the pervasive infiltrations of Owenism, in the later somewhat nebulous teaching or preaching of the Christian Socialists ; and in the early 'eighties there was, above all, throughout all English-speaking countries, the recent gospel of Henry George, who, in *Progress and Poverty*, had achieved a world-success. To us of a somewhat later generation the stir which Henry George created is something of a mystery, for indeed he is in some respects a shallow thinker and an impracticable reformer. Yet for a time he had an ubiquitous influence in popularising a somewhat facile application of the Ricardian Law of Rent. If Fabianism may not be described as a reaction against Marx, since there was virtually no English Marxian school to react against, it may not be an undue strain of language to say that the Fabians were largely instrumental in enabling English socialism to by-pass Marx—at least until Marx came riding home on the shoulders of Lenin.[1]

The Fabian Society represents a picturesque feature in English social and political life in late Victorian and Edwardian days, and its

[1] Perhaps we are at times in danger of forgetting how recent a phenomenon, so far as concerns this country, is the widespread interest in Marx. But occasionally a trifle may bring the point vividly before us. Dr. Joad, in a lecture published in 1944 and obviously delivered shortly before publication, speaking of the intellectuals of our time, says : 'We have, almost all of us, been on the Left. Most of us, especially the younger, have been strongly influenced by Marxism. . . .' The remark suggests an interesting collocation of dates. *The Communist Manifesto*, which contains the clotted cream of Marx, was published in 1848 ; the first volume of *Capital* appeared in 1867 ; Marx died in 1883 ; in 1944, it can at last be said that the younger generation of intellectuals have been strongly influenced by Marxism. This might be interpreted as suggesting that we intellectuals are not very spry in getting off the mark ; but in fact there is another and more plausible explanation.

diverting history has been agreeably chronicled by its secretary, Mr. E. R. Pease. The Fabians, despite their later immersion in sewage, gas, and municipal politics, had, remotely, a somewhat other-worldly, ethical and mystical origin. Thomas Davidson (1840–1900), a wandering scholar of Aberdeen connections, dreaming of 'a community of superior people withdrawn from the world because of its wickedness,' visited London in 1883, and lectured on the Vita Nuova, a Fellowship of the New Life: a touch of a foreign language always adds uplift in these matters.[1] The seed planted by Davidson resulted in the formation of an Association, 'whose ultimate aim shall be the reconstruction of Society in accordance with the highest moral possibilities.' This was the 'Fellowship of the New Life,' of which the ambitious object was declared to be 'the cultivation of a perfect character in each and all.' From the loins of this fellowship, remotely after the manner of what a later generation of national health insurance administrators came to know as a 'separate section,' there sprang on the 4th January, 1884, the Fabian Society. At the same time they redefined the ultimate aim as being, no longer the reconstruction of society as defined above, but as being to 'help on' this reconstruction. It may be that this concession to modesty was bought at the cost of some lucidity of thought, for the purist may perhaps doubt whether, outside the world of hikers, a half-way house can ever be an ultimate aim. Also a collection was made, amounting to 13*s*. 9*d*.[2]

Certain characteristics of Fabianism confront us on the threshold. In the first place, those who think in terms of classes would say that it was essentially a middle-class movement. It was, moreover, not merely middle-class, it was highly intellectual middle-class, free from any infusion of those whose wrongs they were lecturing to right. Fabianism was begotten by highbrows in the drawing-rooms of London. Indeed, not the least curious feature in the earlier days was the wholly disproportionate representation of civil servants, imbued with a natural professional faith in the efficacy and efficiency of higher administration: these were the days when civil servants had leisure, and when the pressure of events had not yet constrained them to develop Section 15 (2) (e) minds. Secondly, the Fabian Society was not, in origin or intention, a socialist society at the outset. So far as its birth and baptismal certificates attest, it sprang from a somewhat vague impulse to moral and ethical regeneration; and it was only as it was borne in upon its members that the desired reconstruction of society was possible only on socialist lines, that they moved to a profession of socialism.[3] At the same time, although it is said that the

[1] Pease: *The History of the Fabian Society*, pp. 26, 28.

[2] *Ibid.* pp. 31–35.

[3] 'Certain members of that circle, modestly feeling that the revolution would have to wait an unreasonably long time if postponed until they personally had attained perfection, set up the banner of socialism militant' (Mr. Bernard Shaw in Tract No. 41).

word 'socialism' does not occur until the third tract,[1] it is impossible to read the first tract without feeling that it ought to be there.

On all the ordinary human probabilities, it might have been prognosticated in January, 1884, that the Fabian Society would lead the anæmic and phthisical life which is the usual lot of a drawing-room coterie. It was saved, because in some rather mysterious way it attracted to its membership in its early days a number of the most remarkable men of their generation, though doubtless this was only obvious to the eye of faith in the years 1884–1886. The men who made Fabianism were not original members. Pre-eminent among the eminent—so pre-eminent that they may almost be called the Big Four—were Sidney Webb, Bernard Shaw, Sydney Olivier and Graham Wallas. With such capable management and such an all-star cast, any production is guaranteed a long run, and the Fabian Society became something of a cult, even if it aimed at being rather an exclusive cult.

The title chosen by the society was intended to present picturesquely its policy and its point of view; but though we have become so familiar with the word 'Fabian' that we scarcely ever stop to ask its meaning, it may be doubted whether the choice was a wholly happy one. Some of the earliest tracts of the Fabian Society bore as a motto what purported to be a quotation in these terms:

> Wherefore it may not be gainsaid that the fruit of this man's long taking of counsel—and (by the many so deemed) untimeous delays—was the safe-holding for all men, his fellow-citizens, of the Common Weal.
>
> For the right moment you must wait, as FABIUS did most patiently when warring against HANNIBAL, though many censured his delays; but when the time comes you must strike hard, as FABIUS did, or your waiting will be in vain, and fruitless.[2]

The quotation appears to be from the works of that versatile author, Anon, who on this occasion was probably a member of the Fabian Society.[3] Many studying the Wardour Street quotation have asked when Fabius struck hard; some may even ask when the Fabians have struck hard, or whether the blow is still pending. But apart from the faintly undergraduatish atmosphere which surrounds the whole business, it may be doubted whether the Society was entirely happy in its baptismal name, since mere opportunism, mere postponement, mere delaying tactics can never provide a map of the path to the Kingdom of Heaven. Nor is it just to the Fabian Society themselves to suggest that they have pursued a purely cunctatious policy. But with this reservation, the origin and the title of the Society give a sufficient preliminary indication of the essence of Fabianism. As Mr. Bernard Shaw said in retrospect in the 41st Tract, 'we were then middle-class all through'; and it is unreasonable to expect a society so constituted to be ardent class-

[1] Pease: *History of the Fabian Society*, p. 38.
[2] Pease: *op. cit.* p. 39.
[3] Tradition assigns the authorship of the 'quotation' to Mr. Frank Podmore.

strugglers and revolutionaries. In a sense it may be said that there was no Fabian doctrine, but only a Fabian policy. Primarily, Fabianism is a method of propaganda, designed to disarm middle-class suspicions and insidiously to facilitate the infiltration of socialist ideas, even when not so recognised, so that it would be ' as easy and matter-of-course for the ordinary respectable Englishman to be a Socialist as to be a Liberal or a Conservative.' [1] For a great part of its history, the Society deliberately restricted its membership, claiming that it was their object to make socialism and not socialists. Their favourite maxim was that of ' permeation,' by which was meant that its members were free to join other political parties where they would operate as Fabian ' cells,' leavening the lump. It was of the essence of Fabian policy to persuade those whom their permeation reached that they were already half-way on the road to socialism without realising it, and that accordingly they might as well be hanged for a sheep as for a lamb. As to what the Fabians meant by socialism, it is perhaps sufficient to say that there never was a Fabian orthodoxy, and the profession of faith exacted from its members enjoyed all the flexibility of interpretation which a tolerant Church grants in the case of a traditional creed. This so-called ' Basis ' is in some ways a curious document.[2] It states that the Society ' works for the transfer to the community of the administration of such industrial capital as can be conveniently managed socially.' The last of the individualists, holding that no industry could be thus ' conveniently ' managed, might have subscribed without undue qualms. The ' Basis ' further indicates the benefits which will flow from these measures, if ' carried out, without compensation (though not without such relief to expropriated individuals as may seem fit to the community) ' ; but again it is not so clear as it might be, in fact it is completely silent, on the rather important question of how relief differs from compensation. Yet, though the most picturesque of the Fabians acknowledged that at the outset they raged at everything that was not socialism, ' without knowing at all clearly what we meant by socialism,' [3] and though they may have had their period of comparative wildness, nevertheless in the course of time they evolved a very precise and in some ways rather restricted view of the content of socialism. Increasingly for the Fabians, State activity became the criterion of socialism, and their gospel was summed up in the largest possible extension of State powers, with, however, a needed reminder that the activity of the State may also be manifested in the functionings of the local authorities.

Yet what constitutes the crown of glory of the Fabians, what indeed

[1] Mr. Bernard Shaw in the Preface to the 1908 reprint of *Fabian Essays*.

[2] It will be found embalmed in the Second Appendix of Pease: *History of the Fabian Society*.

[3] Fabian Tract No. 41.

made them for a generation an indispensable public institution, is that they published tracts, and later much more. Doubtless it took them five years to reach Tract No. 7; but thereafter the floodgates were opened, and the Fabians were ready with a tract on anything. Moreover, though the tracts have the charm of infinite variety, by far the greater number were concerned with horribly concrete questions: municipal pawnshops and slaughterhouses; life in the laundry; the tenant's sanitary catechism; tramways and trusts. The transition from the Rights of Man to the Tenant's Sanitary Catechism is, in its way, symbolical of what Fabianism achieved. The Society became more and more a research laboratory, concerned with the new science of social investigation. They may not have had much faith in the class war, but they believed in the production of an ample supply of controversial ammunition, and in the virtue of keeping it as dry as possible. The cold eye of posterity may look on some of the tracts as rather dud bombs, or Guy Fawkes squibs; but at least the Fabians taught the late Victorian age that on any given question there is much need of digging and delving, much harvesting and gleaning.

It is time to come into closer contact with the Fabians as manifested in some of their more revealing and informative literature. Where Fabian literature begins and ends would be a nice question for discussion; a very considerable section of English literature for a long generation, including much in fields remote from municipal pawnshops, was written by members of the Fabian Society. At one end it would probably be a vain subject of academic research to look for traces of Fabianism in the poetry of Rupert Brooke; at the other extreme, the puritanical and didactic Bernard Shaw has never been able to resist the itch to teach, reprove, correct and instruct, and in consequence his Prefaces, to which he attached Plays, might well be regarded as expositions on particular points of the Fabian way of life. But indeed the Intelligent Woman in a hurry (if, indeed, an intelligent woman ever forgets the dignity of a leisurely carriage) may find all that she requires with regard to Fabianism at its most significant, in relatively small bulk. Apart from Mr. Pease's *History of the Fabian Society*, there are the *Fabian Essays in Socialism*, originally published in 1889, and as many of the tracts (especially the earlier ones) as the nearest public library can disgorge.

The *Fabian Essays in Socialism* has remained a book to be read beyond the generation for whom it was written, though perhaps the later and continuous demand which it has enjoyed may be, in a way, a tribute to its importance as a historical document. Undoubtedly, like everything else with a date, it 'dates'; and prefaces to subsequent editions, written by its admiring authors, are to a considerable extent taken up with drawing attention to what had been concealed from the eyes of the original essayists. An alarming footnote to the *Essays* explains that in the year ending April, 1889, upwards of 700 lectures were given by members of the Fabian Society alone. The *Fabian Essays* are given as a sample of this deluge of oratory; but in the case of such astute salesmen as the Fabians, it is a safe assumption that the sample is drawn from the rosiest and choicest apples on the top of the box. There are in fact eight essays, written by the seven leading Fabians of the time.[1]

Taking as a necessary, and almost as a sufficient, guide the *Fabian Essays* and the earliest tracts, above all Tract No. 70, a *Report on Fabian Policy*, it is possible to arrive at a more precise statement of Fabian views and intentions. It has been said above that Fabianism was primarily a policy, a question of tactics, rather than a body of doctrine; yet obviously they were not without their doctrinal side. Sir Ernest Barker and Mr. Beer have alike stressed the obligation of Mr. Webb to Mill [2]—the later Mill of socialist leanings—and though Mr. Shaw rather demurs,[3] in one passage Mr. Webb speaks as if socialism in England owes its whole existence to Mill.[4] Rather oddly it is recorded that the young Fabians read Proudhon as well as Marx.[5] If they say so, it must be so; but it would be interesting to know what lessons the budding Fabians learned from this most anarchic mind, who boasted that he had never asked the State to do anything for him, and whose pen could drip uninterrupted venom for a page in denunciation of the State as the arch-enemy of mankind. Proudhon and Sidney Webb would indeed be strange bed-fellows.

But indeed the ancestry of Fabianism is sufficiently obvious on the first brush with the *Essays* and the earlier pamphlets, quite apart from the introspective confessions of the Fabians themselves. The first of the essays (one of two by Mr. Bernard Shaw) is very largely a composition based on two themes: one is a restatement of Henry George, with roots in the Ricardian Theory of Rent, and the other is the Jevonian Theory of Value, based on the conception of diminishing utility.[6] With the help of the Ricardian Law, the original owner of the land is shown as growing ever fatter and fatter, leaving no opening for the late arrival, who is accordingly forced to sell himself to the lords of the soil. Mr. Shaw plays with the Jevonian technique with all the

[1] The essayists were Bernard Shaw, Sydney Olivier, William Clarke, Hubert Bland, Sidney Webb, Annie Besant and Graham Wallas.

[2] Barker: *Political Thought in England, from Herbert Spencer to the Present Day*, p. 213. Beer: *History of British Socialism*, vol. 2, p. 281.

[3] Pease: *op. cit.* p. 259.

[4] Fabian Tract No. 15, p. 11. See also Webb: *Socialism in England*, p. 19.

[5] Barker: *op. cit.*, p. 215. Also Fabian Tract No. 41.

[6] This agrees with the considered views of Mr. Shaw: 'Accordingly, the abstract economics of the Fabian Essays are, as regards value, the economics of Jevons. As regards rent they are the economics of Ricardo' (Memorandum by Mr. Shaw, attached to Mr. Pease's *History of the Fabian Society*, p. 261).

gusto one devotes to a new toy. With increasing population, the marginal worker becomes valueless; what he gets is merely his keep: 'for bare subsistence wages you can get as much common labour as you want.'[1] There is no hint here of the possible repercussions of trade unions on the value of workers, who otherwise are little better than superfluous kittens condemned to the bucket, whom you may have if you care to keep them. Indeed, one of the matters on which the Fabians subsequently reproached themselves was that their eyes were at first sealed to the significance and importance of trade unionism. It was a defect for which certain of their number made ample amends later.

Indeed, anyone to-day reading the earlier literature of the Fabians can hardly fail to be impressed by the quite extraordinary importance attached to the Ricardian Law of Rent: it was, of course, the day and the heyday of Henry George, preceding his long crepuscular decline. Moreover, although in theory the Fabians were concerned with every type of rent, not merely with the rent of agricultural land, but extending the terms to cover all differential unearned incomes, again the impression left, and that not merely on a first reading, is that their eyes were on the land. Mr. Shaw proclaimed in the first of his essays that 'public property in land is the basic economic condition of socialism.'[2] In the last of his essays he says with more emphasis of the economists that 'with one law alone—the law of rent—they destroyed the whole series of assumptions upon which private property is based'[3]; though here, it may be urged, he is not specifically, in terms, referring to the law of agricultural rent. Yet in the seventh tract (for instance) it is the nationalisation of land that is put in the forefront, and it is not without significance that in the 'Basis,' that most basic document, the extinction of private property in land takes precedence of place over 'the transfer to the community of the administration of such industrial capital as can conveniently be managed socially.' It is difficult to resist the inference that if the earlier Fabians (or the Fabians in their earlier days—which is not quite the same thing) were fascinated by the Law of Rent, it was primarily in its relationship to land, and that fundamentally, after the manner of Henry George, they were land nationalisers.

But, it may be protested, in theory at least the Fabians did not so limit the interpretation of the word 'rent,' but were also concerned with other forms of rent—rents of ability and what-not. What, it may be asked, is the Law of Rent, and what is a 'rent of ability'—an idea which, when they first stumbled across it, the early Fabians were human enough to find amusing? Though the economists have made a mighty song and dance about the Law of Rent, so that it is impossible to write an economic text-book without devoting to it a

[1] *Fabian Essays*, p. 18. [2] *Ibid.* p. 24. [3] *Ibid.* p. 165.

lengthy chapter, or to deliver a course of lectures without spending at least two on the subject, it is but an obvious deduction from two statements of the obvious, such as might be comprehended even by Mr. Shaw's Intelligent Woman. Looking round the world, it is in the first place obvious that identical commodities are produced at very different costs, whether the commodities be wheat, coal, witches and jumbos, knitted stockings, legal advice or medical attendance. Looking round the market, it is in the second place obvious that substantially identical and indistinguishable commodities are sold at the same price. From these so obvious facts, that things are frequently produced at different costs, and are nevertheless sold at the same price, it is an obvious inference that there must be a surplus (a 'producer's surplus') emerging in the case of the commodity produced under more favourable conditions, which someone will be able to collar, and in fact which someone *must* collar, though of course that someone may be the State. This 'producer's surplus' is rent.

So long as we are moving within Ricardian confines, the position is clear, and the theoretical arguments sufficiently cogent. If society, for its sustenance, requires that inferior land should be cultivated, the price of the product must be such that those who cultivate under unfavourable conditions will at least be able to make ends meet; and such a price will, by hypothesis, yield a surplus to the more fortunate. If the land is worked by the proprietors, the surplus will remain in the pockets of those who are favoured by Nature; if, however, it is a world in which land is leased by owners to those who work it, the 'producer's surplus' will be skimmed off by the landlord as the price of the labourer being allowed to work. Moreover—and we are still following in Ricardo's footsteps—the whack thus appropriated by the landlords will go on mounting; for, as population increases and we are forced for our maintenance to cultivate the Bass Rock and the desolate places of Caithness, rent will rise, since rent rests on differential fertility—the significant difference being between the fertility of the land under consideration and the fertility of the worst land that society is compelled to cultivate. As we depress the margin of cultivation to the waste places, we enlarge this difference, and accordingly there are added to rent continual increments, which owe their origin neither to the anxious care of the proprietor nor the sweat of the farmer. As thus stated, there could scarcely be a stronger argument for the nationalisation of rent than is provided by the Ricardian theory. Perhaps it should be added that the argument is more compelling in theory than in practice, firstly, because it is by no means clear how much of 'rent,' as understood by the vulgar farmer, if indeed any, is in fact the rent of the economic text-book, the payment for that elusive entity 'the original and indestructible qualities of the soil'; and secondly, because owing to changes in population growth, in communications and in agricultural science, we are not in fact being driven to cultivate the ever-more-and-more-barren. On the contrary (war times and war conditions apart) the margin of cultivation rather tends to be pulled in. It follows that the argument is in practice stronger with regard to increments of rent in respect of urban sites; but this lies somewhat apart from the Ricardo-George tradition.

But, after the manner of human ingenuity, the thought dawned on some economist in his obscure lair, that if rent is defined as a 'producer's surplus,' then agricultural rent does not stand alone. The human mind, heedless of the dangers of *als ob*, can never resist an analogy. Throughout the whole of life men making similar efforts get very different results. Anyone who cares to use the jargon of the schools may say, if he chooses, that the good, efficient and rapid worker enjoys a rent of ability denied to his more ordinary comrade. An incompetent doctor with a sunny bedside manner may reap a bounteous crop of patients, far in excess of that harvested by his glum and more competent rival; he may even have them as patients for a longer period of time. He enjoys, if not a rent of ability, then at least a rent which springs from his radiant bearing. But all this, if it may seem ingenious to the ingenuous, is but to feed ourselves on words. Equally one might say, if it meant anything, that the hard-working peasant proprietor (or anyone else) derived a rent from a peculiar kink in his character, from the absence of a normal inhibition, preventing him from reducing his exertions to a minimum. If honesty is the best policy (and anyone who reads Fourier may be forgiven for doubting it), the prosperity of the honest man may with equal justice be described as a rent he draws from his honesty. In essence, all this is in effect a procedure that begs the question. Wherever there is a gain in excess of the ordinary, it may with little effort be described as a rent of some kind, and as rents are something which just happen, these gains should if possible be appropriated for the community. Also in the end this nomenclature leads to a perverse view of the whole human problem. Mr. Shaw, in his airy way, defines a rent of ability as 'the excess of its produce over that of ordinary stupidity.'[1] In any question relating to agriculture, the land least worth cultivating is an ineluctable datum line; but when we begin to play about with rents of ability, it is gradually assumed, as foreshadowed in Mr. Shaw's phrase, that the normal human being, in terms of whom we should think, is a person of ordinary stupidity, very ordinary honesty, and (if possible) more than ordinary aversion to labour; and that anyone who exceeds this marginal and minimal endowment is an exceptional person enjoying a 'rent' to which in

[1] *Fabian Essays*, p. 9.

equity he has no right. There is much to be said for the idea of a 'quasi-rent,' as the term was used by Marshall to indicate the differential gain that may temporarily spring from different 'quality' in machinery; but it would have been well if refinements of the nature of 'rents of ability' had been left undevised.[1]

This digression on rent is, it is hoped, less of a digression than it may appear. The early Fabian theory, so far as there was a theory, was so largely based on the 'Law of Rent'; their practical programme in the early days consisted to so large an extent in the appropriation of rent by the State, that, even at the cost of two pages, it seemed desirable to look at the meaning of rent and its derivatives, and at the dangers that may beset the path.

It is, moreover, of the essence of Fabianism that this process of appropriation and absorption by the State is already far advanced, that it is still making rapid progress and will continue to do so, by entirely constitutional means and without resort to anything remotely resembling violence. 'Slice after slice' has already been taken[2]; and we, of a later generation, can testify that the slices are becoming thicker: as in the nursery tale, we are rapidly moving from 'Top-off' to 'All-gone.' 'Step by step' the process goes on. The transition is gradual and peaceful; it is to a large extent unconscious, directed even by those who imagine that they are free from socialist taint. The distinctive mark of the Fabian Society among rival bodies of socialists was, according to Mr. Shaw, its 'resolute constitutionalism.'[3] At greater length Mr. Webb, already hankering after the inevitability of gradualness, postulated that important organic changes must satisfy four conditions. Somewhat abridged, these conditions are that they must be (i) democratic, acceptable to a majority of the people; (ii) gradual, and thus not causing dislocation; (iii) not regarded as immoral by the mass of the people; and (iv) lastly, in this country at least, constitutional and peaceful.[4]

Two other aspects of this evolutionary process are in a sense linked together. Firstly, the work of socialisation is frequently accomplished by those without the fold, who in their speeches may rail at socialism, yet in their deeds fulfil the observation of Sir William Harcourt (and others) that 'we are all socialists now.' Thus Mr. Webb, surveying the progress of State intervention and State control, is able to say that 'all this has been done by "practical" men, ignorant, that is to say,

[1] Take, as an illustration of the point indicated in this paragraph, the following: 'If those who are never happy unless they are working insist on putting in extra work to please themselves, they must not pretend that this is a painful sacrifice for which they should be paid' (*The Intelligent Woman's Guide to Socialism*, etc., Section 23, on 'Incentive').

[2] Fabian Tract No. 15, p. 13.

[3] Preface to the 1931 reprint of *Fabian Essays*.

[4] *Fabian Essays*, p. 32.

of any scientific sociology believing socialism to be the most foolish of dreams.' [1]

> Glad hearts! Without reproach or blot
> Who do thy work and know it not.

And in the second place, and just for this reason, Mr. Graham Wallas abandons any idea of finality: '. . . the steady introduction of socialistic institutions by men who reject socialist ideas, all incline us to give up any expectation of a final and perfect reform.' [2] This is a frequently recurring idea with the earlier Fabians. The movement to socialism is a continuing process: there is no frontier over which we must pass to enter the promised land. It is not going to be the kind of thing to which a date can be assigned. Mrs. Besant puts the point concisely: 'There will never be a point at which a society crosses from individualism to socialism. The change is ever going forward; and our society is well on the way to socialism.' [3]

Not merely then will the movement to socialism be accomplished by entirely constitutional means; not merely is it a gradual and almost unperceived transition in a direction rather than towards an end; it is a change which is being furthered by those without the fold, who are unconscious of the distance we have already travelled. Moreover, though for very different reasons from those lying behind the Marxian conclusions, the movement is in its way automatic, ineluctable, designed by Fate. The economic evolution going on, 'proceeding silently every day,' is, says Mr. Clarke, 'practically independent of our individual desires or prejudices.' [4] The socialist (above all the Fabian socialist) is thus an interpreter rather than a doer. He is engaged (the phrase is Mr. Bland's) in 'turning instinct into self-conscious reason.' [5] Primarily then, the Fabians regarded themselves as High Priests of the *Zeitgeist*, whose function it was to interpret the spirit and justify the tendencies of the times. Their purpose was to provide a philosophy for changes already taking place, not owing to any feeble action of theirs, but because of the changing outlook of M. Tout le Monde.

As to the direction in which we are being driven or lured by the *Zeitgeist*, whereof the Fabians are the interpreters, it is enough to look round and observe. Already in the preface to the original edition of the *Essays* it had been stated that the writers shared 'a common conviction of the necessity of vesting the organization of industry and the material of production in a State identified with the whole people by complete democracy.' The implication is that in a true democracy the State is a friend of the people; that it is indeed

[1] *Fabian Essays*, p. 46. [2] *Ibid.* p. 123. [3] *Ibid.* p. 141. [4] *Ibid.* p. 58. [5] *Ibid.* p. 195.

the people, and that it is accordingly impossible to ask the State to do too much for the people. On this side Fabianism becomes to a large extent synonymous with a demand for an indefinite extension of State activity. There is a dreadful passage in Mr. Webb's essay wherein he gloatingly chonicles what the State already does; and to this he forthwith adds a list of the activities and other things which it registers, including playing-card makers, hawkers, dogs and cabs, places of worship and dancing-rooms.[1] And if these things were done in the comparatively green tree of 1889, what is being done in the dry of half a century later? It is assumed, it will be observed, that any kind of State activity is an instalment of socialism and to be welcomed accordingly. It is a matter of gratification that the State maintains its own cow-meadows, and that some of the colonial governments deal in guano, quinine and opium. That State activity or control of any kind is tantamount to socialism is a strangely naive view, against which at least one of the essayists, Mr. Bland, had the courage to protest. It is, he held, not so much what the State does, as the end for which it does it, that provides the crucial test; and greatly daring, he adds a derisory footnote on those who adduce the existence of hawkers' licences as an instance of the 'progress of socialism.'[2] But in the main the naivete of Mr. Webb prevailed over the common sense of Mr. Bland; and State activity of any and every kind became the end of their endeavour. This extension of the State into all the available nooks and crannies of life has, moreover, as a natural corollary the disappearance of the individual. It is not merely the capitalist (who calls for no sympathy) who is being 'registered, inspected, controlled, and eventually superseded by the community'[3]; the ultimate aim is that of 'enrolling every able-bodied man directly in the service of the community.'[4] The vision is thus that of an ubiquitous State, acting as the universal employer. The transition, moreover, will be facilitated by the growth of Joint Stock Companies, and their consequent easy transfer to the State in the fullness of time. As Mr. Webb remarks, more than a third of the whole business of England is now done by Joint Stock Companies, and their shareholders could be expropriated by the community with no more dislocation than is occasioned by the daily purchase of shares on the Stock Exchange.[5] Somewhat more picturesquely Mr. Clarke would not seek to undo the work which the capitalists are unconsciously doing for the people (led by Adam Smith's invisible hand?). It is enough to prepare the people 'to take up the threads when they fall from the weak hands of a useless possessing class.'[6] Mrs. Besant is equally emphatic: the capitalists are unconsciously paving the way for their own super-

[1] *Fabian Essays*, pp. 44–45. These two pages must be seen to be believed.
[2] *Ibid.* p. 198. [3] *Ibid.* p. 46. [4] Fabian Tract No. 51.
[5] *Fabian Essays*, p. 45. [6] *Ibid.* pp. 94–95.

session; everything organised as a trust is ripe for appropriation by the community.[1]

In one respect this policy of unlimited *étatisme* calls for a modifying addendum. It is greatly to the honour of the earlier Fabians that they realised, sooner than most, that Westminster and Whitehall do not exhaust the State. There are also the municipalities; and progress to the ultimate heaven of the Fabians' dreams was as likely to be realised through the action of the local authorities as of the central State. At times indeed Fabianism almost became a doctrine of municipal socialism. The most practicable step to advance the control of the community over essential things was, it was held, for the electors to 'capture' the councils. Mr. Webb, calling in aid the example of Mr. Joseph Chamberlain in his Birmingham days, announced a programme of 'unlimited municipalisation of local public services and a wide extension of corporate activity.'[2] 'High rates and a healthy city' was a phrase which epigrammatically presented the means and the end.

This enthusiasm for local authorities, above all the recently created County Councils on which great hopes were set, misled the Fabians into strange Utopian fancies. Much of Mrs. Besant's essay is taken up with what the County Council might do for the unemployed by the establishment of county farms. At least, they begin as county farms, but they end as Heaven knows what—a cross between one of Fourier's *Phalanstères* and a complete outfit of Louis Blanc's workshops. And also, after the manner of Louis Blanc, the private producer will go to the wall in this fierce struggle with a more efficient type of enterprise:

> After a while the private producers will disappear, not because there will be any law against individualist production, but because it will not pay. No one will care to face the worries, the harassments, the anxieties of individual struggling for livelihood, when ease, freedom, and security can be enjoyed in the communal service.[3]

Mr. Shaw, it is interesting to note, is also seduced by a similar vision into re-echoing the soothing assurances of Louis Blanc regarding the imminent capitulation of private enterprise:

> In the market the competition of those industries with the private concern will be irresistible.[4]

As Mr. Webb subsequently acknowledged, the earlier Fabians had not yet realised that local authorities are essentially associations of consumers, not associations of producers.[5]

This concentration of attention on the administrative machine leads in the Fabians to a glorification of efficiency which at times

[1] *Fabian Essays*, p. 146.
[2] Fabian Tract No. 51, p. 7.
[3] *Fabian Essays*, p. 147.
[4] *Ibid.* p. 182.
[5] Introduction (1919) to the *Fabian Essays*.

lives in uneasy harness with their faith in democracy. Democracy, if we be honest with ourselves, does not regard efficiency as the first of virtues ; indeed it may be that—at least in Marshall's short period—democracy and efficiency are rivals. Socialism, as explained by Mr. Shaw in one of the numerous prefaces to successive reprints of the *Essays*, involves the introduction of design, contrivance and co-ordination ; in the past, as he holds, there has been a failure to realise 'the extent to which the very existence of society depends on the skilled work of administrators and experts.'

While the laudation of efficiency pervades the whole of Fabian literature, explicitly or implicitly, there are two passages which are so instructive and so illuminating that they call for special reference. Mr. Webb, in sentences which have a peculiarly Godwinian flavour, remarks that 'there is, at any moment, one particular arrangement of social relations which involves the minimum of human misery then and there possible,' and that such questions as these are a matter for scientific investigation. In the evolution and rivalries of races and nations, what is decisive is no longer the qualities of the individual, but the 'more valuable social organisation.' In the Franco-Prussian war (still a fairly recent memory) the French were beaten, he holds, 'because the German social organism was, for the purposes of the time, superior in efficiency to the French.' And he continues:

> If we desire to hand on to the afterworld our direct influence, and not merely the memory of our excellence, we must take even more care to improve the social organism of which we form part, than to perfect our own individual developments. Or rather, the perfect and fitting development of each individual is not necessarily the utmost and highest cultivation of his own personality, but the filling, in the best possible way, of his humble function in the great social machine.[1]

Here, curiously blended together, is the adoration of the machine and the sacrifice of each individual in order that the machine may be yet more efficient. What matters is not the 'cultivation of personality,' but the smoothness with which each consents to become a cog in the 'great social machine.' Is this the ordered world of Plato? the deceitful harmony of Fascism? the law of the beehive? The Fabians, if they had been called upon to choose between liberty and efficiency, would have had no hesitation in deciding which was the greater good for humanity.

The other passage of great significance in its remoter implications may be found towards the end of an Appendix which Mr. Shaw wrote for later editions of Mr. Pease's *History of the Fabian Society*. Here Mr. Shaw comments on the anomaly that a hawker may not ply his trade without a licence, whereas (though Mr. Shaw would not use such language) any fool may be sent to Parliament.[2] And to

[1] *Fabian Essays*, pp. 53–54. [2] Pease: *op. cit.* p. 268.

remedy this defect, the hope is held out that democracy itself will one day demand that only suitable men shall be presented to its choice: it is in effect, and up to a point, the method adopted in the so-called General Elections in Germany under the Hitler regime. It may be suggested that democracy is no longer democracy, if it is forcibly prevented from choosing fools when it feels so inclined. Assuming that democracy, as we know it, means, or may mean, mess and inefficiency, is it possible to save it from itself, except by means which in one way or another will supersede democracy? 'Without qualified rulers,' says Mr. Shaw, 'a socialist State is impossible': and if the socialist State does not throw up such qualified rulers, what then? Mr. Shaw speaks with the voice of the bureaucratic caste, pursuing efficiency with a single eye, and girding at the obstacles put in its way by foolish people enjoying democratically the right to be foolish.

In conclusion, in supplement of what has already been said, some reference should be made to Fabian Tract No. 70, the *Report on Fabian Policy*, which appeared without any indication of authorship, but which in Mr. Pease's *History* is assigned to Mr. Shaw. For the external student of Fabianism it is probably the most interesting of all the Tracts, since here the Fabians, contemplating themselves in their own mirror, report on what they imagine themselves to be. Most of the characteristic features here acknowledged have already been indicated in the foregoing pages; it is unnecessary to refer further to the question of Fabian tactics, toleration, and readiness to compromise in everything except their uncompromising constitutionalism. On this latter point there is, however, a touching expression of faith in the British Constitution, if suitably and slightly amended, which is of some interest:

> When the House of Commons is freed from the veto of the House of Lords and thrown open to candidates from all classes by an effective system of Payment of Representatives and a more rational method of election, the British parliamentary system will be, in the opinion of the Fabian Society, a first-rate practical instrument of democratic government.

But a creed should not merely be a confession of faith: it should also renounce whatever devil calls for renunciation. From this point of view, some interest attaches to Fabian 'repudiations.' In the first place, they refuse to use the terms 'bourgeois' and 'middle class' as terms of reproach—and in the circumstances, quite right too: 'it's an ill bird that files its ain nest.' This circumspect attitude is, however, not dictated solely by considerations of prudence and self-regard; there is the further restraining thought that hitherto the socialist movement has been 'inspired, instructed and led' by members of the bourgeoisie, whatever that may be. It is profoundly true;

and therefore, if only out of respect for Marx and Lassalle, it is unwise to rail unduly at the middle classes.

Another repudiation relates to wages. Socialism, it is expressly stated, does not involve the abolition of wages, but merely the establishment of 'standard allowances for the maintenance of all workers by the community in its own service.' Even more interesting is the sequel that the Fabian Society 'resolutely opposes all pretensions to hamper the socialisation of industry with equal wages, equal hours of labour, equal official status, or equal authority for everyone.' Such conditions—and it is an ominous phrase—would be 'incompatible with the equality of subordination to the common interest which is fundamental in modern socialism.' Finally, the Fabians explicitly renounce all schemes for securing to any person or group 'the entire product of their labour'—and on good grounds; and they also renounce Utopias in South America or elsewhere, all the prolific brood of New Harmonys, Freelands, Icarias, which are somewhat unkindly repudiated as attempts to establish socialism by private enterprise. The individual may be a nuisance, as the Fabian view uniformly seems to imply, and may deserve all the 'equality of subordination' that can be ladled out to him; but it may be doubted whether he can be eliminated, or whether in the true sense it is possible to circumvent private enterprise. It is not really a debating point to suggest that ultimately everything worth doing is done by some individual, and is therefore an example of private enterprise. Even an Act of Parliament sprouts originally in one mind; even the Minority Report of the Poor Law Commission was effectively the work of one person; even Fabian Tract No. 70 was (as Mr. Pease assures us) written by Mr. Shaw.

Such were the Fabians, most immaculate and least revolutionary of socialists; none were ever less guilty of drinking the wine of violence. In one respect their socialism is the socialism of the simple-minded, signifying, as it does, nothing more than the indefinite extension of State activity, so that the hawker's licence becomes a proof of the progress of socialism, and the existence of a policeman demonstrates that already we are living in a communistic State. On the question of how far the State should go, they were discreetly ambiguous: the path to socialism was a journey, with no assigned destination. They chanted in unison the song of the Pilgrims to Samarkand:

> We shall go
> Always a little further.

Believing that it was better to travel joyfully than to arrive, they travelled; and being blessed with the jocund companionship of Mr. Shaw, they succeeded in travelling very joyfully indeed. Moreover, the vehicle in which they travelled was a highly respectable hackney stage-coach, licensed by the appropriate authority. In place of barricades, rifles and lamp-posts with dependent ropes, they relied on such prosaic machinery as universal suffrage and the ballot-box. They were the cream of the intelligentsia, and they knew it—'a body of highly educated people,' says Mr. Pease, not without satisfaction. Suffering somewhat from the Narcissus complex, they were rather too much given to contemplating themselves. In their missionary zeal for truth or self-advertisement, they were perhaps too apt to winnow with every wind and to go into every way. And perhaps in half-unconscious ways their intellectual top-heaviness reveals itself in a certain aridity. They were more grieved by the world's mess than hurt by the world's wrongs: that the world was run with so little wisdom reflected little credit on the intelligence of *Homo sapiens*.

Yet the Fabians occupy a place in the history of socialism which is in no way commensurate with any contribution they may have made to socialist doctrine or thought. If their primary purpose was to disarm middle-class suspicion and to make socialism respectable, so that even a churchwarden in his most sober moments need not be ashamed to confess a weakness for socialism, then surely they succeeded beyond their wildest dreams. They produced a form of socialism which could be eagerly embraced by the undergraduate, enabling him to give his parents (in the 'nineties) that slight shock which it is so wise to administer from time to time, while at the same time it entailed no upheaval in his present mode of life. For so far from Fabianism imposing any ascetic renunciation on its devotees, it rather implied that while it was permissible to hope that one day the evil Babylon would dissolve into the New Jerusalem, nevertheless so long as Babylon remained the old bad, capitalistic, competitive Babylon, it would be foolish not to live as did the Babylonians.[1] In the end the Fabians not merely took the sting out of socialism, but they gave it an allure of its own. Indeed they almost overshot their target. They not merely made socialism respectable; they came near to making it a fashion, so that a profession of socialism (of a kind), so far from being the mark of a rebel, almost became the done thing.

One last point may be suggested. The Fabians largely based their case on the extent to which the State already controlled, managed, 'interfered,' deducing therefrom that we were already half-way to socialism. Looking back, we may be tempted to think that, compara-

[1] In case this may appear an uncharitable judgment, the reader should refer to Mr. Shaw's chapter on 'Personal Righteousness' addressed to his Intelligent Woman, *e.g.*: 'Should you become a convert to Socialism you will not be committed to any change in your private life, nor indeed will you find yourself able to make any change that would be of the smallest use in that direction.' Neither Jesus of Nazareth nor Lenin, one feels, would have addressed a new disciple in quite these terms; but, of course, neither was a Fabian.

tively speaking, they were chronicling the flow of water in the placid Arun, whereas to-day we are witnesses of the Mississippi in flood. How far the acquiescence of the public in the enormous extension of State activity and control has been facilitated by the insidious preaching and permeation of the Fabians is a question which it is easy to ask, but which no wise man will venture to answer.

(*b*) EDUARD BERNSTEIN AND 'REVISIONISM'

As a pendent to the foregoing discussion of Fabianism, it may be convenient to include here a reference to the Revisionist movement, which in many respects represents in Germany the same influences working to the same conclusions. In each case there is a planing down of the most obvious and the most untenable protuberances of Marx, who, however, is more consciously disowned in the German movement, for the perfectly valid reason that in pre-Fabian days, Marx, neat and undiluted, had counted for so little in Great Britain. In each case, likewise, there is disbelief in revolution as an effective means of progress, and faith in the slow march of events and in the 'inevitability of gradualness,' which perhaps need not be so gradual. We are in each case invited to depose revolution and to enthrone evolution as the goddess who will get us there.

The prime begetter of Revisionism was Eduard Bernstein (1850–1932), who presented his views to the world in a cumbrously entitled volume[1] which appeared in English, somewhat abridged and with a more manageable title-page, as *Evolutionary Socialism.* Bernstein's apparent backslidings had for some time occasioned considerable tumult in the circles affected, and there is incorporated in his volume a letter, written in October, 1898, to the German Social Democratic Party, meeting in Stuttgart, wherein he tersely summarises his doubts, hesitations and disbeliefs. For the ordinary reader this letter is more precious and satisfying than the lengthier statement contained in the *Voraussetzungen*, which, if truth be told, does not always escape dullness.

The problem confronting Bernstein was that which faces all honest souls brought up in orthodoxy. For it is of the essence of orthodoxy that it is dated, and sooner or later it ceases to be a satisfactory explanation of a world which it has ceased to explain. Reality contradicts faith. In the present case, Marx had provided certain economic theories which could no longer hold water, or anything else; he had analysed society, and society had contradicted his analysis; he had prophesied and fulfilment had lagged. What should the discerning faithful do in these circumstances? Should he cling to the old ortho-

[1] *Die Voraussetzungen des Sozialismus und die Aufgaben der Sozialdemokratie* (1899).

doxy, and flatter himself that though not really true, it was nevertheless symbolically true, and therefore true enough to be going on with? Should he turn the revelation into a Sorelian myth, and say that, if not true, it ought to be true; and that, though not true, nevertheless it does him good to imagine it to be true? Or should he frankly acknowledge that the inherited creed is no longer in line with apparent reality, and that accordingly it demands restatement and revision? This was the view of Bernstein and the Revisionists: the Marxian doctrines had to be purged of what time had shown to be fallacious. It is significant that Bernstein did not claim that he was disclosing anything new: the justification of his essay was that it acknowledged what had already been disclosed.[1]

The letter of October, 1898, to which reference was made above, sets out trenchantly the view that things are not developing on lines foreshadowed by Marx, and that therefore a change of tactics is required. Bernstein acknowledges, as a concession to the Marxian faith, that the theory of the evolution of modern society set forth as far back as the *Communist Manifesto* was correct, in so far as it characterised general tendencies: it was mistaken, above all, in its estimate of the time that this evolution would take. In the words of the Prophet Daniel, 'the thing was true, but the time appointed was long' —much longer indeed than Marx had indicated. In short, the revolution which was supposed to be at the door was, if anything, visibly receding. There had not developed that acute opposition of classes which was the basis of the argument of the *Manifesto*:

> It is not only useless, it is the greatest folly to attempt to conceal this from ourselves. The number of members of the possessing classes is to-day not smaller but larger. The enormous increase of social wealth is not accompanied by a decreasing number of large capitalists, but by an increasing number of capitalists of all degrees. The middle classes change their character, but they do not disappear from the social scale.[2]

At the same time Bernstein finds Marx equally at sea in that other prognosis which has generally been regarded as evidence of superior foresight. As he looked round the world, Bernstein saw no evidence that concentration in production was taking place in all its departments with equal thoroughness and at an equal rate. Moreover, if there were concentration, the intermediate and the smaller businesses were not disappearing: 'trade statistics show an extraordinarily elaborated graduation of enterprises in regard to size. No rung of the ladder is disappearing from it.' [3]

Meanwhile, on the other side of the picture, an evolution was taking place in the direction of improving the conditions of the workers; and with increasing democratisation, the needs and the opportuni-

[1] *Evolutionary Socialism* (English version), p. 26.
[2] *Ibid.* p. xi. [3] *Ibid.* p. xi.

ties of political catastrophe were correspondingly diminished. The conclusion of the whole matter was therefore that for the present, and for a long time to come, the task of the socialist would be 'to organise the working classes politically and develop them as a democracy, and to fight for all reforms in the State which are adapted to raise the working classes and transform the State in the direction of democracy.'[1] The vision of a sudden catastrophe and the tactics appropriate on the assumption of an imminent catastrophe thus fade away. A catastrophe would not, indeed, be desirable in the interests of social democracy: 'a greater security for lasting success lies in a steady advance than in the possibilities offered by a catastrophic crash.'[2] Such, largely in his own words, is the substance of Bernstein's somewhat epoch-making letter; and in what is, in effect, comment on his own letter, he declares his faith: 'I strongly believe . . . in the march forward of the working classes, who step by step must work out their own emancipation.'[3] It is an interesting statement and should be compared with the almost identical phraseology of the Fabians. Mr. Sidney Webb and Eduard Bernstein are alike step-by-steppers.

Bernstein's volume is in a sense little more than an elaboration and extension of these and other points, and although of the highest significance as perhaps the earliest critical assessment of Marx from the side of the Marxians, it does not call for any detailed summary or consideration here. Some points may, however, be noted. He repudiates, as had indeed Marx and Engels, the earlier and more extreme statements of the Materialist Conception of History, with its predestinarian implications. In the stage we have reached to-day, he holds that the ideological and ethical factors have greater scope for independent activity than formerly; and it is implicit in this view that there is an increasing power of directing economic evolution.[4] We may be masters of our fate, and determine where we are going. The Marxian theory of value and of surplus value is criticised because surplus value is therein represented as emerging 'exclusively in the sphere of production, where it is the industrial wage-earner who produces it.'[5] Thus, according to Marx, it comes only from 'living labour.'[6] On the Bernstein (and more rational) view, surplus value 'can only be grasped as a concrete fact by thinking of the whole economy of society.'[7] In any case Bernstein writes as if these subtleties of analysis were immaterial: 'a scientific basis for socialism or communism cannot be supported on the fact only that the wage-worker does not receive the full value of the product of his work.'[8] It is a sound point, which, however, strikes at the roots of 'scientific socialism': and it may be observed that if the economic basis is

[1] *Evolutionary Socialism*, p. xiii. [2] *Ibid.* p. xiv.
[3] *Ibid.* p. xxii. [4] *Ibid.* p. 14. [5] *Ibid.* p. 36.
[6] *Ibid.* p. 40. [7] *Ibid.* p. 38. [8] *Ibid.* p. 39.

discarded, socialism must be founded on moral and ethical considerations.

On distribution and concentration, Bernstein in the main elaborates what is contained in his letter. He must have been one of the first to underline that 'the most modern and crass form of capitalist concentration—the Trust'—may have in fact quite a different effect on the distribution of wealth than might at first be assumed, inasmuch as it leads to what he calls 'a splitting up of shares.'[1] In fact, says Bernstein, there is proceeding neither a relative nor an absolute diminution in the number of the possessing classes. So far from society being simplified (into the two extremes foreseen by Marx) there is taking place an increasing differentiation both with regard to incomes and business activities: enterprises of all sizes survive, and there is no development according to a pattern.[2] Indeed, so far as agriculture is concerned (that perpetual stumbling-block in socialist thought), it is argued that the smaller and medium agricultural holding is increasing everywhere, and that the large and very large holding is decreasing.[3] Accordingly, as he suggests, if the collapse of modern society is dependent on the disappearance of the middle classes, and their absorption by the extremes above and below them, then the realisation of the new world, of socialism, 'is no nearer in England, France or Germany to-day than at any earlier time in the nineteenth century.'[4] The squeezing out of the intermediate classes is indeed the unhappiest of all the forecasts of the *Communist Manifesto*; and what was true in the closing decade of last century is still more abundantly true to-day. Society has stubbornly refused to segregate itself in the two pens so assiduously prepared for its reception.

So much for the 'revision'—the less mealy-mouthed might say the 'refutation'—of Marx. It contains little that may not now be regarded as the somewhat hackneyed and obvious criticism of a literal Marxism, but, coming as it did in 1898 from among the ranks of the faithful, it was something of a portent. What is perhaps of greater interest is the general view to be found in Bernstein regarding the immediate and the remoter future of society. He lends no support to the view that society is or can be divided into two sharply antagonistic classes. Modern wage-earners, he says—and with overwhelming rightness—are not a homogeneous mass; there is vast differentiation among the many different kinds of workers.[5] And it follows from this that 'the feeling of solidarity between groups of workers . . . is only very moderate in amount.'[6] Such is his answer to the question of what precisely is meant by this modern proletariat of which so much is spoken. In a sense, he implies, even if he does not so express it,

[1] *Evolutionary Socialism*, p. 43. [2] *Ibid.* pp. 48–49. [3] *Ibid.* p. 71.
[4] *Ibid.* p. 72. [5] *Ibid.* pp. 103–105. [6] *Ibid.* p. 120.

that there is no one 'working class,' bound together as a unity by eternal and inexorable Marxian decree. Inferentially also he answers in advance much of the argumentation of the Syndicalists half a generation later. Above these sectional interests, above the trade unions, he sees something wider which he calls the 'community'; and indeed this point of view leads him to see in the trade unions something potentially antagonistic to the community:

> Even the best productive association, so long as it is only an association for sale and exchange, will always stand in latent opposition to the community. . . . With a productive association which carries on any branch of production or public service on its own account, the community would have the same points of difference as with a capitalist undertaking.[1]

Thus trade unions do not necessarily yield socialism; indeed, a trade union is defined as 'an unsocialistic corporate body.'[2] Trade unions must accordingly be content to be partners: 'associations against the community are as little socialism as is the oligarchic government of the State.'[3] He is equally unsympathetic with the other main battle-cry of the Guild Socialists that there must be democracy in industry, with control from below: 'It is simply impossible that the manager should be the employee of those he manages, that he should be dependent for his position on their favour and bad temper.'[4] Bernstein thus thinks in terms of 'community' and 'partnership' in this community; and democracy is defined negatively as nothing more than an absence of class government, a form of government where political privileges belong to no one class.[5] Doubtless Bernstein expresses what in certain quarters would be regarded as an indefensibly old-fashioned view, when he finds the guarantee of this partnership in a universal suffrage, freely and intelligently exercised: 'The right to vote in a democracy makes its members virtually partners in the community, and this virtual partnership must in the end lead to real partnership.'[6] The most significant point in all this lies in the emphasis with which Bernstein turns his back on the doctrine that the State is necessarily a class organisation, in which the worker—suffrage or no suffrage—necessarily has no part. The State, for him, represents a partnership in which all should, and will yet, share. The conception of the 'dictatorship of the proletariat' which has its roots intertwined with that of the Marxian view of the State as a class organisation is likewise brusquely dismissed: it belongs to a lower civilisation; it is mere 'political atavism.'[7] Further, if there is no substance in the contention that the State is a class organisation, the old tag that the 'proletarian has no fatherland' must be equally untenable. If once true, it is true no longer, and becomes increasingly

[1] *Evolutionary Socialism*, p. 119. [2] *Ibid.* p. 154. [3] *Ibid.* p. 141.
[4] *Ibid.* p. 119. [5] *Ibid.* p. 142. [6] *Ibid.* p. 144.
[7] *Ibid.* pp. 146–147.

void of significance, ' the more the worker, by the influence of socialism, moves from being a proletarian to a citizen.' In what sense, indeed, can a fatherland be denied to a worker, ' whose children the community educates, whose health it protects, whom it secures against injury,' and much more?[1] Had not a potentially honourable phrase been soiled by all ignoble use, Bernstein might very obviously have been described as a National Socialist.

It will be observed how completely the revision, repudiation or refutation of Marx has brought Bernstein round to an old-fashioned, mid-Victorian liberalism, with faith in democracy, safeguarded by education and the intelligence which is supposed to result from the process of education. Democracy is not merely a condition of socialism; it is exalted until it becomes something more than the means—it is indeed the very substance of socialism.[2] Nor is this kinship with an earlier liberalism an attitude of mind remaining inarticulate and unconscious. It is part of Bernstein's confession of faith that socialism is the legitimate heir of liberalism, not only in chronological sequence, but also in its spiritual qualities. There is, he says, no truly liberal thought that does not also have its place among the ideas of socialism; the task of socialism is indeed that of organising liberalism.[3]

Nor does Bernstein, in his adherence to an antiquated liberalism, fail to reveal some of the less lovely aspects of traditional liberalism; and indeed, at the bidding of liberalism, he appears at times to be ready to discard what, rightly or wrongly, are commonly supposed to be ideas dear to the socialist. The liberal, in the era when he flourished, ran the risk of indurating his heart at the behest of *laissez faire*; he was an individualist, believing that every tub should stand on its own bottom, and that Providence had sent every tub a sufficiently broad bottom for the purpose. Also he distrusted the State, holding that any extension of the State's powers—it is Mill who is speaking—' should be regarded with unremitting jealousy.' In both these respects Bernstein is much closer to McCulloch than to Sidney Webb, and it is here that he parts company with the Fabians. The right to work, in its ordinary sense, is, he holds, something that is not in itself even desirable: ' an absolute right to work would simply result in disorganisation.'[4] On the general question of maintenance and relief he is equally, and as surprisingly, emphatic:

> To demand simply the maintenance of all those without employment out of the State money means to commit to the trough of the State not only everyone who cannot find work but everyone that will not find work.

And he adds, in words that mark the final breach with Sidney

[1] *Evolutionary Socialism*, pp. 169–170.
[2] *Ibid.* p. 166.
[3] *Ibid.* pp. 149–154.
[4] *Ibid.* p. 153.

Webb: ‘ One need really be no anarchist in order to find the eternal heaping of duties on the State too much of a good thing.’ [1]

Such is Bernstein, a ‘ radical ’ who had strayed into the cohorts of the Marxians, and whom a liberal conscience (and a sense of reality) drove to a revision of Marx—a task accomplished by the elimination and the extirpation of all the essentially Marxian elements. For him the State represented a universal partnership; all that was required could be obtained by an intelligent use of the ballot-box. And meanwhile the good work was going on: ‘ Everywhere there is action for reform, action for social progress, action for the victory of democracy.’ [2] In England (a country worth looking at) no one now dreamed of an imminent victory for socialism by means of a violent revolution; more and more reliance was being placed on work in the municipalities and other self-governing bodies.[3] It sounds like a well-bred echo from a distant Fabian drawing-room. Let the good work go on, pursuing methods which have already yielded so much. The appeal to a revolution by force has become a meaningless phrase. In words pointedly critical of the theory implicit in the Marxian tradition, there is something wrong with a ‘ doctrine which assumes that progress depends on the deterioration of social conditions.’ [4]

[1] *Evolutionary Socialism*, pp. 168–169.
[2] *Ibid.* p. 199.
[3] *Ibid.* p. 203.
[4] *Ibid.* p. 213.

CHAPTER XV

SYNDICALISM

In the preceding chapter we have witnessed the Revisionists remodelling their Marx, so that socialism has become little better than an attenuated liberalism, a doctrine of progress, and of aspiration towards peace on earth and good-will to men; we have been present, slightly awed, at Fabian receptions in the drawing-rooms of Mayfair. Against all this, syndicalism comes as a many-headed protest. It is a protest against compromise; a protest against the danger that socialism may become respectable; a protest against middle-class vapourings and oleaginous shaking-of-hands. It is a protest against the futility and the ineffectiveness of Parliament and of the parliamentary machine; against all existing authorities; against the accustomed way of doing all things. Into a world in danger of becoming peaceful, syndicalism represents the irruption of violence, the hoarse-voiced clamour for war, and for war without end. It speaks with the voice of Jehu: 'What hast thou to do with peace? turn thee behind me.'

Syndicalism is in its origins an exclusively French movement—with Italian contributions later. Doubtless there were repercussions in America; and in this country, on the 27th March, 1912, the House of Commons devoted an hour and a half of its valuable time to discussing, somewhat ineffectively, the 'grave danger to the State' involved in the growth of syndicalism; and 'it being Eleven of the Clock the Debate stood adjourned'—which, in its way, is almost an adequate epitaph on the syndicalist movement, as a movement, so far as concerns this country. Syndicalism is indeed a manifestation of the Latin races, and it never took root outside the Latin countries. Nevertheless, the underlying ideas, which are perhaps more political than economic, have been an important ingredient in the fermenting pot of the last generation, and to a large extent were embalmed for us later in the doctrines of the Guild Socialist school. Even if syndicalism throughout thus bears the mark of its foreign origin and was obviously designed for foreign use, it is not thereby void of significance for us.

On its first impact, the word 'syndicalism' may have a somewhat mystifying, and indeed misleading, effect on English-hearing ears. That words, common to several languages, may perversely follow a different path in each is a constant vexation of spirit to the hack translator. Heaven alone knows what a syndicate is, and what a syndicate may (or may not) cover in English.[1] But in French a

[1] A Syndicate is a body of syndics. A Syndic is an official of kinds differing in different countries and times (*Concise Oxford Dictionary*). So now we know.

'syndicat' is the everyday word for a trade union. 'Syndicalism,' then, is merely 'trade unionism.' Strictly speaking, one should probably refer to the movement as 'revolutionary syndicalism' to distinguish it from those forms of syndicalism (or trade unionism) which followed a more peaceful path. In short, then, syndicalism ('revolutionary' being understood, or dropped as otiose) is that form of socialism which looks to the achievement of a revolution as the outcome of a class war, waged through the instrumentality of the 'syndicats' or trade unions, which are destined to displace and supplant the State and the machinery of the State.

An exposition of syndicalism, within the limits of a chapter, is confronted with a difficulty which is scarcely encountered elsewhere, or at least not in so acute a form. Syndicalism in its origin was a spontaneous movement among the workers and in the 'syndicats'; it was a natural development of the history of the trade unions and of the working-class movement in France. But alongside this 'proletarian' movement, the sources of which are best found in the records of Trade Union Conferences and in the writings of men actively engaged in the movement, there is a considerable syndicalist literature, written by philosophers, professors and middle-class intelligentsia. It may be that history is in the process of doing an injustice here. The syndicalist movement in its origin owed nothing to its philosophers: and probably while it existed it continued to owe them nothing. They came along later and supplied a philosophy for a movement already in being. Georges Sorel (1847–1922), the most conspicuous of the intellectuals, took no part whatever in the movement, remaining indeed rather ostentatiously aloof. Sorel and Lagardelle alike declared that they had nothing to teach, and everything to learn from, the working classes—a gesture of modesty notably absent from the Guild Socialists later. Yet there has been a tendency to identify Sorel with syndicalism, and indeed in Sombart,[1] if nowhere else, we have hints of 'Sorelism.' In a full-length study of syndicalism it would be necessary to keep these two strands separate; here, with a consciousness of the danger involved, it may be sufficient to give a composite picture. Nor indeed, apart from the injustice of attributing to Sorel the paternity of a child whom he merely explained and justified later, the current view perhaps does no great harm. Except (it may be) on two points, Sorel does not greatly differ from 'proletarian' syndicalism[2]: moreover, whatever may be the rights and the wrongs, it is safe to say that now and hereafter the world, looking back, will see syndicalism through the writings of Sorel and Lagardelle, rather than in the transactions of recurring conferences.

It has been said above that revoluntary syndicalism is a peculiarly

[1] Sombart: *Socialism and the Social Movement*, chapter v.

[2] (i) Sabotage, and (ii) the place assigned to the myth.

French product, explicable only in the light of French traditions and the nature and limitations of French trade unionism. The ordinary man must walk gingerly in this field of social history, threading his way delicately as Agag, among Blanquists, Guesdists, Broussists and Allemanists: and even so, he will probably forget his steps, when he has been removed for a week from his authorities, finding ruefully that his knowledge passeth away as the remembrance of a guest that tarrieth but a day.[1] It is sufficient here to note that the French trade unions, such as they were, were for the most part local bodies; to the Anglo-Saxon eye they appear to have been weak, both in membership and in financial resources. They were late in development, not being fully legalised until the Act of 1884. France never has been a highly industrialised country (despite the vision of Saint-Simon), and its industry has been relatively on a small scale. These considerations are sufficient to explain why French trade unionism, at the beginning of the period with which we are concerned, was largely based on small local unions with a small membership and a restricted field of activity.

On the structure of French trade unionism, the merest hint may here suffice. A large part was played by the 'Bourses du Travail,' of which the first was established in Paris in 1887. The Bourse du Travail was in its origin (or in its revived incarnation) a curious cross between voluntary trade union activity and State encouragement. It was designed to be a headquarters for the *syndicats* of any locality, serving educational and propaganda purposes and equipped with libraries; but also it was in part designed as an employment bureau. In short, it was an amalgam of a Trades Council, a working-men's club, and an employment exchange. In this last capacity their creation was encouraged and they were (at the outset) subsidised by the municipality. Presently, there was established a *Fédération des Bourses du Travail* with, as its secretary, Fernand Pelloutier, one of the leading creators of syndicalism as a movement, and not as a mere philosophy. Meanwhile in 1895 there had been created the *Confédération Générale du Travail*, known as the C.G.T.—letters which later acquired ominous import. At first the C.G.T., despite its ostensible comprehensiveness, was rather ineffective and futile. The union of the Bourses du Travail and the C.G.T., arranged towards the end of 1902, operated from January 1st, 1903. It was in the Bourses du Travail and later, in its period of greatest prominence, in the C.G.T. that revolutionary syndicalism as a working-class theory, with manifestations in working-class practice, was worked out.[2]

[1] On the confused history of French trade unionism and the French labour movement generally, the reader will get all he wants in Levine, *Syndicalism in France*; Estey, *Revolutionary Syndicalism*; and Cole, *The World of Labour*.

[2] This paragraph is, of course, a crudely nude summary. There were other organisations and a network of personalities. The rivalries, the intrigues and the

So far as concerns the working-class end of the movement, the sources of syndicalism are fairly obvious. It is, above all, a manifestation of disillusionment, a reaction of the proletariat against democracy. Much had been promised; much had been expected. The experiment had been made. Democracy had been weighed in the balance and found wanting.[1] Governments had been changed; measures had been passed. The essential injustice of things remained. To the outsider, at a comfortable distance in space and time, it is little short of astounding to note how prominent a place in syndicalist literature is occupied by *l'affaire Millerand.* Revolutionary leaders were obviously bought, seduced by the enemy. Just for a handful of silver he left us: even worse, it may have been a mere ribbon to stick in his coat. And as Lagardelle lugubriously puts it: 'Après Millerand, Briand; après Briand, Viviani; après Viviani, ... d'autres viendront.'[2] Impatient, embittered, disillusioned, the syndicalists exclaimed that it was time to turn their backs on the State and the parliamentary game, and to seek their own salvation in their own way.

With this there is another dominant consideration. It is for the historian to pass judgment on the French character before the nineteenth century; but indubitably and obviously, ever since the French Revolution, the French outlook has been profoundly influenced by the revolutionary tradition, reinforced in 1848 and by the events of the Commune. On the least provocation, they visualise themselves as overturning something; there have perhaps been too many pictures of revolutionary heroes storming the barricades with wide-open mouths. Doubtless for good in many directions—though perhaps for not-so-good in others—the *Marseillaise* is in their blood. It has again been gloriously manifested in the days of August 1944. It is with them second nature to be revolutionary. Syndicalism, viewed as a working-class movement, springs from a realisation of the futility of the parliamentary machine as a means of getting anywhere, combined with the promptings and the stirrings of the revolutionary tradition. The syndicalists demand accordingly that the everlasting struggle be moved to another field, and waged with other weapons of their own forging.

For it is this class struggle—*la lutte de classe*—which in both currents of syndicalism is placed at the centre of things. And indeed, once the reality of the class struggle is conceded as something eternal, it is probable that the whole of syndicalism, in theory and practice, follows with logical necessity. For the intellectuals, the emphasis on

rapprochements of the various sects would have done credit to European diplomacy in its most intricate and subterranean epochs.

[1] Lagardelle: *Le Socialisme Ouvrier*, pp. 271–273.

[2] *Ibid.* p. 274.

the class struggle is merely a belated return to Marx—not to Marx as commonly understood and interpreted, not to the embroideries and frills of Marx, but to the essential Marxian core, whether Marx understood it or not. Sorel tells us that his task was to ascertain 'comment se pourrait réaliser l'essentiel des doctrines marxistes.'[1] It was the function of the syndicalists, so he claimed, to 'purge' traditional Marxism of all that was not specifically Marxist, and to retain what was, according to them, *le noyau*, the kernel of the doctrine.[2] Elsewhere, in a phrase that might intrigue the metaphysicians, he claims that syndicalism retains 'ce qu'il y a de vraiment vrai dans le marxisme' —something transcending all formulas, to wit, that the class struggle is the alpha and omega of socialism.[3] Marx, it is admitted, was not always happily inspired; he allowed a quantity of old rubbish to creep into his writings; he had the disadvantage that 'he did not move in circles which had acquired a satisfactory notion of the General Strike.'[4] But if the dross was washed away from Marx (and dross there unmistakeably is), the pure gold that remains is the doctrine of the class struggle. In this, and in this alone, is the sincere milk of the word.

The idea of the class struggle is thus 'the beginning and the end of socialism.'[5] Nor should it be a matter for regret that there is this warfare at the heart of things. The class struggle is itself a creative force, a prophylactic against sloth and slackness. The two parties in this feud must oppose each other implacably in the interests of both sides, and in the ultimate interests of humanity.[6] There must be no point of contact, no fusion. They must not think alike. 'All our efforts,' says Sorel, 'should aim at preventing bourgeois ideas from poisoning the rising class.'[7]

Those who thus see an eternal and irreducible opposition within society, and whose chief aim is to accentuate and perpetuate the line of demarcation, are obviously not designed for political activity. Along various lines, partly by intuitive impulse in the *Syndicats*, partly by ratiocination among the philosophers, the syndicalists turned their backs on 'reform,' the parliamentary socialist party, democracy and the State.

There is in the first place the very practical point already glanced at, namely, that parliamentary action has not in fact been found to deliver the goods. Parliamentary action, as Godwin had indicated long ago, rests on lobbying, on compromise, on give-and-take; it demands collaboration with other parties; it calls for the qualities

[1] Sorel: *Matériaux d'une théorie du proletariat*, p. 4.
[2] Sorel: *La Décomposition du Marxisme*, p. 63.
[3] Sorel: *Avenir socialiste des Syndicats*, in *Matériaux d'une Théorie*, p. 67.
[4] Sorel: *Reflections on Violence* (English translation), p. 203.
[5] Lagardelle: *Le Socialisme Ouvrier*, p. 283.
[6] Sorel: *Reflections on Violence*, pp. 85–86, and generally.
[7] Sorel: *Les Illusions du Progres*, p. 285.

of the trimmer. It is maddeningly slow. How, asks Lagardelle, can a system ' qui ne vit que des ruses, d'équivoques, de concessions, de compromissions, de conciliations '—how can it evoke the best sentiments of the human soul? [1] Moreover, the would-be revolutionary member breathes an infected and poisoned atmosphere; he is compelled to concern himself with precedents and procedure; he must needs attend receptions; gradually he clothes himself in the physical and mental vestments of the Bourgeoisie and becomes a lost soul: 'il devient un excellent bourgeois avec la plus grande facilité.' [2] He is, in short, a prisoner, a hostage in the hands of the enemy; and the eloquent procession of Millerand, Briand and Viviani provides overwhelming testimony to the dismal conclusion.

All this would be true even if democracy were 'right': but the philosophers at least, even if their arguments may have been too subtle for the ordinary trade unionist, were not slow in producing proof that democracy rests on assumptions that cannot be accepted by the class-strugglers. In his earliest significant work, Sorel argued that government by the totality (*l'ensemble*) of the citizens had never been anything but a fiction: how could the vote of a chaotic majority disclose Rousseau's General Will which is incapable of error? [3] Moreover, along a different line, Marx is invoked to point the same conclusion. Democracy, he argues, is antipathetic to Marxian conceptions ' parce qu'elle recherche toujours l'unité.' [4] It is profoundly true; the ultimate aim of democracy is agreement, even if it be but that makeshift, an agreement to differ. The same point is made by Lagardelle, when he argues at considerable length that democracy places itself above all classes and the conflicts of classes. Its object is to ' reduce differences and destroy antagonisms.' Democracy and the class struggle are therefore conflicting conceptions: democracy pursues the harmony and not the conflict of classes.[5] The ultimate clash between democracy and syndicalism is represented by the incompatibility between collaboration and conflict; and to the syndicalist, whilst collaboration is a delusion, conflict is the mother of all things.[6]

Another line of attack on democracy in its normal operation is significant, because it again reveals a just appreciation of one of the main characteristics of democracy, and at the same time is one of the many pointers to Guild Socialism later. It is of the nature of democracy (so writes Lagardelle) to allow criticism to play unrestrained on every subject. Again, it is an entirely just observation; if the essence

[1] Lagardelle: *Le Socialisme Ouvrier*, p. 373.
[2] Sorel: *La Décomposition du Marxisme*, p. 27.
[3] Sorel: *Avenir socialiste des Syndicats*, in *Matériaux d'une Théorie*, p. 118.
[4] Sorel: *Les Illusions du Progrès*, p. 9.
[5] Lagardelle: *Le Socialisme Ouvrier*, pp. 42, 44.
[6] *Ibid.* p. 63, etc.

of democracy is to be sought for in any single criterion, it must probably be found in the fact that democracy encourages the utmost possible freedom of discussion. Even if democracy must in the end constrain a minority, it aims at allowing all concerned to say all that they have to say before a decision is taken. But, continues Lagardelle, that this criticism playing on all things may be of any value, education is necessary. Unfortunately, he argues, the questions now at issue are so complicated that the masses cannot be sufficiently educated to play their part. The multitude does not govern: it is governed—by its representatives.[1] As against this necessary incompetence of the electorate in the political field, when we turn to industry, 'la masse ouvrière est capable de juger.'[2] It is a frequent plea of the Guild Socialists in their arguments for industrial democracy. Lagardelle does, however, allow a minor part to parliamentary action in the democratic field, on condition that it is recognised as subsidiary. In a rather grotesque metaphor, he admits that the democratic atmosphere is the only one that can be breathed by socialist lungs.[3] Nevertheless, *der Henker steht vor der Thüre*: working-class democracy makes use of political democracy only in order the better to destroy it.[4]

A further reason why parliamentary or political activity is smitten in advance with sterility is to be found in the distinction drawn by the syndicalists between a class and a party. This is an argument particularly dear to Lagardelle, and it is stated repeatedly throughout *Le Socialisme Ouvrier* with varying degrees of felicity. Any *party*, and this applies equally to the Socialist Party, is an artificial aggregate of heterogeneous elements drawn from all classes, and united solely by a *lien de volonté*. The *class*, on the other hand, is a natural product of historical development, comprising elements of the same kind, and whose grouping is accordingly due to a *lien de necessité*. The one represents an intellectual unity; the other rests on homogeneity of origin and of conditions of life. The party comprises men of strangely different social levels. The working class (*la classe ouvrière*), on the other hand, is confined to the proletariat, living the same life, subject to the same eventualities, having the same interests.[5] The one has an economic basis; the other merely an ideological foundation. Another variant of the same point is of interest because it serves to mark the connecting-link between the syndicalists and their enfeebled offspring, the Guild Socialists. The organism of the party (and it is still Lagardelle to whom we are listening) is concerned with the worker in his quality as an elector, as a member of the political society, that

[1] Lagardelle: *Le Socialisme Ouvrier*, pp. 57–58. [2] *Ibid.* p. 344.
[3] *Ibid.* p. 48. [4] *Ibid.* p. 55.
[5] This statement is more or less as given in *Le Socialisme Ouvrier*, pp. 166–167. But for very similar statements, see also pp. 157–161, 256–257, 266, 283–288.

is to say, when he mingles with other citizens belonging to other classes ; the organism of the class seizes him in his quality as a worker, as a member of the economic society, that is to say, at the moment when he separates himself from all the other classes and is opposed to them. Parties act on the *terrain* common to all men ; classes, on the other hand, display their activity only on the *terrain* which separates them from the rest of society.[1] Here, as will be seen in the next chapter, is a significant pointer to certain of the social theories of the earlier days of Guild Socialism.

We see then why a party is so fashioned that it must dissolve in the day of adversity. The Liberal Party may comprise a few earls or even a marquess ; it also includes charwomen and railway porters. The Socialist Party doubtless contains workers ; but it also enrolls in its ranks middle-class intellectuals, journalists and political careerists. They are bound together by, at most, an intellectual creed. They have no common interests ; in a world of economic determinism, no real effective bond unites them. But a class, or so we are told, is based on common interest and nothing but common interest. The class will therefore stand when the party crumbles. It is significant that Sorel regards it as one of the cardinal features of Marxism that it discarded the idea of a party, which was fundamental in the conception of 'classical revolutionaries,' in order to replace it by that of a class.[2]

Yet if one penetrates still deeper, there is an even more fundamental reason for turning away from political activity. It is that the State is a capitalistic State, the tool of the enemy: perhaps, if properly viewed, it may itself be the supreme enemy. Political activity, by its very nature, accepts the State ; 'the socialist parties act within the framework of the existing State.' But clearly, as Lagardelle adds, mere amelioration of the lot of the workers inside capitalistic society has nothing to do with socialism ; socialism is the organisation of working-class revolt against society as we know it.[3] Labriola is abundantly right: it is impossible for socialists or the Socialist Party to accept the responsibility of governing in the existing State, without thereby becoming defenders of the existing State.[4] You cannot by Satan cast out Satan ; a socialist minister, confronted by the prospect of disorder, is compelled to use his utmost endeavour to maintain order.

Sufficient reason for turning one's back on the parliamentary regime, which is the abomination of desolation ; on democracy, which is synonymous with mediocrity and corruption ; on the State,

[1] Lagardelle : *Le Socialisme Ouvrier*, p. 266.
[2] Sorel : *La Décomposition du Marxisme*, p. 51.
[3] Lagardelle ; *Le Socialisme Ouvrier*, pp. 242, 244.
[4] *Syndicalisme et Socialisme*, p. 19.

which is for ever ' unproductive, incompetent and arbitrary.' [1] But if the class struggle is not to be waged under the banner of democracy, with social reform as the fruit of the high contention of parties, what then must men do? The answer is entirely evident from the argument already developed. The working-class movement is essentially revolutionary, and the *lutte de classe* can be conducted only on the *terrain de classe*.[2] The workers must work out their own salvation, creating for the purpose working-class institutions, distinct from and apart from the State. It is idle to ask from the State, cap in hand. The workers must prepare to take what they want—by direct action.

If we ask where we are to find the people, the *classe ouvrière*, the answer is again simple. They are to be found in the trade unions. The Syndicats, the Bourses du Travail, the Federations of Syndicats—these are the peculiar organs of the proletariat, because, as Lagardelle expresses it, they group together workers only, and further because they group them only ' en tant qu'ouvriers '—only workers and only as workers.[3] One of the landmarks in the history of syndicalism on the academic side is represented by Sorel's early work, *L'avenir socialiste des syndicats*, which appeared (in magazine form) as far back as 1898. Writing retrospectively in a later preface, Sorel declared that his purpose had been to draw the attention of socialists to the great rôle which the syndicats might be called upon to play in the modern world.[4] The main idea in this highly significant work is that the trade union, the syndicat, is primarily an instrument of the *guerre sociale*. The unions exist for war, and in this field there is no room for diplomatic action with a view to the establishment or maintenance of peace, such as exists in the corresponding conflicts between States, for the simple reason that the proletariat aims at the destruction of its adversaries.[5] It is a war without truce and without armistice. The syndicats must accordingly consciously remould themselves not merely that they may become more effective instruments of war, but also that they may be fitted to play their part in the world which will result from their triumph. They must therefore prove their political capacity.[6] As against the State, they must pursue a policy analogous to what, with us, was later known as ' encroaching control.' Thus in the case of the *Bureaux de plaçement*, then a matter of current controversy, Sorel argued that if the syndicats could but take over their administration, ' ils auraient arraché à l'autorité politique traditionelle un lambeau de son pouvoir.' [7] So, with regard to other functions of

[1] *E.g.* Sorel: *Reflections on Violence*, p. 19; Lagardelle: *Le Socialisme Ouvrier*, p. 150.

[2] Lagardelle: *Le Socialisme Ouvrier*, pp. 95, 180.

[3] *Ibid.* p. 283.

[4] The 1905 Preface in *Matériaux d'une Théorie du Proletariat*, p. 58.

[5] Sorel: *L'avenir socialiste des Syndicats* in *Matériaux d'une Théorie*, pp. 67–68.

[6] *Ibid.* p. 120.

[7] *Ibid.* p. 121.

the State (*e.g.* Factory Inspection and Public Assistance), ' il faut qu'ils arrachent ces pouvoirs petit à petit, en les réclamant sans cesse.' The struggle for political power is not merely designed to unseat the bourgeois and occupy their vacant places: it is a struggle to divest the existing political organism of all life, and to transfer whatever of value it may have contained to a proletarian organism created concurrently with the development of the proletariat.[1] Thus, like an encroaching and adolescent cuckoo, the syndicat should aim at ousting the State from the nest.

Such is the programme: ' to snatch from the State and from the Commune, one by one, all their attributes in order to enrich the proletarian organisms in process of formation.'[2] But for this task in its fullness the syndicats are not yet prepared. Before the world can be transformed, the workers must first acquire ' a superior degree of moral culture.'[3] Hence the rather pathetic insistence which Sorel lays on the powers of the trade unions to impart uplift: they must become ' puissants mécanismes de moralisation.'[4] If anyone doubts it, let him look at the dockers in England where, under trade union influence, many have abandoned their intemperate habits, ' et quelques-uns sont devenus même teetotalers.' This *même* is an eloquent tribute to the regenerative influence of trade unions. So also the idea of a new education, under trade union guidance and with trade union inspiration, figures largely in Sorel: ' We must bring the young to love their work.'[5] The trade unions, in short, are to become moralising and educational agencies so that their members may be fit for their high task. And if trade unions are equipped and prepared on these lines, then—so Sorel concludes his thesis—the whole future of socialism is to be found in the autonomous development of the workers' unions.[6]

We have succeeded in reducing socialism to the class struggle; and the conduct of this war that knows no armistice has been entrusted to the trade unions, suitably reformed. It remains to say something of the strategy and of the munitions of war, of the tools with which, it was confidently expected, the syndicalists would finish the job. It is scarcely the whole truth, but it is a reasonable approximation to the truth, to say that on this side syndicalism reduced itself to the theory and the advocacy of the General Strike. The conception of the General Strike has a reasonably venerable history. It was a familiar idea in England in the days of Owen. It has been pointed out that it figures in the concluding chapters of Disraeli's *Sybil* under the pleasant euphemism of a ' National Holiday.' In the fat, peaceful, progressive reformist years in the middle of the century, it had faded into the back-

[1] Sorel: *L'avenir socialiste des Syndicats* in *Matériaux d'une Théorie*, p. 123.
[2] *Ibid.* p. 132. [3] *Ibid.* p. 125. [4] *Ibid.* pp. 128–129.
[5] *Ibid.* p. 137. [6] *Ibid.* p. 133.

ground. The re-launching of the idea in the epoch with which we are concerned is attributed by Pouget to a French anarchist, Tortelier, a carpenter, who developed the theory of the General Strike at a meeting of the International in London in November, 1888—*sans grand écho*, as is added.[1] The grand echo was, however, not long in coming; and by 1892 no less a person than Aristide Briand had produced considerable reverberations in inducing the National Federation of Syndicats to approve the principle of the General Strike. Indeed, the conception of the General Strike found its natural home in the Bourses du Travail, and later in the C.G.T.; and though the Guesdists, tainted with reformism, might declare that the General Strike was General Nonsense, it rapidly became the especial badge of the syndicalist school.

In the original form the idea of the General Strike is of a simplicity and a naivete that at least testify to the innocence of mind of those who devised it. This was the *Grève des bras croisés*. How much simpler than the Parliamentary solution, involving delay, intrigue, compromise, uncertainty and defeat! All that is necessary is that the workers in a mass should simultaneously fold their arms, and go for a picnic in the Bois de Vincennes with their wives, families, a lunch-basket and their folded arms. After a few days of this care-free life under a serene heaven, the hated bourgeoisie, crawling supine, will lower the flag, and the revolution will be over. The workers, at last unfolding their arms, will relieve their wives of the luncheon-baskets and return home to a regenerated world. Unimaginative, hard-bitten, 'reformist' trade union leaders, holding with the Guesdists that the General Strike is General Nonsense, have little difficulty in making hay of this idyllic picture. It is unveiling the obvious to observe that while doubtless a General Strike of folded arms would produce chaos, the workers on strike would not be immune from the chaos so produced. They also, when not picnicking in the Bois de Vincennes, would be sitting in houses where the light had failed and where the water-tap (and not merely the water-tap) had ceased to do its duty. Nor might it be an easy matter to replenish the luncheon-basket from day to day in this strange transitional period. 'When toil ceases, the People suffer,' it is recorded in *Sybil*; 'that is the only truth that we have learnt, and it is a bitter one.' Indeed even on syndicalist theory, one is rather impelled to the view that the General Strike, in its naive form, does in fact approximate to General Nonsense. For if the bourgeoisie and the State, the two great enemies, are so powerful for evil as we are led to believe they are, they will not lightly succumb before the serried ranks of folded arms. They will retaliate; they will protect themselves. The picnickers in the Bois will have to unfold their arms sooner than they had intended.

[1] See *La Grève Générale*, p. 42.

Not by such simple means as these will it be possible to fulfil their dignified resolution not to 'expose themselves to the brutalities of the police.' In short, a General Strike, assuming its possibility, would be the mother of chaos on all sides. And who may with confidence undertake in advance to ride the whirlwind and direct the storm to a predestined end?

It should perhaps in fairness be made clear that in certain phases of syndicalist discussion, some ambiguity attaches to the phrase 'General Strike,' which sometimes means a strike of everybody everywhere, and sometimes merely a nation-wide strike in one industry. Yet indubitably the syndicalist movement became more and more attached to strikes on as large a scale as possible, not with the object of attaining any immediate or limited end, but because all strikes are in themselves praiseworthy and desirable as a means of carrying on the class war. The ostensible objects of the strikes and the outcome of the strikes were alike matters of minor significance. And equally beyond question, when the 'proletarian' syndicalist spoke of a General Strike, he meant (like an honest man) what he said, that they were contemplating and moving towards a general cessation of all work which would in fact take place some day not too remote. Turning to the philosophers, however, and above all to Sorel, we find that the General Strike assumes a somewhat different significance; here indeed is one of the points of differentiation between 'proletarian' syndicalism and the syndicalism of the Chair. The Sorelian view of strikes in general, and of the General Strike in particular, is coloured by the rather mystical part assigned in his philosophy to the rôle of violence, and by his somewhat celebrated, not to say notorious, doctrine of myths. Already in one of his (somewhat) later prefaces to the *Avenir Socialiste des Syndicats*, Sorel had emphasised under three headings what the conception of the General Strike did, and in its way this passage provides a convenient introduction to this curious tract of speculation. Firstly, the General Strike usefully and unmistakeably underlines that the time of political revolutions is over and done with (an interesting example of how far out the best of us may be in our guesses regarding the not-so-remote future). Secondly, the General Strike gives concrete expression to the fact that socialism cannot be achieved (*pace* the Revisionists and the Fabians) by easy stages; it has to be a catastrophic and complete change. And thirdly, the conception of the General Strike gives meaning and significance to all the paltry little day-to-day strikes of ordinary industrial life. Each strike, no matter how local it may be, becomes a skirmish in the great battle which we call the General Strike.[1]

On this view, all strikes are educational, disciplinary and symbolic. Every strike is an incident in something larger; it may in itself, and in

[1] Sorel: *Matériaux d'une Théorie du Proletariat*, pp. 59–61.

appearance, be but an affair of outposts, yet it may turn out to be the prologue to the great decisive engagement. The small strike, frequently repeated, cannot fail to 'rejuvenate the socialist idea in the proletariat, reinforce sentiments of heroism, of sacrifice and of union, and keep perpetually alive the hope of the Revolution.'[1] So also it impresses the great truth that the workers are not merely individuals, but that they form a body (*un corps*); otherwise expressed, it gives them solidarity.[2]

One of the characteristic features of Sorel's view of this ceaseless war in which every conflict is a 'vanguard fight' is that the other side also must be compelled to fight, and thus to fulfil its destiny. We are confronted with the 'cowardice of government'; we witness the timidity of the forces of law; a cowardly middle class pursues the chimera of social peace. But just because socialism is destined to be the heir of capitalism, the inheritance must be fully developed. Sorel clearly prefers a middle class 'which would find satisfaction in looking after their own interests.' The world in its upper reaches has gone flabby—terribly ignorant, gapingly stupid, politically impotent—and that it may recover its former energy, the lines of demarcation must be ruthlessly maintained: there must be no fraternising.[3]

The dangers implicit in the existence of a benevolent and philanthropic middle class figure so largely in the Sorelian philosophy that the point almost demands illustration in his own language. 'We are to-day faced with a new and very unforeseen fact—a middle class which seeks to weaken its own strength.' A little later on the same page he goes on:

> A growing and solidly organised working class can compel the capitalist class to remain firm in the industrial war; if a united and revolutionary proletariat confronts a rich middle class, eager for conquest, capitalist society will have reached its historical perfection.[4]

To the same effect:

> Everything may be saved, if the proletariat by their use of violence manage to re-establish the division into classes, and so restore to the middle class something of its former energy.[5]

Elsewhere the attitude of the philosophical syndicalist to the works of social peace is indicated with a rude frankness:

> To repay with black ingratitude the benevolence of those who would protect the workers, to meet with insults the homilies of the defenders of human fraternity, and to reply by blows to the advances of the propagators of social peace . . . is a very practical way of indicating to the middle class that they must mind their own business and only that.[6]

[1] Sorel: *Matériaux d'une Théorie du Proletariat*, pp. 69–71.
[2] *Ibid.* p. 102.
[3] Sorel: *Reflections on Violence*, pp. 69–72, 81–82, etc.
[4] *Ibid.* pp. 90–91. [5] *Ibid.* p. 98. [6] *Ibid.* pp. 88–89.

This point of view is not peculiar to Sorel. Lagardelle likewise, in language which ultimately seems to point to confusion of aim, emphasises the blessedness of struggle as a stimulating force, and the benefits which capitalism itself will derive therefrom. It is not, he says, the debilitating atmosphere of social peace, but the salubrious air of the class struggle that excites the ardour of the masters of production [1]; and in a further sentence which somehow seems to lose its piquancy if removed from its French atmosphere, he says that provided there is

> un proletariat hardi, enivré de l'esprit de conquête, insatiable dans ses réclamations, un proletariat qui ne tolère pas qu'on s'arrête un instant, et voilà le capitalisme marchant, comme malgré lui, de triomphe en triomphe.[2]

The mystified proletarian syndicalist, groping in his trade union, might very pertinently ask: 'But who anyhow (or words to that effect) wants to see capitalism, in spite of itself, marching from triumph to triumph?'

Thus it is the violence of the class war—proletarian violence, 'a very fine and very heroic thing'—that is to save the world from barbarism [3]; and the main vehicle for violence is to be found in the strike and in its universalisation, the General Strike. But for Sorel, the General Strike, so far from having the unsophisticated significance attaching to it in the proletarian mind, fades away into something mysterious and nebulous. It is a myth; it is indeed *the* myth in which socialism is wholly comprised. It would be as well to leave it to Sorel to explain, even in an abbreviated form, what he means by a myth:

> 'Experience shows that the framing of a future, in some indeterminate time, may, when it is done in a certain way, be very effective, and have very few inconveniences.' Such myths 'enclose with them all the strongest inclinations of a people, of a party or of a class.' They 'give an aspect of complete reality to the hopes of immediate action.' Moreover 'these social myths in no way prevent a man profiting by the observations which he makes in the course of his life, and form no obstacle to the pursuit of his normal occupations.' [4]

Such, to avoid misrepresentation on slippery ground, is the Sorelian statement of what is involved in the idea of a myth. A myth is a compelling picture not so much of what we believe, as of what, if we could but believe, would move us to action now. The test of a myth is found in its power to influence action in the present; 'to discuss how far it can be taken literally as future history is devoid of sense.' [5] For the early Christians (says Sorel) the belief in the return

[1] Lagardelle: *Le Socialisme Ouvrier*, pp. 293–294.
[2] *Ibid.* p. 378.
[3] Sorel: *Reflections on Violence*, p. 98.
[4] *Ibid.* p. 133. [5] *Ibid.* p. 135.

of Christ provided the myth which embodied their hopes and explained their actions. Elsewhere Sorel refers incidentally to the Marxian doctrines of the increasing degradation of the proletariat as a ' myth ' ; though perhaps he ought to have said that it was part of a greater myth, for it is of the essence of myths that they must be taken as undivided wholes. In this case one does not *hope* for the increasing degradation of the working classes ; one may not believe it ; it may indeed be statistically disproved. But if the working classes carry about with them a vivid ' body of images ' of their increasing degradation (*whether true or not*), it will move them to action and justify its existence as a myth. This, though it would doubtless have surprised the genuine member of the *Classe Ouvrière*, is what the conception of the General Strike is and does. It provides

> a body of images capable of evoking instinctively all the sentiments which correspond to the different manifestations of the war undertaken by socialism against modern society. Strikes have engendered in the proletariat the noblest, deepest and most moving sentiments they possess ; the general strike groups them all in a co-ordinated picture, and, by bringing them together, gives to each one of them its maximum intensity. . . . We thus obtain that intuition of socialism which language cannot give us with perfect clearness—and we obtain it as a whole, perceived instantaneously.[1]

The great advantage of dealing in myths (no small matter for a philosopher) is that myths cannot be refuted or analysed. Myths are ultimately ' not descriptions of things, but expressions of a determination to act.' [2] People who live in a world of myths are secure from all refutation [3] : how vain then to argue (or even to prove) that the General Strike is General Nonsense. A revolution needs an ideology to give the actors the necessary confidence, and later on to justify the revolution that has taken place.[4] Herein lies the Sorelian justification of the Sorelian myth ; and indeed for these reasons we should apparently, so far as practicable, breathe an atmosphere of myths, at least to this extent that we should be on our guard against formulas ' autres que des formules mythiques.' [5] Lagardelle, though in language less remote from the usage of his clients, gives substantially the same elusive view of the General Strike. He traces its development from the *Grève des bras croisés*, until finally the idea of the General Strike was affirmed ' in all its symbolic purity '—something indeed whose primary purpose is to give a higher meaning to the petty incidents of the daily struggle.[6] Thus with the philosophers, the General Strike, the central conception of syndicalism, fades away

[1] Sorel : *Reflections on Violence*, p. 137. There is said to be a good deal of Bergson in all this ; but that question had better be left to the Bergson expert.
[2] *Ibid.* p. 33.
[3] *Ibid.* p. 35.
[4] Sorel : *Matériaux d'une Théorie du Proletariat*, p. 249.
[5] Sorel : *La Décomposition du Marxisme*, p. 67.
[6] Lagardelle : *Le Socialisme Ouvrier*, p. 378.

into something that may never happen ; nor does it greatly matter if it never does happen. Enough that it is meanwhile a nice thing to think about.[1]

Apart from the cultivation of strikes, for their tonic effect as much as for any immediate end, two other weapons for use in the class war figure with some prominence in the syndicalist armoury. They may be dealt with rather summarily here, because though they may occupy a conspicuous place in the history of syndicalism as a movement, and indeed largely contributed to making syndicalism a word of terror, it may be doubted whether they involve any point of theoretical principle, or anything that is not in a sense obviously implicit in the syndicalist postulates. The first of these is the practice of sabotage, which may doubtless be interpreted to cover a variegated multitude of sins. Assuming that there is a class warfare, then presumably it follows that either party, by the rules of war, is justified in inflicting damage on the other. In its simplest form it is based on the principle of ' poor work for poor pay ' : ' A mauvaise paye, mauvais travail ' ; and it may be achieved by slackness, by what Mr. F. W. Taylor, with a deceitful semblance of classical learning, designated as *Ca canae*. From this to crude wanton destruction there is of course an ascending scale of possibilities. Undoubtedly, sabotage unscrupulously applied might prove a fearful weapon of destruction and confusion. In the days when syndicalism was a power, much perverted ingenuity was applied to discovering irreprehensible ways of reducing output. In certain spheres of activity, it may be possible to bring things to a standstill by carrying out all instructions literally, especially if the instructions are codified in a large folio volume which demands to be consulted ; it may be possible to achieve sabotage by doing conscientiously good work when the management was bargaining on a shoddy output. On all this question of sabotage one point only need be stressed. Sabotage, so far as it was approved, was a weapon of proletarian syndicalism : it never received the blessing of Sorel or the philosophers, except in such eccentric cases as the sabotage which rested on doing too good work. And the reasons for Sorel's disapproval are significant. Firstly, socialism is the heir of capitalism, and he is a foolish heir-presumptive who damages his prospective inheritance. Secondly, syndicalism is an educational and moralising influence, producing the best type of worker for the future ; but you cannot create the perfect worker for the future out of men who meanwhile are encouraged to slovenliness, slackness, indolence and deceit.

[1] In the *Avant-propos* to *La Grève Générale*, Lagardelle distinguishes (i) la grève générale, which is really a cessation of work more or less extended ; and (ii) la grève générale, ' signifiant la révolte suprême.' In this second sense, it fades into the idea of the Social Revolution, and ' devient toujours plus l'acte de foi d'une partie grandissante du proletariat révolutionnaire.'

The other element in syndicalist strategy which calls for brief notice is to be found in its anti-patriotic and anti-militaristic campaign. Again it probably represents no more than a logical inference from the primary syndicalist assumptions. If, as Lagardelle reminds us, the important frontiers for Marx were those between classes and not those between peoples,[1] then the line of division must be drawn accordingly, and the trumpet must sound to the proletariat of all countries. In a well-worn phrase, made familiar though not necessarily made true by much repetition, 'the worker has no *Patrie*.' A school of thought which denies the State and seeks to extinguish the State, which thinks in terms of a world-wide conflict between classes, can hardly be expected to sympathise with the usual manifestations of patriotism. This, however, is not peculiar to syndicalism; and indeed the cult of cosmopolitanism (in the truer sense of the word), of indifference between existing States, is a logical tendency of all liberal and anarchist thought.

The anti-militaristic campaign pursued by the syndicalists, the attempted 'seduction' of the army, is, however, a more peculiar feature. Needless to say, in a school which sanctifies violence and looks on conflict as the mother of progress, this was not due to love of pacifism or 'exaggerated humanitarianism.' On this point Sorel's reassurance is unnecessary. The anti-militaristic aspect of syndicalism is but a phase of its attitude of hostility to the State, due to a realisation of the fact that 'the army is the clearest and the most tangible of all possible manifestations of the State.'[2] This general consideration is, moreover, reinforced by a particular application. Should the State seek to suppress a strike (and this would be a natural stage in the progress and development of the General Strike), it would call out the soldiers and use the army for the purpose. The army is thus (among other things) a strike-breaking agency. This reflection becomes even more galling if one asks who, after all, are these soldiers who, with rifle and bayonet, may bring to naught the sublime work of the General Strike. For these soldiers are the brothers of the strikers. They have been members of the proletariat; they are now doing their period of conscript service; they will return to the ranks of the proletariat. Syndicalist propaganda therefore sought to impress on the recruit that on joining the army he did not thereby lose his old affiliations: he was still of the people. Should the day of trial come, he should remember this, and should act (or, preferably, fail to act) accordingly.

In these ways, then, the class war should be waged—a double warfare against employer and State, though doubtless the campaigns

[1] Lagardelle: *Le Socialisme Ouvrier*, p. 355.
[2] Sorel: *Reflections on Violence*, p. 123.

merge into one. Before drawing together the threads in all this matter of the *lutte de classe*, which finds its almost complete expression in the General Strike (in fact or in myth) there are two questions of tactics which usefully illumine the syndicalist outlook. The first comes with something of a shock to the dull prosaic Anglo-Saxon mind. It is the curious emphasis which the syndicalists lay on the virtue of unpreparedness: perhaps school-day memories of Ethelred the Unready have tilted us too far the other way and have made us somewhat over-conscientious in scanning the future. It may be that in this matter French syndicalism made a virtue of necessity. The syndicats were, to our way of looking at things, grotesquely and absurdly poor, for the quite sufficient reason that the trade union member did not like paying contributions any more than the trade union liked paying contribution to its federation. Sorel (speaking, it is true, of certain English unions which had fallen by the way) says that their members faded out 'quand ils ont trouvé trop dure l'obligation de payer toujours.'[1] The phrase, even if it awakens a sympathetic chord in every heart, explains much in French trade union history. The syndicats were innocent of reserves and resources; and therefore, like the de-tailed fox in the fable,[2] they persuaded themselves that they were better without them :

Que faisons-nous, dit-il, de ce poids inutile ?

Accordingly, and not wholly without reason, it was argued that accumulated funds might represent a debit rather than an asset. For the union which has funds becomes timorous and fearful of losing these funds. It becomes conservative, for there is nothing so effective in quenching the revolutionary spark as a moderate possession of this world's gear. From the higher idealism of penniless adventurousness, it is accordingly possible for the syndicalist to look down his nose across the Channel, at the 'insipidly materialistic conception of a trade unionism concerned solely with high wages and mutual benefits.'[3] Syndicalism, in this as in other things, is profoundly anti-rational. What is required is not foresight, planning, preparation or much goods laid up in barns. What is needed to storm the barricades is *élan, entraînement*, what Lagardelle calls 'adventurous energy.' Syndicalism is a philosophy not of thought but of action, and it gives the first place to 'intuition.'[4] Griffuelhes, in some pages which are not unamusing, contrasts the French worker with his duller German brother, who is sicklied o'er with the pale cast of thought. Those who think too much never do anything; in any case, it is quite impossible to foresee

[1] Sorel: *L'avenir socialiste des Syndicats* in *Matériaux d'une Théorie*, p. 106.
[2] If the Ministry of Food, without audible protest from Mr. A. P. Herbert, may de-feather our geese, La Fontaine may be allowed to present a fox in de-tail.
[3] Lagardelle: *Le Socialisme Ouvrier*, p. 217.
[4] Lagardelle in *Syndicalisme et Socialisme*, p. 8.

everything—so why try? But the French worker!—'Il resiste et proteste; il critique et s'insurge. Et il passe à l'acte immédiatement.' There indeed is the essence of French syndicalism. 'Il ne se laisse pas paralyser, lui, par la peur et la crainte.' Oh no. It consists wholly of action, like the French worker of whom Griffuelhes says: 'Il agit, et voilà tout.'[1] Attack, audacity, surprise—such are the keys of success in the eyes of the syndicalists who, forgetful of the Baconian dictum that boldness is a child of ignorance, accord a place of honour to the untrimmed lamp and the ungirt loin.

Il agit, et voilà tout. It is a picture with pleasing aspects; but cold-blooded people who have drawn into their infant lungs the mists of London or the haar of Eastern Scotland may regard all this as an exquisitely embroidered veil concealing a policy of acting first, and reflecting (and perhaps being sorry) later.

The other point in tactics—if it be tactics—illustrates the anti-democratic bias of syndicalism. It is found in the supremely important part assigned to the 'conscious minority.' This is, of course, a Marxian idea; and it is of the essence of the theory and practice of Leninism. The syndicalists, as indeed all revolutionaries, hold majorities in contempt, and despise representatives, who, once elected, take it upon themselves to do everything that requires to be done, thus losing all contact with those who elect them, and these as a further consequence tend to become 'inert.' All great things, it is claimed, are done by minorities who interpret the views and desires which may as yet be but latent and dormant in the inert mass. And in fact, the syndicalists would be right, if the theory of the 'conscious minority' were merely intended to give a convenient summary of the world's mechanism. Anyone who has had experience knows that if, of a committee of twelve, there are three who from the outset have already a draft report in their portfolio, while the other nine have deplorably virgin minds, the conscious minority have a fair chance of getting there. All great visions have been originally the visions of a few—probably the vision of one. In this sense, we may applaud the services of minorities—whether we call them 'conscious' or 'determined.'

Syndicalist reasoning on this question may, however, give rise to doubt, when they assign to the conscious minority—or at least the conscious minority in whom they are interested—a peculiar sanctity and a position of peculiar privilege. Let Lagardelle (abbreviated) describe the process. Direct action, he says, presupposes the effective intervention of *minorités hardies*. It is no longer mere numbers that form the law. 'Mais il se forme une élite qui, par sa qualité, entraîne la masse et l'oriente dans les chemins du combat.' There takes place a selection of the most courageous, the most audacious, etc., who are drawn in advance at the head of the others.

[1] Griffuelhes in *Syndicalisme et Socialisme*, pp. 56–57.

The only condition imposed is that they shall be 'en correspondance avec l'instinct intime des masses.'[1]

There is much virtue, because much vagueness, in the use of the reflexive in the French language: *Il se forme une élite, il se produit une selection.*[1] 'But how?' is the question to which there is no answer. This élite of the courageous and the audacious is thrown up or throws itself up: the conscious minority, conscious of its superior merit, imposes itself. It is a political theory which, with little modification, may be used to defend any tyranny, any dictatorship, or any other manifestation of gangsterdom.

Syndicalism is almost exclusively a theory of the class struggle, and of the place of the strike (and ultimately of the General Strike) as a weapon of class warfare. The class struggle is not, however, the peculiar property of the syndicalists, and what little may have to he said on this subject by way of comment should perhaps be reserved for a later chapter.[2] But the glorification of the strike is the undisputed pride of the syndicalists, even if there be a pale after-glow in their sucklings, the Guild Socialists. It may therefore be not inappropriate to suggest here on what grounds, as the ordinary man sees things, the syndicalist theory of strikes appears to be psychologically entirely at fault.

When strikes are condemned, the condemnation is generally based on what Sorel would call the ideology of a timorous humanitarian middle class, asking nothing more than to be allowed to live in peace.[3] Strikes involve loss: the Ministry of Labour chronicles how many man-days' productive power are wasted in this way each year; they are very infrequently completely successful; they are quite frequently not successful at all; they leave behind a trail of festering bitterness. None of these consequences would distress Sorel; some he would welcome. But, apart from these grounds of objection, rooted in low considerations of profit-and-loss and in the 'chimera of social peace,' there is another reason (equally one of expediency) for suggesting that strikes are unwise. This springs from the very nature of what a strike is. Now, though doubtless not so intended, a strike is an invitation to the public to find out how they can get along without the services of a particular group of workers; the strikers in effect say not merely to the employers but to the world at large; 'You just try and do without us.' The trouble is that we all tend to overrate our indispensability:

> The weaver's Art, it is renowned so,
> That rich or poor without it cannot go.

[1] Lagardelle: *Le Socialisme Ouvrier*, pp. 370–371.
[2] See concluding chapter, pp. 499–504.
[3] Sorel: *Reflections on Violence*, p. 82.

No doubt; but it is possible, if need arises, to make an old suit serve its primary purpose for a wonderfully long time. If we invite the world to do without us, the world may take us at our word, and may demonstrate that we are not so important as we thought we were. When miners strike, they invite their foreign customers to make arrangements (probably long-term arrangements) with mines in other countries, and their home customers to ascertain in how many ways they can economise in coal from day to day. When railwaymen strike, they invite the public to find out how convenient buses may be; and if road transport should happen at the time to be struggling to its feet, the railway strike may set the buses on a rock, establishing their way. One may not generalise in these matters; but probably there are few large strikes which do not result in a shrinkage (which may sometimes be permanent) in the demand for the strikers' product. The public at large has written down their indispensability. Probably this consideration would not apply to the same extent in a world where the proletariat of all countries had succeeded in uniting; it is a consideration which cannot yet be ignored.

In assessing the syndicalist doctrines in this matter, it is unnecessary to comment further on the strike *des bras croisés*, which, as we have seen, rests on a view of life which the lower grades of the kindergarten should have outgrown. But beyond this, the doctrine of impulsive unpreparedness, of indifference to defeat, and the emphasis on the conscious minority alike betray ignorance of human nature and of human possibilities. An age which has become enamoured of the idea of 'planning' does not need to be told that the world cannot be rebuilt by *élan*. A war cannot be won by relying on the sudden impulse of a private soldier storming a barricade one evening when he feels like it. *Elan* has its uses, but there ought to be somewhere a General Staff with a few ideas about the campaign as a whole. The syndicalists mislead and confuse themselves with the military metaphors in which the whole subject of the class war is steeped. The syndicalist doctrine is that unpreparedness is not merely a virtue, but (what is far better) an asset. They hold that one thing is needful, and that the good part consists in being aglow with passionate enthusiasm; that no heights will be stormed by an army of Marthas troubled about many things. To look upon every encounter as a vanguard action which may lead to the great Napoleonic battle is to make grand strategy depend on the outcome of chance skirmishes; and alike in the military and industrial field such a course is merely to invite disaster.

Equally wrong in its perverseness is the view that all strikes are good, because they provide a bracing tonic, because they teach solidarity, and because all are useful preparations for a still greater engagement. Even if a strike is a failure, it is supposed to possess these educational virtues, and consequently the true syndicalist is indifferent to failure. It is true that a succession of military reverses (if not carried too far) may at times have the effect of making a nation more determined and more resolute. Peoples of a certain temperament and with the right leadership may be tried in adversity and may come forth as gold; though even here defeat is not a matter of indifference. But in the case of strikes and industrial disputes, it may be doubted whether the analogy holds at all. In the industrial field nothing is so discouraging and demoralising as a series of defeats; nothing so quickly turns the revolutionary into a reformist, or so promptly depletes the membership of the union affected. The failure of a big strike has, as an almost inevitable concomitant, the outbreak of bickerings and recriminations among those who have suffered defeat. That a strike, irrespective of its outcome, has a tonic effect is simply not true.

So far as concerns strikes, the emphasis on the conscious and active minority is also a snare and a source of weakness. It has already been conceded that, in the march of things, the minority may be the salt of the earth, leavening the whole lump (if this conjunction of similes be permissible): equally, of course, a minority may be the worst form of public nuisance. In the case of a strike, however, to place reliance on an active conscious minority in the middle of an inert mass is merely to invite failure. The active minority may precipitate a strike; but unless they have got far beyond the stage of being a minority, they will not be able to continue the strike—a reflection which points back to the root principle of democracy that it is the task of the minority to turn itself into the majority as its path to achievement. Indeed, on syndicalist theory, the kind of strike contemplated demands that the whole mass of the workers must be tingling with enthusiasm.

How far the position with regard to the General Strike is clarified, how far the policy of encouraging strikes is strengthened by the Sorelian conception of the myth, might be a matter for argument. Probably the 'myth,' while providing much material for philosophical discussion on the nature and foundations of belief, floated over the heads of the workers, unheeded and uncomprehended. Yet in so far as echoes of Sorelian philosophy penetrated to the proletarian mind, the event can hardly have been without influence in unsettling the ideas of the workers as to what the whole business meant. The myth, as we have seen, is a 'body of images,' capable of moving to action; to enquire into its literal accuracy is wholly otiose. No detail in a myth must be discussed as if it were 'un fait historique previsible.'[1] Myths are not 'astrological almanacs'; nothing that is contained in them may ever come to pass. Though Sorel does not so express it, a myth is, in current jargon, an effective slogan with a picture behind it,

[1] Sorel: *La Décomposition du Marxisme*, p. 58.

whether true or misleading. If it stirs the blood and moves men to act by crystallising their hopes and fears, then it has done its work.

The early socialists, it will be recalled, continually conduct their readers to the outskirts of theological discussion—even if it be a theology of their own. Sorel comes near to reviving the tradition by drawing his illustrations of the functions of myths from the theological as well as from the social field. It may be doubted, on various grounds, whether the expectation held by the early Christians of an imminent return of Christ provides a happy example of the Sorelian myth. He is perhaps on surer ground in invoking 'the myth of the struggle with Satan.' In England, more than in Scotland, it is customary for people to 'renounce the Devil and all his works' when, quite obviously—to judge from their walk and conversation—they have no great living belief in the existence of a subordinate, malevolent, frustrated, but not yet wholly defeated deity. But for the fact that in this country we are still somewhat shy in talking of God it would be interesting, by taking a cross-section of the population, to ascertain what exactly people in general think they are doing when they renounce the devil. Probably most would reply, on Sorelian lines, that the struggle against Satan is a picturesque, convenient and traditional way of expressing a very obvious reality, that somehow there is such a thing as evil, and that evil must be warred against; adding that the effectiveness of the picture is in no way impaired because few of us now visualise Satan as he may be encountered in the first chapter of the Book of Job.[1] Nevertheless, even if some would admit that there is a place for 'symbolic truth,' the conception of the 'myth' as applied to the General Strike is somewhat peculiar, and so far as it had any effect on the ordinary man, must in the long run have produced effects contrary to what was intended. For the essence of the Sorelian myth in this case is that we, the proletariat, are to be inspired from day to day by an apocalyptic vision of the General Strike, which at the same time we are told will in all probability never take place: we should realise that every dispute in which we may engage may, for all we know, be the prelude to an earth-shaking event, which turns out to be the figment of a philosopher's brain—regarding which it is, further, foolishness to ask whether it means what it purports to mean, or whether it means anything at all. If all this were apprehended, hope deferred would soon cool the workers' ardour. If in this life only we have myths, then are we of all men most miserable.

Something, in conclusion, should be said of the syndicalist future: fortunately, at the end of an unduly lengthy chapter, there is sur-

[1] The curious reader may consult the *Report on Doctrine in the Church of England* (1938), and in particular the Note, *On the Application to the Creeds of the Conception of Symbolic Truth.*

prisingly little to say. Doubtless there is in existence a syndicalist Utopia or fairy-tale, explaining *Comment nous ferons la Révolution*, but it is in accordance with the principles of a school whose motto is to act first and think later (if at all), that in the syndicalist scheme of things the future is left to look after itself. Certain points on very broad lines are clear, and have already been indicated incidentally. By a progressive process of encroaching control, the syndicats are to oust the present employers, and place themselves in the warm nest as the legitimate heir: 'it counts on expelling the capitalists from the productive domain, and on taking their place in the workshop created by capitalism.' Likewise it 'proposes to suppress the State.'[1] The same double purpose is expressed by Lagardelle, when he defines the purpose of syndicalist socialism as consisting in the simultaneous suppression of the exploitation of man by man, and of the government of man by man. There is here clearly a strong infusion of anarchism, which admittedly exercised considerable influence in the early days of the formulation of syndicalist policy. It is, however, an anarchism of groups; the individual is not left loose and irresponsible in a disordered world. On the contrary, the individual is to find his responsibilities, his human satisfactions and affiliations in the syndicat. But, so far as can be judged of a prospect where precision is avoided, the syndicats will be left to jostle anarchistically in the void. In a sense, however, it would be truer to say that the syndicalist refused to think of the future. The primary question for them was whether the proletariat has enough strength to *enter on* the struggle.[2] There is repeated emphasis on the fact that not merely is there no need for programmes, it is even folly to plan socialism, since 'tout en lui est imprevisible': it is only a reactionary who would draw up a programme.[3] Lagardelle is particularly scornful of detailed plans: if the *esprit de lutte* is combined with the *esprit positif*, then they may calmly entrust their destiny to the care of history.[4] It is pleasant to encounter this child-like faith. Syndicalism is like the syndicalist worker: *il agit, et voilà tout.*

Syndicalism was, while it lasted—and in retrospect still is—an extremely interesting movement. It is significant that it combined in a peculiar degree two of the most characteristic tendencies of the last generation—and two of the most undesirable tendencies, as it may appear to those of us who are senescent. Syndicalism is anti-democratic; and it is anti-rational and anti-intellectual. Why so large a part of the world has turned its back on democracy, why even

[1] Sorel: *Reflections on Violence*, pp. 189–190.
[2] Sorel: *L'avenir socialiste des Syndicats* in *Matériaux d'une Théorie*, p. 82.
[3] Sorel: *Reflections on Violence*, p. 150; *La Décomposition du Marxisme*, p. 66.
[4] Lagardelle: *Le Socialisme Ouvrier*, pp. 290–292.

democrats agree, sorrowfully, that the theory of democracy needs restatement, may not be considered here. Enough to note that in their irreconcilable antagonism to Parliament and all its ways; in their belief in ' direct action '; in their exaltation of minorities, the syndicalists were, throughout and profoundly, anti-democratic, and were among the first to be so on a large and consistent scale.[1] So also the last generation has to a large extent turned its back on reason, so dear to the eighteenth century. We no longer ask that our poetry, our art, or our music should ' mean ' anything; for many of the younger generation, meaning has ceased to have any meaning. Instinct, intuition, impulse, imagination have displaced reason. It is again a feature profoundly characteristic of the syndicalists who placed enthusiasm in the forefront, scoffed at preparations, relied on their intuitions and refused to think of the future. Georges Sorel, the leading exponent of syndicalism on its philosophical side, is also something of a portent, and a figure who would repay study as a psychological case. He lived long enough to wash his hands of syndicalism because it had failed to fulfil its promise. Indeed, living a placid but increasingly pessimistic life in his villa in the pleasant bourgeois suburb of Boulogne-sur-Seine, he was able in the fullness of time to get a certain kick out of the appearance of Lenin and of Mussolini on the horizon of things. A General Strike (as a myth, and in imagination); a revolution in far-off Russia; a march on Rome (at a distance) were equally welcome as an escape from the slothful slough of modern civilisation. Fundamentally, Sorel detested the mediocrity and drabness of life with an intensity which suggests that life in the villa at Boulogne-sur-Seine was surrounded by a sea of drabness and mediocrity, by an unending fen of stagnant waters. Doubtless there are certain ' bourgeois ' suburbs in which one is instinctively impelled to reflections on violence. Most people work it off by reading, or writing, detective novels.

[1] ' Direct action ' has, of course, at all times been the device of banditti, freebooters and gentlemen of the forest glade. Robin Hood, with the highest motives, believed in effecting a redistribution of purchasing power by a policy of direct action. The theory of direct action may be found admirably interpreted in the conversation of two ruffians in *The Mysteries of Udolpho*. Quoth the first ruffian: ' This is the way to have justice done at once, without more ado. If you go to law, you must stay till the judges please, and may lose your cause at last. Why the best way, then, is to make sure of your right while you can, and execute justice yourself.' Quoth the second ruffian: ' Yes, yes; if you wait till justice is done you . . . you may stay long enough. Why, if I want a friend of mine properly served, how am I to get my revenge? Ten to one, they will tell me he is in the right and I am in the wrong. Or, if a fellow has got possession of property which I think ought to be mine, why I may wait till I starve, perhaps, before the law will give it me, and then, after all, the judge may say—the estate is his. What is to be done then? Why the case is plain enough. I must take it at last.' On her previous form Emily ought to have fainted on overhearing this conversation: she did not, but at least it is recorded that she felt horror.

CHAPTER XVI

GUILD SOCIALISM

We have the highest possible authority for regarding Guild Socialism as representing for this country the essential parallel to syndicalism in France.[1] It may be regarded as a fairly typical example of Anglo-Saxon compromise and of the national instinct to shun excessive theory, when it becomes too obviously and blatantly impracticable. Syndicalism had abolished the State, leaving a cosmos—or perhaps a chaos—of jostling trade unions. Guild Socialism, though in varying degrees according to the interpreter and the time of the interpretation, endeavoured to retain a State, even if it might be a truncated and emasculated State; yet with this presumed concession to practicability, the guildsmen, in their outlook and vision, were close kinsmen to the syndicalists.

That Guild Socialism, in its purest form, represented a significant departure from the older and more orthodox collectivist socialism is indubitable. The nature of the change may be indicated in various ways. On the one hand, it may be said that while the older collectivists (conveniently exemplified by the Fabians) were primarily interested in the consumers, Guild Socialism, holding that man was firstly and for the greater part of his life a worker, approached the problem from the producer's end. Again, though it may be but a variation of the same distinction, collectivism was interested above all in what it regarded as a just distribution of the products of industry, whereas Guild Socialism was more interested in the organisation of industry and in the control of industry by the workers. Further, the collectivists (and the Fabians) looked to the State as the rock of their salvation; the Guild Socialists, realising that for this as for most purposes the State was but a broken reed, and in the great class struggle no better than an enemy agent, looked for deliverance to the trade unions, the organisations of the workers as producers.

From this general setting, it further follows that Guild Socialism was extraordinarily prolific in ideas which, even if not the original property of the Guild Socialists, had nevertheless sufficient freshness to startle and surprise. On the one hand, their preoccupation with the State and the whittling down of the State to its proper place in the scheme of things leads to a vast mass of political speculation, so that one approaches Guild Socialism under the shadow of Rousseau and the general will, with Bodin, Maitland, Austin and many more

[1] Cole: *Self-Government in Industry*, p. 321.

involved in the argument. On the other hand, when the erstwhile Leviathan has been properly pruned and trained and has become sufficiently inoffensive to be drawn out with a hook, there remains the question of fitting its successor, the trade unions, to assume the inheritance. Thus there arose a vast amount of discussion of trade union theory, structure and function. Apart from its criticism of things as they are, which is an ineluctable part of all socialism, Guild Socialism is therefore involved in a considerable volume of speculation relating to general political and social theory, above all with regard to the place of associations in society. Indeed, one of the reasons why Guild Socialism, as a movement, foundered so promptly was that it suffered from too many ideas. It demanded from its devotees a level of mental equipment rarely to be found outside the lonelier altitudes of the more ancient seats of learning.

It has been said above that Guild Socialism is approximately the Anglo-Saxon equivalent of syndicalism, but it would be easy to exaggerate the influence of syndicalism on the formation of the corresponding English school. The process was by no means a mere translation, and indeed, most of the avenues to Guild Socialism were opened before syndicalism was an obvious influence. In the background there is manifest the pervading influence of John Ruskin and William Morris. There was in this country, as elsewhere, a dissatisfaction with the fruits of political action; for, as was argued, the Labour members returned to the 1906 Parliament had, after the shouting had died, been swallowed up in the machine, and had become no better (even if not markedly worse) than Liberal members. In the early development of Guild Socialism much importance is attached to Mr. A. J. Penty's *Restoration of the Gild System*, published in 1906, which, with an infusion of other points of view peculiar to Mr. Penty throughout, did in fact foreshadow most of the dominant ideas of the later Guildsmen. Later, *The New Age* became the centre of propaganda for the ' guild idea ' in articles due to Mr. S. G. Hobson and Mr. A. R. Orage. Mr. G. D. H. Cole can hardly be called one of the original founders of Guild Socialism, though he later became its most obvious leader and most effective exponent. For a time he endeavoured to further the guild idea within the Fabian Society; but indeed the points of divergence were too manifold and too manifest. In 1915 the break took place and the National Guilds League was founded. Popularly, and on the whole justly, Guild Socialism came to be identified with Mr. Cole; but if only because of considerable divergence on certain points, it is wise not to overlook the writings of Mr. Penty, Mr. S. G. Hobson, Mr. Orage, Mr. Stirling Taylor, and a joint work by Mr. Reckitt and Mr. Bechhofer. Beyond this, certain phases of Guild Socialist criticism and ideology are, of course, to be found in writers not intimately connected, or not connected at all, with the Guild Socialist movement. In certain of the writings of Mr. Tawney, Mr. Laski and Mr. MacIver, to mention no more, we get on some points an expression of ideas that have sympathetic kinship with the Guild Socialist outlook.[1]

It may be convenient to attempt, as a framework for a more detailed consideration later, a very summarised statement of the leading ingredients of Guild Socialism. The worker, as a worker—it is urged—is not free. The effect of the wage-contract is that 'labour is a commodity' while the worker renounces all control over the conditions of his labour and the disposal of his product. He is, in short, a wage-slave. That he may be free, the wage-system must be destroyed, and industry must pass under the control of labour. 'Industrial democracy' is no less important than political democracy, which indeed is but an empty phrase, unless industry also is conducted on democratic lines. With wistful glances towards the Middle Ages (seen perhaps through a mist of years), the guild system appears as the ideal; we must therefore revive the spirit and (so far as may be) the structure of the guild system. The obvious nucleus for such transformation to-day can be found only in the trade unions; and therefore trade unions, suitably modified and reorganised, must become the modern guild. These guilds, democratically run from below, will in each case have full and absolute control of the industry concerned. Meanwhile there will of necessity be a corresponding change in the position of the State. Needless to say, no salvation can be expected from the State, or from the collectivest ideal; for the State may be as harsh to its wage-slaves as any ordinary capitalist. We have, however, been in error in any case in our view of the State and its true functions; it does not, in the traditional sense, possess 'sovereign powers.' It is an association, just as a trade union is an association; it is merely one association among many, none of whom can claim 'sovereignty.' Its true and primary purpose (though the statement varies from time to time) should be to represent the consumers. Thus we have a world of self-governing guilds (sprung from the loins of the trade unions) on the producers' side; and on the consumers' side there is left an abridged State, which tended to become ever more abridged as the discussion proceeded. In such a world, the guilds, freed from the lust for profits, will exist solely to render service. Moreover, labour will no longer be a commodity; the worker will no longer be a wage-slave. For the first time there will be true democracy, covering the whole field; and each one, finding joy in his work and realising himself in it, will become 'a man among men.' Such, it is hoped, is a not unfair representation of the

[1] A full-length account of the development and origins of Guild Socialism will be found in Niles Carpenter: *Guild Socialism.*

general position occupied by the Guild Socialists, the further elaboration of which is the purpose of the remainder of this chapter; but it should be remembered that a composite picture is of necessity inaccurate, and that in the present case there were divergencies as to how far the State could or should be reduced, as to whether the Guilds should be few and national or more numerous and local, as to how far we could or should endeavour to return to the thirteenth century.

But before embarking on a more systematic exposition of Guild Socialism there is one point to which, with reluctance, some reference should be made. It is that the Guild Socialists, in the days of their greatest noisiness, suffered from certain obvious defects as controversialists. Some may feel that they tended overmuch to write each book twice over,

> Lest you should think they never could recapture
> Their first wild careful rapture.

That, however, is a small matter, and perhaps pardonable in a world where books are published for profit as well as for use. What is not so excusable is that there has probably never been a school of writers so intolerant of the opinions of others, so violent and unrestrained in their language, so extravagantly contemptuous of all and sundry, so assured of their own righteousness as the possessors of a peculiar illumination, so confident that unto them had been committed the oracles of God.[1] Being in a sense a break-away from the Fabians, their finest invective is reserved for the Fabians (and in particular for Mr. Sidney Webb) because these believed in the State, and for Labour Members of Parliament, because presumably these believed in political action. In a passage frequently quoted, Mr. Cole exclaimed that 'Collectivists may take their choice: they are knaves, who hate freedom, or they are fools, who do not know what freedom means, or they are a bit of both.'[2] Elsewhere we hear of 'the dotards of *The New Statesman*,'[3] and of 'the "Selfridge" State, so loudly heralded these twenty years by Mr. "Callisthenes" Webb'[4]—a reference which will be obscure to the next generation. Mr. and Mrs. Webb become 'the Sir and Lady Oracle of the Socialist movement.'[5] Even in 1917, Mr. Webb was a sufficiently venerable figure to command the outward respect of the very young. As it is counselled in the wisest of books: 'Dishonour not a man in his old age: for even some of us wax old.' But darkness is everywhere. According to the author of *National Guilds*, only a handful of socialists in Great Britain have a clear conception of what socialism means; even worse,

[1] When he gets going, Proudhon runs them hard.
[2] Cole: *Self-Government in Industry*, p. 231.
[3] *Ibid.* p. 208. [4] *Ibid.* p. 122. [5] *Ibid.* p. 114.

there are not half a dozen thinkers in the land who take the trouble to understand the real meaning of wages [1]—which presumably leaves only three, apart from Mr. Cole and the writer. 'Criminal fools,' [2] 'your well-meaning, socially conscientious idiots,' [3] 'that group of honest but stupid men' [4]—such is the world as seen by the Guild Socialist. And there are even more startling side-lights on our contemporaries. The merchant is the 'pimp of industrial prostitution' (whatever that may mean), and the bureaucrat is 'the eunuch in the palace'—though many have mingled with civil servants for a lifetime without noticing it.[5] Lastly, in these few illustrative extracts from what might be a Guide to Bad Manners and Vituperation, it is well to ponder the implications of Mr. Cole's dictum that 'to do good work for a capitalist employer is merely . . . to help a thief to steal more successfully.' [6] The world, it is made to appear, is made up of fools and knaves, of thieves and of people of incredible stupidity; on the other hand, 'we are the world's builders' [7] even if there may not be half a dozen of us who know the meaning of wages. It is a curious phenomenon that a school of socialism which, more than any other, bears the mark of intellectual 'refinement' and high academic equipment should also be pre-eminent in its power of vituperation and abuse. In itself the literary manners of the early Guild Socialists are neither here nor there, except in so far as their intolerance and arrogance contributed greatly to the ineffectiveness of the movement.

In such a vast mass of criticism, theory, and speculation, it is not entirely easy to find the most logical starting-point for purposes of exposition. Probably, however, the initial impulse common to most Guild Socialists is to be found in the degradation of labour resulting from the wage-system. With wearisome reiteration it is asserted that it is universally accepted that labour is a commodity and is treated accordingly, that indeed human beings are treated as commodities, and are bought and sold 'as a grocer sells butter.' [8] As butter is not a sufficiently offensive commodity, Mr. Hobson underlines the point

[1] *National Guilds: An Inquiry into the Wage System and the Way out*, edited by A. R. Orage, pp. 21, 75. This book, which occupies a considerable place in Guild Socialist literature, appeared substantially as a series of articles in *The New Age* during the years 1912–13. As published, it gives no indication of authorship. Mr. Cole, however, says that the articles were written by Mr. Hobson with the collaboration of Mr. Orage (Cole, *Chaos and Order in Industry*, p. 49).

[2] *National Guilds*, p. 291.

[3] Cole: *Labour in the Commonwealth*, p. 137.

[4] *National Guilds*, p. 55. (The reference is to the Labour Party in its entirety.)

[5] *Ibid.* pp. 95, 224.

[6] Cole: *Self-Government in Industry*, p. 235. Fortunately, the volume in which this incitement to universal sabotage appears is in every way a credit to the integrity and the high craftsmanship of all concerned in its production.

[7] *Ibid.* p. 225.

[8] Cole: *Labour in the Commonwealth*, p. 136.

by arguing that the status of labour is 'exactly that of manure.'[1] Labour is, on the contrary, a sacred thing, a sanctified human factor.[2] At present the worker is a slave—a 'wage-slave'—living in conditions which in some respects compare unfavourably with chattel-slavery. On the evils of the wage-system—preferably called 'wagery'—there is no limit to the extravagance of language which Guild Socialist writers allow themselves. The wage-bargain, says Mr. Cole, is still of the essence of slavery.[3] It is cruel and wasteful, says Mr. Hobson; it is devilish and inhuman.[4] To be a wage-earner is in itself dishonourable. In a grotesque flight of the imagination we are assured that every wage-earner carries with him the stigmata of his caste as obviously as if he were a branded slave.[5] Wagery embodies a vile conception of human relationships.[6] It follows that the abolition of 'wagery' (in some respects the immediate objective of the Guild Socialists) will be a greater event than the abolition of slavery.[7] Those who write thus have clearly lost all sense of the meaning of words, and have been singularly unobservant in their journey through life. The British workman is neither a slave, nor does he feel himself to be a slave: he is the least obsequious of animals.[8]

Fortunately Mr. Cole, in one familiar passage, condescends to particulars, and enunciates four points which, taken together, mark the degraded status of labour. Abbreviating them slightly, they are as follows: (i) the wage-system abstracts labour from the labourer, so that the one can be bought and sold without the other; (ii) wages are paid only when profitable to the employer; (iii) in return for his wages, the worker surrenders all control over the organisation of production; and also (iv) he surrenders all claim on the product of his labour. The abolition of the wage-system accordingly requires the removal of these 'marks of degraded status.' Consequently it is the task of National Guilds to assure the worker (i) payment as a human being; (ii) payment in employment and unemployment, in sickness and in health; (iii) control of the organisation of production by the workers; and (iv) a claim upon the product of his work.[9] In more ordinary language these involve (i) remuneration otherwise than by wages; (ii) security, so that a worker is definitely 'on the strength,'

[1] Hobson: *Guild Principles in War and Peace*, p. 85.
[2] *Ibid.* pp. 85, 134.
[3] Cole: *Labour in the Commonwealth*, p. 21.
[4] Hobson: *Guild Principles in War and Peace*, pp. 146, 154.
[5] *National Guilds* (Orage), p. 44.
[6] Reckitt and Bechhofer: *The Meaning of National Guilds*, p. 4 (2nd edition).
[7] Hobson: *Guild Principles in War and Peace*, p. 58.
[8] In the Local Appeal Boards set up to deal with questions under the Essential Work Orders, where employer and worker appear together, nothing is more refreshing than the complete absence of awe shown by the worker in the presence of the employer whom (presumably) God has placed over him, and of the Board whom no less a person than the Minister of Labour has appointed to hear the case.
[9] Cole: *Self-Government in Industry*, pp. 154–155.

irrespective of trade or health conditions: (iii) workers' control over the productive process, and (iv) over the selling process.

These four pointers, if followed up, give some indication of the transformation in the status of labour which it is desired to effect. The reader may experience a curious sense of anti-climax, when he realises that the effect of the abolition of the wage-system will be that in future the worker will receive 'pay' instead of 'wages.' It is astonishing how much effort was devoted to persuading an unconvinced world that 'wages' and 'pay' are worlds apart. Between wages and pay, it is suggested, there is all the difference that there is between slavery and freedom. Again, wages 'are what the capitalist is constrained to give. Pay is what he who renders a service is entitled to receive.' [1] So, somewhat cumbrously and at great length, Mr. Hobson contrasts salaried Robinson, with a 'recognised and recompensed personality' and wage-earner Jones who 'supplies only a non-human quality, from which his personality is *ex hypothesi* excluded,[2] Moreover, and very curiously, attention is frequently drawn to the fact that soldiers receive 'pay' and not 'wages,' and the alleged reason is that 'the work done by the soldier is in no sense a commodity. It is a duty, perhaps a privilege.' [3] Mr. Hobson, with elephantine humour, goes on to an expression of astonishment that Mr. Sidney Webb should not have demanded that soldiers should be put on 'wage-rates, piece-work for preference.' [4] The distinction between the indignity of wages and the honorability of pay bulks so largely in the writings of the Guild Socialists that it may not be ignored; but as presented by them, it is so puerile that any necessary discussion had better be relegated to the smaller type of a footnote.[5]

[1] Reckitt and Bechhofer: *Meaning of National Guilds*, pp. 13–14 (2nd edition).
[2] Hobson: *Guild Principles in War and Peace*, p. 37.
[3] *Ibid.* p. 59. [4] *Ibid.* p. 139.
[5] Like all philological questions, the distinction (if any) between wages and pay is interesting, even if for the present purpose unimportant. The Guild Socialists doubtless wished a change in the method of determination and the conditions of remuneration, but they put themselves on hopelessly weak ground in insisting so vehemently and stridently that the change they desired was represented by the change from wages to pay. No doubt the precise shade of meaning attached to words may vary from one part of the country to another; but in the north-eastern corner of this island the workers probably refer as often to their 'pay' as to their 'wage.' They would say (two generations ago, at any rate) that So-and-so was getting 'gey guid pey.' Perhaps we avoided the word 'wages,' because of its theological connection with sin and death. Also, for what it is worth, the world in general speaks of 'pay-day'; and a 'pay-sheet' is just as common as a 'wages-sheet.' If there is a distinction, it is probably that 'pay' is a more universal word, applicable to all periodic payments; on the other hand, if there were a wage, with overtime or a bonus, probably the whole sum would be described as the week's pay, and not as the week's wage. There is a further consideration tending to make the word 'pay' universally applicable; it is that 'pay' is also (and indeed originally and properly) a verb, while there is no verb corresponding to the word 'wage.' Consequently salaries are *paid*; and wages are *paid*; and but for reasons of euphony, pay would be *paid*. There is something rather ridiculous in the grievance of the Guild Socialists that Mr. and Mrs. Webb 'decline to accept the common

In fact, waving aside the dispute as to the meaning of 'wages' and 'pay' as something of an excrescence, the Guild Socialists see in the abolition of the employer the only hope of escaping from the 'commodity theory of labour' and the consequent degradation of the wage-system. So long as authority derives from 'a power which is external to the workers employed, the system will remain a servile system.' [1] Mr. Cole's desiderata are indeed not four separate demands for four independent transformations. They are closely interconnected, and together they require the fading away of the employer and the transfer of the control of industry in some way to the workers themselves. The workers, banded together, will organise production, and dispose of their produce. There will be no 'wages,' as defined by the Guild Socialists, because, irrespective of the state of trade, everyone will be maintained in sickness and health by the body of which he is a member. Moreover, the pursuit of gain will no longer direct the course of production; everyone will be inspired by the motive of service. In a much-too-familiar tag, production will be for use and not for profit.

Mingled with this line of approach, there are in certain sections of Guild Socialism somewhat curious remnants of undigested Marxian analysis. The author of *National Guilds* in particular is marked by an uncritical acceptance of Marxian ideas and phraseology, which provides him with a somewhat different approach to the attack on the wage-system. It is that 'the profiteer's chief bulwark of defence is the wage-system.' [2] The first step to freedom and economic emancipation must therefore be sought in the abolition of the wage-system, 'for it is by means of wages that rent, interest and profits are exacted.' [3] Strictly speaking, the guild vision does not require the support of Marxian analysis; and in so far as Marxian strands are woven into the texture of the Guild Socialist case, it probably represented in the

meaning of the word "wages"' (*National Guilds*, p. 74), when in fact the distinction they draw is entirely of their own imagining. Presumably Mr. Cole is merely being unpleasant when, in reproving Mr. Webb for his indifference to words, he wonders 'whether it would be equally indifferent to Mr. Webb if his weekly allowance were called "hush money," or to Mrs. Webb if she were paid entirely in "blackmail"' (*The World of Labour*, p. 416). The answer to this is to consult any ordinary dictionary, which will reveal that it finds considerable difficulty in distinguishing 'wages' and 'pay,' but that it has no difficulty at all in giving another and very different meaning to the other two terms. With regard to the repeated emphasis on the fact that the soldier receives 'pay' and not 'wages' it is mildly interesting (though again it is of no importance) to note that the Authorised Version of the Bible, the highest authority on the usage of English, in the only passage where it deals with the remuneration of soldiers, makes no bones about speaking of wages. The reader will recall the advice given by John the Baptist to the soldiers: 'Do violence to no man, neither accuse any falsely; and be content with your wages.' As a contribution to the solution of the wage question, the whole discussion is of an unparalleled irrelevance; but those who seek to appraise Guild Socialism must follow where Guild Socialists lead.

[1] Cole: *Labour in the Commonwealth*, p. 118.

[2] *National Guilds* (edited by Orage), p. 39.

[3] *Ibid.* p. 123.

long run a source of weakness. For the Marxian analysis is of very doubtful validity, unless viewed from afar and with eyes not too critical; nor have we in this country, apart from a few, ever taken to Marxism as to a natural sustenance.

With the abolition of the wage-nexus and the disappearance of the employer, and with the establishment of workers' control, the way is opened to 'democracy in industry'—another of the many phrases to which the Guild Socialists gave currency. If this present sorry scheme of things goes, where—when we seek to remould it nearer to the heart's desire—are we to find the inspiration to provide the spirit, if not the details, of the new order? The answer, perhaps somewhat surprisingly, is in the mediaeval guilds. Not all who have written of mediaeval guilds have been qualified to write competently on what is an abstruse and difficult subject. A very natural nausea with an industrial age inevitably drives a certain type of mind backwards for solace, if only because the past will always win a glory from its being far. Mr. Penty, to whom the Guild Socialist owed so much initial inspiration, was an extreme and consistent mediaevalist, with an uncompromising hatred of inventions and machinery and of division of labour, and with a burning desire to make everyone a skilled craftsman, such as we encounter in the 38th chapter of Ecclesiasticus or in the best historical romances. The Middle Ages certainly represented an era of moderation which frowned on gain and usury and indeed viewed all the things of this world against the background of an eternity to come: it was an age which builded cathedrals which certainly yielded no mundane dividends to their promoters. Its fundamental principle in a sense was that no one, in buying or selling or in any other way, should take advantage of his neighbour. How far Mr. Penty idealised the Middle Ages, seeing in them a Lost Paradise in contrast to the dust and grit, the sweat and dispeace of these times, is a question to be answered only by those who know. Enough that, on the industrial side, Mr. Penty saw in the mediaeval guilds a remedy against our modern sins and deficiencies. In the Middle Ages, as seen through his eyes, industry aimed at service and not at profits; industry was then organised to guarantee quality and a high standard of workmanship, and not merely dividends; and further it was democratic in that there was no sharp cleavage between the worker and the employer.

Where in the world of to-day may we look for something sufficiently similar to the guilds, round which it may be possible to build the world of the future? The Guild Socialists had no hesitation in following the lead of the syndicalists and in replying that for this purpose it is to the trade unions that we must turn. Not indeed that the trade unions as at present constituted are qualified to play the rôle of the mediaeval guilds ; it ought, however, to be the purpose of trade union statesmanship to mould them for this place in the new society. Whether the guilds were in fact the appropriate forerunners of the trade unions in the Guild Socialist world may be doubted. As Mr. Penty himself underlines, ' the mediaeval guilds did not seek to organise industry, but to control it.' [1]

The question of trade union reorganisation thus becomes a large part of Guild Socialist propaganda, mingled with much reproof and correction, which may or may not have been welcome. For, to go no further, are not trade unions guilty of lamentable flabbiness and child-like gullibility, due to the fact that they have neither ideas nor policy ? [2] Trade unions need to be well shaken up [3] ; and the changes to be made in their structure and in the shape of things generally are designed to facilitate two ends, which at first sight might not be thought likely of attainment by the same methods. In the first place, trade unions are to be refashioned, so that they may more readily become polished shafts and pillars in the New Jerusalem ; at the same time they are to be made more apt instruments for carrying on the class struggle in this present evil world. For, like the syndicalists, the Guild Socialists, or most of them, place class warfare at the centre of things.

The changes necessary in trade union organisation must here be disposed of summarily, if we are to avoid the risk of being beguiled into an endless digression on trade union theory and structure.[4] If, in future, guilds are to control industries (and the more orthodox Guild Socialism rejected the local mediaeval guild in favour of a national guild), then trade unions must now be arranged so that their frontiers march with the frontiers of the various industries. This raises the whole question of the appropriate basis of trade unions, which, largely but not entirely because of Guild Socialist propaganda, has been in the centre of discussion for the last generation. Trade unions grew up anyhow, workmen who felt that they had common interests joining together for mutual support. But there are all sorts of reasons which might make men feel that they had common interests, and which might therefore form the basis of their union. In part it might be locality—because they lived in the same neighbourhood ; it might be because they exercised the same craft, though perhaps working in different industries ; it might be because they were engaged in the same industry, though following different crafts therein ; it might even be because they served the same employer, which, in these days of active local authorities and large industrial concerns, might result in combining strange bedfellows.

[1] Penty: *Post-Industrialism*, p. 87.
[2] Cole: *The World of Labour*, Preface to 1917 edition, p. xiii.
[3] Cole: *Labour in the Commonwealth*, p. 62.
[4] The question is dealt with more or less everywhere, but more specifically in Cole, *Self-Government in Industry*, chap. 5 ; and in Cole: *Guild Socialism Restated*, chap. 11.

The main clash of argument and the primary impulse to trade union amalgamations has centred in the conflict between the industrial union, combining all who work in an industry, no matter what they may be doing in that industry, and the craft union, combining all who possess and exercise a given craft, no matter in what industry they may be employed. On this question the Guild Socialist can give but one answer. If society is in future to be founded on industries, then trade unions should refashion themselves on such a basis forthwith. Thus industrial unionism—one comprehensive 'all-grades union' for each industry—becomes the immediate practical objective of the guildsmen. There are in any case too many unions: there is a very long and ineffective tail. Amalgamations should therefore be encouraged in every direction, but they should always be directed towards the replacement of the effete craft union by the industrial union of the future. Moreover, the industrial union provides, it is claimed, a more potent weapon for purposes of the class war. If a craft union goes on strike, it will call out (for example) all the joiners employed in many industries; in consequence it may embarrass many industries, but it will paralyse none. On the other hand, if an industrial union strikes (and if things go according to plan) then the whole industry will come to a standstill at zero hour. Such at least is the theory. But admitting that the industrial union constitutes a heavier bludgeon, there may be a danger that its very weight may cause it to break in the hand when an attempt is made to use it. Possibly all the grades in an industry may not feel community of interest: perhaps the charwomen on the railways, when it comes to the pinch, may refuse to down dusters in order to remedy the grievances of the station-masters.

Secondly, in preparation for the future part assigned to trade unions (and on general principles) the branch of the trade union must be viewed from a different angle. At present the branch is essentially local, so that the members may have little in common apart from the postal address of their sleeping apartment. In a world of industrial democracy the lowest stage of the trade union organisation must combine those who work together. In other words, the branch must be rooted in the 'shop.' The shop is a natural fighting and self-governing unit such as is not provided by a branch based on the place of residence.

Thirdly, and obviously, the trade unions must aim at (and achieve) the widest possible extension of membership. While this is true as a general proposition, special emphasis is laid in the Guild Socialist argument on the importance of winning over the supervisory and technical staff. The chemists, the architects and the engineers have to be taught that they are part of the labour army, and that the enemies of the workers are also their enemies. When the trade unions burgeon into self-governing guilds, the supervisory and technical staff—the experts of every kind—will be needed, and they must be won over now, so that when the time comes the guilds will be qualified for their task. Lastly, in the light of the high destiny awaiting them, the trade unions are weak in that there is no adequate method of formulating trade union policy as a whole. It is a just criticism ; and even after making full allowance for later developments and for the place of the Trade Union Congress in the scheme of things, a friendly critic might suggest that we do not even now possess a trade union movement, but rather a matter of approximately a thousand trade unions, each enjoying autonomy. Nor indeed without radically modifying the accepted view of trade unions (which, of course, would in itself be no obstacle to the Guild Socialist) is it possible to see how individual trade unions can, on occasion, be made to toe the line, against their own wills and desires.

It has been indicated that the modifications in trade union structure designed to bring them into line with guild ideas will also increase their efficiency in the class war. It is perhaps worth noting how entirely Guild Socialism concurs with syndicalism in its emphasis on the class struggle. The class struggle is a 'monstrous and irrefutable fact.' [1] The first purpose of trade unions is to fight the employers, and any other activities in which they may engage are to be regarded as secondary and relatively unimportant.[2] 'The Commonwealth to-day can only express itself in terms of a class struggle.' [3] Moreover, we find undisguised expression given to the view that all strikes under any circumstances are desirable and to be encouraged. As with the syndicalists, 'every strike . . . is a contribution to the education of the worker' [4] —which indeed may be true, if we give a sufficiently wide meaning to the word 'education.' Less ambiguously, 'all strikes, however wrong in their particular circumstances, (are) ultimately right and defensible.' [5] So far from seeking to stop strikes, 'the aim of every right-minded person should be to stimulate and direct them.' Nor is there any place for peace. 'Social peace' is a sham and a trick: 'it is the miserable demand of the narrow-minded egotist to be let alone.' As in other wars, it may at times be to the interest of both sides to call a 'truce'; but it can be no more than a truce, and the class war continues. Industrial peace must not be permanent.[6] The violence of the Guild Socialists is worth noting, as there is an impression that in compromising with some of the extremes of the syndicalists they also sacrificed some of the incendiarism of that school. It is not so: the young Guild

[1] Cole: *The World of Labour*, p. 21.
[2] *Ibid.* p. 259.
[3] Cole: *Labour in the Commonwealth*, p. 46.
[4] Cole: *The World of Labour*, p. 15.
[5] *Ibid.* pp. 33–34.
[6] *Ibid.* chap. 9, in particular pp. 286–288, 319. Also p. 329.

Socialist was determined that in violence of language at least he should in no way fall short of his tutors.

We have seen the trade unions, reshuffled on industrial lines and transmuted into guilds, awaiting to play a larger part in the new order of Guild Socialism. Before considering the relation of these guilds to the State as it will in future be conceived, it may be as well to consider whether there may not be other paths to freedom and a tolerable life. Two such, with the reasons for their dismissal by the Guild Socialists, certainly call for notice. There is, firstly, the possibility of continuous Parliamentary action, the vision of 'Reformers'; and there is, secondly, the dream (Guild Socialists would call it the nightmare) of collectivism or State socialism. The complete inefficacy of Parliamentary action is throughout assumed, rather than proved, by the Guild Socialists. That economic power inevitably shapes, moulds and precedes political power is stated as an axiom every few pages by Mr. Hobson (and not by Mr. Hobson alone). It may be true, but under universal suffrage it can be true only up to a point; and it is certainly not an axiom. A clearer indication of the manner in which this fundamental principle operates would have been welcome. Mr. Cole gives a somewhat overwhelming list of reasons for regarding the ordinary machinery of Parliament and the ballot-box as inept,[1] leading to the conclusion that a revolutionary element is unavoidable in any 'thorough' policy of social transformation. The doctrine taught in *National Guilds* is that the democratic forces must turn resolutely away from political action, inasmuch as 'one of the most disastrous results of political socialism has been to obscure the reality of the class struggle.'[2] According to Mr. Cole, political reforms merely gilded the chains.[3] Legislative reform is condemned to a large extent because it consecrates and accepts the wage-system, and this point of view is revealed in the quite extraordinary bitterness manifested towards the original Insurance Act. Its 'vicious principle,' it was alleged, placed the employee in a clearly dependent status, and gave him a new hall-mark of wage-slavery.[4] So much for well-meaning Parliamentary legislation.

There remains the other possibility of collectivism or nationalisation, to be achieved by vesting industry in the State, This is, of course, the older orthodox socialism, the socialism of the Fabians. Here the

[1] Cole: *Guild Socialism Restated*, pp. 178–179. They are a curious mixture of reasons: (i) there is no chance of the working classes at present voting together; (ii) a class-conscious government (assuming the attainment of the impossible) would take a century to the job, following Parliamentary methods; (iii) the State is unsuited to effect fundamental structural alterations in society; (iv) there would be, before the job was finished, a counter-revolution, based on economic power.

[2] *National Guilds* (edited by Orage), p. 221.

[3] *Self-Government in Industry*, p. 116.

[4] Cole: *Labour in the Commonwealth*, pp. 137–138; *The World of Labour*, Preface to the 1917 edition.

Guild Socialists have a clearer target, even if at times their shafts are dipped in that venom which the young naturally feel towards the pit from which they have been digged. Briefly, their contention is that nationalisation is merely State capitalism, just as municipal socialism is municipal capitalism.[1] It opens a wide field for petty tyranny.[2] It is undemocratic. The accompaniment of State ownership is administrative tyranny.[3] If more is wanted, it is stupid and cruel 'to lure the workmen into a misconceived agitation for mere nationalisation.'[4] State socialism is no remedy for economic servitude: 'on the contrary, it rivets the chains a little more securely.'[5] Fundamentally, the Guild Socialists are right on this point. If nationalisation does no more than displace the private owner in favour of the State, then there need be no change in the position of the worker. If the railways were nationalised, there might be advantages in other directions; but probably not a single ticket-collector would notice the difference. Accordingly, even should Mr. Webb dangle 'the dainty carrot of State intervention before the nose of the Trade Union donkey,' the hope was expressed that the Trade Union would not prove itself quite such an ass as it sometimes seems.[6] It was a favourite theme of Mr. Cole's that syndicalism and collectivism are each statements of an undesirable extreme which are reconciled in the Guild idea; but whereas 'syndicalism is the infirmity of noble minds: collectivism is at best only the sordid dream of a business man with a conscience.'[7]

So far, we have been reshuffling and exalting trade unions, preparing them to become in the ultimate scheme of things 'a controlling force, an industrial republic.'[8] It is now time to turn to the other side of the question and reduce the State to its proper sphere, if only to allow the guilds to attain to the full measure of their stature. In order to avoid embroilment in all the political controversies which have raged since the time of Aristotle, it may be expedient to use an unbecoming brevity in disposing of the political and social background of Guild Socialism.[9] Expressing it summarily, the Guild Socialist theory involved a frontal attack on the venerable doctrine of the sovereignty of the State, accepted more or less unquestioningly since the time of Bodin down to our own day. With this, there is an attempt to show what precisely the State is, the end-result being to reveal it as merely one association among many, with but limited

[1] Cole: *Self-Government in Industry*, p. 195.
[2] *Ibid.* p. 113.
[3] *Ibid.* p. 206.
[4] *National Guilds* (edited by Orage), p. 23.
[5] *Ibid.* pp. 24–25.
[6] Cole: *Self-Government in Industry*, p. 70.
[7] *Ibid.* p. 122.
[8] *Ibid.* p. 117.
[9] It will be found chiefly in Cole: *Social Theory*; but for a shorter statement of essentials, see also *Self-Government in Industry*, chap. 3. The theory, of course, was not static.

functions, and of necessity with no claim to that absolute sovereignty commonly attributed to it.

It is necessary on the threshold to get a clear idea of the meaning of certain terms as used by the Guild Socialists. In their view, as expounded by Mr. Cole, we must be on our guard against the 'facile' identification of the community and the State.[1] A community is defined as a complex of social life; society, as the complex of organised associations and institutions within the community.[2] Associations arise because men have many wants; and an association may be defined as existing when a group of persons pursue a common purpose 'by a course of co-operative action extending beyond a single act.' An association thus requires a common purpose and rules governing common action.[3] So much for the definitions as given by Mr. Cole. There then is the teeming ant-heap in which we live, a maze of associations which men and women have formed in order to give satisfaction to their needs and desires: trade unions of plumbers, of carpenters and of agricultural workers; religious bodies and sects of every shade from the Church of England to Jehovah's Witnesses; associations of master bakers and steam-trawler owners; golf and bridge clubs; right and left clubs; Old Etonians and the 'Co-op.'; societies for the prevention of cruelty to animals and for the relief of decayed gentlewomen; 'la ligue contre les mauvais mots'; societies for the abolition of societies; for the promotion or discouragement of every conceivable object; for the practice, or the prevention of the practice by others, of every conceivable activity.

> Greift nur hinein in's volle Menschenleben!
> Ein jeder lebt's, nicht vielen ist's bekannt,
> Und wo ihr's packt, da ist's interessant.

The contemplation of this entanglement of associations brings us to another word occupying a central place in Guild Socialist phraseology. Every association exists for a purpose, and this purpose will ultimately define the 'function' of the association—what, in more popular language, it exists for. Now it will be observed that this principle of 'function,' which underlies all social organisation, is applicable only to associations, and not to individuals; for the simple reason that, although the Westminster Divines may be so bold as to define the chief end of man, the chief end does not exhaust the sum-total of the ends of man. We are each legion, each 'universal,'[4] with many sides and many interests, in a sense with many purposes. Even with this slight equipment of Guild Socialist phraseology, we are now in a position to begin nibbling at the old doctrine of State sovereignty. For what happens, it is argued, is that we each find

[1] Cole: *Social Theory*, p. 29.
[2] *Ibid.* pp. 25, 29.
[3] *Ibid.* pp. 33–37.
[4] *Ibid.* pp. 48–49.

expression for the various aspects of our personality in the appropriate associations which represent our divergent purposes. In so far as I am a craftsman, I am represented by my trade union; my religious self I entrust to the keeping of the Baptist Church or the Wesleyan Methodists; another bit of myself I give to my bridge club or the association of allotment-holders; and so on. Each of these may represent me, because I surrender to each a part only of myself. In a favourite dictum of the Guild Socialists, true representation must be functional. It follows that any representation that is not functional, but purports to be general and universal, is bound to be merely misrepresentation. Now it is the underlying theory of a comprehensive State with universal competence that the representatives whom we send to Parliament (or, as Proudhon might have said, who are sent to Parliament in spite of our votes) represent us for all purposes. But, so runs the argument, such universal representation is absurd and impossible. Let any Member of Parliament draw out of a bag the names of the first three constituents whom he is supposed to 'represent': A is a plumber, a Plymouth Brother, and a player on the banjo; B is a bookie, a professing atheist, who is happy only in the bar of a music hall; C is the widow of a clergyman who keeps canaries and lodgers, and is interested in the Royal Family. Extend this nucleus of three to a constituency of 30,000, and in what sense can the poor M.P. be said to represent this motley crowd? If it comes to that, is there any rational sense in which it is possible to speak of representing Ipswich or Derby at all? The State fails because it claims to be all-inclusive; Parliament fails because it is based on the hypocrisy of universal representation. In fact, democracy must be functional democracy, and representation must be functional representation.

What then is this State at the mention of which men's knees have quailed? The answer of the most influential section of Guild Socialist teaching is that the State is merely an association like other associations, claiming no doubt 'an important place, but not a solitary grandeur.' [1] Its functions may be ascertained by considering what are its peculiar marks in the galaxy of associations. For it will be observed that the State, whatever it is, is territorial; for whatever purpose it exists, it ropes in everyone. Now, other associations in a sense exist to mark the differences among men. Plumbers, carpenters and teachers join different trade unions, because men differ from each other in being plumbers, carpenters and teachers. Presbyterians, Methodists and Episcopalians join different churches, because men differ from each other in being Presbyterians, Methodists and Episcopalians. But not so the State: it includes everyone, and therefore it must be concerned with the things which all men have in common, by virtue of the fact that they (more or less) live together and are neighbours. And

[1] Cole: *Self-Government in Industry*, p. 82.

apparently what men have in common is that they are all consumers. The State therefore exists to represent the consumers' end of things, and is interested in use and enjoyment.

We have thus got rid of what Mr. Cole calls 'the omnicompetent, omnivorous, omniscient, omnipresent Sovereign State'[1]—which is indeed a very pleasant omnibus phrase. To borrow a convenient phrase from theology, we have witnessed the *kenosis* of the State. It has found its natural level, as one association among others, all existing for certain specific purposes, none claiming supremacy. To these the individual surrenders various aspects of his personality; there may accordingly be a conflict of loyalties, but there is no Leviathan crouching and brooding over everything. The trade unions (to take the type in which we are primarily interested) do not derive their rights from the State; they have an independent existence. Moreover, on this view, the State's exclusive right of legislation also goes. Each functional form of association is its own legislature, and each has its own right to discipline and correct its members.[2]

We are now in a position to bring the two sides of the picture together, even if only in general terms, since Guild Socialist theory had a certain commendable quality of fluidity. Putting aside the position of the Churches, which is a question for the ecclesiastical politician and Dr. J. N. Figgis in particular,[3] and other associations which are less important, we have, on the side which concerns us, production organised in self-governing producers' guilds, run democratically on the basis of the shop, and with election of foremen and others from the ranks. Here, it is claimed, in contrast to our present electoral procedure, people will be voting on what they know about. The guilds, of which there will be surprisingly few, will be linked together in an Industrial Guilds Congress, which would be in effect the Guild legislature, 'laying down and interpreting the essential principles of Guild organisation and practice.'[4] And in this world men will have joy in their work, developing their creative instincts; they will no longer be wage-slaves, but will be free in a true functional democracy, rooted in the shop. As Shakespeare puts it, admittedly in one of his less inspired lines chronicling the happiness of Rome after the banishment of the tyrant, we shall then witness

> our tradesmen singing in their shops, and going
> About their functions friendly.

This picture of the producers ultimately represented by a Central Guild Congress, confronted by a truncated Parliament representing

[1] Cole: *Social Theory*, p. 11.
[2] *Ibid.* pp. 124–127.
[3] J. N. Figgis: *Churches in the Modern State*.
[4] The inter-relationships of the guilds is, however, a subject of admirable complexity (*Guild Socialism Restated*, pp. 67–70).

the consumers, the two being reconciled in some joint body representing both, is admittedly a general impression.[1] For in fact the problem of what to do with the State and of where final sovereignty should be placed was one to which no consistent answer was or could be given. Thus Mr. Hobson was never prepared to sacrifice the State, but his ideas of its functions were rather peculiar. For him ' politics ought to be the expression of the spiritual life of the nation ' [2]; and on this side the contribution of Guild Socialism would be to relieve the State of all economic functions, so that it might ' the more freely devote itself to those spiritual problems the solution of which is the distinguishing mark of a great people.' [3] It is the duty of the State to interpret, express and accept the spiritual impulse behind the national will.[4] In a significant phrase, financial considerations ' corrode ' politics: ' Remove from statesmanship the incubus of financial puzzledom and it may achieve glory in the things that matter.' [5] Needless to say, this is an idealist view of politics and of the State which will hardly bear examination. In his earlier approach to the problem, Mr. Cole's purpose appears to be the relatively modest one of freeing the State from ' the impossible task of regulating all the details of industry ' ; it should still ' allot tasks to the members of the national family.' [6] Later he appears to approach the Marxian view that the State will ' wither away ' to a very considerable extent, and indeed that it will disappear altogether—either after a frontal attack or by atrophy.[7] On the relations of the guilds to each other, and of the guilds to the State (or the rump of the State that might be left), the Guild Socialists indulged in an orgy of constitution-mongering which is at least an eloquent testimony to their enthusiasm. The final vision of the Norwich Commune and of the National Commune presented in *Guild Socialism Restated* is a nightmare which is mildly described by its author as embodying ' a somewhat disagreeable amount of precision.' [8] To enter into these questions to-day would, however, be as unprofitable as to linger unduly over the prophecies of Merlin or of Thomas the Rhymour.

It was the great merit of the Guild Socialists that they acted as an irritant—than which, within limits, there is no more useful public function. They started a multitude of what Mr. Dennis Robertson once called pregnant hares—even if, in the nature of things, these hares were foreordained to miscarriage. Moreover, even if the doctrine of multiple sovereignty was derived from other sources, it is a peculiarity and a merit of the Guild Socialists that, more than any other school,

[1] It represents the stage of *Self-Government in Industry*. See p. 87.
[2] Hobson: *Guild Principles in War and Peace*, p. 112. [3] *Ibid*. p. 61.
[4] Hobson: *National Guilds and the State*, p. 109.
[5] *National Guilds* (edited by Orage), p. 134.
[6] Cole: *The World of Labour*, p. 28.
[7] Cole: *Guild Socialism Restated*, p. 123. [8] *Ibid*. p. 138.

they compelled us to think of our economics and our politics together. In concluding this outline of Guild Socialism, it may be advisable, with the brevity necessary in the tail-end of a longish chapter, to offer a few comments indicating the reaction of the plain man to all this mass of theory and speculation.

Taking first the economic analysis, the most ubiquitous point in Guild Socialist literature is their emphasis on 'wage-slavery,' and their indignant repudiation of the doctrine that labour is a commodity. In the volume edited by Mr. Orage, it is asserted on almost every page that 'economists of every school agree that labour is only a commodity to be bought and sold according to the supply and the demand.'[1] Now despite the author (or authors) of these pages and the economists of every school, and despite the framers of the Treaty of Versailles,[2] labour is not a commodity, and cannot be regarded as such by any sane man. Anyone could reel off a score of reasons showing why labour is not, and cannot be, a commodity. When Mr. Hobson has got his commodity (manure, in his case), he may do what he likes with it. It will not reason or expostulate with him, or insist on the formation of a Whitley Council; it will not indulge in a stay-in strike; it may not refuse to fulfil its appointed function. Labour cannot be separated from the labourer; you may not send it to Penzance or Wick, unless the labourer goes with it: no such consent is required for the transport of Mr. Hobson's manure. Commodities may be stored up in warehouses, barns or granaries; but labour cannot be stored up and used next year. The truth is that the whole of this dismal story about labour being a commodity—raising its head in the strangest places—is merely an illustration of the awful dangers of *als ob*. Within a certain limited sphere, and for certain restricted purposes, labour may be said to fall in the same category as a commodity; and accordingly in that sphere and for that purpose, it may be regarded as if—*als ob*—it were a commodity. Thus, for example, in order that any enterprise may achieve fulfilment, under any system of accounting and in any kind of social organisation, labour must be maintained just as raw material must be acquired. An extremely sensitive soul may accordingly say that to that extent labour is treated *as if* it were on a par with the raw material. In this present sinful world, the claims of debenture holders have also to be met, but that does not confer the status of manure on the debenture-holders, who may happen to be trade unions. Analogies, metaphors, similes—all the tribe of *als ob*'s—are indeed a snare to human weakness; and there is much to be

[1] *National Guilds* (edited by Orage), p. 13.

[2] One of the guiding principles of the I.L.O. (Article 427) is that 'labour should not be regarded as a commodity or an article of commerce.' See also, more recently, the Declaration of Philadelphia (April–May, 1944): 'The Conference reaffirms the fundamental principles on which the Organisation is based and, in particular, that: (i) labour is not a commodity.'

said for banishing poets, the chief traffickers in these wares, from any rational republic. It is so easy to drop out an *als ob*, and forget that it was ever there. When Robert Burns discovered that his love was like a red, red rose, this analogy did not in fact make her a red, red rose; nor did it subsequently justify him in cutting her.

The other battle-cry of the Guild Socialists, that production should be for use and not for profit, relates to a more substantial point which we have already encountered in John Gray. It has therefore a respectable ancestry, though it may be doubted whether the Guild Socialists put it in such a way as to carry persuasion. First of all, be it noted that there is no concept in economics so difficult to define as that of 'profit.' That there is no satisfactory theory of profits has, in fact, recently been singled out by Mr. Hawtrey as one of the points on which economic science has failed to give effective guidance.[1] At one stage of his development, Lord Keynes identified profits with windfalls, as something there by accident, and argued that the conditions of equilibrium required that profits should be nil. Without following these refinements, and talking the language of ordinary men, it may be suggested, though with natural trepidation, that there is nothing wrong in aiming at a profit, if thereby is meant that we ought to avoid unprofitable enterprises and entanglements. After all, 'What shall it profit a man?' is the supreme question applied to the supreme issue; and to walk after things that do not profit is the supreme condemnation. There is a scriptural injunction contained in the Gospel written by the most communistic of the Apostles, to the effect that before building a tower, we should first sit down and count the cost. The principle is of universal applicability, and is not confined to building towers. In any system of society there ought to be an estimate before an adventure is embarked upon; and at the end (or periodically) there ought to be a balancing of accounts to ascertain whether the venture has been justified. Doubtless the science of accounting and the science of finance may in future collaborate in order to justify an enterprise which on crude nineteenth-century principles would not have 'paid.' At present it may be worth while for a State or a municipality to run a business at an apparent financial loss. But it is essential that accounts be kept and audited to show whether an enterprise is worth while, whatever test of worth-whileness be adopted; and as things are at present there is nothing sinful in a business being run at (or for) a profit, nor will it be an easy matter to convince the world at large that there is. Moreover, undue emphasis on the contrast between 'use' and 'profit,' as if they were for ever diametrically opposed, has the disadvantage of distracting attention from the real point of criticism. May not a business be run, the plain man asks, both for use *and* profit?

For the real point of criticism is that in a society marked by pro-

[1] Hawtrey: *Economic Destiny*.

nounced inequality, the price-system does not act as the divinely inspired guide to production, as was rather postulated in the complacent orthodoxy of a former generation. The wealthy have an undue influence in the market, and production is therefore directed to satisfy their desires in the first place. Their whims are satisfied before the urgent desires of others are considered. A millionaire who acquires half a county may divert all the building resources of the area to enclosing each of his green fields with a substantial wall fit for a mediaeval keep. Inequality of wealth, as soon as it becomes immoderate, must mean that resources may well be applied in directions which are less socially desirable than some other possible ways of expenditure. This presumably is what the Guild Socialists meant by production being for profit and not for use. In substance they are obviously right; the criticism implied in the preceding paragraph is that they state their proposition in a form which appears to imply something more, and which, so far from inviting assent, rather tends to provoke an uncomprehending stare from ordinary people who do not see why, in their day-to-day occupations, they should not endeavour to avoid a loss.

The political theories associated with Guild Socialism may only be glanced at here. The doctrine of multiple sovereignty is not their special creation, but doubtless they popularised it, or at least made it known. Probably no one in these days holds the State in undue reverence, as the incarnation of the doctrine of sovereignty after the manner of Bodin or Austin, or quakes before the great monster conceived by Hobbes. The State is a human device designed for human needs; and an act of State may be merely the off-hand decision of a very ordinary civil servant, who lives at Balham, where he eats cheese and pickled onions and frequents the Balham Hippodrome. Without qualms, therefore, we may put aside any idea of the divine nature of the State. But having said so much, it may be doubted whether the State is an association exactly like other associations, a little higher than the Lossiemouth Golf Club or the Ramsgate Sea Anglers' Association, but essentially the same in character. One point the Guild Socialists do not seem to meet adequately lies in the inevitability and the comprehensiveness of the State. Membership of all other associations is now optional, even if at one time membership of the Church may have been in effect compulsory (sometimes, significantly, by injunction of the State). Not only is it possible to go through life without being a member of any of these other numerous associations, but in fact quite a number of surly individualists attain a degree of comparative immunity. But there is no escaping the State: we are born into it without being consulted, and though apparently nowadays there are some who are nationals of no State, it would be difficult to advise a man born and continuing to live in Hackney just precisely how he ought to set about getting rid of his British nationality without acquiring another. This does not in itself, of course, establish the doctrine of sovereignty, but it does point to the State being in some way unique among associations.

Nor can one accept the implications of the argument that other associations also possess coercive powers over their members and may impose penalties upon them. They do and they can; but these coercive powers do not merely differ in degree, they differ in kind from the corresponding powers possessed by the State. If I offend my golf club in any of the usual ways, they may fine me; but if I elect not to pay the fine, and decide to play golf elsewhere or take to billiards, they are powerless to collect the fine. In other words they have disciplinary powers over me for only so long as I choose to submit to their discipline. They may, of course, expel me; but expulsion is not a method of disciplining a member; it is a confession of failure to discipline a member. So also a trade union member who falls into arrears used to be said, in a vivid and picturesque phrase, 'to run out of the union'; but failure to pay our income tax does not enable us to run out of the State in quite the same way. Also it should be noted that if the reason why I was expelled from my club was that I had pinched a box of the club's cigars, and if the club thinks that, in order to discourage the others, something more drastic than expulsion is necessary, they have to fall back on the machinery of justice provided by the State. They at least cannot send me to prison for fourteen days.

But indeed it may be doubted whether the idea of sovereignty can be so easily exorcised. In the first place, it is difficult to imagine any kind of society where there will not be somewhere, *de jure* or *de facto*, an ultimate authority. Nor in fact does Guild Socialist theory, in spite of its repudiation of the State's sovereignty, free itself from the necessity of some kind of sovereignty. In the simpler version there will be some sort of co-ordinating body, representing the guilds and the rump of the State; in the later version of *Guild Socialism Restated*, there is the rather appalling *Commune* which, like a seven-cup pudding, containing a bit of everything, is supposed to hold everything together. In the second place, doubts arise as to whether the State is not bound to be something more than a mere expression of the interests of the consumers treated, to use a rather curious phrase, 'on a basis of neighbourhood or inhabitancy.' [1] The earlier Mr. Cole was perhaps nearer the truth when he visualised the State's functions as including that of 'allotting tasks.' And if it allots tasks, it must define tasks, and it must delimit tasks. Even in a world of guilds, there is need of some authority, other than themselves, to define, *e.g.* the conditions under which all associations (and not merely trade unions or guilds) may exist, may hold property and so on. Ultimately (though

[1] Cole: *Self-Government in Industry*, p. 78.

heaven forbid that we should be engulfed in the discussion of such depths) the State is probably an expression of protection, and of what men gropingly, and for want of a better word, call justice. It certainly is, and must be, more than an expression of 'inhabitancy,' resting on the assumption that consumption is the sole link among men.

Lastly, there are certain questions that arise in connection with the framework and the operation of the guilds. To discuss the habitability of a house that will never be built is a peculiarly unprofitable employment; and there are accordingly many questions once prominent in Guild Socialist controversy which may be ranked with conjectures as to what name Achilles assumed when he hid himself among women. Whether these guilds—a handful in number, dwarfing in potency the greatest capitalist combine of these days—would develop selfish instincts and exploit the public [1]; how redundant labour could be disposed of, or transferred from one guild to another; how they could be restrained if necessary, or whether it would be sufficient to 'put them on their honour'; what form taxation would take in the new world—these and many more questions may once have been interesting, but are so no longer. But the underlying ideas are of more permanent vitality, and have not been interred with the defunct body of Guild Socialism.

To a few such points reference may be made, even without discussion, but rather in the manner of what Mably called *Doutes Proposées.* On the whole question of democracy, it is probable that we shall have to redefine and reformulate our ideas in the light of the experience of the last generation. He would be a pessimist who alleged that democracy had broken down or had proved unworkable; but clearly the assumptions underlying the mid-Victorian conception of democracy have not been fulfilled. The Guild Socialists in their criticisms of

[1] That is, of course, on the assumption of 'National' guilds, which perhaps, because of the dominance of Mr. Cole, became in a sense the orthodox theory. Indeed, in the earlier stages, National Guilds were hardly big enough for Mr. Cole: 'our modern Guilds must be national and even, in many respects, international and world-wide. . . . The epoch of world-commerce calls for national and international Guilds' (*Chaos and Order in Industry*, p. 44). The disputes regarding the rival claims of national and of small local guilds have been avoided in the text; but (if only in illustration of the divergences in the school, and as a warning against the danger of accepting an over-simplified statement), it should perhaps be made clear that Mr. Stirling Taylor regarded the small guild as essential, if the evils of bureaucracy were to be avoided: 'Self-management under the national system would be little more than a name' (*The Guild State*, p. 84). Generally, his views of Guild Socialism were tainted with relics of the evil past. He visualised 'sane competition' among a reasonable number of guilds in the same area (*ibid.* p. 93). Also the guilds were to be the creation of the State, by charter, on the petition of those concerned. For Mr. Taylor, in fact, the State remained pretty well intact: 'We will leave everything to the State which the guilds cannot conduct with greater skill as professionals' (*ibid.* p. 113). But indeed Mr. Stirling Taylor's world comes rather near a glorified state of co-operation and copartnership.

Parliament and in their views on the nature of representation have, on the intellectual side, been as influential as any in undermining the old attitude towards democracy. The general theory of democracy must then be restated and reassessed. But, apart from this large question, it is perhaps doubtful whether democracy in industry can be placed on quite the same footing as political democracy. This, in effect, is the argument of Mr. Field.[1] Without entirely accepting his point of view, there is this to be said. In industry there must be those who give orders and those who execute them. Legitimate doubts arise as to whether a foreman elected by the workers and liable to recall (*i.e.*, dismissal) by them would be in a position to exercise his authority, undeterred by distracting thoughts and speculations. It is somewhat analogous to the position that would arise if students elected their examiners: the common-sense of the world would not be surprised if under such conditions the standard slowly deteriorated. The flight from authority in fact leads logically to philosophical anarchism, where each man is his own law and his own authority. For, be it noted, my foreman will not be endeared to me merely because he has been elected by the senseless votes of my senseless fellow-workers who, despite my protests, insisted on choosing the wrong man.

Further it may be doubted whether working in an industry does in fact give one an insight into the management of that industry. An engine-driver or a ticket-collector is not really concerned with the kind of work that flows into the ' In-tray ' of a railway manager. A compositor in the Clarendon Press, though presumably he knows his Greek alphabet, is hardly in a position to decide whether they should or should not issue a new edition of Hesiod—not that he is any the worse for that.

Moreover, the whole idea that an industry should be run solely by those employed within it is open to doubt; and even if accepted, must be accepted with limitations. There is a venerable tag, originally applicable to bees, which begins ' Sic vos non vobis.' There are few details in the running of an industry which are not a matter of public concern, and which ought not to be a possible subject of public and general criticism. Doubtless we are not, but we all ought to be, interested in everything. It is not enough to say of an educational matter: ' We must leave this to the Teachers' Guild.' They might raise the leaving age to 25, and decree that no teacher should have a class exceeding three in number—both excellent reforms and in the right direction, but not immediately practicable. It is possibly a libel, and it is dangerous to repeat libels; but it is frequently suggested that not a little reduplication of work in the legal profession is ultimately due to the fact that lawyers, more than most, approximate to a self-governing corporation.

[1] Field: *Guild Socialism.*

One last *Doute* leads to a large question on which something has already been said in an earlier chapter on the Anarchists; but a few further observations may be offered here on those aspects that relate to Guild Socialism. In effect, it amounts to a hesitant enquiry whether the Guild Socialists knew anything about the psychology of the wage-slaves whose liberation was the end of their crusade, or about what this thing called ' work ' really is. There is a great deal in Guild Socialism (especially among the mediaevalists) about self-expression, and the creative instinct, and the joy of doing good things well, and much more. Now no one ought to speak lightly of the creative instinct, or of the nobility of craftsmanship.

> I too will something make
> And joy in the making.

This, if you like, is the highest of all impulses. But the creative instinct, in the true sense, is the possession of but few. Nor is this the result of suppression or of the lack of education. The finest flower of the most ancient seats of learning have frequently little inclination to ' create ' anything, or any great desire to give expression to such personality as may have survived. Nor can the world's work, as at present run, afford an opening for such self-expression. Short of a collapse of the sum of things, we are not going back to the days when every man clouted his own shoon, and was proud to see that they were clouted as no one else could clout them. To-day a man's job is to punch tramway tickets, or slice bacon to the sixteenth of an inch, or push a revolting mass of putrescent cods' heads and entrails a stage further on in its transforming journey to fishmeal, or periodically clean out the pig-sty of a pig that is not too particular. It does not follow that life is therefore intolerable; it does not follow that there may not be room somewhere for personality or the creative instinct where it exists. But it is idle to hope that the worker can ' express his personality ' in these ways, or find in these things a ' joy,' the prospect of which will make him spring from his bed in delirious excitement that once again yesterday's ecstatic experiences will be repeated. To plan the world's work on the assumption that everyone may find in it the joy of creative work, and that everyone is dying to express himself in his work and is capable of doing so, is merely to court disappointment.

The Guild Socialists are perhaps unique in that they stirred so many waters simultaneously; that they cast their net so wide must be the plea for this disproportionately long section. And though Guild Socialism has passed away, it has been a fertilising influence. The whole trade union movement has become more ' industrially ' minded, in part because of their doctrines; we tend to think more of ' function ' because of them; some of our doubts about democracy have been strengthened by their criticisms of our electoral system. So far as concerns the socialist movement as a whole, perhaps their influence has been rather curious. Socialism to-day is rather like a lost child at the cross-roads, not quite sure where it has come from, and not knowing where exactly it wants to go. For this the Guild Socialists are to a considerable extent responsible. They killed, and killed rather effectively, the old idea of State socialism, meaning thereby straightforward nationalisation; and they showed that it was rather a poor and unimaginative ideal. But having destroyed the old faith of socialism, they have provided no new abiding faith to take its place.

If their merit was that they brought to jaded minds the stimulus which a Brains Trust brings, only to minds that are jaded, their defects are no less obvious. Even more than over the Fabians there weighs upon them the incubus of their middle-class origin and of their over-intellectualised upbringing. They would have been more successful as propagandists, if they had been somewhat less prejudiced, not quite so obviously determined to see evil in everything, and generally more tolerant, and with more regard to the graces and courtesies of controversy. In the end the final word on Guild Socialism may be spoken by Mr. Cole himself:

> Some of us, who find a large part of our happiness in congenial work, have been too ready to assume that all the world's work can be made as pleasant and as satisfying as our own. We have built Utopias on the assumption that all the irksomeness of this work arises from defects of social organisation, and that in a world rightly organised each man will find pleasure and some measure of self-realisation in the work which he does on the common behalf. What is more—we have sometimes felt rather proud of ourselves for asserting this, on the ground that our ideal was a higher ideal of pleasure in service than our critics could appreciate. That has been our particular form of cant, and it had for a time a great appeal. But the modern world has seen through it.[1]

This is most admirably, courageously and honestly spoken. But did ever a stoic Roman father conduct with less visible sign of emotion the obsequies of his offspring? Of course, it may be said that it never had been a viable child.

[1] Cole: *The Next Ten Years in British Social and Economic Policy*, p. 16.

CHAPTER XVII

LENIN

To write of Vladimir Ilyich Ulyanov (1870–1924)—known in history as Lenin—while ignoring as far as may be the titanic upheaval of the Russian Revolution, may at first sight appear an odd, but it is by no means an indefensible, procedure. We are still too near the events of 1917 to know just what happened then, or to have any clear comprehension of what has happened since; and though there has never been any lack of testimony, most of those who have gone to Russia have seen what they went to see, and have reported accordingly. In the intervening years, there has obviously been much tacking and trimming, an infinite readiness to compromise—in accordance, be it observed, with Lenin's own teaching. How far the principles and the programme of 1917 are being observed a generation later is a matter for the enlightened and documented historian, in his due season. There are those who would suggest that the U.S.S.R. is gradually sliding back into individualism and capitalism, marked by class distinctions, even if somewhat differently oriented from the old; indeed that there may be taking place a drift to something like that imperialism so detested by Lenin.

Here, however, we are concerned with the history of socialist thought, and irrespective of the repercussions of Lenin's speeches and writings, the fact remains that Lenin was, in the quaint language of Mr. Bukharin's translator, 'a genius theoretician.'[1] Moreover, the written word remains. There may be considerable obscurity as to the development of Lenin's legacy in Russia; there can be no doubt as to what he said in putting the finishing touches on the Marxian structure. A somewhat misguided piety has ordained that all that Lenin ever said or wrote should be given the immortality of publication; and it may yet be Lenin's ultimate fate to be drowned beneath the unbridled torrent of his own words. Even if we may not yet bask in the thirty (large) volumes of his Collected Works, there is ample room, even for the most enterprising, to get lost in the twelve (substantial) volumes of his Selected Works. As a matter of fact, a surprisingly adequate viaticum for the pilgrim to the world of communism may be obtained in a judicious selection from among the twenty-five volumes in the Little Lenin Library.'[2]

[1] Bukharin: *Lenin as a Marxist*, p. 5.

[2] Because of the greater accessibility of the 'Little Lenin Library,' references have, as far as possible, been confined to the volumes in that series, designated 'L.L.L.' in the footnotes.

Not wholly without injustice, the student-in-a-hurry might conclude that Leninism is merely Marxism over again, and that Lenin was exclusively concerned in preserving the pristine purity of Marx, and in translating Marxian theory into Leninist practice. And it is certainly true that Lenin regards every utterance of Marx with that reverence which elsewhere is paid to a sacred and divine revelation. Engels and Marx (whom, justly, he regards as twin-stars) belonged, he says, to that class of 'rare and very rare authors whose every sentence in every one of their great works was of remarkably profound content.'[1] In Lenin's eyes any departure from Marxism is wrong, and that concludes the argument. Yet the student-in-a-hurry would not be wholly justified in side-tracking Lenin as merely a restatement of Marx, and that for two reasons. In the first place, despite the sanctity with which Lenin invested every Marxian utterance, it is of the essence of Leninism that Marxism is a living force and therefore, as a theory, not something fixed and inviolable, but on the contrary calling for development 'to keep pace with life.'[2] Marx did not really know monopoly capitalism; he may have foreseen, but he had no living knowledge of imperialism. Lenin may not have modified Marxism in any material, or even immaterial, respect; but it is the accepted view of the school of Lenin that he added to Marxism by unfolding its applications to the age of imperialism. In this respect, Leninism represents an extension of the Marxism of Marx.

In the second place, Lenin was pre-eminently a Defender of the Faith, and like other defenders of other faiths he was more concerned with the backslidings of renegades from within than with the frontal attacks of declared enemies from without. The writings of Lenin are an unceasing and embittered campaign against 'opportunism' and 'social chauvinism,' and a further heresy, mysteriously called 'economism'—in short, against all the evils resulting from the 'flabby philistinism and sober political bargaining'[3] of the Second International. He himself in *The Tasks of the Proletariat* calls on his followers to go back to *The Communist Manifesto*, which in the intervening period had been perverted by Social Democrats and the Second International on two points. The selected points of perversion throw a flood of light on the essential elements of Leninism. They relate, firstly, to the old doctrine that 'the workers have no country,' which had been destroyed by the supine acceptance on the part of the bulk of the Second International of the doctrine of national defence; and, secondly, to the whole Marxian theory of the State and of the replacement of the bourgeois State by the dictatorship of the proletariat, which in large measure had come to be numbered among the 'for-

[1] '*Left Wing*' *Communism*, p. 49 (L.L.L. No. 16).

[2] *Lenin*: the Official Biography prepared by the Marx-Engels-Lenin Institute, p. 32, quoting an article, *Our Programme*.

[3] Stalin: *Foundations of Leninism*, p. 20 (Little Stalin Library).

gotten words' of Marx.[1] It follows that Leninism is a one-sided restatement of certain aspects of Marx—with most damnable emphasis and reiteration. Doubtless, when he writes an article on *The Teachings of Karl Marx*, he 'covers the ground,' to use the phrase appropriate to all laudable text-books. But in the main, he has the good sense to show little interest in (for example) the Marxian theory of value. With the single eye of a fanatic, he fixes his attention on the revolutionary side of Marxism, so that in the end he becomes primarily a political writer, concerned on the theoretical side with the problems of the State and of the successive stages of its annihilation. 'Leninism,' in a somewhat too familiar definition due to Stalin, 'is Marxism of the era of imperialism and of the proletarian revolution. To be more exact, Leninism is the theory and tactics of the proletarian revolution in general, the theory and tactics of the dictatorship of the proletariat in particular.'[2] More successfully than most such definitions, this states concisely the two points to be borne in mind in relating Lenin to the general Marxian tradition.

Stalin's definition has a further merit, in that it points to a third significant feature in Lenin's achievement, which cannot be passed over in silence, even if perhaps, in strictness, it falls outside our special territory. It is that Lenin is a master of strategy and tactics. He is never tired of repeating that revolution is an art, of which he clearly regards himself as a master. He is indeed an engineer of revolution; and much of his writings—and not merely *What is to be Done?*—is devoted to developing the technique of manœuvring a revolution and of training a body of professional revolutionaries for the purpose. In reading Lenin, it is difficult at times to shake off the feeling that the spirit of Machiavelli is not far distant. His Italian forerunner was also a supreme exponent of the art of attaining the desired end, looking at all political problems as a game played on a strictly non-moral chess-board. But whereas Machiavelli, apart from one flaming chapter, is the aloof and dispassionte instructor of others who may think it worth while to play this kind of chess, Lenin is himself a player against principalities and powers in a game where the stakes are nothing less than the future of the world and of humanity. Broadly, then, these are the three aspects of Leninism which are adequately significant for all but the extreme specialist. He applies Marxism to the age of imperialism; he restates the Marxian theory of the State, placing the doctrine of the dictatorship of the proletariat in the centre of all things; apart from the theory of socialism, he provides a tactical handbook for the use of all revolutionaries.

Lenin's analysis of imperialism provides a convenient starting-

[1] *The Tasks of the Proletariat in our Revolution*, p. 48 (L.L.L. No. 9).
[2] Stalin: *Foundations of Leninism*, p. 10.

point for an exposition of the essentials of his doctrine. Imperialism is defined, somewhat too tersely, as the monopoly stage of capitalism.[1] It is the culminating point, 'the highest stage of capitalism,' and its place in the general scheme of things is that it is 'the eve of the proletarian social revolution.[2] Much of the picture drawn by Lenin is familiar even to reasonably elementary students of economics, above all if they have been guided in the direction of our Mr. J. A. Hobson, who in this matter furnished considerable inspiration to Lenin. The new type of capitalism, it is argued, is that in which monopoly prevails; nor is this merely a continuation of the Marxian law of the concentration of capital. The characteristic feature of the age is the dependence of the industrial capitalist on the banks. There has emerged, in Bukharin's unlovely phrase which Lenin quotes with approval, a 'concrescence of bank and industrial capital.' [3] Banks have become institutions of a 'universal character.' This, it need hardly be said, is true—so far as it is true—of continental rather than of British experience. Thus there emerges the domination of finance capital, represented by a financial oligarchy.[4]

In this transition to monopoly, capitalism becomes 'over-ripe.' [5] It lacks opportunities for profiable investment, and this leads to an intensification of the struggle for the partition of the world.[6] Thus Capitalism passes from 'peaceful expansion to armed struggle for the *re-division* of colonies and spheres of influence.' [7] War is thus represented as the inevitable result of gigantic large-scale capitalism. Once capital reaches the monopoly stage, it is impossible by any means to avoid the erà of imperialistic wars.[8]

[1] *Imperialism, the Highest Stage of Capitalism*, p. 80 (L.L.L. No. 15).
[2] *Ibid.* p. 14. [3] *Ibid.* p. 41. [4] *Ibid.* p. 43.
[5] *Ibid.* p. 58. [6] *Ibid.* p. 71.
[7] *The War and the Second International*, p. 23 (L.L.L. No. 2).
[8] In one passage Lenin gives an attempted concise summary of the leading features of Imperialism which must be covered by any definition. In view of the importance attached to Imperialism in the theories of Lenin, it may be worth while to reproduce them here, even at the cost of a lengthy footnote. There are five essential features:

'1. The concentration of production and capital, developed to such a high stage that it has created monopolies which play a decisive rôle in economic life.
2. The merging of bank capital with industrial capital and the creation, on the basis of this 'finance capital,' of a financial oligarchy.
3. The export of capital, as distinguished from the export of commodities, becomes of particularly great importance.
4. International monopoly combines of capitalists are formed which divide up the world.
5. The territorial division of the world by the greatest capitalist powers is completed.'

Accordingly, this definition is offered: 'Imperialism is capitalism in that stage of development in which the domination of monopolies and finance capital has taken shape; in which the export of capital has acquired pronounced importance; in which the division of the world by the international trusts has begun, and in which the partition of all the territory of the earth by the greatest capitalist countries has been completed' (*Imperialism*, p. 81 (L.L.L. No. 15)).

It is almost unnecessary to observe that, in Lenin's view, the war of 1914–18 was such a war. It was an imperialist predatory war, and it retained this character to the end.[1] That it was looked upon as a war of this nature—a war between two gangs of equally criminal robbers—explains the attitude of Lenin, and much of the history of the Bolshevist Party during the critical year, 1917. 'It is not the business of socialists,' he observes pleasantly, 'to help the younger and stronger robber (Germany) to rob the older and fatter bandits.'[2]

One further stage of development should be noted. Over-ripe capitalism passes into 'a state of parasitic decaying capitalism'—part of that 'tendency towards stagnation and decay, inherent in monopoly,' an odd phrase which might be invoked as involving an unwilling concession to the individualist point of view.[3] This parasitic tendency is evidenced by the fact that the few wealthy States where accumulation has been carried furthest have made themselves 'the oppressors and subjugators of the majority of the populations of the entire globe.'[4] Thus there arises the Rentier-State (the *Rentnerstaat*) riding securely on the backs of an oppressed Asia and Africa.[5]

From this analysis of imperialism as the final stage of decaying and parasitic capitalism, two inferences follow which are of significance in connection with the general body of Leninist tenets. The first is hinted at by Stalin when he claims that Lenin 'linked the national problem with the problem of the colonies.'[6] But this is hardly an adequate expression of what is involved. No doubt it is true that Marx had called upon the proletarians of all countries to unite; but the view of capital underlying Lenin's interpretation of imperialism leads much more emphatically to a vision of an enemy internationally integrated, not merely throughout Europe and America, but with tentacles stretching to the utmost ends of the earth. It follows quite logically that the war in which Lenin was engaged was not one which could be confined within the frontiers of any one country; perhaps not immediately, but inevitably and ineluctably, and sooner rather than later, the dictatorship of the proletariat had to be a world-wide phenomenon.

The second inference from the theory of imperialism is perhaps more germane to a later part of this chapter; but cross-references are not without their use. It is that the world-wide development of imperialism has led to a division in the ranks of the proletariat itself. For it is not merely the capitalists who are interested in the exploitation, the continued plundering of Africa and Asia. A section of what should be the proletariat are bribed by the bourgeoisie and become themselves

[1] *War and the Workers*, p. 15 (L.L.L. No. 20).
[2] *Socialism and War*, p. 13 (L.L.L. No. 3).
[3] *Imperialism*, pp. 90, 92 (L.L.L. No. 15).
[4] *Socialism and War*, p. 13 (L.L.L. No. 3).
[5] *Opportunism and Social-Chauvinism*, p. 9 (L.L.L. No. 22).
[6] Stalin: *Foundations of Leninism*, p. 68.

interested in the maintenance of imperialist oppression.[1] This explains the progressive ' bourgeoisification ' of a section of the proletariat, above all in Great Britain, as was noted long ago by Engels, and in our own day by Mr. Cole. The solidarity of the working class is thus undermined, since a privileged upper stratum of the workers is enabled to live at the expense of oppressed nations.[2]

In such a summary statement as is here imposed, more may not be said on this side of Lenin, where he is regarded as having supplemented Marx by applying Marxism to the problems of a new age, the age of imperialism. The only escape from war, rendered inevitable by large-scale imperialistic capitalism, lies of course in the complete abolition of capitalism by the proletarian revolution. This leads conveniently to the other, and vastly more extensive, aspect of Lenin where he reveals himself as a defender of the Marxian faith, above all against back-sliders within the fold, and with special underlinings of the revolutionary elements in the Marx-Engels tradition.

Here Lenin's crusade is largely against revisionism and the Second International, with special reference to Bernstein and Kautsky as the villains of the piece. True, the renegade Bernstein is ' a mere puppy compared with the renegade Kautsky,' [3] for whom accordingly the choicest vituperation is reserved. Kautsky is a scoundrel who has sold himself to the bourgeoisie[4]; his arguments are ' repulsive in a person who has not yet been officially certified as being feeble-minded.' [5] Let it not be imagined, however, that Lenin ever restricted his invective to specially selected objects of his aversion. He seems to have shared with Marx the peculiar misfortune that life brought him into contact with an incredibly large number of people who sooner or later turned out to be knaves or nit-wits. It is probably a characteristic of all who, in the true sense of the word, are single-eyed fanatics.

What, in the eyes of Lenin, constitutes the degradation of these degenerate years between Marx and his own renewed annunciation of the Marxian gospel? Broadly, in one form or another, all backsliding is attributable to the taint of the Second International, elegantly described by Rosa Luxemburg as a ' stinking corpse.' Lenin, doubtless with the same metaphor circulating in his nostrils, diagnoses the situation by observing that ' an intolerable putrid stench is issuing from somewhere.' [6] In less picturesque language the offence of the Second International was that it had gone over to the side of the bourgeoisie against the proletariat. As has already been indicated, the betrayal of the revolutionary cause assumed various forms which

[1] *Imperialism*, p. 97 (L.L.L. No. 15).
[2] *Opportunism and Social-Chauvinism*, p. 6 (L.L.L. No. 22).
[3] *The Proletarian Revolution and the Renegade Kautsky*, p. 25 (L.L.L. No. 18).
[4] *Ibid.* p. 46. [5] *Ibid.* p. 53.
[6] *The War and the Second International*, p. 6 (L.L.L. No. 2).

nevertheless interlocked. The essence of 'opportunism,' the most conspicuous form of backsliding, is the idea of class-collaboration, the alliance of a section of the workers with the bourgeoisie against the proletariat.[1] In nothing is the apostacy (or the 'renegacy') of Kautsky more clearly shown than in the fact that he 'adopts the position of an advocate of conciliation, compromise and collaboration between the proletariat and the bourgeoisie.'[2] Bukharin, with his gift of making every point clear to the lowest intelligence, calls this pretext 'the defence of the (plundering) fatherland.'[3] The doctrine of defencism, however, —States being what we know them to be—is 'tantamount to supporting the imperialist predatory bourgeoisie, it is tantamount to the utter betrayal of socialism.'[4] The character of a war, as Lenin frequently emphasises, is determined by the *class* that is waging it,[5] and those who arm for the defence of a plundering fatherland (and in a capitalist world all 'fatherlands' are thieves) forget that the only struggle that matters is international in character between world bourgeoisie and world proletariat and that the only war worth fighting is a civil war. The third insidious and sapping influence is represented by the 'economists'—a misleading term since, in the pages of Lenin, an economist is, as often as not, an exponent of 'economism,' and 'economism' is the faith of those who prefer the economic to the political struggle. In other words, they are those who fall from virtue to what is merely a trade union conception of the everlasting struggle.[6] Now the trade union struggle is necessarily a struggle according to trade, a restricted affair which may even generate selfishness.[7] For the 'economists' aim at 'palpable results'—adding a kopek to a rouble, as Lenin contemptuously observes. At best these are but reforms, and 'reforms' should not be regarded as particularly important.[8] To the true revolutionary, the main thing is revolution, and not reform.

Against all who in these three directions reveal their inability to continue in the faith grounded and settled, Lenin is instant in preaching. But in a sense these are but different aspects of the same apostacy, and when we realise what is common to Lenin's three major antipathies, we reach the core of Leninism. The common factor in these three heresies is that they all recognise the existing State and the machinery of the existing State. They abandon revolutionary aims 'for the sake of preserving the legal organisations'[9]; they are marked by a 'servile

[1] *The War and the Second International*, p. 37 (L.L.L. No. 2).
[2] *The Proletarian Revolution and the Renegade Kautsky*, p. 50 (L.L.L. No. 18).
[3] Bukharin: *Programme of the World Revolution*, p. 89.
[4] *The Proletarian Revolution and the Renegade Kautsky*, p. 62 (L.L.L. No. 18).
[5] *Ibid.* p. 66.
[6] *What is to be Done?* p. 54 (L.L.L. No. 4).
[7] *Ibid.* p. 60. [8] *Ibid.* p. 62.
[9] *The War and the Second International*, p. 45 (L.L.L. No. 2).

worship of legalism.'[1] Stalin puts the point explicitly: the mortal sin of the Second International was that it regarded parliamentary forms of struggle as virtually the only forms.[2] The supreme act of apostacy is in recognising the State. It is because he did so that Kautsky is condemned as a 'first-class hypocrite and a virtuoso in the art of prostituting Marxism,'[3] which at the same time, and elsewhere, he is accused of having castrated.[4] The diversity of metaphor may be confusing but the general intention is clear. The central core of Marxism which calls for restatement and defence is the theory of the State.

We have already glanced at this theory in the chapter on Marx and Engels. Needless to say, Lenin accepts all that his great forerunners had said on the subject, but it would not be quite just to regard Lenin's contribution as a mere restatement. The difference rather is that whereas in Marx and Engels the references to the dictatorship of the proletariat and the 'withering away' of the State are, all things considered, remarkably rare, so that it is possible to quote them all (as in fact Lenin virtually does in *State and Revolution*), in the later writer these questions are moved into the centre of things, and indeed made the supreme issue and the only criterion of a true Marxian. There is nothing peculiarly Marxian, he says in one place, about the conception of the class struggle. Others had thought of that before. 'Those who recognise *only* the class struggle are not yet Marxists'; but, he adds, 'a Marxist is one who *extends* the acceptance of the class struggle to the acceptance of the *dictatorship of the proletariat*.'[5] Here then, in Lenin's eyes, is the acid test of what Marxism means in theory and practice; and doubtless because he was the begetter of a revolution which was supposed to conform strictly to Marxian prescriptions—leading to communism through the dictatorship of the proletariat—the writings of Lenin and of those who follow him contain a wealth of speculation and of theorising regarding the sequence of stages in an orthodox Marxian revolution for which the reader will search in vain in the large and vague hints given by Marx and Engels.

Let us recall briefly the essentials of the Marxian theory of the State, in order to serve as a basis for Lenin's elaboration on the same theme. The State is fundamentally the product of the irreconcilability of class antagonism. There was a time when there was no State: it emerged with the emergence of classes, as the apparatus used by one class for the subjugation of another. Also (a point emphasised by Engels) the State is a power which places itself above society, and becomes more

[1] *Socialism and War*, p. 19 (L.L.L. No. 3).
[2] Stalin: *Foundations of Leninism*, p. 78.
[3] *The War and the Second International*, p. 51 (L.L.L. No. 2).
[4] *Socialism and War*, p. 21 (L.L.L. No. 3).
[5] *State and Revolution*, p. 28 (L.L.L. No. 14).

and more alienated from society. It is thus an external repressive force, resting on ' special bodies ' of men. In a useful phrase due to Stalin, the instruments of the State's authority are concentrated in the army, the punitive organs, the espionage service, the prisons.[1] Such is the State: a class organisation, standing outside society, owned by one class for the rigorous repression of all others. Moreover, by its very nature and origin, the State cannot be anything but a repressive force. One other point may be recalled from an earlier chapter. The ultimate object of all endeavour is the abolition of all classes: do not let us say ' the creation of the classless state,' since such a phrase would involve a contradiction in terms. If we have defined the State—as we have done—as an organism or an apparatus which has no meaning nor reason for existence apart from the idea of classes, then the abolition of classes will mean the abolition of the State. The nearer we are to classlessness, the more will the State have withered away.

There then are the two termini of this great adventure. We are now living in a capitalist world where all the machinery, the resources and the trappings of the bourgeois State are directed to perpetuating the dominance of the bourgeoisie and to the suppression and the oppression of the proletariat. A few, a mere handful, own the State, and tyrannise over the many. Far, far away, we are destined to reach a stage when there will be neither bond nor free—putting it otherwise, when the State will have completed the process of withering away. Much of Leninism is concerned with a consideration of the various stages in this transition and an elaboration of the characteristics of the various succeeding phases.

Let us approach more closely to the revolution and its *sequelae.* But first, on the threshold, it is necessary to bear in mind that revolutions differ from each other in character, in their inner significance and in their results. Above all we must distinguish between the bourgeois and the proletarian revolution, which may be conveniently exemplified (as they are throughout by Lenin) by reference to the Russian Revolution of February 1917, and that in November of the same year. The former is a middle-class affair, leading to the democratic republic; and this, as Lenin wrote as far back as 1905, is by no means a matter of indifference to the proletariat.[2] But such a revolution is not the real thing, though with skilful guidance one may be a step to the other, as indeed Lenin contrived it should be in the Russia of 1917. Stalin, writing considerably later, drew up an imposing list of five points of distinction between the bourgeois and the proletarian revolution.[3] Of these the most significant for our purpose are probably, firstly, that the bourgeois revolution is consummated with the seizure of power.

[1] *Lenin and Stalin on the State*, p. 45 (L.L.L. No. 23).
[2] *Two Tactics*, p. 38 (L.L.L. No. 17).
[3] *On the Problems of Leninism*, p. 124 in Stalin: *Leninism.*

It is the end, whereas the proletarian revolution is but the beginning of a long political pilgrimage. And secondly, the bourgeois revolution consists merely in the substitution of one group of exploiters for another; the old machine is merely taken over. There may be new management; but, so far as concerns the proletariat, the bourgeois revolution can amount to no more. In the proletarian revolution, the old State machine is broken up.

Clearly, however, we are concerned with the proletarian revolution, and with what happens on the morrow of the revolution after the proletariat has seized power. Here, in contradiction to a milk-and-water bourgeois revolution, the first step is to ' smash ' the old State machine and all its organs; and no doubt is ever left as to the thoroughness with which this preliminary duty of destruction must be carried through: ' The workers, having conquered political power, will smash the old bureaucratic apparatus, they will shatter it to its very foundations, they will not leave a single stone of it standing.' Thus is the old State ' smashed ' (it is the word almost invariably used)—without any question of ' withering away.' In its place there will be established a new State, the dictatorship of the proletariat; and to avoid any misunderstanding, such as has in fact sometimes been manifested, let it be repeated that it is of this new State, and not of the old bourgeois State now done to death, that there can be any question of a process of ' withering away.'

To those who are still so innocent as to be able to approach the question with unsullied minds, the whole idea of the ' dictatorship of the proletariat ' must at first sight appear odd and topsy-turvy to the verge of meaninglessness. For what sense is there, asks the tyro in these matters—holding a dictionary in his hands—what sense can there be in a dictatorship exercised apparently by virtually the whole population over such remnants of the remainder of the population as have not yet been liquidated? Indeed, is it possible to think of a dictatorship in connection with every man, and in what way may the summation of every man, approximating to all men, exercise the dictatorship vested jointly in them? Here is a problem more elusive than that of ascertaining what exactly is meant by the general will, and how it manifests itself. Lenin's lively controversy with Kautsky, the renegade, on all these questions provides one of the livelier subsections of the literature of Leninism.[1] Kautsky suggests that Marx used the mysterious phrase only once; and that when he did use the phrase, the mere fact that he spoke of the dictatorship of a class and not of a single person ' excludes the inference that Marx thought of dictatorship in the literal sense.'[2] The first of these suggestions is clearly untenable; on the

[1] Lenin: *State and Revolution*; followed by Kautsky: *The Dictatorship of the Proletariat*; followed by Lenin: *The Proletarian Revolution and the Renegade Kautsky*.

[2] Kautsky: *The Dictatorship of the Proletariat*, p. 43.

second, as we have already seen, it is by no means easy for anyone, even for a Kautsky, to declare What Marx Really Meant.

Here, however, we can but seek with all humility to ascertain, if possible, what Lenin understood by the dictatorship of the proletariat, and what place, in his theory, it holds in the general evolution to the stateless society of the far future. Firstly, we ought to know what is meant by 'dictatorship,' even if we may never be quite sure that we know the meaning of 'proletariat.' Lenin, in his castigation of Kautsky, gives a definition of 'dictatorship' which is admirable in its clarity:

> Dictatorship is power, based directly upon force, and unrestricted by any laws.
>
> The revolutionary dictatorship of the proletariat is power won and maintained by the violence of the proletariat against the bourgeoisie, power that is unrestricted by any laws.[1]

Waiving for the present the question of the manner of the exercise of this dictatorship, we have here absolute, irresponsible power vested in the proletariat. We have not, it will be observed, escaped from the State. To dream that such a development is possible forthwith is the folly of the anarchists with whom Lenin carried on that feud which is a legacy from the days of Marx and Bakunin. As a general principle Lenin may declare that 'we Marxists are opposed to all and every kind of State' [2]; yet he is never tired of emphasising that after unseating the bourgeoisie, 'we need revolutionary *power*, we need (for a certain period of transition) the *State*.' [3] The error of the anarchists lies, not in favouring the abolition of the State (for on this point Lenin is at one with them), but in preaching that the State can be abolished overnight [4]; and with a touch of impatience in his voice and a liberal sprinkling of italics on the printed page, he chides them for denying the necessity for a State and for State power in the period of transition, 'whereas I,' he continues, 'with a precision that excludes all possibility of misunderstanding, *insist* on the necessity of a State in this period.' [5]

A State then is needed, even if ostensibly a 'transitional' State, and the need is supplied by the dictatorship of the proletariat. Why a dictatorship is still needed was known long ago to Marx and Engels, even if Kautsky 'with the learned air of a most learned armchair fool, or with the innocent air of a ten-year-old girl' pretends not to know. Though we may have a majority, we still need a dictatorship to break down the resistance of the bourgeoisie; to inspire the reactionaries with fear; to maintain the authority of the armed people against the

[1] *The Proletarian Revolution and the Renegade Kautsky*, p. 19 (L.L.L. No. 18).
[2] *The Tasks of the Proletariat in Our Revolution*, p. 48 (L.L.L. No. 9).
[3] *News from Afar*, p. 27 (L.L.L. No. 8).
[4] *State and Revolution*, p. 46 (L.L.L. No. 14).
[5] *The Tasks of the Proletariat in our Revolution*, p. 16 (L.L.L. No. 9).

bourgeoisie.[1] Thus, true to the old definition of the State, this new State is a class organisation, an instrument of repression. This reproach—and as such Kautsky had endeavoured to represent it—is gladly accepted as a badge of honour. Of course, there is repression; but whereas it used to be repression of the majority by a minority, it is now the repression of a mere minority by the majority; and 'it is clear that where there is suppression there is also violence, there is no freedom, no democracy.'[2] In the course of his controversy with Kautsky, Lenin becomes even more explicit, pointing out that

> the proletariat cannot achieve victory without breaking the resistance of the bourgeoisie, without forcibly suppressing its enemies, and that, where there is 'forcible suppressing,' where there is no 'freedom,' there, of course, is no democracy.[3]

The extent of this suppression is made clear later in the same argument against Kautsky:

> If you exploiters attempt to offer resistance to our proletarian revolution we shall ruthlessly suppress you; we shall deprive you of your rights; more than that, we shall not give you any bread, for in our proletarian republic the exploiters will have no rights, they will be deprived of fire and water, for we are socialists in real earnest, and not the Scheidemann or Kautskian type of socialist.[4]

The new transitional State of the dictatorship of the proletariat has clearly nothing to learn from the old in its essential feature of being a class organisation and an instrument of suppression. But indeed from the moment the dictatorship of the proletariat is acknowledged to be a 'kind' of State, freedom is excluded: 'While the State exists there is no freedom. When freedom exists, there will be no State.'[5]

One might have thought that with such sharp measures of suppression as the denial of bread and fire and water, the contest would be short, and that the dictatorship of the proletariat, a transitional form, might with reasonable expedition be outgrown. On the contrary, the theory contemplates that the establishment of the dictatorship of the proletariat, even if it be the end of one stage of the struggle, is but the beginning of another and a longer. 'The dictatorship of the proletariat,' Stalin tells us encouragingly, 'must not be regarded as a fleeting period of "super-revolutionary" acts and decrees, but as an entire historical era, replete with civil wars and external conflicts.'[6] Lenin, writing considerably earlier, when greater optimism might have been expected, is in no ways more encouraging. Classes have remained,

[1] *The Proletarian Revolution and the Renegade Kautsky*, p. 34 (L.L.L. No.18).
[2] *State and Revolution*, p. 67 (L.L.L. No. 14).
[3] *The Proletarian Revolution and the Renegade Kautsky*, p. 38 (L.L.L. No. 18).
[4] *Ibid.* pp. 60–61.
[5] *State and Revolution*, p. 73 (L.L.L. No. 14).
[6] Stalin: *Foundations of Leninism*, p. 45 (Little Stalin Library).

he observes, and everywhere they will remain for years after the conquest of power by the proletariat. The dictatorship of the proletariat is a persistent struggle against the forces and traditions of the old society. To which he adds, rather sombrely, 'the force of habit of millions and of tens of millions is a very terrible force.' [1]

Thus the dictatorship of the proletariat is not the end of the class struggle but its continuation in new forms.[2] The reason for this, and it is now Stalin who testifies, is that the bourgeoisie for a long time after its overthrow remains stronger than the proletariat which has overthrown it.[3] Even when full allowance is made for the 'reasons annexed'—the international connections of the bourgeoisie, their numerous advantages in education, organisation and what-not, the force of habit, and the multitude of small producers—it may appear an odd and indeed illogical argument to anyone who has grasped the significance of the suppression of the enemies of the revolution by the denial of bread and water. If they have been so rigorously suppressed, clearly they will be no longer there to invite suppression during the subsequent 'historical era'—unless indeed the revolutionary State, like all other States, engenders ever new opponents with the march of time and events. The argument does, however, give some support to the suggestion of the miserable Kautsky that the emphasis on dictatorship rather implies that those supporting it are still in a minority and have not yet converted a majority of their fellows.[4] There is further implicit the claim of the dictatorship of the proletariat, during the indefinite period of its transitory existence, to suppress all opposition (or criticism) from any quarter by the simple but extremely effective device of withholding ration cards.

So far we have spoken of the dictatorship of the proletariat as a 'State,' and looked at it in the large without enquiring too curiously about its machinery or the manner of its functioning. One of the most significant observations in *State and Revolution* is that, just because this transition stage seeks to rope the whole population into the discharge of State functions, there is necessarily imposed 'some reversion to primitive democracy.' [5] The consequence is that the dictatorship of the proletariat, although a State, is 'not a State in the ordinary sense of that word.' The example of the French Commune plays a large part in the writings of Lenin [6]: in particular, it was regarded as being a kind of State, distinguished by the fact that it had shed most of what

[1] '*Left Wing*' *Communism*, pp. 27–28 (L.L.L. No. 16).
[2] Preface to *The Deception of the People*, p. 6 (L.L.L. No. 19).
[3] Stalin: *Foundations of Leninism*, p. 44.
[4] Kautsky: *Dictatorship of the Proletariat*, p. 91.
[5] *State and Revolution*, p. 35 (L.L.L. No. 14).
[6] E.g. *The April Conference*, p. 22 (L.L.L. No 10).

are ordinarily regarded as the organs of a State. And in theory it is possible to give a very simple explanation of the fact that the proletarian State can dispense with a large part of the machinery of the bourgeois State. All States are exclusively instruments of suppression; but in the capitalist State it is the very few who suppress the overwhelming majority, and for this a very elaborate State machinery is required; whereas in the proletarian State (the dictatorship of the proletariat) the people, now the suppressors, are many, while the exploiters, now due for suppression, are few. Now this is a relatively simple task, which can be done 'with a very simple "machine," almost without a "machine," without a special apparatus, by the simple organisation of the armed masses.'[1] The police are merged in a universally armed people; and accordingly, lacking a special army, an organised police and all the other instruments of repression, the State 'is no longer a State in the proper sense.'[2] It invokes and rests upon the activity of the masses of the people.

In tracing the development of this State which is not quite a State in the ordinary sense of the word, we must, however, distinguish between two well-defined stages on the long journey from capitalism to the communist society. Developing certain hints in Marx's *Critique of the Gotha Programme*, Lenin speaks of a 'first or lower phase' and of a 'higher phase' of communist society. The lower phase, which is what emerges when society has just issued from 'the womb of capitalism.' is not really communism at all. It is what is generally called 'socialism,' where the means of production belong to the whole of society, and where 'bourgeois' right is not abolished in its entirety.[3] And when Lenin speaks of this early stage of the dictatorship of the proletariat, one almost catches at times what seems like a whiff of detestable Fabianism. The immediate task, it is said, is 'to organise the whole of national economy on the lines of the postal system'; all citizens are to be converted into 'workers and employees of one huge "syndicate"—the whole State.'[4] This process of nationalisation is, of course, much more simple in Lenin's eyes by reason of his extraordinary view of what is involved in the transaction of the world's affairs. He shares to the full Marx's naive view that business runs itself, and that there is really nothing in it for anyone to do. It is merely a matter of accounts, and the frequency of his reference to accurate accounting as the sum and substance of all business at times almost suggests an obsession or a complex. The accounting and control necessary have been so simplified by capitalism itself 'that they have become the extraordinarily simple operations of checking, recording

[1] *State and Revolution*, p. 69 (L.L.L. No. 14).
[2] *Ibid*. See also *Letters from Afar*, p. 28 (L.L.L. No. 8).
[3] *State and Revolution*, pp. 70–71 (L.L.L. No. 14).
[4] *Ibid*. pp. 40, 74.

and issuing receipts, which anyone who can read and write and who knows the first four rules of arithmetic can perform.' [1]

Here we come to the soviets, and their relationship, in theory, to the dictatorship of the proletariat. How the soviets have in fact worked in practice must be left to the competent observer. Be it noted that Lenin is emphatic that the machinery of the banks and syndicates, while it must be freed from subjection to the capitalists, must not be broken up. All things considered, Lenin has a surprising respect for the potentialities of the banking system, whatever may be his views of its past record. 'Without the big banks socialism could not be realised,' he observes; and that it may arrest the attention, the whole sentence is italicised. Not only so, but one State bank, as huge as possible, is already nine-tenths of the socialist apparatus.[2] But in the management of all this legacy of capitalism, there must be 'control "from below," control of the workers and the poorest peasants *over* the capitalists' [3]; in fact, control by the spontaneously generated soviets of workers, soldiers and peasants.

Here we come within bowing distance of certain aspects of Syndicalism and Guild Socialism. Writing in May 1917, Lenin spoke in terms of 'soviets and congresses'; and such soviets and congresses of bank employees were to be convened, and directed to 'work out at once practical measures for ensuring the merger of all banking and credit establishments into one general State bank, and for establishing the most scrupulous control over all banking operations.' Similarly soviets and congresses of the employees of all syndicates and trusts were to devote their attention to 'measures for control and accounting'; and in the same way, the right of control was to be given to the soviets of workers in every big factory.[4] How soviets in fact came into being is something of a mystery; but being there, it is clear that Leninism established them securely as the foundation of society, controlling industry from below.

We are in search of the elusive proletariat in whom this nebulous dictatorship is vested. Presumably the soviets might be candidates for recognition as being, or as representing, the proletariat; but are there, by any chance, other claimants either in opposition to, or in conjunction with, the soviets? On this point more informative guidance may be obtained from Stalin, writing in January 1926, when the dictatorship of the proletariat was something more than a theoretical concept to be realised in the future. In his essay, *On the Problems of Leninism*, there is a passage of unusual interest, written against a heretic called Sorin, who had advanced the view that the dictatorship

[1] *State and Revolution*, p. 77. Equally emphatic is the passage in *Will the Bolsheviks Maintain Power?* p. 21 (L.L.L. No. 12).

[2] *Will the Bolsheviks Maintain Power?* p. 20 (L.L.L. No. 12).

[3] *The Threatening Catastrophe*, p. 33 (L.L.L. No. 11).

[4] *Ibid.* pp. 46–47.

of the proletariat was in fact nothing other than the dictatorship of the communist party. In a section, consisting of what to the outsider may appear to be extremely casuistical argumentation, Stalin gives the official view of the structure of the dictatorship of the proletariat and of its mechanism, with due regard to the necessary 'transmission belts,' 'levers,' and 'directing force.'[1] Waiving the picturesque metaphors, there are certain mass organisations of the proletariat, without whose aid the dictatorship could not be realised. In brief, there are trade unions; there are soviets, glanced at above; and there are co-operative societies, all of which are classed as non-party organisations. There is also the Young Communist League, which, while strictly a non-party organisation, is yet associated with the party. In addition there is the party, whose function is 'to *combine* the work of all the mass organisations of the proletariat without exception and to *direct* their activities towards a single goal, the goal of the emancipation of the proletariat.'[2] All these together provide the mechanism of the dictatorship of the proletariat, in such wise that while the party exercises the dictatorship, it does so, not directly, but through and with the help of the trade unions, the soviets and the other mass organisations as 'transmission belts.'[3]

On this view, the place assigned to the party ('the rallying centre of the finest elements in the working class') with regard to the dictatorship is that it provides the inspiration and the leadership. And indeed the party would appear to be omnipresent in its power of veto and sanction: 'Not a single important political or organizational question is decided by our Soviet and other mass organizations without guiding directions from the Party.'[4] Stalin indeed is prepared to accept (because Lenin had already accepted) the formula that 'the dictatorship of the proletariat is *in essence* the dictatorship of the Party.' Yet even this, he argues, does not justify the view that the dictatorship of the proletariat *is* the dictatorship of the party. For, as he opines, when we say 'in essence' we do not mean 'wholly'; and things which are in essence the same are not identical. It is unnecessary to pursue the argument which, as it proceeds, becomes more and more reminiscent of mediaeval theology. Doubtless, it is admitted that on five occasions (which are enumerated) Lenin did in fact speak of the dictatorship of the party; but when he spoke thus, he really meant 'leadership,' speaking figuratively and metaphorically, as he clearly showed by placing in inverted commas the word which has occasioned all the pother. Oddly, it is pretty much what Kautsky had said about Marx's original use of the phrase! From all this, two conclusions emerge for the ordinary man; firstly, that Stalin attached quite extraordinary importance to branding as heretical the view that the dictatorship of

[1] Stalin: *On the Problems of Leninism*, section v, p. 131 in *Leninism*.
[2] *Ibid.* p. 133. [3] *Ibid.* pp. 134–135. [4] *Ibid.* p. 135.

the proletariat was vested in the party; and secondly, he was prepared to accept the view that *in essence* it came to the same thing as the dictatorship of the party. After this long journey in the wilderness, the ordinary man will probably conclude that the mysterious ' dictatorship of the proletariat ' only begins to have a meaning when it is identified with the dictatorship of the communist party.[1]

Should it be thought that this lengthy pursuit of an abstraction calls for an apology, the plea in mitigation must be that the ' dictatorship of the proletariat ' is almost the sum and substance of Leninism, just as Lenin regarded it as the crux of Marxism, and faith in it as the test of a good Marxian. In the end (*in essence*, if the scrupulous reader cares to retain the safeguarding phrase) we have found the seat of this dictatorship, of this ' power, based directly upon force, and unrestricted by any laws,' in the party, a self-appointed and self-perpetuating body, whose existence is based solely on their assumed greater class-consciousness.

The establishment of the dictatorship of the proletariat on the debris of the bourgeois State represents the point as from which the State should, in theory, begin to ' wither away.' From that moment classes begin to disappear, and with the progressive disappearance of classes, the State, and indeed the party itself, suffer atrophy *pari passu*.[2] But there are two reservations, one express and the other a matter of inference, to be found in the commentaries of Stalin on this subject, which must inevitably tend to delay the beginning of the withering-away process. The first is found in the contention that, while Engels' original formulation of the theory is correct, it is so, only on the assumption that socialism is already victorious in the majority of countries. Otherwise, the ostensibly transitional form of the socialist State dare not wither away; and it follows that the State will of necessity have to continue, ' unless the capitalist encirclement is liquidated, and unless the danger of foreign military attack has disappeared.'[3]

This touches on a question of considerable interest in the earlier expositions of Leninism which can, however, merely be glanced at

[1] Machiavelli, it may be recalled, supports the view that for an effective and total revolution a dictatorship is necessary, but it is the dictatorship of one man and of one mind: ' E debbesi pigliare questo per una regola generale, che non mai, o di rado occorre che alcuna repubblica o regno sia da principio ordinato bene, o al tutto di nuovo fuori degli ordini vecchi riformato, se non è ordinato da uno; anzi e necessario che uno solo sia quello che dia il modo e dalla cui mente dipenda qualunque simile ordinazione ' (*Discorsi sopra la prima Deca di Tito Livio*, Book I, chap. 9). Machiavelli, however, was no indiscriminate ' Smasher ' of the old State. He who desires to refashion or remake a State, he observes, ' e necessitato a ritenere l'ombra almanco dei modi antichi, accio che ai popoli non paja avere mutato ordine, ancora che in fatto gli ordini nuovi fossero al tutto alieni dai passati ' (*Discorsi*, Book I, chap. 25). The leisured reader might very advantageously read Machiavelli and Lenin together.

[2] Stalin: *Foundations of Leninism*, p. 105.

[3] *Lenin and Stalin on the State*, pp. 43, 48 (L.L.L. No. 23).

here. What is, or should be, the relationship of the proletarian revolution in one country to the wider issue of a world proletarian revolution? It was one of Kautsky's criticisms that 'the Bolshevist revolution was based on the supposition that it would be the starting-point of a general European revolution, and that the bold initiative of Russia would summon the proletariat of all Europe to rise.'[1] Lenin, of course, snorted with unusual vigour at this suggestion; but, viewed dispassionately, Kautsky was not so far wrong. Lenin always regarded the Russian revolution as part of a much larger picture, which would inevitably be completed. Away back at the relative beginning of things (1905–1906), he argued that the Russian proletariat required, as a condition of its success, that the European socialist proletariat should come to its assistance.[2] Even in *Letters from Afar* (Spring, 1917), he acknowledges that the Russian proletariat single-handed could not bring the socialist revolution to a victorious conclusion; they might start the revolution, but for the decisive battles they required the collaboration of the European and the American socialist proletariat.[3] This realisation of the need of aid from other countries is accompanied by a firm conviction that we are (or were, in 1917) on the threshold of a world proletariat revolution.[4] Earlier in the same year (April 1917) Lenin had supported the view that before the war could be ended 'the entire state power in at least several of the belligerent countries' would have to pass to the proletarians.[5] He regarded it as part of his job to 'carry the revolutionary conflagration into Europe,'[6] and he had little doubt that the world revolution was at the door. Later, with the passage of years, the emphasis was rather shifted. While it was realised that the victory of the workers in at least several countries was a necessary condition for fully guaranteeing the first victorious country, nevertheless the orthodox view as presented by Stalin was that there was a primary duty to establish socialism in one country, even if no aid from elsewhere were forthcoming. Any suggestion to the contrary indeed implied lack of faith.[7] The bearing of all this on the 'withering away' of the State is obvious. To those who might be inclined to ask why this transitional State was showing no disposition to wither away, the answer is simple. It is that a socialist State, surrounded by capitalist States, cannot afford to follow its natural bent to wilt and droop. And (waiving the whole absurdity of the State 'withering away') it is a perfectly good answer.

The second reason why the State may not proceed to wither away forthwith according to plan, is not explicitly stated by Stalin, but is

[1] Kautsky: *The Dictatorship of the Proletariat*, p. 62.
[2] *The Revolution of* 1905, p. 59 (L.L.L. No. 6).
[3] *Letters from Afar*, p. 47 (L.L.L. No. 8).
[4] *On the Eve of October*, p. 12 (L.L.L. No. 13).
[5] *The April Conference*, p. 39 (L.L.L. No. 10).
[6] *Two Tactics*, p. 45 (L.L.L. No. 17).
[7] Stalin: *On the Problems of Leninism*, pp. 155–158, in *Leninism*.

rather a matter of inference from certain remarks regarding the functions of the dictatorship of the proletariat. It is a trite and well-known observation that a party in opposition subtly changes its views on becoming a party in power. It is easy (and pleasant) to criticise, when someone else is running the show; the responsibility of responsibility has a sobering effect. In the Marxian tradition, expressed with all the freedom of an opposition party, the State is solely, exclusively and entirely an organ of repression. A soldier, a policeman, a hangman, a prison warder and a tax-collector exhausted its functions; and if happier days enable us to reduce the army to a size appropriate to Lippe-Detmold, to replace our hangman by a more and more markedly part-time functionary, then, these being the State, the State will wither away. But what is to happen if it slowly dawns on those who have come to power, holding this theory, that the State is, or can be, something more than this?

It is significant that when Stalin does come to power, and has a State to do his bidding, the State is found to develop qualities quite outside the old Marxian definition. Doubtless, the repressive side remains, but a place is now made for 'the peaceful, organizational, and cultural work of the dictatorship,' for the task of organising construction.[1] But if the State is thus found to be capable of positive constructive work, is there any need for it to languish, unreprieved, under sentence of withering-away? Thus the time is not yet ripe for the State to redden to its fall; and there is just a chance that when the time is ripe, the eclipse of the Marxian view of the State by an opposed view which might almost be inspired by the Fabians may alter the whole situation.

Yet despite these possibilities of indefinitely delayed action, it may not be unprofitable to consider how long the way is to this land of Beulah and how we, or our remote descendants, may fare when we get there. It is true that in a moment of exuberance, Lenin in addressing the young assured them that the generation then fifteen years old (in 1920) would see the communist society, and would itself help to build it; indeed, in warming to his task, he guaranteed that in ten or twenty years' time, they would be living in communist society.[2] But no one should be held wholly responsible for what he says in addressing a company of students: it is so easy to be carried away. Elsewhere, writing in solitude, he is much more cautious. How long the journey will be, 'we do not and *cannot* know.' The question, alike of the time required for the transition, and the concrete forms to be assumed by the withering away, must be left entirely open, since 'no material is available to enable us to answer these questions.'[3]

[1] Stalin: *On the Problems of Leninism*, p. 131, in *Leninism. Foundations of Leninism*, p. 43.

[2] *Lenin and Stalin on Youth*, p. 35 (L.L.L. No. 21).

[3] *State and Revolution*, p. 73: see also p. 64 (L.L.L. No. 14).

But that there can be no short-cut to Beulah is reasonably obvious to anyone who reflects on the work of moral regeneration that must first be accomplished. On the economic side, the antithesis between mental and physical labour must first disappear.[1] This, however, is only a small part of the complete disappearance of all division of labour —for not in vain has Lenin read his Engels. The first stage will be the replacement of craft unions by large industrial unions. The later development Lenin may be allowed to express in his own words:

> Later, these industrial unions will, in their turn, lead to the abolition of division of labour among people, to the education, training and preparation of people who will have versatile development and versatile training, people who *will be able to do everything*. Communism is marching, must march to this goal; *and it will reach it*, but only after very many years.[2]

On the moral side (if that be the phrase) the necessity for restraint or compulsion will disappear because everyone will do that which is right as a mere matter of habit. People are to become accustomed to observing the elementary rules of social life 'without compulsion, without subordination, without the special apparatus for compulsion which is called the State.'[3] Not without a touch of absurdity, Lenin states that when all have learned to keep accounts (and admittedly do some other things as well), 'very soon the *necessity* of observing the simple, fundamental rules of human intercourse will become a *habit*.'[4] The path to Lenin's heaven is paved with good accountants.

In this paradise, moreover, the question of work will not arise, for all will voluntarily work according to their ability: unpaid work for the general good will become the general phenomenon. On the other side, there will be no need of exact calculation of what each may receive: 'each will take freely according to his needs.'[5] Having glimpsed this better world through a door held ajar, it is somewhat dashing to learn that all this presupposes 'a person unlike the present man-in-the-street.' A perfect society demands that it be made out of perfect men; and unfortunately, we are not yet perfect. We may see the promised land from afar, but we may not enter therein.

A reference to an earlier chapter will satisfy the reader that this is substantially a repetition of the vision that cheered Engels in the fog and smoke of his exile. It may, of course, be the mere repetition of a devout and pious disciple, on the principle that the revelation vouchsafed to Marx and Engels must also be seen of Lenin. Yet even so, the recurrence of this tepidly-emotional, adolescently-sentimental Utopia as the final crown and achievement of the Marxian system is more than astonishing. More than either of his two great predecessors, Lenin might claim to be a hard-boiled realist. Yet his vision, borrowed

[1] *State and Revolution*, p. 73 (L.L.L. No. 14).
[2] '*Left Wing*' *Communism*, p. 33 (L.L.L. No. 16).
[3] *State and Revolution*, pp. 63, 68 (L.L.L. No. 14).
[4] *Ibid.* p. 78. [5] *Ibid.* p. 74.

or inherited from Engels, rests on the extraordinary assumption that a time will come when men will habitually and automatically agree ; when men (and even women) will go through life, miracles of lamb-like docility, murmuring ' After you.' In order to people his Utopia, Lenin has to imagine a race of men as unlike himself as it is possible for them to be. To persuade one's self, or to seek to persuade others that with the help of something called the ' administration of things ' replacing the ' government of men,' all occasion of controversy and all conflict of ideals will cease, is merely puerile. Charles Fourier, in his confusion of mind, was in this matter a vastly profounder psychologist than Lenin, Marx or Engels. The totality of mankind never will agree, and it would be an insipid world if they did. Men always will take sides—whether this is in accordance with God's deliberate purpose, as Fourier would have added, is here immaterial. Perhaps the sincere fanatic is so convinced of his own obvious rightness that he cannot imagine anyone differing from him. Yet the fanatics with whom we are concerned ought to have known better. The biographies of Marx and Lenin show that they regarded themselves as surrounded by scoundrels, renegades and nincompoops. Perhaps they regarded these as aberrations and monstrosities, the spawn of evil days, and they may have cherished the hope that, once the world was put in order, there would be no more double-dealers like Lassalle, no more renegades like Kautsky. Then all men would be brothers, saying ' Yes, Sir,' or preferably, ' Yes, Comrade ' ; and the greatest of all human qualities—that of asking questions and groping for an answer—would wither away. It will not happen that way. Even in a communistic world there will be heretics who will flirt with ' dangerous thoughts.' Perhaps even some old man may dream dreams, and some young men may imagine that they see visions of what it would be like to live in an individualistic competitive world, replete with glittering prizes.

In so far as we are concerned with Lenin's additions to, or changes of emphasis in, the statement of Marxian socialism, this chapter might almost conclude at this point. Nevertheless, if only in the broadest terms, something ought to be said regarding that aspect of Leninist teaching, indicated at the outset of this survey—that, namely, in which we are concerned less with socialist theory than with the tactics of revolutionary socialism. The chief authority in this is the relatively early work, *What is to be Done?* (1902), a book which, while not of absorbing interest for the alien, was a pamphlet of enormous and indeed decisive creative influence during the next fifteen years. To this should perhaps be added *' Left Wing ' Communism* (1920), for the light it throws on tactical problems at a much later period of the struggle, indeed after the reputed establishment of the dictatorship of the proletariat.

The fundamental point to be grasped in Lenin's theory of tactics lies in his continually reiterated view that insurrection is an art. If insurrection is an art, then it is something that can be taught: it is even something which in a sense is capable of being reduced to copy-book maxims.[1] Moreover, if an art, it is primarily a matter for the artist in revolution, the professional revolutionary, who must be no less professionally trained than the police to whom he is opposed.[2] Waiving the maxims, which sometimes tend to be trite, these conditions almost provide the essentials of Leninism on this point. He was constantly opposed to a large, diffuse party, where a window-display of numerical strength would offer but poor compensation for the loss of zeal which comes from a flabby membership swollen by the influx of the Laodiceans. What was required was a compact, militant party. Putting it otherwise, this means the leadership of a self-constituted vanguard, whose duty it is to lead the broad masses, described, in not too complimentary terms, as ' now, for the most part, slumbering, apathetic, hidebound, inert and dormant.'[3] In the very nature of things, it follows that the organisation of professional revolutionaries, in contradistinction to organisations of workmen, must be not too extensive and must be as secret as possible.[4] As a further consequence it follows that in this sphere there is no room for the characteristics of democracy which rest on publicity and the devices of elections.[5] In place of democracy and all that, the binding force must be sought elsewhere, in ' complete, comradely, mutual confidence among revolutionists.'[6] And if anyone suggests that in such an organisation ' control ' is lacking, Lenin in a sinister sentence observes that ' an organisation of real revolutionists will stop at nothing to rid itself of an undesirable member.'[7] All this is a plea for ' Leadership,' the irresponsible *Führerprinzip*; and it is justified because the working classes themselves will get nowhere, without a vanguard guided by advanced theory.[8] The so-called ' spontaneous ' labour movement lapses into mere trade unionism and the restricted outlook of ' economism.'[9] And like some other things, trade unionism is not enough.

One other aspect of Leninist tactics is notable; it is the emphasis laid on the duty of compromise as against the ultra-rigidity of those

[1] *E.g.* '(1) Never *play* at uprising, but once it is begun, remember firmly that you have to *go to the very end.*

(2) It is necessary to gather *a great preponderance of forces* in a decisive place at a decisive moment, otherwise the enemy, being better prepared and organized, will annihilate the insurgents. . . .

(4) One must strive to take the enemy by surprise, to take advantage of a moment when his troops are scattered ' (*Official Biography of Lenin*, p. 125).

[2] *What is to be Done?* p. 117 (L.L.L. No. 4).

[3] ' *Left Wing* ' *Communism*, p. 74 (L.L.L. No. 16).

[4] *What is to be Done?* pp. 105–106 (L.L.L. No. 4).

[5] *Ibid.* p. 128. [6] *Ibid.* p. 131. [7] *Ibid.* p. 131.

[8] *Ibid.* pp. 27–28. [9] *Ibid.* p. 41.

who represented the extreme left-wing. In Lenin's own words, they should be prepared to enter into practical compromises ' even with the Devil and his grandmother '—whoever she may have been.[1] As he insisted, the history of Bolshevism had been full of instances of ' manœuvring, temporising and compromising with other parties, bourgeois parties included.' [2] To reject compromises on principle was merely childish; and political leaders who could not tack were good for nothing.[3] Here indeed is high praise for the character of a trimmer! There are three particular applications of this general theory of compromise, of the counsel to ' take advantage of every fissure.' [4] Firstly, communists, so far from boycotting trade unions because of their proneness to ' economism,' must get inside them and use them to their advantage.[5] Secondly, whatever the communist party might think of the democratic machine, it was obligatory on its members to participate in parliamentary elections. Indeed, it was their duty to get inside Parliament and work inside Parliament. The ' dispersion of Parliament ' (an odd phrase) would in fact be facilitated ' by the presence of a Soviet opposition *within* the counter-revolutionary parliament.' [6] Here, mixed up with a good deal of unconscious Fabian permeation is, undisguisedly and consciously, the policy of fifth columnism, applied in an unusual field. The third application relates to the question of ' allies.' It follows from the general doctrine of compromise that no political party can exist without entering into alliances.[7] In the literature of Lenin, much is said with regard to possible allies at different stages—liberals, peasants, the proletariat of other countries and so on—and of the order in which they should be ranked as allies. All this, in a different sphere, is merely lobbying, playing for position. But Lenin, the realist, had learned as early as 1905, and he never forgot, that we must always watch our ally as if he were an enemy.

One other question may be viewed in relation to the tactics of Lenin, though in some ways it is perhaps a subject which merits independent consideration, although probably not in this volume. It is the attitude of Leninism (and of Marxism) to religion. The anonymous writer of the introduction to the small volume entitled *Lenin and Religion* in the Little Lenin Library states unhesitatingly that ' Atheism is a natural and inseparable part of Marxism, of the theory and practice of scientific socialism.' [8] Indeed, before he exhausts his introduction, he supplements and strengthens his opening statement. While Marxism cannot

[1] *Official Biography*, p. 166.
[2] ' *Left Wing* ' *Communism*, p. 52 (L.L.L. No. 16).
[3] *Ibid.* p. 21.
[4] *Ibid.* p. 53.
[5] *Ibid.* p. 38.
[6] *Ibid.* p. 44.
[7] *What is to be Done?* p. 21 (L.L.L. No. 4).
[8] *Lenin on Religion*, p. 5 (L.L.L. No. 7).

be conceived without atheism, he adds that it is equally true that atheism without Marxism is incomplete and inconsistent.[1] The formula: 'No Marxism without atheism, and no atheism without Marxism' is obviously absurd.[2] It is easy enough to be an atheist without being a Marxian—always assuming that atheists can and do exist. The proposition that Marxism connotes atheism is in a different case. It is at least a proposition which has been accepted as a commonplace and a platitude by all the best Marxians.

It is unnecessary to go back to Engels and Marx and the somewhat too notorious aphorism that 'Religion is the opium of the people.' It is sufficient here to note Lenin's attitude. Firstly, he assumes as a matter of course, as a proposition on which it is not worth while wasting printer's ink, that all (Marxian) socialists are atheists—'an atheist, as every socialist usually is'; 'Social-Democrats (who are, it stands to reason, atheists),' etc.[3] The reason for this tacit and pervading assumption that atheism is part of the creed of a Marxian is that religion (all religions and not merely Christianity) is one of the many forms of spiritual oppression devised everywhere by the exploiters to keep down the exploited, one of the many devices to keep them quiet. Ultimately, in the Marxian tradition, everything that is, is explicable in terms of the class struggle, which is the process in which the materialist conception of history manifests itself. Religion is a weapon in the class struggle, and is explicable only by reference to the materialist conception of history—'men make their religion; religion does not make men.' It follows (and it is Lenin who is writing in 1905) that 'our programme thus necessarily includes the propaganda of atheism.'[4] This, be it again observed, is not merely opposition to Christianity, or to any Christian Church, but to all and every religion. This being so, the question not unnaturally arose as to why the party did not in its programme declare itself to be atheist, and why it did not exact a profession of atheism from its members. The answer which Lenin gives is significant, and provides the justification for including this slight discussion here as a pendent to a consideration of Lenin's 'tactics.' It is that the religious question must not be pushed into the foreground where it does not belong; the party must not allow its forces to be 'broken up for the sake of opinions and dreams that are of third-rate importance'—and which are in any case relegated to the rubbish heap by the normal course of economic development.[5] To declare war on religion is a mere anarchist pose, which in the end merely helps the

[1] *Lenin on Religion*, p. 9.

[2] The formula 'No A without B; and no B without A' is an undeniably effective way of presenting a proposition when it is true: but that is no justification for expressing in this, or a similar manner, a proposition which is either untrue or absurd. Marx, in *La Misère de la Philosophie,* quotes a forgotten economist who is alleged to have said: Jésus-Christ, c'est le free-trade; le free-trade, c'est Jésus-Christ.' Theology and economics have strange meeting-places.

[3] *Lenin on Religion*, pp. 12, 20. [4] *Ibid.* p. 14. [5] *Ibid.* p. 15.

priests, and diverts the attention of the working classes from the really urgent tasks of class and revolutionary struggle.[1] A frontal attack on religion is therefore unwise. Religion to-day has its roots in the social oppression of the working classes; and, in effect, religion is best attacked by paying no attention to it, but by removing the social oppression which feeds it.[2]

Thus Lenin on religion, isolating one of the enemies of revolutionary socialism, and applying for its destruction the devices of his tactical strategy. In a former chapter, it was suggested that anarchism was in its essence almost bound to be atheistic; and it is interesting to compare the divergent roots and character of anarchistic and Marxian atheism—if one may, for convenience, continue to use a word which is as difficult to define as 'bourgeois,' and which should perhaps, for this reason, be replaced by 'irreligion.' The anarchistic atheism of Proudhon and Bakunin is merely part of a revolt against all authority. God and the State are the two great dictators; and the anarchist accordingly scales the high walls of heaven in order to unseat a tyrant who, being a tyrant, is necessarily an odious tyrant. It is, in the words of Lenin, a frontal attack. They might each have expressed themselves in the words of another rebel against the Almighty, one of the confederates of Satan:

> My sentence is for open war. Of wiles,
> More inexpert, I boast not.

The attitude, if the phrase be not misunderstood, compels a certain measure of admiration. Proudhon and Bakunin—but especially Bakunin—have in them something of Milton's Satan, who, in spite of Milton's best intentions, ends up by being the hero of *Paradise Lost*. But, it may be said, this is not atheism. Nor is it. Milton's Satan had the best of reasons for not being an atheist. The mere act of rebellion against God implies belief that there is a God. The devils also believe and tremble.

It is different with Marxian atheism, a less admirable product, more in line with John Bunyan's conception of what an atheist should be. When all good Marxians say that they are 'of course' atheists, this obviously does not imply that belief in the Marxian theory of value necessarily undermines one's belief in the existence of God. The roots of Marxian atheism are to be found, as we have seen, in the materialist conception of history, as understood by the strict Marxian school, and not as castrated (if Lenin will lend us the word for a moment) by evangelical dons in England. How religion arises in the Marxian view, and on the materialistic conception of history, may be found at its crudest in Bukharin, who can always be relied upon to vulgarise anything capable of vulgarisation. It is, as he verbosely explains, in

[1] *Lenin on Religion*, p. 17. [2] *Ibid.* p. 19.

the material conditions of our life that we must seek for the cause of our ideal imaginings ; and our ideas of God are therefore but a reflection of our daily experiences. As the bulk of humanity has admittedly had for countless ages a pretty thin time, the human race has imagined a God who is ' a vicious old man who chastises his subjects severely.' [1] With the materialist conception of history, men's views of things thus resolve themselves into the reflection of the conditions under which they make their living, and the idea of God accordingly evaporates, being merely a distorted image of some lord of the manor, or of some petty tyrant who, in Victorian phraseology, ' flourished ' in a prehistoric age. The Leninist (and it is also the Marxian) attitude to religion logically follows from this view. Religion is really no more than a symptom of a deeper disease—the disease being class inequality and the exploitation flowing therefrom. The social surgeon, like other surgeons, should not worry overmuch about symptoms, which might merely distract him from his primary task of extirpating or excising the root of the trouble.[2]

Enough has been said to indicate the place of Lenin in the socialist tradition and, so far as one may in a single chapter, just what he did with the legacy which he inherited from Marx and Engels. In some ways, while accepting the whole *corpus* of Marxian theory, he nevertheless in fact considerably restricted its content. In the end Leninism very largely resolves itself into the theory of the dictatorship of the proletariat. The peculiar position which Lenin occupies among his companions in this volume is that somehow he got things done ; for a time, and within limits, he contrived that events should march according to his Marxian blue-prints. Doubtless the Russian scene was set for a revolution, and it may be that he guided rather than created

[1] Bukharin : *Programme of the World Revolution*, p. 74.

[2] The Bukharin view, of course—to come nearer home—is substantially in agreement with the opinions expressed by Thomas Paine, who might, with some reason, complain of his total exclusion from this volume. Though not a professing atheist, he would have concurred with Owen regarding the erroneousness (or worse) of all ' known ' religions. ' All national institutions of Churches,' he says, ' whether Jewish, Christian, or Turkish, appear to me no other than human inventions set up to terrify and enslave mankind, and monopolise power and profit.' Paine, discoursing on the Scriptures in *The Age of Reason*, is a curious spectacle in these days : but, as he is chiefly engaged in barking up insignificant and immaterial trees, he cannot be regarded as a very successful disturber of the faith, unless indeed where faith is already so disturbed as to be non-existent. Few, to take one example at random, will be impressed by the argument based on Joshua's astronomical ignorance as revealed by his action in ordering the sun and moon about, whereas ' he should have commanded the earth to have stood still.' This more enlightened procedure, as a matter of fact, was the course adopted by Mr. Wells' hero who worked miracles—with disastrous results, as will be recalled by those who have seen the film which embodies the fable. Or again, take his comments on the ' ignorance ' of the author (or authors) of the first chapter of the Book of Genesis, in speaking of three days and three nights before there was any sun, ' when it is the presence or the absence of the sun that is the cause of day and night.' This is indeed the ' higher criticism.'

the storm. The sources of his strength and the nature of his limitations are alike fairly obvious. His strength lay in his singleness of purpose, in the intensity with which he kept his mind fixed on the end to be attained. He was a man set apart, ruthless and undeviating in the fulfilment of a mission. Also he knew his Russia and his fellow-Russians. Beyond this, however, he suffered from those defects which too frequently make the saint near kin to the persecutor. Mr. Christopher Hollis is probably right in suggesting that despite his long periods of exile spent abroad, he never acquired any real intimate knowledge of the reactions of Western Europe. His references to the life and politics of this country—and they are many—do not suggest that he ever began to get the hang of things.[1] In particular, of course, Lenin fails—as the whole of the Marxian tradition fails—in his complete refusal to allow, in his assessment of things, for the influence of patriotism and religion. The materialist conception of history requires that both should be resolved into devices of the ruling classes, maintained for sinister ends—delusions which men will shed when, in their enfranchisement, they attain to the measure of the stature of the fullness of which they are capable. That is as it may be. Meanwhile, whether it be foolish or not, most of us are more attached to our own parish pump at Inversnecky than to the probably equally efficient parish pump which adorns the Market Square at Tomsk.

> Hier sind die starken Wurzeln deiner Kraft;
> Dort in der fremden Welt stehst du allein,
> Ein schwankes Rohr.

So likewise the bulk of humanity serve some God, though it may be a god of their own creation, bearing a name no more explicit than a fragment of the verb 'to be.' To visualise multitudes, multitudes, in the valley of decision, and to excise from their make-up two of the most fundamental and widespread instincts in human nature, is but to court disillusionment sooner or later. Here in a way is the significance and the interest of the very lively Lenin-Kautsky feud. Kautsky may have been a 'renegade'; so in a sense is everyone who, in his journey through life, reassesses his scale of values. But (at least on the evidence) he was no 'scoundrel.' He was merely a man who, in a season of calm weather, miscalculated the relative strength of the various emotions

[1] It may be too trivial for the larger type of the text; yet Lenin's references to (*e.g.*) the Fabians are interesting and illustrating. When he describes them as a 'band of bourgeois humbugs,' there may be no sudden outcry of dissent, especially from those who have recently been sharing a school-bench with the Intelligent Woman. Besides, we are probably all humbugs, and in that universal 'bourgeoisification' which is one of England's most disquieting features, we are most certainly all bourgeois. When he calls Fabianism 'the lowest and vilest form of social chauvinism,' we feel that he is just going too far. But to call them 'filthy froth on the surface of the world labour movement' is just to betray a complete lack of all sense of proportion. No doubt the greatest of all the Fabians has been accused of froth before now—but not of this kind of froth.

by which he would be rent in time of crisis. The backsliding of the Second International, instead of leading Lenin and Rosa Luxemburg to speak in terms of stinking corpses, should rather have induced them to enquire humbly whether, by any chance, there might not have been something in all this patriotism-and-defence-of-the-(plundering)-fatherland racket which they had overlooked. Time, however, brings its curious reverses. It is not improbable that a legend may yet develop, presenting Lenin as a national hero and as a torch of Russian patriotism.[1]

For the rest, Lenin was a man of many bourgeois, and indeed puritanical, virtues. No one ever worked harder, or lived more ascetically ; no one ever spared himself less. He was a man of extraordinarily strong family affections. Never was there such a tender and solicitously anxious son-in-law.

[1] That a socialism which begins by denying the 'Fatherland' may nevertheless in the end develop a new and stronger patriotism is perhaps not a new phenomenon. Riccardo Bacchelli, who, in his novel *Il Diavolo al Pontelungo*, has presented a fascinating study of Bakunin in his old age, draws attention to the point in connection with the influence of Italian socialism of the 'seventies of last century : 'Finalmente l'amore del popolo ebbe una nuova patria da quelle idee che s'eran mosse per distruggerne pure il concetto' (vol. 2, p. 17).

CHAPTER XVIII

POSTFACE

It is out of respect for the memory of Charles Fourier that this concluding section has been designated a 'Postface.' In the foregoing chapters, some attempt has been made to present the sources and origins of socialist thought, and to consider the leading and most influential figures in this long line of development. Before concluding, it may be as well to bring the threads together; to ascertain, if possible, what it all comes to; and—with our eyes more especially on our own country—to ask in what directions we are being led to-day.

It was observed in the Prologue that it is easier to say who are, by common consent, the 'great socialists,' than to give a neat definition of socialism which will embrace all socialists and exclude all non-socialists. The internecine feuds between the various socialist schools and sects provide ample testimony that one man's socialism is another man's heresy, and that a dissentient comrade is usually regarded as more worthy of hatred and contempt than is the common enemy. Waiving for the present the possibility of framing a tentative definition of socialism, or (should that prove too difficult and delicate a task) the possibility of at least expiscating the more positive elements commonly found in socialism, a first stage may be reached if we consider what socialism is *not*. As the words are commonly understood, socialism is ordinarily regarded as opposed to individualism; nor, despite certain reservations that might be made, is the contrast unjustified. In the classical expressions of individualism and *laissez faire*, the underlying assumption is that each individual is competent to look after himself; that he is the best judge of what is good for him; that, without instruction from any outside authority, he best knows how to run his own business; and that the best service he can render to his day and generation is to look after his own affairs. All unconsciously, we serve others best when we allow ourselves to be guided by enlightened self-interest. We are each led by an invisible hand to promote an end that is no part of our intention. God, thus adroitly concealed behind an invisible hand, is in his heaven; and all's right with a world governed by competition and enlightened self-interest. St. Paul, who in some respects was a rather hardened individualist, comes rather near the core of the matter when he lays on the Thessalonians the injunction 'that ye study to be quiet, and to do your own business.'

On this question of the relation of individualism to socialism, there is, however, this to be said. While it may be convenient to contrast individualism and socialism, they are not so much opposed as complementary principles. There is no one who is completely and exclusively an individualist, just as there is no one who is completely and exclusively a socialist. We are each of us an individual *in* society. We express ourselves as individuals through society and (whether we like it or not) we depend on society. At times and in certain circumstances, above all at the great crises of life, we all recognise, or should recognise, the supreme importance of ourselves to ourselves, the necessity of fulfilling our own lives in our own way, though the whole world be against us. 'Necessity is laid upon me,' said the Apostle, meaning thereby pretty much what Luther meant in various expressions which have become almost proverbial, namely, that in the matter in question, powers and principalities notwithstanding, he would obey the dictates of his own inner self. 'Kirk and State may gae to Hell,' said Robert Burns, when embarking on a less laudable enterprise. This is the self-regarding motive which leads each one to regard himself as an 'end' to be realised; it is present in all, though it may be long dormant in the docile and the downtrodden. In the extreme case, it may become the right of rebellion, counting the world and life itself well lost, if the price otherwise exacted involves disobedience to the necessity laid upon us.

The other instinct common to all is, of course, that of kinship with our fellows, the feeling that we are parts of a larger whole, that we need society and that we need a healthy society. It is the instinctive realisation of the Aristotelian maxim that man outside society, or apart from the State, is less than a man. Whether these two fundamental instincts be defined as the self-regarding and the other-regarding motives; whether they be classed as egotism and altruism is immaterial; by whatever name they may be called, they are present in all. Moreover, the line between them is neither sharp nor well-defined. In a society still based on the family, each one obviously projects his personality into his family; but the care and love of children and grandchildren, though obviously it is rooted in the self, has clearly altruistic infusions. A Père Goriot, who starves himself for the sake of his daughters, exhibits at worst a modified egotism. But beyond the family, there are groups and relationships (Church membership; trade union membership, etc.), where such sacrifices as we may make for others are nevertheless undergone for a group with which we are already identified. An appeal is admitted to have 'a claim upon us,' in proportion as we have already identified ourselves with the cause on behalf of which the appeal is made. In this way the transition from extreme egotism to pure altruism is marked by a long series of gradations.

One other point may be noted on the threshold of these general observations. It is agreed—and the point is not worth discussing—

that a society whose members were governed exclusively by self-regarding motives could not exist. It would be a war of all against all, in which life would indeed be nasty, brutish and short. But it is equally true that a world in which altruism and the other-regarding motives had completely displaced the self-regarding motives would be an intolerable nightmare. If, on an over-literal interpretation of Godwin's fundamental principle, we were all to divest ourselves of our trousers every time we met anyone whose need was greater than ours, the business of life in street and market-place would make but slow progress; and even if (still on Godwinian principles) the exchange were not finally effected, the discussion of the issues involved would nevertheless be a time-devouring and obstructive process. A person, moved solely by altruistic motives would be on the rates in a fortnight and a burden to the community at large, having exchanged for naught the glorious privilege of being independent. Let 'every man shift for all the rest,' exclaimed the befuddled Stephano, 'and let no man take care for himself.' It is a sentiment which he probably restated with greater lucidity when he returned to sobriety; for in itself it is a principle which leads to chaos as surely as does its opposite extreme.

In this broad sense, it may be said that the difference between the individualist and the socialist is not that they stand for uncompromisingly opposed and non-intermingling principles, but that they each represent a fusion of these two principles in varying proportions. According as the one or the other predominates, a man for the time being may be conveniently described as a socialist or an individualist. On the whole, socialism places society first, and points to the chaos and conflicts which may result from an unbridled individualism, pleading for an ordered State in which the community, or some authority representing the community, would have the ordering of things. On the whole, individualism places in the forefront the supreme importance of the personality of each citizen, pleading that he be given the opportunity of self-development, and (so far as may be) untrammelled freedom in his lawful enterprises. In the one case, society comes first, and the individual is (or should be) of no importance as against the claims of society; in the other, the individual is what matters, and the State (avoiding for the present the question of the relation of the State to the community) exists for the individual, and finds its justification in the life of the individual. This is doubtless a somewhat generalised and idealised contrast, subject to many reservations; it is also upset by the existence of the anarchist tradition which tends to nullify all easy generalisations. Within limits, however, it is a defensible statement as a first stage on the journey towards a closer elucidation of the essence of various types of socialism.

Indeed, it is probably wise to refrain from searching with undue diligence for any precision in the matter of a definition, warned in advance by the cloud of wholly inadequate definitions that clutter up the ordinary sources of illumination in these matters. The older writers (such as Flint and Graham) [1] amused themselves and instructed their readers by assembling representative definitions, which are sometimes of interest inillustrating the path by which we have come. Proudhon is quoted as having defined socialism as consisting of ' every aspiration towards the amelioration of society.' 'In that case,' said the examining magistrate, anticipating Sir William Harcourt by a good half-century, ' we are all socialists.' [2] Proudhon should have done better than this. Sidgwick in one place appears to make socialism equivalent to ' the mitigation of the harshest inequalities in the present distribution of incomes.' [3] There is an interesting line of French thought which extends from Janet, through Leroy-Beaulieu and de Laveleye to Emile Faguet which finds the whole essence, the *idée mère*, of Socialism in a striving for equality. 'Every socialistic doctrine,' says M. de Laveleye, ' aims at introducing greater equality into social conditions; and, secondly, it tries to realise these reforms by the action of the law or the State.' Socialism for him is essentially ' égalitaire et niveleur.' [4] With characteristic incisiveness, Faguet opens his discussion by asserting: ' J'appelle socialisme toute tendance ayant pour objet l'égalite *réelle* entre les hommes.' [5]

On all this type of definition, two observations are necessary in order to get ideas in their proper perspective. Firstly, definitions of the nature of that offered by M. de Laveleye point merely to reform, and there is no one who does not at least profess to be a reformer. Now there is doubtless an evolutionary as well as a revolutionary socialism (though the former would be disowned by the latter as spurious), yet even the evolutionary socialist aims at something more than mere reform. He aims at a complete transformation of the social order, and though he hopes to attain this by constitutional means, nevertheless the final result is meant to be an uprooting of the existing scheme of things and its replacement by another. The socialist is, or ought to be, something more than a reformer. The second general observation is suggested by the unusually fatuous definition given in an idle moment by Proudhon, though indeed there are many other pegs on which it might be hung. It is that there is nothing peculiarly

[1] Robert Flint: *Socialism*; William Graham: *Socialism, Old and New.*

[2] Flint: *Socialism*, p. 23.

[3] Sidgwick: *Elements of Politics*, p. 160. Sidgwick, of course, belonged to a generation when property was still property and a bulwark of liberty. There is much food for reflection on the changes wrought by time (and not so very much time) in his explanation of his use of the word ' socialistic ': ' the requirement that one sane adult, apart from contract or claim to reparation, shall contribute positively by money or services to the support of others I shall call " socialistic " ' (*Elements of Politics*, p. 42).

[4] De Laveleye: *Le Socialisme Contemporain*, Introduction.

[5] Faguet: *Le Socialisme en 1907*, p. 1.

socialistic in an aspiration for a better world, or in sensitiveness towards the houseless heads and unfed sides of the poor. There is indeed a very real, and doubtless sincere, type of benevolence, associated with what may be called Tory despotism. One need not be a socialist in order to feel indignation against those who sow upon the furrows of unrighteousness, or who buy the poor for silver and the needy for a pair of shoes. It requires more than indignation to make a socialist; and not all who are indignant are socialists. It ought not to be necessary to say this, but apparently it is.

Socialism, in short, beyond indignation and reform, demands the abolition of the private ownership of much (if not all) wealth, and requires that the wealth so transferred should in some way be vested in, and operated by the community as a whole. Always remembering that anarchism is in a class by itself, a definition which did good service in its time represents what may be fairly taken as the orthodox view in this country during the period when there was an approach to socialist orthodoxy: 'Socialism denies individual private property, and affirms that Society organised as the State should own all wealth, direct all labour and compel the equal distribution of all produce.' [1]

Lastly, in this attempt to find something approaching to a definition which will cover much, if not the whole, of the field, we may, though without undue approval, note what M. Hubert Bourgin has to say on the subject. M. Bourgin has spent a lifetime closeted with *Les Systèmes Socialistes*, and he is therefore entitled to be listened to with more than respect. In groping for the criteria which determine whether a system of thought should or should not be allowed to pass the barrier into the enclosure reserved for his *Systèmes Socialistes*, he formulates four points which he enumerates, gracefully but peremptorily, in a series of paragraphs beginning: *N'est pas socialiste tout système qui ne . . .*[2] He thus proceeds by a system of exclusion. In the first place he excludes any system which does not imply 'a system of total reconstitution of society'; to be socialist, a system of thought must extend to the sum-total of social relationships, to the whole of the institutions which make up society at the time when the system was conceived. Secondly, although to the ordinary man it seems implied in the foregoing, he excludes all systems which do not involve a radical criticism of existing social institutions; on this critical side, it must put in question 'l'institution sociale toute entière, dans son existence, dans son organisation ou dans son fonctionnement.' Thirdly, he excludes all systems which do not imply the idea of a 'régime social coordonné'; and fourthly, all systems which do not contain 'un principe social d'intervention dans les rélations entre les individus.'

[1] Bradlaugh. [2] Bourgin: *Les Systèmes Socialistes*, pp. 3–6.

Thus M. Bourgin, in his gropings for a dividing line between what is socialist and what is not socialist. He is perhaps unduly strict. The first and second test-questions emphasise that socialism is no mere matter of reform, no mere 'tinkering'; but that *all* things must be questioned and *all* things made new. It is, however, probable that there are some institutions that do not necessarily call for reconstitution. Marriage, for example, would be regarded by most as one of the institutions, 'dont la société se compose'; yet socialists do not necessarily desire the *réconstitution* of marriage—nor are those who may desire the abolition of marriage necessarily socialists. The third of M. Bourgin's conditions points to what in to-day's phraseology would be called 'planning'; and the fourth calls for some central authority with powers of intervention and regulation. In sum, M. Bourgin, while wisely eschewing any crisp definition, postulates a wholesale criticism of all aspects of the existing order; a fundamental transformation of all things; something for convenience called 'planning'; and a central authority with powers of intervention, regulation and control. Whether in fact all the types of socialism discussed in M. Bourgin's *Systèmes Socialistes* passed all these tests on their merits, or (like some other candidates) through the kindly indulgence of the examiner, is another question.

Leaving aside the quest for a water-tight definition as an enlightening journey that leads nowhere, it may be profitable, before seeking to classify *types* of socialism, to confront certain fundamental questions relating to the ultimate ideals of socialism. In certain respects, it may be suggested that socialism aims at ends, and is actuated by motives that are ultimately incompatible. Broadly speaking, one would not be far wrong in saying that socialism has two main springs of inspiration. It is, in the first place, a protest against the injustice of this world; witnessing the grinding of the faces of the poor and the monstrous inequalities in the conditions of men, it contrasts this repulsive reality with a better world where justice will prevail. But socialism is also a protest against the inefficiency, the mess, and the incompetence of this present competitive world. The Fabians, seeing whole cohorts of individualistic milk-carts delivering milk in each street; Fourier, seeing every miserable housewife cooking her miserable dinner on her individualistic fire, exclaim that this is not how things should be done. We compete when we ought to co-operate. We get in each other's way, and we waste our efforts, because we never see the tasks of life steadily nor do we see them whole. Now justice (if we only knew what it was) is an admirable ideal, and so is efficiency; but they are wholly distinct 'values.' Justice concerns the individual, and is something that is promised to the individual, that he should, for example, have a 'fair deal'—purposely keeping to appropriately nebulous language. It is in the working of the whole machine that the socialist looks for efficiency: society is to be an efficient organism. But not only are efficiency and justice distinct values; they represent ideals which may conflict. To attain to an efficient society, one may have to be unjust to the individual: part of the price of justice may be a certain measure of inefficiency. At one time the right to the whole produce of labour was one of the leading catchwords of socialism, springing from the side of socialism that is based on justice; but at least in some of its interpretations, it was the most individualistic of all catch-words, and the most anti-social principle imaginable. Justice, inasmuch as it is a protest against injustice, is a humanitarian principle; but efficiency and humanitarianism are not easy bed-companions. In the extreme case efficiency may require that the individual should be entirely suppressed, which, in its way, is the height or depth of injustice. In some countries and in some quarters, and at certain times, it has even been suggested that the old and the useless should be liquidated as a contribution to national and social efficiency, just as in the bee-hive the drones are eliminated when their opportunities of usefulness are exhausted.

The same point may be put from a somewhat different angle. It may be a hard saying, yet it is true, that of all systems of government that which is most austere, that which demands most *from* the individual, is the socialist commonwealth. By its very name it proclaims that what comes first is society, the commonwealth; that the individual is subordinate and must be prepared, if need be, to be sacrificed for a higher good. It should be a gospel of sacrifice, of surrender, of renunciation. Needless to say, it has not proceeded on these lines, above all in popular propaganda. Instead of imposing burdens on the individual, it has rather tended to promise all things to all men. Another possible conflict of ultimate ideals is that involved in the incompatibility between liberty and order—which may indeed be but a subhead of the point already considered. Socialism, in its leading exponents, almost invariably represents itself as a liberating force; its purpose is to deliver the proletarian from his chains, to give *real* content to rights which may be ineffective and nominal in present conditions. Nor can it be denied that the influence of socialism has indubitably been in this direction. But it is equally clear that socialism cannot be a society of free men, guaranteeing to all the right to a full life, the development of their personality and all the rest of it, consistently with the pursuit of its other object, that of being an ordered society intent on ends to which all are subordinate. The one ideal excludes the other. In some visions, the ordered state to be attained under socialism must involve a grave curtailment of liberty.

It may indeed be doubted whether socialism gains—or indeed whether any system of thought gains—from being mixed up overmuch with the idea of justice, so fundamental in Proudhon, to mention one name only. It was somewhat of an obsession with Emile Faguet that with the idea of abstract justice we get nowhere, and although he expressed his views so uncompromisingly that they almost became an 'odious paradox'[1] he was substantially justified. Love we know; efficiency we think we know; 'kindness,' which Mr. Hawtrey has recently sanctified, we can guess at; but what is justice? God Almighty himself does not aim at justice, so far as the human eye may descry; nor has official theological dogma made any such claim on his behalf, either with regard to this world or the next. 'I will have mercy on whom I will have mercy.' One is sent into the world with normal equipment; another is born a cripple, or blind, or an idiot, burdened with the seeds of disease. We enter this world with different capacities, endowments, defects and deformities, and we suffer very different afflictions in our journey through life. In all this, there is no 'justice': we can but reflect that the economy of heaven is dark. We may ask despairingly whether they of Babylon are then better than they of Sion; but the only answer we can get is that 'on ne raisonne pas avec Dieu,' as Proudhon remarked somewhere, coming nearer the mark than he usually did when he trespassed into theology, and, as it happens, almost echoing one of the grievances of Job. Nor in the ordinary affairs of this world is it possible to give 'justice' any satisfying meaning, or indeed any meaning other than that it is that to which a man is entitled under contract or by virtue of the law of the country. Even a Court of Justice does not ordinarily administer 'justice'; it determines rights in certain conditions, but whether the contract which it enforces is just, whether the Act which it administers is just, is not ordinarily before it. When Portia said: 'The Jew shall have all justice,' she knew and everyone else knew that justice here merely meant the unduly literal enforcement of a badly drawn contract, and that in fact the Jew was going to get what was coming to him. But is this justice?

We are now perhaps in a position to classify the various types of socialism. If their differences can be carefully catalogued, what they have in common may also become apparent. It is not impossible that the different types of socialism represent different attempted answers to the same question. If so, what is that question? This exercise in classification is all the more necessary, because there prevails in the use of certain terms not a little confusion which it is now doubtless impossible to eradicate. In particular, one of the most important of all, 'communism,' has in fact changed its meaning with the passage of time, and has at different stages had very different associations.

Waiving, as irrelevant for our present purpose, certain movements

[1] Faguet: *Le Socialisme en 1907*, p. 322: *e.g.* 'la plupart des idées rigoureusement déduites de l'idée de justice étant abominablement fausses.'

which have socialist infusions, though they are themselves doubtfully socialist—such as the co-operative movement—the socialist systems which have been prominent in the last generation fall broadly into four groups. There is, firstly, anarchism; secondly, collectivism; thirdly, communism; and fourthly, there is the type represented by syndicalism and Guild Socialism, for which no convenient name is in existence. In the early days, Faguet suggested for the fourth type 'Appropriationism,' which is an ungainly word, and, as things have developed, is now inaccurate. Perhaps we may call this fourth type 'trade union socialism' which, as it happens, is more or less a translation of 'syndicalism' without, however, the associations which that word has acquired. As briefly as may be, how do these types differ?

Of anarchism little need be said. Strictly speaking, it is hardly entitled to appear as a socialist system at all; and nothing is easier than to show, in the lecture room or on paper, that anarchism, so far from being a type of socialism, is the complete antithesis of most forms of socialism. An anarchist is a liberal who carries his distrust of the State so far that he desires to abolish it altogether. Yet in practice anarchism works out as an extreme form of socialism. It has its roots in that side of socialism which seeks for freedom; and as the State is the greatest of all tyrants, the State (if we may waive the Almighty) is the chief enemy. Having abolished the State, the work of the world will be carried on by voluntary associations—spontaneously hatched like mayflies and with something of the mayfly's delightful evanescence. Anarchism is rather the charming dream of an innocent child. It postulates the passing of all political bones of contention; the evaporation of all passion; the reign of reason. In the matter of the relation existing between anarchism and other forms of socialism, it is of extreme significance that the ultimate long-term ideal of the Marx-Engels-Lenin tradition, after the State has withered away, is a condition of anarchy, indistinguishable from other dreams of anarchism. If Marx and Lenin detested anarchism, it was not because they disapproved of the ultimate vision, but because the anarchists were so foolish as to imagine that the vision could be realised forthwith, as the result of a mere act of volition.

Collectivism and communism may conveniently be considered together. 'Communism' is the word with the longer pedigree, as witness *The Communist Manifesto*; J. S. Mill's use of the word is also of interest. 'Collectivism,' as a word, is a much more recent arrival. Collectivism has gradually come to denote that type of socialism which concentrates attention on the side of production. At its purest it is seen in the Fabians. By the nationalisation of industry all enterprise is ultimately vested in the State. The private capitalist goes; the critics suggest that State capitalism arrives. All, or nearly all, would ultimately become employees of the State, which, as the unquestioned monopolist in every industry, would be exalted to a place of peculiar power. But collectivism need not aim at equality : as there is a hierarchy and much inequality in the Civil Service now, so in that extended Civil Service which will be represented by the nationalised industries of the collectivist State, there will be grades and ranks, marked by appropriate differences of rewards.

Communism is much more elusive ; but it may be seen, *inter alia,* in More's *Utopia,* and in the brief glimpse which Lenin allows his readers of a far-off distant paradise. Communism is the socialism of consumption : it is the socialism in which all, metaphorically speaking, eat out of a common pot, sharing as members of a family. It would be wrong to regard communism as involving distribution on an equal basis, for nothing is less equal than formal equality. Rather is it distribution according to needs. Assume—and it is an easy assumption—that more than enough has been produced for all, through the love that all men have for their work ; assume—and again it is an easy assumption—that in a world cured of its unreason, all men will be reasonable. Then, if reasonable, they will not take more than they require, and the problem of distribution can be solved by allowing all to take what they require ' from the Halls.' Collectivism then, we may say, is the socialism of ordered production, prompted by the desire for efficiency, not necessarily unduly revolutionary in the matter of distribution. Communism is the socialism of consumption, prompted by the impulse to equality and justice, and not unduly curious of how the goods are in fact being produced.

There the matter might rest, but for the confusion which has resulted in the last generation owing to the adoption of the word ' communist ' by the dominant party in Russia. For sufficient reasons, Lenin desired to change the name of his party ; for quite plausible reasons, he selected a name honourably associated with Marx's earlier days. The result, however, has been anything but fortunate, for the communist party is in no way a communist party—yet. As has been noted in the chapter on Lenin, there is a long journey to be traversed before that stage is reached. There is, firstly, the dictatorship of the proletariat, which is a régime of rigorous repression, followed by a long process of the withering away of the State—a process the very beginning of which is necessarily, according to Stalin, indefinitely delayed. Then, when the State has finally withered away, we may expect communism. The communism of the communist party is thus postponed to almost as remote a future as it is possible to contemplate. It is rather important to realise this, because orthodox ' bourgeois ' labour parties have at times shown little inclination to be identified with ' communism,' and have in certain quarters been harshly criticised and misunderstood in consequence. Communism is a great ideal : it is the vision of the brotherhood of man at last realised, of mankind living as a family.

Even if they are impractical, it is the communist and the anarchist who have the loftiest vision. When, however, the bourgeois Labour M.P. avoids too close contact with communism, it is not that he wishes to disown the poetic vision of an ultra-remote future: what disconcerts him is the dictatorship of the proletariat of the immediate present, in which the dictatorship is more prominent than the proletariat. Enough, however, to note here that in the commonest use of the word in the last generation, 'communist' has, strictly speaking, been a misnomer.

The fourth general group corresponds to Faguet's 'appropriationism,' a word devised when this tendency was still at the elementary stage of 'the Mine to the Miners,' 'the Railways to the Railwaymen,' 'the Sewers to the Scavengers,' and so on. In this phase, it is best regarded as an attempt to find a plausible solution to the problem of property. For if the objection to the absentee landowner, the absentee mineowner, the absentee shareholder generally, is that he is in fact an absentee-owner, doing nothing and living prosperously notwithstanding, it is a fairly obvious suggestion that justice will be done and the unjust rights of property extirpated, if the land is given to the peasant, the mine to the mine-worker, and generally the tools and instruments to those who in fact are doing the work. But syndicalism and Guild Socialism are a great deal more than such 'appropriation' of the means of production by the workers concerned; indeed Guild Socialism would deny that it is appropriationist in this sense at all. Trade union socialism is best viewed as resulting from Marxian hatred of the class State, seen as a potent instrument in the class war, combined with an infusion from anarchist sources, suggesting that perhaps the State is not really necessary. Putting aside the State, can the working classes build up their own machine to displace the State, or—if the State may not be wholly displaced—to reduce the State to its proper and comparatively insignificant rôle? The answer is that in the one case there are the syndicats, the trade unions; in the other that there may be guilds, obtained by a slight refashioning of trade unions, and if something like a State is left, it need be but a shadow of its former self, with its functions delimited and defined. And thus a world arises in which the government, so far as government is necessary, shall be upon the shoulders of the workers' organisations, and in these the workers will enjoy freedom from tyranny.

In the light of this classification of the four main types of socialism, it is not difficult to arrive at what is the central question of socialism. We saw at the outset of this section that socialism and individualism are complementary in this sense, that socialism tends to place society first and to subordinate the individual, whereas individualism underlines the importance of the individual and only thinks secondarily of society. It is a question of the relative emphasis placed on the obvious right (or duty) of self-expression, and the equally ineluctable fact that there are others who make claims (and hampering claims) upon us. In short, the contrast between individualism and socialism springs from the eternal question of the relation of the individual to society. Now it has been sufficiently hammered into us in the last generation that we must not confuse society and the State; nor should we. But just precisely what the State is, and what should be the relation of the State to society are questions which are not easily to be answered. Heaven forbid that at what (it is hoped) is the fag-end of a chapter which is itself the fag-end, we should allow ourselves to be enticed into the unending labyrinth of sociological and political theory. It is clear, however, that here we touch on the core of socialism, and above all of modern socialism. Increasingly, as we approach Leninism, socialism merges into the general, fundamental, eternal questions of politics. Do we need a State? What is the State anyhow? Can we cunningly side-track the existing State, and arrive at something 'functional'? Can we make use of the State, such as it is, and with its help fashion a better world? Or is there a canker at the heart of the State, of any State known to us, which makes it for ever an enemy and an instrument of oppression, so that the only remedy is to 'smash' it and replace it by something which will be, not a State in the ordinary sense, but—a dictatorship?—a State, born to wither away? These, in various combinations, are the problems that more or less lie at the heart of recent socialism. In its modern forms, socialism has largely become a dissatisfied and sceptical questioning of the theory of the nature and the functions of the State.

It was of the essence of the teaching of Aristotle on the subject that the State had a natural existence. In a too frequently quoted dictum: 'as the State was formed to make life possible, so it exists to make life good.' It may be that if we are so hardy as to ask whose life it is that the State exists to make good, we may get an answer which will deter us from quoting Aristotle to Lenin: for assuredly, Lenin would have been more interested in the many unconsidered slaves than in the few consecrated to the good life. Nevertheless on the inevitability, the naturalness of the State, the teaching of Aristotle is as relevant to-day as ever. The conditions necessary for anarchism, whether it be the straightforward, immediate anarchism of Godwin and Kropotkin, or the indefinitely postponed 'statelessness' of the Marx-Engels-Lenin tradition which will come with the final withering away of the State, are so remote from actuality that anarchism must remain a doctrinaire and academic plaything. Not till the nature of man has changed, as Lenin expressly realised, shall we be ready for the ultimate withering-away of the State. Till then the State (or *a* State) remains.

With somewhat more hesitation, the same may be said of trade union socialism. The leading exemplars here are hybrids, the daughter or the grand-daughter of anarchy, and, like other hybrids, they are deprived of the hope of posterity. In its attitude to the State, syndicalism is almost entirely anarchist; Guild Socialism somewhat less so. Alike they leave unanswered a multitude of questions of co-ordination and what-not, which for their answer would recall the State (or its equivalent) from the semi-limbo to which trade union socialism would consign it. Doubtless ideas with kinship to those of syndicalism and Guild Socialism will periodically recur to enliven and fertilise discussion; but with some assurance it may be said that the future of socialism does not lie in the direction of trade union socialism.

There remains as the central question of socialism to-day the choice between the pessimistic view of the State inherent in the Marxian tradition, and the more hopeful and optimistic attitude represented conveniently by Bernstein and the Revisionists, and by the Fabians. The contrasted views have already been expounded in the relevant chapters, and a mere cross-reference is sufficient here. The Marxian view is that the State always has been, is now, and always will be an engine of repression; that in consequence nothing good can come out of it, or be achieved through it; that it is the instrument through which the dominant class exercises its domination; that accordingly it is necessary to 'smash' it, and replace it by something entirely different. This is the socialism of revolution, according to which socialism can be realised only as the result of a revolution. The contrary view is that the State is not so black as it is painted; that it can in fact be used, as it has been used, to effect reform—and indeed, indefinitely and without any assignable frontier, including reform in the State itself; that, in consequence, revolution is not an ineluctable necessity, but on the contrary would probably be an uncertain gamble. This, in short, is evolutionary socialism, making use of the existing State and of the existing State machinery.

The Marxian theory of the State is itself, of course, merely an inference from the dogma of the class struggle. In the Marxian tradition, history is nothing but the record of class struggles; with the emergence of class distinctions, the State itself emerged; when, after the coming revolution, we approximate to a classless society, the end of the State will also be at hand. The State and the class struggle are, in short, almost interchangeable terms; or (more accurately) the State is merely part, though perhaps the most important part, of the armoury used in the class struggle. In this sense the syndicalists were right in seeing in the class struggle the innermost core of Marx. In foregoing chapters, the views of Marx, the syndicalists and others on the class struggle, have been stated without undue comment, and without attempting to assess how far this society of ours is in fact rent by a class struggle (between the bourgeoisie and the proletariat) which goes on and on, for ever and ever—or at least will do so until it is ended! Here, in drawing the threads together, especially as this class struggle is the begetter of the Marxian theory of the State, it may be as well to look more closely at this 'class war,' which, as we are assured, lies at the heart of all things.

Now it is obvious that at any time and in any society known to history, there have been conflicting interests; and in the extreme case where there is an unbridgeable gulf between one section and another, a barrier which none may pass, there may be something like a class war and the State may quite properly be viewed as a class organisation. Even in the Great Britain of the eighteenth and early nineteenth centuries (to come no later), when the bulk of the population was disfranchised, the State, conforming to the Marxian formula, represented the interests of the small fraction enjoying suffrage rights. To-day, however, while there are admittedly conflicting interests, these conflicting interests are in a condition of perpetual flux, and there is nothing to justify the assumption of a perpetual war between two classes, eternally divided and eternally struggling. Before it is possible to speak, with even a semblance of symbolic accuracy, of a class war, it is necessary to postulate that there are in fact classes in opposition, and strictly one should also postulate that the classes never intermingle. One must assume that all on one side of the fence have common interests, that there is in fact 'solidarity' among all workers over the whole range of the battle, which means, ultimately, a solidarity of interest uniting the proletariat of the whole world, just as equally it must be assumed that there is solidarity among all employers. All workers must have common interests against all employers. That there may be a really effective class war, both sides should also be aware of their community of interests. There must be no confusion along the battle-front: if the trumpet give an uncertain sound, who shall prepare himself to the battle?

In fact, of course, there never was a battle where the trumpet, most raucous of wind-instruments, so triumphantly succeeded in giving forth so uncertain a sound. The assumed solidarity of interest uniting all workers, an essential condition of a class war, is a mere delusion. In a given industry there may be a conflict of interest between the different grades. Station-masters, signalmen, engine-drivers and ticket-collectors may have certain interests in common, springing from their common employment; but equally, and for the same reason, they may have divergent interests. If the station-masters are over-paid, the ticket-collectors may have to do without. Strippers, brushers and oncost workers may be divided by jealousy as well as united by love. It is equally and glaringly true that workers in different industries may have sharply contrasted interests. A coal strike which successfully raises the wages of miners may lead to dearer coal, hampering employment in countless dependent industries. There is, tucked away in the files of the Ministry of Labour, the records of a dispute where the trade union and the employers' association in industry A. waged a bitter feud in a demarcation wrangle with the trade union and the employers' association in industry B. On each side the workers' dearest friends were their corresponding employers' association; their bitterest enemies (for the time being) were in the opposite trade union. In fact, the frequent alliance between trade unions and employers' associations, gratifying though it may be in certain respects, is one of the disturbing features of these times, representing, as it does, the danger of an anti-social conspiracy directed against the consumers. When we approach the assumed solidarity of workers in different countries, the whole argument lamentably collapses. Here the economic struggle tends to conform to the example just cited. Competition between countries is reflected in competition between the workers of different countries, and employers and workers have a joint interest in manipulating the tariff (and in doing other things) so that they may keep what they have at the expense of others. Nor is it any answer to say that these things should not be so, and that if the workers were better educated to a higher stage of class consciousness, they would behave otherwise. The point is that the class war is represented as something that is now raging, and has been raging as far back as the memory of man runneth; but the class war postulates solidarity of interests among the workers, and at this moment such solidarity of interest does not exist.

The fatuity of this assumed eternal, unremitting class-war between the bourgeoisie and the proletariat becomes obvious along another line of approach. It is a curiously significant fact, indicating how alien the whole idea is to us in this country, that in these matters the English language reveals its bankruptcy, and we are compelled to resort to a foreign language which we imperfectly understand. It may be that in other countries they know just exactly what the bourgeoisie is; in this country it is hardly too much to say that, outside the compositors' room, no one has any clear conception of the idea that he intends to convey to another, or that in fact will be conveyed to another, when he uses the word 'bourgeois.'[1] It may be a term of contempt or abuse for that which is contemptible or worthy of abuse. So are other words.

> How beastly the bourgeois is,
> especially the male of the species,

as the modern poet sings in characteristically modern cadences. 'Bourgeois,' says Lenin somewhere with less than his usual lucidity,

[1] Mr. Hawtrey has endeavoured to familiarise us with 'Burgessry'; but even if 'Burgessry,' with Mr. Hawtrey's help, contrives to acquire letters of naturalisation, like some other naturalised aliens it will continue to speak with a horrible foreign accent.

'means an owner of property. . . . A big bourgeois is the owner of big property. A petty bourgeois is the owner of small property.' Who then, indeed, shall be saved? 'Bourgeois' entirely, and 'proletariat' somewhat less so, mean (in English) just what anyone cares to make them mean. This ambiguity in the definition of the two contending parties is paralleled by the fact that in practice (quite apart from terminology) no frontiers can be drawn. Society discloses an infinite series of almost undiscernible gradations. Almost equally significant is the fact that society is perpetually in flux; it is never static. Even when you have caught your unmistakably typical proletarian family, there is no saying where they will be in half a generation's time. It is the fate of many a good bourgeois to experience a proletarian sunset to his days. The difficulty is felt by all honest enquirers who seek to force society into categories to which society in fact refuses to conform. Mr. Cole, in wrestling with the *petite bourgeoisie*, asks himself and his readers what is meant to be a searching conundrum:

> How are we to classify a family in which the father is a local grocer, the mother the daughter of a works manager in a big factory, one of the sons a garage proprietor, another a municipal official, and a third a technician in a large-scale business, while one daughter has married a schoolmaster, one a small-scale employer with a tiny workshop of his own, and another a trade union official? [1]

Happy is the man that hath his quiver full of them. Apart from regretting that there is apparently no one to carry on the grocer's business, the obvious answer would probably be that there is no urgent necessity to classify them, and that none of them, probably not even the trade union son-in-law, had ever realised that they lived under sentence of classification. But indeed Mr. Cole is singularly modest in the dispersal he allows his grocer's family. It may be that in Scotland, where proverbially we are 'a' Jock Tamson's bairns' (whoever Jock Tamson may have been), the general environment and tradition facilitate a greater movement throughout society than is readily seen elsewhere. But on all this question of the assumed dichotomy of society, two tests are illuminating and at times surprisingly instructive. Wander into any village of Scotland, and ask the first person of reasonable age for the tale of his cousins—assuming always that he knows about them, and assuming also that he belongs to a generation when families were large, and cousins correspondingly abundant. In a surprisingly large number of cases, the result will give a picture of all society in miniature. The other test—a favourite device of the novelists—is to look at the movement through two or three generations. One of the few advantages of growing old is that we begin to see the grandchildren of those whose grandfathers we dimly remember. The story of the years

[1] Cole: *What Marx Really Meant*, p. 127.

tells the same thing. Society is in perpetual movement; and if in perpetual movement, there can be no rigid classes between which eternal warfare must be waged.

The class war is so much at the root of the Marxian view of the State and is so potent an influence in determining the shape of Marxian politics, that one last method of approach may be permissible in considering how far in these days the class struggle does or does not exist as an actual fact. Nowhere in the Marxian tradition is the class war so prominent as in the syndicalists, and it is of unusual interest to look somewhat more closely at the implications of certain of Sorel's pronouncements on the subject. Labriola may say with vigour that 'the only reality we recognise is the existence of the class struggle'[1]; yet it is obvious that, at least for the intellectuals, this 'reality' fades away into a mere myth—one of those things which, even if untrue, are nevertheless good to think about. There is an illuminating sequence of paragraphs in the *Préface pour Colajanni* on this point. The Marxian theory of classes is, Sorel here remarks, an abstraction. Admittedly, the middle classes are not disappearing; and indeed, as he rightly observes, it is from the middle classes that most of the leaders of socialism come. What Marx did was to present the conflict of juridical ideas 'sous la forme de luttes engagées entre couples antagonistes.' Without this dichotomic division of society, it would have been impossible for socialist propaganda to get the revolutionary idea across to their public—*de faire comprendre l'idée révolutionnaire*. The class struggle is thus merely a picturesque and symbolic abstraction, the justification of which is to be found in its effectiveness for propaganda purposes.[2]

Even more significant, because expressed in simpler language, is the corresponding passage in *Reflections on Violence*. Speaking of the Marxian division of society into two fundamentally antagonistic groups, Sorel concedes that 'a certain effort of will is necessary before we can find it verified in the phenomena of everyday life.' You have to make up your mind in advance that you are going to see the class struggle, before the vision will be vouchsafed. But, rather oddly, any dullness of sight may be overcome by introducing the conception of the general strike: for society is plainly divided into two camps, and only into two, on a field of battle.[3] Thus may one myth give support and sustenance to another, by a curious process of blood transfusion which strengthens him that gives and him that takes. The clear inference from such statements as these is that the class struggle, so far from being the 'only reality,' is merely, after the manner of myths, a vividly pictorial way of visualising something that some of us (apparently) would like to believe.

[1] *Syndicalisme et Socialisme*, p. 17.
[2] Sorel: *Matériaux d'une Théorie du Proletariat*, pp. 184–188.
[3] Sorel: *Reflections on Violence*, pp. 143–144.

Without undue fastidiousness one may trace in all Sorel's references to the class struggle that process of circular reasoning which infests the whole of this question: it is the purpose of syndicalism to produce that sharp division of classes which syndicalism has already postulated as the sole ground for its existence. On a survey of the syndicalist philosophers, one may say that the class war exists only for those who are prepared to make the necessary effort of will required to see the class war. The greatest of all the syndicalists has said it.

It may be that in all this class-war business, there is something that eludes us of Anglo-Saxon stock, and disqualifies us from passing judgment. It is wisdom to realise that we never understand our neighbours. Sorel laments that the English and the Americans alike have no proper comprehension of the class war. In the case of America his comment is extraordinarily suggestive. In America, he says, *la vie ouvrière* is not looked upon as a condition peculiar to any section of the people; but rather it is regarded as 'a preparation, a school, a means of selection for everyone': the fundamental idea is that every citizen should regard himself as under obligation to pass through this apprenticeship.[1] This may or may not be a valid analysis of the American situation; it is certainly a happy and healthy contrast to the squalor of the class war. And, be it noted, in no country is capitalism so fully developed. With regard to contemporary England, Sorel can merely record, rather ruefully, that 'the English are distinguished by an extraordinary lack of understanding of the class war [2]; and there is a naive footnote in which he contrasts English and French trade union leaders: 'the English trade union leaders rapidly become gentlemen, without any one blaming them for it.' Assuredly, we do not understand the class war.[3]

This somewhat lengthy digression has been necessary because the assumption of classes, leading to the everlasting class struggle, explains the Marxian conception of the class state. But if, speaking for this country and relying on Sorel for support, the Marxian dichotomising of society in no way corresponds to reality, but is, at best, a vividly

[1] Sorel: *Préface pour Gatti*, in *Matériaux d'une Théorie du proletariat*, p. 213.

[2] *Reflections on Violence*, p. 132.

[3] Perhaps the last word on the class war, and on history as the record of class wars may, quite properly, be left to a philosopher. Croce's final summary is not unamusing:

'I should be inclined to say that history is a class war (1) when there are classes; (2) when they have antagonistic interests; (3) when they are aware of this antagonism, which would give us, in the main, the humorous equivalence that history is a class war only when it is a class war.'

He goes on to add that 'in fact sometimes classes have not had antagonistic interests, and very often they are not conscious of them; of which the socialists are well aware when they endeavour by efforts not always crowned with success . . . to arouse this consciousness in the modern proletariat' (Croce: *Historical Materialism and the Economics of Karl Marx*, p. 85).

effective symbol with considerable propagandist value, then the 'class State' also goes. The State, as we have known it in the last two generations, has been anything but the organ of a class. It has given surprising evidence of adaptability, and of power to give effect to changes considered desirable—to changes, moreover, that may be far-reaching in their scope and consequences. The State can be used; unless in the eyes of those to whom a violent revolution is in itself a desirable experience, there is no occasion to 'smash' it.

This means that we may eliminate Marxism from the paths of development which may be commended to British socialism to-day. We have not in this country suffered overmuch from Marx, and, it may be suggested, it is in no way a matter of regret that he has succeeded so ill in becoming acclimatised. Marx has been so large a part of the history of the last two generations that it is perhaps more than usually futile to speculate on how the world would have got along without him. It may be that we are now tending to exaggerate Marx's influence in his own lifetime; it is fairly clear that at the time of his death he counted for little in the eyes of the world at large. Ultimately, however, without doubt he brought socialism something that it had hitherto lacked—a driving force, a revolutionary power, a daemonic energy. Yet it is equally true that wherever the Marxian tradition has prevailed, something has gone out of socialism, leaving it poorer. The case against Marx is simple. It is that he built socialism on class warfare, and set hatred, and not love, at the centre of all things. In his hands, socialism lost its vision, and it lost its breadth; for however useful hatred may be as the inspiration of a short-term policy, the doctrine of eternal rancour, of class warfare and undying bitterness provides too narrow a basis for a philosophy of life. And perhaps just here we find one reason why Marxism has shown itself so little congenial to the English temperament. For the English (and it is more an English than a Scots virtue) are of all peoples the least inclined to cherish malice, and to feed present hatred on the memory of past grievances. It was a Scots and not an English poet who pictured the neglected wife 'nursing her wrath to keep it warm.' That it is, however, a virtue not unrecognised in Scotland, a land of long memories, certain of our own poets remind us:

> What signifies 't for folks to chide
> For what was done before them?

By a process of elimination we are thus forced back to the use of the existing State and the machinery of the existing State. But, for the socialist cherishing socialist ideals, the question of how the existing State should be used is by no means simple; and very probably—and indeed most certainly—the answer given to-day would be very different from that which would have been given forty years ago.

Then the answer was simple. The ideal then of orthodox socialists was the completely collectivist State, arrived at by nationalising as rapidly as possible all the industries of the country, and putting each one under a Minister, sitting on an indefinitely elongated front bench. This vision has rather faded, partly under criticism, and partly under the pressure of changing events. For the difficulties of the completely collectivist State are enormous. The State could be the universal employer; everyone would be an employee of the State. Life would be a civil service examination, in which there would be no failures. There would be no outer limbo, into which to toss the incompetents and the insubordinate, in the hope that they would be brought to their senses by being left to fend for themselves for a time. Also the completely collectivist State would in practice be the 'horridest tyranny.' The State being everything, there would be nothing outside the State; and though this does not seem to have unduly perturbed some of the socialists of the unadulterated collectivist era, a later generation has begun to wonder whether there would be quite enough fresh air about such an arrangement. The State may be as tough a taskmaster as any ordinary capitalist, and in a world of 'State capitalism,' where there would not even be the satisfaction of changing one's boss, life might be even less pleasant than at present.

Here, however, as not infrequently happens in life, the great change in the attitude to complete undiluted collectivism is due to the fact that in this long controversy, each side has to a very considerable extent succeeded in convincing its opponents. It would probably not be true to say, in the well-worn phrase, that 'we are all socialists now': Lenin would certainly not admit that we were. But what may plausibly be suggested is that much of what the socialists contended for forty years ago has passed into fairly general acceptance in the minds of the population at large. We would certainly, with but few exceptions, all be regarded as socialists—and indeed as dangerous socialists, past praying for—by the startled eyes of Sudre and Thonissen. On the other hand, the socialist has to a large extent been convinced by the arguments of his opponents, reinforced (perhaps oddly) by those of the anarchists, that unrelieved collectivism would be not merely an unlovely and stifling world, but that in fact it would not work.

Why a nationalised industry need not necessarily be an efficient industry raises some curious questions. No subject in our time seems to provide such a perennial fountain of discussion wherever men meet, and whenever they are moved to write to the Press, as this problem of the incompetence of Government departments, compared with the greater assumed efficiency that distinguishes business circles. The lack of zeal which Adam Smith noted as the natural badge of employees of joint stock companies, deprived of the spur which comes from managing one's own business, may be ignored. Few of us to-day manage our own affairs; yet zeal (or some zeal) survives. The whole discussion tends to overlook the fact that it involves a comparison between work which is carried on under conditions which are wholly dissimilar. So long as we live under a system of Parliamentary government, and so long as the transaction of Parliamentary business is subject to the principle of Parliamentary responsibility, the servant of the State must of necessity perform his work under restraining conditions from which the business man is happily free. The business man is responsible only to himself and his shareholders, who are not unduly hard to placate, if things are going reasonably well; the Government is responsible to the House, the public, the Press and anyone who may care to ask questions. Business is relatively informal and confidential; the Government, in normal times, must be prepared to live in the open and to defend all that it does. For we now engage an official leader of the opposition to be critical in advance, and to search diligently with a candle for every flaw in the Government's record. It is a natural consequence of the party system, as we have known it, that in the work of government every item is looked at in isolation; the minutest point in administration may be detached and given an unholy prominence. The standard tacitly set up is that the Government must not make any mistake anywhere. Again, it is exacted of the Government that it must attain absolute uniformity in time and place. It must treat all alike at any given time; not only so, the answer it gives to-day—in the absence of changed legislation or other authorised modification of policy—must be consistent with all the answers it has given in the last ten years. There must be regard for precedent; and regard for precedent and the precedent-book means delay and red-tape (which is now white). From all this, business in the great outside world is relatively free. Above all, however, the principle of Ministerial responsibility has far-reaching effects in producing an atmosphere of caution and prudence in Government activity. The Minister (we are speaking of days of healthy political warfare) is there to be shot at; whatever he does, he will be attacked. Some Ministers may enjoy this; temperamentally others may not, and may accordingly seek to expose as small a surface as possible to the blows they are there to receive. But it reaches far beyond this. Everything that any civil servant does is in theory the act of the Minister; the ideal civil servant is, as nearly as may be, non-existent; he is, as nearly as may be, merely one of the many vehicles through which the Minister lives and moves, signs letters, makes statutory orders and has his being. He must conform to what he knows or believes to be the will of the Minister. But, to pursue the question no further, what is a poor civil servant to do if he has no clear guidance, or if no clear guidance is obtainable, and he has the choice of doing something spectacular and inspired (but of which the chances are that the Minister would disapprove) or of doing something humdrum and conventional, which if uninspired is well within the frontiers of safety? If he is a good civil servant he will not splash; his first duty is to his Minister, and, relying on such lights as he may possess, he must not get his Minister into a hole. Other differences might be noted; there are, for example, the fundamentally different financial positions of Government and private enterprise, the transience of Ministers, and so on; but enough has been said to indicate that, so long as we live under a Parliamentary regime, the Government machine and the business machine operate in entirely different atmospheres. The administrative machine in this country is in the highest degree efficient, but we have hedged it about with conditions which impel it to be cautious, to aim at formal correctness, to avoid undue risk, and to be forearmed against criticism. These are not the qualities which make for success in business; and few business men, however scathing they may be in their criticisms of Government incompetence, would care to conduct their affairs under an incessant barrage of Parliamentary questions and with several hundred Members of Parliament yapping on their flanks.

It is this highly practical consideration that provides the real argument against collectivism in the older sense. The State—or at least the Parliamentary State—does not provide the appropriate machine for the day-to-day running of a great industry. The consequence is that the demand for 'nationalisation' has curiously faded into the background; already the word has a somewhat old-fashioned flavour about it. Mr. Cole is here the most illuminating of commentators:

> The idea of socialisation remains; but perhaps we shall find that we no longer want to 'nationalise' any industry at all, in quite the old sense.[1]

Elsewhere in the same argument he remarks:

> What the Socialist does essentially set out to nationalise, or perhaps better to socialise, is, not this or that particular industry, but the control and direction of the economic life of the community.[2]

Control, then, takes the place of the older, rather too facile suggestion of nationalisation; and the underlying reason is in some ways an acknowledgment of the individualistic argument. Things are better run by people whose job it is to know how to run them; and therefore, always assuming that they can be kept in order, it is better to leave the actual conduct of business to those who bring to it something of the virtues of individual enterprise. The importance of national ownership recedes, as Mr. Cole expressly acknowledges:

> Let the State control the nation's industries, and it need not care who owns them, as long as it has the unfettered power of taxation in its hands.[3]

[1] Cole: *The Next Ten Years*, p. 134.
[2] *Ibid.* p. 131. [3] *Ibid.* p. 143.

Herein lies the significance of the various half-way houses devised, or stumbled upon, in the inter-war period ; and likewise it gives a clue to the periodic demand that one thing or another should be 'taken out of politics.'[1] The London Passenger Transport Board gives, in its way, a fairly perfect example of the curious hybrid form which is supposed to combine the advantages of private enterprise with the advantages of social control, the elimination of the cruder forms of the profit motive with emphasis on the idea of service. With these we must take the various special Commissions—sugar, coal, white fish, and heaven knows what else—with doubtless very diverse functions, but all in a way attempts to do things on behalf of the State, but not directly through the State. There have been attempts to mould the General Post Office more on business lines, and the original Unemployment Assistance Board was not meant to be, and theoretically its successor, the Assistance Board, is not yet, a straightforward Government department. In part, this last example has its roots in the foolish belief, which we have seen periodically cropping up, that the economics and the politics of life may be kept apart, that the 'administration of things' differs from the government of men, and that therefore anything that represents the routine doing of things may be taken out of politics. On all this question of the development of subordinate quasi-governmental activity, we are at present confronted with a curious spectacle. More and more the State 'interferes' or 'controls' (according to the political bias of the observer) ; but the more it interferes and controls, the less does it show a disposition to accept ultimate and direct responsibility for what is done.[2]

[1] Cf. Chapter VI, on Saint-Simon, p. 144.

[2] That the New Leviathan is really a somewhat diffident and reticent Leviathan may be illustrated by two trivial examples. Sometimes more illumination can be derived from the relatively trivial than from the consideration of a major issue.

(i) The London Passenger Transport Act, 1933 (23 Geo. 5, Ch. 14), made provision for the establishment of the London Passenger Transport Board. Even if the Government wished to decline all responsibility for the work of the Board, one would have thought that they might at least have pulled up their socks, and accepted responsibility for the appointment of the Board. But no: under section 1 of the Act this duty is entrusted to a body of 'Appointing Trustees,' comprising the Chairman of the London County Council, the Chairman of the Committee of London Clearing Banks, the President of the Law Society, and the President of the Institute of Chartered Accountants in England and Wales. The Poet Laureate is an obvious and inexplicable omission from the list. Thus the Government not merely wash their hands of the work of the Board: they even disclaim the responsibility of choosing the right men for the job.

(ii) When the Broadcasting Committee presided over by Lord Ullswater reported (1935), they pointed out that in the early days the Postmaster-General was a natural choice as Minister responsible for broadcasting services. But, in the intervening years, the service had acquired 'a high and certainly unforeseen degree of educative and cultural importance,' and accordingly they suggested that 'responsibility for the cultural side of broadcasting should be transferred to a Cabinet Minister in the House of Commons, preferably a senior member of the Government, and free from any heavy Departmental responsibilities' (Cmd. 5091). The Memorandum of the Postmaster-General, embodying the conclusions of the Govern-

The 'half-way houses' have produced quite an extensive literature on the economic and administrative side, but they have not yet been sufficiently studied by the constitutional lawyer. The London Passenger Transport Board, for instance, has very extensive powers and, if it chose, it might exercise these somewhat arbitrarily. To whom it is responsible and how that responsibility can be enforced are questions which it is by no means easy to answer. Needless to say, these examples are cited merely in illustration of the argument. If we elect to adhere to the existing State, and yet turn away from the serfdom of universal nationalisation, one of the tasks of the next generation will be to explore the ways whereby the State—itself in the background—may yet exercise control through bodies which are sanctioned by the State, yet are not of the State. Moreover, it may be necessary in the process to rewrite certain sections of our Dicey, or perhaps even add a new chapter.

The doubts regarding collectivism expressed in the foregoing paragraphs are based on the contention that a Government department is not an appropriate machine for running much of the business of the country, so long as Ministerial responsibility is maintained. There are few to-day who would openly or consciously suggest that Ministers should in normal times be freed from the shackles of Parliamentary responsibility; although it may be observed that all the half-way houses are in one sense devices for diminishing or sharing the Minister's responsibility. If anyone doubts, let him study the answers given in the House in reply to questions regarding the B.B.C. It is true that an irresponsible Government, should we choose that path, might in the short period be an efficient Government; it is significant that, in the Marxian theory, after the revolution the first stage in the building of socialism is a dictatorship. After all, the irresponsible Government can plan; and an organised and planned system of production has always been a large part of the socialist vision. It is important in these days to consider how far 'planning' calls for irresponsibility: how far it can be fitted into the machinery of democratic responsibility.

In so far as a planned economy is the antithesis of a competitive economy, it is primarily a socialist ideal; and the almost universal clamour for a planned economy to-day may very properly be cited as an illustration of the general acceptance of much that socialism has

ment (Cmd. 5207), is significant. On this issue, it is recorded that 'the Government consider that if a Minister "free from heavy Departmental responsibilities" were specially appointed to be "responsible in respect of broad questions of policy and culture," he would find himself more and more obliged to exercise actual control.' In less official language, responsibility (such as it is) for the B.B.C. is better entrusted to an over-worked Minister, who will probably be compelled to take his responsibility lightly; if entrusted to one of the ornamental Ministers, without portfolio (worth mentioning), he might in his ample leisure be in danger of taking his responsibilities seriously, and might even become interested in the B.B.C.

In essence and despite appearances, a timorous and faint-hearted Leviathan.

stood for. In any case he is a fool who does not plan, if the contrary means doing things without foresight and without calculation. Yet the present mania for planning has its dangers, and it may indeed be doubted whether 'planning,' as understood by the zealous, is consistent with our freedom and our liberties. It may indeed be a short cut to a dictatorship. Let no one delude himself that it is possible to have an economic plan in an isolated chamber, kept rigidly apart from the political life of the country. If we agree to adopt a plan, then either we may not criticise the plan, once it is adopted, in which case the plan becomes our dictator during its currency; or we may reserve the right to criticise and modify the plan, in which case the plan ceases to be a plan, as now understood in many quarters. One simple-minded enthusiast has spoken quite cheerfully of a long-term 75-years plan. Who are we to expect from our great-grandchildren a measure of respect and docility which we ourselves would never dream of according to our own great-grandfathers? Can anyone seriously contend that, if somewhere round about 1875 a plan had been evolved by the greatest minds of the day, the subsequent years would have regarded it as sacrosanct, or—even with the best intentions—could possibly have lived within the blue-print? Democracy, the critic may say, means the right to change views with indefinite frequency: it also means the right to shake off the fetters forged by our fathers. Even under the name of Planning, we cannot bind our successors. Socialism in the next generation may be tempted to play planning as its long suit. It should be very sure that its plan is a servant liable to statutory notice, not a master concealing a hidden dictatorship.[1]

[1] The naive idea that in order to still the voice of political controversy, it is merely necessary to turn questions over to a Planning Commission, finds extreme expression in Mr. Lipson's treatment of the issue in *A Planned Economy or Free Enterprise* (pp. 296–297). Twelve large proliferations of problems are *included* in the scope of his Planning Commission, so presumably the list is not exhaustive. Even so, if we may abridge and condense, the Commission is to (i) direct the resources of the country; (ii) look to national security; (iii) take steps to avoid booms and slumps; (iv) divert labour and capital from declining industries; . . . (vii) 'frame a comprehensive labour code relating to wages, hours, holidays, technical training, housing, and general conditions of work'; (viii) supervise trade associations; (ix) set up public corporations in industries not left to private enterprise; (x) formulate monetary policy, etc.; (xi) control investment abroad; (xii) develop international economic co-operation. It is assumed that these proposals will have 'the merit of taking national planning out of the arena of party strife,' and that such a planning commission 'would be detached from politics and so exert an influence which parties and governments would be bound to respect.' If we (and Parliament) may not decently discuss these things because the Planning Commission has spoken or is about to speak, what on earth is left for us to talk about? But indeed there is not one of these headings which would not, very properly, provoke Parliament to the utterance of furlongs of Hansards. Take, for example, No. 7, which alone has been quoted in full in the foregoing condensation. What chance is there that the parties concerned would seal their mouths on such a code, merely on the assurance that thus-and-thus had the Planning Commission decided?

It is assumed in the text, and probably most plain citizens assume, that a plan implies a period of currency. It may be a short-period plan, designed to take us

It is on the whole an idle pastime to conjecture the shape of things to come. At the present moment the individual is under an eclipse—perhaps unduly and even dangerously so. Society in the last generation has undergone a curious process of coagulation. We express ourselves through the group to which we belong. A worker tends to be nothing unless he is a member of his union; an employer is an outcast unless he belongs to his association. Even the individualists have formed an individualist society—an ominous indication of the sapping of their individualist faith. From the point of view of industrial negotiations, trade agreements and much more, this coagulation of society is probably highly advantageous. It makes it possible to achieve an organisation of industry such as could not be dreamed of in an atomistic society. But without doubt it renders the individual of small account. Nor does the individual get back his self-respect when, as an elector, he contemplates the working of the political machine. It would be idle to deny that democracy has not worked out just quite as was anticipated. Putting aside Hitler and Lenin as somewhat violent and prejudiced witnesses, there is an uneasy feeling that the individual elector counts for nothing and can do nothing. He may have the option periodically of indicating his preference between two (or three) candidates, among whom in fact he feels no preference. The claim constantly made by Lenin that the soviets gave each worker a feeling that he counted for something may, or may not, be justified: few can speak of Russia with any grounded knowledge. But it would be foolish to deny that the implied criticism of the working of democracy has foundation. The headquarters party machine may count for much; the local party machine may count for a little; but the lone elector, no longer enthusiastic for any of the prevailing political creeds, counts for nothing, and he feels that he counts for nothing. This is in part the explanation of the apathy increasingly manifested at elections, so frequently deplored by the righteous. And very properly deplored: for an electorate that abdicates is already opening the door invitingly to a dictatorship in one form or another. Democracy, if it is to face the future with equanimity, must contrive some means whereby the ordinary elector will attain to a better conceit of himself.

In pursuing the aim of reconciling social control with the spontaneity of individual initiative, it is probable that for some time to come the eclipse of the individual will become more pronounced.

to an objective not so remote; or it may be a long-period plan, which seeks to fix our eyes on a more distant future. But acts of decision, taken singly or in conjunction, do not constitute a plan. Mrs. Wootton, in the essay contributed to the Fabian publication *Can Planning be Democratic?* interprets planning as meaning that major economic decisions (on certain types of questions which are not specified) 'are made *deliberately* by someone acting on behalf of all the people concerned' (*Op. cit.* p. 38). But surely a plan should be something more than this.

The curious speculator may be invited to consider what will be the effect, on our changing view of the State's functions, of the imminent and inevitable decline in our population, for which the stage is now completely set. It might be reasoned with much force (though not here) that a shrinking population will raise such difficult and delicate questions in every direction as may not be left to solve themselves *ambulando*, by the march of time, and with reliance on the surviving remnants of *laissez faire*. In an expanding world, with expanding markets and expanding industries, the individualist comes into his own, and a policy of *laissez faire* may in a sense be imposed. On the other hand, nothing is so difficult as to shrink gracefully and proportionately, while avoiding yawning maladjustments in the body social and economic. Here, within the next generation is a task which will require of our governors a most unusual combination of firmness of purpose and delicacy of touch. Nor will the problems be presented in a field that can be delimited. If we are to get through the years of shrinkage, we shall need a State professing an obligation to exercise a guiding and controlling influence in every sphere of the national life, and prepared to act accordingly. In the end, it may well be found that the population factor, as that will be increasingly revealed in the next fifty years, will be the chiefest cause urging in the direction of what, for convenience, we may call the Socialist State.

But, even if it be recognised that for all manner of reasons the tide is still flowing, and is likely to continue for some time to flow, so strongly in the direction of a more ubiquitous State and a less significant individual, it may just for that reason be all the more necessary to emphasise the other side in order that a proper balance may be maintained. It is of the essence of democracy that there should be someone to point out the dangers inherent in the views of the prevailing majority, and to draw attention to the pitfalls along the path by which we are being led. Quite apart from the economics and the politics of the matter—which perhaps in the light of eternity are the least important parts of life—we are to-day too much lost in the crowd; we are too much mass-produced. The race of eccentrics, the salt of the world, has perished from the earth. Where is there to-day a Saint-Simon or a Fourier? Who would listen to them if they were to arise and speak? The great need of the present day is for a prophet of liberalism: not because liberalism, any more than any other tenable political creed, is an exclusive repository of wisdom and truth, but precisely because liberalism, in so far as it stands for the pre-eminent worth of the individual, is an essential ingredient in any balanced view of things, and because liberalism at the present moment is dangerously in eclipse. For the strength of liberalism or individualism, or whatever it may be called, is that all great things are conceived in solitude—however they may be executed—by men who have relied on themselves, and not on their fellows or the State. There may be a divinely inspired man; there may even be a heaven-sent statesman; but there was never a divinely inspired State. In the great moments of life, man is necessarily, and perhaps lamentably, alone. For every life is a pilgrimage, and every true pilgrimage ends in solitude. As John Bunyan shrewdly observed, a man may have company when he sets out for heaven, and yet go thither alone. The danger involved in the drift or urge in the direction of an ever more actively controlling and intervening State, is that at the end of that path—however it may be disguised—lies totalitarianism, with the individual even less than the Guild Socialist's manure, even less than a thing of naught. The very great and deserved welcome accorded to Mr. Hayek's warnings regarding *The Road to Serfdom* may perhaps be interpreted as an indication that the public mind and conscience are not wholly at ease on the question.

INDEX

R